Get the eBook FREE!

(PDF, ePub, Kindle, and liveBook all included)

We believe that once you buy a book from us, you should be able to read it in any format we have available. To get electronic versions of this book at no additional cost to you, purchase and then register this book at the Manning website.

Go to https://www.manning.com/freebook and follow the instructions to complete your pBook registration.

That's it!
Thanks from Manning!

Praise for the second edition

Slices through the complexity of AWS using examples and visuals to cement knowledge in the minds of readers.

—From the foreword by Ben Whaley, AWS community hero and author

The authors' ability to explain complex concepts is the real strength of the book.

—Antonio Pessolano, Consoft Sistemi

Useful examples, figures, and sources to help you learn efficiently.

—Christof Marte, Daimler-Benz

Does a great job of explaining some of the key services in plain English so you have the knowledge necessary to dig deeper.

—Ryan Burrows, Rooster Park Consulting

This is a great book that covers all aspects of Amazon Web Services, from top to bottom.

—Ariel Gamino, Northwestern Medicine

A great way to learn AWS step by step, using the Free Tier.

—Jose San Leandro, DevOps, OSOCO.es

A perfect journey to the world of Amazon Web Services.

—Jean-Pol Landrain, Agile Partner

Amazon Web Services in Action

THIRD EDITION
AN IN-DEPTH GUIDE TO AWS

ANDREAS WITTIG
MICHAEL WITTIG

MANNING

SHELTER ISLAND

For online information and ordering of this and other Manning books, please visit
www.manning.com. The publisher offers discounts on this book when ordered in quantity.
For more information, please contact

    Special Sales Department
    Manning Publications Co.
    20 Baldwin Road
    PO Box 761
    Shelter Island, NY 11964
    Email: orders@manning.com

Manning Publications Co.
20 Baldwin Road
PO Box 761
Shelter Island, NY 11964

Development editor:	Frances Lefkowitz
Review editor:	Aleksandar Dragosavljević
Production editor:	Kathleen Rossland
Copy editor:	Pamela Hunt
Proofreader:	Keri Hales
Technical proofreader:	Shawn Bolan
Typesetter:	Dennis Dalinnik
Cover designer:	Marija Tudor

ISBN: 9781633439160
Printed in the United States of America

brief contents

contents

      Private Cloud (VPC)   158

      *Creating the VPC and an internet gateway (IGW)   160 ▪ Defining
      the public proxy subnet   160 ▪ Adding the private backend
      subnet   163 ▪ Launching virtual machines in the subnets   166
      Accessing the internet from private subnets via a NAT gateway   167*

6 *Automating operational tasks with Lambda   172*

      6.1   Executing your code with AWS Lambda   173

            *What is serverless?   173 ▪ Running your code on AWS
            Lambda   174 ▪ Comparing AWS Lambda with virtual
            machines (Amazon EC2)   175*

      6.2   Building a website health check with AWS Lambda   176

            *Creating a Lambda function   177 ▪ Use CloudWatch to search
            through your Lambda function's logs   181 ▪ Monitoring a
            Lambda function with CloudWatch metrics and alarms   184
            Accessing endpoints within a VPC   189*

      6.3   Adding a tag containing the owner of an EC2 instance
            automatically   190

            *Event-driven: Subscribing to EventBridge events   191
            Implementing the Lambda function in Python   193 ▪ Setting
            up a Lambda function with the Serverless Application Model
            (SAM)   195 ▪ Authorizing a Lambda function to use other
            AWS services with an IAM role   196 ▪ Deploying a Lambda
            function with SAM   197*

      6.4   What else can you do with AWS Lambda?   198

            *What are the limitations of AWS Lambda?   198 ▪ Effects of the
            serverless pricing model   199 ▪ Use case: Web application   201
            Use case: Data processing   202 ▪ Use case: IoT backend   202*

PART 3   STORING DATA IN THE CLOUD 205

7 *Storing your objects: S3   207*

      7.1   What is an object store?   208
      7.2   Amazon S3   209
      7.3   Backing up your data on S3 with AWS CLI   210
      7.4   Archiving objects to optimize costs   213
      7.5   Storing objects programmatically   216

            *Setting up an S3 bucket   218 ▪ Installing a web application that
            uses S3   218 ▪ Reviewing code access S3 with SDK   218*

preface

When we started our career as software developers in 2008, we didn't care about operations. We wrote code, and someone else was responsible for deployment and operations. A huge gap existed between software development and IT operations back then. On top of that, releasing new features was risky because it was impossible to test all the changes to software and infrastructure manually. Every six months, when new features needed to be deployed, we experienced a nightmare.

Then, in 2012, we became responsible for a product: an online banking platform. Our goal was to iterate quickly and to be able to release new features for the product every week. Our software was responsible for managing money, so the quality and security of the software and infrastructure were as important as the ability to innovate. But the inflexible on-premises infrastructure and the outdated process of deploying software made those goals impossible to reach. We started to look for a better way.

Our search led us to Amazon Web Services, which offered a flexible and reliable way to build and operate our applications. The possibility of automating every part of our infrastructure struck us as fascinating and innovative. Step by step, we dove into the different AWS services, from virtual machines to distributed message queues. Being able to outsource tasks like operating an SQL database or a load balancer saved us a lot of time. We invested this time in automating the testing and operations for our entire infrastructure.

The changes that took place during this transformation to the cloud went beyond the technical. After a while, the software architecture changed from a monolithic application to microservices, and the separation between software development and operations got very blurry—and, in some cases, disappeared altogether. Instead, we built our organization around the core principle of DevOps: you build it, you run it.

Since 2015, we have worked as independent consultants, helping our clients get the most out of AWS. We have accompanied startups, midsized companies, and enterprise corporations on their journey to the cloud. Along the way, we have identified—and solved—the common challenges that confront companies of all sizes as they move to the cloud. In fact, we ended up turning some of our solutions into products to sell on the AWS Marketplace.

We enjoyed writing the first edition of our book in 2015. The astonishing support from Manning and our MEAP readers allowed us to finish the whole book in only nine months. Above all, it was a pleasure to observe you—our readers—using our book to get started with AWS or deepen your knowledge with the platform.

AWS is always innovating and constantly releasing new features or whole new services. So, in 2018, we released a second edition of the book, updated and revised based on the feedback of our readers. The second edition added three more chapters to cover newer developments—Lambda, EFS, and ElastiCache—and updated all the previous chapters.

Now, in 2023, it is time to update our book once again. In this third edition, we meticulously reviewed every chapter, updating the text and screenshots so they match the current way things work on the AWS platform. We've also added new content, including a chapter on containerized architectures as well as sections about CodeDeploy, Packer, and more.

We hope you enjoy the third edition of *Amazon Web Services in Action* as much as we do!

acknowledgments

Writing a book is time consuming. We invested our time, and other people did as well. Thank you to everyone involved!

We want to thank all the readers who bought the MEAP edition of this book. Thanks for overlooking the rough edges and focusing on learning about AWS instead. Your feedback helped us polish the final version of the book that you are now reading.

Thank you to all the people who posted comments in the book's liveBook forum and who provided excellent feedback, which improved the book.

Thanks to all the reviewers of the third, second, and first editions who provided detailed comments from the first to the last page. To all the reviewers of this edition: Adrian Rossi, Alessandro Campeis, Amitabh P. Cheekoth, Andres Sacco, Ashley Eatly, Bobby Lin, Brent Honadel, Chris Villanueva, Darnell Gadberry, Edin Kapic, Ernesto Cardenas Cangahuala, Floris Bouchot, Franklin Neves, Frans Oilinki, Ganesh Swaminathan, George Onofrei, Gilberto Taccari, Jeffrey Chu, Jeremy Chen, John Larsen, John Zoetebier, Jorge Bo, Kamesh Ganesan, Kent Spillner, Matteo Battista, Matteo Rossi, Mohammad Shahnawaz Akhter, Philip Patterson, Rahul Modpur, Roman Levchenko, Simeon Leyzerzon, Simone Sguazza, Uziel Linares, Venkatesh Rajagopal, and Vidhya Vinay—your feedback helped shape this book. We hope you like it as much as we do.

Special thanks to Michael Labib for his input and feedback on chapter 11 covering AWS ElastiCache.

Furthermore, we want to thank the technical editors, John Hyaduck and Jonathan Thoms. Your unbiased and technical view on Amazon Web Services helped to perfect our book.

Shawn P. Bolan made sure all the examples in this third edition work as expected. Thanks for proofing the technical parts of our book. Thanks to David Fombella Pombal and Doug Warren for proofing the technical parts in previous editions.

We also want to thank Manning Publications for placing their trust in us. Especially, we want to thank the following staff at Manning for their excellent work:

- Frances Lefkowitz, our development editor, who guided us through the process of writing the second and third editions. Her writing and teaching expertise is noticeable in every part of our book. Thanks for your support.
- Dan Maharry, our development editor for the first edition. Thanks for taking us by the hand from writing the first pages to finishing our first book.
- Aleksandar Dragosavljević, our review editor, who organized the reviews of our book. Thanks for making sure we got valuable feedback from our readers.
- Tiffany Taylor, our copyeditor, who perfected our English in the first two editions, and Pamela Hunt, who copyedited the third edition. We know you had a hard time with us, but our mother tongue is German, and we thank you for your efforts.
- Charlotte Harborne, Ana Romac, and Christopher Kaufmann, who helped us to promote this book.
- Ivan Martinović, who answered our many questions regarding the technical aspects of writing a book in Asciidoc.
- And thanks to the production staff, who worked behind the scenes to take our rough draft and turn it into a real book.

Last but not least, we want to thank the significant people in our lives who supported us as we worked on the book.

about this book

Our book guides you from creating an AWS account to building fault-tolerant and autoscaling applications. You will learn about services offering compute, network, and storage capacity. We get you started with everything you need to run web applications on AWS: load balancers, virtual machines, containers, file storage, database systems, and in-memory caches.

The first part of the book introduces you to the principles of Amazon Web Services and gives you a first impression of the possibilities in the cloud. Next, in part 2, you will learn about fundamental compute and network services. In part 3, we demonstrate six different ways to store your data. Finally, part 4 focuses on architecting on AWS: highly available or even fault-tolerant architectures using load balancers and queues, containerized applications, deployment options, and autoscaling strategies to scale your infrastructure dynamically as well.

Amazon offers a wide variety of services—more than 200 services in 25 categories at last count, with more added regularly. Unfortunately, the number of pages within a book is limited. Therefore, you will not find instructions for all AWS services in this book. What you *will* find is a collection of the most important and universally popular services. We consider these services the essential toolkit, the ones you need to get up and running and get your business done. You could operate fine with just these services, but once you have mastered them, we hope you will have the confidence and curiosity to explore what else is out there—for instance: Machine Learning as a Service, anyone?

Automation sneaks in throughout the book, so by the end, you'll be comfortable with using AWS CloudFormation, an Infrastructure as Code tool that allows you to manage your cloud infrastructure in an automated way; this will be one of the most important things you will learn from our book.

Most of our examples use popular web applications to demonstrate important points. We use tools offered by AWS instead of third-party tools whenever possible, because we appreciate the quality and support offered by AWS. Our book focuses on the different aspects of security in the cloud, for example, by following the "least-privilege" principle when accessing cloud resources.

We focus on Linux as the operating system for virtual machines. Our examples are based on open source software.

Amazon operates data centers in various geographic regions around the world. To simplify the examples, we use the region US East (N. Virginia). You will also learn how to switch to another region to use resources in the region Asia Pacific (Sydney).

About the third edition

In this third edition, we have revised all of the previous 17 chapters. AWS has made significant progress since the second edition in 2018. As a result, we incorporated countless new features into the third edition. Of course, we also updated all the examples.

The most significant change is the addition of chapter 18, "Building modern architecture for the cloud: ECS, Fargate, and App Runner." The brand-new chapter discusses deploying a web application using containers. We start with a simple example based on App Runner and end the chapter with a cloud-native architecture based on ALB, ECS, Fargate, and S3. We also rewrote chapter 15, "Automating deployment: CloudFormation, CodeDeploy, and Packer," to provide you the tools to deploy your applications to AWS.

Who should read this book

Amazon Web Services is a toolbox. You can find tools to run a website that can sell goods and services to the general public, but you can also host private applications securely and economically, which a corporation with thousands of customers depends on. Tools are also available to crunch numbers or to train your ML models. The possibilities go on and on. Reading this book should help you get used to the most common tools. Once you are familiar with the common tools, you are equipped to explore the rest of the toolbox on your own.

You don't need much training to read, understand, and adapt the lessons from this book to your own needs. Familiarity with Linux computers, the markup language YAML, and an understanding of basic networking concepts are all you need to get started. You don't even need an AWS account—we'll show you how to sign up for one in chapter 1.

How this book is organized: A road map

Chapter 1 introduces cloud computing and Amazon Web Services. You'll learn about key concepts and basics, and you'll create and set up your AWS account.

Chapter 2 brings Amazon Web Services into action. You'll spin up and dive into a complex cloud infrastructure with ease.

Chapter 3 is about working with a virtual machine. You'll learn about the key concepts of the Elastic Compute Service (EC2) with the help of a handful of practical examples.

Chapter 4 presents different approaches for automating your infrastructure: the AWS Command Line Interface (CLI) from your terminal, the AWS SDKs to program in your favorite language, and AWS CloudFormation, an Infrastructure as Code tool.

Chapter 5 is about security. You'll learn how to secure your networking infrastructure with private networks and firewalls. You'll also learn how to protect your AWS account and your cloud resources.

Chapter 6 is about automating operational tasks with AWS Lambda. You will learn how to execute small code snippets in the cloud without needing to launch a virtual machine.

Chapter 7 introduces the Amazon Simple Storage Service (S3), a service offering object storage, and Amazon Glacier, a service offering long-term storage. You'll learn how to integrate object storage into your applications to implement a stateless server by creating an image gallery.

Chapter 8 is about storing data from your virtual machines on hard drives with Amazon Elastic Block Storage (EBS) and instance storage. To get an idea of the different options available, you'll take some performance measurements.

Chapter 9 explains how to use a networking filesystem to share data among multiple machines. Therefore, we introduce the Amazon Elastic File System (EFS).

Chapter 10 introduces Amazon Relational Database Service (RDS), offering managed relational database systems like MySQL, PostgreSQL, Oracle, and Microsoft SQL Server. You will learn how to connect an application to an RDS database instance, for example.

Chapter 11 is about adding a cache to your infrastructure to speed up your application and save costs due to minimizing load on the database layer. Specifically, you will learn about Amazon ElastiCache, which provides Redis or Memcached as a service, as well as Amazon MemoryDB for Redis.

Chapter 12 introduces Amazon DynamoDB, a NoSQL database offered by AWS. DynamoDB is typically not compatible with legacy applications. You need to rework your applications to use DynamoDB. You'll implement a to-do application in this chapter.

Chapter 13 explains what's needed to make your infrastructure highly available. You'll learn how to recover automatically from a failed virtual machine or even a whole data center.

Chapter 14 introduces the concept of decoupling your system to increase reliability. You'll learn how to use synchronous decoupling with the help of Elastic Load Balancing (ELB). Asynchronous decoupling is also part of this chapter; we explain how to use the Amazon Simple Queue Service (SQS), a distributed queuing service, to build a fault-tolerant system.

Chapter 15 introduces three different ways to deploy software to AWS. You'll use each of the tools to deploy an application to AWS in an automated fashion.

Chapter 16 dives into building fault-tolerant applications based on the concepts explained in chapters 13 and 14. You'll create a fault-tolerant image-processing web service within this chapter.

Chapter 17 is all about flexibility. You'll learn how to scale the capacity of your infrastructure based on a schedule or based on the current load of your system.

Chapter 18 explains ways to deploy containers on AWS. You'll learn to use ECS with Fargate and App Runner to run your containerized application.

AWS costs

AWS offers a Free Tier, which allows you to experiment with a number of services for at least a full year at no charge. Most of the projects we walk you through in this book can be done within the Free Tier. For the few processes we teach that do go beyond the Free Tier, we provide a clear warning for you, so you can opt out if you do not want to incur charges. In chapter 1, you'll learn much more about how AWS charges for services, what's covered in the Free Tier, and how to set budgets and alerts so you don't receive any unexpected bills from AWS.

About the code

You'll find four types of code listings in this book: bash, YAML, Python, and Node.js/ JavaScript. We use bash to create tiny scripts to interact with AWS in an automated way. YAML is used to describe infrastructure in a way that AWS CloudFormation can understand. In addition, we use Python to manage our cloud infrastructure. Also, we use the Node.js platform to create small applications in JavaScript to build cloud-native applications.

All source code in listings or in text is in a `fixed-width font like this` to separate it from ordinary text. Code annotations accompany many of the listings, highlighting important concepts. In some cases, numbered bullets link to explanations that follow the listing, and sometimes we needed to break a line into two or more to fit on the page. In our bash code, we used the continuation backslash. The $ at the beginning indicates that the following line was an input. If you are using Windows, you have to make the following adjustments: the leading $ can be ignored. In PowerShell: replace the continuation backslash \ with a `. At the command prompt: replace \ with a ^. An artificial line break is indicated by this symbol: ⇒.

You can get executable snippets of code from the liveBook (online) version of this book at https://livebook.manning.com/book/amazon-web-services-in-action-third-edition. The complete code for the examples in the book is available for download from the Manning website at https://www.manning.com/books/amazon-web-services-in-action -third-edition, and from GitHub at https://github.com/AWSinAction/code3/.

liveBook discussion forum

Purchase of *Amazon Web Services in Action, Third Edition,* includes free access to liveBook, Manning's online reading platform. Using liveBook's exclusive discussion features, you can attach comments to the book globally or to specific sections or paragraphs. It's a snap to make notes for yourself, ask and answer technical questions, and receive help from the author and other users. To access the forum, go to https://livebook.manning.com/book/amazon-web-services-in-action-third-edition/discussion. You can also learn more about Manning's forums and the rules of conduct at https://livebook.manning.com/discussion.

Manning's commitment to our readers is to provide a venue where a meaningful dialogue between individual readers and between readers and the author can take place. It is not a commitment to any specific amount of participation on the part of the authors, whose contribution to the forum remains voluntary (and unpaid). We suggest you try asking them some challenging questions lest their interest stray! The forum and the archives of previous discussions will be accessible from the publisher's website as long as the book is in print.

about the authors

ANDREAS WITTIG and **MICHAEL WITTIG** are software engineers and consultants, focusing on Amazon Web Services. The brothers started building on AWS in 2013 when migrating the IT infrastructure of a German bank to AWS—the first bank in Germany to do so. Since 2015, Andreas and Michael have worked as consultants, helping their clients migrate and run their workloads on AWS. They focus on Infrastructure as Code, continuous deployment, serverless applications based on AWS Lambda, containers, and security. Andreas and Michael are building SaaS products on top of Amazon's cloud as well. On top of that, Andreas and Michael love to share their knowledge and teach others how to use Amazon Web Services through their book, *Amazon Web Services in Action*, as well as their blog, podcast, and YouTube channel at cloudonaut.io.

about the cover illustration

The figure on the cover of *Amazon Web Services in Action, Third Edition,* is "Paysan du Canton de Lucerne," or "A Peasant from the Canton of Lucerne," taken from a collection by Jacques Grasset de Saint-Sauveur, published in 1797. Each illustration is finely drawn and colored by hand.

In those days, it was easy to identify where people lived and what their trade or station in life was just by their dress. Manning celebrates the inventiveness and initiative of the computer business with book covers based on the rich diversity of regional culture centuries ago, brought back to life by pictures from collections such as this one.

Part 1

Getting started

Have you watched a blockbuster on Netflix, bought a gadget on Amazon .com, or booked a room on Airbnb today? If so, you have used Amazon Web Services (AWS) in the background. Because Netflix, Amazon.com, and Airbnb all use AWS for their business.

AWS is the biggest player in the cloud computing markets. According to analysts, AWS maintains a market share of more than 30%.[1] Another impressive number: AWS accounts for net sales of $20.5 billion year-over-year (a 27% increase).[2] AWS data centers are distributed worldwide in North America, South America, Europe, Africa, Asia, and Australia. But the cloud does not consist of hardware and computing power alone. Software is part of every cloud platform and makes the difference for you, as a customer who aims to provide a valuable experience to your service's users. The research firm Gartner has yet again classified AWS as a leader in their Magic Quadrant for Cloud Infrastructure & Platform Services in 2022. Gartner's Magic Quadrant groups vendors into four quadrants—niche players, challengers, visionaries, and leaders—and provides a quick overview of the cloud computing market.[3] Being recognized as a leader attests to AWS's high speed and high quality of innovation.

---

[1] Statista, "Global Cloud Infrastructure Market Share 2022," http://mng.bz/Popv.
[2] Amazon, "Amazon.com Announces Third Quarter Results 2022," http://mng.bz/JVXa.
[3] AWS Blog, "AWS Named as a Leader in the 2022 Gartner Cloud Infrastructure & Platform Services (CIPS) Magic Quadrant for the 12th Consecutive Year," http://mng.bz/wy7a.

The first part of this book will guide you through your initial steps with AWS. You will get an impression of how you can use AWS to improve your IT infrastructure.

Chapter 1 introduces cloud computing and AWS. This will get you familiar with the big-picture basics of how AWS is structured.

Chapter 2 brings Amazon Web Service into action. Here, you will spin up and dive into a complex cloud infrastructure with ease.

What is Amazon Web Services?

This chapter covers

- Overview of Amazon Web Services
- The benefits of using Amazon Web Services
- What you can do with Amazon Web Services
- Creating and setting up an AWS account

Almost every IT solution gets labeled with the term *cloud computing* or even just *cloud* nowadays. Buzzwords like these may help sales, but they're hard to work with when trying to teach—or learn—how to work with these technologies. So, for the sake of clarity, let's start this book by defining some terms.

Cloud computing, or the cloud, is a metaphor for supply and consumption of IT resources. The IT resources in the cloud aren't directly visible to the user; layers of abstraction exist in between. The level of abstraction offered by the cloud varies, from offering virtual machines (VMs) to providing Software as a Service (SaaS) based on complex distributed systems. Resources are available on demand in enormous quantities, and you pay for what you use.

The official definition from the National Institute of Standards and Technology follows:

> *Cloud computing is a model for enabling ubiquitous, convenient, on-demand network access to a shared pool of configurable computing resources (networks, virtual machines, storage, applications, and services) that can be rapidly provisioned and released with minimal management effort or service provider interaction.*

> —National Institute of Standards and Technology

Also, NIST defines the following five essential characteristics for cloud computing:

- *On-demand self-service*—The cloud enables us to provision resources ad hoc with the click of a button or an API call.
- *Broad network access*—Capabilities are available over the network.
- *Resource pooling*—The cloud assigns resources based on a multitenant model, which means consumers share the same physical and virtual resources.
- *Rapid elasticity*—The cloud allows us to expand and shrink the provisioned capacity on demand.
- *Measured service*—The cloud provides metrics allowing consumers to gain insights into the utilization of their resources.

Besides that, offerings are often divided into the following three types:

- *Public*—A cloud managed by an organization and open to use by the general public
- *Private*—A cloud that virtualizes and distributes the IT infrastructure for a single organization
- *Hybrid*—A mixture of a public and a private cloud

Amazon Web Services (AWS) is a public cloud. By combining your on-premises data center with AWS, you are building a hybrid cloud.

Cloud computing services also have several classifications, described here:

- *Infrastructure as a Service (IaaS)*—Offers fundamental resources like computing, storage, and networking capabilities, using virtual machines such as Amazon EC2, Google Compute Engine, and Microsoft Azure Virtual Machines.
- *Platform as a Service (PaaS)*—Provides platforms to deploy custom applications to the cloud, such as AWS Lambda, AWS App Runner, Google App Engine, and Heroku.
- *Software as a Service (SaaS)*—Combines infrastructure and software running in the cloud, including office applications like Amazon WorkSpaces, Google WorkSpace, and Microsoft 365.

AWS is a cloud-computing provider with a wide variety of IaaS, PaaS, and SaaS offerings. Let's go into a bit more detail about what AWS is and does.

1.1   What is Amazon Web Services (AWS)?

Amazon Web Services (AWS) is a platform of web services that offers solutions for computing, storing, and networking, at different layers of abstraction. For example, you can attach volumes to a virtual machine—a low level of abstraction—or store and retrieve data via a REST API—a high level of abstraction. Use the services provided by AWS to host websites, run enterprise applications, and mine tremendous amounts of data. *Web services* are accessible via the internet by using typical web protocols (such as HTTP) and are used by machines or by humans through a UI. The most prominent services provided by AWS are *EC2*, which offers virtual machines, and *S3*, which offers storage capacity. Services on AWS work well together: you can use them to migrate existing on-premises infrastructures or build from scratch. The pricing model for services is pay-per-use.

As an AWS customer, you can choose among different *data centers*. AWS data centers are distributed worldwide. For example, you can start a virtual machine in Japan in exactly the same way as you would start one in Ireland. This enables you to serve customers worldwide.

The map in figure 1.1 shows AWS's data centers. Access to some of them is limited: some data centers are accessible for US government organizations only, and special conditions apply for the data centers in China. Additional data centers have been announced for Canada, Spain, Switzerland, Israel, UAE, India, Australia, and New Zealand.

* Limited access

Figure 1.1   AWS data center locations

Now that we have defined the most important terms, the question is: what can you do with AWS?

1.2   What can you do with AWS?

You can run all sorts of application on AWS by using one or a combination of services. The examples in this section will give you an idea of what you can do.

1.2.1   *Hosting a web shop*

John is CIO of a medium-sized e-commerce business. He wants to develop a fast, reliable, and scalable web shop. He initially decided to host the web shop on-premises, and three years ago, he rented machines in a data center. A web server handles requests from customers, and a database stores product information and orders. John is evaluating how his company can take advantage of AWS by running the same setup on AWS, as shown in figure 1.2.

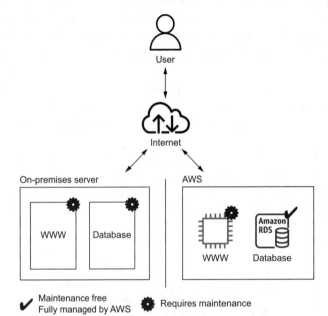

✔ Maintenance free
  Fully managed by AWS   ✿ Requires maintenance

Figure 1.2   Running a web shop on-premises vs. on AWS

John not only wants to lift-and-shift his current on-premises infrastructure to AWS, he wants to get the most out of the advantages the cloud is offering. Additional AWS services allow John to improve his setup as follows:

- The web shop consists of dynamic content (such as products and their prices) and static content (such as the company logo). Splitting these up would reduce the load on the web servers and improve performance by delivering the static content over a content delivery network (CDN).
- Switching to maintenance-free services, including a database, an object store, and a DNS system, would free John from having to manage these parts of the system, decreasing operational costs and improving quality.
- The application running the web shop can be installed on virtual machines. Using AWS, John can run the same amount of resources he was using on his on-premises machine but split them into multiple, smaller virtual machines at no extra cost. If one of these virtual machines fails, the load balancer will send customer requests to the other virtual machines. This setup improves the web shop's reliability.

Figure 1.3 shows how John enhanced his web shop setup with AWS.

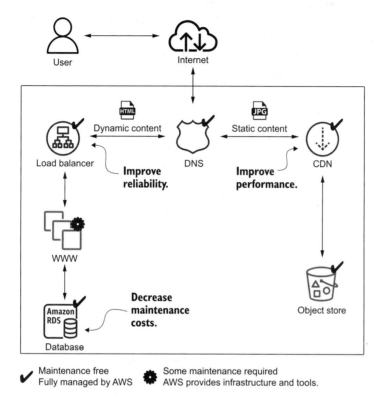

Figure 1.3   Running a web shop on AWS with CDN for better performance,
a load balancer for high availability, and a managed database to decrease
maintenance costs

John is happy with running his web shop on AWS. By migrating his company's infrastructure to the cloud, he was able to increase the reliability and performance of the
web shop.

1.2.2   Running a Java EE application in your private network

Maureen is a senior system architect in a global corporation. She wants to move parts
of her company's business applications to AWS when the data center contract expires
in a few months, to reduce costs and gain flexibility. She would like to run enterprise
applications (such as Java Enterprise Edition [EE] applications) consisting of an application server and an SQL database on AWS. To do so, she defines a virtual network in
the cloud and connects it to the corporate network through a virtual private network
(VPN) connection. She installs application servers on virtual machines to run the Java
EE application. Maureen also wants to store data in an SQL database service (such as
Oracle Database EE or Microsoft SQL Server EE).

For security, Maureen uses subnets to separate systems with different security levels from each other. By using access-control lists, she can control ingoing and outgoing traffic for each subnet. For example, the database is accessible only from the Java EE server's subnet, which helps to protect mission-critical data. Maureen controls traffic to the internet by using network address translation (NAT) and firewall rules as well. Figure 1.4 illustrates Maureen's architecture.

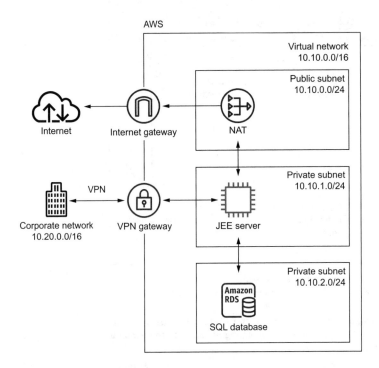

Figure 1.4   Running a Java EE application with enterprise networking on AWS improves flexibility and lowers costs.

Maureen has managed to connect the local data center with a private network running remotely on AWS to enable clients to access the Java EE server. To get started, Maureen uses a VPN connection between the local data center and AWS, but she is already thinking about setting up a dedicated network connection to reduce network costs and increase network throughput in the future.

The project was a great success for Maureen. She was able to reduce the time needed to set up an enterprise application from months to hours because AWS provides virtual machines, databases, and even the networking infrastructure on demand within a few minutes. Maureen's project also benefits from lower infrastructure costs on AWS, compared to using its own infrastructure on-premises.

1.2.3 *Implementing a highly available system*

Alexa is a software engineer working for a fast-growing startup. She knows that Murphy's Law applies to IT infrastructure: anything that can go wrong *will* go wrong. Alexa is working hard to build a highly available system to prevent outages from ruining the business. All services on AWS are either highly available or can be used in a highly available way. So, Alexa builds a system like the one shown in figure 1.5 with a high availability architecture. The database service is offered with replication and fail-over handling. In case the primary database instance fails, the standby database is promoted as the new primary database automatically. Alexa uses virtual machines acting as web servers. These virtual machines aren't highly available by default, but Alexa launches multiple virtual machines in different data centers to achieve high availability. A load balancer checks the health of the web servers and forwards requests to healthy machines.

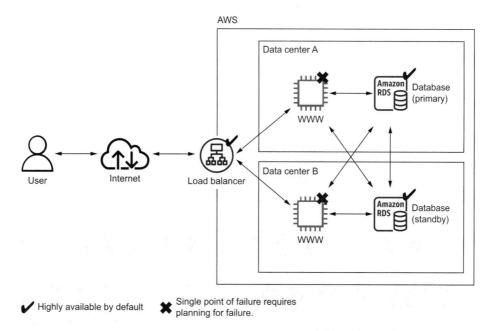

Figure 1.5   Building a highly available system on AWS by using a load balancer, multiple virtual machines, and a database with primary-standby replication

So far, Alexa has protected the startup from major outages. Nevertheless, she and her team are always planning for failure and are constantly improving the resilience of their systems.

1.2.4 *Profiting from low costs for batch processing infrastructure*

Nick is a data scientist who needs to process massive amounts of measurement data collected from gas turbines. He needs to generate a daily report containing the maintenance condition of hundreds of turbines. Therefore, his team needs a computing infrastructure to analyze the newly arrived data once a day. Batch jobs are run on a schedule and store aggregated results in a database. A business intelligence (BI) tool is used to generate reports based on the data stored in the database.

Because the budget for computing infrastructure is very small, Nick and his team have been looking for a cost effective solution to analyze their data. He finds the following ways to make clever use of AWS's price model:

- *AWS bills virtual machines per second with a minimum of 60 seconds.* So Nick launches a virtual machine when starting a batch job and terminates it immediately after the job finishes. Doing so allows him to pay for computing infrastructure only when actually using it. This is a big game changer compared to the traditional data center where Nick had to pay a monthly fee for each machine, no matter how much it was used.
- *AWS offers spare capacity in their data centers at a substantial discount.* It is not important for Nick to run a batch job at a specific time. He can wait to execute a batch job until there is enough spare capacity available, so AWS offers him a virtual machine with a discount of 75%.

Figure 1.6 illustrates how Nick benefits from the pay-per-use price model for virtual machines.

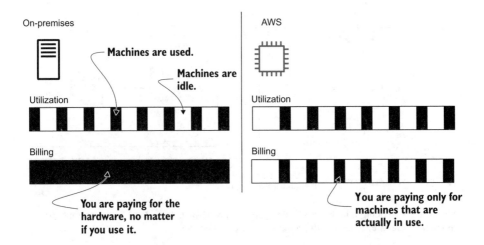

Figure 1.6   Making use of the pay-per-use price model of virtual machines

Nick is happy to have access to a computing infrastructure that allows his team to analyze data at low costs. You now have a broad idea of what you can do with AWS. Generally speaking, you can host any application on AWS. The next section explains the nine most important benefits AWS has to offer.

1.3   How you can benefit from using AWS

What's the most important advantage of using AWS? Cost savings, you might say. But saving money isn't the only advantage. Let's see how else you can benefit from using AWS by looking at some of its key features.

1.3.1   Innovative and fast-growing platform

AWS is announcing new services, features, and improvements constantly. Go to https://aws.amazon.com/about-aws/whats-new/ to get an impression of the speed of innovation. We counted 2,080 announcements in 2021. Making use of the innovative technologies provided by AWS helps you to generate valuable solutions for your customers and thus achieve a competitive advantage.

Amazon reported net sales of $62 billion for 2021. See http://mng.bz/lRqB if you are interested in the full report. We expect AWS to expand the size and extent of its platform in the upcoming years, for example, by adding additional services and data centers.

1.3.2   Services solve common problems

As you've learned, AWS is a platform of services. Common problems such as load balancing, queuing, sending email, and storing files are solved for you by services. You don't need to reinvent the wheel. It's your job to pick the right services to build complex systems. Let AWS manage those services while you focus on your customers.

1.3.3   Enabling automation

Because AWS is API driven, you can automate everything: write code to create networks, start virtual machine clusters, or deploy a relational database. Automation increases reliability and improves efficiency.

The more dependencies your system has, the more complex it gets. A human can quickly lose perspective, whereas a computer can cope with interconnected systems of any size. You should concentrate on tasks humans are good at—such as describing a system—while the computer figures out how to resolve all those dependencies to create the system. Setting up an environment in the cloud based on your blueprints can be automated with the help of infrastructure as code, covered in chapter 4.

1.3.4   Flexible capacity (scalability)

Flexible capacity reduces overcapacity. You can scale from one virtual machine to thousands of virtual machines. Your storage can grow from gigabytes to petabytes. You no longer need to predict your future capacity needs for the coming months and years to purchase hardware.

If you run a web shop, you have seasonal traffic patterns, as shown in figure 1.7. Think about day versus night, and weekday versus weekend or holiday. Wouldn't it be nice if you could add capacity when traffic grows and remove capacity when traffic

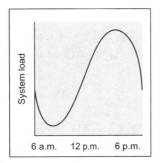 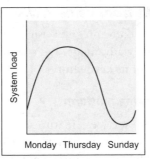 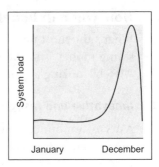

Figure 1.7   Seasonal traffic patterns for a web shop

shrinks? That's exactly what flexible capacity is about. You can start new virtual machines within minutes and throw them away a few hours after that.

The cloud has almost no capacity constraints. You no longer need to think about rack space, switches, and power supplies—you can add as many virtual machines as you like. If your data volume grows, you can always add new storage capacity.

Flexible capacity also means you can shut down unused systems. In one of our last projects, the test environment ran only from 7 a.m. to 8 p.m. on weekdays, allowing us to save 60%.

1.3.5   *Built for failure (reliability)*

Most AWS services are highly available or fault tolerant by default. If you use those services, you get reliability for free. Also, AWS provides tooling allowing you to build systems in a reliable way. It provides everything you need to create your own highly available or even fault-tolerant systems.

1.3.6   *Reducing time to market*

In AWS, you request a new virtual machine, and a few minutes later, that virtual machine is booted and ready to use. The same is true with any other AWS service available. You can use them all on demand.

Your development process will be faster because of the shorter feedback loops. You can eliminate constraints such as the number of test environments available; if you need another test environment, you can create it for a few hours.

1.3.7   *Benefiting from economies of scale*

AWS is increasing its global infrastructure constantly, and, therefore, AWS benefits from an economy of scale. As a customer, you will benefit partially from these effects.

AWS reduces prices for their cloud services every now and then. A few examples follow:

- In January 2019, AWS reduced the price for running containers on Fargate by 20% for vCPU and 65% for memory.

- In November 2020, AWS reduced prices for EBS volumes of type Cold HDD by 40%.
- In November 2021, AWS reduced prices for S3 storage by up to 31% in three storage classes.
- In April 2022, AWS removed additional costs for network traffic between data centers when using AWS PrivateLink, AWS Transit Gateway, and AWS Client VPN.

1.3.8   Global infrastructure

Are you serving customers worldwide? Making use of AWS's global infrastructure has the following advantages: having low network latencies between your customers and your infrastructure, being able to comply with regional data protection requirements, and benefiting from different infrastructure prices in different regions. AWS offers data centers in North America, South America, Europe, Africa, Asia, and Australia, so you can deploy your applications worldwide with little extra effort.

1.3.9   Professional partner

When you use AWS services, you can be sure that their quality and security follow the latest standards and certifications, such as the following:

- *ISO 27001*—A worldwide information security standard certified by an independent and accredited certification body.
- *ISO 9001*—A standardized quality management approach used worldwide and certified by an independent and accredited certification body.
- *PCI DSS Level 1*—A data security standard (DSS) for the payment card industry (PCI) to protect cardholders data.

Go to https://aws.amazon.com/compliance/ if you want to dive into the details. If you're still not convinced that AWS is a professional partner, you should know that Expedia, Volkswagen, FINRA, Airbnb, Slack, and many more are running serious workloads on AWS. To read about AWS customer success, go to https://aws.amazon .com/solutions/case-studies/.

We have discussed a lot of reasons to run your workloads on AWS. But what does AWS cost? You will learn more about the pricing models in the next section.

1.4   How much does it cost?

A bill from AWS is similar to an electric bill. Services are billed based on use. You pay for the time a virtual machine was running, the used storage from the object store, or the number of running load balancers. Services are invoiced on a monthly basis. The pricing for each service is publicly available; if you want to calculate the monthly cost of a planned setup, you can use the AWS Pricing Calculator (https://calculator.aws/).

1.4.1   *Free Tier*

You can use some AWS services for free within the first 12 months of signing up. The idea behind the Free Tier is to enable you to experiment with AWS and get some experience using its services. Here is a taste of what's included in the Free Tier:

- 750 hours (roughly a month) of a small virtual machine running Linux or Windows. This means you can run one virtual machine for a whole month, or you can run 750 virtual machines for one hour.
- 750 hours (or roughly a month) of a classic or application load balancer.
- Object store with 5 GB of storage.
- Small relational database with 20 GB of storage, including backup.
- 25 GB of data stored on NoSQL database.

If you exceed the limits of the Free Tier, you start paying for the resources you consume without further notice. You'll receive a bill at the end of the month. We'll show you how to monitor your costs before you begin using AWS.

After your one-year trial period ends, you pay for all resources you use. But some resources are free forever. For example, the first 25 GB of the NoSQL database are free forever.

You get additional benefits, as detailed at http://aws.amazon.com/free. This book will use the Free Tier as much as possible and will clearly state when additional resources are required that aren't covered by the Free Tier.

1.4.2   *Billing example*

As mentioned earlier, you can be billed in the following ways:

- *Based on time of use*—A virtual machine is billed per second. A load balancer is billed per hour.
- *Based on traffic*—Traffic is measured in gigabytes or in number of requests, for example.
- *Based on storage usage*—Usage can be measured by capacity (e.g., 50 GB volume no matter how much you use) or real usage (such as 2.3 GB used).

Remember the web shop example from section 1.2? Figure 1.8 shows the web shop and adds information about how each part is billed.

Let's assume your web shop started successfully in January, and you ran a marketing campaign to increase sales for the next month. Lucky you: you were able to increase the number of visitors to your web shop fivefold in February. As you already know, you have to pay for AWS based on usage. Table 1.1 shows your bill for February. The number of visitors increased from 100,000 to 500,000, and your monthly bill increased from $112 to $473, which is a 4.2-fold increase. Because your web shop had to handle more traffic, you had to pay more for services, such as the CDN, the web servers, and the database. Other services, like the amount of storage needed for static files, didn't change, so the price stayed the same.

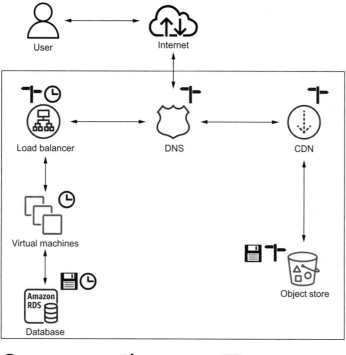

Based on time of use   Based on traffic   Based on storage usage

Figure 1.8 Some services are billed based on time of use, others by throughput or consumed storage.

Table 1.1 How an AWS bill changes if the number of web shop visitors increases

Service	January usage	February usage	February charge	Increase
Visits to website	100,000	500,000		
CDN	25 M requests + 25 GB traffic	125 M requests + 125 GB traffic	$115.00	$100.00
Static files	50 GB used storage	50 GB used storage	$1.15	$0.00
Load balancer	748 hours + 50 GB traffic	748 hours + 250 GB traffic	$19.07	$1.83
Web servers	1 virtual machine = 748 hours	4 virtual machines = 2,992 hours	$200.46	$150.35
Database (748 hours)	Small virtual machine + 20 GB storage	Large virtual machine + 20 GB storage	$133.20	$105.47
DNS	2 M requests	10 M requests	$4.00	$3.20
Total cost			*$472.88*	*$360.85*

With AWS, you can achieve a linear relationship between traffic and costs. And other opportunities await you with this pricing model.

1.4.3 *Pay-per-use opportunities*

The AWS pay-per-use pricing model creates new opportunities. For example, the barrier for starting a new project is lowered, because you no longer need to invest in infrastructure up front. You can start virtual machines on demand and pay only per second of usage. You can stop using those virtual machines whenever you like, and you no longer have to pay for them. You don't need to make an upfront commitment regarding how much storage you'll use.

Another example: a big virtual machine costs exactly as much as two smaller ones with the same capacity. Thus, you can divide your systems into smaller parts, because the cost is the same. This makes fault tolerance affordable not only for big companies but also for smaller budgets.

1.5 *Comparing alternatives*

AWS isn't the only cloud computing provider. Microsoft Azure and Google Cloud Platform (GCP) are major players as well. The three major cloud providers share a lot in common. They all have the following:

- A worldwide infrastructure that provides computing, networking, and storage capabilities
- An IaaS offering that provides virtual machines on-demand: Amazon EC2, Azure Virtual Machines, Google Compute Engine
- Highly distributed storage systems able to scale storage and I/O capacity without limits: Amazon S3, Azure Blob Storage, Google Cloud Storage
- A pay-as-you-go pricing model

But what are the differences between the cloud providers?

AWS is the market leader in cloud computing, offering an extensive product portfolio. Although AWS has expanded into the enterprise sector during recent years, it is still obvious that AWS started with services to solve internet-scale problems. Overall, AWS is building great services based on innovative, mostly open source, technologies. AWS offers complicated but rock-solid ways to restrict access to your cloud infrastructure.

Microsoft Azure provides Microsoft's technology stack in the cloud, recently expanding into web-centric and open source technologies as well. It seems like Microsoft is putting a lot of effort into catching up with Amazon's market share in cloud computing.

The Google Cloud Platform (GCP) is focused on developers looking to build sophisticated distributed systems. Google combines their worldwide infrastructure to offer scalable and fault-tolerant services (such as Google Cloud Load Balancing). The GCP seems more focused on cloud-native applications than on migrating your locally hosted applications to the cloud, in our opinion.

There are no shortcuts to making an informed decision about which cloud provider to choose. Each use case and project is different—the devil is in the details. Also don't forget where you are coming from. (Are you using Microsoft technology heavily? Do you have a big team consisting of system administrators or are you a developer-centric company?) Overall, in our opinion, AWS is the most mature and powerful cloud platform available at the moment.

1.6   Exploring AWS services

In this section, you will get an idea of the range of services that AWS offers. We'll also construct a mental model, with the help of some diagrams, to give you a high-level look at where those services sit in relation to the AWS setup as a whole.

Let's start with the mental model overview. Hardware for computing, storing, and networking is the foundation of the AWS cloud. AWS runs services on this hardware, as shown in figure 1.9.

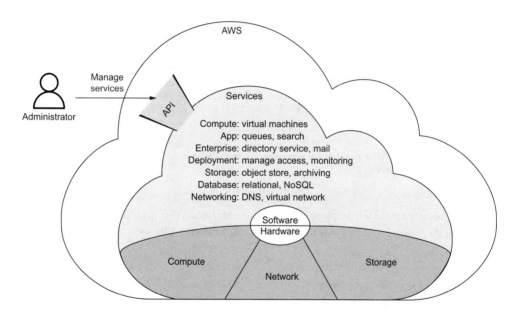

Figure 1.9   The AWS cloud is composed of hardware and software services accessible via an API.

You can manage services by sending requests to the API manually via a web-based GUI like the Management Console, a command-line interface (CLI), or programmatically via an SDK. Virtual machines have a special feature: you can connect to virtual machines through SSH, for example, and gain administrator access. This means you can install any software you like on a virtual machine. Other services, like the NoSQL database service, offer their features through an API and hide everything that's going on behind the scenes. Figure 1.10 shows an administrator installing a custom PHP web application on a virtual machine and managing dependent services such as a NoSQL database used by the application.

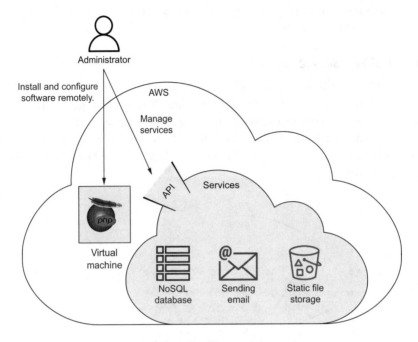

Figure 1.10   Managing a custom application running on a virtual machine and cloud-native services

Users send HTTP requests to a virtual machine. This virtual machine is running a web server along with a custom PHP web application. The web application needs to talk to AWS services to answer HTTP requests from users. For example, the application might need to query data from a NoSQL database, store static files, and send email. Communication between the web application and AWS services is handled by the API, as figure 1.11 shows.

The number of services available can be scary at the outset. When logging into AWS's web interface, you are presented with an overview listing around 200 services in 25 categories. On top of that, new services are announced constantly during the year and at the big conference in Las Vegas, AWS re:Invent, which takes place annually in November.

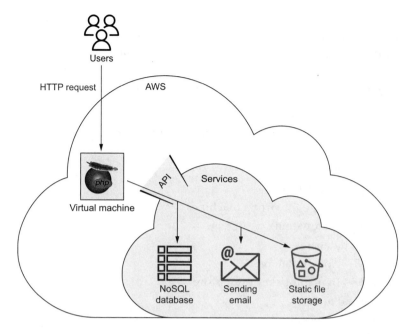

Figure 1.11   Handling an HTTP request with a custom web application using additional AWS services

AWS offers services in the following categories:

▪ Analytics	▪ Application integration	▪ AR and VR
▪ AWS cost management	▪ Blockchain	▪ Business applications
▪ Compute	▪ Containers	▪ Customer enablement
▪ Database	▪ Developer tools	▪ End-user computing
▪ Frontend web and mobile	▪ Game Development	▪ Internet of Things
▪ Machine learning	▪ Management and governance	▪ Media services
▪ Migration and transfer	▪ Networking and content delivery	▪ Quantum technologies
▪ Robotics	▪ Satellite	▪ Security, identity, and compliance
▪ Storage		

Obviously, it is impossible for us to cover all the services offered by AWS in one book. Therefore, in this book, we have selected for you the services that will help you get started quickly to build a fully capable, responsive, and dependable system, and then to grow and maintain that system. These are the most widely used services and will address most of your needs. After you've become more adept at working with AWS on these must-have services, feel free to investigate the nice-to-have services available to you.

The following services are covered in detail in our book:

- *EC2*—Virtual machines
- *ECS and Fargate*—Running and managing containers
- *Lambda*—Executing functions
- *S3*—Object store
- *Glacier*—Archiving data
- *EBS*—Block storage for virtual machines
- *EFS*—Network filesystem
- *RDS*—SQL databases
- *DynamoDB*—NoSQL database
- *ElastiCache*—In-memory key-value store
- *VPC*—Virtual network
- *ELB*—Load balancers
- *Simple Queue Service*—Distributed queues
- *CodeDeploy*—Automating code deployments
- *CloudWatch*—Monitoring and logging
- *CloudFormation*—Automating your infrastructure
- *IAM*—Restricting access to your cloud resources

We are missing at least three important topics that could fill their own books: continuous delivery, machine learning, and analytics. In fact, Manning has a whole book on doing machine learning and data analysis on AWS: *AI as a Service: Serverless Machine Learning with AWS* by Peter Elger and Eóin Shanaghy (https://www.manning.com/books/ai-as-a-service). You can read the first chapter free by following this link: http://mng.bz/BZvr. We suggest you do so after you've finished our book, because we provide the foundational knowledge you need to work with any of these more advanced services.

Let's return to a more immediate question: how exactly do you interact with an AWS service? The next section explains how to use the web interface, the CLI, and SDKs to manage and access AWS resources.

1.7   *Interacting with AWS*

When you interact with AWS to configure or use services, you make calls to the API. The API is the entry point to AWS, as figure 1.12 demonstrates.

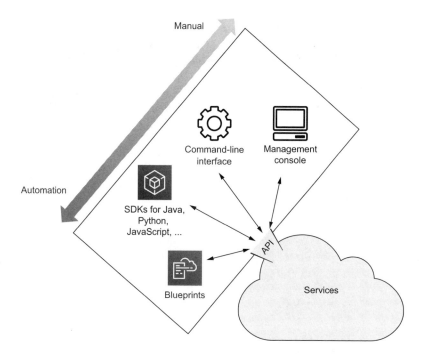

Figure 1.12   Different ways to access the AWS API, allowing you to manage and access AWS services

Next, we'll give you an overview of the tools available for communicating with AWS's APIs: the Management Console, the command-line interface, the SDKs, and infrastructure blueprints. We will compare the different tools, and you will learn how to use all of them while working your way through the book.

1.7.1   *Management Console*

The AWS Management Console allows you to manage and access AWS services through a graphical user interface (GUI), which works with modern browsers on desktop computers, laptops, and tablets. See figure 1.13.

When getting started or experimenting with AWS, the Management Console is the best place to start. It helps you to gain a quick overview of the different services. The Management Console is also a good way to set up a cloud infrastructure for development and testing.

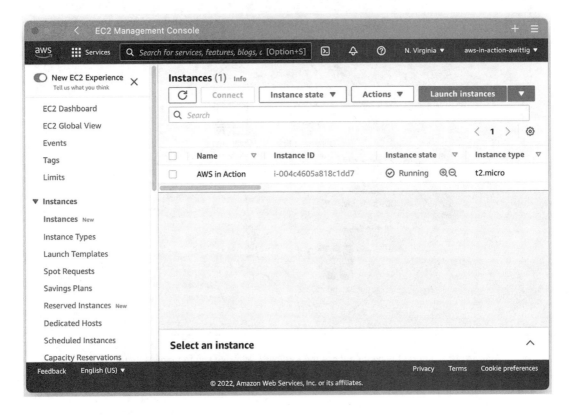

Figure 1.13   The AWS Management Console offers a GUI to manage and access AWS services.

1.7.2   *Command-line interface*

The command-line interface (CLI) allows you to manage and access AWS services within your terminal. Because you can use your terminal to automate or semi-automate recurring tasks, the CLI is a valuable tool. You can use the terminal to create new cloud infrastructures based on blueprints, upload files to the object store, or get the details of your infrastructure's networking configuration regularly. Figure 1.14 shows the CLI in action.

If you want to automate parts of your infrastructure with the help of a continuous integration server, like Jenkins, the CLI is the right tool for the job. The CLI offers a convenient way to access the API and combine multiple calls into a script.

You can even begin to automate your infrastructure with scripts by chaining multiple CLI calls together. The CLI is available for Windows, Mac, and Linux, as well as PowerShell.

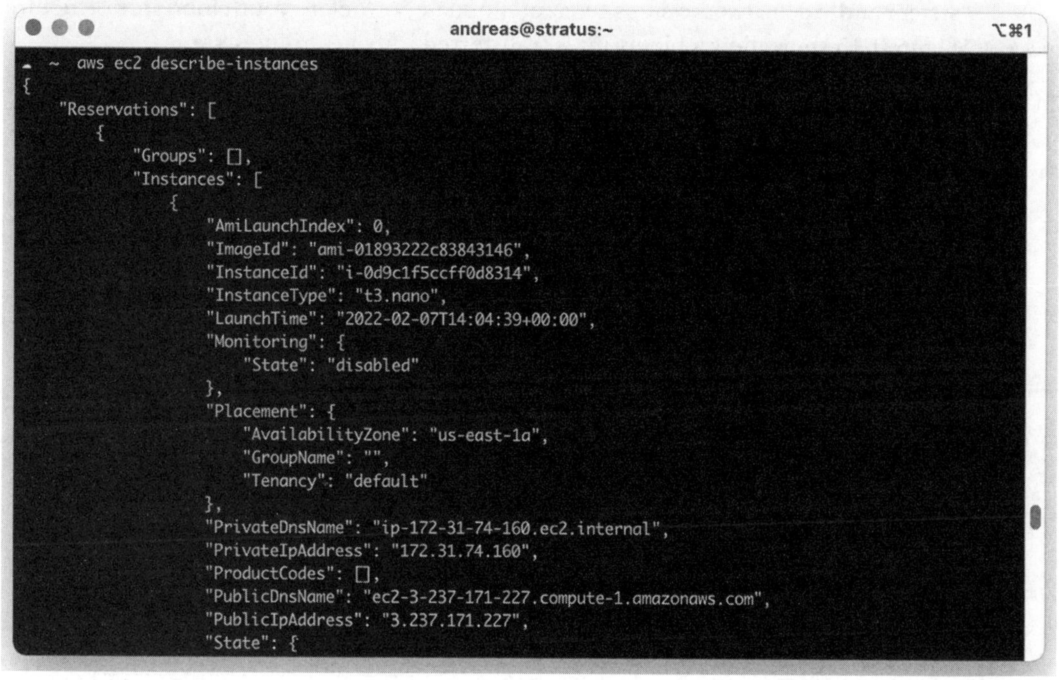

Figure 1.14 The CLI allows you to manage and access AWS services from your terminal.

1.7.3 SDKs

Use your favorite programming language to interact with the AWS API. AWS offers SDKs for the following platforms and languages:

▪ JavaScript	▪ Python	▪ PHP
▪ .NET	▪ Ruby	▪ Java
▪ Go	▪ Node.js	▪ C++

SDKs are typically used to integrate AWS services into applications. If you're doing software development and want to integrate an AWS service like a NoSQL database or a push-notification service, an SDK is the right choice for the job. Some services, such as queues and topics, must be used with an SDK.

1.7.4 Blueprints

A *blueprint* is a description of your system containing all resources and their dependencies. An Infrastructure as Code tool compares your blueprint with the current system and calculates the steps to create, update, or delete your cloud infrastructure. Figure 1.15 shows how a blueprint is transferred into a running system.

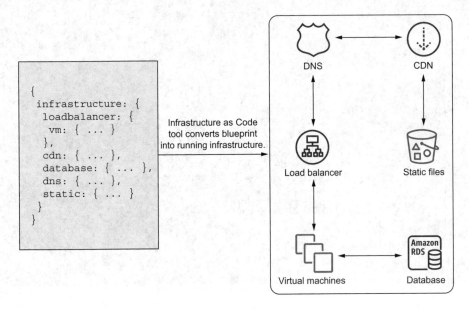

```
{
  infrastructure: {
    loadbalancer: {
      vm: { ... }
    },
    cdn: { ... },
    database: { ... },
    dns: { ... },
    static: { ... }
  }
}
```

Infrastructure as Code tool converts blueprint into running infrastructure.

DNS   CDN

Load balancer   Static files

Virtual machines   Database

Figure 1.15   Infrastructure automation with blueprints

Consider using blueprints if you have to control many or complex environments. Blueprints will help you to automate the configuration of your infrastructure in the cloud. You can use them to set up a network and launch virtual machines, for example.

Automating your infrastructure is also possible by writing your own source code with the help of the CLI or the SDKs. Doing so, however, requires you to resolve dependencies, to make sure you are able to update different versions of your infrastructure, and to handle errors yourself. As you will see in chapter 4, using a blueprint and an Infrastructure-as-Code tool solves these challenges for you. It's time to get started creating your AWS account and exploring AWS practice after all that theory.

1.8   *Creating an AWS account*

Before you can start using AWS, you need to create an account, which is a basket for all your cloud resources. You can attach multiple users to an account if multiple people need access to it; by default, your account will have one AWS account root user. To create an account, you need the following:

- A telephone number to validate your identity
- A credit card to pay your bills

USING AN OLD ACCOUNT?   It is possible to use your existing AWS account while working through this book. In this case, your usage might not be covered by the Free Tier, so you might have to pay for the use.

Also, if you created your existing AWS account before December 4, 2013, please create a new one, because some legacy problems might cause trouble when following our examples.

MULTIPLE AWS ACCOUNTS?   It is fine to create more than one AWS account. AWS even encourages you to do so, to isolate different workloads.

1.8.1   Signing up

The sign-up process consists of five steps:

1   Providing login credentials
2   Providing contact information
3   Providing payment details
4   Verifying your identity
5   Choosing a support plan

Point your favorite web browser to https://aws.amazon.com, and click the Create an AWS Account button.

1. PROVIDING LOGIN CREDENTIALS

Creating an AWS account starts with defining a unique AWS account name, as shown in figure 1.16. The AWS account name has to be globally unique among all AWS customers. Try `aws-in-action-$yourname` and replace `$yourname` with your name. In addition

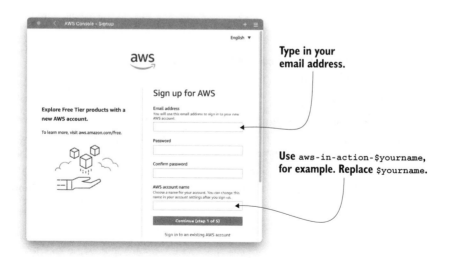

Figure 1.16   First step of creating an AWS account: account name and password

to the account name, you have to specify an email address and a password used to authenticate the root user of your AWS account.

We advise you to choose a strong password to prevent misuse of your account. *Use a password consisting of at least 20 characters.* Protecting your AWS account from unwanted access is crucial to avoid data breaches, data loss, or unwanted resource usage on your behalf.

2. PROVIDING CONTACT INFORMATION

The next step, as shown in figure 1.17, is adding your contact information. Fill in all the required fields, and continue.

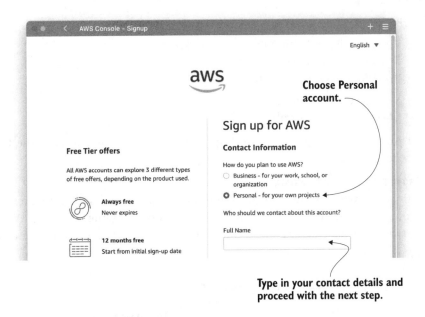

Figure 1.17   Second step of creating an AWS account: contact details

3. PROVIDING PAYMENT DETAILS

Next, the screen shown in figure 1.18 asks for your payment information. Provide your credit card information. There's an option to change the currency setting from USD to AUD, BRL, CAD, CHF, CNY, DKK, EUR, GBP, HKD, JPY, KRW, NOK, NZD, SEK, SGD, or ZAR later if that's more convenient for you. If you choose this option, the amount in USD is converted into your local currency at the end of the month.

Figure 1.18 Third step of creating an AWS account: payment details

4. VERIFYING YOUR IDENTITY

The next step is to verify your identity. Figure 1.19 shows the first step of the process.

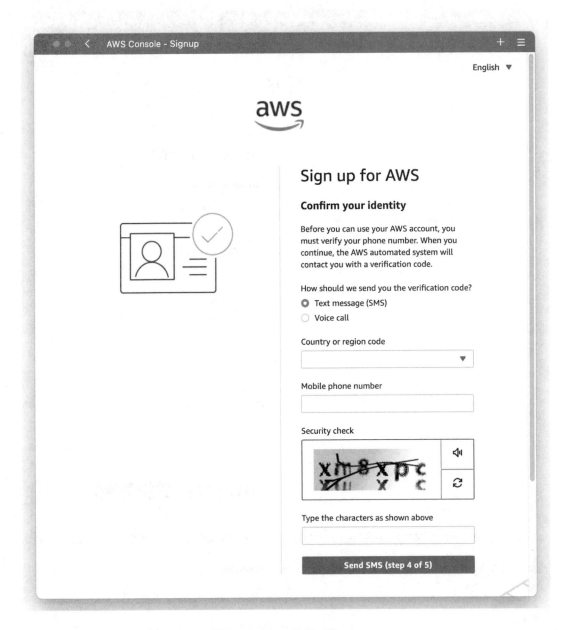

Figure 1.19   Fourth step of creating an AWS account: verify identity

After you complete the first part of the form, you'll receive a text message or call from AWS. All you need to do is to type in the verification code.

5. CHOOSING A SUPPORT PLAN

The last step is to choose a support plan; see figure 1.20. For now, select the Basic plan, which is free. When running a production workload an AWS, we recommend at least a Developer plan to be able to ask questions about upcoming issues.

Figure 1.20   Fifth step of creating an AWS account: choose a support plan

High five! You're done. Click Go to the AWS Management Console, as shown in figure 1.21, to sign in to your AWS account for the first time.

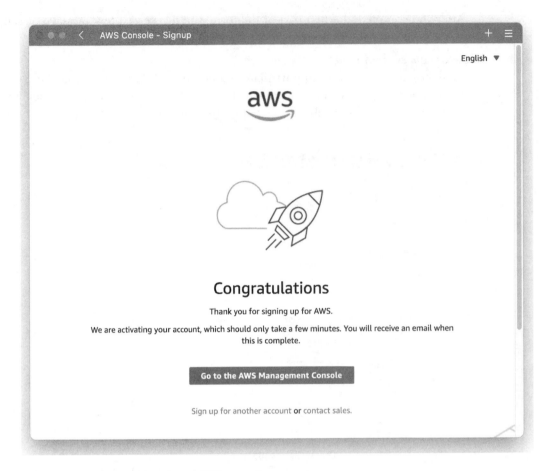

Figure 1.21   Fifth step of creating an AWS account: success!

1.8.2   Signing in

You now have an AWS account and are ready to sign in to the AWS Management Console. As mentioned earlier, the Management Console is a web-based tool you can use to control AWS resources; it makes most of the functionality of the AWS API available to you. Figure 1.22 shows the sign-in form at https://console.aws.amazon.com. Choose Root User and enter your email address, click Next, and then enter your password to sign in.

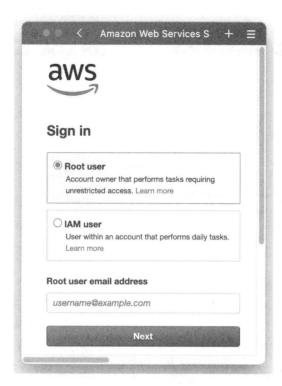

Figure 1.22 Sign in with the AWS account root user.

After you have signed in successfully, you are forwarded to the start page of the Management Console, as shown in figure 1.23.

The most important part is the navigation bar at the top, shown in figure 1.24. It consists of the following eight sections:

- *AWS*—The dashboard of the Management Console shows an overview of your AWS account.
- *Services*—Provides access to all AWS services.
- *Search*—Allows you to search for services, features, and more.
- *Terminal*—Spin up a terminal with access to your cloud resources in the browser.
- *Notifications*—View alerts and notifications by AWS, for example, planned downtimes or outages.
- *Help*—Get support by the community, experts, or AWS support.
- *Region*—Select the region you want to manage.
- *Account*—Manage your AWS account.

Next, you'll make sure to avoid unwanted AWS costs.

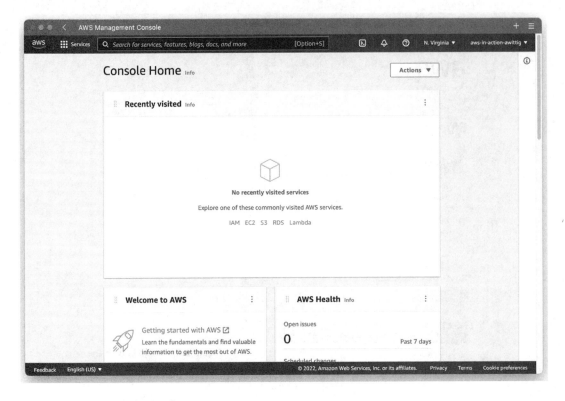

Figure 1.23   The dashboard after logging in for the first time

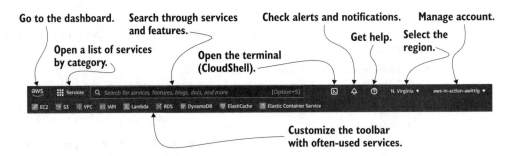

Figure 1.24   AWS Management Console navigation bar

1.9   *Creating a budget alert to keep track of your AWS bill*

At first, the pay-per-use pricing model of AWS might feel unfamiliar to you, because it is not 100% foreseeable what your bill will look like at the end of the month. Most of the examples in this book are covered by the Free Tier, so AWS won't charge you anything. Exceptions are clearly marked. To provide you with the peace of mind needed to learn about AWS in a comfortable environment, you will create a budget next. The budget will notify you via email in case your AWS bill will exceed $5 so you can react quickly.

Before creating a budget, configure a Free Tier usage alert as follows:

1. Open the billing preferences of your AWS account at http://mng.bz/5m8D.
2. Enable Receive Free Tier Usage Alerts, and type in your email address as shown in figure 1.25.
3. Press the Save Preferences button.

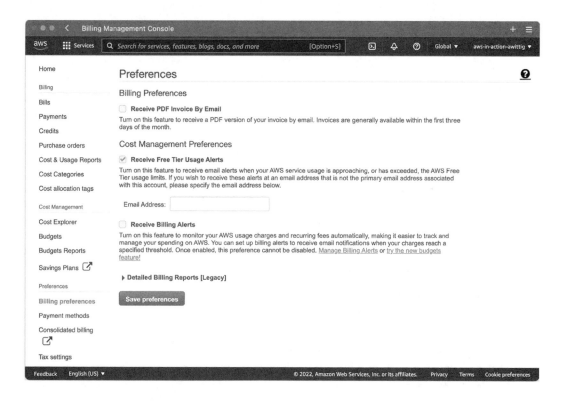

Figure 1.25   Creating a Free Tier usage alert to avoid unwanted costs

Next, you will create a budget that monitors costs incurred and forecasts costs to the end of the month, as described here:

1. Search and open Budgets in the Management Console's navigation bar.
2. Click Create Budget.
3. Select Cost Budget, as shown in figure 1.26.
4. Click Next.

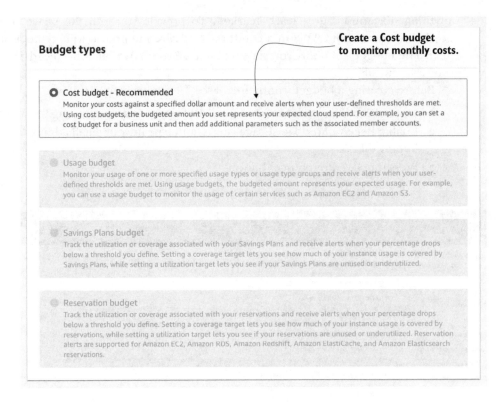

Figure 1.26   Creating a cost budget to monitor incurred and forecasted costs

Next, configure the cost budget as illustrated in figure 1.27 and described next:

1. Choose period Monthly.
2. Select Recurring Budget.
3. Choose the current month and year as start month.
4. Select Fixed to use the same budget for every month of the year.
5. Type in 5 to set the budget to $5 per month.
6. Click Next.

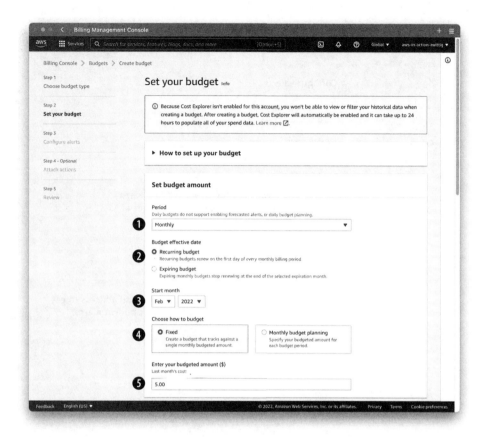

Figure 1.27   Creating a cost budget to monitor incurred and forecasted costs

After defining the budget, it is time to create alerts that will notify you via email as follows (figure 1.28):

1 Click Add Alert Threshold.
2 Type in 100% of budgeted amount.
3 Select trigger Actual to get notified when the incurred costs increase the budget.
4 Type in your email address.
5 Click Add Alert Threshold.
6 Type in 100% of budgeted amount.
7 Select trigger Forecasted to get notified when the forecasted costs increase the budget.
8 Type in your email address.
9 Click Next to proceed.
10 Review the budget, and click Create Budget.

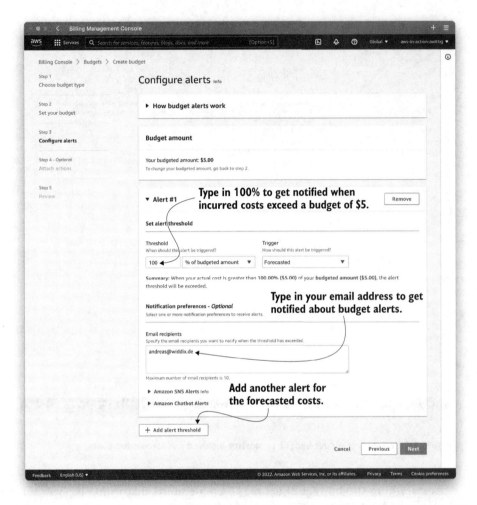

Figure 1.28   **Define alerts to get notified when incurred or forecasted costs exceed your monthly budget.**

That's it—you are ready to get started learning all the services and approaches we cover in the rest of this book. When you forget to shut down or delete resources when following our examples, AWS will notify you in case your monthly bill will exceed $5.

Summary

- Cloud computing, or the cloud, is a metaphor for supply and consumption of IT resources.
- Amazon Web Services (AWS) offers Infrastructure as a Service (IaaS), Platform as a Service (PaaS), and Software as a Service (SaaS).

- AWS is a platform of web services for computing, storing, and networking that work well together.
- Cost savings aren't the only benefit of using AWS. You'll also profit from an innovative and fast-growing platform with flexible capacity, fault-tolerant services, and a worldwide infrastructure.
- Almost any use case can be implemented on AWS, whether it's a widely used web application or a specialized enterprise application with an advanced networking setup.
- You can interact with AWS in many different ways. Control the different services by using the web-based user interface, use code to manage AWS programmatically from the command line or SDKs, or use blueprints to set up, modify, or delete your infrastructure on AWS.
- Pay-per-use is the pricing model for AWS services. Computing power, storage, and networking services are billed similarly to electricity.
- To create an AWS account, all you need is a telephone number and a credit card.
- Creating budget alerts allows you to keep track of your AWS bill and get notified whenever you exceed the Free Tier.

A simple example: WordPress in 15 minutes

This chapter covers

- Creating a cloud infrastructure for WordPress
- Exploring a cloud infrastructure consisting of a load balancer, virtual machines, a database, and a network filesystem
- Estimating costs of a cloud infrastructure
- Shutting down a cloud infrastructure

Having looked at why AWS is such a great choice to run web applications in the cloud, in this chapter, you'll explore migrating a simple web application to AWS by setting up a sample cloud infrastructure within 15 minutes. Over the course of the book, we will revisit the WordPress example to understand the concepts in more detail. For example, we will take a look at the relational database in chapter 10 and learn how to add and remove virtual machines based on the current load in chapter 17.

> **NOTE** The example in this chapter is totally covered by the Free Tier (see section 1.4.1 for details). As long as you don't run this example longer than a few days, you won't pay anything for it. Keep in mind that this applies only if you created a fresh AWS account for this book and there is

38

nothing else going on in your AWS account. Try to complete the chapter within a few days, because you'll clean up your account at the end of the chapter.

Imagine you work for a mid-sized company that runs a blog to attract new software and operations engineers and uses WordPress as the content management system. Around 1,000 people visit the blog daily. You are paying $250 per month for the on-premises infrastructure. This seems expensive to you, particularly because at the moment, the blog suffers from several outages per month.

To leave a good impression on potential candidates, the infrastructure should be highly available, which is defined as an uptime of 99.99%. Therefore, you are evaluating new options to operate WordPress reliably. AWS seems to be a good fit. As a proof of concept, you want to evaluate whether a migration is possible, so you need to do the following:

- Set up a highly available infrastructure for WordPress.
- Estimate the monthly costs of the infrastructure.
- Come to a decision and delete the infrastructure afterward.

WordPress is written in PHP and uses a MySQL database to store data. Besides that, data like user uploads is stored on disk. Apache is used as the web server to serve the pages. With this information in mind, it's time to map your requirements to AWS services.

2.1 Creating your Infrastructure

You'll use the following five AWS services to copy the old infrastructure to AWS:

- *Elastic Load Balancing (ELB)*—AWS offers a load balancer as a service. The load balancer distributes traffic to a bunch of virtual machines and is highly available by default. Requests are routed to virtual machines as long as their health check succeeds. You'll use the Application Load Balancer (ALB), which operates on layer 7 (HTTP and HTTPS).
- *Elastic Compute Cloud (EC2)*—The EC2 service provides virtual machines. You'll use a Linux machine with an optimized distribution called Amazon Linux to install Apache, PHP, and WordPress. You aren't limited to Amazon Linux; you could also choose Ubuntu, Debian, Red Hat, or Windows. Virtual machines can fail, so you need at least two of them. The load balancer will distribute the traffic between them. In case a virtual machine fails, the load balancer will stop sending traffic to the failed VM, and the remaining VM will need to handle all requests until the failed VM is replaced.
- *Relational Database Service (RDS) for MySQL*—WordPress relies on the popular MySQL database. AWS provides MySQL with its RDS. You choose the database size (storage, CPU, RAM), and RDS takes over operating tasks like creating backups and installing patches and updates. RDS can also provide a highly available MySQL database using replication.

- *Elastic File System (EFS)*—WordPress itself consists of PHP and other application files. User uploads—for example, images added to an article—are stored as files as well. By using a network filesystem, your virtual machines can access these files. EFS provides a scalable, highly available, and durable network filesystem using the NFSv4.1 protocol.
- *Security groups*—Control incoming and outgoing traffic to your virtual machine, your database, or your load balancer with a firewall. For example, use a security group allowing incoming HTTP traffic from the internet to port 80 of the load balancer. Or restrict network access to your database on port 3306 to the virtual machines running your web servers.

Figure 2.1 shows all the parts of the infrastructure in action. Sounds like a lot of stuff to set up, so let's get started!

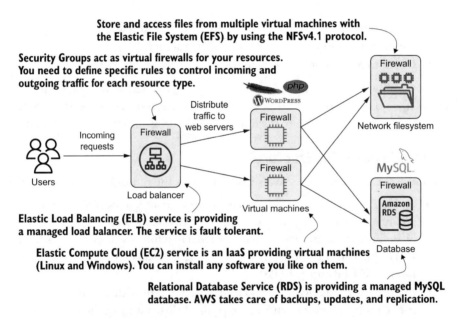

Figure 2.1   The company's blogging infrastructure consists of two load-balanced web servers running WordPress, a network filesystem, and a MySQL database server.

If you expect pages of instructions, you'll be happy to know that you can create all of this with just a few clicks using a service called AWS CloudFormation, which you will learn about in detail in chapter 4. AWS CloudFormation does all of the following automatically in the background:

1 Creates a load balancer (ELB)
2 Creates a MySQL database (RDS)
3 Creates a network filesystem (EFS)
4 Creates and attaches firewall rules (security groups)

5   Creates two virtual machines running web servers:
   a   Creates two virtual machines (EC2)
   b   Mounts the network filesystem (EFS)
   c   Installs Apache and PHP
   d   Downloads and extracts the 4.8 release of WordPress
   e   Configures WordPress to use the created MySQL database (RDS)
   f   Starts the Apache web server

To create the infrastructure for your proof of concept, open the AWS Management Console at https://console.aws.amazon.com. Click Services in the navigation bar, and select CloudFormation. You can use the search function to find CloudFormation more easily.

> **DEFAULT REGION FOR EXAMPLES**   All examples in this book use N. Virginia (also called us-east-1) as the default region. Exceptions are indicated. Please make sure you switch to the region N. Virginia before starting to work on an example. When using the AWS Management Console, you can check and switch the region on the right side of the main navigation bar at the top.

Click Create Stack, and choose With New Resources (Standard) to start the four-step wizard, as shown in figure 2.2. Choose Template Is Ready, and enter the Amazon S3

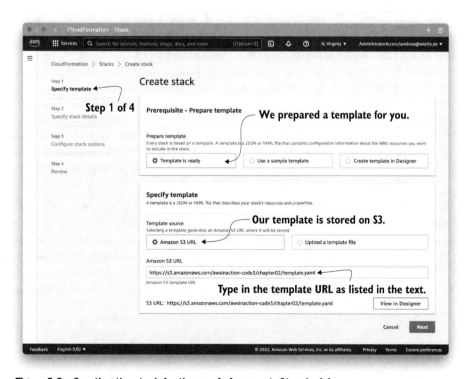

Figure 2.2   Creating the stack for the proof of concept: Step 1 of 4

URL https://s3.amazonaws.com/awsinaction-code3/chapter02/template.yaml to use the template prepared for this chapter. Proceed with the next step of the wizard.

Specify wordpress as the Stack name and, in the Parameters section, set the WordpressAdminPassword to a password of your choice that you are not using somewhere else, as shown in figure 2.3.

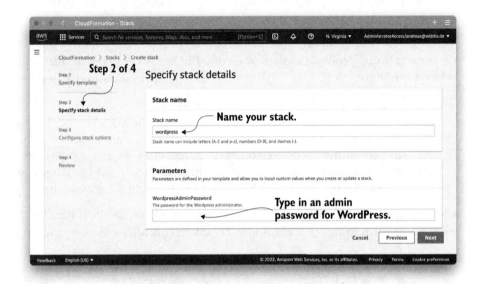

Figure 2.3   Creating the stack for the proof of concept: Step 2 of 4

The next step is to specify tags for your infrastructure, as illustrated in figure 2.4. A *tag* consists of a key and a value and can be used to add metadata to all parts of your infrastructure. You can use tags to differentiate between testing and production resources, add a cost center to easily track costs in your organization, or mark resources that belong to a certain application if you host multiple applications in the same AWS account.

Figure 2.4 shows how to configure the tag. In this example, you'll use a tag to mark all resources that belong to the wordpress system. This will help you to easily find all the parts of your infrastructure later. Use a custom tag consisting of the key—system—and the value—wordpress. Afterward, press the Next button to proceed to the next step.

You can define your own tags as long as the key name is less than 128 characters and the value is less than 256 characters.

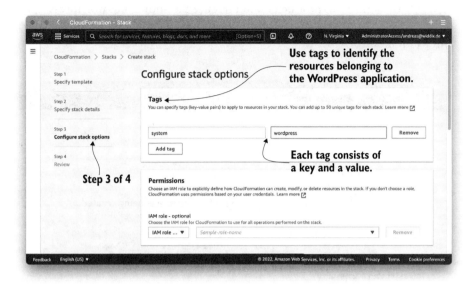

Figure 2.4 Creating the stack for the proof of concept: Step 3 of 4

Additional CloudFormation stack options

It is possible to define specific permissions used to manage resources, as well as to set up notifications and other advanced options. You won't need these options for 99% of the use cases, so we don't cover them in our book. Have a look at the Cloud-Formation User Guide (http://mng.bz/deqv) if you're interested in the details.

Figure 2.5 illustrates that all you need to do is to acknowledge that CloudFormation will create IAM resources and click Create Stack.

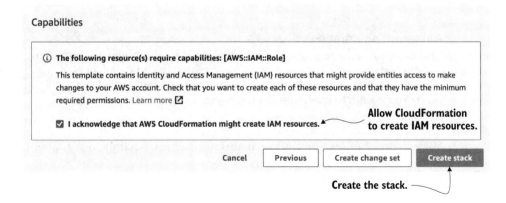

Figure 2.5 Creating the stack for the proof of concept: Step 4 of 4

Your infrastructure will now be created. Figure 2.6 shows that wordpress is in the state of CREATE_IN_PROGRESS. It's a good time to take a break; come back in 15 minutes, and you'll be surprised.

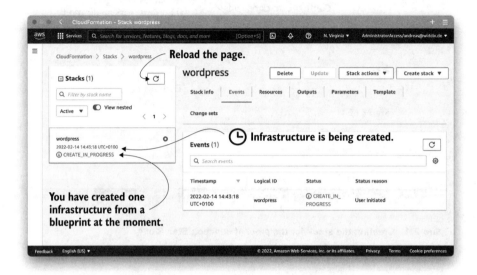

Figure 2.6   CloudFormation is creating the resources needed for WordPress.

After all the needed resources have been created, the status will change to CREATE _COMPLETE. Be patient and click the refresh button from time to time if your status continues to show CREATE_IN_PROGRESS.

Select the check box at the beginning of the row containing your wordpress stack. Switch to the Outputs tab, as shown in figure 2.7. There you'll find the URL to your WordPress installation; click the link to open it in your browser.

You may ask yourself, how does this work? The answer is *automation*.

Automation references

One of the key concepts of AWS is automation. You can automate everything. In the background, your cloud infrastructure was created based on a blueprint. You'll learn more about blueprints and the concept of programming your infrastructure in chapter 4. You'll learn to automate the deployment of software in chapter 15.

You'll explore the blogging infrastructure in the next section to get a better understanding of the services you're using.

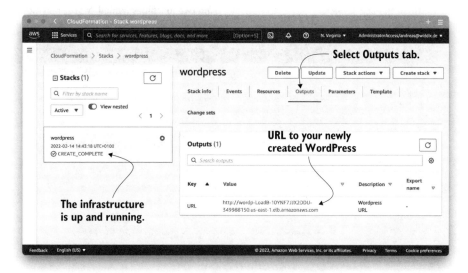

Figure 2.7   The blogging infrastructure has been created successfully.

2.2   Exploring your infrastructure

Now that you've created your blogging infrastructure, let's take a closer look at it. Your infrastructure consists of the following:

- Web servers running on virtual machines
- Load balancer
- MySQL database
- Network filesystem

2.2.1   Virtual machines

First, use the navigation bar to open the EC2 service as shown in figure 2.8. Next, select Instances from the subnavigation options. A list showing two virtual machines named wordpress shows up. When you select one of those instances, details about the virtual machine appear below.

You're now looking at the details of your virtual machine, also called an EC2 instance. Some interesting details follow:

- *Instance ID*—The ID of the virtual machine.
- *Instance type*—The size of the virtual machine (CPU and memory).
- *IPv4 Public IP*—The IP address that is reachable over the internet.
- *AMI ID*—Remember that you used the Amazon Linux OS. If you click the AMI ID, you'll see the version number of the OS, among other things.

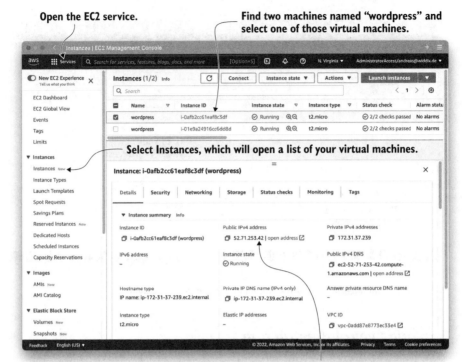

Figure 2.8   **The virtual machines are running a web server to deliver WordPress.**

Select the Monitoring tab to see how your virtual machine is used. This tab is essential if you really want to know how your infrastructure is doing. AWS collects some metrics and shows them here. For example, if the CPU is using more than 80% of its capacity, it might be a good time to add another virtual machine to prevent increasing response times. You will learn more about monitoring virtual machines in section 3.2.

2.2.2   *Load balancer*

Next, have a look at the load balancer, shown in figure 2.9, which is part of the EC2 service as well. There is no need to switch to a different service in the Management Console—just click Load Balancer in the subnavigation options on the left-hand side of the screen. Select your load balancer from the list to show more details. Your *internet-facing* load balancer is accessible from the internet via an automatically generated DNS name.

The load balancer forwards an incoming request to one of your virtual machines. A target group is used to define the targets for a load balancer. You'll find your target

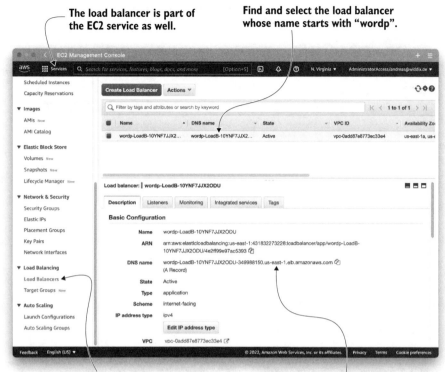

The load balancer is part of the EC2 service as well.

Find and select the load balancer whose name starts with "wordp".

Select Load Balancers to look at the load balancer distributing incoming requests to one of the VMs.

Shows details about the virtual machine, for example, its public DNS name

Figure 2.9   Get to know the load balancer.

group after switching to Target Groups through the subnavigation options of the EC2 service, as shown in figure 2.10.

The load balancer performs health checks to ensure requests are routed only to healthy targets. Two virtual machines are listed as targets for the target group. As you can see in the figure, the status of both virtual machines is healthy.

As before, on the Monitoring tab you can find interesting metrics that you should watch in production. If the traffic pattern changes suddenly, this indicates a potential problem with your system. You'll also find metrics indicating the number of HTTP errors, which will help you to monitor and debug your system.

2.2.3   *MySQL database*

The MySQL database is an important part of your infrastructure; you'll look at it next. To do so, open the Relational Database Service (RDS) via the main navigation. Afterward, select Databases from the subnavigation options. Select the database using the engine called MySQL community, as illustrated in figure 2.11.

Find and select the target group whose name starts with "wordp".

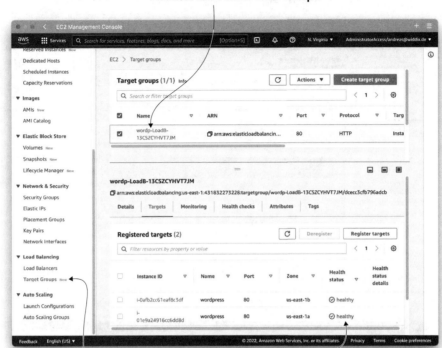

Select Target Groups, which is used by the load balancer to identify the targets when forwarding incoming requests.

Remember those two VMs you just took a closer look at? Both are listed here as targets for the load balancer. As long as the status is "healthy," the load balancer forwards requests to the machine.

Figure 2.10   Details of target group belonging to the load balancer

Open the RDS service.

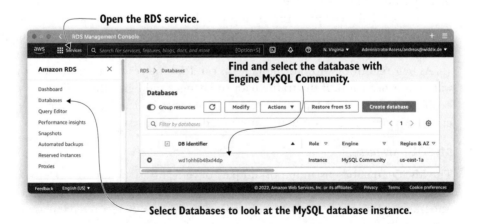

Find and select the database with Engine MySQL Community.

Select Databases to look at the MySQL database instance.

Figure 2.11   Finding the MySQL database

WordPress requires a MySQL database, so you have launched a database instance with the MySQL engine as noted in figure 2.12. Your blog receives a low amount of traffic, so the database doesn't need to be very powerful. A small instance class with a single virtual CPU and 1 GB memory is sufficient. Instead of using SSD storage, you are using magnetic disks, which is cheaper and sufficient for a web application with around 1,000 visitors per day.

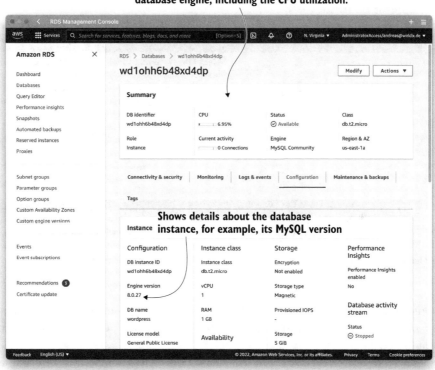

Figure 2.12   Details of the MySQL database storing data for the blogging infrastructure

As you'll see in chapter 10, other database engines, such as PostgreSQL or Oracle Database, are available, as well as more powerful instance classes, offering up to 96 cores with 768 GB memory, for example.

Common web applications use a database to store and query data. That is true for WordPress as well. The content management system (CMS) stores blog posts, comments, and more within a MySQL database.

WordPress also stores data outside the database on disk. For example, if an author uploads an image for their blog post, the file is stored on disk. The same is true when you are installing plug-ins and themes as an administrator.

2.2.4 *Network filesystem*

The Elastic File System (EFS) is used to store files and access them from multiple virtual machines. EFS is a storage service accessible through the NFS protocol. To keep things simple, all files that belong to WordPress, including PHP, HTML, CSS, and PNG files, are stored on EFS so they can be accessed from all virtual machines.

Open the EFS service via the main navigation as shown in figure 2.13. Next, select the filesystem whose name starts with "wordpress".

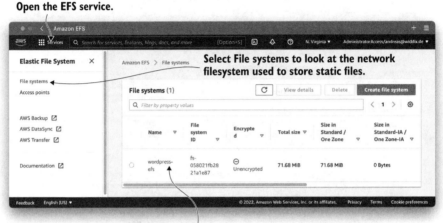

Figure 2.13   The NFS used to store the WordPress application and user uploads

Figure 2.14 shows the details of the filesystem. For example, the throughput mode *bursting* is used, to allow high I/O throughput for small periods of time during the day at low cost.

To mount the Elastic File System from a virtual machine, mount targets are needed. You should use two mount targets for fault tolerance. The network filesystem is accessible using a DNS name for the virtual machines.

Now it's time to evaluate costs. You'll analyze the costs of your blogging infrastructure in the next section.

2.3 *How much does it cost?*

Part of evaluating AWS is estimating costs. We recommend using the AWS Pricing Calculator to do so. We created a cost estimation including the load balancer, the virtual machines, the database, and the network file system. Go to http://mng.bz/VyEW to check out the results, which are also shown in figure 2.15. We estimate costs of about $75 for hosting WordPress on AWS in a highly available manner, which means all components are distributed among at least two different data centers. Don't worry—the

Shows details about the filesystem, for example, the throughput mode Bursting,
which allows high I/O throughout for short periods of time during the day

Figure 2.14   The details of the EFS

example in this chapter is covered by the Free Tier. Our cost estimation does not consider the Free Tier, because it applies for only the first 12 months.

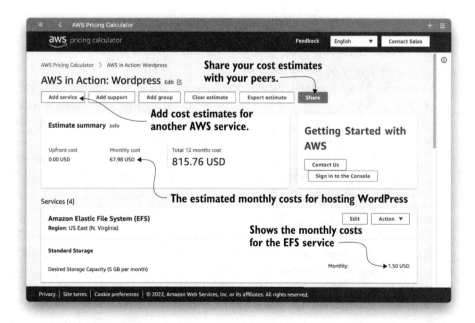

Figure 2.15   Blogging infrastructure cost calculation

Table 2.1 summarizes the results from the AWS Pricing Calculator.

Table 2.1   More detailed cost calculation for blogging infrastructure

AWS service	Infrastructure	Pricing	Monthly cost
EC2	Virtual machines	2 * 730 hours * $0.0116 (t2.micro)	$16.94
EC2	Storage	2 * 8 GB * $0.10 per month	$1.60
Application Load Balancer	Load balancer	730 hours * $0.0225 (load balancer hour) 200 GB per month	$18.03
Application Load Balancer	Outgoing traffic	100 GB * $0.00 (first 100 GB) 100 GB * $0.09 (up to 10 TB)	$9.00
RDS	MySQL database instance (primary + standby)	732.5 hours * $0.017 * 2	$24.82
RDS	Storage	5 GB * $0.115 * 2	$2.30
EFS	Storage	5 GB * $0.3	$1.50
			$74.19

Keep in mind that this is only an estimate. You're billed based on actual use at the end of the month. Everything is on demand and usually billed by seconds or giga-byte of usage. The following factors might influence how much you actually use this infrastructure:

- *Traffic processed by the load balancer*—Expect costs to go down in December and in the summer when people are on vacation and not looking at your blog.
- *Storage needed for the database*—If your company increases the amount of content in your blog, the database will grow, so the cost of storage will increase.
- *Storage needed on the NFS*—User uploads, plug-ins, and themes increase the amount of storage needed on the NFS, which will also increase the cost.
- *Number of virtual machines needed*—Virtual machines are billed by seconds of usage. If two virtual machines aren't enough to handle all the traffic during the day, you may need a third machine. In that case, you'll consume more seconds of virtual machines.

Estimating the cost of your infrastructure is a complicated task, but that is also true if your infrastructure doesn't run in AWS. The benefit of using AWS is that it's flexible. If your estimated number of virtual machines is too high, you can get rid of a machine and stop paying for it. You will learn more about the pricing model of the different AWS services throughout the course of this book.

You have completed the proof of concept for migrating your company's blog to AWS. It's time to shut down the infrastructure and complete your migration evaluation.

2.4   Deleting your infrastructure

Your evaluation has confirmed that you can migrate the infrastructure needed for the company's blog to AWS from a technical standpoint. You have estimated that a load balancer, virtual machines, and a MySQL database, as well as a NFS capable of serving 1,000 people visiting the blog per day, will cost you around $75 per month on AWS. That is all you need to come to a decision.

Because the infrastructure does not contain any important data and you have finished your evaluation, you can delete all the resources and stop paying for them.

Go to the CloudFormation service in the Management Console, and take the following steps, as shown in figure 2.16:

1 Select your wordpress stack.
2 Click the Delete button.

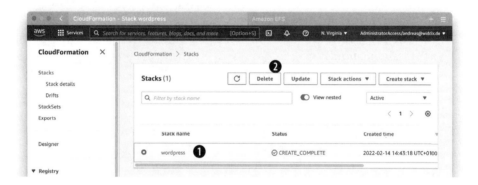

Figure 2.16   **Deleting your blogging infrastructure**

After you confirm the deletion of the infrastructure, as shown in figure 2.17, it takes a few minutes for AWS to delete all of the infrastructure's dependencies.

Figure 2.17   **Confirming deletion of your blogging infrastructure**

This is an efficient way to manage your infrastructure. Just as the infrastructure's creation was automated, its deletion is also. You can create and delete infrastructure on demand whenever you like. You pay for infrastructure only when you create and run it.

Summary

- Creating a cloud infrastructure for WordPress and any other application can be fully automated.
- AWS CloudFormation is a tool provided by AWS for free. It allows you to automate the managing of your cloud infrastructure.
- The infrastructure for a web application like WordPress can be created at any time on demand, without any up-front commitment for how long you'll use it.
- You pay for your infrastructure based on usage. For example, you pay for a virtual machine per second of usage.
- The infrastructure required to run WordPress consists of several parts, such as virtual machines, load balancers, databases, and network filesystems.
- The whole infrastructure can be deleted with one click. The process is powered by automation.

Part 2

Building virtual infrastructure consisting of computers and networking

Computing power and network connectivity have become a basic need for private households, medium-sized enterprises, and big corporations. Operating hardware in data centers that are in-house or outsourced has covered these needs in the past. Now the cloud is revolutionizing the way you can access computing power.

Virtual machines can be started and stopped on demand to fulfill your computing needs within minutes. Being able to install software on virtual machines enables you to execute your computing tasks without needing to buy or rent hardware.

If you want to understand AWS, you have to dive into the possibilities of the API working behind the scenes. You can control every single service on AWS by sending requests to a REST API. Based on this, a variety of solutions can help you automate your overall infrastructure. Infrastructure automation is a big advantage of the cloud compared to hosting on-premises. This part will guide you into infrastructure orchestration and the automated deployment of applications.

Creating virtual networks allows you to build closed and secure network environments on AWS and to connect these networks with your home or corporate network.

Chapter 3 covers working with virtual machines. You will learn about the key concepts of the EC2 service.

Chapter 4 contains different approaches to automate your infrastructure. You will learn how to make use of Infrastructure as Code.

Chapter 5 is about networking. You will learn how to secure your system with a virtual private network and firewalls.

Chapter 6 is about a new way of computing: functions. You will learn how to automate operational tasks with AWS Lambda.

Using virtual machines: EC2

This chapter covers

- Launching a virtual machine with Linux
- Controlling a virtual machine remotely via the Session Manager
- Monitoring and debugging a virtual machine
- Saving costs for virtual machines

It's impressive what you can achieve with the computing power of the smartphone in your pocket or the laptop in your bag. But if your task requires massive computing power or high network traffic, or needs to run reliably 24/7, a virtual machine is a better fit. With a virtual machine, you get access to a slice of a physical machine located in a data center. On AWS, virtual machines are offered by the service called Elastic Compute Cloud (EC2).

In this chapter, you will learn how to launch and manage a virtual machine on AWS. Also, we will show you how to connect to a virtual machine to install or configure applications. On top of that, you will learn how to monitor a virtual machine. Last but not least, we will introduce the different pricing options of the Elastic Compute Cloud (EC2) to make sure you get the most computing power for your money.

Not all examples are covered by Free Tier

The examples in this chapter are not all covered by the Free Tier. A special warning message appears when an example incurs costs. As for the other examples, as long as you don't run them longer than a few days, you won't pay anything for them. Keep in mind that this applies only if you created a fresh AWS account for this book and nothing else is going on in your AWS account. Try to complete the chapter within a few days; you'll clean up your account at the end.

3.1   *Exploring a virtual machine*

A virtual machine (VM) runs on a physical machine isolated from other virtual machines by the hypervisor; it consists of CPUs, memory, networking interfaces, and storage. The physical machine is called the *host machine*, and the VMs running on it are called *guests*. A *hypervisor* is responsible for isolating the guests from each other and for scheduling requests to the hardware by providing a virtual hardware platform to the guest system. Figure 3.1 shows these layers of virtualization.

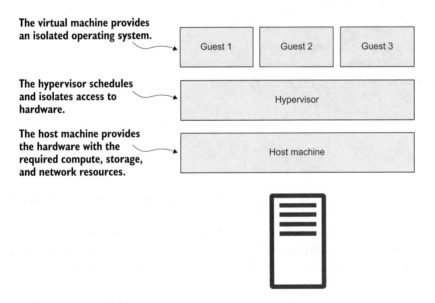

Figure 3.1   Layers of virtualization

Typical use cases for a virtual machine follow:

- Hosting a web application such as WordPress
- Operating an enterprise application, such as an ERP (enterprise resource planning) application
- Transforming or analyzing data, such as encoding video files

3.1.1 Launching a virtual machine

In the following example, you will launch a virtual machine to run a tool called *Link-Checker* that checks a website for broken links. Checking for links resulting in "404 Not Found" errors improves the usability and SEO score of your website. You could run LinkChecker on your local machine as well, but an EC2 instance in Amazon's data center offers more compute and networking capacities. As shown here, it takes only a few clicks to launch a virtual machine, which AWS calls an EC2 instance:

1 Open the AWS Management Console at https://console.aws.amazon.com.
2 Make sure you're in the N. Virginia (US East) region (see figure 3.2), because we optimized our examples for this region.
3 Click Services and search for EC2.
4 Click Launch Instance to start the wizard for launching a virtual machine, as shown in figure 3.2.

Figure 3.2 The EC2 dashboard gives you an overview of all parts of the service.

A form will appear, guiding you through the following details needed to create a virtual machine:

1 Naming the virtual machine
2 Selecting the operating system (OS)
3 Choosing the size of your virtual machine

4   Configuring details

5   Adding storage

6   Configuring a firewall

7   Granting the virtual machine permissions to access other AWS services

NAMING THE VIRTUAL MACHINE

To make it easy to find your virtual machine later, it is recommended you assign a name to it. That's especially important when other people have access to the same AWS account. Figure 3.3 shows the details.

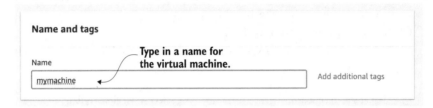

Figure 3.3   Naming the virtual machine

SELECTING THE OPERATING SYSTEM

Next, you need to choose an operating system (OS). In AWS, the OS comes bundled with preinstalled software for your virtual machine; this bundle is called an *Amazon Machine Image* (AMI). Select Amazon Linux 2 AMI (HVM), as shown in figure 3.4.

Figure 3.4   Choose the OS for your virtual machine.

The AMI is the basis for your virtual machine starts. AMIs are offered by AWS, third-party providers, and by the community. AWS offers the Amazon Linux AMI, which is based on Red Hat Enterprise Linux and optimized for use with EC2. You'll also find popular Linux distributions and AMIs with Microsoft Windows Server as well as more AMIs with preinstalled third-party software in the AWS Marketplace.

When choosing an AMI, start by thinking about the requirements of the application you want to run on the VM. Your knowledge and experience with a specific operating system are other important factors when deciding which AMI to start with. It's also important that you trust the AMI's publisher. We prefer working with Amazon Linux, because it's maintained and optimized by AWS.

Virtual appliances on AWS

As shown in the following figure, a virtual appliance is an image of a virtual machine containing an OS and preconfigured software. Virtual appliances are used when the hypervisor starts a new VM. Because a virtual appliance contains a fixed state, every time you start a VM based on a virtual appliance, you'll get exactly the same result. You can reproduce virtual appliances as often as needed, so you can use them to eliminate the cost of installing and configuring complex stacks of software. Virtual appliances are used by virtualization tools from VMware, Microsoft, and Oracle, and for Infrastructure as a Service (IaaS) offerings in the cloud.

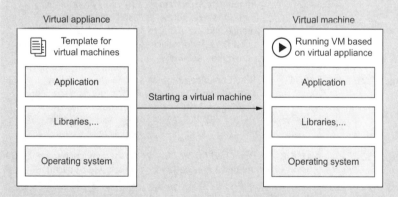

A virtual appliance contains a template for a virtual machine.

The AMI is a special type of virtual appliance for use with the EC2 service. An AMI technically consists of a read-only filesystem including the OS, additional software, and configuration. You can also use AMIs for deploying software on AWS, but the AMI does not include the kernel of the OS. The kernel is loaded from an Amazon Kernel Image (AKI).

Nowadays, AWS uses a virtualization called Nitro. Nitro combines a KVM-based hypervisor with customized hardware (ASICs), aiming to provide a performance that is indistinguishable from bare metal machines.

(continued)

The current generations of VMs on AWS use hardware-assisted virtualization. The technology is called a hardware virtual machine (HVM). A virtual machine run by an AMI based on HVM uses a fully virtualized set of hardware and can take advantage of extensions that provide fast access to the underlying hardware.

CHOOSING THE SIZE OF YOUR VIRTUAL MACHINE

It's now time to choose the computing power needed for your virtual machine. AWS classifies computing power into instance types. An instance type primarily describes the number of virtual CPUs and the amount of memory.

Table 3.1 shows examples of instance types for different use cases. The prices represent the actual prices in USD for a Linux VM in the US East (N. Virginia) region, as recorded April 5, 2022.

Table 3.1   Examples of instance families and instance types

Instance type	Virtual CPUs	Memory	Description	Typical use case	Monthly cost (USD)
t2.nano	1	0.5 GiB	Small and cheap instance type, with moderate baseline performance and the ability to burst CPU performance above the baseline	Testing and development environments and applications with very low traffic	$4
m6i.large	2	8 GiB	Has a balanced ratio of CPU, memory, and networking performance	All kinds of applications, such as medium databases, web servers, and enterprise applications	$69
r6i.large	2	16 GiB	Optimized for memory-intensive applications with extra memory	In-memory caches and enterprise application servers	$90

Instance families are optimized for different kinds of use cases, as described next:

- *T family*—Cheap, moderate baseline performance with the ability to burst to higher performance for short periods of time
- *M family*—General purpose, with a balanced ration of CPU and memory
- *C family*—Computing optimized, high CPU performance
- *R family*—Memory optimized, with more memory than CPU power compared to the M family
- *X family*—Extensive capacity with a focus on memory, up to 1952 GB memory and 128 virtual cores

- *D family*—Storage optimized, offering huge HDD capacity
- *I family*—Storage optimized, offering huge SSD capacity
- *P, G, and CG family*—Accelerated computing based on GPUs (graphics processing units)
- *F family*—Accelerated computing based on FPGAs (field-programmable gate arrays)

Additional instance families are available for niche workloads like high-performance computing, in-memory databases, MacOS workloads, and more. See https://aws .amazon.com/ec2/instance-types/ for a full list of instance types and families.

Our experience indicates that you'll overestimate the resource requirements for your applications. We recommend that you try to start your application with a smaller instance type than you think you need at first—you can change the instance family and type later if needed.

Instance types and families

The names for different instance types are all structured in the same way. The instance family groups instance types with similar characteristics. AWS releases new instance types and families from time to time; the different versions are called generations. The instance size defines the capacity of CPU, memory, storage, and networking. For example, the instance type `t2.micro` tells you the following:

- The instance family is called `t`. It groups small, cheap virtual machines with low-baseline CPU performance but the ability to burst significantly over baseline CPU performance for a short time.
- You're using generation 2 of this instance family.
- The size is micro, indicating that the EC2 instance is very small.

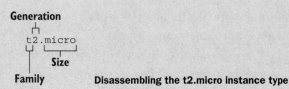

Disassembling the t2.micro instance type

Computer hardware is getting faster and more specialized, so AWS is constantly introducing new instance types and families. Some of them are improvements of existing instance families, and others are focused on specific workloads. For example, the instance family `R6i`, introduced in November 2021, provides instances for memory-intensive workloads and replaces the `R5` instance types.

One of the smallest and cheapest VMs will be enough for your first experiments. Choose the instance type `t2.micro`, as shown in figure 3.5, which is eligible for the Free Tier.

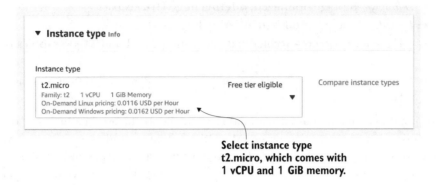

Figure 3.5   Choosing the size of your virtual machine

You might have already heard about Apple switching from Intel processors to ARM processors. The reason for this is that custom-built ARM processors achieve higher performance with lower energy consumption. This is, of course, exciting not only for laptops but also for servers in the data center.

AWS offers machines based on custom-built ARM processors called *Graviton* as well. As a customer, you will notice similar performance at lower costs. However, you need to make sure that the software you want to run is compiled for the ARM64 architecture. We migrated workloads from EC2 instances with Intel processors to virtual machines with ARM processors a few times already, typically within one to four hours. We would have liked to use Graviton instances for the third edition of this book, but, unfortunately, these were not yet part of the Free Tier at that time. We highly recommend you check out the following Graviton instance types offered by AWS:

- T4g—Burstable and cost-effective instance types
- M6g, M6gd—General-purpose instance types
- C6g, C6gd, C6gn, C7g—Compute-optimized instance types
- R6g, R6gd, X2gd—Memory-optimized instance types
- Im4gn, Is4gen—Instance types providing built-in storage
- G5g—A special instance type optimized for Android game streaming

CONFIGURING THE KEY PAIR FOR LOGIN

As an administrator of a Linux machine, you used a username and password or username and a public/private key pair to authenticate yourself in the past. By default, AWS uses a username and a key pair for authentication. That's why the next section of the wizard asks you about defining a key pair for the EC2 instance you are going to launch. We try to avoid this approach, because it works only for a single user, and it is not possible to change the key pair externally after launching an EC2 instance.

Therefore, we recommend a different approach to authenticate to an EC2 instance that we will introduce shortly. There is no need to configure the key pair now, so please select Proceed without a Key Pair, as shown in figure 3.6.

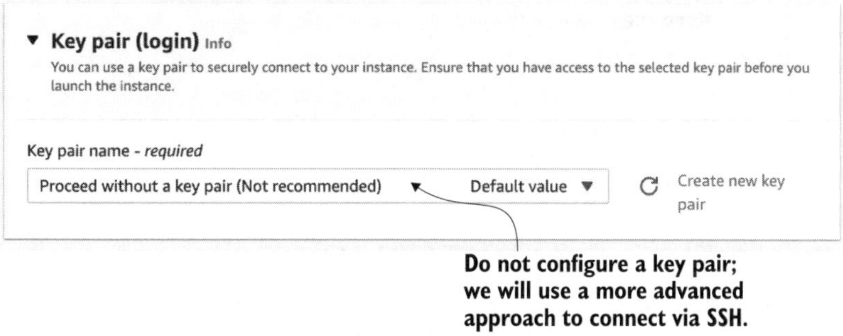

Figure 3.6   Proceeding without a key pair

DEFINING NETWORK AND FIREWALL SETTINGS

In the next section of the setup process, you can configure the network and firewall settings for the EC2 instance. The default settings are fine for now. You will learn more about networking on AWS in chapter 5. The only thing you should change is to deselect the Allow SSH Traffic option. As promised before, you will learn about a new approach to connect to EC2 instances that does not require inbound SSH connectivity. With the configuration shown in figure 3.7, the firewall does not allow any incoming connections at all.

ATTACHING STORAGE

Next, attach some storage to your virtual machine for the root filesystem. It is fine to keep the defaults and attach a volume with 8 GB of type gp2, which consists of network-attached SSDs, as illustrated in figure 3.8.

SETTING ADVANCED DETAILS

Last but not least, you need to configure an advanced detail for the EC2 instance you are going to launch: an IAM role. You will learn more about IAM in chapter 5. For now, all you need to know is that an IAM role grants processes running on the virtual machine access to other AWS services. This is needed because you will use AWS services called Systems Manager and EC2 Instance Connect to establish an SSH connection with your virtual machine later.

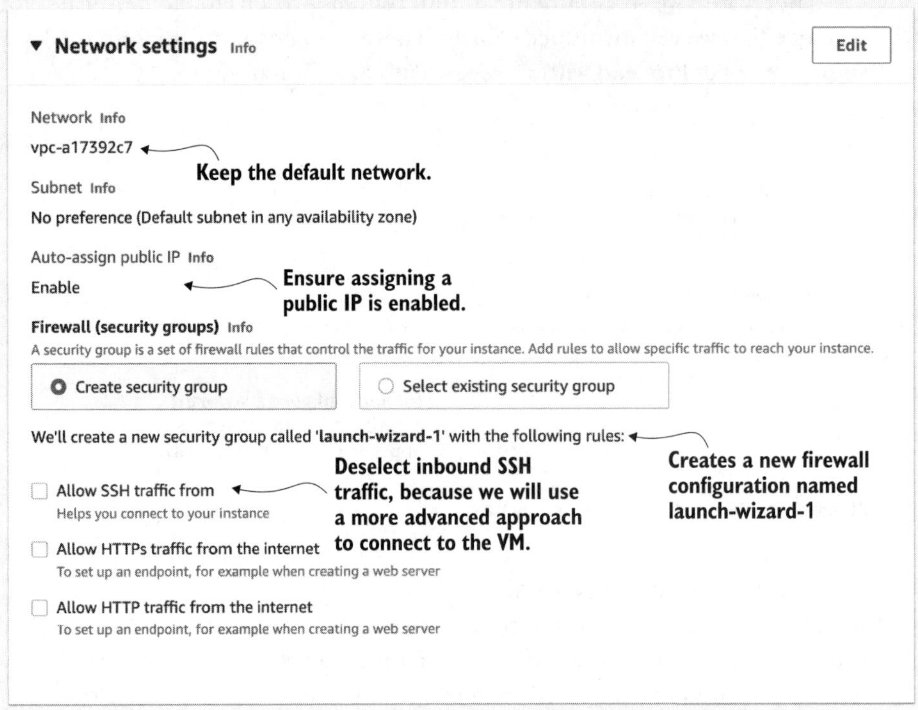

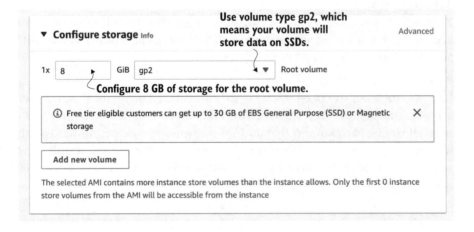

Figure 3.7   Configuring the network and firewall settings for the EC2 instance

Figure 3.8   Adding storage to the virtual machine

CREATING AN **IAM** ROLE

Before you proceed configuring your EC2 instance, you need to create an IAM role. To do so open https://console.aws.amazon.com/iam/ in a new tab in your browser and do the following:

1 Select Roles from the subnavigation options.
2 Click the Create Role button.
3 Select the trusted entity type AWS Service and EC2, as shown in figure 3.9.
4 Proceed to the next step.

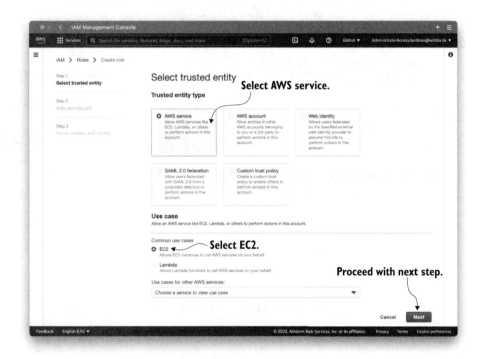

Figure 3.9   Creating an IAM role: Select trusted entity

Add permissions to the IAM role by filtering and selecting the policies named Amazon-SSMManagedInstanceCore, as demonstrated in figure 3.10. Doing so is required so that the Systems Manager agent running on the EC2 instance, which you will use to connect to the EC2 instance later, works properly. Afterward, proceed to the next step.

To create the IAM role, type the name ec2-ssm-core—please use this exact name because later chapters depend on it—and a description, as shown in figure 3.11. After doing so, click the Create Role button at the bottom of the page.

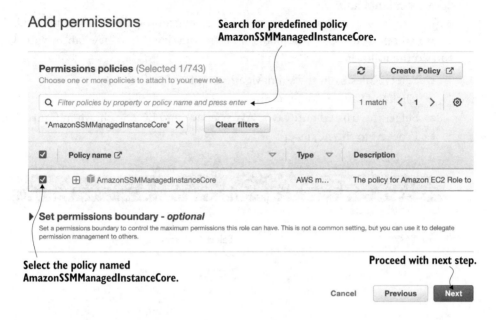

Figure 3.10   Creating an IAM role: Add permissions

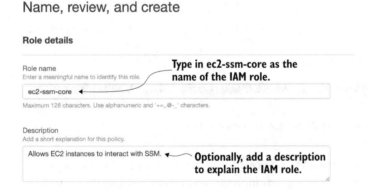

Figure 3.11   Creating an IAM role: Role details

Switch back to the EC2 browser tab. We have a lot to configure in the Advanced Details section. Keep the default setting for everything except the IAM instance profile. Click the Reload button next to the dropdown list and select the IAM instance profile named `ec2-ssm-core` (see figure 3.12).

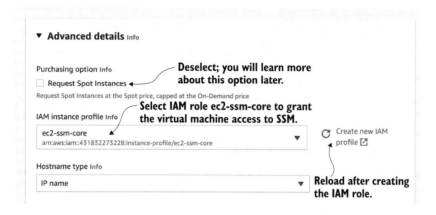

Figure 3.12   Configuring the IAM role for the EC2 instance

LAUNCHING THE EC2 INSTANCE

You are now ready to launch your virtual machine. To do so, just click the Launch Instance button, as illustrated in figure 3.13.

Figure 3.13   Launching the EC2 instance

Mark this day on your calendar: you've just launched your first EC2 instance. Many more will follow!

3.1.2 *Connecting to your virtual machine*

To be able to do something with the running virtual machines, you have to log in next. After connecting to your E2 instance, you will install and run LinkChecker to check a website for broken links. Of course, this exercise is just an example. When you get administrator access to the virtual machine, you have full control and are able to install the application and configure the operating system as needed.

You will learn how to connect to an EC2 instance by using the AWS Systems Manager Session Manager. The advantages of this approach follow:

- You do not need to configure key pairs upfront but use temporary key pairs instead.
- You don't need to allow inbound SSH or RDP connectivity, which limits the attack surface.

Using AWS Systems Manager Session Manager comes with the following requirements:

- Works with virtual machines based on Amazon Linux 2, CentOS, Oracle Linux, Red Hat Enterprise Linux, SUSE Linux Enterprise Server, macOS, and Windows Server.
- Requires the SSM agent, which is preinstalled on Amazon Linux 2, macOS >10.14, SUSE Linux Enterprise Server 12/15, Ubuntu Server >16.04, and Windows Server 2008–2012/2016/2019/2022.
- Requires an IAM role that grants permissions to the AWS Systems Manager service; see the previous section.

The following instructions guide you through the steps necessary to connect to the EC2 instance you launched in the previous section, which fulfills all of the following requirements:

1 Choose Instances from the subnavigation options of the EC2 service, in case you are not looking at the list of EC2 instances already, as shown in figure 3.14.
2 Select the instance named `mymachine`.
3 Wait until the instance reaches the status `Running`.
4 Click the Connect button.
5 Select the Session Manager tab.
6 Press the Connect button as shown in figure 3.15.

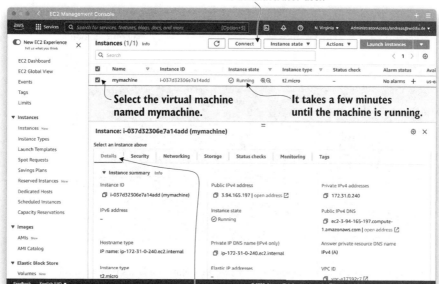

Figure 3.14 Listing all EC2 instances running in the region N. Virginia

Figure 3.15 Connecting to an EC2 instance via Session Manager

After a few seconds, a terminal appears in your browser window, as shown in figure 3.16.

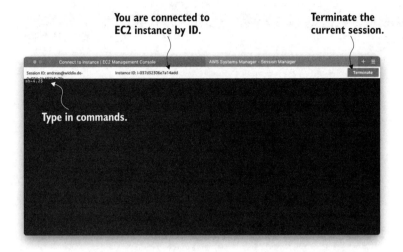

Figure 3.16   The terminal connected with your EC2 instance is waiting for input.

SSH and SCP

Accessing an EC2 instance directly from the browser is great, but sometimes you might prefer a good old SSH connection from your local machine, for example, to copy files with the help of SCP (secure file copy via SSH). Doing so is possible as well. If you're interested in the details, see http://mng.bz/JleK and http://mng.bz/wPw2.

You are now ready to enter the first commands into the terminal of your virtual machine.

3.1.3   *Installing and running software manually*

Back to our example: you launched a virtual machine to run LinkChecker to find broken links on a website. First, you need to install LinkChecker. Also, the tool requires a Python runtime environment.

In general, Amazon Linux 2 comes with the package manager yum, which allows you to install additional software. Besides that, Amazon Linux 2 comes with an extras library, covering additional software packages. Run the following command to install Python 3.8. Press y when prompted to acknowledge the changes:

```
$ sudo amazon-linux-extras install python3.8
```

Next, execute the following command to install the LinkChecker tool, which allows you to find broken links on a website:

```
$ pip3 install linkchecker
```

Now you're ready to check for links pointing to websites that no longer exist. To do so, choose a website and run the following command. The `-r` option limits the recursion level that the tool will crawl through:

```
$ ~/.local/bin/linkchecker -r 2 https://
```

The output of checking the links looks something like this:

```
[...]
URL          `/images/2022/02/terminal.png'
Name         `Connect to your EC2 instance using SSH the modern way'
Parent URL https://cloudonaut.io, line 379, col 1165
Real URL   https://cloudonaut.io/images/2022/02/terminal.png
Check time 2.959 seconds
Size       0B
Result     Error: 404 Not Found
10 threads active,     5 links queued,    72 links in  87 URLs checked, ...
 1 thread active,      0 links queued,    86 links in  87 URLs checked, ...

Statistics:
Downloaded: 66.01KB.
Content types: 26 image, 29 text, 0 video, 0 audio, 3 application, ...
URL lengths: min=21, max=160, avg=56.

That's it. 87 links in 87 URLs checked. 0 warnings found. 1 error found.
Stopped checking at 2022-04-04 09:02:55+000 (22 seconds)
[...]
```

Depending on the number of web pages, the crawler may need some time to check all of them for broken links. At the end, it lists the broken links and gives you the chance to find and fix them.

3.2 Monitoring and debugging a virtual machine

If you need to find the reason for an error or determine why your application isn't behaving as you expect, it's important to have access to tools that can help with monitoring and debugging. AWS provides tools that let you monitor and debug your virtual machines. One approach is to examine the virtual machine's logs.

3.2.1 Showing logs from a virtual machine

If you need to find out what your virtual machine was doing during and after startup, you have a simple solution. AWS allows you to see the EC2 instance's logs with the help of the Management Console (the web interface you use to start and stop virtual machines). Follow these steps to open your VM's logs:

1 Go to EC2 in the AWS Management Console: https://console.aws.amazon .com/ec2/.
2 Open the list of all virtual machines by selecting Instances from the subnavigation options.

3   Select the running virtual machine by clicking the row in the table.

4   In the Actions menu, select Monitor and Troubleshoot > Get System Log.

5   A screen showing the system logs from your VM that would normally be displayed on a physical monitor during startup, as shown in figure 3.17, appears.

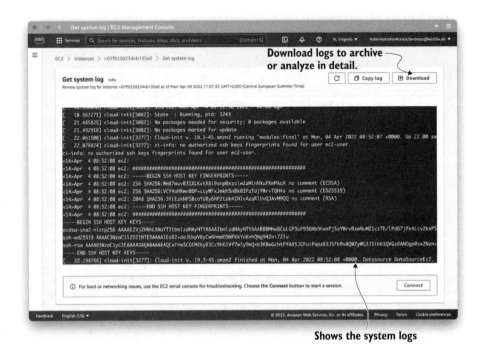

Figure 3.17   Debugging a virtual machine with the help of system logs

The log contains all log messages that would be displayed on the monitor of your machine if you were running it on-premises. Watch for any log messages stating that an error occurred during startup. If the error message is not obvious, you should contact the vendor of the AMI or AWS Support, or post your question to the official AWS community at https://repost.aws.

This is a simple and efficient way to access your system logs without needing an SSH connection. Note that it will take several minutes for a log message to appear in the log viewer.

3.2.2   *Monitoring the load of a virtual machine*

AWS can help you answer another question: is your virtual machine close to its maximum capacity? Follow these steps to open the EC2 instance's metrics:

1   Go to EC2 in the AWS Management Console: https://console.aws.amazon.com/ec2/.

2   Open the list of all virtual machines by choosing Instances from the subnavigation options.

3   Select the running virtual machine by clicking the row in the table.

4   Select the Monitoring tab in the lower-right corner.

5   Click the three dots at the upper-right corner of the Network in (Bytes) metric
and choose Enlarge.

You'll see a graph that shows the virtual machine's use of incoming networking traffic,
similar to figure 3.18, with metrics for CPU, network, and disk usage. As AWS is looking at your VM from the outside, there is no metric indicating the memory usage. You
can publish a memory metric yourself, if needed. The metrics are updated every five
minutes if you use basic monitoring, or every minute if you enable detailed monitoring of your virtual machine, which costs extra.

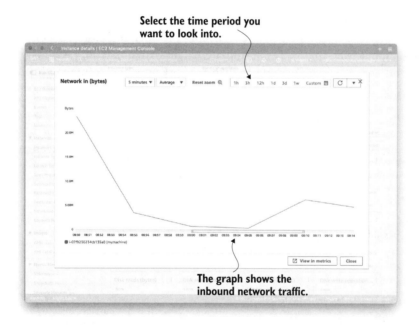

**Figure 3.18   Gaining insight into a virtual machine's incoming network traffic with
the CloudWatch metric**

Checking the metrics of your EC2 instance is helpful when debugging performance
problems. You will also learn how to increase or decrease your infrastructure based on
these metrics in chapter 17.

Metrics and logs help you monitor and debug your virtual machines. Both tools
can help ensure that you're providing high-quality services in a cost-efficient manner.
Look at "Monitor Amazon EC2" in the AWS documentation at http://mng.bz/xMqg
for more detailed information about monitoring your virtual machines.

3.3   *Shutting down a virtual machine*

To avoid incurring charges, you should always turn off virtual machines when you're not using them. You can use the following four actions to control a virtual machine's state:

- *Start*—You can always start a stopped virtual machine. If you want to create a completely new machine, you'll need to launch another virtual machine.
- *Stop*—You can always stop a running virtual machine. A stopped virtual machine doesn't incur charges, except for attached resources like network-attached storage. A stopped virtual machine can be started again but likely on a different host. If you're using network-attached storage, your data persists.
- *Reboot*—Have you tried turning off your virtual machine, then turning it on again? If you need to reboot your virtual machine, this action is what you want. You won't lose any persistent data when rebooting a virtual machine because it stays on the same host.
- *Terminate*—Terminating a virtual machine means deleting it. You can't start a virtual machine that you've terminated. The virtual machine is deleted, usually together with its dependencies, like network-attached storage and public and private IP addresses. A terminated virtual machine doesn't incur charges.

> **WARNING**   The difference between *stopping* and *terminating* a virtual machine is important. You can start a stopped virtual machine. This isn't possible with a terminated virtual machine. If you terminate a virtual machine, you delete it.

Figure 3.19 illustrates the difference between stopping and terminating an EC2 instance, with the help of a flowchart.

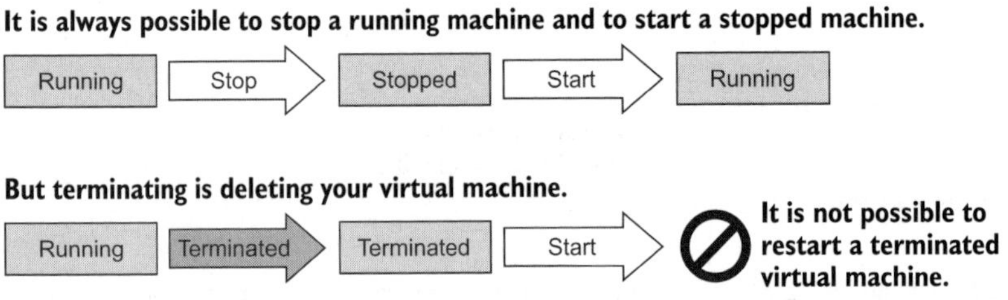

It is always possible to stop a running machine and to start a stopped machine.

| Running | Stop | Stopped | Start | Running |

But terminating is deleting your virtual machine.

| Running | Terminated | Terminated | Start | It is not possible to restart a terminated virtual machine. |

Figure 3.19   The difference between stopping and terminating a virtual machine

Stopping or terminating unused virtual machines saves costs and prevents you from being surprised by an unexpected bill from AWS. You may want to stop or terminate unused virtual machines when the following situations arise:

- You have launched virtual machines to implement a proof of concept. After finishing the project, the virtual machines are no longer needed. Therefore, you can terminate them.

- You are using a virtual machine to test a web application. Because no one else uses the virtual machine, you can stop it before you knock off work and start it back up again the following day.
- One of your customers canceled their contract. After backing up the relevant data, you can terminate the virtual machines that had been used for your former customer.

After you terminate a virtual machine, it's no longer available and eventually disappears from the list of virtual machines.

Cleaning up

Terminate the virtual machine named `mymachine` that you started at the beginning of this chapter by doing the following:

1 Go to EC2 in the AWS Management Console: https://console.aws.amazon .com/ec2/.
2 Open the list of all virtual machines and select Instances from the subnavigation options.
3 Select the running virtual machine by clicking the row in the table.
4 Click the Instance State button and select Terminate Instance.

3.4 Changing the size of a virtual machine

It is always possible to change the size of a virtual machine. This is one of the advantages of using the cloud, and it gives you the ability to scale vertically. If you need more computing power, increase the size of the EC2 instance, or vice versa.

In this section, you'll learn how to change the size of a running virtual machine. To begin, follow these steps to start a small virtual machine:

1 Go to EC2 in the AWS Management Console: https://console.aws.amazon .com/ec2/.
2 Click the Launch Instances button.
3 Enter growingup as the name of the virtual machine.
4 Choose the Amazon Linux 2 AMI.
5 Select instance type `t2.micro`.
6 Select the option Proceed without a Key Pair.
7 Keep the default for network and storage.
8 Select the IAM instance profile `ec2-ssm-core` under Advanced Details.
9 Launch the instance.

You've now started an EC2 instance of type `t2.micro`. This is one of the smallest virtual machines available on AWS.

Use the Session Manager to connect to the instance as demonstrated in the previous section, and execute `cat /proc/cpuinfo` and `free -m` to see information about the machine's capabilities. The output should look similar to this:

```
$ cat /proc/cpuinfo
processor       : 0
vendor_id       : GenuineIntel
cpu family      : 6
model           : 63
model name      : Intel(R) Xeon(R) CPU E5-2676 v3 @ 2.40GHz
stepping        : 2
microcode       : 0x46
cpu MHz         : 2399.915
cache size      : 30720 KB
[...]

$ free -m
          total     used     free     shared     buff/cache     available
Mem:        965       93      379          0            492           739
Swap:         0        0        0
```

Your virtual machine provides a single CPU core and 965 MB of memory. If your application is having performance problems, increasing the instance size can solve this. Use your machine's metrics as described in section 3.2 to find out whether you are running out of CPU or networking capacity. Would your application benefit from additional memory? If so, increasing the instance size will improve the application's performance as well.

If you need more CPUs, more memory, or more networking capacity, you can choose from many other sizes. You can even change the virtual machine's instance family and generation. To increase the size of your VM, you first need to stop it as follows:

1 Go to EC2 in the AWS Management Console: https://console.aws.amazon .com/ec2/.
2 Click Instances in the submenu to jump to an overview of your virtual machines.
3 Select your running VM from the list by clicking it.
4 Click Instance State > Stop Instance.

WARNING Starting a virtual machine with instance type `m5.large` incurs charges. Go to http://aws.amazon.com/ec2/pricing if you want to see the current on-demand hourly price for an `m5.large` virtual machine.

After waiting for the virtual machine to stop, you can change the instance type as follows:

1 Click the Actions button and select Instance Settings.
2 Click Change Instance Type.

3 Select `m5.large` as the new instance type and click the Apply button, as shown in figure 3.20.

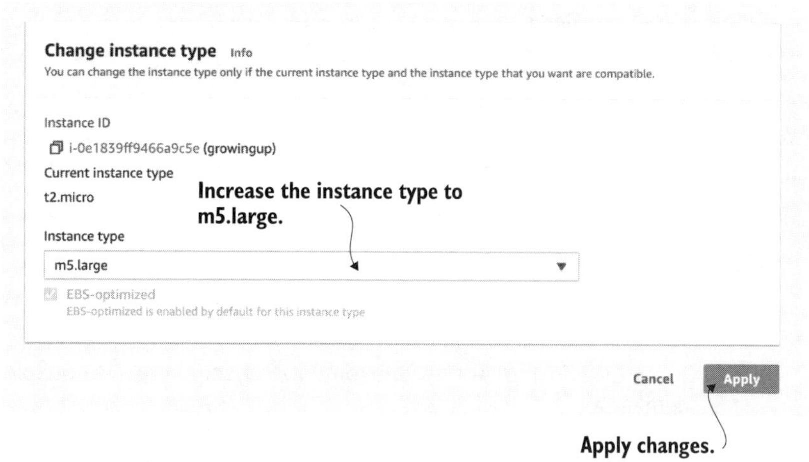

Change instance type Info
You can change the instance type only if the current instance type and the instance type that you want are compatible.

Instance ID
☐ i-0e1839ff9466a9c5e (growingup)
Current instance type
t2.micro
Instance type

| m5.large | ▼ |

Increase the instance type to m5.large.

☑ EBS-optimized
EBS-optimized is enabled by default for this instance type

Cancel   Apply

Apply changes.

Figure 3.20   Increasing the size of your virtual machine by selecting `m4.large` **as the instance type**

You've now changed the size of your virtual machine and are ready to start it again. To do so, select your EC2 instance and click Start Instance under Instance State. Your VM will start with more CPUs, more memory, and increased networking capabilities.

Use the Session Manager to connect to your EC2 instance, and execute `cat /proc/cpuinfo` and `free -m` to see information about its CPU and memory again. The output should look similar to this:

```
$ cat /proc/cpuinfo
processor       : 0
vendor_id       : GenuineIntel
cpu family      : 6
model           : 85
model name      : Intel(R) Xeon(R) Platinum 8259CL CPU @ 2.50GHz
stepping        : 7
microcode       : 0x500320a
cpu MHz         : 3117.531
cache size      : 36608 KB
[...]

processor       : 1
vendor_id       : GenuineIntel
cpu family      : 6
model           : 85
model name      : Intel(R) Xeon(R) Platinum 8259CL CPU @ 2.50GHz
stepping        : 7
microcode       : 0x500320a
```

```
cpu MHz        : 3100.884
cache size     : 36608 KB
[...]

$ free -m
            total    used    free    shared   buff/cache   available
Mem:         7737     108    7427         0          202        7406
Swap:           0       0       0
```

Your virtual machine can use two CPU cores and offers 7,737 MB of memory, compared to a single CPU core and 965 MB of memory before you increased the VM's size.

Cleaning up

Terminate the EC2 instance named growingup of type m5.large to stop paying for it as follows:

1 Go to EC2 in the AWS Management Console: https://console.aws.amazon .com/ec2/.
2 Open the list of all virtual machines by selecting Instances from the subnavigation options.
3 Select the running virtual machine by clicking the row in the table.
4 In the Actions menu, select Instance State > Terminate Instance.

3.5 *Starting a virtual machine in another data center*

AWS offers data centers all over the world. Take the following criteria into account when deciding which region to choose for your cloud infrastructure:

- *Latency*—Which region offers the shortest distance between your users and your infrastructure?
- *Compliance*—Are you allowed to store and process data in that country?
- *Service availability*—AWS does not offer all services in all regions. Are the services you are planning to use available in the region? Check out the service availability region table at https://aws.amazon.com/about-aws/global-infrastructure/regional -product-services/ or https://awsservices.info.
- *Costs*—Service costs vary by region. Which region is the most cost-effective region for your infrastructure?

Let's assume you have customers not just in the United States but in Australia as well. At the moment you are operating EC2 instances only in N. Virginia (US). Customers from Australia complain about long loading times when accessing your website. To make your Australian customers happy, you decide to launch an additional VM in Australia.

Changing a data center is simple. The Management Console always shows the current data center you're working in on the right side of the main navigation menu. So far, you've worked in the data centers located in N. Virginia (US), called us-east-1.

To change the data center, click N. Virginia and select Asia Pacific (Sydney) from the menu. Figure 3.21 shows how to jump to the data center in Sydney, also called `ap-southeast-2`.

Switch to other data centers located somewhere different.

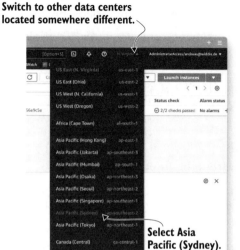

Select Asia Pacific (Sydney).

Figure 3.21   Changing the data center's location from N. Virginia to Sydney in the Management Console

AWS groups its data centers into these regions:

■ US East, N. Virginia (us-east-1)	■ US East, Ohio (us-east-2)
■ US West, N. California, us-west-1	■ US West, Oregon (us-west-2)
■ Africa, Cape Town (af-south-1)	■ Asia Pacific, Hong Kong (ap-east-1)
■ Asia Pacific, Jakarta (ap-southeast-3)	■ Asia Pacific, Mumbai (ap-south-1)
■ Asia Pacific, Osaka (ap-northeast-3)	■ Asia Pacific, Seoul (ap-northeast-2)
■ Asia Pacific, Singapore (ap-southeast-1)	■ Asia Pacific, Sydney (ap-southeast-2)
■ Asia Pacific, Tokyo (ap-northeast-1)	■ Canada, Central (ca-central-1)
■ Europe, Frankfurt (eu-central-1)	■ Europe, Ireland (eu-west-1)
■ Europe, London (eu-west-2)	■ Europe, Milan (eu-south-1)
■ Europe, Paris (eu-west-3)	■ Europe, Stockholm (eu-north-1)
■ Middle East, Bahrain (me-south-1)	■ South America, São Paulo (sa-east-1)

You can specify the region for most AWS services. The regions are independent of each other; data isn't transferred between regions. Typically, a region is a collection of three or more data centers located in the same area. Those data centers are well connected to each other and offer the ability to build a highly available infrastructure, as you'll discover later in this book. Some AWS services—like IAM, where you created the ec2-ssm-core role, or the CDN and the Domain Name System (DNS) service—act globally on top of these regions and even on top of some additional data centers.

Next, start a virtual machine in a data center in Sydney following these steps:

1. Go to EC2 in the AWS Management Console: https://console.aws.amazon .com/ec2/.
2. Click the Launch Instances button.
3. Enter sydney as the name of the virtual machine.
4. Choose the Amazon Linux 2 AMI.
5. Select the instance type t2.micro.
6. Select the option Proceed without a Key Pair.
7. Select the Allow HTTP Traffic from the Internet option.
8. Keep the defaults for storage.
9. Select the IAM instance profile ec2-ssm-core under Advanced Details.
10. Launch the instance.

You did it! Your virtual machine is now running in a data center in Sydney. Let's proceed with installing a web server on it. To do so, you have to connect to your virtual machine via Session Manager as you did in the previous sections.

Use the following commands to install and start an Apache web server on your virtual machine:

```
$ sudo yum install httpd -y
```

Next, start the web server and make sure it will get started whenever the machine starts automatically.

```
$ sudo systemctl start httpd
$ sudo systemctl enable httpd
```

To access the default website served by Apache, you need to know the public IPv4 address of your EC2 instance. Get this information by selecting your virtual machine and looking into the details via the Management Console. You can also execute the following command in the terminal of your EC2 instance:

```
$ curl http:/ /169.254.169.254/latest/meta-data/public-ipv4
```

Open http://$PublicIp in your browser. Don't forget to replace $PublicIp with the public IPv4 address of your EC2 instance, for example, http://52.54.202.9. A demo website appears.

The public IPv4 address assigned to your EC2 instance is subject to change. For example, when you stop and start your instance, AWS assigns a new public IPv4 address. Therefore, you will learn how to attach a fixed public IP address to the virtual machine in the following section.

3.6 Allocating a public IP address

You've already launched some virtual machines while reading this book. Each VM was connected to a public IP address automatically. But every time you launched or stopped a VM, the public IP address changed. If you want to host an application under a fixed IP address, this won't work. AWS offers a service called *Elastic IPs* for allocating fixed public IP addresses.

Using a fixed public IP address is useful, in case clients aren't able to resolve a DNS name, a firewall rule based on IP addresses is required, or you don't want to update DNS records to avoid the delay until all clients resolve to the new IP address. Therefore, allocate a public IP address and associate with your EC2 instance named `sydney` as follows:

1 Open the Management Console, and go to the EC2 service.
2 Choose Elastic IPs from the submenu. You'll see an overview of public IP addresses allocated by you.
3 Allocate a public IP address by clicking Allocate Elastic IP Address, as shown in figure 3.22.

Figure 3.22   An overview of public IP addresses connected to your account in the current region

4 Select Amazon's Pool of IPv4 Addresses, and click the Allocate button, as shown in figure 3.23.
5 To associate the Elastic IP with your EC2 instance, select the public IP address you just allocated, click the Actions button, and select Associate Elastic IP Address.

Figure 3.23   Allocating a public IPv4 address

6   Select the resource type Instance, and select your EC2 instance named `sydney` from the dropdown list, as shown in figure 3.24.

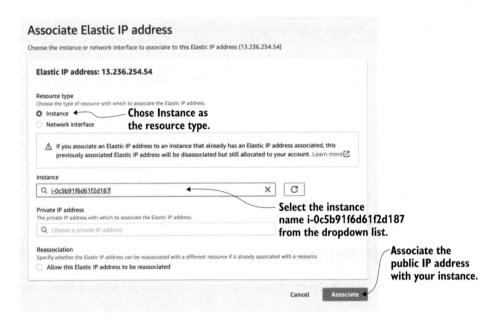

Figure 3.24   Associating an Elastic IP address with an EC2 instance

7   Click the Associate button.

Hurray! Your virtual machine is now accessible through the public IP address you allocated at the beginning of this section. Point your browser to this IP address, and you should see the placeholder page as you did in section 3.5.

Allocating a static public IP address can be useful if you want to make sure the endpoint to your application doesn't change, even if you have to replace the virtual machine behind the scenes. For example, assume that virtual machine A is running and has an associated Elastic IP. The following steps let you replace the virtual machine with a new one without changing the public IP address:

1 Start a new virtual machine B to replace the running virtual machine A.
2 Install and start applications as well as all dependencies on virtual machine B.
3 Disassociate the Elastic IP from virtual machine A, and associate it with virtual machine B.

Requests using the Elastic IP address will now be routed to virtual machine B, with a short interruption while moving the Elastic IP. You can also connect multiple public IP addresses with a virtual machine by using multiple network interfaces, as described in the next section. This method can be useful if you need to host different applications running on the same port, or if you want to use a unique fixed public IP address for different websites.

> **WARNING** IPv4 addresses are scarce. To prevent stockpiling Elastic IP addresses, AWS will charge you for Elastic IP addresses that aren't associated with a virtual machine. You'll clean up the allocated IP address at the end of the next section.

3.7 Adding an additional network interface to a virtual machine

In addition to managing public IP addresses, you can control your virtual machine's network interfaces. It is possible to add multiple network interfaces to a VM and control the private and public IP addresses associated with those network interfaces. Here are some typical use cases for EC2 instances with multiple network interfaces:

- Your web server needs to answer requests by using multiple TLS/SSL certificates, and you can't use the Server Name Indication (SNI) extension due to legacy clients.
- You want to create a management network separated from the application network, and, therefore, your EC2 instance needs to be accessible from two networks. Figure 3.25 illustrates an example.
- Your application requires or recommends the use of multiple network interfaces (e.g., network and security appliances).

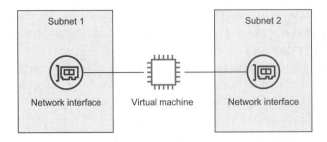

Figure 3.25   A virtual machine with two network interfaces in two different subnets

In the next procedure, you will use an additional network interface to connect a second public IP address to your EC2 instance. Follow these steps to create an additional networking interface for your virtual machine:

1   Open the Management Console, and go to the EC2 service.
2   Select Network Interfaces from the submenu. The default network interface of your virtual machine is shown in the list. Note the subnet ID of this network interface.
3   Click Create Network Interface.
4   Enter 2nd interface as the description, as shown in figure 3.26.
5   Choose the subnet you noted in step 3.
6   Select Auto-Assign Private IPv4 Address.
7   Chose the security group named `launch-wizard-1`.
8   Click Create Network Interface.

After the new network interface's state changes to `Available`, you can attach it to your virtual machine. Select the new 2nd interface network interface, and select Attach from the Actions menu. A dialog opens like the one shown in figure 3.27. Choose the only available Instance ID, and click Attach.

You've attached an additional networking interface to your virtual machine. Next, you'll associate an additional public IP address to the additional networking interface. To do so, note the network interface ID of the 2nd interface shown in the overview—eni-0865886f80fcc31a9 in our example—and follow these steps:

1   Open the AWS Management Console, and go to the EC2 service.
2   Choose Elastic IPs from the submenu.
3   Click Allocate Elastic IP Address as you did in section 3.6.
4   Select the newly created public IP address, and select Associate Elastic IP Address from the Actions menu.

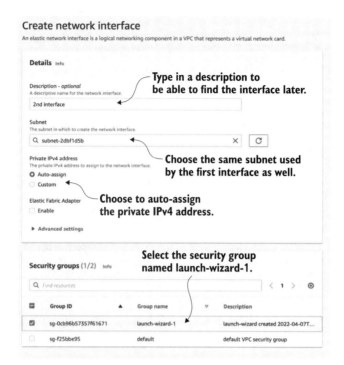

Figure 3.26   Creating an additional networking interface for your virtual machine

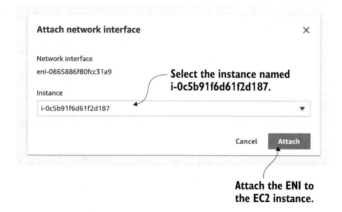

Figure 3.27   Attaching an additional networking interface to your virtual machine

5   Select Network Interface as the resource type, as shown in figure 3.28.

6   Select your 2nd interface's ID.

7   Select the only available private IP of your network interface.

8   Click Associate to finish the process.

Your virtual machine is now reachable under two different public IP addresses. This enables you to serve two different websites, depending on the public IP address. You

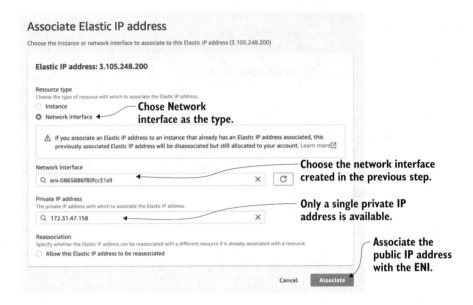

Figure 3.28   Associating a public IP address with the additional networking interface

need to configure the web server to answer requests depending on the public IP address. Use the Session Manager to connect to your EC2 instance named sydney and execute ifconfig in the terminal, which will output the network configuration of your virtual machine, shown here:

```
$ ifconfig
eth0: flags=4163<UP,BROADCAST,RUNNING,MULTICAST>  mtu 9001
    inet 172.31.33.219  netmask 255.255.240.0  broadcast 172.31.47.255    ◄──┐
    inet6 fe80::495:5fff:fea6:abde  prefixlen 64  scopeid 0x20<link>          │
    ether 06:95:5f:a6:ab:de  txqueuelen 1000  (Ethernet)                      │
    RX packets 68382  bytes 80442006 (76.7 MiB)
    RX errors 0  dropped 0  overruns 0  frame 0
    TX packets 35228  bytes 4219870 (4.0 MiB)
    TX errors 0  dropped 0 overruns 0  carrier 0  collisions 0

eth1: flags=4163<UP,BROADCAST,RUNNING,MULTICAST>  mtu 9001
    inet 172.31.47.158  netmask 255.255.240.0  broadcast 172.31.47.255    ◄──┐
    inet6 fe80::4a2:8fff:feea:bbba  prefixlen 64  scopeid 0x20<link>          │
    ether 06:a2:8f:ea:bb:ba  txqueuelen 1000  (Ethernet)                      │
    RX packets 22  bytes 1641 (1.6 KiB)
    RX errors 0  dropped 0  overruns 0  frame 0
    TX packets 33  bytes 2971 (2.9 KiB)
    TX errors 0  dropped 0 overruns 0  carrier 0  collisions 0
[...]
```

The primary network interface uses the private IP address 172.31.33.219.

The secondary network interface uses the private IP address 172.31.47.158.

Each network interface is connected to a private and a public IP address. You'll need to configure the web server to deliver different websites, depending on the IP address.

Your virtual machine doesn't know anything about its public IP address, but you can distinguish the requests based on the private IP addresses.

First you need two websites. Run the following commands on your virtual machine in Sydney via the Session Manager to download two simple placeholder websites:

```
$ sudo -s
$ mkdir /var/www/html/a
$ wget -P /var/www/html/a \
➟ https://raw.githubusercontent.com/AWSinAction/code3/main/chapter03
➟ /a/index.html
$ mkdir /var/www/html/b
$ wget -P /var/www/html/b \
➟ https://raw.githubusercontent.com/AWSinAction/code3/main/chapter03
➟ /b/index.html
```

Next, you need to configure the web server to deliver the websites, depending on which IP address is called. To do so, add a file named a.conf under /etc/httpd/conf.d. The following example uses the editor `nano`:

```
$ nano /etc/httpd/conf.d/a.conf
```

Copy and paste the following file content. Change the IP address from 172.31.x.x to the IP address from the `ifconfig` output for the networking interface `eth0`:

```
<VirtualHost 172.31.x.x:80>
  DocumentRoot /var/www/html/a
</VirtualHost>
```

Press CTRL + X and select y to save the file.

Repeat the same process for a configuration file named b.conf under /etc/httpd/conf.d with the following content. Change the IP address from 172.31.y.y to the IP address from the `ifconfig` output for the networking interface `eth1`:

```
<VirtualHost 172.31.y.y:80>
  DocumentRoot /var/www/html/b
</VirtualHost>
```

To activate the new web server configuration, execute `systemctl restart httpd`.

Next, go to the Elastic IP overview in the Management Console. Copy both public IP addresses, and open them with your web browser. You should get the answer "Hello A!" or "Hello B!," depending on the public IP address you're calling. Thus, you can deliver two different websites, depending on which public IP address the user is calling. Congrats—you're finished!

> **NOTE** You switched to the AWS region in Sydney earlier. Now you need to switch back to the region US East (N. Virginia). You can do so by selecting US East (N. Virginia) from the region chooser in the main navigation menu of the Management Console.

Cleaning up

It's time to clean up your setup:

1 Terminate the virtual machine, and wait until it is terminated.
2 Go to Networking Interfaces, and select and delete the 2nd networking interface.
3 Change to Elastic IPs, and select and release the two public IP addresses by clicking Release Elastic IP Address from the Actions menu.
4 Go to Security Groups, and delete the `launch-wizard-1` security group you created.

That's it. Everything is cleaned up, and you're ready for the next section.

3.8   *Optimizing costs for virtual machines*

Usually you launch virtual machines *on demand* in the cloud to gain maximum flexibility. AWS calls them on-demand instances, because you can start and stop VMs on demand, whenever you like, and you're billed for every second or hour the machine is running.

Billing unit: Seconds

Most EC2 instances running Windows or Linux (such as Amazon Linux or Ubuntu) are billed per second. The minimum charge per instance is 60 seconds. For example, if you terminate a newly launched instance after 30 seconds, you have to pay for 60 seconds. But if you terminate an instance after 61 seconds, you pay exactly for 61 seconds.

Other instances are billed per hour. See https://aws.amazon.com/ec2/pricing/ for details.

Besides stopping or downsizing EC2 instances, you have two options to reduce costs: *Spot Instances* and *Savings Plans*. Both help to reduce costs but decrease your flexibility. With a Spot Instance, you take advantage of unused capacity in an AWS data center. A Spot Instance comes with a discount of up to 90% compared to on-demand instances. However, AWS might terminate a Spot Instance at anytime when the resources are needed for someone else, so this type of instance is for stateless and fault-tolerant workloads only. With Savings Plans, you commit to a certain amount of resource consumption for one or three years and get a discount in turn. Therefore, Savings Plans are a good fit if you are running workloads with planning security. Table 3.2 summarizes the differences between the pricing options.

Table 3.2   Differences between on-demand instances, Savings Plans, and Spot Instances

	On-demand instances	Savings Plans	Spot Instances
Price	High	Medium	Low
Flexibility	High	Low	Medium
Reliability	High	High	Low
Scenarios	Dynamic workloads (e.g., for a news site) or proof of concept	Predictable and static workloads (e.g., for a business application)	Batch workloads (e.g., for data analytics, media encoding, etc.)

3.8.1   Commit to usage, get a discount

AWS offers the following two types of Savings Plans for EC2:

- Compute Savings Plans do not apply only to EC2 but also to Fargate (Container) and Lambda (Serverless) as well.
- EC2 Instance Savings Plans apply to EC2 instances only.

When purchasing a Compute Savings Plan, you need to specify the following details:

- *Term*—One year or three years
- *Hourly commitment*—In USD
- *Payment option*—All/partial/no upfront

For example, when committing to $1 per hour for one year and paying $8,760.00 upfront, you will get an `m5.large` EC2 instance at a discount of 31% in US East (N. Virginia). As you might have guessed already, the discount between on-demand and Savings Plans differs based on term, payment option, and even region. Find more details at https://aws.amazon.com/savingsplans/compute-pricing/.

An EC2 Instance Savings Plan applies to EC2 instances only. Therefore, it does not provide the flexibility to migrate a workload from virtual machines (EC2) to containers (Fargate). However, EC2 Instance Savings Plans offer a higher discount compared to Compute Savings Plans.

When purchasing an EC2 Instance Savings Plan, you need to specify the following details:

- *Term*—One year or three years
- *Region*—US East (N. Virginia), for example.
- *Instance family*—`m5`, for example
- *Hourly commitment*—In USD
- *Payment Option*—All/partial/no upfront

So the Savings Plan applies only to EC2 instances of a certain instance family in a certain region. Note that you are able to modify the instance family of a Savings Plan later, if needed.

Let's look at the earlier example again. When committing to $1 per hour for one year of `m5` instances running in `us-east-1` and paying $8,760.00 upfront, you will get an `m5.large` EC2 instance at a discount of 42% in US East (N. Virginia). Compare that to the 31% discount when purchasing a Compute Savings Plan instead.

> **WARNING**   Buying a reservation will incur costs for one or three years. That's why we did not add an example for this section.

Think of Savings Plans as a way to optimize your AWS bill. Buying a Savings Plan does not have any effect on your running EC2 instances. Also, an on-demand instance gets billed under the conditions of a Savings Plan automatically. There is no need to restart or modify an EC2 instance.

Capacity Reservations

As mentioned, Savings Plans do not have any effect on EC2 instances, only on billing. In contrast, EC2 Capacity Reservations allow you to reserve capacities in AWS's data centers. A Capacity Reservation comes with an hourly fee. For example, when you reserve the capacity for an `m5.large` instance, you will pay the typical on-demand fee of $0.096 per hour, no matter whether or not an EC2 instance of that type is running. In return, AWS guarantees the capacity to launch an `m5.large` instance at anytime.

With on-demand instances, you might run into the case that AWS cannot fulfill your request of spinning up a virtual machine. This type of situation might happen for rare instance types, during peak hours, or in special cases like outages causing many AWS customers to replace their failed instances.

If you need to guarantee that you are able to spin up an EC2 instance at anytime, consider EC2 Capacity Reservations.

In summary, we highly recommend purchasing Savings Plans for workloads, where predicting the resource consumption for the next year is possible. It is worth noting that it is not necessary to cover 100% of your usage with Savings Plans. Reducing costs is also possible by committing to a smaller fraction of your workload.

3.8.2   *Taking advantage of spare compute capacity*

AWS is operating data centers at large scale, which results in spare capacity because it has to build and provision data centers and machines in advance to be able to fulfill future needs for on-demand capacity. But spare capacity does not generate revenue. That's why AWS tries to reduce spare capacity within its data centers. One way of doing so is offering Spot Instances.

Here is the deal. With Spot Instances, you get a significant discount on the on-demand price without the need to commit to using capacity in advance. In turn, a Spot Instance will start only when AWS decides that there is enough spare capacity available. In addition, a Spot Instance might be terminated by AWS at any time on short notice.

For example, when writing this on April 8, 2022, the price for an `m5.large` Spot Instance in US East (N. Virginia) is $0.039 per hour. That's a discount of about 60% compared to the $0.096 on-demand price. The spot price for EC2 instances used to be very volatile. Nowadays, it changes much more slowly.

But who is crazy enough to use virtual machines that might be terminated by AWS at any time with notice of only two minutes before the machine gets interrupted? Here are a few scenarios:

- Scanning objects stored on S3 for viruses and malware, by processing tasks stored in a queue
- Converting media files into different formats, where the process orchestrator will restart failed jobs automatically
- Processing parts of the requests for a web application, when the system is designed for fault tolerance

On top of that, we use Spot Instances for test systems where dealing with short outages is worth the cost savings.

As discussed in the previous section, using Savings Plans does not require any changes to your EC2 instances. But to use Spot Instances, you have to launch new EC2 instances and also plan for interrupted virtual machines.

Next, you will launch your first spot instance as follows:

1 Go to EC2 in the AWS Management Console: https://console.aws.amazon.com/ec2/.
2 Select Spot Requests from the subnavigation options.
3 Click the Request Spot Instances button.
4 Select Manually Configure Launch Parameters, as shown in figure 3.29.

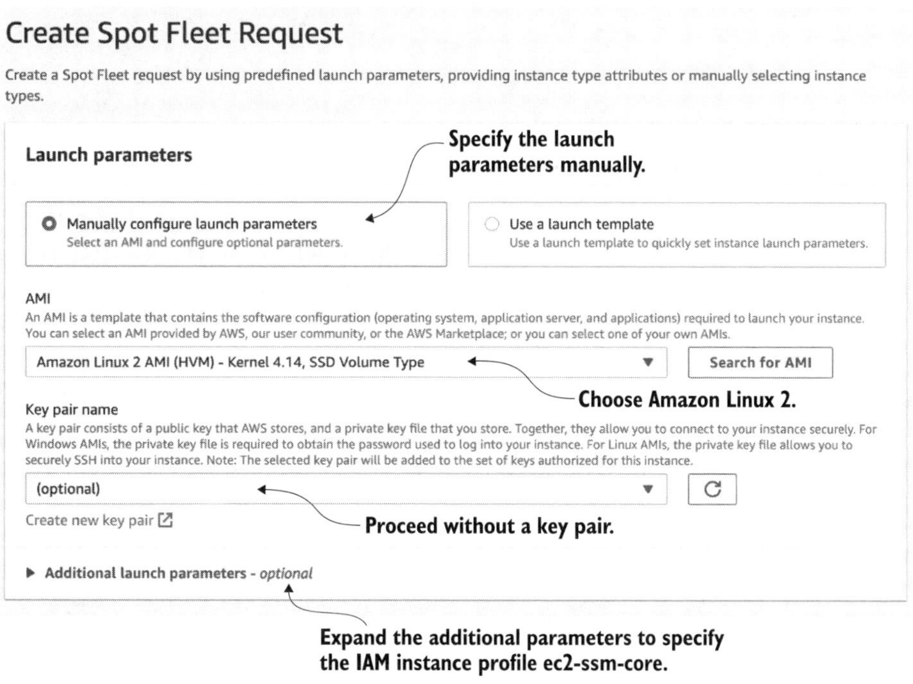

Create Spot Fleet Request

Create a Spot Fleet request by using predefined launch parameters, providing instance type attributes or manually selecting instance types.

Launch parameters   Specify the launch
                                                parameters manually.

◉ Manually configure launch parameters   ○ Use a launch template
   Select an AMI and configure optional parameters.   Use a launch template to quickly set instance launch parameters.

AMI
An AMI is a template that contains the software configuration (operating system, application server, and applications) required to launch your instance.
You can select an AMI provided by AWS, our user community, or the AWS Marketplace; or you can select one of your own AMIs.

Amazon Linux 2 AMI (HVM) - Kernel 4.14, SSD Volume Type   ▼   Search for AMI

Key pair name   Choose Amazon Linux 2.
A key pair consists of a public key that AWS stores, and a private key file that you store. Together, they allow you to connect to your instance securely. For Windows AMIs, the private key file is required to obtain the password used to log into your instance. For Linux AMIs, the private key file allows you to securely SSH into your instance. Note: The selected key pair will be added to the set of keys authorized for this instance.

(optional)   ▼   ⟳
Create new key pair ↗   Proceed without a key pair.

▶ Additional launch parameters - *optional*

                        Expand the additional parameters to specify
                        the IAM instance profile ec2-ssm-core.

Figure 3.29   Step 1 of creating a spot fleet request

5   Choose an Amazon Linux 2 AMI.

6   Do not configure a key pair; select (optional) instead.

7   Expand the Additional Launch Parameters section.

8   Select the IAM instance profile `ec2-ssm-core` to be able to connect to the Spot Instance using the Session Manager.

9   Keep the defaults for Addition Request Details.

10   Set the total target capacity to one instance, as demonstrated in figure 3.30.

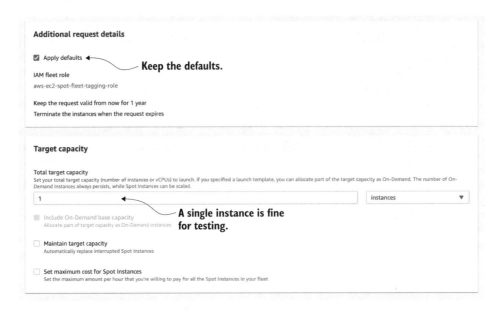

Figure 3.30   Step 2 of creating a spot fleet request

11   Chose Manually Select Instance Types, as shown in figure 3.31.

12   Empty the list of prepopulated instance types by selecting all instance types and clicking the Delete button.

13   Click the Add Instance Types button and select `t2.micro` from the list.

14   Choose the allocation strategy Capacity Optimized to increase the availability of a spot instance, as shown in figure 3.32.

15   Press the Launch button to create a spot fleet request.

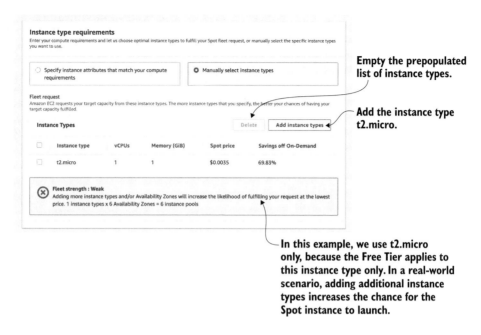

Empty the prepopulated list of instance types.

Add the instance type t2.micro.

In this example, we use t2.micro only, because the Free Tier applies to this instance type only. In a real-world scenario, adding additional instance types increases the chance for the Spot instance to launch.

Figure 3.31   Step 3 of creating a spot fleet request

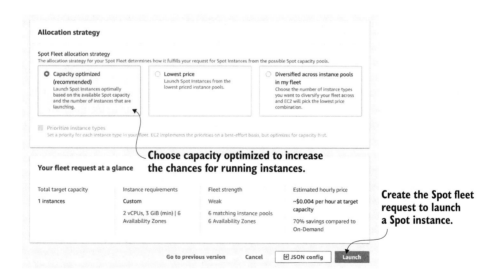

Choose capacity optimized to increase the chances for running instances.

Create the Spot fleet request to launch a Spot instance.

Figure 3.32   Step 4 of creating a spot fleet request

16 Two items appear in the list of spot requests. Wait until both the instance and fleet request reach status `Fulfilled`, as shown in figure 3.33.

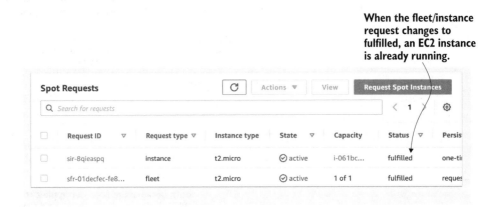

Figure 3.33   Step 5 of creating a spot fleet request

17 Select Instances from the subnavigation options. The list of EC2 instances includes your first Spot Instance.

The Spot Instance is ready for your workload. But be aware that AWS might terminate the Spot Instance at any time to free capacity for other workloads. AWS notifies you two minutes before terminating a Spot Instance.

One way to get notified about an interruption is to ask the EC2 metadata service about planned instance actions. Use the Session Manager to connect with your EC2 instance and execute the following command to send an HTTP request to the EC2 metadata service, which is accessible only from your virtual machine. Most likely, the HTTP request will result in a 404 error, which is a good sign, because that means AWS did not mark your Spot Instance for termination:

```
$ curl http://169.254.169.254/latest/meta-data/spot/instance-action
<?xml version="1.0" encoding="iso-8859-1"?><!DOCTYPE html PUBLIC "-//W3C//DTD
    XHTML 1.0 Transitional//EN"
        "http://www.w3.org/TR/xhtml1/DTD/xhtml1-transitional.dtd">
<html xmlns="http://www.w3.org/1999/xhtml" xml:lang="en" lang="en">
 <head>
  <title>404 - Not Found</title>
 </head>
 <body>
  <h1>404 - Not Found</h1>
 </body>
</html>
sh-4.2$
```

If the HTTP request results into something like that shown in the following snippet, your instance will be terminated within two minutes:

```
{"action": "stop", "time": "2022-04-08T12:12:00Z"}
```

In summary, Spot Instances help AWS to reduce spare capacity in their data centers and save us costs. However, you need to make sure that your application tolerates interruptions of Spot Instances, which might cause increased engineering effort.

> **Cleaning up**
> Terminate the Spot Instance as follows:
>
> 1 Go to the list of Spot Requests.
> 2 Select the fleet request.
> 3 Click the Action button and then the Cancel Request button.
> 4 Make sure to select the Terminate Instances check box and then click the Confirm button.

Summary

- When launching a virtual machine on AWS, you chose between a wide variety of operating systems: Amazon Linux, Ubuntu, Windows, and many more.
- Modifying the size of a virtual machine is simple: stop the virtual machine, modify the instance type—which defines the number of CPUs as well as the amount of memory and storage—and start the virtual machine.
- Using logs and metrics can help you to monitor and debug your virtual machine.
- AWS offers data centers all over the world. Starting VMs in Sydney, Australia, works the same as starting a machine in northern Virginia.
- Choose a data center by considering network latency, legal requirements, and costs, as well as available features.
- Allocating and associating a public IP address to your virtual machine gives you the flexibility to replace a VM without changing the public IP address.
- Committing to a certain compute usage for one or three years reduces the cost of virtual machines through buying Savings Plans.
- Use spare capacity at significant discount but with the risk of AWS terminating your virtual machine in case the capacity is needed elsewhere.

Programming
your infrastructure:
The command line, SDKs,
and CloudFormation

This chapter covers

- Starting a virtual machine with the command-line interface (CLI)
- Starting a virtual machine with JavaScript SDK for Node.js
- Understanding the idea of infrastructure as code
- Using CloudFormation to start a virtual machine

Imagine that we want to provide room lighting as a service. To switch off the lights in a room using software, we need a hardware device like a relay connected to the light circuit. This hardware device must have some kind of interface that lets us send commands via software. With a relay and an interface, we can offer room lighting as a service.

To run a virtual machine, we need a lot of hardware and software—power supply, networking gear, host machine, operating system, virtualization layer, and much more. Luckily, AWS runs the hardware and software for us. Even better, we can control all of that with software. AWS provides an *application programming interface* (API) that we can use to control every part of AWS with HTTPS requests. In the end, you can write software that spins up VMs on AWS as well as in-memory caches, data warehouses, and much more.

Calling the HTTP API is a low level task and requires a lot of repetitive work, like authentication, data (de)serialization, and so on. That's why AWS offers tools on top of the HTTP API that are easier to use. Those tools follow:

- *Command-line interface (CLI)*—Use the CLI to call the AWS API from your terminal.
- *Software development kit (SDK)*—SDKs, available for most programming languages, make it easy to call the AWS API from your programming language of choice.
- *AWS CloudFormation*—Templates are used to describe the state of the infrastructure. AWS CloudFormation translates these templates into API calls.

Not all examples are covered by the Free Tier

The examples in this chapter are not all covered by the Free Tier. A special warning message appears when an example incurs costs. As for the other examples, as long as you don't run them longer than a few days, you won't pay anything. Keep in mind that this applies only if you created a fresh AWS account for this book and nothing else is going on in your AWS account. Try to complete the chapter within a few days; you'll clean up your account at the end.

On AWS, you control everything via an API. You interact with AWS by making calls to the REST API using the HTTPS protocol, as figure 4.1 illustrates. Everything is available through the API. You can start a virtual machine with a single API call, create 1 TB of storage, or start a Hadoop cluster over the API. By everything, we really mean *everything*.

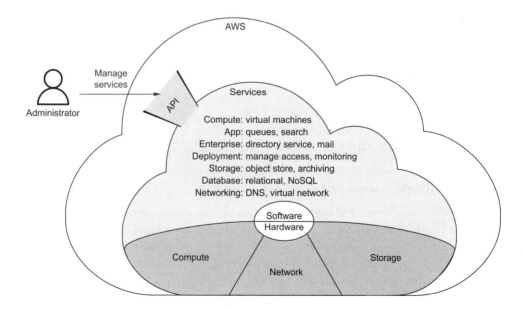

Figure 4.1   The AWS cloud is composed of hardware and software services accessible via an API.

You'll need some time to understand the consequences. By the time you finish this book, you'll ask why the world wasn't always this easy.

Let's look at how the API works. Imagine you uploaded a few files to the object store S3 (you will learn about S3 in chapter 7). Now you want to list all the files in the S3 object store to check whether the upload was successful. Using the raw HTTP API, you send a GET request to the API endpoint using the following HTTP protocol:

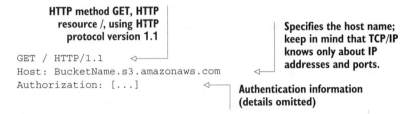

The HTTP response will look like this:

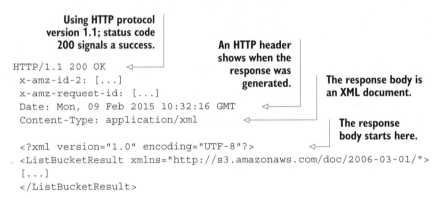

Calling the API directly using plain HTTPS requests is inconvenient. The easy way to talk to AWS is by using the CLI or SDKs, as you'll learn in this chapter. The API, however, is the foundation of all these tools.

4.1 Automation and the DevOps movement

The *DevOps movement* aims to bring software development and operations together. This usually is accomplished in one of two ways:

- Using mixed teams with members from both operations and development. Developers become responsible for operational tasks like being on call. Operators are involved from the beginning of the software development cycle, which helps make the software easier to operate.
- Introducing a new role that closes the gap between developers and operators. This role communicates a lot with both developers and operators and cares about all topics that touch both worlds.

The goal is to develop and deliver software to the customer rapidly without negatively affecting quality. Communication and collaboration between development and operations are, therefore, necessary.

The trend toward automation has helped DevOps culture bloom, because it codifies the cooperation between development and operations. You can do multiple deployments per day only if you automate the whole process. If you commit changes to the repository, the source code is automatically built and tested against your automated tests. If the build passes the tests, it's automatically installed in your testing environment, which triggers some acceptance tests. After those tests have passed, the change is propagated into production. But this isn't the end of the process: now you need to carefully monitor your system and analyze the logs in real time to ensure that the change was successful.

If your infrastructure is automated, you can spawn a new system for every change introduced to the code repository and run the acceptance tests isolated from other changes that were pushed to the repository at the same time. Whenever a change is made to the code, a new system is created (virtual machine, databases, networks, and so on) to run the change in isolation.

4.1.1 Why should you automate?

Why should you automate instead of using the graphical AWS Management Console? A script or a blueprint can be reused and will save you time in the long run. You can build new infrastructures quickly with ready-to-use modules from your former projects, or automate tasks that you will have to do regularly. Automating your infrastructure also enhances your software development process, for example, by using a deployment pipeline.

Another benefit is that a script or blueprint is the most detailed documentation you can imagine (even a computer understands it). If you want to reproduce on Monday what you did last Friday, a script is worth its weight in gold. If you're sick and a coworker needs to take care of your tasks, they will appreciate your blueprints.

You're now going to install and configure the CLI. After that, you can get your hands dirty and start scripting. The AWS CLI is one tool for automating AWS. Read on to learn how it works.

4.2 Using the command-line interface

The AWS CLI is a convenient way to interact with AWS from your terminal. It runs on Linux, macOS, and Windows and provides a unified interface for all AWS services. Unless otherwise specified, the output is by default in JSON format.

4.2.1 Installing the CLI

How you proceed depends on your OS. If you're having difficulty installing the CLI, consult http://mng.bz/AVng for a detailed description of many installation options.

LINUX X86 (64-BIT)

In your terminal, execute the following commands:

```
$ curl "https://awscli.amazonaws.com/awscli-exe-linux-x86_64.zip" \
  -o "awscliv2.zip"
$ unzip awscliv2.zip
$ sudo ./aws/install
```

Verify your AWS CLI installation by running aws --version in your terminal. The version should be at least 2.4.0.

LINUX ARM

In your terminal, execute the following commands:

```
$ curl "https://awscli.amazonaws.com/awscli-exe-linux-aarch64.zip" \
  -o "awscliv2.zip"
$ unzip awscliv2.zip
$ sudo ./aws/install
```

Verify your AWS CLI installation by running aws --version in your terminal. The version should be at least 2.4.0.

MACOS

The following steps guide you through installing the AWS CLI on macOS using the installer:

1 Download the AWS CLI installer at https://awscli.amazonaws.com/AWSCLIV2 .pkg.
2 Run the downloaded installer, and install the CLI by going through the installation wizard for **all users**.
3 Verify your AWS CLI installation by running aws --version in your terminal. The version should be at least 2.4.0.

WINDOWS

The following steps guide you through installing the AWS CLI on Windows using the MSI Installer:

1 Download the AWS CLI installer at https://awscli.amazonaws.com/AWSCLIV2 .msi.
2 Run the downloaded installer, and install the CLI by going through the installation wizard.
3 Run PowerShell as administrator by searching for "PowerShell" in the Start menu and choosing Run as Administrator from its context menu.
4 Type Set-ExecutionPolicy Unrestricted into PowerShell, and press Enter to execute the command. This allows you to execute the unsigned PowerShell scripts from our examples.

5 Close the PowerShell window; you no longer need to work as administrator.
6 Run PowerShell by choosing PowerShell from the Start menu.
7 Verify whether the CLI is working by executing `aws --version` in PowerShell. The version should be at least 2.4.0.

WARNING   Setting the PowerShell execution policy to `Unrestricted` allows you to run unsigned scripts. There is a risk of running malicious scripts. Use it to run the scripts provided in our examples only. Check about Execution Policies (http://mng.bz/1MK1) to learn more.

4.2.2   Configuring the CLI

To use the CLI, you need to authenticate. Until now, you've been using the root AWS account. This account can do everything, good and bad. It's strongly recommended that you not use the AWS root account (you'll learn more about security in chapter 5), so let's create a new user. To create a new user, use the following steps, which are illustrated in figure 4.2:

1 Open the AWS Management Console at https://console.aws.amazon.com.
2 Click Services and search for IAM.
3 Open the IAM service.

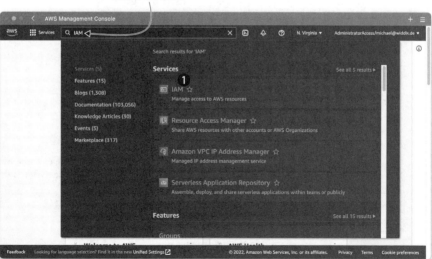

Figure 4.2   Open the IAM service

A page opens as shown in figure 4.3; select Users at the left.

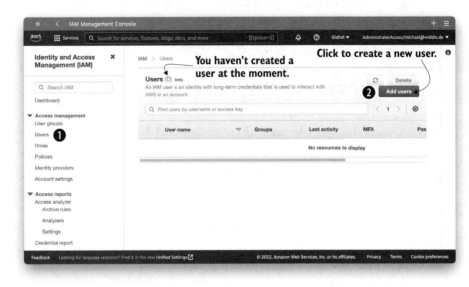

Figure 4.3   IAM users (empty)

Follow these steps to create a user:

1   Click Add Users to open the page shown in figure 4.4.
2   Enter mycli as the user name.

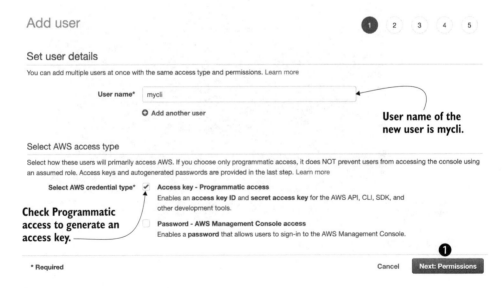

Figure 4.4   Creating an IAM user

3 Under AWS credential type, select Access Key—Programmatic Access.

4 Click the Next: Permissions button.

In the next step, you have to define the permissions for the new user, as shown in figure 4.5:

1 Click Attach Existing Policies Directly.

2 Select the AdministratorAccess policy.

3 Click the Next: Tags button.

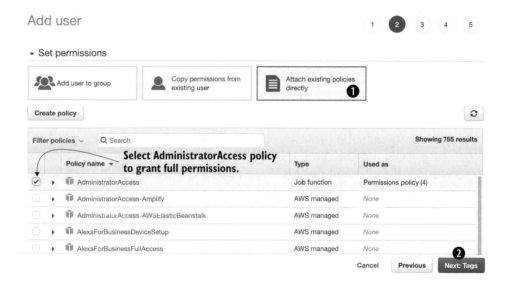

Figure 4.5   Setting permissions for an IAM user

No tags are needed (you learned about tags in chapter 2), so click the Next: Review button.

The review page sums up what you have configured. Click the Create User button to save. Finally, you will see the page shown in figure 4.6. Click the Show link to display the secret value. You now need to copy the credentials to your CLI configuration. Read on to learn how this works.

> **WARNING**   Treat the access key ID and secret access key as top secret. Anyone who gets access to these credentials will have administrator access to your AWS account.

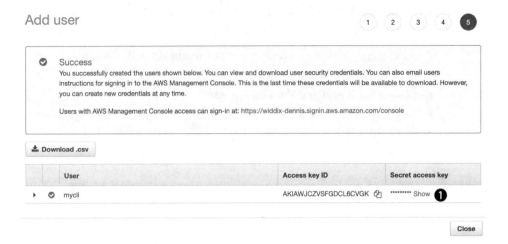

Figure 4.6   Showing the access key of an IAM user

Open the terminal on your computer (PowerShell on Windows or a shell on Linux and macOS; not the AWS Management Console), and run `aws configure`. You're asked for the next four pieces of information:

1   *AWS access key ID*—Copy and paste this value from the Access key ID column (your browser window).
2   *AWS secret access key*—Copy and paste this value from the Secret access key column (your browser window).
3   *Default region name*—Enter us-east-1.
4   *Default output format*—Enter json.

In the end, the terminal should look similar to this:

```
$ aws configure
 AWS Access Key ID [None]:  AKIAIRUR3YLPOSVD7ZCA
 AWS Secret Access Key [None]:
➥ SSKIng7jkAKERpcT3YphX4cD87sBYgWVw2enqBj7
 Default region name [None]: us-east-1
 Default output format [None]: json
```

Your value will be different! Copy it from your browser window.

Your value will be different! Copy it from your browser window.

The CLI is now configured to authenticate as the user `mycli`. Switch back to the browser window, and click Close to finish the user-creation wizard.

It's time to test whether the CLI works. Switch to the terminal window, and enter `aws ec2 describe-regions` to get a list of all available regions, as shown here:

```
$ aws ec2 describe-regions
{
  "Regions": [
    {
      "Endpoint": "ec2.eu-north-1.amazonaws.com",
```

```
      "RegionName": "eu-north-1",
      "OptInStatus": "opt-in-not-required"
    },
    [...]
    {
      "Endpoint": "ec2.us-west-2.amazonaws.com",
      "RegionName": "us-west-2",
      "OptInStatus": "opt-in-not-required"
    }
  ]
}
```

It works! You can now begin to use the CLI.

4.2.3 Using the CLI

Suppose you want to get a list of all running EC2 instances of type `t2.micro` so you can see what is running in your AWS account. Execute the following command in your terminal:

```
$ aws ec2 describe-instances --filters "Name=instance-type,Values=t2.micro"
{
  "Reservations": []          ◁─────  The list is empty because
}                                      you haven't created an
                                       EC2 instance.
```

> ### Dealing with long output
>
> By default, the AWS CLI returns all output through your operating system's default pager program (on my system this is `less`). This method is helpful to avoid massive amounts of data being printed to your terminal.
>
> There is one thing to know: **to quit less**, press q and you will be taken back to where you issued the AWS CLI command.

To use the AWS CLI, you need to specify a service and an action. In the previous example, the service is `ec2` and the action is `describe-instances`. You can add options with `--name value` as follows:

```
$ aws <service> <action> [--name value ...]
```

One important feature of the CLI is the help keyword. You can get help at the following three levels of detail:

- `aws help`—Shows all available services
- `aws <service> help`—Shows all actions available for a certain service
- `aws <service> <action> help`—Shows all options available for the particular service action

4.2.4   Automating with the CLI

> **IAM role ec2-ssm-core**
>
> The following script requires an IAM role named `ec2-ssm-core`. You created the role in the section "Creating an IAM role" in chapter 3.

Sometimes you need temporary computing power, like a Linux machine to test something. To do this, you can write a script that creates a virtual machine for you. The script will run on your local computer and does the following:

1. Starts a virtual machine.
2. Helps you to connect to the VM via the Session Manager.
3. Waits for you to finish your temporary usage of the VM.
4. Terminates the virtual machine.

The script is used like this:

```
$ ./virtualmachine.sh
waiting for i-08f21510e8c4f4441 ...          ◁──┐ Waits until
i-08f21510e8c4f4441 is up and running             started
connect to the instance using Session Manager
https://console.aws.amazon.com/systems-manager/ses[...]441
Press [Enter] key to terminate i-08f21510e8c4f4441 ...
terminating i-08f21510e8c4f4441 ...          ◁──┐ Waits until
done.                                             terminated
```

Your virtual machine runs until you press the Enter key. When you press Enter, the virtual machine is terminated. The CLI solution solves the following use cases:

- Creating a virtual machine
- Getting the ID of a virtual machine to connect via the Session Manager
- Terminating the virtual machine if it's no longer needed

Depending on your OS, you'll use either Bash (Linux and macOS) or PowerShell (Windows) to script.

One important feature of the CLI needs explanation before you can begin. The `--query` option uses JMESPath syntax, which is a query language for JSON, to extract data from the result. Doing this can be useful because usually you need only a specific field from the result. The following CLI command gets a list of all AMIs in JSON format:

```
$ aws ec2 describe-images --filters \
    "Name=name,Values=amzn2-ami-hvm-2.0.202*-x86_64-gp2"     ◁──┐ The filter returns
{                                                                 only Amazon
  "Images": [                                                     Linux 2 images
    {                                                             for AMD/Intel.
      "ImageId": "ami-0ce1e3f77cd41957e",
      "State": "available"
```

```
    [...]
  },
  [...]
  {
    "ImageId": "ami-08754599965c30981",
    "State": "available"
  }
 ]
}
```

The output is overwhelming. To start an EC2 instance, you need the `ImageId` without all the other information. With JMESPath, you can extract just that information, like so:

```
$ aws ec2 describe-images --filters \
➡  "Name=name,Values=amzn2-ami-hvm-2.0.202*-x86_64-gp2" \
➡  --query "Images[0].ImageId"          ◁─── Returns the first image
"ami-146e2a7c"                                 ID from the list
```

The output is wrapped in quotes. This is caused by the default setting of the AWS CLI to output all data in JSON format and JSON strings are enclosed in quotes. To change that, use the `--output text` option as follows to format the output as multiple lines of tab-separated string values. This setting can be useful to pass the output to a text processor, like `grep`, `sed`, or `awk`:

```
$ aws ec2 describe-images --filters \
➡  "Name=name,Values=amzn2-ami-hvm-2.0.202*-x86_64-gp2" \
➡  --query "Images[0].ImageId" --output text     ◁─── Sets the output
ami-146e2a7c                                            format to plain text
```

With this short introduction to JMESPath, you're well equipped to extract the data you need.

> **Where is the code located?**
>
> All code can be found in the book's code repository on GitHub: https://github.com/AWSinAction/code3. You can download a snapshot of the repository at https://github.com/AWSinAction/code3/archive/main.zip.

Linux and macOS can interpret Bash scripts, whereas Windows prefers PowerShell scripts. So, we've created two versions of the same script.

LINUX AND MACOS

You can find the following listing in /chapter04/virtualmachine.sh in the book's code folder. You can run it either by copying and pasting each line into your terminal or by executing the entire script via the following:

```
chmod +x virtualmachine.sh    ◁─── Ensures that the script is
./virtualmachine.sh                 executable (only required once)
```

Listing 4.1   Creating and terminating a virtual machine from the CLI (Bash)

> **-e makes Bash abort if a command fails.**

> **Gets the ID of Amazon Linux AMI**

> **Gets the default VPC ID**

> **Gets the default subnet ID**

> **Creates and start the virtual machine**

> **Waits until the virtual machine is started**

> **Terminates the virtual machine**

> **Waits until the virtual machine is terminated**

```bash
#!/bin/bash -e
AMIID="$(aws ec2 describe-images --filters \
 "Name=name,Values=amzn2-ami-hvm-2.0.202*-x86_64-gp2" \
 --query "Images[0].ImageId" --output text)"
VPCID="$(aws ec2 describe-vpcs --filter "Name=isDefault, \
 Values=true" \
 --query "Vpcs[0].VpcId" --output text)"
SUBNETID="$(aws ec2 describe-subnets --filters \
 "Name=vpc-id, Values=$VPCID" --query "Subnets[0].SubnetId" \
 --output text)"
INSTANCEID="$(aws ec2 run-instances --image-id "$AMIID" \
 --instance-type t2.micro --subnet-id "$SUBNETID" \
 --iam-instance-profile "Name=ec2-ssm-core" \
 --query "Instances[0].InstanceId" --output text)"
echo "waiting for $INSTANCEID ..."
aws ec2 wait instance-running --instance-ids "$INSTANCEID"
echo "$INSTANCEID is up and running"
echo "connect to the instance using Session Manager"
echo "https://console.aws.amazon.com/systems-manager/
 session-manager/$INSTANCEID"
read -r -p "Press [Enter] key to terminate $INSTANCEID ..."
aws ec2 terminate-instances --instance-ids
 "$INSTANCEID" > /dev/null
echo "terminating $INSTANCEID ..."
aws ec2 wait instance-terminated --instance-ids
 "$INSTANCEID"
echo "done."
```

Cleaning up

Make sure you terminate the virtual machine before you go on by pressing the Enter key!

WINDOWS

You can find the following listing in /chapter04/virtualmachine.ps1 in the book's code folder. Right-click the virtualmachine.ps1 file, and select Run with PowerShell to execute the script.

Listing 4.2   Creating and terminating a virtual machine from the CLI (PowerShell)

> **Aborts if the command fails**

> **Gets the ID of Amazon Linux AMI**

> **Gets the default VPC ID**

```powershell
$ErrorActionPreference = "Stop"

$AMIID=aws ec2 describe-images --filters \
 "Name=name,Values=amzn2-ami-hvm-2.0.202*-x86_64-gp2" \
 --query "Images[0].ImageId" --output text
$VPCID=aws ec2 describe-vpcs --filter
 "Name=isDefault, Values=true" \
```

```
➡ --query "Vpcs[0].VpcId" --output text
$SUBNETID=aws ec2 describe-subnets \                    ⟵⎯⎤  Gets the default subnet ID
➡ --filters "Name=vpc-id, Values=$VPCID" --query "Subnets[0].SubnetId" \
➡ --output text
$INSTANCEID=aws ec2 run-instances --image-id $AMIID \   ⟵⎯⎤  Creates and
➡ --instance-type t2.micro --subnet-id $SUBNETID \           starts the virtual
➡ --iam-instance-profile "Name=ec2-ssm-core" \               machine
➡ --query "Instances[0].InstanceId" --output text
Write-Host "waiting for $INSTANCEID ..."                       ⎤ Waits until the
aws ec2 wait instance-running --instance-ids $INSTANCEID  ⟵⎯⎤   virtual machine
Write-Host "$INSTANCEID is up and running"                     ⎦ is started
Write-Host "connect to the instance using Session Manager"
Write-Host "https://console.aws.amazon.com/systems-manager
➡ /session-manager/$INSTANCEID"
Write-Host "Press [Enter] key to terminate $INSTANCEID ..."   ⎤ Terminates the
Read-Host                                                      ⎦ virtual machine
aws ec2 terminate-instances --instance-ids $INSTANCEID    ⟵⎯⎤
Write-Host "terminating $INSTANCEID ..."
aws ec2 wait instance-terminated --instance-ids $INSTANCEID  ⟵⎯⎤
Write-Host "done."
                                                         Waits until the virtual
                                                         machine is terminated
```

> **Cleaning up**
> Make sure you terminate the virtual machine before you go on.

The limitations of the CLI solution follow:

- It can handle only one virtual machine at a time.
- There is a different version for Windows than for Linux and macOS.
- It's a command-line application, not a graphical one.

Next, learn how to improve the CLI solution using the AWS SDK.

4.3   Programming with the SDK

AWS offers SDKs for the following programming languages and platforms:

- JavaScript/Node.js
- Java
- .NET
- PHP
- Python
- Ruby
- Go
- C++

An AWS SDK is a convenient way to make calls to the AWS API from your favorite programming language. The SDK takes care of things like authentication, retry on error,

HTTPS communication, and XML or JSON (de)serialization. You're free to choose the SDK for your favorite language, but in this book, most examples are written in JavaScript and run in the Node.js runtime environment.

> ### Installing and getting started with Node.js
>
> Node.js is a platform for executing JavaScript in an event-driven environment so you can easily build network applications. To install Node.js, visit https://nodejs.org and download the package that fits your OS. All examples in this book are tested with Node.js 14.
>
> After Node.js is installed, you can verify that everything works by typing node –version into your terminal. Your terminal should respond with something similar to v14.*. Now you're ready to run JavaScript examples, like the Node Control Center for AWS. Your Node.js installation comes with a important tool called npm, which is the package manager for Node.js. Verify the installation by running npm --version in your terminal.
>
> To run a JavaScript script in Node.js, enter node script.js in your terminal, where script.js is the name of the script file. We use Node.js in this book because it's easy to install, it requires no IDE, and the syntax is familiar to most programmers.
>
> Don't be confused by the terms *JavaScript* and *Node.js*. If you want to be precise, JavaScript is the language and Node.js is the runtime environment. But don't expect anybody to make that distinction. Node.js is also called node.
>
> Do you want to get started with Node.js? We recommend *Node.js in Action* (second edition) by Alex Young et al. (Manning, 2017), or the video course *Node.js in Motion* by PJ Evans (Manning, 2018).

To understand how the AWS SDK for Node.js (JavaScript) works, let's create a Node.js (JavaScript) application that controls EC2 instances via the AWS SDK. The name of the application is *Node Control Center for AWS* or *nodecc* for short.

4.3.1   *Controlling virtual machines with SDK: nodecc*

The *Node Control Center for AWS* (nodecc) is for managing multiple temporary EC2 instances using a text UI written in JavaScript. nodecc offers the following features:

- It can handle multiple virtual machines.
- It's written in JavaScript and runs in Node.js, so it's portable across platforms.
- It uses a textual UI.

Figure 4.7 shows what nodecc looks like.

> ### IAM role ec2-ssm-core
>
> nodecc requires an IAM role named ec2-ssm-core. You created the role in the "Creating an IAM Role" section in chapter 3.

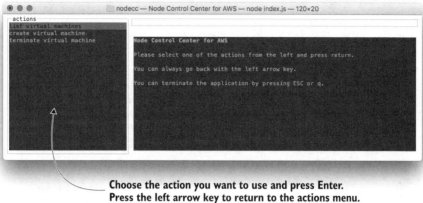

Choose the action you want to use and press Enter.
Press the left arrow key to return to the actions menu.

Figure 4.7   nodecc: Start screen

You can find the nodecc application at /chapter04/nodecc/ in the book's code folder. Switch to that directory, and run npm install in your terminal to install all needed dependencies. To start nodecc, run node index.js. You can always go back by pressing the left arrow key. You can quit the application by pressing Esc or q. The SDK uses the same settings you created for the CLI, so you're using the mycli user when running nodecc.

4.3.2   *How nodecc creates a virtual machine*

Before you can do anything with nodecc, you need at least one virtual machine. To start a virtual machine, choose the AMI you want, as figure 4.8 shows.

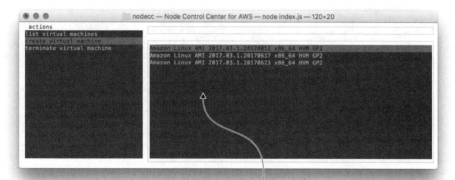

Choose the AMI you want to use for the new EC2 server.

Figure 4.8   nodecc: Creating a virtual machine (step 1 of 2)

The code shown in the next listing, which fetches the list of the available AMIs, is located at lib/listAMIs.js.

Listing 4.3   Fetching the list of available AMIs: /lib/listAMIs.js

API call to
list AMIs

require is used to
load modules.

Creates an
EC2 client

```
const AWS = require('aws-sdk');
const ec2 = new AWS.EC2({region: 'us-east-1'});

module.exports = (cb) => {
    ec2.describeImages({
        Filters: [{
            Name: 'name',
            Values: ['amzn2-ami-hvm-2.0.202*-x86_64-gp2']
        }]
    }, (err, data) => {
        if (err) {
            cb(err);
        } else {
            const amiIds = data.Images.map(image => image.ImageId);
            const descriptions = data.Images.map(image => image.Description);
            cb(null, {amiIds: amiIds, descriptions: descriptions});
        }
    });
};
```

module.exports makes this
function available to users of
the listAMIs module.

Otherwise, data
contains all AMIs.

In case of
failure, err
is set.

The code is structured in such a way that each action is implemented in the lib folder. The next step to create a virtual machine is to choose which subnet the virtual machine should be started in. You haven't learned about subnets yet, so for now, select one randomly; see figure 4.9.

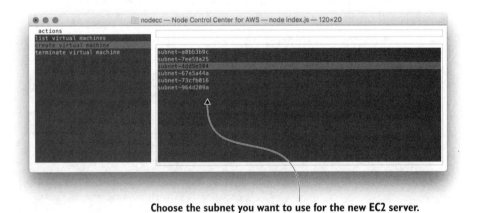

Choose the subnet you want to use for the new EC2 server.

Figure 4.9   nodecc: Creating a virtual machine (step 2 of 2)

The corresponding script, shown in the next listing, is located at lib/listSubnets.js.

Listing 4.4   Fetching the list of available default subnets: /lib/listSubnets.js

```
const AWS = /* ... */;
const ec2 = /* ... */;

module.exports = (cb) => {
  ec2.describeVpcs({                          ◁  API call to
    Filters: [{                                  list VPCs
      Name: 'isDefault',        ◁─────  The filter selects
      Values: ['true']                   default VPCs only.
    }]
  }, (err, data) => {
    if (err) {
      cb(err);                                      There can be
    } else {                                        only one default
      const vpcId = data.Vpcs[0].VpcId;      ◁     VPC.
      ec2.describeSubnets({            ◁─────  API call to list
        Filters: [{               ◁              subnets
          Name: 'vpc-id',
          Values: [vpcId]
        }]                          The filter selects
      }, (err, data) => {          subnets from the
        if (err) {                 default VPC only.
          cb(err);
        } else {
          const subnetIds = data.Subnets.map(subnet => subnet.SubnetId);
          cb(null, subnetIds);
        }
      });
    }
  });
};
```

After you select the subnet, the virtual machine is created by lib/createVM.js, and you see a starting screen, as shown in the following listing.

Listing 4.5   Launching an EC2 instance: /lib/createVM.js

**The IAM role and instance profile
ec2-ssm-core was created in chapter 3.**

```
module.exports = (amiId, subnetId, cb) => {
  ec2.runInstances({                 ◁─────  API call to launch
    IamInstanceProfile: {                    an EC2 instance
      Name: 'ec2-ssm-core'
    },                           │  Passes the selected AMI
    ImageId: amiId,        ◁─────┘
    MinCount: 1,              Launches one instance...
    MaxCount: 1,
    InstanceType: 't2.micro',     ◁    ...of type t2.micro
    SubnetId: subnetId        ◁         to stay in the
  }, cb);                                Free Tier
};                         Passes the
                         selected subnet
```

Now it's time to find out some details of the newly created virtual machine. Use the left arrow key to switch to the navigation section.

4.3.3   *How nodecc lists virtual machines and shows virtual machine details*

One important use case that nodecc must support is showing the details of a VM that you can use to connect via the Session Manager. Because nodecc handles multiple virtual machines, the first step is to select a VM, as shown in figure 4.10.

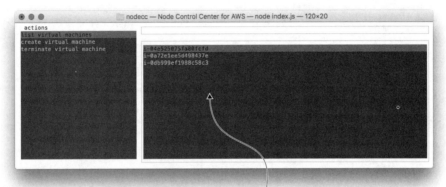

All running servers are listed by their EC2 instance ID.

Figure 4.10   nodecc: Listing virtual machines

Look at lib/listVMs.js, shown in the next listing, to see how a list of virtual machines can be retrieved with the AWS SDK.

Listing 4.6   Listing EC2 instances: /lib/listVMs.js

```
module.exports = (cb) => {                          API call to list
  ec2.describeInstances({                           EC2 instances
    Filters: [{
      Name: 'instance-state-name',                  The filter selects
      Values: ['pending', 'running']                starting and running
    }],                                             instances only.
    MaxResults: 10                  Shows at most
  }, (err, data) => {               10 instances
    if (err) {
      cb(err);
    } else {
      const instanceIds = data.Reservations
        .map(r => r.Instances.map(i => i.InstanceId))
        .flat();
      cb(null, instanceIds);
    }
  });
};
```

After you select the VM, you can display its details; see figure 4.11. You could use the `LaunchTime` to find old EC2 instances. You can also connect to an instance using the Session Manager. Press the left arrow key to switch back to the navigation section.

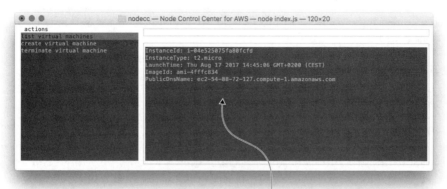

The launch time can help to find old instances.

Figure 4.11   nodecc: Showing virtual machine details

4.3.4   How nodecc terminates a virtual machine

To terminate a virtual machine, you first have to select it. To list the virtual machines, use lib/listVMs.js again. After you select the VM, lib/terminateVM.js takes care of termination, as shown in the following code snippet.

Listing 4.7   Terminating an EC2 instance: /lib/terminateVM.js

```
module.exports = (instanceId, cb) => {          API call to list
  ec2.terminateInstances({                       EC2 instances
    InstanceIds: [instanceId]
  }, cb);                                        Passes the selected
};                                               instance ID
```

That's nodecc: a text UI program for controlling temporary EC2 instances. Take some time to think about what you could create by using your favorite language and the AWS SDK. Chances are high that you might come up with a new business idea!

> **Cleaning up**
> Make sure you terminate all started virtual machines before you go on! You learned to use nodecc to terminate instances in the previous section.

The hard parts about using the SDK follow:

- The SDK (or, better, Node.js) follows an imperative approach. You provide all instructions, step by step, in the right order, to get the job done.

- You have to deal with dependencies (e.g., wait for the instance to be running before connecting to it).
- There is no easy way to update the instances that are running with new settings (e.g., change the instance type).

It's time to enter a new world by leaving the imperative world and entering the declarative world.

4.4   Infrastructure as Code

Infrastructure as Code is the idea of using a high-level programming language to control infrastructures. Infrastructure can be any AWS resource, like a network topology, a load balancer, a DNS entry, and so on. In software development, tools like automated tests, code repositories, and build servers increase the quality of software engineering. If your infrastructure is defined as code, then you can apply these types of software development tools to your infrastructure and improve its quality.

> **WARNING**   Don't mix up the terms Infrastructure as Code and *Infrastructure as a Service* (IaaS)! IaaS means renting virtual machines, storage, and network with a pay-per-use pricing model.

4.4.1   Inventing an infrastructure language: JIML

For the purposes of learning the concepts behind Infrastructure as Code, let's invent a new language to describe infrastructure: JSON Infrastructure Markup Language (JIML). Figure 4.12 shows the infrastructure that will be created in the end.

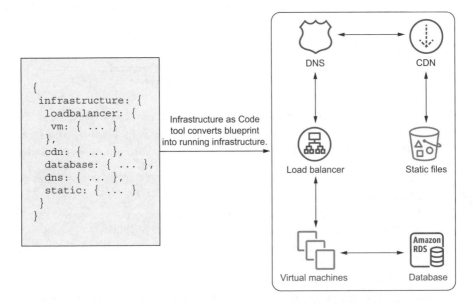

Figure 4.12   From JIML blueprint to infrastructure: Infrastructure automation

The infrastructure consists of the following:

- Load balancer (LB)
- Virtual machines (VMs)
- Database (DB)
- DNS entry
- Content delivery network (CDN)
- Storage for static files

To reduce problems with syntax, let's say JIML is based on JSON. The following JIML code creates the infrastructure shown in figure 4.12. The $ indicates a reference to an ID.

Listing 4.8 Infrastructure description in JIML

```
{
    "region": "us-east-1",
    "resources": [{
        "type": "loadbalancer",              ←—  A load balancer
        "id": "LB",                               is needed.
        "config": {
            "virtualmachines": 2,             ←—  Needs two VMs
            "virtualmachine": {      ←—┐
                "cpu": 2,                     VMs are Ubuntu
                "ram": 4,                     Linux (4 GB memory,
                "os": "ubuntu"                2 cores).
            }
        },
        "waitFor": "$DB"             ←—┘  LB can be created only if
    }, {                                  the database is ready.
        "type": "cdn",
        "id": "CDN",                 ←————
        "config": {                       A CDN is used that caches
            "defaultSource": "$LB",       requests to the LB or fetches
            "sources": [{                 static assets (images, CSS
                "path": "/static/*",      files, ...) from a bucket.
                "source": "$BUCKET"
            }]
        }
    }, {
        "type": "database",
        "id": "DB",                  ←—┐  Data is stored
        "config": {                       within a MySQL
            "password": "***",            database.
            "engine": "MySQL"
        }
    }, {
        "type": "dns",               ←—┤  A DNS entry points
        "config": {                       to the CDN.
            "from": "www.mydomain.com",
            "to": "$CDN"
        }                            ┌—  A bucket is used to store
    }, {                                static assets (images,
        "type": "bucket",            ←——  CSS files, ...).
```

```
    "id": "BUCKET"
  }]
}
```

How can we turn this JSON into AWS API calls?

1 Parse the JSON input.
2 The JIML tool creates a dependency graph by connecting the resources with their dependencies.
3 The JIML tool traverses the dependency graph from the bottom (leaves) to the top (root) and a linear flow of commands. The commands are expressed in a pseudo language.
4 The commands in pseudo language are translated into AWS API calls by the JIML runtime.

The AWS API calls have to be made based on the resources defined in the blueprint. In particular, you must send the AWS API calls in the correct order. Let's look at the dependency graph created by the JIML tool, shown in figure 4.13.

You traverse the dependency graph in figure 4.13 from bottom to top and from left to right. The nodes at the bottom have no children and therefore no dependencies: DB, VM, and bucket.

The LB node depends on the DB node and the two VM nodes. The CDN node depends on the LB and the bucket node. Finally, the DNS node depends on the CDN node.

The JIML tool turns the dependency graph into a linear flow of commands using pseudo language, as shown in the next listing. The pseudo language represents the steps needed to create all the resources in the correct order. The nodes are easy to create because they have no dependencies, so they're created first.

Listing 4.9 Linear flow of commands in pseudo language

```
$DB = database create {"password": "***",          ◁──┐  Creates the database
➥  "engine": "MySQL"}
$VM1 = virtualmachine create {"cpu": 2, "ram": 4,   ◁─┐  Creates the virtual machine
➥  "os": "ubuntu"}
$VM2 = virtualmachine create {"cpu": 2, "ram": 4,
➥  "os": "ubuntu"}
$BUCKET = bucket create {}          ◁──┘  Creates the bucket

await [$DB, $VM1, $VM2]                    ◁──┘  Waits for the dependencies
$LB = loadbalancer create {"virtualmachines":       ◁─┐  Creates the load balancer
➥  [$VM1, $VM2]}

await [$LB, $BUCKET]
$CDN = cdn create {...}          ◁──┐  Creates the CDN

await $CDN
$DNS = dns create {...}          ◁──┐  Creates the DNS entry

await $DNS
```

JIML code   **JIML dependency graph**

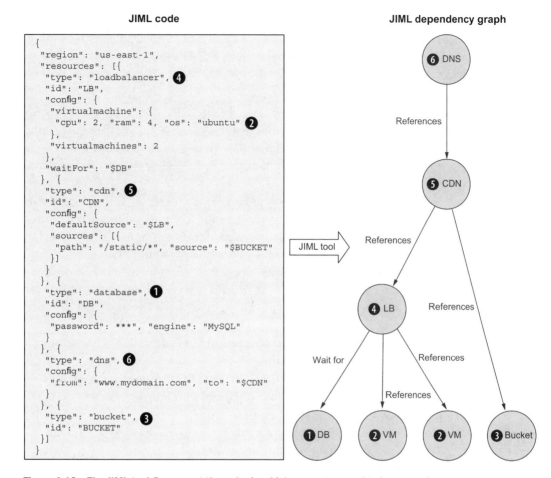

Figure 4.13 The JIML tool figures out the order in which resources need to be created.

We'll skip the last step—translating the commands from the pseudo language into AWS API calls. You've already learned everything you need to know about infrastructure as code: it's all about dependencies. Let's apply those newly learned ideas in practice.

4.5 Using AWS CloudFormation to start a virtual machine

In the previous section, we created JIML to introduce the concept of infrastructure as code. Luckily, AWS already offers a tool that does much better than our JIML: *AWS CloudFormation*.

NOTE When using CloudFormation, what we have been referring to as a blueprint so far is actually referred to as a CloudFormation template.

A *template* is a description of your infrastructure, written in JSON or YAML, that can be interpreted by CloudFormation. The idea of describing something rather than listing the necessary actions is called a *declarative approach*. Declarative means you tell CloudFormation how your infrastructure should look. You aren't telling CloudFormation what actions are needed to create that infrastructure, and you don't specify the sequence in which the actions need to be executed. The benefits of CloudFormation follow:

- *It's a consistent way to describe infrastructure on AWS.* If you use scripts to create your infrastructure, everyone will solve the same problem differently. This is a hurdle for new developers and operators trying to understand what the code is doing. CloudFormation templates provide a clear language for defining infrastructure.
- *It handles dependencies.* Ever tried to register a web server with a load balancer that wasn't yet available? When you first start trying to automate infrastructure creation, you'll miss a lot of dependencies. Trust us: never try to set up complex infrastructure using scripts. You'll end up in dependency hell!
- *It's reproducible.* Is your test environment an exact copy of your production environment? Using CloudFormation, you can create two identical infrastructures. It is also possible to apply changes to both the test and production environment.
- *It's customizable.* You can insert custom parameters into CloudFormation to customize your templates as you wish.
- *It's testable.* If you can create your architecture from a template, it's testable. Just start a new infrastructure, run your tests, and shut it down again.
- *It's updatable.* CloudFormation supports updates to your infrastructure. It will figure out the parts of the template that have changed and apply those changes as smoothly as possible to your infrastructure.
- *It minimizes human failure.* CloudFormation doesn't get tired—even at 3 a.m.
- *It's the documentation for your infrastructure.* A CloudFormation template is a JSON or YAML document. You can treat it as code and use a version control system like Git to keep track of the changes.
- *It's free.* Using CloudFormation comes at no additional charge. If you subscribe to an AWS support plan, you also get support for CloudFormation.

We think CloudFormation is the most powerful tool available for managing infrastructure on AWS.

4.5.1   *Anatomy of a CloudFormation template*

A basic CloudFormation template consists of the following five parts:

1   *Format version*—The latest template format version is 2010-09-09, and this is currently the only valid value. Specify this version; the default is to use the latest version, which will cause problems if new versions are introduced in the future.

2   *Description*—What is this template about?

3 *Parameters*—Parameters are used to customize a template with values, for example, domain name, customer ID, and database password.

4 *Resources*—A resource is the smallest block you can describe. Examples are a virtual machine, a load balancer, or an Elastic IP address.

5 *Outputs*—An output is comparable to a parameter, but the other way around. An output returns details about a resource created by the template, for example, the public name of an EC2 instance.

A basic template looks like the following listing.

Listing 4.10   CloudFormation template structure

```
---                    ◁─┘ Start of a document
AWSTemplateFormatVersion: '2010-09-09'    ◁─┘ The only valid version
Description: 'CloudFormation template structure'    ◁─┐ What is this
Parameters:                                              template about?
  # [...]      ◁─┐ Defines the parameters
Resources
  # [...]      ◁─┐ Defines the resources
Outputs:
  # [...]      ◁─┐ Defines the outputs
```

Let's take a closer look at parameters, resources, and outputs.

FORMAT VERSION AND DESCRIPTION

The only valid `AWSTemplateFormatVersion` value at the moment is 2010-09-09. Always specify the format version. If you don't, CloudFormation will use whatever version is the latest one. As mentioned earlier, this means if a new format version is introduced in the future, you'll end up using the wrong format and get into serious trouble.

`Description` isn't mandatory, but we encourage you to take some time to document what the template is about. A meaningful description will help you in the future to remember what the template is for. It will also help your coworkers.

PARAMETERS

A parameter has at least a name and a type. We encourage you to add a description as well, as shown in the next listing.

Listing 4.11   CloudFormation parameter structure

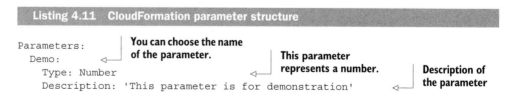

```
Parameters:          │ You can choose the name
  Demo:      ◁─┘      │ of the parameter.
    Type: Number                         │ This parameter
    Description: 'This parameter is for demonstration'    ◁─┘ represents a number.
                                                           │ Description of
                                                           │ the parameter
```

Valid types are listed in table 4.1.

Table 4.1 CloudFormation parameter types

Type	Description
String CommaDelimitedList	A string or a list of strings separated by commas
Number List<Number>	An integer or float, or a list of integers or floats
AWS::EC2::AvailabilityZone::Name List<AWS::EC2::AvailabilityZone::Name>	An Availability Zone, such as us-west-2a, or a list of Availability Zones
AWS::EC2::Image::Id List<AWS::EC2::Image::Id>	An AMI ID or a list of AMIs
AWS::EC2::Instance::Id List<AWS::EC2::Instance::Id>	An EC2 instance ID or a list of EC2 instance IDs
AWS::EC2::KeyPair::KeyName	An Amazon EC2 key-pair name
AWS::EC2::SecurityGroup::Id List<AWS::EC2::SecurityGroup::Id>	A security group ID or a list of security group IDs
AWS::EC2::Subnet::Id List<AWS::EC2::Subnet::Id>	A subnet ID or a list of subnet IDs
AWS::EC2::Volume::Id List<AWS::EC2::Volume::Id>	An EBS volume ID (network attached storage) or a list of EBS volume IDs
AWS::EC2::VPC::Id List<AWS::EC2::VPC::Id>	A VPC ID (virtual private cloud) or a list of VPC IDs
AWS::Route53::HostedZone::Id List<AWS::Route53::HostedZone::Id>	A DNS zone ID or a list of DNS zone IDs

In addition to using the Type and Description properties, you can enhance a parameter with the properties listed in table 4.2.

Table 4.2 CloudFormation parameter properties

Property	Description	Example
Default	A default value for the parameter	Default: 'm5.large'
NoEcho	Hides the parameter value in all graphical tools (useful for secrets)	NoEcho: true
AllowedValues	Specifies possible values for the parameter	AllowedValues: [1, 2, 3]
AllowedPattern	More generic than AllowedValues because it uses a regular expression	AllowedPattern: '[a-zA-Z0-9]*' allows only a–z, A–Z, and 0–9 with any length
MinLength, MaxLength	Defines how long a parameter can be	MinLength: 12

Table 4.2 CloudFormation parameter properties *(continued)*

Property	Description	Example
MinValue, MaxValue	Used in combination with the Number type to define lower and upper bounds	MaxValue: 10
ConstraintDescription	A string that explains the constraint when the constraint is violated	ConstraintDescription: 'Maximum value is 10.'

A parameter section of a CloudFormation template could look like this:

```
Parameters:
  KeyName:
    Description: 'Key Pair name'
    Type: 'AWS::EC2::KeyPair::KeyName'        ←──  Only key-pair
  NumberOfVirtualMachines:                          names are allowed.
    Description: 'How many virtual machine do you like?'
    Type: Number                    The default is one
    Default: 1          ←────────   virtual machine.
    MinValue: 1
    MaxValue: 5         ←────────   Prevents massive costs
  WordPressVersion:                 with an upper bound
    Description: 'Which version of WordPress do you want?'
    Type: String
    AllowedValues: ['4.1.1', '4.0.1']       ←──  Restricted to
                                                 certain versions
```

Now you should have a better feel for parameters. If you want to know everything about them, see the documentation at http://mng.bz/ZpB5, or follow along in the book and learn by doing.

RESOURCES

A resource has at least a name, a type, and some properties, as shown in the next listing.

Listing 4.12 CloudFormation resources structure

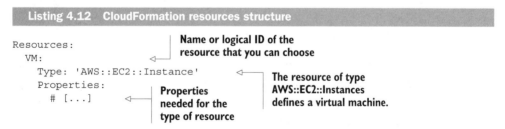

When defining resources, you need to know about the type and that type's properties. In this book, you'll get to know a lot of resource types and their respective properties. An example of a single EC2 instance appears in the following code snippet.

Listing 4.13 CloudFormation EC2 instance resource

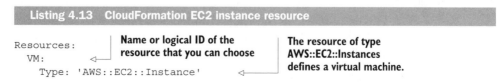

The AMI defines the operating system of the vm.

```
Properties:
  ImageId: 'ami-6057e21a'
  InstanceType: 't2.micro'
  SecurityGroupIds:
  - 'sg-123456'
  SubnetId: 'subnet-123456'
```

The instance type defines the number of vCPUs, memory, and more.

You'll learn about this in chapter 5.

Now you've described the virtual machine, but how can you output its public name?

OUTPUTS

A CloudFormation template's output includes at least a name (like parameters and resources) and a value, but we encourage you to add a description as well, as illustrated in the next listing. You can use outputs to pass data from within your template to the outside.

Listing 4.14   CloudFormation outputs structure

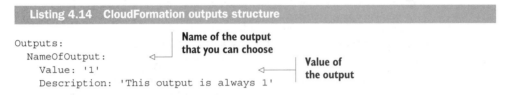

```
Outputs:
  NameOfOutput:
    Value: '1'
    Description: 'This output is always 1'
```

Name of the output that you can choose

Value of the output

Static outputs like this one aren't very useful. You'll mostly use values that reference the name of a resource or an attribute of a resource, like its public name. If you see `!Ref NameOfSomething`, think of it as a placeholder for what is referenced by the name. A `!GetAtt 'NameOfSomething.AttributeOfSomething'`, shown in the next code, is similar to a ref but you select a specific attribute of the referenced resource.

Listing 4.15   CloudFormation outputs example

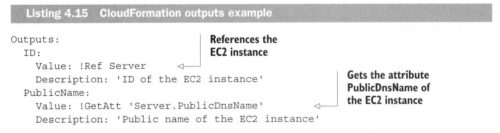

```
Outputs:
  ID:
    Value: !Ref Server
    Description: 'ID of the EC2 instance'
  PublicName:
    Value: !GetAtt 'Server.PublicDnsName'
    Description: 'Public name of the EC2 instance'
```

References the EC2 instance

Gets the attribute PublicDnsName of the EC2 instance

You'll get to know the most important attributes of `!GetAtt` while reading this book.

Now that we've taken a brief look at the core parts of a CloudFormation template, it's time to make one of your own.

4.5.2   Creating your first template

How do you create a CloudFormation template? Different options are available, as shown here:

- Use a text editor or IDE to write a template from scratch.
- Start with a template from a public repository that offers a default implementation, and adapt it to your needs.
- Use a template provided by your vendor.

AWS and its partners offer CloudFormation templates for deploying popular solutions: AWS Partner Solutions at https://aws.amazon.com/quickstart/. Furthermore, we have open sourced the templates we are using in our day-to-day work on GitHub: https://github.com/widdix/aws-cf-templates.

Suppose you've been asked to provide a VM for a developer team. After a few months, the team realizes the VM needs more CPU power, because the usage pattern has changed. You can handle that request with the CLI and the SDK, but before the instance type can be changed, you must stop the EC2 instance. The process follows:

1 Stop the instance.
2 Wait for the instance to stop.
3 Change the instance type.
4 Start the instance.
5 Wait for the instance to start.

A declarative approach like that used by CloudFormation is simpler: just change the `InstanceType` property and update the template. `InstanceType` can be passed to the template via a parameter, as shown in the next listing. That's it! You can begin creating the template.

Listing 4.16   A template to create an EC2 instance with CloudFormation

```
---
AWSTemplateFormatVersion: '2010-09-09'
Description: 'AWS in Action: chapter 4'
Parameters:
  VPC:
    Type: 'AWS::EC2::VPC::Id'
  Subnet:                                      The user
    Type: 'AWS::EC2::Subnet::Id'              defines the
  InstanceType:                               instance type.
    Description: 'Select one of the possible instance types'
    Type: String
    Default: 't2.micro'
    AllowedValues: ['t2.micro', 't2.small', 't2.medium']
Resources:
  SecurityGroup:
    Type: 'AWS::EC2::SecurityGroup'
    Properties:
      # [...]                          Defines a minimal
  VM:                                  EC2 instance
    Type: 'AWS::EC2::Instance'
    Properties:
      ImageId: 'ami-061ac2e015473fbe2'
      InstanceType: !Ref InstanceType              By referencing the
      IamInstanceProfile: 'ec2-ssm-core'          security group, an implicit
      SecurityGroupIds: [!Ref SecurityGroup]      dependency is declared.
      SubnetId: !Ref Subnet
Outputs:
  InstanceId:                    Returns the ID of
    Value: !Ref VM               the EC2 instance
    Description: 'Instance id (connect via Session Manager)'
```

You'll learn about this in chapter 5.

You can find the full code for the template at /chapter04/virtualmachine.yaml in the book's code folder. Please don't worry about VPC, subnets, and security groups at the moment; you'll get to know them in chapter 5.

> **Where is the template located?**
> You can find the template on GitHub. You can download a snapshot of the repository at https://github.com/AWSinAction/code3/archive/main.zip. The file we're talking about is named chapter04/virtualmachine.yaml. On S3, the same file is located at https://s3.amazonaws.com/awsinaction-code3/chapter04/virtualmachine.yaml.

If you create an infrastructure from a template, CloudFormation calls it a *stack*. You can think of *template* versus *stack* much like *class* versus *object*. The template exists only once, whereas many stacks can be created from the same template. The following steps will guide you through creating your stack:

1 Open the AWS Management Console at https://console.aws.amazon.com.
2 Click Services and search for CloudFormation.
3 Open the CloudFormation service.
4 Select Stacks at the left.

Figure 4.14 shows the empty list of CloudFormation stacks.

1 Click Create Stack and select With New Resources (Standard) to start a four-step wizard.
2 Select Template Is Ready.

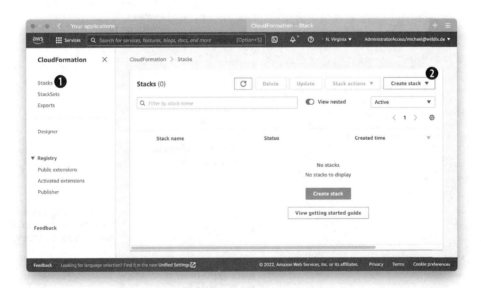

Figure 4.14   Overview of CloudFormation stacks

3　Select Amazon S3 URL as your template source, and enter the value https://
s3.amazonaws.com/awsinaction-code3/chapter04/virtualmachine.yaml, as shown
in figure 4.15.

4　Continue by clicking Next.

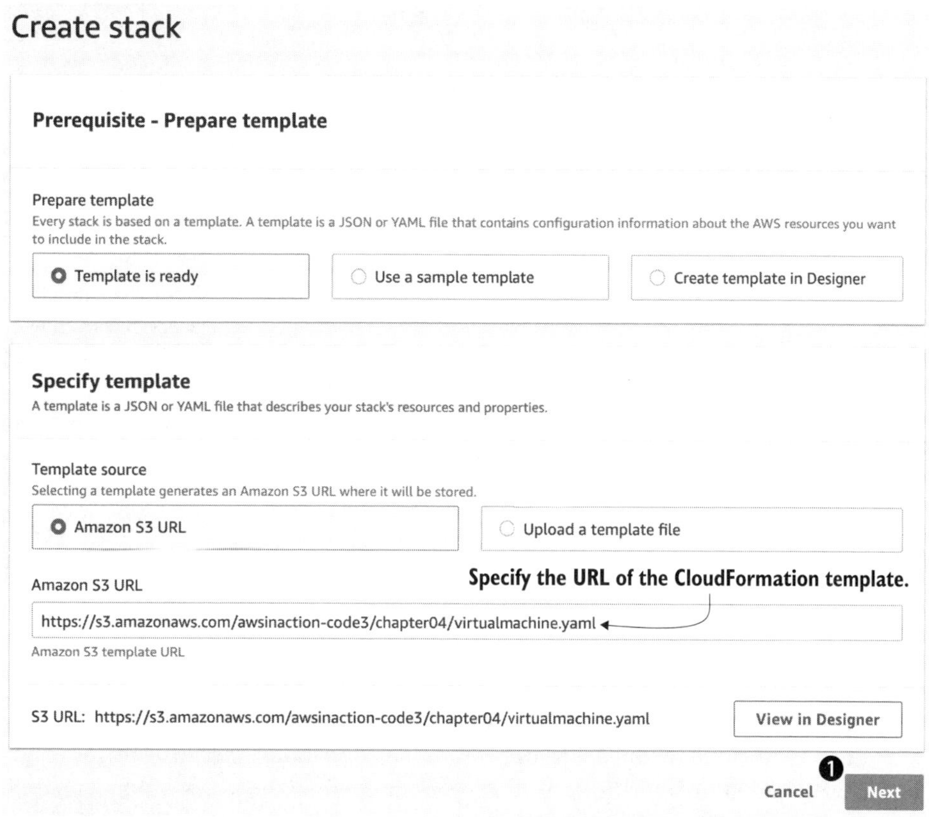

Create stack

Prerequisite - Prepare template

Prepare template
Every stack is based on a template. A template is a JSON or YAML file that contains configuration information about the AWS resources you want
to include in the stack.

　◉ Template is ready　　　　　○ Use a sample template　　　　　○ Create template in Designer

Specify template
A template is a JSON or YAML file that describes your stack's resources and properties.

Template source
Selecting a template generates an Amazon S3 URL where it will be stored.

　◉ Amazon S3 URL　　　　　○ Upload a template file

Specify the URL of the CloudFormation template.

Amazon S3 URL

https://s3.amazonaws.com/awsinaction-code3/chapter04/virtualmachine.yaml ◄

Amazon S3 template URL

S3 URL: https://s3.amazonaws.com/awsinaction-code3/chapter04/virtualmachine.yaml　　　[View in Designer]

Cancel　❶　**Next**

Figure 4.15　Creating a CloudFormation stack: Selecting a template (step 1 of 4)

In the second step, you define the stack name and parameters. Give the stack a name
like myvm, and fill out the parameter values as follows:

1　`InstanceType`—Select t2.micro.
2　`Subnet`—Select the first value in the drop-down list. You'll learn about subnets
later.
3　`VPC`—Select the first value in the drop-down list. You'll learn about VPCs later.

Figure 4.16 shows the second step. Click Next after you've chosen a value for the stack
name and every parameter, to proceed with the next step.

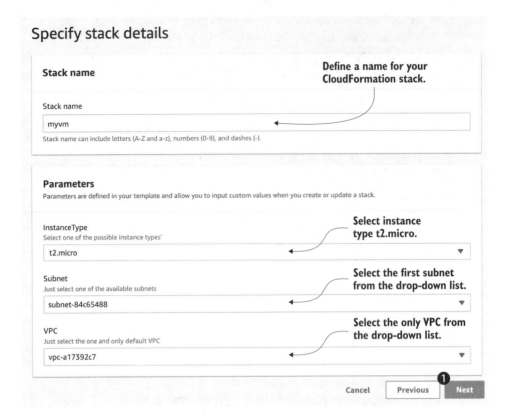

Figure 4.16   Creating a CloudFormation stack: Defining parameters (step 2 of 4)

In the third step, you can define optional tags for the stack and advanced configuration. You can skip this step at this point in the book, because you will not use any advanced features for now. All resources created by the stack will be tagged by CloudFormation by default. Click Next to go to the last step.

The fourth step displays a summary of the stack. At the bottom of the page, you are asked to Acknowledge the Creation of IAM Resources as figure 4.17 shows. You can safely allow CloudFormation to create IAM resources for now. You will learn more about them in chapter 5.

Click Create Stack. CloudFormation now starts to create the stack. If the process is successful, you'll see the screen shown in figure 4.18. As long as status is CREATE_IN_PROGRESS, you need to be patient and click the reload button from time to time. When the status is CREATE_COMPLETE, click the Outputs tab to see the ID of the EC2 instance. Double-check the instance type in the EC2 Management Console.

Your stack is now created. But that's not the end of the story. CloudFormation supports updating and deleting stacks as well.

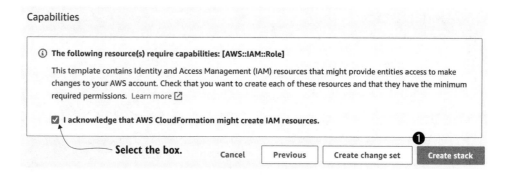

Figure 4.17 Creating a CloudFormation stack: Summary (step 4 of 4)

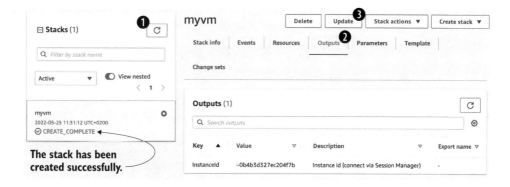

Figure 4.18 The CloudFormation stack has been created

4.5.3 *Updating infrastructure using CloudFormation*

It's time to test whether we can modify the instance type. Click the Update button. The wizard that starts is similar to the one you used during stack creation. Figure 4.19 shows the first step of the wizard. Select Use Current Template, and proceed with the next step by clicking the Next button.

In step 2, you need to change the `InstanceType` parameter value: choose `t2.small` to double or `t2.medium` to quadruple the computing power of your EC2 instance.

> **WARNING** Starting a virtual machine with instance type t2.small or t2.medium will incur charges. See https://aws.amazon.com/ec2/pricing/ to find out the current hourly price.

Step 3 is about sophisticated options during the update of the stack. You don't need any of these features now, so skip the step by clicking Next. Step 4 is a summary; acknowledge the creation of IAM resources and click Update Stack. The stack now has the status `UPDATE_IN_PROGRESS`. If you are quickly jumping to the EC2 Management

Update stack

Prerequisite - Prepare template

Prepare template
Every stack is based on a template. A template is a JSON or YAML file that contains configuration information about the AWS resources you want to include in the stack.

- ● Use current template
- ○ Replace current template
- ○ Edit template in designer

Use the current template.

Cancel   **❶ Next**

Figure 4.19   Updating the CloudFormation stack: Summary (step 1 of 4)

Console, you can see the instance to be stopped and started again with the new instance type. After a few minutes, the status should change to UPDATE_COMPLETE.

> **Alternatives to CloudFormation**
>
> If you don't want to write plain JSON or YAML to create templates for your infrastructure, a few alternatives to CloudFormation exist.
>
> The AWS Cloud Development Kit (CDK) (https://aws.amazon.com/cdk/) allows you to use a general-purpose programming language to define your infrastructure. Under the hood, the CDK generates CloudFormation templates.
>
> Another popular option is Terraform (https://www.terraform.io), which supports AWS as well as other cloud and service providers.

When you changed the parameter, CloudFormation figured out what needed to be done to achieve the end result. That's the power of a declarative approach: you say what the end result should look like, not how the end result should be achieved.

> **Cleaning up**
> Delete the stack by selecting it and clicking the Delete button.

Summary

- Use the CLI, one of the SDKs, or CloudFormation to automate your infrastructure on AWS.
- Infrastructure as Code describes the approach of programming the creation and modification of your infrastructure, including virtual machines, networking, storage, and more.

- You can use the CLI to automate complex processes in AWS with scripts (Bash and PowerShell).
- You can use SDKs for nine programming languages and platforms to embed AWS into your applications and create applications like nodecc.
- CloudFormation uses a declarative approach in JSON or YAML: you define only the end state of your infrastructure, and CloudFormation figures out how this state can be achieved. The major parts of a CloudFormation template are parameters, resources, and outputs.

Securing your system: IAM, security groups, and VPC

This chapter covers

- Who is responsible for security?
- Keeping your software up-to-date
- Controlling access to your AWS account with users and roles
- Keeping your traffic under control with security groups
- Using CloudFormation to create a private network

If security is a wall, you'll need a lot of bricks to build that wall, as shown in figure 5.1. This chapter focuses on the following four most important bricks to secure your systems on AWS:

1. *Installing software updates*—New security vulnerabilities are found in software every day. Software vendors release updates to fix those vulnerabilities, and it's your job to install those updates as quickly as possible after they're released on your systems. Otherwise, your systems will be an easy victim for hackers.

2. *Restricting access to your AWS account*—This becomes even more important if you aren't the only one accessing your AWS account, such as when coworkers and automated processes need access to your AWS account as well. A buggy

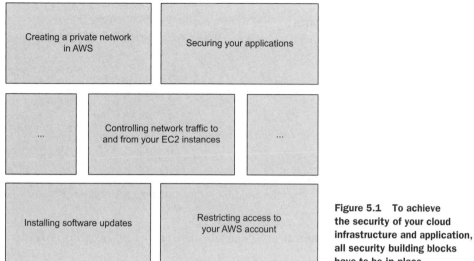

Figure 5.1 **To achieve the security of your cloud infrastructure and application, all security building blocks have to be in place.**

script could easily terminate all your EC2 instances instead of only the one you intended. Granting only the permissions needed is the key to securing your AWS resources from accidental or intended disastrous actions.

3 *Controlling network traffic to and from your EC2 instances*—You want ports to be accessible only if they must be. If you run a web server, the only ports you need to open to the outside world are ports 80 for HTTP traffic and 443 for HTTPS traffic. Do not open any other ports for external access.

4 *Creating a private network in AWS*—Control network traffic by defining subnets and routing tables. Doing so allows you to specify private networks that are not reachable from the outside.

One important brick is missing: securing your applications. We do not cover application security in our book. When buying or developing applications, you should follow security standards. For example, you need to check user input and allow only the necessary characters, don't save passwords in plain text, and use TLS/SSL to encrypt traffic between your virtual machines and your users.

This is going to be a long chapter—security is such an important topic, there's a lot to cover. But don't worry, we'll take it step by step.

Not all examples are covered by Free Tier

The examples in this chapter are not all covered by the Free Tier. A special warning message appears when an example incurs costs. As for the other examples, as long as you don't run them longer than a few days, you won't pay anything for them. Keep in mind that this applies only if you created a fresh AWS account for this book and nothing else is going on in your AWS account. Try to complete the chapter within a few days; you'll clean up your account at the end.

Chapter requirements

To fully understand this chapter, you should be familiar with the following networking concepts:

- Subnet
- Route tables
- Access control lists (ACLs)
- Gateway
- Firewall
- Port
- Access management
- Basics of the Internet Protocol (IP), including IP addresses

Before we look at the four bricks, let's talk about how responsibility is divided between you and AWS.

5.1   *Who's responsible for security?*

The cloud is a shared-responsibility environment, meaning responsibility is shared between you and AWS. AWS is responsible for the following:

- Protecting the network through automated monitoring systems and robust internet access, to prevent distributed denial of service (DDoS) attacks
- Performing background checks on employees who have access to sensitive areas
- Decommissioning storage devices by physically destroying them after end of life
- Ensuring the physical and environmental security of data centers, including fire protection and security staff

The security standards are reviewed by third parties; you can find an up-to-date overview at https://aws.amazon.com/compliance/.

What are your responsibilities? See the following:

- Configuring access management that restricts access to AWS resources like S3 and EC2 to a minimum, using AWS IAM
- Encrypting network traffic to prevent attackers from reading or manipulating data (e.g., using HTTPS)
- Configuring a firewall for your virtual network that controls incoming and outgoing traffic with security groups and NACLs
- Encrypting data at rest. For example, enable data encryption for your database or other storage systems
- Managing patches for the OS and additional software on virtual machines

Security involves an interaction between AWS and you, the customer. If you play by the rules, you can achieve high security standards in the cloud. Want to dive into more details? Check out https://aws.amazon.com/compliance/shared-responsibility-model/.

5.2   *Keeping the operating system up-to-date*

Not a week goes by without the release of an important update to fix security vulnerabilities in some piece of software or another. Sometimes the kernel is affected or libraries, like OpenSSL. Other times, it's affecting an environment like Java, Apache, and PHP, or an application like WordPress. If a security update is released, you must install it quickly, because the exploit may have already been released, or because unscrupulous people could look at the source code to reconstruct the vulnerability. You should have a working plan for how to apply updates to all running virtual machines as quickly as possible.

Amazon Linux 2 installs critical or important security updates automatically on startup while `cloud-init` is running. We highly recommend you install all the other updates as well. The following options are available:

- *Install all updates at the end of the boot process*—Include `yum -y` update in your user-data script. `yum` is the package manager used by Amazon Linux 2.
- *Install security updates at the end of the boot process only*—Include the `yum -y --security` update in your user-data script.
- Use the *AWS Systems Manager Patch Manager*—Install updates based on a patch baseline.

The first two options can be easily included in the user data of your EC2 instance. You can find the code in /chapter05/ec2-yum-update.yaml in the book's code folder. You install all updates as follows:

```
Instance:
  Type: 'AWS::EC2::Instance'
  Properties:
    # [...]
    UserData: !Base64 |
      #!/bin/bash -ex
      yum -y update        <──┐  Installs all
                               │  updates
```

To install only security updates, do the following:

```
Instance:
  Type: 'AWS::EC2::Instance'
  Properties:
    # [...]
    UserData: !Base64 |
      #!/bin/bash -ex
      yum -y --security update   <──┐  Installs only
                                     │  security updates
```

The following challenges are still waiting for a solution:

- The problem with installing all updates is that your system might still be vulnerable. Some updates require a reboot (most notably kernel updates)!
- Installing updates on startup is not enough. Updates need to be installed continuously.

Before reinventing the wheel, it is a good strategy to research whether AWS provides the building blocks needed to get the job done. Luckily, AWS Systems Manager (SSM) Patch Manager is a good choice to make patching more robust and stable.

The AWS Systems Manager provides a toolbox that includes a core set of features bundled into capabilities. Patch Manager is one such capability. The following core SSM features are bundled together in the Patch Manager, as figure 5.2 shows:

- *Agent*—Preinstalled and autostarted on Amazon Linux 2 (also powers the Session Manager).
- *Document*—Think of a document as a script on steroids. We use a prebuild document named `AWS-RunPatchBaseline` to install patches.
- *Run Command*—Executes a document on an EC2 instance.
- *Association*—Sends commands (via Run Command) to EC2 instances on a schedule or during startup (bundled into the capability named State Manager).
- *Maintenance Window*—Sends commands (via Run Command) to EC2 instances on a schedule during a time window.
- *Patch baseline*—Set of rules to approve patches for installation based on classification and severity. Luckily, AWS provides predefined patch baselines for various operating systems including Amazon Linux 2. The predefined patch baseline for Amazon Linux 2 approves all security patches that have a severity level of critical or important and all bug fixes. A seven-day waiting period exists after the release of a patch before approval.

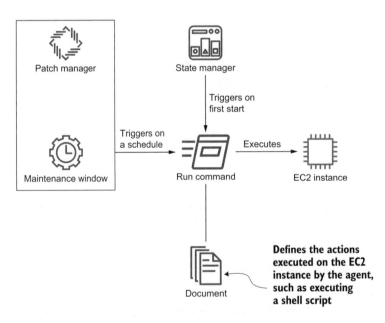

Figure 5.2   SSM features required for Patch Manager capability

The following CloudFormation snippet defines a maintenance window to patch on a schedule as well as an association to patch on startup:

The maintenance window is two hours long. You can patch more than one EC2 instance if you wish.

```
MaintenanceWindow:
  Type: 'AWS::SSM::MaintenanceWindow'
  Properties:
    AllowUnassociatedTargets: false
    Duration: 2
    Cutoff: 1
    Name: !Ref 'AWS::StackName'
    Schedule: 'cron(0 5 ? * SUN *)'
    ScheduleTimezone: UTC
MaintenanceWindowTarget:
  Type: 'AWS::SSM::MaintenanceWindowTarget'
  Properties:
    ResourceType: INSTANCE
    Targets:
    - Key: InstanceIds
      Values:
      - !Ref Instance
    WindowId: !Ref MaintenanceWindow
MaintenanceWindowTask:
  Type: 'AWS::SSM::MaintenanceWindowTask'
  Properties:
    MaxConcurrency: '1'
    MaxErrors: '1'
    Priority: 0
    Targets:
    - Key: WindowTargetIds
      Values:
      - !Ref MaintenanceWindowTarget
    TaskArn: 'AWS-RunPatchBaseline'
    TaskInvocationParameters:
      MaintenanceWindowRunCommandParameters:
        Parameters:
          Operation:
          - Install
    TaskType: 'RUN_COMMAND'
    WindowId: !Ref MaintenanceWindow
AssociationRunPatchBaselineInstall:
  Type: 'AWS::SSM::Association'
  Properties:
    Name: 'AWS-RunPatchBaseline'
    Parameters:
      Operation:
      - Install
    Targets:
    - Key: InstanceIds
      Values:
      - !Ref Instance
```

The last hour is reserved for commands to finish (all commands are started in the first hour).

The maintenance window is scheduled every Sunday morning at 5am UTC time. Learn more about the syntax at http://mng.bz/zmRZ.

Assigns one EC2 instance to the maintenance window. You can also assign EC2 instances based on tags.

The AWS-RunPatchBaseline document is executed.

The document supports parameters. Operation can be set to Install or Scan. By default, a reboot happens if required by any patch.

The association ensures that patches are installed on startup. The same document with the same parameters are used.

There is one prerequisite missing: the EC2 instance needs read access to a set of S3 buckets for Patch Manager to work, which is granted in the next snippet. Learn more at https://mng.bz/0ynz:

```
InstanceRole:
  Type: 'AWS::IAM::Role'
  Properties:
    #[...]
    Policies:
    - PolicyName: PatchManager
      PolicyDocument:
        Version: '2012-10-17'
        Statement:
        - Effect: Allow
          Action: 's3:GetObject'
          Resource:
          - !Sub 'arn:aws:s3:::patch-baseline-snapshot-${AWS::Region}/*'
          - !Sub 'arn:aws:s3:::aws-ssm-${AWS::Region}/*'
```

Patch Manager can also visualize the patches that are waiting for installation. To gather the data, another association is needed, as shown next:

Do not run on startup. Unfortunately, the document AWS-RunPatchBaseline crashes when running more than once at the same time. It avoids a conflict with the association defined in AssociationRunPatchBaselineInstall.

```
AssociationRunPatchBaselineScan:
  Type: 'AWS::SSM::Association'
  Properties:
    ApplyOnlyAtCronInterval: true
    Name: 'AWS-RunPatchBaseline'
    Parameters:
      Operation:
      - Scan
    ScheduleExpression: 'cron(0 0/1 * * ? *)'
    Targets:
    - Key: InstanceIds
      Values:
      - !Ref Instance
```

Uses the same document AWS-RunPatchBaseline...

...but this time, Operation is set to Scan.

Runs every hour

It's time for a demo. Create the CloudFormation stack with the template located at https://s3.amazonaws.com/awsinaction-code3/chapter05/ec2-os-update.yaml by clicking the CloudFormation Quick-Create Link (http://mng.bz/KlXn). Pick the default Virtual Private Cloud (VPC) and subnet, then wait for the stack creation to finish.

Visit the AWS Systems Manager management console at https://console.aws.amazon.com/systems-manager/. Open Patch Manager in the navigation bar, and you see a nice dashboard, as shown in figure 5.3.

You can also patch instances manually by pressing the Patch Now button, if needed.

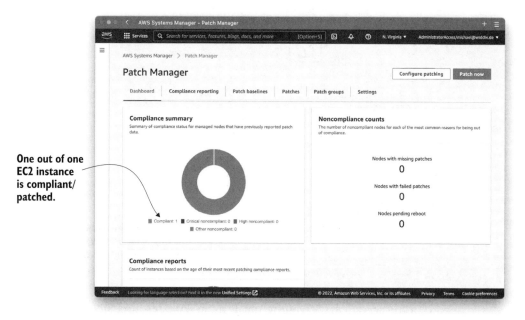

One out of one EC2 instance is compliant/ patched.

Figure 5.3   AWS Systems Manager Patch Manager dashboard

Cleaning up

Don't forget to delete your stack `ec2-os-update` after you finish this section, to clean up all used resources. Otherwise, you'll likely be charged for the resources you use.

5.3 *Securing your AWS account*

Securing your AWS account is critical. If someone gets access to your AWS account, they can steal your data, use resources at your expense, or delete all your data. As figure 5.4 shows, an AWS account is a basket for all the resources you own: EC2 instances, CloudFormation stacks, IAM users, and so on. Each AWS account comes with a root user granted unrestricted access to all resources. So far, you've used the AWS account root user to log in to the Management Console and the user `mycli`—created in section 4.2—when using the CLI. In this section, you will create an additional user to log in to the Management Console to avoid using the AWS account root user at all. Doing so allows you to manage multiple users, each restricted to the resources that are necessary for their roles.

To access your AWS account, an attacker must be able to authenticate to your account. There are three ways to do so: using the AWS account root user, using an IAM user, or authenticating as an AWS resource like an EC2 instance. To authenticate as a AWS account root user or IAM user, the attacker needs the username and

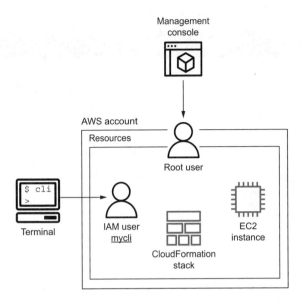

Figure 5.4   An AWS account contains all the AWS resources and comes with an AWS account root user by default.

password or the access keys. To authenticate as an AWS resource like an EC2 instance, the attacker needs access to the machine to communicate with the instance metadata service (IMDS).

To protect yourself from an attacker stealing or cracking your passwords or access keys, in the following section, you will enable multifactor authentication (MFA) for your AWS account root user to add an additional layer of security to the authentication process.

5.3.1   *Securing your AWS account's root user*

We advise you to enable MFA for the AWS account root user of your AWS account. After MFA is activated, you'll need a password and a temporary token to log in as the root user. Follow these steps to enable MFA, as shown in figure 5.5:

1   Click your name in the navigation bar at the top right of the Management Console.
2   Select Security Credentials.
3   Install an MFA app on your smartphone that supports the TOTP standard (such as Google Authenticator).
4   Expand the Multi-Factor Authentication (MFA) section.
5   Click Activate MFA.
6   Select Virtual MFA Device, and proceed with the next step.
7   Follow the instructions. Use the MFA app on your smartphone to scan the QR code that is displayed.

If you're using your smartphone as a virtual MFA device, it's a good idea not to log in to the Management Console from your smartphone or to store the AWS account root

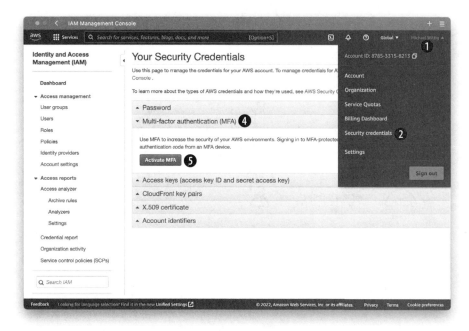

Figure 5.5 Protect your AWS account root user with multifactor authentication (MFA).

user's password on the phone. Keep the MFA token separate from your password. YubiKeys and hardware MFA tokens are also supported.

5.3.2 *AWS Identity and Access Management (IAM)*

Figure 5.6 shows an overview of all the core concepts of the *Identity and Access Management* (IAM) service. This service provides authentication and authorization for the AWS API. When you send a request to the AWS API, IAM verifies your identity and checks whether you are allowed to perform the action. IAM controls who (authentication) can do what (authorization) in your AWS account. For example, is the user allowed to launch a new virtual machine? The various components of IAM follow:

- An *IAM user* is used to authenticate people or workloads running outside of AWS.
- An *IAM group* is a collection of IAM users with the same permissions.
- An *IAM role* is used to authenticate AWS resources, for example, an EC2 instance.
- An *IAM identity policy* is used to define the permissions for a user, group, or role.

Table 5.1 shows the differences between users and roles. Roles authenticate AWS entities such as EC2 instances. IAM users authenticate the people who manage

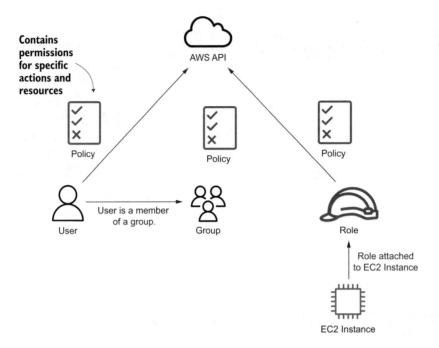

Figure 5.6   IAM concepts

AWS resources, for example, system administrators, DevOps engineers, or software developers.

Table 5.1   Differences among an AWS account root user, IAM user, and IAM role

	AWS account root user	IAM user	IAM role
Can have a password (needed to log in to the AWS Management Console)	Always	Yes	No
Can have access keys (needed to send requests to the AWS API (e.g., for CLI or SDK)	Yes (not recommended)	Yes	No
Can belong to a group	No	Yes	No
Can be associated with an EC2 instance, ECS container, Lambda function	No	No	Yes

By default, users and roles can't do anything. You have to create an identity policy stating what actions they're allowed to perform. IAM users and IAM roles use identity policies for authorization. Let's look at identity policies next.

5.3.3 *Defining permissions with an IAM identity policy*

By attaching one or multiple IAM identity policies to an IAM user or role, you are granting permissions to manage AWS resources. Identity policies are defined in JSON and contain one or more statements. A statement can either allow or deny specific actions on specific resources. You can use the wildcard character * to create more generic statements.

> **Identity vs. resource policies**
>
> IAM policies come in two types. *Identity policies* are attached to users, groups, or roles. *Resource policies* are attached to resources. Very few resource types support resource policies. One common example is the S3 bucket policy attached to S3 buckets.
>
> If a policy contains the property `Principal`, it is a resource policy. The `Principal` defines who is allowed to perform the action. Keep in mind that the principal can be set to public.

The following identity policy has one statement that allows every action for the EC2 service, for all resources:

```
                        Specifies 2012-10-17
                        to lock down the
                        version
{
  "Version": "2012-10-17",        ◁──      This statement allows
  "Statement": [{                          access to actions and
    "Effect": "Allow",            ◁──      resources.
    "Action": "ec2:*",            ◁──
    "Resource": "*"               ◁──      Any action offered by
  }]                                        the EC2 service
}              ...on any                    (wildcard *)...
               resource
```

If you have multiple statements that apply to the same action, `Deny` overrides `Allow`. The following identity policy allows all EC2 actions except terminating EC2 instances:

```
{
  "Version": "2012-10-17",
  "Statement": [{
    "Effect": "Allow",
    "Action": "ec2:*",
    "Resource": "*"
  }, {
    "Effect": "Deny",                      ◁──   Action is denied.
    "Action": "ec2:TerminateInstances",    ◁──   Terminate EC2
    "Resource": "*"                              instances.
  }]
}
```

The following identity policy denies all EC2 actions. The `ec2:TerminateInstances` statement isn't crucial, because `Deny` overrides `Allow`. When you deny an action, you can't allow that action with another statement:

```
{
  "Version": "2012-10-17",
  "Statement": [{
    "Effect": "Deny",              ⟵┐ Denies every
    "Action": "ec2:*",             ⟵┘ EC2 action
    "Resource": "*"
  }, {
    "Effect": "Allow",                      ┐ Allow isn't
    "Action": "ec2:TerminateInstances",  ⟵┤ crucial; Deny
    "Resource": "*"                         ┘ overrides Allow.
  }]
}
```

So far, the `Resource` part has been set to * to apply to every resource. Resources in AWS have an Amazon Resource Name (ARN); figure 5.7 shows the ARN of an EC2 instance.

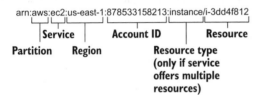

Figure 5.7   Components of an Amazon Resource Name (ARN) identifying an EC2 instance

To find out the account ID, you can use the CLI as follows:

```
$ aws sts get-caller-identity --query "Account" --output text
111111111111              ⟵┐ Account ID always
                            ┘ has 12 digits.
```

If you know your account ID, you can use ARNs to allow access to specific resources of a service like this:

```
{
  "Version": "2012-10-17",
  "Statement": [{
    "Effect": "Allow",
    "Action": "ec2:TerminateInstances",
    "Resource":
➥  "arn:aws:ec2:us-east-1:111111111111:instance/i-0b5c991e026104db9"
  }]
}
```

The list of all IAM actions of a service and possible resource ARNs can be found at http://mng.bz/Po0g.

The following two types of identity policies exist:

- *Managed policy*—If you want to create identity policies that can be reused in your account, a managed policy is what you're looking for. There are two types of managed policies:
  - *AWS managed policy*—An identity policy maintained by AWS. There are identity policies that grant admin rights, read-only rights, and so on.
  - *Customer managed*—An identity policy maintained by you. It could be an identity policy that represents the roles in your organization, for example.
- *Inline policy*—An identity policy that belongs to a certain IAM role, user, or group. An inline identity policy can't exist without the IAM role, user, or group that it belongs to.

With CloudFormation, it's easy to maintain inline identity policies; that's why we use inline identity policies most of the time in this book. One exception is the `mycli` user: this user has the AWS managed policy `AdministratorAccess` attached.

> **WARNING** Using managed policies can often conflict with following the least-privilege principal. Managed policies usually set the `Resource` property to `*`. That's why we attach our own inline policies to IAM roles or users.

5.3.4 *Users for authentication and groups to organize users*

A user can authenticate using either a username and password or access keys. When you log in to the Management Console, you're authenticating with your username and password. When you use the CLI from your computer, you use access keys to authenticate as the `mycli` user.

You're using the AWS account root user at the moment to log in to the Management Console. You should create an IAM user instead, for the following reasons:

- Creating IAM users allows you to set up a unique user for every person who needs to access your AWS account.
- You can grant access only to the resources each user needs, allowing you to follow the least-privilege principle.

To make things easier if you want to add users in the future, you'll first create a group for all users with administrator access. Groups can't be used to authenticate, but they centralize authorization. So, if you want to stop your admin users from terminating EC2 instances, you need to change the identity policy only for the group instead of changing it for all admin users. A user can be a member of zero, one, or multiple groups.

It's easy to create groups and users with the CLI, as shown here. Replace `$Password` in the following with a secure password:

```
$ aws iam create-group --group-name "admin"
$ aws iam attach-group-policy --group-name "admin" \
➥ --policy-arn "arn:aws:iam::aws:policy/AdministratorAccess"
$ aws iam create-user --user-name "myuser"
```

```
$ aws iam add-user-to-group --group-name "admin" --user-name "myuser"
$ aws iam create-login-profile --user-name "myuser" --password '$Password'
```

The user myuser is ready to be used. But you must use a different URL to access the Management Console if you aren't using the AWS account root user: https://$accountId .signin.aws.amazon.com/console. Replace $accountId with the account ID that you extracted earlier with the aws sts get-caller-identity command.

Enabling MFA for IAM users

We encourage you to enable MFA for all users. To enable MFA for your users, follow these steps:

1 Open the IAM service in the Management Console.
2 Choose Users at the left.
3 Click the myuser user.
4 Select the Security Credentials tab.
5 Click the Manage link near the Assigned MFA Device.
6 The wizard to enable MFA for the IAM user is the same one you used for enabling MFA for the AWS account root user.

We recommend enabling MFA for all users, especially for users granted administrator access to all or some services.

WARNING   Stop using the AWS account root user from now on. Always use myuser and the new link to the Management Console.

WARNING   You should never copy a user's access keys to an EC2 instance; use IAM roles instead! Don't store security credentials in your source code. And never ever check them into your source code repository. Try to use IAM roles instead whenever possible, as described in the next section.

5.3.5   *Authenticating AWS resources with roles*

Various use cases exist where an EC2 instance needs to access or manage AWS resources. For example, an EC2 instance might need to do the following:

- Back up data to the object store S3
- Terminate itself after a job has been completed
- Change the configuration of the private network environment in the cloud

To be able to access the AWS API, an EC2 instance needs to authenticate itself. You could create an IAM user with access keys and store the access keys on an EC2 instance for authentication. But doing so is a hassle and violates security best practices, especially if you want to rotate the access keys regularly.

Instead of using an IAM user for authentication, you should use an IAM role whenever you need to authenticate AWS resources like EC2 instances. When using an IAM role, your access keys are injected into your EC2 instance automatically.

If an IAM role is attached to an EC2 instance, all identity policies attached to those roles are evaluated to determine whether the request is allowed. By default, no role is attached to an EC2 instance, and, therefore, the EC2 instance is not allowed to make any calls to the AWS API.

The following example will show you how to use an IAM role for an EC2 instance. Do you remember the temporary EC2 instances from chapter 4? What if we forgot to terminate those VMs? A lot of money would have been wasted because of that. You'll now create an EC2 instance that stops itself automatically. The following snippet shows a one-liner terminating an EC2 instance after five minutes. The command `at` is used to execute the `aws ec2 stop-instances` with a five-minute delay:

```
$ echo "aws ec2 stop-instances --instance-ids i-0b5c991e026104db9" \
   | at now + 5 minutes
```

The EC2 instance needs permission to stop itself. Therefore, you need to attach an IAM role to the EC2 instance. The role contains an inline identity policy granting access to the `ec2:StopInstances` action. Unfortunately, we can't lock down the action to the EC2 instance resource itself due to a cyclic dependency. Luckily, we can grant permissions with additional conditions. One such condition is that a specific tag must be present. The following code shows how you define an IAM role with the help of CloudFormation:

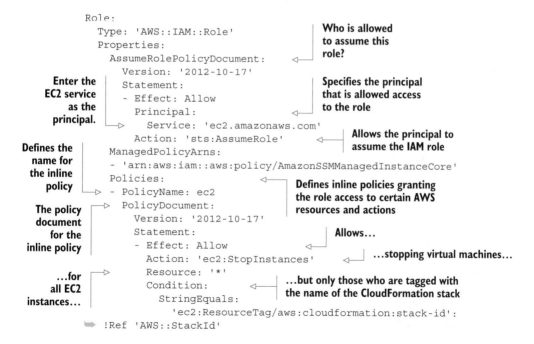

To attach an inline role to an instance, you must first create an instance profile, as shown in the following code snippet:

```
InstanceProfile:
  Type: 'AWS::IAM::InstanceProfile'
  Properties:
    Roles:
    - !Ref Role
```

The next code snippet shows how to attach the IAM role to the virtual machine:

```
Instance:
  Type: 'AWS::EC2::Instance'
  Properties:
    # [...]
    IamInstanceProfile: !Ref InstanceProfile
    UserData:
      'Fn::Base64': !Sub |
        #!/bin/bash -ex
        TOKEN=`curl -X PUT "http://169.254.169.254/latest/api/token" \
 -H "X-aws-ec2-metadata-token-ttl-seconds: 21600"`
        INSTANCEID=`curl -H "X-aws-ec2-metadata-token: $TOKEN" \
 -s "http://169.254.169.254/latest/meta-data/instance-id"`
        echo "aws ec2 stop-instances --region ${AWS::Region} \
 --instance-ids $INSTANCEID" | at now + ${Lifetime} minutes
```

Create the CloudFormation stack with the template located at https://s3.amazonaws
.com/awsinaction-code3/chapter05/ec2-iam-role.yaml by clicking the CloudFormation
Quick-Create Link (http://mng.bz/JVeP). Specify the lifetime of the EC2 instance via
the parameter, and pick the default VPC and subnet as well. Wait until the amount of
time specified as the lifetime has passed, and see whether your EC2 instance is
stopped in the EC2 Management Console. The lifetime begins when the server is fully
started and booted.

> **Cleaning up**
>
> Don't forget to delete your stack `ec2-iam-role` after you finish this section, to clean
> up all used resources. Otherwise, you'll likely be charged for the resources you use
> (even when your EC2 instance is stopped, you pay for the network-attached storage).

You have learned how to use IAM users to authenticate people and IAM roles to
authenticate EC2 instances or other AWS resources. You've also seen how to grant
access to specific actions and resources by using an IAM identity policy. The next section will cover controlling network traffic to and from your virtual machine.

5.4 Controlling network traffic to and from your virtual machine

You want traffic to enter or leave your EC2 instance only if it has to do so. With a firewall, you control ingoing (also called *inbound* or *ingress*) and outgoing (also called *outbound* or *egress*) traffic. If you run a web server, the only ports you need to open to the

outside world are ports 80 for HTTP traffic and 443 for HTTPS traffic. All other ports should be closed down. You should only open ports that must be accessible, just as you grant only the permissions you need with IAM. If you are using a firewall that allows only legitimate traffic, you close a lot of possible security holes. You can also prevent yourself from human failure—for example, you prevent accidentally sending email to customers from a test system by not opening outgoing SMTP connections for test systems.

Before network traffic enters or leaves your EC2 instance, it goes through a firewall provided by AWS. The firewalls inspects the network traffic and uses rules to decide whether the traffic is allowed or denied.

> **IP vs. IP address**
> The abbreviation IP is used for Internet Protocol, whereas an IP address describes a specific address like 84.186.116.47.

Figure 5.8 shows how an SSH request from a source IP address 10.0.0.10 is inspected by the firewall and received by the destination IP address 10.10.0.20. In this case, the firewall allows the request because a rule is in place that allows TCP traffic on port 22 between the source and the destination.

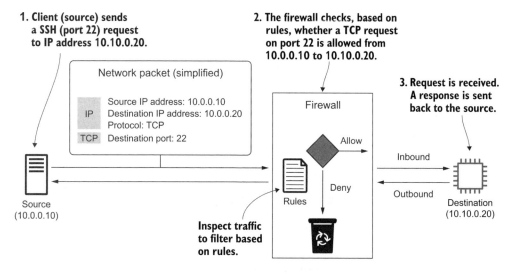

Figure 5.8 How an SSH request travels from source to destination, controlled by a firewall

AWS is responsible for the firewall, but you're responsible for the rules. By default, a security group does not allow any inbound traffic. You must add your own rules to allow specific incoming traffic. A security group contains a rule allowing all outbound traffic by default. If your use case requires a high level of network security, you should remove the rule and add your own rules to control outgoing traffic.

> **Debugging or monitoring network traffic**
>
> Imagine the following problem: your EC2 instance does not accept SSH traffic as you
> want it to, but you can't spot any misconfiguration in your firewall rules. The following
> two strategies are helpful:
>
> - Use the VPC Reachability Analyzer to simulate the traffic and see if the tool
>   finds the configuration problem. Learn more at http://mng.bz/wyqW.
> - Enable VPC Flow Logs to get access to aggregated log messages containing
>   rejected connections. Learn more at http://mng.bz/qoqE.

5.4.1 Controlling traffic to virtual machines with security groups

A security group acts as a firewall for virtual machines and other services. You will associate a security group with AWS resources, such as EC2 instances, to control traffic. It's
common for EC2 instances to have more than one security group associated with
them and for the same security group to be associated with multiple EC2 instances.

A security group consists of a set of rules. Each rule allows network traffic based on
the following:

- Direction (inbound or outbound)
- IP protocol (TCP, UDP, ICMP)
- Port
- Source/destination based on IP address, IP address range, or security group
  (works only within AWS)

In theory, you could define rules that allow all traffic to enter and leave your virtual
machine; AWS won't prevent you from doing so. But it's a best practice to define your
rules so they are as restrictive as possible.

Security group resources in CloudFormation are of type `AWS::EC2::Security-`
`Group`. The following listing is in /chapter05/firewall1.yaml in the book's code folder;
the template describes an empty security group associated with a single EC2 instance.

Listing 5.1 CloudFormation template: Security group

```
---
[..]
Parameters:
  VPC:
    # [..]              <--  You'll learn about
  Subnet:                   this in section 5.5.
    # [..]              <--
Resources:
  SecurityGroup:        <--  Defines the security group without
    Type: 'AWS::EC2::SecurityGroup'   any rules (by default, inbound traffic
    Properties:                       is denied and outbound traffic is
      GroupDescription: 'Learn how to protect your EC2 Instance.'  allowed). Rules will be added in
      VpcId: !Ref VPC               the following sections.
```

```
    Tags:
    - Key: Name
      Value: 'AWS in Action: chapter 5 (firewall)'
Instance:                          ◁——  Defines the
  Type: 'AWS::EC2::Instance'             EC2 instance
  Properties:
    # [...]
    SecurityGroupIds:                    Associates the
    - !Ref SecurityGroup       ◁——       security group with
    SubnetId: !Ref Subnet                the EC2 instance
```

To explore security groups, you can try the CloudFormation template located at https://s3.amazonaws.com/awsinaction-code3/chapter05/firewall1.yaml. Create a stack based on that template by clicking the CloudFormation Quick-Create Link (http://mng.bz/91e8), and then copy the `PublicIpAddress` from the stack output.

5.4.2 Allowing ICMP traffic

If you want to ping an EC2 instance from your computer, you must allow inbound Internet Control Message Protocol (ICMP) traffic. By default, all inbound traffic is blocked. Try `ping $PublicIpAddress` to make sure `ping` isn't working, like this:

```
$ ping 34.205.166.12
PING 34.205.166.12 (34.205.166.12): 56 data bytes
Request timeout for icmp_seq 0
Request timeout for icmp_seq 1
[...]
```

You need to add a rule to the security group that allows inbound traffic, where the protocol equals ICMP. The following listing is in /chapter05/firewall2.yaml in the book's code folder.

Listing 5.2 CloudFormation template: Security group that allows ICMP

```
SecurityGroup:
  Type: 'AWS::EC2::SecurityGroup'
  Properties:
    GroupDescription: 'Learn how to protect your EC2 Instance.'
    VpcId: !Ref VPC
    Tags:
    - Key: Name
      Value: 'AWS in Action: chapter 5 (firewall)'            Rules allowing
    SecurityGroupIngress:                          ◁——        incoming traffic
    - Description: 'allowing inbound ICMP traffic'
      IpProtocol: icmp                             ◁——        Specifies
      FromPort: '-1'        ◁——                               ICMP as the
      ToPort: '-1'               ICMP does not use            protocol
   ▷  CidrIp: '0.0.0.0/0'        ports. -1 means
                                 every port.
Allows traffic
from any source
IP address
```

Update the CloudFormation stack with the template located at https://s3.amazonaws
.com/awsinaction-code3/chapter05/firewall2.yaml and retry the ping command. It
should work now:

```
$ ping 34.205.166.12
PING 34.205.166.12 (34.205.166.12): 56 data bytes
64 bytes from 34.205.166.12: icmp_seq=0 ttl=234 time=109.095 ms
64 bytes from 34.205.166.12: icmp_seq=1 ttl=234 time=107.000 ms
[...]
round-trip min/avg/max/stddev = 107.000/108.917/110.657/1.498 ms
```

Everyone's inbound ICMP traffic (every source IP address) is now allowed to reach
your EC2 instance.

5.4.3 *Allowing HTTP traffic*

Once you can ping your EC2 instance, you want to run a web server. To do so, you
must create a rule to allow inbound TCP requests on port 80, as shown in the next listing. You also need a running web server.

> **Listing 5.3 CloudFormation template: Security group that allows HTTP**

```
SecurityGroup:
  Type: 'AWS::EC2::SecurityGroup'
  Properties:
    GroupDescription: 'Learn how to protect your EC2 Instance.'
    VpcId: !Ref VPC
    # [...]
    SecurityGroupIngress:          ← Adds a rule to allow incoming HTTP traffic
    # [...]
    - Description: 'allowing inbound HTTP traffic'
      IpProtocol: tcp              ← HTTP is based on the TCP protocol.
      FromPort: '80'               ← You can allow a range of ports or set FromPort = ToPort.
      ToPort: '80'                    The default HTTP port is 80.
      CidrIp: '0.0.0.0/0'          ← Allows traffic from any source IP address
Instance:
  Type: 'AWS::EC2::Instance'
  Properties:
    # [...]
    UserData:
      'Fn::Base64': |
        #!/bin/bash -ex
        yum -y install httpd          ← Installs Apache HTTP Server on startup
        systemctl start httpd         ← Starts Apache HTTP Server
        echo '<html>...</html>' > /var/www/html/index.html
```

Update the CloudFormation stack with the template located at https://s3.amazonaws
.com/awsinaction-code3/chapter05/firewall3.yaml. Enter the public IP address in your
browser to see a very basic test page.

5.4.4 *Allowing HTTP traffic from a specific source IP address*

So far, you're allowing inbound traffic on port 80 (HTTP) from every source IP address. It is possible to restrict access to only your own IP address for additional security as well.

What's the difference between public and private IP addresses?

On my local network, I'm using private IP addresses that start with 192.168.0.*. My laptop uses 192.168.0.10, and my iPad uses 192.168.0.20. But if I access the internet, I have the same public IP address (such as 79.241.98.155) for my laptop and iPad. That's because only my internet gateway (the box that connects to the internet) has a public IP address, and all requests are redirected by the gateway. (If you want to know more about this, search for network address translation.) Your local network doesn't know about this public IP address. My laptop and iPad only know that the internet gateway is reachable under 192.168.0.1 on the private network.

To find your public IP address, visit https://checkip.amazonaws.com/. For some of us, our public IP address changes from time to time, usually when you reconnect to the internet (which happens every 24 hours in my case).

Hardcoding the public IP address into the template isn't a good solution because your public IP address can change from time to time. You already know the solution: parameters. You need to add a parameter that holds your current public IP address, and you need to modify the Security Group. You can find the following listing in /chapter05/firewall4.yaml in the book's code folder.

Listing 5.4 Security group allows traffic from source IP

```
Parameters:
  WhitelistedIpAddress:                          ◀── Public IP address
    Description: 'Whitelisted IP address'            parameter
    Type: String
    AllowedPattern: '^[0-9]{1,3}\.[0-9]{1,3}\.[0-9]{1,3}\.[0-9]{1,3}$'
    ConstraintDescription: 'Enter a valid IPv4 address'
Resources:
  SecurityGroup:
    Type: 'AWS::EC2::SecurityGroup'
    Properties:
      GroupDescription: 'Learn how to protect your EC2 Instance.'
      VpcId: !Ref VPC
      # [...]
      SecurityGroupIngress:
      # [...]
      - Description: 'allowing inbound HTTP traffic'
        IpProtocol: tcp
        FromPort: '80'
        ToPort: '80'                                    Uses WhitelistedIpAddress/32
        CidrIp: !Sub '${WhitelistedIpAddress}/32'  ◀──  as a value to turn the IP
                                                        address input into a CIDR
```

Update the CloudFormation stack with the template located at https://s3.amazonaws
.com/awsinaction-code3/chapter05/firewall4.yaml. When asked for parameters, type
in your public IP address for `WhitelistedIpAddress`. Now only your IP address can
open HTTP connections to your EC2 instance.

Classless Inter-Domain Routing (CIDR)

You may wonder what `/32` means. To understand what's going on, you need to switch
your brain into binary mode. An IP address is 4 bytes or 32 bits long. The `/32` defines
how many bits (32, in this case) should be used to form a range of addresses. If you
want to define the exact IP address that is allowed, you must use all 32 bits.

Sometimes it makes sense to define a range of allowed IP addresses. For example,
you can use `10.0.0.0/8` to create a range between 10.0.0.0 and 10.255.255.255,
`10.0.0.0/16` to create a range between 10.0.0.0 and 10.0.255.255, or `10.0.0.0/24`
to create a range between 10.0.0.0 and 10.0.0.255. You aren't required to use the
binary boundaries (8, 16, 24, 32), but they're easier for most people to understand.
You already used `0.0.0.0/0` to create a range that contains every possible IP address.

Now you can control network traffic that comes from outside a virtual machine or goes
outside a virtual machine by filtering based on protocol, port, and source IP address.

5.4.5 *Allowing HTTP traffic from a source security group*

It is possible to control network traffic based on whether the source or destination
belongs to a specific security group. For example, you can say that a MySQL database
can be accessed only if the traffic comes from your web servers, or that only your
proxy servers are allowed to access the web servers. Because of the elastic nature of the
cloud, you'll likely deal with a dynamic number of virtual machines, so rules based on
source IP addresses are difficult to maintain. This process becomes easy, however, if
your rules are based on source security groups.

To explore the power of rules based on a source security group, let's look at the
concept of a load balancer/ingress router/proxy. The client sends requests to the
proxy. The proxy inspects the request and forwards it to the backend. The backend
response is then passed back to the client by the proxy. To implement the concept of
an HTTP proxy, you must follow these two rules:

- Allow HTTP access to the proxy from 0.0.0.0/0 or a specific source address.
- Allow HTTP access to all backends only if the traffic source is the proxy.

Figure 5.9 shows that only the proxy is allowed to communicate with the backend over
HTTP.

A security group allowing incoming HTTP traffic from anywhere needs to be attached
to the proxy. All backend VMs are attached to a security group allowing HTTP traffic
only if the source is the proxy's security group. Listing 5.5 shows the security groups
defined in a CloudFormation template.

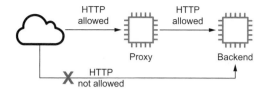

Figure 5.9 The proxy is the only HTTP entry point to the system (realized with security groups).

Listing 5.5 CloudFormation template: HTTP from proxy to backend

```
SecurityGroupProxy:                          ◁──┐ Security group
  Type: 'AWS::EC2::SecurityGroup'               │ attached to the proxy
  Properties:
    GroupDescription: 'Allowing incoming HTTP and ICPM from anywhere.'
    VpcId: !Ref VPC
    SecurityGroupIngress:
    - Description: 'allowing inbound ICMP traffic'
      IpProtocol: icmp
      FromPort: '-1'
      ToPort: '-1'
      CidrIp: '0.0.0.0/0'
    - Description: 'allowing inbound HTTP traffic'
      IpProtocol: tcp
      FromPort: '80'                        ┐ Security group
      ToPort: '80'                          │ attached to
      CidrIp: '0.0.0.0/0'                   │ the backend
SecurityGroupBackend:                       ◁─┘
  Type: 'AWS::EC2::SecurityGroup'
  Properties:
    GroupDescription: 'Allowing incoming HTTP from proxy.'
    VpcId: !Ref VPC
    SecurityGroupIngress:
    - Description: 'allowing inbound HTTP traffic from proxy'
      IpProtocol: tcp
      FromPort: '80'                            ┐ Allows incoming
      ToPort: '80'                              │ HTTP traffic only
      SourceSecurityGroupId: !Ref SecurityGroupProxy ◁─┘ from proxy
```

Update the CloudFormation stack with the template located at https://s3.amazonaws
.com/awsinaction-code3/chapter05/firewall5.yaml. After the update is completed,
the stack will show the following two outputs:

- `ProxyPublicIpAddress`—Entry point into the system. Receives HTTP requests
  from the outside world.

- `BackendPublicIpAddress`—You can connect to this EC2 instance only from
  the proxy.

Copy the `ProxyPublicIpAddress` output and open it in your browser. A Hello AWS in
Action! page shows up.

But when you copy the `BackendPublicIpAddress` output and try to open it in
your browser, an error message will appear. That's because the security group of the
backend instance allows incoming traffic only from the proxy instance, not from your
IP address.

The only way to reach the backend instance is through the proxy instance. The Hello AWS in Action! page that appears when opening http://$ProxyPublicIpAddress in your browser originates from the backend instance but gets passed through the proxy instance. Check the details of the HTTP request, for example, with `curl`, as shown in the following code. You'll find a `x-backend` response header indicating that the proxy forwarded your request to the backend named `app1`, which points to the backend instance:

```
$ curl -I http://$ProxyPublicIpAddress
< HTTP/1.1 200 OK
[...]
< accept-ranges: bytes
< content-length: 91
< content-type: text/html; charset=UTF-8
< x-backend: app1
<html><title>Hello AWS in Action!</title><body>
➥ <h1>Hello AWS in Action!</h1></body></html>
```

The x-backend header is injected by the proxy and indicates the backend answered the request.

> **Cleaning up**
> Don't forget to delete your stack after you finish this section to clean up all used resources. Otherwise, you'll likely be charged for the resources you use.

5.5 Creating a private network in the cloud: Amazon Virtual Private Cloud (VPC)

When you create a VPC, you get your own private network on AWS. *Private* means you can use the address ranges 10.0.0.0/8, 172.16.0.0/12, or 192.168.0.0/16 to design a network that isn't necessarily connected to the public internet. You can create subnets, route tables, network access control lists (NACLs), and gateways to the internet or a VPN endpoint.

> **IPv6**
> Amazon Virtual Private Cloud supports IPv6 as well. You can create IPv4 only, IPv6 only, or IPv4 and IPv6 VPCs. To reduce complexity, we are sticking to IPv4 in this chapter.

Subnets allow you to separate concerns. We recommend to create at least the following two types of subnets:

- *Public subnets*—For all resources that need to be reachable from the internet, such as a load balancer of a internet-facing web application
- *Private subnets*—For all resources that should not be reachable from the internet, such as an application server or a database system

What's the difference between a public and private subnet? A public subnet has a route to the internet; a private subnet doesn't.

For the purpose of understanding how a VPC works, you'll create a VPC to replicate the example from the previous section. You'll implement the proxy concept from
the previous section by creating a public subnet that contains only the proxy. You'll
also create a private subnet for the backend servers. You will not be able to access a
backend server directly from the internet because it will sit on a private subnet. The
backend servers will be accessible only via the proxy server running in a public subnet.

The VPC uses the address space 10.0.0.0/16. To isolate different parts of the system, you'll add the next two public subnets and one private subnet to the VPC:

- *10.0.0.0/24*—Public subnet used later in this section to deploy a NAT gateway
- *10.0.1.0/24*—Public proxy subnet
- *10.0.2.0/24*—Private backend subnet

> **What does 10.0.0.0/16 mean?**
>
> 10.0.0.0/16 represents all IP addresses in 10.0.0.0 and 10.0.255.255. It's using
> CIDR notation (explained earlier in the chapter).

Figure 5.10 shows the architecture of the VPC.

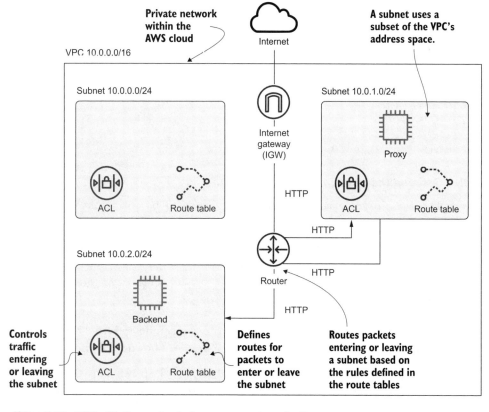

Figure 5.10   VPC with three subnets to secure a web application

You'll use CloudFormation to describe the VPC with its subnets. The template is split into smaller parts to make it easier to read in the book. As usual, you'll find the code in the book's code repository on GitHub: https://github.com/AWSinAction/code3. The template is located at /chapter05/vpc.yaml.

5.5.1   Creating the VPC and an internet gateway (IGW)

The first resources listed in the template are the VPC and the internet gateway (IGW). In the next code snippet, the IGW will translate the public IP addresses of your virtual machines to their private IP addresses using network address translation (NAT). All public IP addresses used in the VPC are controlled by this IGW:

```
VPC:
  Type: 'AWS::EC2::VPC'                          The IP address space
  Properties:                                    used for the private
    CidrBlock: '10.0.0.0/16'      ◁───           network
    EnableDnsHostnames: 'true'          Adds a Name
    Tags:                         ◁───  tag to the VPC
    - Key: Name
      Value: 'AWS in Action: chapter 5 (VPC)'
InternetGateway:                      ◁───       An IGW is needed to
  Type: 'AWS::EC2::InternetGateway'              enable traffic to and
  Properties: {}                                 from the internet.
VPCGatewayAttachment:
  Type: 'AWS::EC2::VPCGatewayAttachment'
  Properties:
    VpcId: !Ref VPC
    InternetGatewayId: !Ref InternetGateway
```

**Attaches the internet
gateway to the VPC**

Next you'll define the subnet for the proxy.

5.5.2   Defining the public proxy subnet

The EC2 instance running the proxy needs to be reachable via the internet. To achieve that, you'll need to complete the next four steps:

1 Create a subnet spanning a subsection of the IP address range assigned to the VPC.
2 Create a route table, and attach it to the subnet.
3 Add the 0.0.0.0/0 route pointing to the internet gateway to the route table.
4 Create an NACL, and attach it to the subnet.

To allow traffic from the internet to the proxy machine and from the proxy to the backend servers, you'll need the following NACL rules, shown in the next code snippet:

- Internet to proxy: HTTP from 0.0.0.0/0 to 10.0.1.0/24 is allowed.
- Proxy to backend: HTTP from 10.0.1.0/24 to 10.0.2.0/24 is allowed.

```
SubnetPublicProxy:
  Type: 'AWS::EC2::Subnet'
  Properties:
    AvailabilityZone: !Select [0, !GetAZs '']
    CidrBlock: '10.0.1.0/24'
    MapPublicIpOnLaunch: true
    VpcId: !Ref VPC
    Tags:
    - Key: Name
      Value: 'Public Proxy'
RouteTablePublicProxy:
  Type: 'AWS::EC2::RouteTable'
  Properties:
    VpcId: !Ref VPC
RouteTableAssociationPublicProxy:
  Type: 'AWS::EC2::SubnetRouteTableAssociation'
  Properties:
    SubnetId: !Ref SubnetPublicProxy
    RouteTableId: !Ref RouteTablePublicProxy
RoutePublicProxyToInternet:
  Type: 'AWS::EC2::Route'
  Properties:
    RouteTableId: !Ref RouteTablePublicProxy
    DestinationCidrBlock: '0.0.0.0/0'
    GatewayId: !Ref InternetGateway
  DependsOn: VPCGatewayAttachment
NetworkAclPublicProxy:
  Type: 'AWS::EC2::NetworkAcl'
  Properties:
    VpcId: !Ref VPC
SubnetNetworkAclAssociationPublicProxy:
  Type: 'AWS::EC2::SubnetNetworkAclAssociation'
  Properties:
    SubnetId: !Ref SubnetPublicProxy
    NetworkAclId: !Ref NetworkAclPublicProxy
```

Annotations:
- Picks the first availability zone in the region. (You'll learn about availability zones in chapter 16.)
- IP address space
- Route table
- Associates the route table with the subnet
- Routes everything (0.0.0.0/0) to the IGW
- Network access control list (NACL)
- Associates the NACL with the subnet

There's an important difference between security groups and NACLs: security groups are stateful, but NACLs aren't. If you allow an inbound port on a security group, the corresponding response to requests on that port are allowed as well. A security group rule will work as you expect it to. If you open inbound port 80 on a security group, you can connect via HTTP.

That's not true for NACLs. If you open inbound port 80 on an NACL for your subnet, you still may not be able to connect via HTTP. In addition, you need to allow outbound ephemeral ports, because the web server accepts connections on port 80 but uses an ephemeral port for communication with the client. Ephemeral ports are selected from the range starting at 1024 and ending at 65535. If you want to make an HTTP connection from within your subnet, you have to open outbound port 80 and inbound ephemeral ports as well.

Another difference between security group rules and NACL rules is that you have to define the priority for NACL rules. A smaller rule number indicates a higher priority.

When evaluating an NACL, the first rule that matches a package is applied; all other rules are skipped.

The proxy subnet allows clients sending HTTP requests on port 80. The following NACL rules are needed:

- Allow inbound port 80 (HTTP) from 0.0.0.0/0.
- Allow outbound ephemeral ports to 0.0.0.0/0.

We also want to make HTTP and HTTPS requests from the subnet to the internet. The following NACL rules are needed:

- Allow inbound ephemeral ports from 0.0.0.0/0.
- Allow outbound port 80 (HTTP) to 0.0.0.0/0.
- Allow outbound port 443 (HTTPS) to 0.0.0.0/0.

Find the CloudFormation implementation of the previous NACLs next:

```
NetworkAclEntryInPublicProxyHTTP:                    ◁          Allows inbound
  Type: 'AWS::EC2::NetworkAclEntry'                             HTTP from
  Properties:                                                   everywhere
    NetworkAclId: !Ref NetworkAclPublicProxy
    RuleNumber: '110'            ◁
    Protocol: '6'                          Rules are evaluated
    PortRange:                             starting with the
      From: '80'                           lowest-numbered rule.
      To: '80'
    RuleAction: 'allow'
    Egress: 'false'          ◁———————— Inbound
    CidrBlock: '0.0.0.0/0'
NetworkAclEntryInPublicProxyEphemeralPorts:          ◁          Ephemeral ports
  Type: 'AWS::EC2::NetworkAclEntry'                             used for short-lived
  Properties:                                                   TCP/IP connections
    NetworkAclId: !Ref NetworkAclPublicProxy
    RuleNumber: '200'
    Protocol: '6'
    PortRange:
      From: '1024'
      To: '65535'
    RuleAction: 'allow'
    Egress: 'false'                     Allows outbound
    CidrBlock: '0.0.0.0/0'        ◁      HTTP to everywhere
NetworkAclEntryOutPublicProxyHTTP:            ◁
  Type: 'AWS::EC2::NetworkAclEntry'
  Properties:
    NetworkAclId: !Ref NetworkAclPublicProxy
    RuleNumber: '100'
    Protocol: '6'
    PortRange:
      From: '80'
      To: '80'
    RuleAction: 'allow'               Outbound
    Egress: 'true'          ◁————————
    CidrBlock: '0.0.0.0/0'
```

```
NetworkAclEntryOutPublicProxyHTTPS:          ◄──┐   Allows outbound
  Type: 'AWS::EC2::NetworkAclEntry'              │   HTTPS to everywhere
  Properties:
    NetworkAclId: !Ref NetworkAclPublicProxy
    RuleNumber: '110'
    Protocol: '6'
    PortRange:
      From: '443'
      To: '443'
    RuleAction: 'allow'
    Egress: 'true'
    CidrBlock: '0.0.0.0/0'                              Ephemeral
NetworkAclEntryOutPublicProxyEphemeralPorts: ◄──┘      ports
  Type: 'AWS::EC2::NetworkAclEntry'
  Properties:
    NetworkAclId: !Ref NetworkAclPublicProxy
    RuleNumber: '200'
    Protocol: '6'
    PortRange:
      From: '1024'
      To: '65535'
    RuleAction: 'allow'
    Egress: 'true'
    CidrBlock: '0.0.0.0/0'
```

We recommend you start with using security groups to control traffic. If you want to add an extra layer of security, you should use NACLs on top. But doing so is optional, in our opinion.

5.5.3   Adding the private backend subnet

As shown in figure 5.11, the only difference between a public and a private subnet is that a private subnet doesn't have a route to the IGW.

Traffic between subnets of a VPC is always routed by default. You can't remove the routes between the subnets. If you want to prevent traffic between subnets in a VPC, you need to use NACLs attached to the subnets, as shown here. The subnet for the web server has no additional routes and is, therefore, private:

```
SubnetPrivateBackend:
  Type: 'AWS::EC2::Subnet'
  Properties:
    AvailabilityZone: !Select [0, !GetAZs '']
    CidrBlock: '10.0.2.0/24'        ◄──┐   Address
    VpcId: !Ref VPC                     │   space
    Tags:
    - Key: Name
      Value: 'Private Backend'
RouteTablePrivateBackend:           ◄──    No route to
  Type: 'AWS::EC2::RouteTable'             the IGW
  Properties:
    VpcId: !Ref VPC
```

```
RouteTableAssociationPrivateBackend:
  Type: 'AWS::EC2::SubnetRouteTableAssociation'
  Properties:
    SubnetId: !Ref SubnetPrivateBackend
    RouteTableId: !Ref RouteTablePrivateBackend
NetworkAclPrivateBackend:
  Type: 'AWS::EC2::NetworkAcl'
  Properties:
    VpcId: !Ref VPC
SubnetNetworkAclAssociationPrivateBackend:
  Type: 'AWS::EC2::SubnetNetworkAclAssociation'
  Properties:
    SubnetId: !Ref SubnetPrivateBackend
    NetworkAclId: !Ref NetworkAclPrivateBackend
```

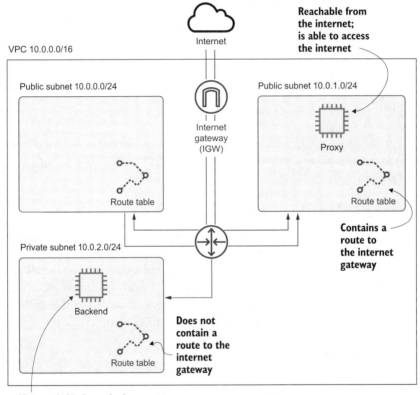

Figure 5.11   Private and public subnets

The backend subnet allows HTTP requests from the proxy subnet. The following NACLs are needed:

- Allow inbound port 80 (HTTP) from 10.0.1.0/24.
- Allow outbound ephemeral ports to 10.0.1.0/24.

We also want to make HTTP and HTTPS requests from the subnet to the internet. Keep in mind that we have no route to the internet yet. There is no way to access the internet, even with the NACLs. You will change this soon. The following NACLs are needed:

- Allow inbound ephemeral ports from 0.0.0.0/0.
- Allow outbound port 80 (HTTP) to 0.0.0.0/0.
- Allow outbound port 443 (HTTPS) to 0.0.0.0/0.

Find the CloudFormation implementation of the previous NACLs here:

```
NetworkAclEntryInPrivateBackendHTTP:          ◁────┐  Allows inbound HTTP
  Type: 'AWS::EC2::NetworkAclEntry'                 │  from proxy subnet
  Properties:
    NetworkAclId: !Ref NetworkAclPrivateBackend
    RuleNumber: '110'
    Protocol: '6'
    PortRange:
      From: '80'
      To: '80'
    RuleAction: 'allow'
    Egress: 'false'
    CidrBlock: '10.0.1.0/24'                              ┐  Ephemeral
NetworkAclEntryInPrivateBackendEphemeralPorts:  ◁────     ┘  ports
  Type: 'AWS::EC2::NetworkAclEntry'
  Properties:
    NetworkAclId: !Ref NetworkAclPrivateBackend
    RuleNumber: '200'
    Protocol: '6'
    PortRange:
      From: '1024'
      To: '65535'
    RuleAction: 'allow'
    Egress: 'false'
    CidrBlock: '0.0.0.0/0'                     ◁────  Allows outbound
NetworkAclEntryOutPrivateBackendHTTP:                 HTTP to everywhere
  Type: 'AWS::EC2::NetworkAclEntry'
  Properties:
    NetworkAclId: !Ref NetworkAclPrivateBackend
    RuleNumber: '100'
    Protocol: '6'
    PortRange:
      From: '80'
      To: '80'
    RuleAction: 'allow'
    Egress: 'true'
    CidrBlock: '0.0.0.0/0'                     ◁────  Allows outbound
NetworkAclEntryOutPrivateBackendHTTPS:                HTTPS to everywhere
  Type: 'AWS::EC2::NetworkAclEntry'
  Properties:
    NetworkAclId: !Ref NetworkAclPrivateBackend
    RuleNumber: '110'
    Protocol: '6'
```

```
    PortRange:
      From: '443'
      To: '443'
    RuleAction: 'allow'
    Egress: 'true'
    CidrBlock: '0.0.0.0/0'                          ⎤  Ephemeral
NetworkAclEntryOutPrivateBackendEphemeralPorts:  ⟵⎦  ports
  Type: 'AWS::EC2::NetworkAclEntry'
  Properties:
    NetworkAclId: !Ref NetworkAclPrivateBackend
    RuleNumber: '200'
    Protocol: '6'
    PortRange:
      From: '1024'
      To: '65535'
    RuleAction: 'allow'
    Egress: 'true'
    CidrBlock: '10.0.1.0/24'
```

5.5.4   *Launching virtual machines in the subnets*

Your subnets are ready, and you can continue with the EC2 instances. First you describe
the proxy, like this:

```
SecurityGroup:
  Type: 'AWS::EC2::SecurityGroup'
  Properties:
    GroupDescription: 'Allowing all incoming and outgoing traffic.'
    VpcId: !Ref VPC
    SecurityGroupIngress:
    - IpProtocol: '-1'
      FromPort: '-1'
      ToPort: '-1'
      CidrIp: '0.0.0.0/0'
    SecurityGroupEgress:
    - IpProtocol: '-1'
      FromPort: '-1'
      ToPort: '-1'
      CidrIp: '0.0.0.0/0'
Proxy:
  Type: AWS::EC2::Instance
  Properties:
    ImageId: 'ami-061ac2e015473fbe2'          ⎤  This security group
    InstanceType: 't2.micro'                       allows everything.
    IamInstanceProfile: 'ec2-ssm-core'
    SecurityGroupIds:
    - !Ref SecurityGroup                ⟵          Launches in the
    SubnetId: !Ref SubnetPublicProxy    ⟵          proxy subnet
    Tags:
    - Key: Name                                We need to manually tell CloudFormation about
      Value: Proxy                             a dependency here. Without the attachment
    UserData: # [...]                          being created, the instance could launch but
  DependsOn: VPCGatewayAttachment   ⟵          without access to the internet.
```

The private backend has a different configuration, as shown next:

```
Backend:
  Type: 'AWS::EC2::Instance'
  Properties:
    ImageId: 'ami-061ac2e015473fbe2'
    InstanceType: 't2.micro'
    IamInstanceProfile: 'ec2-ssm-core'
    SecurityGroupIds:
    - !Ref SecurityGroup
    SubnetId: !Ref SubnetPrivateBackend          Launches in the
    Tags:                                         private backend
    - Key: Name                                   subnet
      Value: Backend
    UserData:                    Installs Apache
      'Fn::Base64': |            from the internet
        #!/bin/bash -ex
        yum -y install httpd                   Starts the Apache
        systemctl start httpd                  web server
        echo '<html>...</html>' > /var/www/html/index.html
```

You're now in serious trouble: installing Apache won't work because your private sub-net has no route to the internet. Therefore, the `yum install` command will fail, because the public Yum repository is not reachable without access to the internet.

5.5.5 Accessing the internet from private subnets via a NAT gateway

Public subnets have a route to the internet gateway. You can use a similar mechanism to provide outbound internet connectivity for EC2 instances running in private sub-nets without having a direct route to the internet: create a NAT gateway in a public subnet, and create a route from your private subnet to the NAT gateway. This way, you can reach the internet from private subnets, but the internet can't reach your private subnets. A NAT gateway is a managed service provided by AWS that handles network address translation. Internet traffic from your private subnet will access the internet from the public IP address of the NAT gateway.

> **Reducing costs for NAT gateway**
>
> You have to pay for the traffic processed by a NAT gateway (see VPC Pricing at https://aws.amazon.com/vpc/pricing/ for more details). If your EC2 instances in private subnets will have to transfer huge amounts of data to the internet, you have two options to decrease costs:
>
> - Moving your EC2 instances from the private subnet to a public subnet allows them to transfer data to the internet without using the NAT gateway. Use firewalls to strictly restrict incoming traffic from the internet.
> - If data is transferred over the internet to reach AWS services (such as Amazon S3 and Amazon DynamoDB), use gateway VPC endpoints. These endpoints allow your EC2 instances to communicate with S3 and DynamoDB directly and at no additional charge. Furthermore, most other services are accessible from private subnets via interface VPC endpoints (offered by AWS PrivateLink) with an hourly and bandwidth fee.

WARNING   NAT gateways are finite resources. A NAT gateway processes up to 100 Gbit/s of traffic and up to 10 million packets per second. A NAT gateway is also bound to an availability zone (introduced in chapter 16).

To keep concerns separated, you'll create a subnet for the NAT gateway as follows:

```
SubnetPublicNAT:
  Type: 'AWS::EC2::Subnet'
  Properties:
    AvailabilityZone: !Select [0, !GetAZs '']
    CidrBlock: '10.0.0.0/24'          ⟵  10.0.0.0/24 is
    MapPublicIpOnLaunch: true              the NAT subnet.
    VpcId: !Ref VPC
    Tags:
    - Key: Name
      Value: 'Public NAT'
RouteTablePublicNAT:
  Type: 'AWS::EC2::RouteTable'
  Properties:
    VpcId: !Ref VPC
RouteTableAssociationPublicNAT:
  Type: 'AWS::EC2::SubnetRouteTableAssociation'
  Properties:
    SubnetId: !Ref SubnetPublicNAT
    RouteTableId: !Ref RouteTablePublicNAT
RoutePublicNATToInternet:              ⟵  The NAT subnet is
  Type: 'AWS::EC2::Route'                  public with a route
  Properties:                             to the internet.
    RouteTableId: !Ref RouteTablePublicNAT
    DestinationCidrBlock: '0.0.0.0/0'
    GatewayId: !Ref InternetGateway
  DependsOn: VPCGatewayAttachment
NetworkAclPublicNAT:
  Type: 'AWS::EC2::NetworkAcl'
  Properties:
    VpcId: !Ref VPC
SubnetNetworkAclAssociationPublicNAT:
  Type: 'AWS::EC2::SubnetNetworkAclAssociation'
  Properties:
    SubnetId: !Ref SubnetPublicNAT
    NetworkAclId: !Ref NetworkAclPublicNAT
```

We need a bunch of NACL rules to make the NAT gateway work.

To allow all VPC subnets to use the NAT gateway for HTTP and HTTPS, perform the following steps:

1 Allow inbound ports 80 (HTTP) and 443 (HTTPS) from 10.0.0.0/16.
2 Allow outbound ephemeral ports to 10.0.0.0/16.

To allow the NAT gateway to reach out to the internet on HTTP and HTTPS, perform these steps:

- Allow outbound ports 80 (HTTP) and 443 (HTTPS) to 0.0.0.0/0.
- Allow inbound ephemeral ports from 0.0.0.0/0.

Find the CloudFormation implementation of the previous NACL rules next:

```
NettworkAclEntryInPublicNATHTTP:            ◁─┐  Allows inbound
  Type: 'AWS::EC2::NetworkAclEntry'              HTTP from all
  Properties:                                    VPC subnets
    NetworkAclId: !Ref NetworkAclPublicNAT
    RuleNumber: '100'
    Protocol: '6'
    PortRange:
      From: '80'
      To: '80'
    RuleAction: 'allow'
    Egress: 'false'                         ┌─  Allows inbound
    CidrBlock: '10.0.0.0/16'                │   HTTPS from all
NetworkAclEntryInPublicNATHTTPS:          ◁─┘   VPC subnets
  Type: 'AWS::EC2::NetworkAclEntry'
  Properties:
    NetworkAclId: !Ref NetworkAclPublicNAT
    RuleNumber: '110'
    Protocol: '6'
    PortRange:
      From: '443'
      To: '443'
    RuleAction: 'allow'
    Egress: 'false'                         ┌─  Ephemeral
    CidrBlock: '10.0.0.0/16'                │   ports
NetworkAclEntryInPublicNATEphemeralPorts: ◁─┘
  Type: 'AWS::EC2::NetworkAclEntry'
  Properties:
    NetworkAclId: !Ref NetworkAclPublicNAT
    RuleNumber: '200'
    Protocol: '6'
    PortRange:
      From: '1024'
      To: '65535'
    RuleAction: 'allow'
    Egress: 'false'                         ┌─  Allows
    CidrBlock: '0.0.0.0/0'                  │   outbound HTTP
NetworkAclEntryOutPublicNATHTTP:          ◁─┘   to everywhere
  Type: 'AWS::EC2::NetworkAclEntry'
  Properties:
    NetworkAclId: !Ref NetworkAclPublicNAT
    RuleNumber: '100'
    Protocol: '6'
    PortRange:
      From: '80'
      To: '80'
    RuleAction: 'allow'
    Egress: 'true'
    CidrBlock: '0.0.0.0/0'                  ┌─  Allows
NetworkAclEntryOutPublicNATHTTPS:         ◁─┘   outbound HTTPS
  Type: 'AWS::EC2::NetworkAclEntry'             to everywhere
  Properties:
    NetworkAclId: !Ref NetworkAclPublicNAT
    RuleNumber: '110'
```

```
      Protocol: '6'
      PortRange:
        From: '443'
        To: '443'
      RuleAction: 'allow'
      Egress: 'true'
      CidrBlock: '0.0.0.0/0'                          Ephemeral
NetworkAclEntryOutPublicNATEphemeralPorts:             ports
  Type: 'AWS::EC2::NetworkAclEntry'
  Properties:
    NetworkAclId: !Ref NetworkAclPublicNAT
    RuleNumber: '200'
    Protocol: '6'
    PortRange:
      From: '1024'
      To: '65535'
    RuleAction: 'allow'
    Egress: 'true'
    CidrBlock: '10.0.0.0/16'
```

Finally, you can add the NAT gateway itself. The NAT gateway comes with a fixed public IP address (also called an Elastic IP address). All traffic that is routed through the NAT gateway will come from this IP address. We also add a route to the backend's route table to route traffic to 0.0.0.0/0 via the NAT gateway, as shown here:

```
EIPNatGateway:                        A static public IP address is
  Type: 'AWS::EC2::EIP'               used for the NAT gateway.
  Properties:
    Domain: 'vpc'                     The NAT gateway is placed into the
NatGateway:                           private subnet and associated with
  Type: 'AWS::EC2::NatGateway'        the static public IP address.
  Properties:
    AllocationId: !GetAtt 'EIPNatGateway.AllocationId'
    SubnetId: !Ref SubnetPublicNAT
RoutePrivateBackendToInternet:
  Type: 'AWS::EC2::Route'
  Properties:                              Route from the
    RouteTableId: !Ref RouteTablePrivateBackend   Apache subnet to
    DestinationCidrBlock: '0.0.0.0/0'       the NAT gateway
    NatGatewayId: !Ref NatGateway
```

Last, one small tweak to the already covered backend EC2 instance is needed to keep dependencies up-to-date, shown here:

```
Backend:
  Type: 'AWS::EC2::Instance'         Helps CloudFormation to
  Properties:                        understand that the route
    # [...]                          is needed before the EC2
  DependsOn: RoutePrivateBackendToInternet   instance can be created
```

WARNING   The NAT gateway included in the example is not covered by the Free Tier. The NAT gateway will cost you $0.045 per hour and $0.045 per GB of data processed when creating the stack in the US East (N. Virginia) region. Go to https://aws.amazon.com/vpc/pricing/ to have a look at the current prices.

Now you're ready to create the CloudFormation stack with the template located at https://s3.amazonaws.com/awsinaction-code3/chapter05/vpc.yaml by clicking the CloudFormation Quick-Create Link (http://mng.bz/jmR9). Once you've done so, copy the `ProxyPublicIpAddress` output and open it in your browser. You'll see an Apache test page.

Cleaning up
Don't forget to delete your stack after finishing this section to clean up all used resources. Otherwise, you'll likely be charged for the resources you use.

Summary

- AWS is a shared-responsibility environment in which security can be achieved only if you and AWS work together. You're responsible for securely configuring your AWS resources and your software running on EC2 instances, whereas AWS protects buildings and host systems.
- Keeping your software up-to-date is key and can be automated.
- The Identity and Access Management (IAM) service provides everything needed for authentication and authorization with the AWS API. Every request you make to the AWS API goes through IAM to check whether the request is allowed. IAM controls who can do what in your AWS account. To protect your AWS account, grant only those permissions that your users and roles need.
- Traffic to or from AWS resources like EC2 instances can be filtered based on protocol, port, and source or destination.
- A VPC is a private network in AWS where you have full control. With VPCs, you can control routing, subnets, NACLs, and gateways to the internet or your company network via a VPN. A NAT gateway enables access to the internet from private subnets.
- You should separate concerns in your network to reduce potential damage, for example, if one of your subnets is hacked. Keep every system in a private subnet that doesn't need to be accessed from the public internet, to reduce your attackable surface.

Automating operational tasks with Lambda

This chapter is about adding a new tool to your toolbox. The tool we're talking about, AWS Lambda, is as flexible as a Swiss Army knife. You don't need a virtual machine to run your own code anymore, because AWS Lambda offers execution environments for C#/.NET Core, Go, Java, JavaScript/Node.js, Python, and Ruby. All you have to do is implement a function, upload your code, and configure the execution environment. Afterward, your code is executed within a fully managed computing environment. AWS Lambda is well integrated with all parts of AWS, enabling you to easily automate operations tasks within your infrastructure. We use AWS to automate our infrastructure regularly, such as to add and remove instances to a container cluster based on a custom algorithm and to process and analyze log files.

AWS Lambda offers a maintenance-free and highly available computing environment. You no longer need to install security updates, replace failed virtual machines, or manage remote access (such as SSH or RDP) for administrators. On top of that, AWS Lambda is billed by invocation. Therefore, you don't have to pay for idling resources that are waiting for work (e.g., for a task triggered once a day).

In our first example, you will create a Lambda function that performs periodic health checks for your website. This will teach you how to use the Management Console to get started with AWS Lambda quickly. In our second example, you will learn how to write your own Python code and deploy a Lambda function in an automated way using CloudFormation, which we introduced in chapter 4. Your Lambda function will automatically add a tag to newly launched EC2 instances. At the end of the chapter, we'll show you additional use cases like building web applications and Internet of Things (IoT) backends and processing data with AWS Lambda.

> **Examples are almost all covered by the Free Tier**
>
> The examples in this chapter are mostly covered by the Free Tier. There is one exception: AWS CloudTrail. In case you already created a trail in your account, additional charges—most likely just a few cents—will apply. For details, please see https://aws .amazon.com/cloudtrail/pricing/.
>
> You will find instructions on how to clean up the examples at the end of each section.

You may be asking a more basic question: what exactly is AWS Lambda? Before diving into our first real-world example, let us introduce you, briefly, to Lambda and explain why it's often mentioned in the context of an architecture that's being called *serverless*.

6.1 *Executing your code with AWS Lambda*

Computing capacity is available at different layers of abstraction on AWS: virtual machines, containers, and functions. You learned about the virtual machines offered by Amazon's EC2 service in chapter 3. Containers offer another layer of abstraction on top of virtual machines; you will learn about containers in chapter 18. AWS Lambda provides computing power, as well, but in a fine-grained manner: it is an execution environment for small functions, rather than a full-blown operating system or container.

6.1.1 *What is serverless?*

When reading about AWS Lambda, you might have stumbled upon the term *serverless*. In his book *Serverless Architectures on AWS* (Manning, 2022; http://mng.bz/wyr5), Peter Sbarski summarizes the confusion created by this catchy and provocative phrase:

[…] the word serverless is a bit of a misnomer. Whether you use a compute service such as AWS Lambda to execute your code, or interact with an API, there are still servers running in the background. The difference is that these servers are hidden from you. There's no infrastructure for you to think about and no way to tweak the underlying operating system. Someone else takes care of the nitty-gritty details of infrastructure management, freeing your time for other things.

—Peter Sbarski

We define a serverless system as one that meets the following criteria:

- No need to manage and maintain virtual machines
- Fully managed service offering scalability and high availability
- Billed per request and by resource consumption

AWS Lambda certainly fits these definitions and is indeed a serverless platform in that AWS handles server configurations and management so the server is essentially invisible to you and takes care of itself. AWS is not the only provider offering a serverless platform. Google (Cloud Functions) and Microsoft (Azure Functions) are other competitors in this area. If you would like to read more about serverless, here is a free chapter from *Serverless Architectures on AWS,* second edition: http://mng.bz/qoEx.

6.1.2   *Running your code on AWS Lambda*

AWS Lambda is the basic building block of the serverless platform provided by AWS. The first step in the process is to run your code on Lambda instead of on your own server.

As shown in figure 6.1, to execute your code with AWS Lambda, follow these steps:

1 Write the code.
2 Upload your code and its dependencies (such as libraries or modules).
3 Create a function determining the runtime environment and configuration.
4 Invoke the function to execute your code in the cloud.

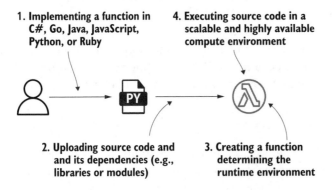

1. Implementing a function in C#, Go, Java, JavaScript, Python, or Ruby

4. Executing source code in a scalable and highly available compute environment

2. Uploading source code and and its dependencies (e.g., libraries or modules)

3. Creating a function determining the runtime environment

Figure 6.1   Executing code with AWS Lambda

Currently, AWS Lambda offers runtime environments for the following languages:

- C#/.NET Core
- Go
- Java
- JavaScript/Node.js
- Python
- Ruby

Besides that, you can bring your own runtime by using a custom runtime. In theory, a custom runtime supports any programming language. You need to bring your own container image and follow conventions for initializing the function and processing tasks. Doing so adds extra complexity, so we recommend going with one of the available runtimes.

Next, we will compare AWS Lambda with EC2 virtual machines.

6.1.3   *Comparing AWS Lambda with virtual machines (Amazon EC2)*

What is the difference between using AWS Lambda and virtual machines? First is the granularity of virtualization. Virtual machines provide a full operating system for running one or multiple applications. In contrast, AWS Lambda offers an execution environment for a single function, a small part of an application.

Furthermore, Amazon EC2 offers virtual machines as a service, but you are responsible for operating them in a secure, scalable, and highly available way. Doing so requires you to put a substantial amount of effort into maintenance. In contrast, when building with Lambda, AWS manages the underlying infrastructure for you and provides a production-ready infrastructure.

Beyond that, AWS Lambda is billed per execution, and not per second like when a virtual machine is running. You don't have to pay for unused resources that are waiting for requests or tasks. For example, running a script to check the health of a website every five minutes on a virtual machine would cost you about $3.71 per month. Executing the same health check with AWS Lambda will cost about $0.04 per month.

Table 6.1 compares AWS Lambda and virtual machines in detail. You'll find a discussion of AWS Lambda's limitations at the end of the chapter.

Table 6.1   AWS Lambda compared to Amazon EC2

	AWS Lambda	**Amazon EC2**
Granularity of virtualization	Small piece of code (a function).	An entire operating system.
Scalability	Scales automatically. A throttling limit prevents you from creating unwanted charges accidentally and can be increased by AWS support if needed.	As you will learn in chapter 17, using an Auto Scaling group allows you to scale the number of EC2 instances serving requests automatically, but configuring and monitoring the scaling activities is your responsibility.

Table 6.1 AWS Lambda compared to Amazon EC2 *(continued)*

	AWS Lambda	Amazon EC2
High availability	Fault tolerant by default. The computing infrastructure spans multiple machines and data centers.	Virtual machines are not highly available by default. Nevertheless, as you will learn in chapter 13, it is possible to set up a highly available infrastructure based on EC2 instances as well.
Maintenance effort	Almost zero. You need only to configure your function.	You are responsible for maintaining all layers between your virtual machine's operating system and your application's runtime environment.
Deployment effort	Almost zero due to a well-defined API	Rolling out your application to a fleet of virtual machines is a challenge that requires tools and know-how.
Pricing model	Pay per request as well as execution time and allocated memory	Pay for operating hours of the virtual machines, billed per second

Looking for limitations and pitfalls of AWS Lambda? Stay tuned: you will find a discussion of Lambda's limitations at the end of the chapter.

That's all you need to know about AWS Lambda to be able to go through the first real-world example. Are you ready?

6.2 *Building a website health check with AWS Lambda*

Are you responsible for the uptime of a website or application? We do our best to make sure our blog https://cloudonaut.io is accessible 24/7. An external health check acts as a safety net, making sure we, and not our readers, are the first to know when our blog goes down. AWS Lambda is the perfect choice for building a website health check, because you do not need computing resources constantly but only every few minutes for a few milliseconds. This section guides you through setting up a health check for your website based on AWS Lambda.

In addition to AWS Lambda, we are using the Amazon CloudWatch service for this example. Lambda functions publish metrics to CloudWatch by default. Typically, you inspect metrics using charts and create alarms by defining thresholds. For example, a metric could count failures during the function's execution. On top of that, EventBridge provides events that can be used to trigger Lambda functions as well. Here we are using a rule to publish an event every five minutes.

As shown in figure 6.2, your website health check will consist of the following three parts:

1 *Lambda function*—Executes a Python script that sends an HTTP request to your website (e.g., GET https://cloudonaut.io) and verifies that the response includes specific text (such as cloudonaut).
2 *EventBridge rule*—Triggers the Lambda function every five minutes. This is comparable to the cron service on Linux.

3 *Alarm*—Monitors the number of failed health checks and notifies you via email whenever your website is unavailable.

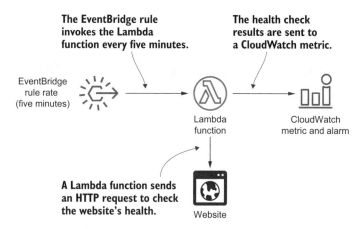

Figure 6.2 The Lambda function performing the website health check is executed every five minutes by a scheduled event. Errors are reported to CloudWatch.

You will use the Management Console to create and configure all the necessary parts manually. In our opinion, this is a simple way to get familiar with AWS Lambda. You will learn how to deploy a Lambda function in an automated way in section 6.3.

6.2.1 Creating a Lambda function

The following step-by-step instructions guide you through setting up a website health check based on AWS Lambda. Open AWS Lambda in the Management Console: https://console.aws.amazon.com/lambda/home. Click Create a Function to start the Lambda function wizard, as shown in figure 6.3.

Figure 6.3 Welcome screen: Ready to create your first Lambda function

AWS provides blueprints for various use cases, including the code and the Lambda function configuration. We will use one of these blueprints to create a website health check. Select Use a Blueprint, and search for canary. Next, choose the lambda-canary blueprint. Figure 6.4 illustrates the details.

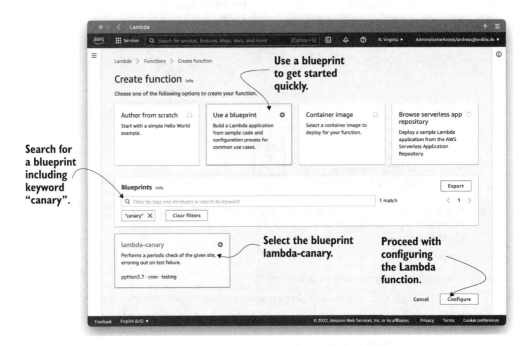

Figure 6.4   Creating a Lambda function based on a blueprint provided by AWS

In the next step of the wizard, you need to specify a name for your Lambda function, as shown in figure 6.5. The function name needs to be unique within your AWS account and the current region US East (N. Virginia). In addition, the name is limited to 64 characters. To invoke a function via the API, you need to provide the function name. Type in website-health-check as the name for your Lambda function.

Continue with creating an IAM role. Select Create a New Role with Basic Lambda Permissions, as shown in figure 6.5, to create an IAM role for your Lambda function. You will learn how your Lambda function uses the IAM role in section 6.3.

Next, configure the scheduled event that will trigger your health check repeatedly. We will use an interval of five minutes in this example. Figure 6.6 shows the settings you need:

1   Select Create a New Rule to create a scheduled event rule.
2   Type in website-health-check as the name for the rule.
3   Enter a description that will help you to understand what is going on if you come back later.

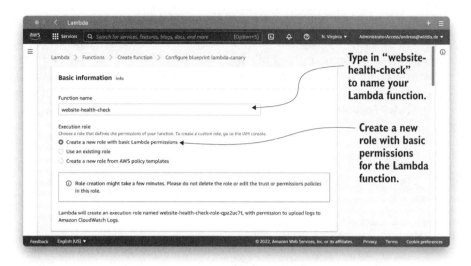

Figure 6.5   Creating a Lambda function: Choose a name and define an IAM role.

4   Select Schedule Expression as the rule type. You will learn about the other
option, Event Pattern, at the end of this chapter.
5   Use rate(5 minutes) as the schedule expression.

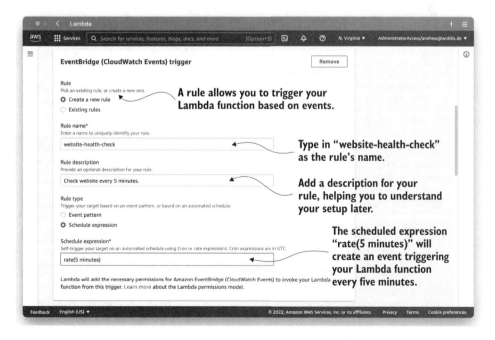

Figure 6.6   Configuring a scheduled event triggering your Lambda function every five minutes

Define recurring tasks using a *schedule expression* in form of rate($value $unit). For example, you could trigger a task every five minutes, every hour, or once a day. $value needs to be a positive integer value. Use minute, minutes, hour, hours, day, or days as the unit. For example, instead of triggering the website health check every five minutes, you could use rate(1 hour) as the schedule expression to execute the health check every hour. Note that frequencies of less than one minute are not supported.

It is also possible to use the crontab format, shown here, when defining a schedule expression:

```
cron($minutes $hours $dayOfMonth $month $dayOfWeek $year)

 # Invoke a Lambda function at 08:00am (UTC) everyday
 cron(0 8 * * ? *)

 # Invoke a Lambda function at 04:00pm (UTC) every Monday to Friday
 cron(0 16 ? * MON-FRI *)
```

See "Schedule Expressions Using Rate or cron" at http://mng.bz/7ZnQ for more details.

Your Lambda function is missing an integral part: the code. Because you are using a blueprint, AWS has inserted the Python code implementing the website health check for you, as shown in figure 6.7.

The Python code references two environment variables: site and expected. Environment variables are commonly used to dynamically pass settings to your function. An environment variable consists of a key and a value. Specify the following environment variables for your Lambda function:

- site—Contains the URL of the website you want to monitor. Use https:// cloudonaut.io if you do not have a website to monitor yourself.
- expected—Contains a text snippet that must be available on your website. If the function doesn't find this text, the health check fails. Use cloudonaut if you are using https://cloudonaut.io as your website.

The Lambda function is reading the environment variables during its execution, as shown next:

```
SITE = os.environment['site']
 EXPECTED = os.environment['expected']
```

After defining the environment variables for your Lambda function, click the Create Function button at the bottom of the screen.

Congratulations—you have successfully created a Lambda function. Every five minutes, the function is invoked automatically and executes a health check for your website.

You could use this approach to automate recurring tasks, like checking the status of a system, cleaning up unused resources like EBS snapshots, or to send recurring reports.

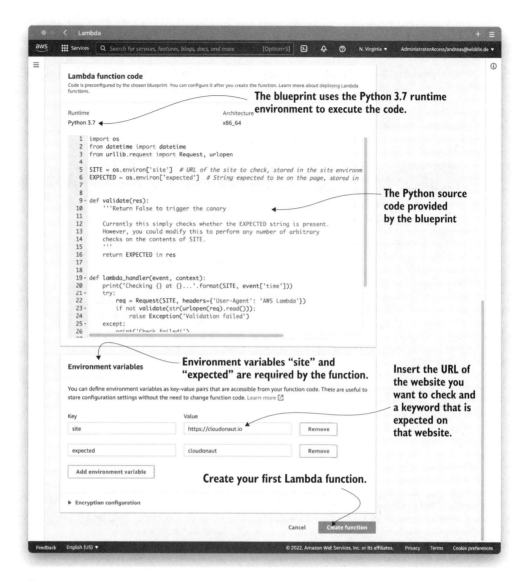

Figure 6.7 The predefined code implementing the website health check and environment variables to pass settings to the Lambda function

So far, you have used a predefined template. Lambda gets much more powerful when you write your own code. But before we look into that, you will learn how to monitor your Lambda function and get notified via email whenever the health check fails.

6.2.2 Use CloudWatch to search through your Lambda function's logs

How do you know whether your website health check is working correctly? How do you even know whether your Lambda function has been executed? It is time to look at how to monitor a Lambda function. You will learn how to access your Lambda function's log messages first. Afterward, you will create an alarm notifying you if your function fails.

Open the Monitor tab in the details view of your Lambda function. You will find a chart illustrating the number of times your function has been invoked. Reload the chart after a few minutes, in case the chart isn't showing any invocations. To go to your Lambda function's logs, click View Logs in CloudWatch, as shown in figure 6.8.

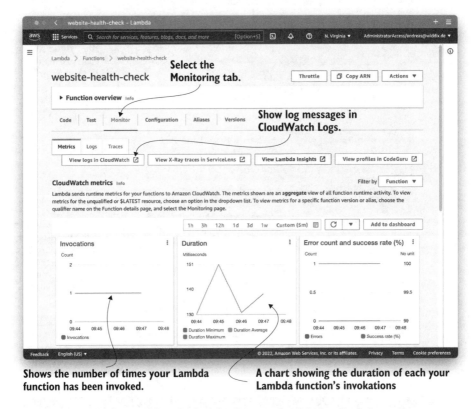

Figure 6.8   Monitoring overview: Get insights into your Lambda function's invocations.

By default, your Lambda function sends log messages to CloudWatch. Figure 6.9 shows the log group named /aws/lambda/website-health-check that was created automatically and collects the logs from your function. Typically, a log group contains multiple log streams, allowing the log group to scale. Click Search Log Group to view the log messages from all streams in one view.

All log messages are presented in the overview of log streams, as shown in figure 6.10. You should be able to find a log message `Check passed!`, indicating that the website health check was executed and passed successfully, for example.

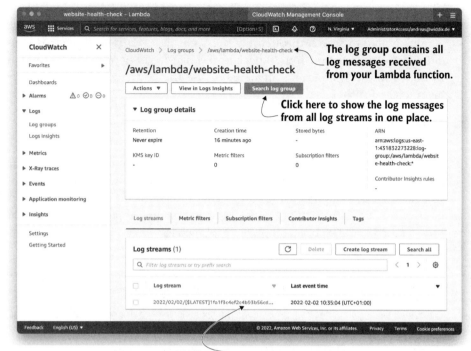

Figure 6.9   A log group collects log messages from a Lambda function stored in multiple log streams.

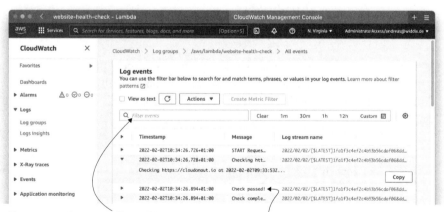

Figure 6.10   CloudWatch shows the log messages of your Lambda function.

The log messages show up after a delay of a few minutes. Reload the table if you are missing any log messages.

Being able to search through log messages in a centralized place is handy when debugging Lambda functions, especially if you are writing your own code. When using Python, you can use `print` statements or use the `logging` module to send log messages to CloudWatch.

6.2.3   *Monitoring a Lambda function with CloudWatch metrics and alarms*

The Lambda function now checks the health of your website every five minutes, and a log message with the result of each health check is written to CloudWatch. But how do you get notified via email if the health check fails? Each Lambda function publishes metrics to CloudWatch by default. Table 6.2 shows important metrics. Check out http://mng.bz/m298 for a complete list of metrics.

Table 6.2   The CloudWatch metrics published by each Lambda function

Name	Description
Invocations	Counts the number of times a function is invoked. Includes successful and failed invocations.
Errors	Counts the number of times a function failed due to errors inside the function, for example, exceptions or timeouts.
Duration	Measures how long the code takes to run, from the time when the code starts executing to when it stops executing.
Throttles	As discussed at the beginning of the chapter, there is a limit for how many copies of your Lambda function can run at one time. This metric counts how many invocations have been throttled due to reaching this limit. Contact AWS support to increase the limit, if needed.

Whenever the website health check fails, the Lambda function returns an error, which increases the count of the Errors metric. You will create an alarm notifying you via email whenever this metric counts more than zero errors. In general, we recommend creating an alarm on the Errors and Throttles metrics to monitor your Lambda functions.

The following steps guide you through creating a CloudWatch alarm to monitor your website health checks. Your Management Console still shows the CloudWatch service. Select Alarms from the subnavigation menu. Next, click Create Alarm, as shown in figure 6.11.

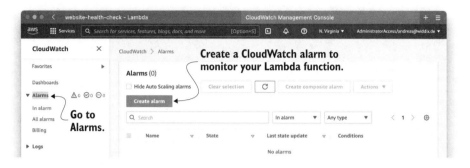

Figure 6.11   Starting the wizard to create a CloudWatch alarm to monitor a Lambda function

The following three steps guide you through the process of selecting the Error metric of your `website-health-check` Lambda function, as illustrated in figure 6.12:

1 Click Select Metric.
2 Choose the Lambda namespace.
3 Select metrics with dimension Function Name.

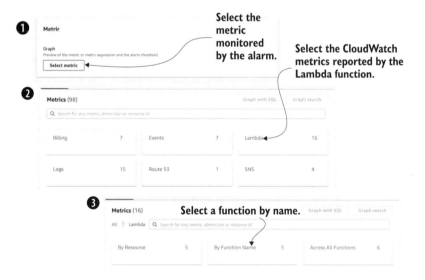

Figure 6.12   Searching the CloudWatch metric to create an alarm

Last but not least, select the Error metric belonging to the Lambbda function `website-health-check` as shown in figure 6.13. Proceed by clicking the Select Metric button.

Figure 6.13   Selecting the Error metric of the Lambda function

Next, you need to configure the alarm, as shown in figure 6.14. To do so, specify the statistic, period, and threshold as follows:

1 Choose the statistic Sum to add up all the errors that occurred during the evaluation period.
2 Define an evaluation period of five minutes.
3 Select the Static Threshold option.
4 Choose the Greater operator.
5 Define a threshold of zero.
6 Click the Next button to proceed.

In other words, the alarm state will change to ALARM when the Lambda function reports any errors during the evaluation period of five minutes. Otherwise, the alarm state will be OK.

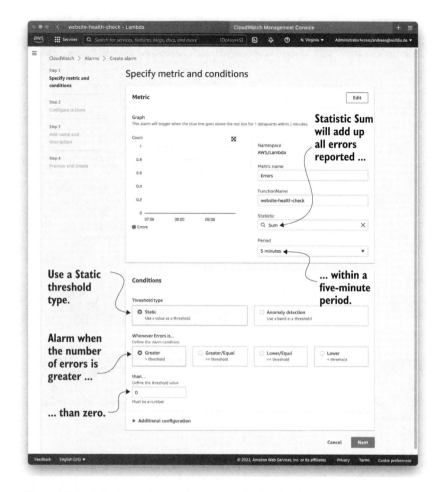

Figure 6.14   Selecting and preparing the metric view for the alarm

The next step, illustrated in figure 6.15, configures the alarm actions so you will be notified via e-mail:

1 Select In Alarm as the state trigger.
2 Create a new SNS topic by choosing Create New Topic.
3 Type in website-health-check as the name for the SNS topic.
4 Enter your email address.
5 Click the Next button to proceed.

In the following step, you need to enter a name for the CloudWatch alarm. Type in website-health-check-error. Afterward, click the Next button to proceed.

After reviewing the configuration, click the Create Alarm button. Shortly after creating the alarm, you will receive an email including a confirmation link for SNS. Check your inbox and click the link to confirm your subscription to the notification list.

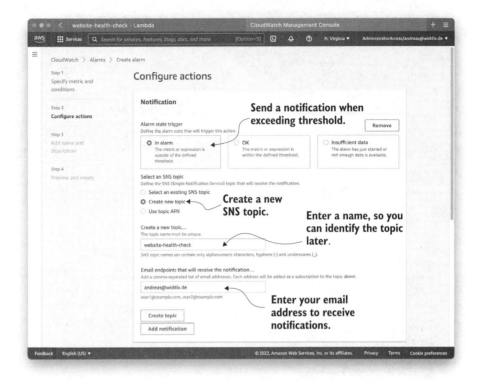

Figure 6.15 Creating an alarm by defining a threshold and defining an alarm action to send notifications via email

To test the alarm, go back to the Lambda function and modify the environment variable expected. For example, modify the value from cloudonaut to FAILURE. This will cause the health check to fail, because the word FAILURE does not appear on the website. It might take up to 15 minutes before you receive a notification about the failed website health check via email.

Cleaning up

Open your Management Console and follow these steps to delete all the resources you have created during this section:

1 Go to the AWS Lambda service and delete the function named website-health-check.

2 Open the AWS CloudWatch service, select Logs from the subnavigation options, and delete the log group /aws/lambda/website-health-check.

3 Go to the EventBridge service, select Rules from the subnavigation menu, and delete the rule website-health-check.

4 Open the CloudWatch service, select Alarms from the subnavigation menu, and delete the alarm website-health-check-error.

5 Jump to the AWS IAM service, select Roles from the subnavigation menu, and delete the role whose name starts with website-health-check-role-.

6 Go to the SNS service, select Topics from the subnavigation menu, and delete the rule website-health-check.

6.2.4 *Accessing endpoints within a VPC*

As illustrated in figure 6.16, by default Lambda functions run outside your networks defined with VPC. However, Lambda functions are connected to the internet and, therefore, are able to access other services. That's exactly what you have been doing when creating a website health check: the Lambda function was sending HTTP requests over the internet.

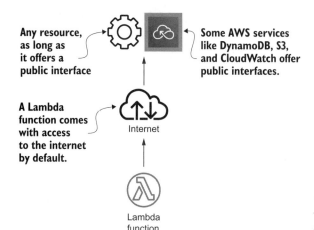

Figure 6.16 By default a Lambda function is connected to the internet and running outside your VPCs.

So, what do you do when you have to reach a resource running in a private network within your VPC, for example, if you want to run a health check for an internal website? If you add network interfaces to your Lambda function, the function can access resources within your VPCs, as shown in figure 6.17.

To do so, you have to define the VPC and the subnets, as well as security groups for your Lambda function. See "Configuring a Lambda Function to Access Resources in an Amazon VPC" at http://mng.bz/5m67 for more details. We have been using the ability to access resources within a VPC to access databases in various projects.

We do recommend connecting a Lambda function to a VPC only when absolutely necessary because it introduces additional complexity. However, being able to connect with resources within your private networks is very interesting, especially when integrating with legacy systems.

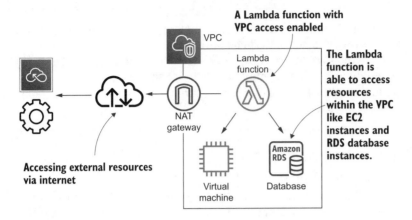

Figure 6.17   Deploying a Lambda function into your VPC allows you to access internal resources (such as database, virtual machines, and so on).

6.3   Adding a tag containing the owner of an EC2 instance automatically

After using one of AWS's predefined blueprints to create a Lambda function, you will implement the function from scratch in this section. We are strongly focused on setting up your cloud infrastructure in an automated way. That's why you will learn how to deploy a Lambda function and all its dependencies without needing the Management Console.

Are you working in an AWS account together with your colleagues? Have you ever wondered who launched a certain EC2 instance? Sometimes you need to find out the owner of an EC2 instance for the following reasons:

- Double-checking whether it is safe to terminate an unused instance without losing relevant data
- Reviewing changes to an instance's configuration with its owner (such as making changes to the firewall configuration)
- Attributing costs to individuals, projects, or departments
- Restricting access to an instance (e.g., so only the owner is allowed to terminate an instance)

Adding a tag that states who owns an instance solves all these use cases. A tag can be added to an EC2 instance or almost any other AWS resource and consists of a key and a value. You can use tags to add information to a resource, filter resources, attribute costs to resources, and restrict access. See "Tag your Amazon EC2 resources" at http://mng.bz/69oR for more details.

It is possible to add tags specifying the owner of an EC2 instance manually. But, sooner or later, someone will forget to add the owner tag. There is a better solution! In the following section, you will implement and deploy a Lambda function that automatically adds a tag containing the name of the user who launched an EC2 instance.

But how do you execute a Lambda function every time an EC2 instance is launched so that you can add the tag?

6.3.1 Event-driven: Subscribing to EventBridge events

EventBridge is an event bus used by AWS, third-party vendors, and customers like you, to publish and subscribe to events. In this example, you will create a rule to listen for events from AWS. Whenever something changes in your infrastructure, an event is generated in near real time and the following things occur:

- CloudTrail emits an event for every call to the AWS API if CloudTrail is enabled in the AWS account and region.
- EC2 emits events whenever the state of an EC2 instances changes (such as when the state changes from Pending to Running).
- AWS emits an event to notify you of service degradations or downtimes.

Whenever you launch a new EC2 instance, you are sending a call to the AWS API. Subsequently, CloudTrail sends an event to EventBridge. Our goal is to add a tag to every new EC2 instance. Therefore, we are executing a function for every event that indicates the launch of a new EC2 instance. To trigger a Lambda function whenever such an event occurs, you need a rule. As illustrated in figure 6.18, the rule matches incoming events and routes them to a target, a Lambda function in our case.

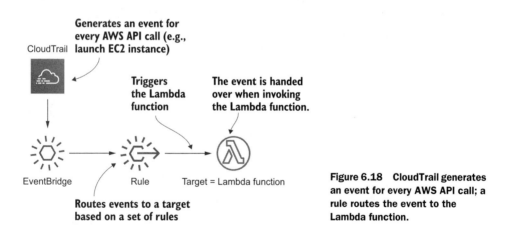

Figure 6.18   CloudTrail generates an event for every AWS API call; a rule routes the event to the Lambda function.

Listing 6.1 shows some of the event details generated by CloudTrail whenever someone launches an EC2 instance. For our case, we're interested in the following information:

- detail-type—The event has been created by CloudTrail.
- source—The EC2 service is the source of the event.
- eventName—The event name RunInstances indicates that the event was generated because of an AWS API call launching an EC2 instance.
- userIdentity—Who called the AWS API to launch an instance?

- responseElements—The response from the AWS API when launching an instance. This includes the ID of the launched EC2 instance; we will need to add a tag to the instance later.

Listing 6.1   Event generated by CloudTrail when launching an EC2 instance

```
{
  "version": "0",
  "id": "2db486ef-6775-de10-1472-ecc242928abe",
  "detail-type": "AWS API Call via CloudTrail",          ◁── CloudTrail generated the event.
  "source": "aws.ec2",                                   ◁── Someone sent a call to the AWS API, affecting the EC2 service.
  "account": "XXXXXXXXXXXX",
  "time": "2022-02-03T11:42:25Z",
  "region": "us-east-1",
  "resources": [],
  "detail": {
    "eventVersion": "1.08",                              Information about the user who launched the EC2 instance
    "userIdentity": {                                    ◁──
      "type": "IAMUser",
      "principalId": "XXXXXXXXXXXX",                     ID of the user who launched the EC2 instance
      "arn": "arn:aws:iam::XXXXXXXXXXXX:user/myuser",    ◁──
      "accountId": "XXXXXXXXXXXX",
      "accessKeyId": "XXXXXXXXXXXX",
      "userName": "myuser"
    },
    "eventTime": "2022-02-03T11:42:25Z",                 Event was generated because a RunInstances call (used to launch an EC2 instance) was processed by the AWS API.
    "eventSource": "ec2.amazonaws.com",
    "eventName": "RunInstances",                         ◁──
    "awsRegion": "us-east-1",
    "sourceIPAddress": "109.90.107.17",
    "userAgent": "aws-cli/2.4.14 Python/3.9.10 Darwin/21.2.0
        ⇨ source/arm64 prompt/off command/ec2.run-instances",
    "requestParameters": {
      [...]
    },
    "responseElements": {                                ◁── Response of the AWS API when launching the instance
      "requestId": "d52b86c7-5bf8-4d19-86e8-112e59164b21",
      "reservationId": "r-08131583e8311879d",
      "ownerId": "166876438428",
      "groupSet": {},
      "instancesSet": {
        "items": [                                       ID of the launched EC2 instance
          {
            "instanceId": "i-07a3c0d78dc1cb505",         ◁──
            "imageId": "ami-01893222c83843146",
            [...]
          }
        ]
      }
    },
    "requestID": "d52b86c7-5bf8-4d19-86e8-112e59164b21",
    "eventID": "8225151b-3a9c-4275-8b37-4a317dfe9ee2",
    "readOnly": false,
    "eventType": "AwsApiCall",
```

```
      "managementEvent": true,
      "recipientAccountId": "XXXXXXXXXXXX",
      "eventCategory": "Management",
      "tlsDetails": {
        [...]
      }
    }
  }
}
```

A rule consists of an event pattern for selecting events, along with a definition of one or multiple targets. The following pattern selects all events from CloudTrail generated by an AWS API call affecting the EC2 service. The pattern matches four attributes from the event described in the next listing: source, detail-type, eventSource, and eventName.

Listing 6.2   The pattern to filter events from CloudTrail

```
{
  "source": [                              ──┐  Filters events from
    "aws.ec2"                         ◁──────┘  the EC2 service
  ],
                                                    Filters events from
  "detail-type": [                                  CloudTrail caused
    "AWS API Call via CloudTrail"    ◁──────┐  by AWS API calls
  ],                                        ──┘
  "detail": {
    "eventSource": [                         ──┐ Filters events from
      "ec2.amazonaws.com"            ◁─────────┘ the EC2 service
    ],
    "eventName": [
      "RunInstances"                 ◁──┐  Filters events with event name
    ]                                   └──  RunInstances, which is the AWS
  }                                          API call to launch an EC2 instance
}
```

Defining filters on other event attributes is possible as well, in case you are planning to write another rule in the future. The rule format stays the same.

When specifying an event pattern, we typically use the following fields, which are included in every event:

- source—The namespace of the service that generated the event. See "Amazon Resource Names (ARNs)" at http://mng.bz/o5WD for details.
- detail-type—Categorizes the event in more detail.

See "EventBridge Event Patterns" at http://mng.bz/nejd for more detailed information.

You have now defined the events that will trigger your Lambda function. Next, you will implement the Lambda function.

6.3.2   *Implementing the Lambda function in Python*

Implementing the Lambda function to tag an EC2 instance with the owner's user name is simple. You will need to write no more than 10 lines of Python code. The programming model for a Lambda function depends on the programming language you choose. Although we are using Python in our example, you will be able to apply what you've learned when implementing a Lambda function in C#/.NET Core, Go, Java, JavaScript/Node.js, Python, or Ruby. As shown in the next listing, your function written in Python needs to implement a well-defined structure.

Listing 6.3   Lambda function written in Python

The name of the Python function, which is referenced by the AWS Lambda as the function handler. The event parameter is used to pass the CloudWatch event, and the context parameter includes runtime information.

```
def lambda_handler(event, context):
    # Insert your code
    return
```

It is your job to implement the function.

Use return to end the function execution. It is not useful to hand over a value in this scenario, because the Lambda function is invoked asynchronously by a CloudWatch event.

Where is the code located?

As usual, you'll find the code in the book's code repository on GitHub: https://github .com/AWSinAction/code3. Switch to the chapter06 directory, which includes all files needed for this example.

Time to write some Python code! Listing 6.4 for `lambda_function.py` shows the function, which receives an event from CloudTrail indicating that an EC2 instance has been launched recently, and adds a tag including the name of the instance's owner. The AWS SDK for Python 3.9, named `boto3`, is provided out of the box in the Lambda runtime environment for Python 3.9. In this example, you are using the AWS SDK to create a tag for the EC2 instance `ec2.create_tags(…)`. See the Boto3 documentation at https://boto3.readthedocs.io/en/latest/index.html if you are interested in the details of `boto3`.

Listing 6.4   Lambda function adding a tag to EC2 instance

Creates an AWS SDK client for EC2

The name of the function used as entry point for the Lambda function

Logs the incoming event for debugging

Extracts the user's name from the CloudTrail event

```
import boto3
ec2 = boto3.client('ec2')

def lambda_handler(event, context):
    print(event)
    if "/" in event['detail']['userIdentity']['arn']:
        userName = event['detail']['userIdentity']['arn'].split('/')[1]
    else:
        userName = event['detail']['userIdentity']['arn']
    instanceId = event['detail']['responseElements']['instancesSet']
```

```
['items'][0]['instanceId']
print("Adding owner tag " + userName + " to instance " + instanceId + ".")
ec2.create_tags(Resources=[instanceId,],
    Tags=[{'Key': 'Owner', 'Value': userName},])
return
```

Extracts the instance's ID from the CloudTrail event

Adds a tag to the EC2 instance using the key owner and the user's name as value

After implementing your function in Python, the next step is to deploy the Lambda function with all its dependencies.

6.3.3 Setting up a Lambda function with the Serverless Application Model (SAM)

You have probably noticed that we are huge fans of automating infrastructures with CloudFormation. Using the Management Console is a perfect way to take the first step when learning about a new service on AWS. But leveling up from manually clicking through a web interface to fully automating the deployment of your infrastructure should be your second step.

AWS released the *Serverless Application Model* (SAM) in 2016. SAM provides a framework for serverless applications, extending plain CloudFormation templates to make it easier to deploy Lambda functions. The next listing shows how to define a Lambda function using SAM and a CloudFormation template.

Listing 6.5   Defining a Lambda function with SAM within a CloudFormation template

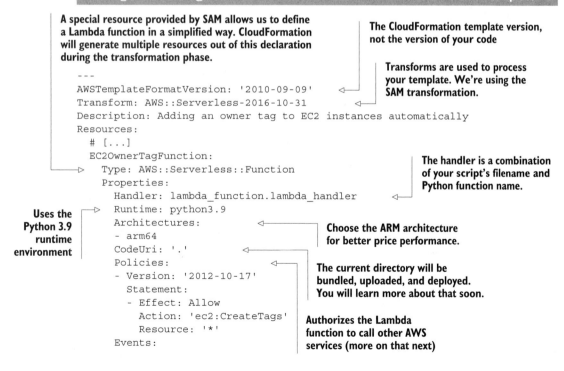

A special resource provided by SAM allows us to define a Lambda function in a simplified way. CloudFormation will generate multiple resources out of this declaration during the transformation phase.

The CloudFormation template version, not the version of your code

Transforms are used to process your template. We're using the SAM transformation.

```
---
AWSTemplateFormatVersion: '2010-09-09'
Transform: AWS::Serverless-2016-10-31
Description: Adding an owner tag to EC2 instances automatically
Resources:
  # [...]
  EC2OwnerTagFunction:
    Type: AWS::Serverless::Function
    Properties:
      Handler: lambda_function.lambda_handler
      Runtime: python3.9
      Architectures:
      - arm64
      CodeUri: '.'
      Policies:
      - Version: '2012-10-17'
        Statement:
        - Effect: Allow
          Action: 'ec2:CreateTags'
          Resource: '*'
      Events:
```

The handler is a combination of your script's filename and Python function name.

Uses the Python 3.9 runtime environment

Choose the ARM architecture for better price performance.

The current directory will be bundled, uploaded, and deployed. You will learn more about that soon.

Authorizes the Lambda function to call other AWS services (more on that next)

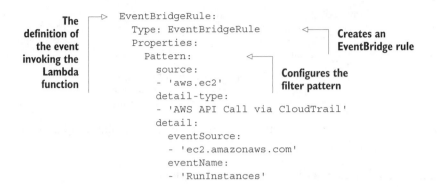

The definition of the event invoking the Lambda function

```
EventBridgeRule:
    Type: EventBridgeRule
    Properties:
        Pattern:
            source:
            - 'aws.ec2'
            detail-type:
            - 'AWS API Call via CloudTrail'
            detail:
                eventSource:
                - 'ec2.amazonaws.com'
                eventName:
                - 'RunInstances'
```

Creates an EventBridge rule

Configures the filter pattern

Please note: this example uses CloudTrail, which records all the activity within your AWS account. The CloudFormation template creates a trail to store an audit log on S3. That's needed because the EventBridge rule does not work without an active trail.

6.3.4   *Authorizing a Lambda function to use other AWS services with an IAM role*

Lambda functions typically interact with other AWS services. For instance, they write log messages to CloudWatch allowing you to monitor and debug your Lambda function. Or they create a tag for an EC2 instance, as in the current example. Therefore, calls to the AWS APIs need to be authenticated and authorized. Figure 6.19 shows a Lambda function assuming an IAM role to be able to send authenticated and authorized requests to other AWS services.

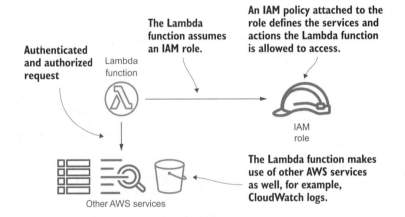

The Lambda function assumes an IAM role.

An IAM policy attached to the role defines the services and actions the Lambda function is allowed to access.

Authenticated and authorized request

Lambda function

IAM role

Other AWS services

The Lambda function makes use of other AWS services as well, for example, CloudWatch logs.

Figure 6.19
A Lambda function assumes an IAM role to authenticate and authorize requests to other AWS services.

Temporary credentials are generated based on the IAM role and injected into each invocation via environment variables (such as AWS_ACCESS_KEY_ID, AWS_SECRET_ACCESS_KEY, and AWS_SESSION_TOKEN). Those environment variables are used by the AWS SDK to sign requests automatically.

You should follow the least-privilege principle: your function should be allowed to access only services and actions that are needed to perform the function's task. You should specify a detailed IAM policy granting access to specific actions and resources.

Listing 6.6 shows an excerpt from the Lambda function's CloudFormation template based on SAM. When using SAM, an IAM role is created for each Lambda function by default. A managed policy that grants write access to CloudWatch logs is attached to the IAM role by default as well. Doing so allows the Lambda function to write to CloudWatch logs.

So far the Lambda function is not allowed to create a tag for the EC2 instance. You need a custom policy granting access to the `ec2:CreateTags`.

Listing 6.6   A custom policy for adding tags to EC2 instances

```
# [...]
EC2OwnerTagFunction:
  Type: AWS::Serverless::Function
  Properties:
    Handler: lambda_function.lambda_handler
    Runtime: python3.9
    CodeUri: '.'
    Policies:                                   Defines a custom IAM policy
    - Version: '2012-10-17'                      that will be attached to the
                                                 Lambda function's IAM role
      Statement:
        - Effect: Allow                          The statement allows ...
          Action: 'ec2:CreateTags'               ...creating tags...
          Resource: '*'
    # [...]                                      ...for all resources.
```

If you implement another Lambda function in the future, make sure you create an IAM role granting access to all the services your function needs to access (e.g., reading objects from S3, writing data to a DynamoDB database). Revisit section 5.3 if you want to recap the details of IAM.

6.3.5   *Deploying a Lambda function with SAM*

To deploy a Lambda function, you need to upload the deployment package to S3. The deployment package is a zip file including your code as well as additional modules. Afterward, you need to create and configure the Lambda function as well as all the dependencies (the IAM role, event rule, and so on). Using SAM in combination with the AWS CLI allows you to accomplish both tasks.

First, you need to create an S3 bucket to store your deployment packages. Use the following command, replacing $yourname with your name to avoid name conflicts with other readers:

```
$ aws s3 mb s3://ec2-owner-tag-$yourname
```

Execute the following command to create a deployment package and upload the package to S3. Please note: the command creates a copy of your template at output.yaml, with a reference to the deployment package uploaded to S3. Make sure your working directory is the code directory chapter06 containing the template.yaml and lambda_function.py files:

```
$ aws cloudformation package --template-file template.yaml \
  ➡ --s3-bucket ec2-owner-tag-$yourname --output-template-file output.yaml
```

By typing the following command in your terminal, you are deploying the Lambda function. This results in a CloudFormation stack named ec2-owner-tag:

```
$ aws cloudformation deploy --stack-name ec2-owner-tag \
  ➡ --template-file output.yaml --capabilities CAPABILITY_IAM
```

You are a genius! Your Lambda function is up and running. Launch an EC2 instance, and you will find a tag with your username myuser attached after a few minutes.

Cleaning up

If you have launched an EC2 instance to test your Lambda function, don't forget to terminate the instance afterward. Otherwise, it is quite simple to delete the Lambda function and all its dependencies. Just execute the following command in your terminal. Replace $yourname with your name:

```
$ CURRENT_ACCOUNT=$(aws sts get-caller-identity --query Account \
  ➡ --output text)
$ aws s3 rm --recursive s3://ec2-owner-tag-${CURRENT_ACCOUNT}/
$ aws cloudformation delete-stack --stack-name ec2-owner-tag
$ aws s3 rb s3://ec2-owner-tag-$yourname --force
```

6.4   *What else can you do with AWS Lambda?*

In the last part of the chapter, we would like to share what else is possible with AWS Lambda, starting with Lambda's limitations and insights into the serverless pricing model. We will end with three use cases for serverless applications we have built for our consulting clients.

6.4.1   *What are the limitations of AWS Lambda?*

Executing a Lambda function cannot exceed 15 minutes. This means the problem you are solving with your function needs to be small enough to fit into the 900-second limit. It is probably not possible to download 10 GB of data from S3, process the data, and insert parts of the data into a database within a single invocation of a Lambda function. But even if your use case fits into the 900-second constraint, make sure that it will fit under all circumstances. Here's a short anecdote from one of our first serverless projects: we built a serverless application that preprocessed analytics data from news sites. The Lambda functions typically processed the data within less than 180 seconds.

But when the 2017 US elections came, the volume of the analytics data exploded in a way no one expected. Our Lambda functions were no longer able to complete within 300 seconds—which was the maximum back then. It was a show-stopper for our serverless approach.

AWS Lambda provisions and manages the resources needed to run your function. A new execution context is created in the background every time you deploy a new version of your code, go a long time without any invocations, or when the number of concurrent invocations increases. Starting a new execution context requires AWS Lambda to download your code, initialize a runtime environment, and load your code. This process is called a *cold start*. Depending on the size of your deployment package, the runtime environment, and your configuration, a cold start could take from a few milliseconds to a few seconds.

In many scenarios, the increased latency caused by a cold start is not a problem at all. The examples demonstrated in this chapter—a website health check and auto-mated tags for EC2 instances—are not negatively affected by a cold start. To minimize cold-start times, you should keep the size of your deployment package as small as possible, provision additional memory, and use a runtime environment like JavaScript/Node.js or Python.

However, when processing real-time data or user interactions, a cold start is unde-sirable. For those scenarios, you could enable provisioned concurrency for a Lambda function. With provisioned concurrency, you tell AWS to keep a certain amount of execution contexts warm, even when the Lambda function is not processing any requests. As long as the provisioned concurrency exceeds the required number of execution contexts, you will not experience cold starts. The downside is you pay $0.0000041667 for every provisioned GB per second, whether or not you use the capacity. However, you will get a discount on the cost incurred for the actual term of the Lambda function.

Another limitation is the maximum amount of memory you can provision for a Lambda function: 10,240 MB. If your Lambda function uses more memory, its execu-tion will be terminated.

It is also important to know that CPU and networking capacity are allocated to a Lambda function based on the provisioned memory as well. So, if you are running computing- or network-intensive work within a Lambda function, increasing the provi-sioned memory will probably improve performance.

At the same time, the default limit for the maximum size of the compressed deploy-ment package (zip file) is 250 MB. When executing your Lambda function, you can use up to 512 MB nonpersistent disk space mounted to /tmp. Look at "Lambda Quotas" at http://mng.bz/vXda if you want to learn more about Lambda's limitations.

6.4.2 Effects of the serverless pricing model

When launching a virtual machine, you have to pay AWS for every operating hour, billed in second intervals. You are paying for the machines whether or not you are using the resource they provide. Even when nobody is accessing your website or using your application, you are paying for the virtual machine.

That's totally different with AWS Lambda. Lambda is billed per request. Costs occur only when someone accesses your website or uses your application. That's a game changer, especially for applications with uneven access patterns or for applications that are used rarely. Table 6.3 explains the Lambda pricing model in detail. Please note: when creating a Lambda function, you select the architecture. As usual, the Arm architecture based on AWS Graviton is the cheaper option.

Table 6.3 AWS Lambda pricing model

	Free Tier	x86	Arm
Number of Lambda function invocations	First 1 million requests every month are free.	$0.0000002 per request	$0.0000002 per request
Duration billed in 1 ms increments based on the amount of memory you provisioned for your Lambda function	Using the equivalent of 400,000 seconds of a Lambda function with 1 GB is free of charge provisioned memory every month.	$0.0000166667 for using 1 GB for one second	$0.0000133334 for using 1 GB for one second

Free Tier for AWS Lambda

The Free Tier for AWS Lambda does not expire after 12 months. That's a huge difference compared to the Free Tier of other AWS services (such as EC2) where you are eligible for the Free Tier only within the first 12 months, after creating an AWS account.

Sounds complicated? Figure 6.20 shows an excerpt of an AWS bill. The bill is from November 2017 and belongs to an AWS account we are using to run a chatbot (see https://marbot.io). Our chatbot implementation is 100% serverless. The Lambda functions were executed 1.2 million times in November 2017, which results in a charge of $0.04. All our Lambda functions are configured to provision 1536 MB memory. In total, all our Lambda functions have been running for 216,000 seconds, or around 60 hours, in November 2017. That's still within the Free Tier of 400,000 seconds with 1 GB provisioned memory every month. So, in total we had to pay $0.04 for using AWS Lambda in November 2017, which allowed us to serve around 400 customers with our chatbot.

This is only a small piece of our AWS bill, because other services we used together with AWS Lambda—for example, to store data—add more significant costs to our bill.

Don't forget to compare costs between AWS Lambda and EC2. Especially in a high-load scenario with more than 10 million requests per day, using AWS Lambda will probably result in higher costs compared to using EC2. But comparing infrastructure costs is only one part of what you should be looking at. Consider the total cost of

▾ Lambda		$0.04
▾ **US East (Northern Virginia) Region**		**$0.04**
AWS Lambda Lambda-GB-Second		$0.00
AWS Lambda - Compute Free Tier - 400,000 GB-Seconds - US East (Northern Virginia)	331,906.500 seconds	$0.00
AWS Lambda Request		$0.04
0.0000000367 USD per AWS Lambda - Requests Free Tier - 1,000,000 Requests - US East (Northern Virginia) (blended price)*	1,209,096 Requests	$0.04

Figure 6.20   Excerpt from our AWS bill from November 2017 showing costs for AWS Lambda

ownership (TOC), including costs for managing your virtual machines, performing load and resilience tests, and automating deployments. Our experience has shown that the total cost of ownership is typically lower when running an application on AWS Lambda compared to Amazon EC2.

The last part of the chapter focuses on additional use cases for AWS Lambda besides automating operational tasks, as you have done thus far.

6.4.3   Use case: Web application

A common use case for AWS Lambda is building a backend for a web or mobile application. As illustrated in figure 6.21, an architecture for a serverless web application typically consists of the following building blocks:

- *Amazon API Gateway*—Offers a scalable and secure REST API that accepts HTTPS requests from your web application's frontend or mobile application.
- *AWS Lambda*—Lambda functions are triggered by the API gateway. Your Lambda function receives data from the request and returns the data for the response.

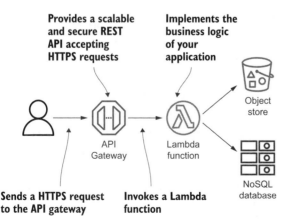

Figure 6.21   A web application build with API Gateway and Lambda

- *Object store and NoSQL database*—For storing and querying data, your Lambda functions typically use additional services offering object storage or NoSQL databases, for example.

Do you want to get started building web applications based on AWS Lambda? We recommend *AWS Lambda in Action* from Danilo Poccia (Manning, 2016).

6.4.4   Use case: Data processing

Another popular use case for AWS Lambda follows: event-driven data processing. Whenever new data is available, an event is generated. The event triggers the data processing needed to extract or transform the data. Figure 6.22 shows an example:

1 The load balancer collects access logs and uploads them to an object store periodically.
2 Whenever an object is created or modified, the object store triggers a Lambda function automatically.
3 The Lambda function downloads the file, including the access logs, from the object store and sends the data to an Elasticsearch database to be available for analytics.

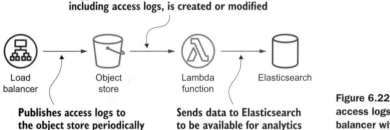

Triggers the Lambda function whenever a file, including access logs, is created or modified

Load balancer — Object store — Lambda function — Elasticsearch

Publishes access logs to the object store periodically

Sends data to Elasticsearch to be available for analytics

Figure 6.22   Processing access logs from a load balancer with AWS Lambda

We have successfully implemented this scenario in various projects. Keep in mind the maximum execution limit of 900 seconds when implementing data-processing jobs with AWS Lambda.

6.4.5   Use case: IoT backend

The AWS IoT service provides building blocks needed to communicate with various devices (things) and build event-driven applications. Figure 6.23 shows an example. Each thing publishes sensor data to a message broker. A rule filters the relevant messages and triggers a Lambda function. The Lambda function processes the event and decides what steps are needed based on the business logic you provide.

We built a proof of concept for collecting sensor data and publishing metrics to a dashboard with AWS IoT and AWS Lambda, for example.

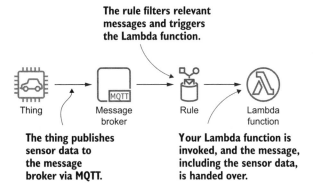

The rule filters relevant messages and triggers the Lambda function.

Thing   Message broker   Rule   Lambda function

The thing publishes sensor data to the message broker via MQTT.

Your Lambda function is invoked, and the message, including the sensor data, is handed over.

Figure 6.23   Processing events from an IoT device with AWS Lambda

We have gone through three possible use cases for AWS Lambda, but we haven't covered all of them. AWS Lambda is integrated with many other services as well. If you want to learn more about AWS Lambda, we recommend the following books:

- *AWS Lambda in Action* by Danilo Poccia (Manning, 2016) is an example-driven tutorial that teaches how to build applications using an event-based approach on the backend.
- *Serverless Architectures on AWS*, second edition, by Peter Sbarski (Manning, 2022) teaches how to build, secure, and manage serverless architectures that can power the most demanding web and mobile apps.

Summary

- AWS Lambda allows you to run your C#/.NET Core, Go, Java, JavaScript/Node.js, Python and Ruby code within a fully managed, highly available, and scalable environment.
- The Management Console and blueprints offered by AWS help you to get started quickly.
- By using a schedule expression, you can trigger a Lambda function periodically. This is comparable to triggering a script with the help of a cron job.
- CloudWatch is the place to go when it comes to monitoring and debugging your Lambda functions.
- The Serverless Application Model (SAM) enables you to deploy a Lambda function in an automated way with AWS CloudFormation.
- Many event sources exist for using Lambda functions in an event-driven way. For example, you can subscribe to events triggered by CloudTrail for every request you send to the AWS API.
- The most important limitation of a Lambda function is the maximum duration of 900 seconds per invocation.
- AWS Lambda can be used to built complex services as well, from typical web applications, to data analytics, and IoT backends.

## Part 3

Storing data in the cloud

There is one guy named Singleton in your office who knows all about your file server. If Singleton is out of office, no one else can maintain the file server. As you can imagine, while Singleton is on vacation, the file server crashes. No one else knows where the backup is located, but the boss needs a document now or the company will lose a lot of money. If Singleton had stored his knowledge in a database, coworkers could look up the information. But because the knowledge and Singleton are tidily coupled, the information is unavailable.

Imagine a virtual machine where important files are located on hard disk. As long as the virtual machine is up and running, everything is fine. But everything fails all the time, including virtual machines. If a user uploads a document on your website, where is it stored? Chances are high that the document is persisted to hard disk on the virtual machine. Let's imagine that the document was uploaded to your website but persisted as an object in an independent object store. If the virtual machine fails, the document will still be available. If you need two virtual machines to handle the load on your website, they both have access to that document because it is not tightly coupled with a single virtual machine. If you separate your state from your virtual machine, you will be able to become fault tolerant and elastic. Let highly specialized solutions like object stores and databases persist your state.

AWS offers many ways to store your data. The following table can help you decide which service to use for your data at a high level. The comparison is only a rough overview. We recommend that you choose two or three services that best fit your use case and then jump into the details by reading the chapters to make your decision.

Table 1   Overview of data storage services

Service	Access	Maximum storage volume	Latency	Storage cost
S3	AWS API (SDKs, CLI), third-party tools	Unlimited	High	Very low
EBS (SSD)	Attached to an EC2 instance via network	16 TiB	Low	Low
EC2 Instance Store (SSD)	Attached to an EC2 instance directly	305 TB	Very low	Very low
EFS	NFSv4.1, for example, from an EC2 instance or on-premises	Unlimited	Medium	Medium
RDS (MySQL, SSD)	SQL	64 TiB	Medium	Low
ElastiCache	Redis/Memcached protocol	635 GiB	Low	High
DynamoDB	AWS API (SDKs, CLI)	Unlimited	Medium	Medium

Chapter 7 will introduce S3, a service offering object storage. You will learn how to integrate the object storage into your applications to implement a stateless server.

Chapter 8 is about block-level storage for virtual machines offered by AWS. You will learn how to operate legacy software on block-level storage.

Chapter 9 covers highly available block-level storage that can be shared across multiple virtual machines offered by AWS.

Chapter 10 introduces RDS, a service that offers managed relational database systems like PostgreSQL, MySQL, Oracle, or Microsoft SQL Server. If your applications use such a relational database system, this is an easy way to implement a stateless server architecture.

Chapter 11 introduces ElastiCache, a service that offers managed in-memory database systems like Redis or Memcached. If your applications need to cache data, you can use an in-memory database to externalize ephemeral state.

Chapter 12 will introduce DynamoDB, a service that offers a NoSQL database. You can integrate this NoSQL database into your applications to implement a stateless server.

Storing your objects: S3

This chapter covers

- Transferring files to S3 using the terminal
- Integrating S3 into your applications with SDKs
- Archiving data at low costs
- Hosting a static website with S3
- Diving into the internals of the S3 object store

Storing data comes with two challenges: dealing with ever-increasing volumes of data and ensuring durability. Solving the challenges is hard, or even impossible, if using disks connected to a single machine. For this reason, this chapter covers a revolutionary approach: a distributed data store consisting of a large number of machines connected over a network. This way, you can store nearly unlimited amounts of data by adding additional machines to the distributed data store. And because your data is always stored on more than one machine, you dramatically reduce the risk of losing that data.

You will learn about how to store images, videos, documents, executables, or any other kind of data on Amazon S3 in this chapter. Amazon S3 is a simple-to-use, fully managed distributed data store provided by AWS. Data is managed as objects, so the storage system is called an *object store*. We will show you how to use S3 to back up your data, how to archive data at low cost, and how to integrate S3 into your own application for storing user-generated content, as well as how to host static websites on S3.

Not all examples are covered by the Free Tier

The examples in this chapter are not all covered by the Free Tier. A warning message appears when an example incurs costs. As for the other examples, as long as you follow the instructions and don't run them longer than a few days, you won't pay anything.

7.1   *What is an object store?*

Back in the old days, data was managed in a hierarchy consisting of folders and files. The file was the representation of the data. In an *object store*, data is stored as objects. Each object consists of a globally unique identifier, some metadata, and the data itself, as figure 7.1 illustrates. An object's *globally unique identifier* (GUID) is also known as its *key*; you can address the object from different devices and machines in a distributed system using the GUID.

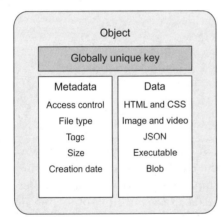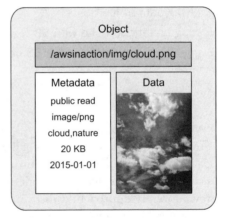

Figure 7.1   Objects stored in an object store have three parts: a unique ID, metadata describing the content, and the content itself (such as an image).

Typical examples for object metadata are:

- Date of last modification
- Object size
- Object's owner
- Object's content type

It is possible to request only an object's metadata without requesting the data itself. This is useful if you want to list objects and their metadata before accessing a specific object's data.

7.2 Amazon S3

Amazon S3 is a distributed data store, and one of the oldest services provided by AWS. *Amazon S3* is an acronym for *Amazon Simple Storage Service*. It's a typical web service that lets you store and retrieve data organized as objects via an API reachable over HTTPS. Here are some typical use cases:

- *Storing and delivering static website content*—For example, our blog https://cloudonaut.io is hosted on S3.
- *Backing up data*—For example, you can back up your photo library from your computer to S3 using the AWS CLI.
- *Storing structured data for analytics, also called a data lake*—For example, you can use S3 to store JSON files containing the results of performance benchmarks.
- *Storing and delivering user-generated content*—For example, we built a web application—with the help of the AWS SDK—that stores user uploads on S3.

Amazon S3 offers virtually unlimited storage space and stores your data in a highly available and durable way. You can store any kind of data, such as images, documents, and binaries, as long as the size of a single object doesn't exceed 5 TB. You have to pay for every GB you store in S3, and you also incur costs for every request and for all transferred data. As figure 7.2 shows, you can access S3 via the internet using HTTPS to upload and download objects. To access S3, you can use the Management Console, the CLI, SDKs, or third-party tools.

Figure 7.2   Uploading and downloading an object to S3 via HTTPS

S3 uses *buckets* to group objects. A bucket is a container for objects. It is up to you to create multiple buckets, each of which has a globally unique name, to separate data for different scenarios. By *unique,* we really mean unique—you have to choose a bucket name that isn't used by any other AWS customer in any other region. Figure 7.3 shows the concept.

You will learn how to upload and download data to S3 using the AWS CLI next.

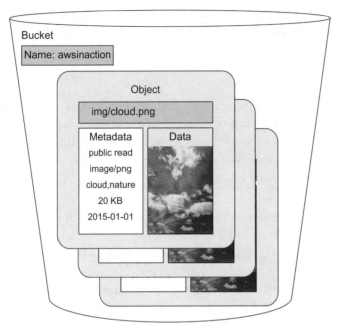

Figure 7.3   **S3 uses buckets
with globally unique names to
group objects.**

7.3   *Backing up your data on S3 with AWS CLI*

Critical data needs to be backed up to avoid loss. Backing up data at an offsite location
decreases the risk of losing data, even during extreme conditions like natural disaster.
But where should you store your backups? S3 allows you to store any data in the form
of objects. The AWS object store is a perfect fit for your backup, allowing you to
choose a location for your data as well as storing any amount of data with a pay-per-use
pricing model.

In this section, you'll learn how to use the AWS CLI to upload data to and download data from S3. This approach isn't limited to offsite backups; you can use it in
many other scenarios as well, such as the following:

- Sharing files with your coworkers or partners, especially when working from different locations
- Storing and retrieving artifacts needed to provision your virtual machines (such
  as application binaries, libraries, or configuration files)
- Outsourcing storage capacity to lighten the burden on local storage systems—
  in particular, for data that is accessed infrequently

First, you need to create a bucket for your data on S3. As we mentioned earlier, the
name of the bucket must be unique among all other S3 buckets, even those in other
regions and those of other AWS customers. To find a unique bucket name, it's useful
to use a prefix or suffix that includes your company's name or your own name. Run
the following command in the terminal, replacing $yourname with your name:

```
$ aws s3 mb s3://awsinaction-$yourname
```

Your command should look similar to this one:

```
$ aws s3 mb s3://awsinaction-awittig
```

In the unlikely event that you or another AWS customer has already created a bucket with this name, you will see the following error:

```
[... ] An error occurred (BucketAlreadyExists) [...]
```

In this case, you'll need to use a different value for $yourname.

Everything is ready for you to upload your data. Choose a folder you'd like to back up, such as your Desktop folder. Try to choose a folder with a total size less than 1 GB, to avoid long waiting times and exceeding the Free Tier. The following command uploads the data from your local folder to your S3 bucket. Replace $path with the path to your folder and $yourname with your name. sync compares your folder with the /backup folder in your S3 bucket and uploads only new or changed files:

```
$ aws s3 sync $path s3://awsinaction-$yourname/backup
```

Your command should look similar to this one:

```
$ aws s3 sync /Users/andreas/Desktop s3://awsinaction-awittig/backup
```

Depending on the size of your folder and the speed of your internet connection, the upload can take some time.

After uploading your folder to your S3 bucket to back it up, you can test the restore process. Execute the following command in your terminal, replacing $path with a folder you'd like to use for the restore (don't use the folder you backed up) and $yourname with your name. Your Downloads folder would be a good place to test the restore process:

```
$ aws s3 cp --recursive s3://awsinaction-$yourname/backup $path
```

Your command should look similar to this one:

```
$ aws s3 cp --recursive s3://awsinaction-awittig/backup/ \
➡ /Users/andreas/Downloads/restore
```

Again, depending on the size of your folder and the bandwidth of your internet connection, the download may take a while.

Versioning for objects

By default, S3 versioning is disabled for every bucket. Suppose you use the following steps to upload two objects:

1 Add an object with key A and data 1.
2 Add an object with key A and data 2.

(continued)

If you download the object with key A, you'll download data 2. The old data 1 doesn't exist any more.

You can change this behavior by turning on versioning for a bucket. The following command activates versioning for your bucket. Don't forget to replace $yourname:

```
$ aws s3api put-bucket-versioning --bucket awsinaction-$yourname \
➥ --versioning-configuration Status=Enabled
```

If you repeat the previous steps, the first version of object A consisting of data 1 will be accessible even after you add an object with key A and data 2. The following command retrieves all objects and versions:

```
$ aws s3api list-object-versions --bucket awsinaction-$yourname
```

You can now download all versions of an object.

Versioning can be useful for backing up and archiving scenarios. Keep in mind that the size of the bucket you'll have to pay for will grow with every new version.

You no longer need to worry about losing data. S3 is designed for 99.999999999% durability of objects over a year. For instance, when storing 100,000,000,000 objects on S3, you will lose only a single object per year on average.

After you've successfully restored your data from the S3 bucket, it's time to clean up. Execute the following command to remove the S3 bucket containing all the objects from your backup. You'll have to replace $yourname with your name to select the right bucket. rb removes the bucket; the force option deletes every object in the bucket before deleting the bucket itself:

```
$ aws s3 rb --force s3://awsinaction-$yourname
```

Your command should look similar to this one:

```
$ aws s3 rb --force s3://awsinaction-awittig
```

You're finished—you've uploaded and downloaded files to S3 with the help of the CLI.

Removing a bucket causes a `BucketNotEmpty` error

If you turn on versioning for your bucket, removing the bucket will cause a `Bucket-NotEmpty` error. Use the Management Console to delete the bucket in this case as follows:

1 Open the Management Console with your browser.
2 Go to the S3 service using the main navigation menu.
3 Select the bucket you want to delete.

4 Click the Empty button, and confirm permanently deleting all objects.
5 Wait until objects and versions have been deleted, and click the Exit button.
6 Select the bucket you want to delete.
7 Click the Delete button, and confirm deleting the bucket.

7.4 Archiving objects to optimize costs

In the previous section, you learned about backing up your data to S3. Storing 1 TB of data on S3 costs about $23 per month. Wouldn't it be nice to reduce the costs for storing data by 95%? Besides, by default, S3 comes with storage classes designed to archive data for long time spans.

Table 7.1 compares the storage class *S3 Standard* with storage classes intended for data archival.

Table 7.1   Differences between storing data with S3 and Glacier

	S3 Standard	S3 Glacier Instant Retrieval	S3 Glacier Flexible Retrieval	S3 Glacier Deep Archive
Storage costs for 1 GB per month in US East (N. Virginia)	$0.023	$0.004	$0.0036	$0.00099
Costs for 1,000 write requests	$0.005	$0.02	$0.03	$0.05
Costs for retrieving data	Low	High	High	Very High
Accessibility	Milliseconds	Milliseconds	1–5 minutes/ 3–5 hours/ 5–12 hours	12 hours/ 48 hours
Durability objective	99.999999999%	99.999999999%	99.999999999%	99.999999999%
Availability objective	99.99%	99.9%	99.99%	99.99%

The potential savings for storage costs are enormous. So what's the catch?

First, accessing data stored on S3 by using the storage classes S3 Glacier Instant Retrieval, S3 Glacier Flexible Retrieval, and S3 Glacier Deep Archive is expensive. Let's assume, you are storing 1 TB of data on S3 and decided to use storage type S3 Glacier Deep Archive. It will cost you about $120 to restore 1 TB of data stored in 1,000 files.

Second, fetching data from S3 Glacier Flexible Retrieval and S3 Glacier Deep Archive takes something between 1 minute and 48 hours, depending on the storage class and retrieval option.

Using the following example, we would like to explain what it means not to be able to access archived data immediately. Let's say you want to archive a document for five years. You do not expect to access the document more than five times during this period.

Start by creating an S3 bucket that you will use to archive documents, as shown next. Replace $yourname with your name to get a unique bucket name:

```
$ aws s3 mb s3://awsinaction-archive-$yourname
```

Next, copy a document from your local machine to S3. The `--storage-class` parameter overrides the default storage class with `GLACIER`, which maps to the S3 Glacier Flexible Retrieval storage class. Replace $path with the path to a document, and $yourname with your name. Note the key of the object:

```
$ aws s3 cp --storage-class GLACIER $path \
➥ s3://awsinaction-archive-$yourname/
```

For instance, I run the following command:

```
$ aws s3 cp --storage-class GLACIER \
➥ /Users/andreas/Desktop/taxstatement-2022-07-01.pdf \
➥ s3://awsinaction-archive-awittig/
```

The key point is that you can't download the object. Replace $objectkey with the object's key that you noted down after uploading the document, and $path with the Downloads folder on your local machine:

```
$ aws s3 cp s3://awsinaction-archive-$yourname/$objectkey $path
```

For example, I'm getting the following error when trying to download my document taxstatement-2022-07-01.pdf:

```
$ aws s3 cp s3://awsinaction-archive-awittig/taxstatement-2022-07-01.pdf \
➥ ~/Downloads
warning: Skipping file s3://awsinaction-archive-awittig/
➥ taxstatement-2022-07-01.pdf. Object is of storage class GLACIER.
➥ Unable to perform download operations on GLACIER objects. You must
➥ restore the object to be able to perform the operation.
```

As mentioned in the error message, you need to restore the object before download-ing it. By default, doing so will take three to five hours. That's why we will pay a little extra—just a few cents—for expedited retrieval. Execute the following command after replacing $yourname with your name, and $objectkey with the object's key:

```
$ aws s3api restore-object --bucket awsinaction-archive-$yourname \
➥ --key $objectkey \
➥ --restore-request Days=1,,GlacierJobParameters={"Tier"="Expedited"}
```

This results in the following command in my scenario:

```
$ aws s3api restore-object --bucket awsinaction-archive-awittig \
➥ --key taxstatement-2022-07-01.pdf
➥ --restore-request Days=1,,GlacierJobParameters={"Tier"="Expedited"}
```

As you are using expedited retrieval, you need to wait one to five minutes for the object to become available for download. Use the following command to check the status of the object and its retrieval. Don't forget to replace $yourname with your name, and $objectkey with the object's key:

```
$ aws s3api head-object --bucket awsinaction-archive-$yourname \
➥ --key $objectkey
{
    "AcceptRanges": "bytes",
    "Expiration": "expiry-date=\"Wed, 12 Jul 2023 ...\", rule-id=\"...\"",
    "Restore": "ongoing-request=\"true\"",              ◀── Restoration of
    "LastModified": "2022-07-11T09:26:12+00:00",            the object is still
    "ContentLength": 112,                                   ongoing.
    "ETag": "\"c25fa1df1968993d8e647c9dcd352d39\"",
    "ContentType": "binary/octet-stream",
    "Metadata": {},
    "StorageClass": "GLACIER"
}
```

Repeat fetching the status of the object until ongoing-request flips to false:

```
{
    "AcceptRanges": "bytes",
    "Expiration": "expiry-date=\"Wed, 12 Jul 2023 ...\", rule-id=\"...\"",
    "Restore": "ongoing-request=\"false\", expiry-date=\"...\"",    ◀──
    "LastModified": "2022-07-11T09:26:12+00:00",
    "ContentLength": 112,                              The restoration is
    "ETag": "\"c25fa1df1968993d8e647c9dcd352d39\"",    finished, with no
    "ContentType": "binary/octet-stream",              ongoing restore
    "Metadata": {},                                    requests.
    "StorageClass": "GLACIER"
}
```

After restoring the object, you are now able to download the document using the next code snippet. Replace $objectkey with the object's key that you noted down after uploading the document, and $path with the Downloads folder on your local machine:

```
$ aws s3 cp s3://awsinaction-archive-$yourname/$objectkey $path
```

In summary, the Glacier storage types are intended for archiving data that you need to access seldom, which means every few months or years. For example, we are using the S3 Glacier Deep Archive to store a remote backup of our MacBooks. Because we store another backup of our data on an external hard drive, the chances that we need to restore data from S3 are very low.

> **Cleaning up**
>
> Execute the following command to remove the S3 bucket containing all the objects from your backup. You'll have to replace `$yourname` with your name to select the right bucket. `rb` removes the bucket; the `force` option deletes every object in the bucket before deleting the bucket itself:
>
> ```
> $ aws s3 rb --force s3://awsinaction-archive-$yourname
> ```

You've learned how to use S3 with the help of the CLI. We'll show you how to integrate S3 into your applications with the help of SDKs in the next section.

7.5   *Storing objects programmatically*

S3 is accessible using an API via HTTPS. This enables you to integrate S3 into your applications by making requests to the API programmatically. Doing so allows your applications to benefit from a scalable and highly available data store. AWS offers free SDKs for common programming languages like C++, Go, Java, JavaScript, .NET, PHP, Python, and Ruby. You can execute the following operations using an SDK directly from your application:

- Listing buckets and their objects
- Creating, removing, updating, and deleting (CRUD) objects and buckets
- Managing access to objects

Here are examples of how you can integrate S3 into your application:

- *Allow a user to upload a profile picture.* Store the image in S3, and make it publicly accessible. Integrate the image into your website via HTTPS.
- *Generate monthly reports (such as PDFs), and make them accessible to users.* Create the documents and upload them to S3. If users want to download documents, fetch them from S3.
- *Share data between applications.* You can access documents from different applications. For example, application A can write an object with the latest information about sales, and application B can download the document and analyze the data.

Integrating S3 into an application is one way to implement the concept of a *stateless server*. We'll show you how to integrate S3 into your application by diving into a simple web application called Simple S3 Gallery next. This web application is built on top of Node.js and uses the AWS SDK for JavaScript and Node.js. You can easily transfer what you learn from this example to SDKs for other programming languages; the concepts are the same.

Installing and getting started with Node.js

Node.js is a platform for executing JavaScript in an event-driven environment so you can easily build network applications. To install Node.js, visit https://nodejs.org and download the package that fits your OS. All examples in this book are tested with Node.js 14.

After Node.js is installed, you can verify that everything works by typing `node --version` into your terminal. Your terminal should respond with something similar to `v14.*`. Now you're ready to run JavaScript examples like the Simple S3 Gallery.

Do you want to get started with Node.js? We recommend *Node.js in Action* (second edition) by Alex Young et al. (Manning, 2017), or the video course *Node.js in Motion* by PJ Evans (Manning, 2018).

Next, we will dive into a simple web application called the Simple S3 Gallery. The gallery allows you to upload images to S3 and displays all the images you've already uploaded. Figure 7.4 shows Simple S3 Gallery in action. Let's set up S3 to start your own gallery.

Figure 7.4   The Simple S3 Gallery app lets you upload images to an S3 bucket and then download them from the bucket for display.

7.5.1 Setting up an S3 bucket

To begin, you need to set up an empty bucket. Execute the following command, replacing $yourname with your name:

```
$ aws s3 mb s3://awsinaction-sdk-$yourname
```

Your bucket is now ready to go. Installing the web application is the next step.

7.5.2 Installing a web application that uses S3

You can find the Simple S3 Gallery application in /chapter07/gallery/ in the book's code folder. Switch to that directory, and run `npm install` in your terminal to install all needed dependencies.

To start the web application, run the following command. Replace $yourname with your name; the name of the S3 bucket is then passed to the web application:

```
$ node server.js awsinaction-sdk-$yourname
```

> **Where is the code located?**
> You can find all the code in the book's code repository on GitHub: https://github .com/AWSinAction/code3. You can download a snapshot of the repository at https:// github.com/AWSinAction/code3/archive/main.zip.

After you start the server, you can open the gallery application. To do so, open http:// localhost:8080 with your browser. Try uploading a few images.

7.5.3 Reviewing code access S3 with SDK

You've uploaded images to the Simple S3 Gallery and displayed images from S3. Inspecting parts of the code will help you understand how you can integrate S3 into your own applications. It's not a problem if you don't follow all the details of the programming language (JavaScript) and the Node.js platform; we just want you to get an idea of how to use S3 via SDKs.

UPLOADING AN IMAGE TO S3

You can upload an image to S3 with the SDK's `putObject()` function. Your application will connect to the S3 service and transfer the image via HTTPS. The next listing shows how to do so.

Listing 7.1   Uploading an image with the AWS SDK for S3

```
const AWS = require('aws-sdk');          ◁─── Loads the
const uuid = require('uuid');                  AWS SDK

const s3 = new AWS.S3({                   ◁─── Instantiates the S3
  'region': 'us-east-1'                        client with additional
});                                            configurations
```

```
const bucket = process.argv[2];

async function uploadImage(image, response) {
  try {
    await s3.putObject({                    ◁── Uploads the
      Body: image,                               image to S3
      Bucket: bucket,
      Key: uuid.v4(),
      ACL: 'public-read',                   Allows everybody to read
      ContentLength: image.byteCount,            the image from bucket
      ContentType: image.headers['content-type']
    }).promise();
    response.redirect('/');
  } catch (err) {                           Catching
    console.error(err);                     errors
    response.status(500);
    response.send('Internal server error.');
  }
}
```

Image content — Image content
Name of the bucket — Name of the bucket
Generates a unique key for the object — Generates a unique key for the object
Size of image in bytes
Content type of the object (image/png)
Returns an error with the HTTP status code 500

The AWS SDK takes care of sending all the necessary HTTPS requests to the S3 API in the background.

LISTING ALL THE IMAGES IN THE S3 BUCKET

To display a list of images, the application needs to list all the objects in your bucket. This can be done with the S3 service's listObjects() function. The next code listing shows the implementation of the corresponding function in the server.js JavaScript file, acting as a web server.

Listing 7.2 Retrieving all the image locations from the S3 bucket

```
const bucket = process.argv[2];              ◁── Reads the bucket name from
                                                  the process arguments
async function listImages(response) {
  try {
    let data = await s3.listObjects({        ◁── Lists the objects
      Bucket: bucket                             stored in the bucket
    }).promise();
    let stream = mu.compileAndRender(        ◁── Renders an HTML
      'index.html',                              page based on
      {                                          the list of objects
        Objects: data.Contents,
        Bucket: bucket
      }
    );
    stream.pipe(response);                   Streams the
  } catch (err) {                            response
    console.error(err);                      Handles
    response.status(500);                    potential errors
    response.send('Internal server error.');
  }
}
```

The bucket name is the only required parameter.

Listing the objects returns the names of all the images from the bucket, but the list doesn't include the image content. During the uploading process, the access rights to the images are set to public read. This means anyone can download the images with the bucket name and a random key. The following listing shows an excerpt of the index.html template, which is rendered on request. The `Objects` variable contains all the objects from the bucket.

Listing 7.3   Template to render the data as HTML

```
[...]
<h2>Images</h2>
{{#Objects}}               Iterates
  <p><img src=           over all         Puts together the URL
                          objects          to fetch an image from
                                           the bucket
  "https://s3.amazonaws.com/{{Bucket}}/{{Key}}"
  width="400px" ></p>
{{/Objects}}
[...]
```

You've now seen the three important parts of the Simple S3 Gallery integration with S3: uploading an image, listing all images, and downloading an image.

Cleaning up

Don't forget to clean up and delete the S3 bucket used in the example. Use the following command, replacing $yourname with your name:

```
$ aws s3 rb --force s3://awsinaction-sdk-$yourname
```

You've learned how to use S3 using the AWS SDK for JavaScript and Node.js. Using the AWS SDK for other programming languages is similar.

The next section is about a different scenario: you will learn how to host static websites on S3.

7.6   *Using S3 for static web hosting*

We started our blog https://cloudonaut.io in May 2015. The most popular blog posts, like "ECS vs. Fargate: What's the Difference?" (http://mng.bz/Xa2E), "Advanced AWS Networking: Pitfalls That You Should Avoid" (http://mng.bz/yaxe), and "Cloud-Formation vs. Terraform" (https://cloudonaut.io/cloudformation-vs-terraform/) have been read more than 200,000 times. But we did not need to operate any VMs to publish our blog posts. Instead, we used S3 to host our static website built with a static site generator, Hexo (https://hexo.io). This approach provides a cost-effective, scalable, and maintenance-free infrastructure for our blog.

You can host a static website with S3 and deliver static content like HTML, JavaScript, CSS, images (such as PNG and JPG), audio, and videos. Keep in mind, however, that you can't execute server-side scripts like PHP or JSP. For example, it's not possible to host WordPress, a content management system based on PHP, on S3.

Increasing speed by using a CDN

Using a content-delivery network (CDN) helps reduce the load time for static web content. A CDN distributes static content like HTML, CSS, and images to nodes all around the world. If a user sends out a request for some static content, the request is answered from the nearest available node with the lowest latency. Various providers offer CDNs. Amazon CloudFront is the CDN offered by AWS. When using Cloud-Front, users connect to CloudFront to access your content, which is fetched from S3 or other sources. See the CloudFront documentation at http://mng.bz/M0m8 if you want to set this up; we won't cover it in this book.

In addition, S3 offers the following features for hosting a static website:

- *Defining a custom index document and error documents*—For example, you can define index.html as the default index document.
- *Defining redirects for all or specific requests*—For example, you can forward all requests from /img/old.png to /img/new.png.
- *Setting up a custom domain for an S3 bucket*—For example, Andreas might want to set up a domain like mybucket.andreaswittig.info pointing to his bucket.

7.6.1   Creating a bucket and uploading a static website

First you need to create a new S3 bucket. To do so, open your terminal and execute the following command, replacing $BucketName with your own bucket name. As we've mentioned, the bucket name has to be globally unique. If you want to link your domain name to S3, you must use your entire domain name as the bucket name:

```
$ aws s3 mb s3://$BucketName
```

The bucket is empty; you'll place an HTML document in it next. We've prepared a placeholder HTML file. Download it to your local machine from the following URL: http://mng.bz/aPyX. You can now upload the file to S3. Execute the following command to do so, replacing $pathToPlacerholder with the path to the HTML file you downloaded in the previous step and $BucketName with the name of your bucket:

```
$ aws s3 cp $pathToPlaceholder/helloworld.html \
⮞ s3://$BucketName/helloworld.html
```

You've now created a bucket and uploaded an HTML document called helloworld .html. You need to configure the bucket next.

7.6.2 *Configuring a bucket for static web hosting*

By default, only you, the owner, can access files from your S3 bucket. Because you want to use S3 to deliver your static website, you'll need to allow everyone to view or download the documents included in your bucket. A *bucket policy* helps you control access to bucket objects globally. You already know from chapter 5 that policies are defined in JSON and contain one or more statements that either allow or deny specific actions on specific resources. Bucket policies are similar to IAM policies.

Download our bucket policy from the following URL: http://mng.bz/gROG. You need to edit the bucketpolicy.json file next, as shown in the following listing. Open the file with the editor of your choice, and replace $BucketName with the name of your bucket.

Listing 7.4 Bucket policy allowing read-only access to every object in a bucket

```
{
  "Version":"2012-10-17",
  "Statement":[
    {
      "Sid":"AddPerm",                              Allows access...
      "Effect":"Allow",                             ...for anyone
      "Principal": "*",
      "Action":["s3:GetObject"],                    Reads objects
      "Resource":["arn:aws:s3:::$BucketName/*"]      Your
    }                                                bucket
  ]
}
```

You can add a bucket policy to your bucket with the following command. Replace $BucketName with the name of your bucket and $pathToPolicy with the path to the bucketpolicy.json file:

```
$ aws s3api put-bucket-policy --bucket $BucketName \
➥ --policy file://$pathToPolicy/bucketpolicy.json
```

Every object in the bucket can now be downloaded by anyone. You need to enable and configure the static web-hosting feature of S3 next. To do so, execute the following command, replacing $BucketName with the name of your bucket:

```
$ aws s3 website s3://$BucketName --index-document helloworld.html
```

Your bucket is now configured to deliver a static website. The HTML document helloworld.html is used as index page. You'll learn how to access your website next.

7.6.3 Accessing a website hosted on S3

You can now access your static website with a browser. To do so, you need to choose the right endpoint. The endpoints for S3 static web hosting depend on your bucket's region. For us-east-1 (US East N. Virginia), the website endpoint looks like this:

```
http://$BucketName.s3-website-us-east-1.amazonaws.com
```

Replace `$BucketName` with your bucket. So if your bucket is called `awesomebucket` and was created in the default region us-east-1, your bucket name would be:

```
http://awesomebucket.s3-website-us-east-1.amazonaws.com
```

Open this URL with your browser. You should be welcomed by a Hello World website.

Please note that for some regions, the website endpoint looks a little different. Check S3 endpoints and quotas at http://mng.bz/epeq for details.

Linking a custom domain to an S3 bucket

If you want to avoid hosting static content under a domain like awsinaction.s3-website-us-east-1.amazonaws.com, you can link a custom domain to an S3 bucket, such as `awsinaction.example.com`. All you have to do is to add a CNAME record for your domain, pointing to the bucket's S3 endpoint. The domain name system provided by AWS allowing you to create a CNAME record is called Route 53.

The CNAME record will work only if you comply with the following rules:

- *Your bucket name must match the CNAME record name.* For example, if you want to create a CNAME for awsinaction.example.com, your bucket name must be awsinaction.example.com as well.
- *CNAME records won't work for the primary domain name (such as example.com).* You need to use a subdomain for CNAMEs like awsinaction or www. If you want to link a primary domain name to an S3 bucket, you need to use the Route 53 DNS service from AWS.

Linking a custom domain to your S3 bucket works only for HTTP. If you want to use HTTPS (and you probably should), use AWS CloudFront together with S3. AWS Cloud-Front accepts HTTPS from the client and forwards the request to S3.

Cleaning up

Don't forget to clean up your bucket after you finish the example. To do so, execute the following command, replacing `$BucketName` with the name of your bucket:

```
$ aws s3 rb --force s3://$BucketName
```

7.7 *Protecting data from unauthorized access*

Not a week goes by without a frightening announcement that an organization has leaked confidential data from Amazon S3 accidentally. Why is that?

While reading through this chapter, you have learned about different scenarios for using S3. For example, you used S3 to back up data from your local machine. Also, you hosted a static website on S3. So, S3 is used to store sensitive data as well as public data. This can be a dangerous mix because a misconfiguration might cause a data leak.

To mitigate the risk, we recommend you enable Block Public Access for all your buckets as illustrated in figure 7.5 and shown next. By doing so, you will disable public access to all the buckets belonging to your AWS account. This will break S3 website hosting or any other form of accessing S3 objects publicly.

1 Open the AWS Management Console and navigate to S3.
2 Select Block Public Access Settings for This Account from the subnavigation menu.
3 Enable Block All Public Access, and click the Save Changes button.

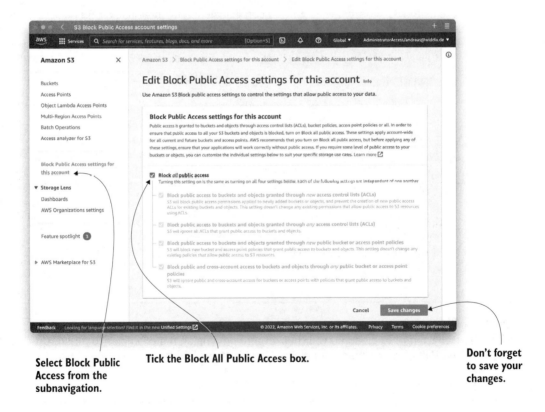

Select Block Public Access from the subnavigation.

Tick the Block All Public Access box.

Don't forget to save your changes.

Figure 7.5   Enable Block Public Access for all S3 buckets to avoid data leaks.

In case you really need buckets with both sensitive data and public data, you should enable Block Public Access not on the account level but for all buckets with sensitive data individually instead.

Check out our blog post "How to Avoid S3 Data Leaks?" at https://cloudonaut .io/s3-security-best-practice/ if you are interested in further advice.

7.8 *Optimizing performance*

By default, S3 handles 3,500 writes and 5,500 reads per second. If your workload requires higher throughput, you need to consider the following when coming up with the naming scheme for the object keys.

Objects are stored without a hierarchy on S3. There is no such thing as a directory. All you do is specify an object key, as discussed at the beginning of the chapter. However, using a prefix allows you to structure the object keys.

By default, the slash character (/) is used as the prefix delimiter. So, `archive` is the prefix in the following example of object keys:

```
archive/image1.png
archive/image2.png
archive/image3.png
archive/image4.png
```

Be aware that the maximum throughput per partitioned prefix is 3,500 writes and 5,500 reads per second. Therefore, you cannot read more than 5,500 objects from the prefix `archive` per second.

To increase the maximum throughput, you need to distribute your objects among additional prefixes. For example, you could organize the objects from the previous example like this:

```
archive/2021/image1.png
archive/2021/image2.png
archive/2022/image3.png
archive/2022/image4.png
```

By doing so, you can double the maximum throughput when reading from archive/2021 and archive/2022 as illustrated in figure 7.6.

In summary, the structure of your object keys has an effect on the maximum read and write throughput.

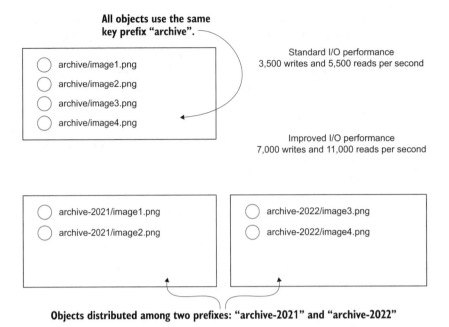

All objects use the same key prefix "archive".

- archive/image1.png
- archive/image2.png
- archive/image3.png
- archive/image4.png

Standard I/O performance
3,500 writes and 5,500 reads per second

Improved I/O performance
7,000 writes and 11,000 reads per second

- archive-2021/image1.png
- archive-2021/image2.png

- archive-2022/image3.png
- archive-2022/image4.png

Objects distributed among two prefixes: "archive-2021" and "archive-2022"

Figure 7.6   To improve I/O performance, distribute requests among multiple object key prefixes.

Summary

- An object consists of a unique identifier, metadata to describe and manage the object, and the content itself. You can save images, documents, executables, or any other content as an object in an object store.

- Amazon S3 provides endless storage capacity with a pay-per-use model. You are charged for storage as well as read and write requests.

- Amazon S3 is an object store accessible only via HTTP(S). You can upload, manage, and download objects with the CLI, SDKs, or the Management Console. The storage classes Glacier Instant Retrieval, Glacier Flexible Retrieval, and Glacier Deep Archive are designed to archive data at low cost.

- Integrating S3 into your applications will help you implement the concept of a stateless server, because you don't have to store objects locally on the server.

- Enable Block Public Access for all buckets, or at least those buckets that contain sensitive information to avoid data leaks.

- When optimizing for high performance, make sure to use many different key prefixes instead of similar ones or the same prefix for all objects.

Storing data on hard drives: EBS and instance store

This chapter covers

- Attaching persistent storage volumes to an EC2 instance
- Using temporary storage attached to the host system
- Backing up volumes
- Testing and tweaking volume performance
- Differences between persistent (EBS) and temporary volumes (instance store)

Imagine your task is to migrate an enterprise application being hosted on-premises to AWS. Typically, legacy applications read and write files from a filesystem. Switching to object storage, as described in the previous chapter, is not always possible or easy. Fortunately, AWS offers good old block-level storage as well, allowing you to migrate your legacy application without the need for expensive modifications.

Block-level storage with a disk filesystem (FAT32, NTFS, ext3, ext4, XFS, and so on) can be used to store files as you would on a personal computer. A *block* is a sequence of bytes and the smallest addressable unit. The OS is the intermediary between the application that needs to access files and the underlying filesystem and block-level storage. The disk filesystem manages where (at what block address) your files are stored. You can use block-level storage only in combination with an EC2 instance where the OS is running.

The OS provides access to block-level storage via open, write, and read system calls. The simplified flow of a read request goes like this:

1 An application wants to read the file /path/to/file.txt and makes a read system call.

2 The OS forwards the read request to the filesystem.

3 The filesystem translates /path/to/file.txt to the block on the disk where the data is stored.

Applications like databases that read or write files by using system calls must have access to block-level storage for persistence. You can't tell a MySQL database to store its files in an object store because MySQL uses system calls to access files.

> ### Not all examples are covered by the Free Tier
>
> The examples in this chapter are not all covered by the Free Tier. A warning message appears when an example incurs costs. Nevertheless, as long as you don't run all other examples longer than a few days, you won't pay anything for them. Keep in mind that this applies only if you created a fresh AWS account for this book and nothing else is going on in your AWS account. Try to complete the chapter within a few days; you'll clean up your account at the end.

AWS provides two kinds of block-level storage:

- A persistent block-level storage *volume connected via network*—This is the best choice for most problems, because it is independent of your virtual machine's life cycle and replicates data among multiple disks automatically to increase durability and availability.

- A temporary block-level storage *volume physically attached to the host system of the virtual machine*—This is interesting if you're optimizing for performance, because it is directly attached to the host system and, therefore, offers low latency and high throughput when accessing your data.

The next three sections will introduce and compare these two solutions by connecting storage with an EC2 instance, doing performance tests, and exploring how to back up the data.

8.1   Elastic Block Store (EBS): Persistent block-level storage attached over the network

Elastic Block Store (EBS) provides persistent block-level storage with built-in data replication. Typically, EBS is used in the following scenarios:

- Operating a relational database system on a virtual machine
- Running a (legacy) application that requires a filesystem to store data on EC2
- Storing and booting the operating system of a virtual machine

An EBS volume is separate from an EC2 instance and connected over the network, as shown in figure 8.1. EBS volumes have the following characteristics:

- They aren't part of your EC2 instances; they're attached to your EC2 instance via a network connection. If you terminate your EC2 instance, the EBS volumes remain.
- They are either not attached to an EC2 instance or attached to exactly one EC2 instance at a time.
- They can be used like typical hard disks.
- They replicate your data on multiple disks to prevent data loss due to hardware failures.

To use an EBS volume, it must be attached to an EC2 instance over the network.

EC2 instance   EBS volume

Figure 8.1   EBS volumes are independent resources but can be used only when attached to an EC2 instance.

EBS volumes have one big advantage: they are not part of the EC2 instance; they are an independent resource. No matter whether you stop your virtual machine or your virtual machine fails because of a hardware defect, your volume and your data will remain.

By default, AWS sets the `DeleteOnTermination` attribute to `true` for the root volume of each EC2 instance. This means, whenever you terminate the EC2 instance, the EBS volume acting as the root volume gets deleted automatically. In contrast, AWS sets the `DeleteOnTermination` attribute to `false` for all other EBS volumes attached to an EC2 instance. When you terminate the EC2 instance, those EBS volumes will remain. If you need to modify the default behavior, it is possible to override the initial value for the `DeleteOnTermination` attribute.

> **WARNING**   You can't easily attach the same EBS volume to multiple virtual machines! If you are still interested in attaching an EBS volume to many EC2 instances, read http://mng.bz/p68w carefully and see if the many limitations

still support your workload. See chapter 9 if you are looking for a network filesystem.

8.1.1   *Creating an EBS volume and attaching it to your EC2 instance*

Let's return to the example from the beginning of the chapter. You are migrating a legacy application to AWS. The application needs to access a filesystem to store data. Because the data contains business-critical information, durability and availability are important. Therefore, you create an EBS volume for persistent block storage. The legacy application runs on a virtual machine, and the volume is attached to the EC2 instance to enable access to the block-level storage.

The following bit of code demonstrates how to create an EBS volume and attach it to an EC2 instance with the help of CloudFormation:

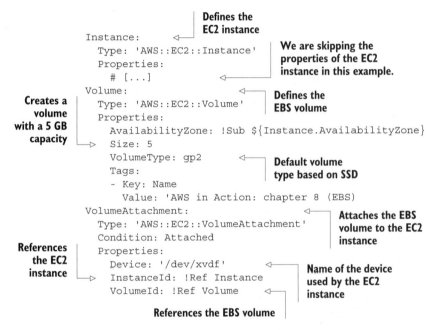

An EBS volume is a standalone resource. This means your EBS volume can exist without an EC2 instance, but you need an EC2 instance to access the EBS volume.

8.1.2   *Using EBS*

To help you explore EBS, we've prepared a CloudFormation template located at https://s3.amazonaws.com/awsinaction-code3/chapter08/ebs.yaml. Create a stack based on that template by clicking the CloudFormation Quick-Create Link (http://mng.bz/O6la), select the default VPC and a random subnet, and set the AttachVolume parameter to yes. Don't forget to check the box marked "I Acknowledge That AWS CloudFormation Might Create IAM Resources." After creating the stack, use the SSM Session Manager to connect to the instance.

You can see the attached EBS volumes using `lsblk`. Usually, EBS volumes can be found somewhere in the range of /dev/xvdf to /dev/xvdp. The root volume (/dev/xvda) is an exception—it's based on the AMI you choose when you launch the EC2 instance and contains everything needed to boot the instance (your OS files), as shown here:

```
$ lsblk
NAME    MAJ:MIN RM SIZE RO TYPE MOUNTPOINT
xvda    202:0    0   8G  0 disk
└─xvda1 202:1    0   8G  0 part /
xvdf    202:80   0   5G  0 disk
```

The root volume, an EBS volume with a size of 8 GiB

An additional volume, an EBS volume with a size of 5 GiB

The first time you use a newly created EBS volume, you must create a filesystem. You could also create partitions, but in this case, the volume size is only 5 GB, so you probably don't want to split it up further. Because you can create EBS volumes in any size and attach multiple volumes to your EC2 instance, partitioning a single EBS volume is uncommon. Instead, you should create volumes at the size you need (1 GB to 16 TB); if you need two separate scopes, create two volumes. In Linux, you can create a filesystem on the additional volume with the help of `mkfs`. The following example creates an XFS filesystem:

```
$ sudo mkfs -t xfs /dev/xvdf
meta-data=/dev/xvdf              isize=512    agcount=4, agsize=327680 blks
         =                       sectsz=512   attr=2, projid32bit=1
         =                       crc=1        finobt=1, sparse=0
data     =                       bsize=4096   blocks=1310720, imaxpct=25
         =                       sunit=0      swidth=0 blks
naming   =version 2              bsize=4096   ascii-ci=0 ftype=1
log      =internal log           bsize=4096   blocks=2560, version=2
         =                       sectsz=512   sunit=0 blks, lazy-count=1
realtime =none                   extsz=4096   blocks=0, rtextents=0
```

After the filesystem has been created, you can mount the device as follows:

```
$ sudo mkdir /data
$ sudo mount /dev/xvdf /data
```

To see mounted volumes, use `df` like this:

```
$ df -h
Filesystem      Size  Used Avail Use% Mounted on
devtmpfs        484M     0  484M   0% /dev
tmpfs           492M     0  492M   0% /dev/shm
tmpfs           492M  348K  491M   1% /run
tmpfs           492M     0  492M   0% /sys/fs/cgroup
/dev/xvda1      8.0G  1.5G  6.6G  19% /
/dev/xvdf       5.0G   38M  5.0G   1% /data
```

Root volume

Additional volume

EBS volumes are independent of your virtual machine. To see this in action, as shown in the next code snippet, you will save a file to a volume, unmount, and detach the volume. Afterward, you will attach and mount the volume again. The data will still be available!

```
$ sudo touch /data/testfile      ⟵┐ Creates testfile
$ sudo umount /data      ⟵┐        in /data
                          └ Unmounts
                            the volume
```

Open the AWS Management Console and update the CloudFormation stack named ebs. Keep the current template, but update the AttachVolume parameter from yes to no and update the stack. This will detach the EBS volume from the EC2 instance. After the update is completed, only your root device is left, as shown here:

```
$ lsblk
NAME    MAJ:MIN RM SIZE RO TYPE MOUNTPOINT
xvda    202:0    0  8G  0 disk
└─xvda1 202:1    0  8G  0 part /
```

The testfile in /data is also gone, illustrated next:

```
$ ls /data/testfile
ls: cannot access /data/testfile: No such file or directory
```

Next, attach the EBS volume again. Open the AWS Management Console and update the CloudFormation stack named ebs. Keep the current template but set the Attach-Volume parameter to yes. Then, update the CloudFormation stack and wait for the changes to be applied. The volume /dev/xvdf is available again, as shown here:

```
                                     Mounts the attached
$ sudo mount /dev/xvdf /data  ⟵┐     volume again
$ ls /data/testfile      ⟵┐
/data/testfile            └ Checks whether testfile
                            is still in /data
```

Voilà! The file testfile that you created in /data is still there.

8.1.3   Tweaking performance

Performance testing of hard disks is divided into read and write tests. To test the performance of your volumes, you will use a simple tool named dd, which can perform block-level reads and writes between a source if=/path/to/source and a destination of=/path/to/destination, shown next. For comparison, you'll run a performance test for a temporary block-level storage volume in the following section:

```
$ sudo dd if=/dev/zero of=/data/tempfile bs=1M count=1024 \  ⟵┐ Writes 1 MB
⮡ conv=fdatasync,notrunc                                        1,024 times
1024+0 records in
1024+0 records out
1073741824 bytes (1.1 GB) copied, 15.8331 s, 67.8 MB/s  ⟵┐ 67.8 MB/s write
                                                            performance
$ echo 3 | sudo tee /proc/sys/vm/drop_caches  ⟵┐ Flushes
3                                                 caches
```

```
$ sudo dd if=/data/tempfile of=/dev/null bs=1M            ◁──┐  Reads 1 MB
  count=1024                                                 │  1,024 times
1024+0 records in
1024+0 records out                                           ┌  68.0 MB/s read
1073741824 bytes (1.1 GB) copied, 15.7875 s, 68.0 MB/s  ◁──┤  performance
```

Keep in mind that performance can be different depending on your actual workload. This example assumes that the file size is 1 MB. If you're hosting websites, you'll most likely deal with lots of small files instead.

EBS performance is more complicated. Performance depends on the type of EC2 instance as well as the EBS volume type. EC2 instances with EBS optimization benefit by having dedicated bandwidth to their EBS volumes. Table 8.1 gives an overview of EC2 instance types that are EBS-optimized by default. Some older instance types can be optimized for an additional hourly charge whereas others do not support EBS optimization at all. Input/output operations per second (IOPS) are measured using a standard 16 KB I/O operation size.

Table 8.1   What performance can be expected from modern instance types? Your mileage may vary.

Use case	Instance type	Baseline bandwidth (Mbps)	Maximum bandwidth (Mbps)
General purpose	m6a.large–m6a.48xlarge	531–40,000	6,666–40,000
Compute optimized	c6g.medium–c6g.16xlarge	315– 9,000	4,750–19,000
Memory optimized	r6i.large–r6i.32xlarge	650–40,000	10,000–40,000
Memory and net-work optimized	x2idn.16xlarge–x2idn.32xlarge	40,000–80,000	40,000–80,000

WARNING   Performance depends heavily on your workload: read versus write, as well as the size of your I/O operations (a bigger operation size equates to more throughput).

Depending on your storage workload, you must choose an EC2 instance that can deliver the bandwidth you require. Additionally, your EBS volume must be balanced with the amount of bandwidth. Table 8.2 shows the different EBS volume types and how they perform.

Table 8.2   How EBS volume types differ

Volume type	Volume size	MiB/s	IOPS	Performance burst	Price
General Purpose SSD (gp3)	1 GiB–16 TiB	1,000	3,000 per default, plus as much as you provision (up to 500 IOPS per GiB or 16,000 IOPS)	n/a	$$$$

Table 8.2   How EBS volume types differ *(continued)*

Volume type	Volume size	MiB/s	IOPS	Performance burst	Price
General Purpose SSD (gp2)	1 GiB–16 TiB	250	3 per GiB (up to 16,000)	3,000 IOPS	$$$$$
Provisioned IOPS SSD (io2 Block Express)	4 GiB–64 TiB	4000	As much as you provision (up to 500 IOPS per GiB or 256,000 IOPS)	n/a	$$$$$$
Provisioned IOPS SSD (io2)	4 GiB–16 TiB	1000	As much as you provision (up to 500 IOPS per GiB or 64,000 IOPS)	n/a	$$$$$$
Provisioned IOPS SSD (io1)	4 GiB–16 TiB	1000	As much as you provision (up to 50 IOPS per GiB or 64,000 IOPS)	n/a	$$$$$$$
Throughput Optimized HDD (st1)	125 GiB–16 TiB	40 per TiB (up to 500)	500	250 MiB/s per TiB (up to 500 MiB/s)	$$
Cold HDD (sc1)	125 GiB–16 TiB	12 per TiB (up to 250)	250	80 MiB/s per TiB (up to 250 MiB/s)	$
EBS Magnetic HDD (standard)	1 GiB–1 TiB	40-90	40-200 (100 on average)	Hundreds	$$$

Here are typical scenarios for the different volume types:

- Use General Purpose SSD (gp3) as the default for most workloads with medium load and a random access pattern. For example, use this as the boot volume or for all kinds of applications with low to medium I/O load.
- I/O-intensive workloads access small amounts of data randomly. Provisioned IOPS SSD (io2) offers throughput guarantees, for example, for large and business-critical database workloads.
- Use Throughput Optimized HDD (st1) for workloads with sequential I/O and huge amounts of data, such as Big Data workloads. Don't use this volume type for workloads in need of small and random I/O.
- Cold HDD (sc1) is a good fit when you are looking for a low-cost storage option for data you need to access infrequently and sequentially. Don't use this volume type for workloads in need of small and random I/O.
- EBS Magnetic HDD (standard) is an older volume type from a previous generation. It might be a good option when you need to access your data infrequently.

> **Gibibyte (GiB) and Tebibyte (TiB)**
>
> The terms gibibyte (GiB) and tebibyte (TiB) aren't used often; you're probably more familiar with gigabyte and terabyte. But AWS uses them in some places. Here's what they mean:
>
> | | |
> |---|---|
> | 1 TiB = 2^{40} bytes = 1,099,511,627,776 bytes | 1 TB = 10^{12} bytes = 1,000,000,000,000 bytes |
> | 1 GiB = 2^{30} bytes = 1,073,741,824 bytes | 1 GB = 10^9 bytes = 1,000,000,000 bytes |
>
> Or, in other words, 1 TiB is 1.0995 TB and 1 GiB is 1.074 GB.

EBS volumes are charged based on the size of the volume, no matter how much data you store in the volume. If you provision a 100 GiB volume, you pay for 100 GiB, even if you have no data on the volume. If you use EBS Magnetic HDD (standard) volumes, you must also pay for every I/O operation you perform. Provisioned IOPS SSD (io1) volumes are additionally charged based on the provisioned IOPS. Use the AWS Simple Monthly Calculator at https://calculator.aws/ to determine how much your storage setup will cost.

We advise you to use general-purpose (SSD) volumes as the default. If your workload requires more IOPS, then go with provisioned IOPS (SSD). You can attach multiple EBS volumes to a single EC2 instance to increase overall capacity or for additional performance.

8.1.4 Backing up your data with EBS snapshots

EBS volumes replicate data on multiple disks automatically and are designed for an annual failure rate (AFR) of 0.1% and 0.2%. This means on average you should expect to lose 0.5–1 of 500 volumes per year. To plan for an unlikely (but possible) failure of an EBS volume, or more likely a human failure, you should create backups of your volumes regularly. Fortunately, EBS offers an optimized, easy-to-use way to back up EBS volumes with EBS snapshots. A *snapshot* is a block-level incremental backup. If your volume is 5 GiB in size, and you use 1 GiB of data, your first snapshot will be around 1 GiB in size. After the first snapshot is created, only the changes will be persisted, to reduce the size of the backup. EBS snapshots are charged based on how many gigabytes you use.

You'll now create a snapshot using the CLI. Before you can do so, you need to know the EBS volume ID. You can find it as the `VolumeId` output of the CloudFormation stack, or by running the following:

```
$ aws ec2 describe-volumes \
➥ --filters "Name=size,Values=5" --query "Volumes[].VolumeId" \
➥ --output text
vol-043a5516bc104d9c6          ⟵──┤ The output shows
                                   │ the $VolumeId.
```

With the volume ID, you can go on to create a snapshot like this:

```
$ aws ec2 create-snapshot --volume-id $VolumeId          ◁──┐  Replace $VolumeId
{                                                            │  with the ID of your
  "Description": "",                                         │  volume.
  "Encrypted": false,
  "OwnerId": "163732473262",
  "Progress": "",
  "SnapshotId": "snap-0babfe807decdb918",        ◁──┐  Note the ID of
  "StartTime": "2022-08-25T07:59:50.717000+00:00",  │  the snapshot:
  "State": "pending",               ◁──┐            │  $SnapshotId.
  "VolumeId": "vol-043a5516bc104d9c6", │  EBS is still
  "VolumeSize": 5,                     │  creating your
  "Tags": []                           │  snapshot.
}
```

Creating a snapshot can take some time, depending on how big your volume is and how many blocks have changed since the last backup. You can see the status of the snapshot by running the following:

```
$ aws ec2 describe-snapshots --snapshot-ids $SnapshotId    ◁──┐  Replace $VolumeId
{                                                              │  with the ID of your
  "Snapshots": [                                               │  snapshot.
    {
      "Description": "",
      "Encrypted": false,
      "OwnerId": "163732473262",
      "Progress": "100%",          ◁──┐  Progress of
      "SnapshotId": "snap-0babfe807decdb918",  │  your snapshot
      "StartTime": "2022-08-25T07:59:50.717000+00:00",
      "State": "completed",        ◁──┐  The snapshot has
      "VolumeId": "vol-043a5516bc104d9c6", │  reached the state
      "VolumeSize": 5,                     │  completed.
      "StorageTier": "standard"
    }
  ]
}
```

Creating a snapshot of an attached, mounted volume is possible but can cause problems with writes that aren't flushed to disk. You should either detach the volume from your instance or stop the instance first. If you absolutely must create a snapshot while the volume is in use, you can do so safely as follows:

1 Freeze all writes by running `sudo fsfreeze -f /data` on the virtual machine.
2 Create a snapshot and wait until it reaches the pending state.
3 Unfreeze to resume writes by running `sudo fsfreeze -u /data` on the virtual machine.
4 Wait until the snapshot is completed.

Unfreeze the volume as soon as the snapshot reaches the state `pending` . You don't have to wait until the snapshot has finished.

With an EBS snapshot, you don't have to worry about losing data due to a failed EBS volume or human failure. You are able to restore your data from your EBS snapshot.

To restore a snapshot, you must create a new EBS volume based on that snapshot. Execute the following command in your terminal, replacing $SnapshotId with the ID of your snapshot:

```
$ aws ec2 create-volume --snapshot-id $SnapshotId \           ◁─┐  The ID of your
⮑  --availability-zone us-east-1a                   ◁──┐       │  snapshot used to
{                                                 Choose       │  create the volume
    "AvailabilityZone": "us-east-1a",             data
    "CreateTime": "2022-08-25T08:08:49+00:00",    center.
    "Encrypted": false,
    "Size": 5,
    "SnapshotId": "snap-0babfe807decdb918",
    "State": "creating",
    "VolumeId": "vol-0bf4fdf3816f968c5",          ◁─┐  The $RestoreVolumeId
    "Iops": 100,                                     │  of the volume restored
    "Tags": [],                                      │  from your snapshot
    "VolumeType": "gp2",
    "MultiAttachEnabled": false
}
```

Cleaning up

Don't forget to delete the snapshot, the volume, and your stack. The following code will delete the snapshot and volume. Don't forget to replace $SnapshotId with the ID of the EBS snapshot you created earlier and $RestoreVolumeId with the ID of the EBS volume you created by restoring the snapshot:

```
$ aws ec2 delete-snapshot --snapshot-id $SnapshotId
$ aws ec2 delete-volume --volume-id $RestoreVolumeId
```

Also delete your CloudFormation stack named ebs after you finish this section to clean up all used resources as follows:

```
$ aws cloudformation delete-stack --stack-name ebs
```

8.2   *Instance store: Temporary block-level storage*

An *instance store* provides block-level storage directly attached to the physical machine hosting the virtual machine. Figure 8.2 shows that the instance store is part of an EC2 instance and available only if your instance is running; it won't persist your data if you stop or terminate the instance. You don't pay separately for an instance store; instance store charges are included in the EC2 instance price.

In comparison to an EBS volume, which is connected to your EC2 instance over the network, the instance store depends upon the EC2 instance and can't exist without it. The instance store will be deleted when you stop or terminate the virtual machine.

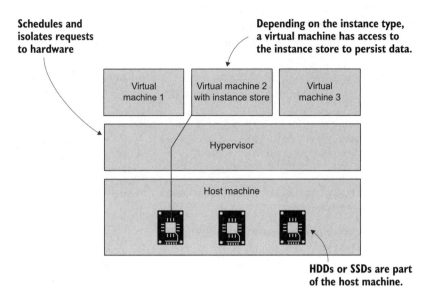

Figure 8.2   The instance store is part of your EC2 instance and uses the host machine's HDDs or SSDs.

Don't use an instance store for data that must not be lost; use it for temporary data only. For example, it is not a big deal to cache data on instance store, because you are able to restore the data from its origin anytime.

In rare cases, it is also advisable to persist data on instance storage, such as whenever the application is replicating data among multiple machines by default. For example, many NoSQL database systems use a cluster of machines to replicate data. The benefit of doing so is low latency and high throughput. But be warned, this is for experts in the field of distributed systems and storage only. If in doubt, use EBS instead.

> **WARNING**   If you stop or terminate your EC2 instance, the instance store is lost. *Lost* means all data is destroyed and can't be restored!

Note that most EC2 instance types do not come with instance storage. Only some instance families come with instance storage included. AWS offers SSD and HDD instance stores from 4 GB up to 335,520 GB. Table 8.3 shows a few EC2 instance families providing instance stores.

Table 8.3   Instance families with instance stores

Use case	Instance type	Instance store type	Instance store size in GB
General purpose	m6id.large m6id.32xlarge	SSD	118 7600
Compute optimized	c6id.large c6id.32xlarge	SSD	118 7600

Table 8.3   Instance families with instance stores *(continued)*

Use case	Instance type	Instance store type	Instance store size in GB
Memory optimized	r6id.large r6id.32xlarge	SSD	118 7600
Storage optimized	i4i.large i4i.32xlarge	SSD	468 30000
Storage optimized	d3.xlarge d3.8xlarge	HDD	5940 47520
Storage optimized	d3en.xlarge d3en.12xlarge	HDD	27960 335520

The following listing demonstrates how to use an instance store with CloudFormation. Instance stores aren't standalone resources like EBS volumes; the instance store is part of your EC2 instance.

Listing 8.1   Using an instance store with CloudFormation

```
Instance:
  Type: 'AWS::EC2::Instance'
  Properties:
    IamInstanceProfile: 'ec2-ssm-core'
    ImageId: 'ami-061ac2e015473fbe2'
    InstanceType: 'm6id.large'          ◁───┐  Chooses an instance
    SecurityGroupIds:                        │  type with an instance
    - !Ref SecurityGroup                     │  store
    SubnetId: !Ref Subnet
```

Read on to see how you can use the instance store.

8.2.1   Using an instance store

To help you explore instance stores, we created the CloudFormation template located at https://s3.amazonaws.com/awsinaction-code3/chapter08/instancestore.yaml. Create a CloudFormation stack based on the template by clicking the CloudFormation Quick-Create Link (http://mng.bz/YK5a).

> **WARNING**   Starting a virtual machine with instance type m6id.large will incur charges. See https://aws.amazon.com/ec2/pricing/on-demand/ if you want to find out the current hourly price.

Create a stack based on that template, and select the default VPC and a random subnet. After creating the stack, use the SSM Session Manager to connect to the instance and explore the available devices, as shown in the following code snippet.

> **WARNING**   You might run into the following error: "Your requested instance type (m6id.large) is not supported in your requested Availability Zone." Not

all regions/availability zones support `m6id.large` instance types. Select a different subnet and try again.

```
$ lsblk
NAME          MAJ:MIN RM   SIZE RO TYPE MOUNTPOINT
nvme1n1       259:0    0 109.9G  0 disk
nvme0n1       259:1    0     8G  0 disk
├─nvme0n1p1   259:2    0     8G  0 part /
└─nvme0n1p128 259:3    0     1M  0 part
```

The instance store device

The EBS root volume device

To see the mounted volumes, use this command:

```
$ df -h
Filesystem      Size  Used Avail Use% Mounted on
devtmpfs        3.9G     0  3.9G   0% /dev
tmpfs           3.9G     0  3.9G   0% /dev/shm
tmpfs           3.9G  348K  3.9G   1% /run
tmpfs           3.9G     0  3.9G   0% /sys/fs/cgroup
/dev/nvme0n1p1  8.0G  1.5G  6.6G  19% /
```

The EBS root volume contains the OS.

Your instance store volume is not yet usable. You have to format the device and mount it as follows:

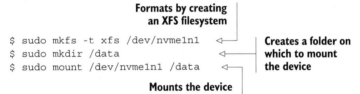

Formats by creating an XFS filesystem

```
$ sudo mkfs -t xfs /dev/nvme1n1
$ sudo mkdir /data
$ sudo mount /dev/nvme1n1 /data
```

Creates a folder on which to mount the device

Mounts the device

You can now use the instance store by reading and writing to /data like this:

```
$ df -h
Filesystem      Size  Used Avail Use% Mounted on
[...]
/dev/nvme1n1    110G  145M  110G   1% /data
```

110 GB are available.

> **Windows**
>
> For Windows instances, instance store volumes are NTFS formatted and mounted automatically.

8.2.2   Testing performance

Let's take the same performance measurements we took in section 8.1.3 to see the difference between the instance store and EBS volumes, as shown next:

```
$ sudo dd if=/dev/zero of=/data/tempfile bs=1M count=1024 \
⇒ conv=fdatasync,notrunc
1024+0 records in
1024+0 records out
1073741824 bytes (1.1 GB) copied, 13.3137 s, 80.6 MB/s
```

18% faster compared with EBS from section 8.1.3

```
$ echo 3 | sudo tee /proc/sys/vm/drop_caches
3

$ sudo dd if=/data/tempfile of=/dev/null bs=1M count=1024
1024+0 records in
1024+0 records out
1073741824 bytes (1.1 GB) copied, 5.83715 s, 184 MB/s
sh-4.2$ echo 3 | sudo tee /proc/sys/vm/drop_caches
```

170% faster compared with EBS from section 8.1.3

Keep in mind that performance can vary, depending on your actual workload. This example assumes a file size of 1 MB. If you're hosting websites, you'll most likely deal with lots of small files instead. The performance characteristics show that the instance store is running on the same hardware as the virtual machine. The volumes are not connected to the virtual machine over the network as with EBS volumes.

> **Cleaning up**
> Don't forget to delete your stacks after you finish this section to clean up all used resources. Otherwise, you'll be charged for the resources you use.

8.2.3 *Backing up your data*

There is no built-in backup mechanism for instance store volumes. Based on what you learned in section 7.3, you can use a combination of scheduled jobs and S3 to back up your data periodically, as shown here:

```
$ aws s3 sync /path/to/data s3://$YourCompany-backup/instancestore-backup
```

If you need to back up data, you should probably use more durable, block-level storage like EBS. An instance store is better used for ephemeral persistence requirements.

You will learn about another option to store your data in the next chapter: a network filesystem.

Summary

- Block-level storage can be used only in combination with an EC2 instance because the OS is needed to provide access to the block-level storage (including partitions, filesystems, and read/write system calls).
- When creating an EBS volume, you need to specify the volume size. AWS charges you for the provisioned storage, no matter whether or not you are using all the storage. Also, it is possible to increase the size of a volume later.
- EBS volumes are connected to a single EC2 instance via network. Depending on your instance type, this network connection can use more or less bandwidth.
- There are different types of EBS volumes available: General Purpose SSD (gp3), Provisioned IOPS SSD (io2), Throughput Optimized HDD (st1), and Cold HDD (sc1) are the most common.

- EBS snapshots are a powerful way to back up your EBS volumes because they use a block-level, incremental approach.
- An instance store provides low latency and high throughput. However, as you are using storage directly attached to the physical machine running your virtual machine, data is lost if you stop or terminate the instance.
- Typically, an instance store is used only for temporary data that does not need to be persisted.

Sharing data volumes
between machines: EFS

This chapter covers

- Creating a highly available network filesystem
- Mounting a network filesystem on multiple EC2 instances
- Sharing files between EC2 instances
- Tweaking the performance of your network filesystem
- Monitoring possible bottlenecks in your network filesystem
- Backing up your shared filesystem

Many legacy applications store state in a filesystem on disk. Therefore, using Amazon S3—an object store, described in chapter 7—isn't possible without modifying the application. Using block storage as discussed in the previous chapter might be an option, but it doesn't allow you to access files from multiple machines. Because block storage persists data in a single data center only, AWS promises an uptime of only 99.9%.

If you need to share a filesystem between virtual machines or require high availability, the Elastic File System (EFS) might be an option. EFS is based on the NFSv4.1 protocol, which allows you to mount and access the filesystem on one or multiple machines in parallel. EFS distributes data among multiple data centers, called availability zones, and promises an uptime of 99.99%. In this chapter, you learn how to set up EFS, tweak the performance, and back up your data.

EFS WORKS ONLY WITH LINUX   At this time, EFS isn't supported by Windows EC2 instances. The Amazon FSx for Windows File Server is an alternative to EFS for Windows workloads. See http://mng.bz/zmq1 to learn more.

Let's take a closer look at how EFS works compared to Elastic Block Store (EBS) and the instance store, introduced in chapter 8. An EBS volume is tied to a data center and can be attached to only a single EC2 instance from the same data center. Typically, EBS volumes are used as the root volumes that contain the operating system, or, for relational database systems, to store the state. An instance store consists of a hard drive directly attached to the hardware the virtual machine is running on. An instance store can be regarded as ephemeral storage and is, therefore, used only for temporary data, caching, or for systems with embedded data replication, like many NoSQL databases, for example. In contrast, the EFS filesystem supports reads and writes by multiple EC2 instances from different data centers in parallel. In addition, the data on the EFS filesystem is replicated among multiple data centers and remains available even if a whole data center suffers an outage, which isn't true for EBS and instance stores. Figure 9.1 shows the differences: EBS is a virtual disk, instance store is a local disk, and EFS is a shared folder.

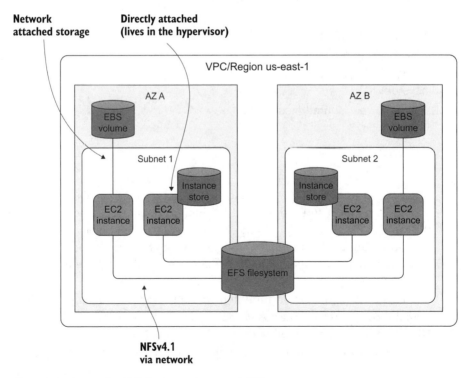

Figure 9.1   Comparing EBS, instance stores, and EFS

All examples are covered by the Free Tier

All examples in this chapter are covered by the Free Tier. As long as you follow the instructions and don't run them longer than a few days, you won't pay anything. You will find instructions to delete all resources at the end of the chapter.

EFS consists of two components:

- *Filesystem*—Stores your data
- *Mount target*—Makes your data accessible

The filesystem is the resource that stores your data in an AWS region, but you can't access it directly. To do so, you must create an EFS mount target in a subnet. The mount target provides a network endpoint that you can use to mount the filesystem on an EC2 instance via NFSv4.1. The EC2 instance must be in the same subnet as the EFS mount target, but you can create mount targets in multiple subnets. Figure 9.2 demonstrates how to access the filesystem from EC2 instances running in multiple subnets.

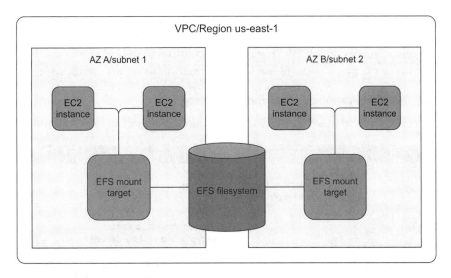

Figure 9.2   Mount targets provide an endpoint for EC2 instances to mount the filesystem in a subnet.

Equipped with the knowledge about filesystems and mount targets, we will now continue to practice.

Linux is a multiuser operating system. Many users can store data and run programs isolated from each other. Each user has a home directory, which is usually stored under /home/$username. For example, the user michael owns the home directory /home/michael. Of course, only user michael is allowed to read and write in /home/michael. The ls -d -l /home/* command lists all home directories, as shown next:

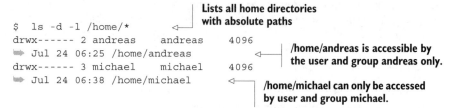

```
$  ls -d -l /home/*
drwx------ 2 andreas     andreas     4096
➡ Jul 24 06:25 /home/andreas
drwx------ 3 michael     michael     4096
➡ Jul 24 06:38 /home/michael
```

Lists all home directories with absolute paths

/home/andreas is accessible by the user and group andreas only.

/home/michael can only be accessed by user and group michael.

When using multiple EC2 instances, your users will have a separate home folder on each EC2 instance. If a Linux user uploads a file on one EC2 instance, they can't access the file on another EC2 instance. To solve this problem, create a filesystem and mount EFS on each EC2 instance under /home. The home directories are then shared across all your EC2 instances, and users will feel at home no matter which machine they log in to. In the following sections, you will build this solution step-by-step. First, you will create the filesystem.

9.1   Creating a filesystem

The filesystem is the resource that stores your files, directories, and links. Like S3, EFS grows with your storage needs. You don't have to provision the storage up front. The filesystem is located in an AWS region and replicates your data under the covers across multiple data centers. You will use CloudFormation to set up the filesystem next.

9.1.1   Using CloudFormation to describe a filesystem

First, configure the filesystem. The next listing shows the CloudFormation resource.

Listing 9.1   CloudFormation snippet of an EFS filesystem resource

```
Resources:
  [...]
  FileSystem:
    Type: 'AWS::EFS::FileSystem'
    Properties:
      Encrypted: true
      ThroughputMode: bursting
      PerformanceMode: generalPurpose
      FileSystemPolicy:
        Version: '2012-10-17'
        Statement:
        - Effect: 'Deny'
          Action: '*'
```

Specifies the stack resources and their properties

We recommend to enable encryption at rest by default.

The default throughput mode is called bursting. We'll cover more on the throughput mode for I/O intensive workloads later.

The default performance mode is general purpose. We'll cover more on the performance mode later.

It's a security best practice to encrypt data in transit. The filesystem policy ensures that all access uses secure transport.

```
Principal:
  AWS: '*'
Condition:
  Bool:
    'aws:SecureTransport': 'false'
```

That's it. The filesystem is ready to store data. Before we do so, let's talk about the costs.

9.1.2 *Pricing*

Estimating costs for storing data on EFS is not that complicated. The following three factors affect the price:

- The amount of stored data in GB per month
- The frequency that the data is accessed
- Whether you want to trade in availability for cost

When accessing data frequently choose the Standard Storage or One Zone Storage storage class, which comes with the lowest latency. When accessing data less than daily, consider Standard–Infrequent Access Storage or One Zone–Infrequent Access Storage to reduce storage costs. Keep in mind that doing so increases the first-byte latency. Also, when using the Infrequent Access Storage classes, accessing the data comes with a fee.

If you do not need the high availability of 99.99% provided by the Standard Storage and Standard–Infrequent Access Storage, consider choosing the One Zone Storage or One Zone–Infrequent Access Storage storage classes. Those storage classes do not replicate your data among multiple data centers, which reduces the promised availability to 99.9%. It is worth mentioning that all storage classes are designed for a durability of 99.999999999%. However, you should back up your data stored with One Zone to be able to recover in the event of a data center destruction. You will learn more about backing up an EFS filesystem at the end of the chapter.

Table 9.1 shows EFS pricing when storing data in US East (N. Virginia), also called us-east-1.

Table 9.1 EFS storage classes affect the monthly costs for storing data.

Storage class	Price per GB/month	Access requests per GB transferred
Standard Storage	$0.30	$0.00
Standard–Infrequent Access Storage	$0.025	$0.01
One Zone Storage	$0.16	$0.00
One Zone–Infrequent Access Storage	$0.0133	$0.01

Let's briefly estimate the costs for storing 5 GB of data on EFS. Assuming the data is accessed multiple times per day and high availability is required, we choose the

Standard Storage class. So, the cost for storing data is 5 GB × $0.30, which results in a total of $1.50 a month.

Please note: the first 5 GB (Standard Storage) per month are free in the first year of your AWS account (Free Tier). For more details about EFS pricing go to https://aws.amazon.com/efs/pricing/.

After configuring an EFS filesystem with the help of CloudFormation and estimating costs, you will learn how to mount the NFS share on an EC2 instance. To do so, you need to create a mount target first.

9.2   Creating a mount target

An EFS mount target makes your data available to EC2 instances via the NFSv4.1 protocol in a subnet. The EC2 instance communicates with the mount target via a TCP/IP network connection. As you learned in section 6.4, you control network traffic on AWS using security groups. You can use a security group to allow inbound traffic to an EC2 instance or an RDS database, and the same is true for a mount target. Security groups control which traffic is allowed to enter the mount target. The NFS protocol uses port 2049 for inbound communication. Figure 9.3 shows how mount targets are protected.

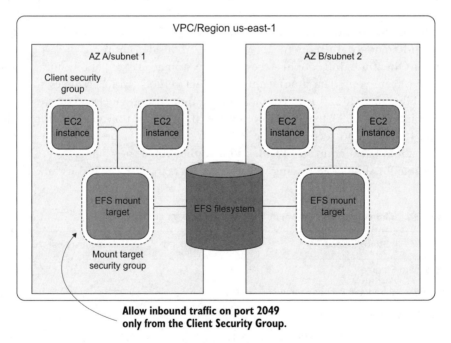

Figure 9.3   EFS mount targets are protected by security groups.

In our example, to control traffic as tightly as possible, you won't grant traffic based on IP addresses. Instead, you'll create two security groups. The client security group will be attached to all EC2 instances that want to mount the filesystem. The mount target security group allows inbound traffic on port 2049 only for traffic that comes from the client security group. This way, you can have a dynamic fleet of clients who are allowed to send traffic to the mount targets.

> **EFS IS NOT ONLY ACCESSIBLE FROM EC2 INSTANCES** In this chapter, we are focusing on mounting an EFS filesystem on EC2 instances. In our experience, that's the most typical use case for EFS. However, EFS can also be used in the following other scenarios:
>
> - Containers (ECS and EKS)
> - Lambda functions
> - On-premises servers

Next, use CloudFormation to manage an EFS mount target. The mount target references the filesystem, needs to be linked to a subnet, and is also protected by at least one security group. You will first describe the security groups, followed by the mount target, as shown in the following listing.

Listing 9.2 CloudFormation snippet of an EFS mount target and security groups

```yaml
Resources:
  [...]
  EFSClientSecurityGroup:          # This security group needs no rules.
                                   # It's just used to mark outgoing
                                   # traffic from EC2 instances.
    Type: 'AWS::EC2::SecurityGroup'
    Properties:
      GroupDescription: 'EFS Mount target client'
      VpcId: !Ref VPC
  MountTargetSecurityGroup:        # This security group is linked
                                   # to the mount target.
    Type: 'AWS::EC2::SecurityGroup'
    Properties:
      GroupDescription: 'EFS Mount target'
      SecurityGroupIngress:
      - IpProtocol: tcp
        FromPort: 2049             # Allows traffic on port 2049
        ToPort: 2049
        SourceSecurityGroupId: !Ref EFSClientSecurityGroup   # Only allows traffic from the security group linked to the EC2 instances
      VpcId: !Ref VPC
  MountTargetA:
    Type: 'AWS::EFS::MountTarget'
    Properties:                    # Attaches the mount target to the filesystem
      FileSystemId: !Ref FileSystem
      SecurityGroups:              # Assigns the security group
      - !Ref MountTargetSecurityGroup
      SubnetId: !Ref SubnetA       # Links the mount target with subnet A
```

Copy the `MountTargetA` resource and also create a mount target for `SubnetB` as shown in listing 9.3.

Listing 9.3   CloudFormation snippet of an EFS mount target and security groups

```
Resources:
  [...]
  MountTargetB:
    Type: 'AWS::EFS::MountTarget'
    Properties:
      FileSystemId: !Ref FileSystem
      SecurityGroups:
      - !Ref MountTargetSecurityGroup
      SubnetId: !Ref SubnetB
```

Attaches the
mount target
to subnet B

Next, you will finally mount the /home directory on an EC2 instance.

9.3   *Mounting the EFS filesystem on EC2 instances*

EFS creates a DNS name for each filesystem following the schema `$FileSystemID`
`.efs.$Region.amazonaws.com`. From an EC2 instance, this name resolves to the
mount target of the instance's subnet.

We recommend using the EFS mount helper to mount EFS filesystems because the
tool comes with two features: secure transport with TLS and authentication with IAM.
Besides that, the EFS mount helper applies the recommended defaults for mounting
EFS filesystems.

On Amazon Linux 2, which we are using for our examples, installing the EFS
mount helper is quite simple, as shown here:

```
$ sudo yum install amazon-efs-utils
```

With the EFS mount util installed, the following command mounts an EFS filesystem.
This snippet shows the full mount command:

```
$ sudo mount -t efs -o tls,iam $FileSystemID $EFSMountPoint
```

Replace `$FileSystemID` with the EFS filesystem, such as `fs-123456`, and `$EFSMount-`
`Point` with the local path where you want to mount the filesystem. The following code
snippet shows an example:

```
$ sudo mount -t efs -o tls,iam fs-123456 /home
```

1 `tls` initiates a TLS tunnel from the EC2 instance to the EFS filesystem to
   encrypt data in transit.
2 `iam` enables authentication via IAM using the IAM role attached to the EC2
   instance.

Of course, it is also possible to use the /ets/fstab config file to automatically mount on
startup. Again, you need to replace `$FileSystemID` and `$EFSMountPoint` as described
in the previous example:

```
$FileSystemID:/ $EFSMountPoint efs _netdev,noresvport,tls,iam 0 0
```

You are already familiar with the options `tls` and `iam`. The two other options have the following meanings:

- `_netdev`—Identifies a network filesystem
- `noresvport`—Ensures that a new TCP source port is used when reestablishing a connection, which is required when recovering from network problems

It's now time to add two EC2 instances to the CloudFormation template. Each EC2 instance should be placed in a different subnet and mount the filesystem to /home. The /home directory will exist on both EC2 instances, and it will also contain some data (such as the folder ec2-user). You have to ensure that you're copying the original data the first time before you mount the EFS filesystem, which is empty by default. The following listing describes the EC2 instance that copies the existing /home folder before the shared home folder is mounted.

Listing 9.4 Using CloudFormation to launch an EC2 instance and mount an EFS filesystem

```
Resources:
  [...]
  EC2InstanceA:                                           Creates an EC2 instance
    Type: 'AWS::EC2::Instance'
    Properties:
      ImageId: !FindInMap [RegionMap, !Ref 'AWS::Region', AMI]
      InstanceType: 't2.micro'
      IamInstanceProfile: !Ref IamInstanceProfile          The IAM role grants access
      NetworkInterfaces:                                   to the EFS filesystem (see
      - AssociatePublicIpAddress: true                     the next listing).
        DeleteOnTermination: true          Attaches the security
        DeviceIndex: 0                     group, which is used
        GroupSet:                          to identify outgoing
        - !Ref EFSClientSecurityGroup      traffic to the filesystem
        SubnetId: !Ref SubnetA
      UserData:                            Adds a Bash script to the user data of the virtual
        'Fn::Base64': !Sub |               machine, which is executed automatically at the
          #!/bin/bash -ex                  end of the first boot process
          trap '/opt/aws/bin/cfn-signal -e 1 --stack ${AWS::StackName}
 --resource EC2InstanceA --region ${AWS::Region}' ERR

          # install dependencies
          yum install -y nc amazon-efs-utils
          pip3 install botocore
                                                          After creating a new
          # copy existing /home to /oldhome               filesystem, it takes a
          mkdir /oldhome                                  few minutes until its
          cp -a /home/. /oldhome                          DNS name resolves to
                                                          the mount targets.
          # wait for EFS mount target
          while ! (echo > /dev/tcp/${FileSystem}.efs.${AWS::Region}.
 amazonaws.com/2049) >/dev/null 2>&1; do sleep 5; done

          # mount EFS filesystem
          echo "${FileSystem}:/ /home efs _netdev,noresvport,tls,iam 0 0"
```

Places the EC2 instance into subnet A

Backs up all home directories to /oldhome

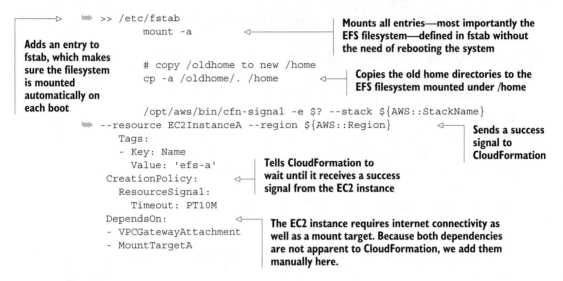

```
    >>  /etc/fstab
            mount -a

        # copy /oldhome to new /home
        cp -a /oldhome/. /home

        /opt/aws/bin/cfn-signal -e $? --stack ${AWS::StackName}
--resource EC2InstanceA --region ${AWS::Region}
    Tags:
    - Key: Name
        Value: 'efs-a'
    CreationPolicy:
        ResourceSignal:
            Timeout: PT10M
    DependsOn:
    - VPCGatewayAttachment
    - MountTargetA
```

Adds an entry to fstab, which makes sure the filesystem is mounted automatically on each boot

Mounts all entries—most importantly the EFS filesystem—defined in fstab without the need of rebooting the system

Copies the old home directories to the EFS filesystem mounted under /home

Sends a success signal to CloudFormation

Tells CloudFormation to wait until it receives a success signal from the EC2 instance

The EC2 instance requires internet connectivity as well as a mount target. Because both dependencies are not apparent to CloudFormation, we add them manually here.

To prove that the EFS filesystem allows you to share files across multiple instances, we are adding a second EC2 instance, as shown next.

Listing 9.5   Mounting an EFS filesystem from a second EC2 instance

```
Resources:
  [...]
  EC2InstanceB:
    Type: 'AWS::EC2::Instance'
    Properties:
      ImageId: !FindInMap [RegionMap, !Ref 'AWS::Region', AMI]
      InstanceType: 't2.micro'
      IamInstanceProfile: !Ref IamInstanceProfile
      NetworkInterfaces:
      - AssociatePublicIpAddress: true
        DeleteOnTermination: true
        DeviceIndex: 0
        GroupSet:
        - !Ref EFSClientSecurityGroup
        SubnetId: !Ref SubnetB
      UserData:
        'Fn::Base64': !Sub |
          #!/bin/bash -ex
          trap '/opt/aws/bin/cfn-signal -e 1 --stack ${AWS::StackName}
--resource EC2InstanceB --region ${AWS::Region}' ERR

          # install dependencies
          yum install -y nc amazon-efs-utils
          pip3 install botocore

          # wait for EFS mount target
          while ! (echo > /dev/tcp/${FileSystem}.efs.${AWS::Region}
.amazonaws.com/2049) >/dev/null 2>&1; do sleep 5; done
```

Places the EC2 instance into subnet B

The old /home folder is not copied here. This is already done on the first EC2 instance in subnet A.

```
        # mount EFS filesystem
        echo "${FileSystem}:/ /home efs _netdev,noresvport,tls,iam 0 0"
⇒ >> /etc/fstab
        mount -a

        /opt/aws/bin/cfn-signal -e $? --stack ${AWS::StackName}
⇒ --resource EC2InstanceB --region ${AWS::Region}
    Tags:
    - Key: Name
      Value: 'efs-b'
  CreationPolicy:
    ResourceSignal:
      Timeout: PT10M
  DependsOn:
  - VPCGatewayAttachment
  - MountTargetB
```

To make things easier, you can also add outputs to the template to expose the IDs of your EC2 instances like this:

```
Outputs:
  EC2InstanceA:
    Value: !Ref EC2InstanceA
    Description: 'Id of EC2 Instance in AZ A (connect via Session Manager)'
  EC2InstanceB:
    Value: !Ref EC2InstanceB
    Description: 'Id of EC2 Instance in AZ B (connect via Session Manager)'
```

The CloudFormation template is now complete. It contains the following:

- The EFS filesystem
- Two mount targets in subnet A and subnet B
- Security groups to control traffic from the EC2 instances to the mount targets
- EC2 instances in both subnets, including a `UserData` script to mount the filesystem

> **Where is the template located?**
>
> You can find the template on GitHub. Download a snapshot of the repository at
> https://github.com/AWSinAction/code3/archive/main.zip. The file we're talking about
> is located at chapter09/efs.yaml. On S3, the same file is located at https://s3
> .amazonaws.com/awsinaction-code3/chapter09/efs.yaml.

It's now time to create a stack based on your template to create all the resources in your AWS account. Use the AWS CLI to create the stack like this:

```
$ aws cloudformation create-stack --stack-name efs \
⇒ --template-url https://s3.amazonaws.com/awsinaction-code3/\
⇒ chapter09/efs.yaml --capabilities CAPABILITY_IAM
```

Once the stack is in the state CREATE_COMPLETE, two EC2 instances are running. Both mounted the EFS share to /home. You also copied the existing home directories to the EFS share. It's time to connect to the instances via the Session Manager and do some tests to see whether users can really share files between the EC2 instances in their home directory.

9.4   *Sharing files between EC2 instances*

Use the Session Manager to connect to the virtual machine named EC2InstanceA. Use the following command to get the EC2 instance IDs of EC2InstanceA and EC2InstanceB:

```
$ aws cloudformation describe-stacks --stack-name efs \
   --query "Stacks[0].Outputs"
[{
  "Description": "[...]",
  "OutputKey": "EC2InstanceA",
  "OutputValue": "i-011a050b697d12e7a"
}, {
  "Description": "[...]",
  "OutputKey": "EC2InstanceB",
  "OutputValue": "i-a22b67b2a4d25a2b"
}]
```

Then, establish a second connection to the virtual machine EC2InstanceB with the help of the Session Manager and switch to the user's home directory, as shown in the next code snippet. By the way, the default user on Amazon Linux 2 is the ec2-user. But when using the Session Manager via the AWS Management Console, you are logged in with another user named ssm-user:

```
$ cd $HOME          ◁——  Changes to the home directory
                          of the current user
```

Also check whether there are any files or folders in your home directory as follows:

```
$ ls          ◁——  If no data is returned, the folder
                    /home/ec2-user is empty.
```

Now, create a file on one of the machines like this:

```
$ touch i-was-here          ◁——  The touch command creates an
                                  empty file named i-was-here.
```

On the other machine, confirm that you can see the new file as follows:

```
$ cd $HOME                        The file created on
$ ls                              the other machine
i-was-here          ◁——           appears here.
```

This simple experiment proves that you have access to the same home directory on both machines. You could add hundreds of machines to this example. All would share the same home directory, and users would be able to access the same home directory on all EC2 instances. You can apply the same mechanism to share files between a fleet of web servers, for example, mounting the folder /var/www/html from an EFS filesystem. A similar example is building a highly available Jenkins server by putting /var/lib/jenkins on EFS.

To run the solution successfully, you also need to take care of backups, performance tuning, and monitoring. You will learn about this in the following sections.

9.5   Tweaking performance

EFS makes it easy for us to mount a network filesystem from many machines. However, we can say from our own experience that we repeatedly have problems with the performance of EFS in everyday practice. Therefore, in the following section, we describe what you should consider to get the maximum performance out of EFS.

The following factors affect latency, throughput, and I/O operations per second of an EFS filesystem:

- *The performance mode*—General Purpose or Max I/O
- *The throughput mode*—Bursting or Provisioned
- *The storage class*—Standard or One Zone

Let's dive into the details.

9.5.1   Performance mode

EFS comes with two performance modes:

- *General Purpose mode*—Supports up to 35,000 IOPS
- *Max I/O mode*—Supports 500,000+ IOPS

IOPS stands for read or write operations per second. When reading or writing a file, EFS accounts for one I/O operation for every 4 KB with a minimum of one I/O operation.

So, when to choose which option? So far, you've used the General Purpose performance mode, which is fine for most workloads, especially latency-sensitive ones where small files are served most of the time. The /home directory is a perfect example of such a workload. Typical files like documents are relatively small, and users expect low latency when fetching files.

But sometimes, EFS is used to store massive amounts of data for analytics. For data analytics, latency is not important. Throughput is the metric you want to optimize instead. If you want to analyze gigabytes or terabytes of data, it doesn't matter if your time to first byte takes 1 ms or 100 ms. Even a small increase in throughput will decrease the time it will take to analyze the data. For example, analyzing 1 TB of data with 100 MB/second throughput will take 167 minutes. That's almost three hours, so the first few milliseconds don't really matter. Optimizing for throughput can be achieved using the Max I/O performance mode.

Please note: the performance mode being used by an EFS filesystem cannot be changed—you set it when the filesystem is created. Therefore, to change the performance mode, you have to create a new filesystem. We recommend you start with the General Purpose performance mode if you are unsure which mode fits best for your workload. You will learn how to check whether you made the right decision by monitoring data, which is covered in the following section.

As most AWS services do, EFS sends metrics to CloudWatch, allowing us to get insight into the performance of a filesystem. We recommend creating a CloudWatch alarm to monitor filesystems with General Purpose performance mode. The metric `PercentIOLimit` tells you whether a filesystem is approaching its I/O limit. By migrating your data to a filesystem with Max I/O mode, you can increase the I/O limit from 35,000 IOPS to 500,000+ IOPS. Keep in mind, however, that doing so increases read latency from around 600 microseconds to single-digit milliseconds. The next listing shows the CloudWatch alarm to monitor the `PercentIOLimit` metric.

> **Listing 9.6   Monitoring the `PercentIOLimit` metric using a CloudWatch alarm**

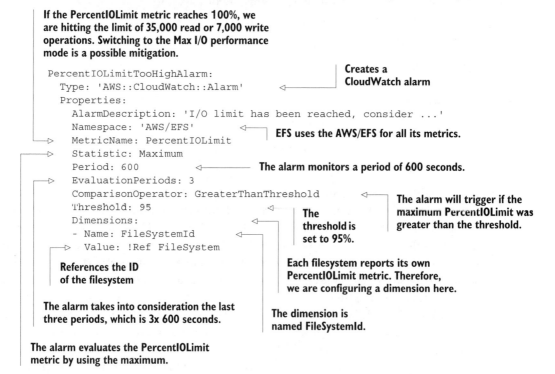

If the PercentIOLimit metric reaches 100%, we are hitting the limit of 35,000 read or 7,000 write operations. Switching to the Max I/O performance mode is a possible mitigation.

```
PercentIOLimitTooHighAlarm:
  Type: 'AWS::CloudWatch::Alarm'            Creates a
  Properties:                               CloudWatch alarm
    AlarmDescription: 'I/O limit has been reached, consider ...'
    Namespace: 'AWS/EFS'        EFS uses the AWS/EFS for all its metrics.
    MetricName: PercentIOLimit
    Statistic: Maximum
    Period: 600          The alarm monitors a period of 600 seconds.
    EvaluationPeriods: 3
    ComparisonOperator: GreaterThanThreshold
    Threshold: 95              The            The alarm will trigger if the
    Dimensions:                threshold is   maximum PercentIOLimit was
    - Name: FileSystemId       set to 95%.    greater than the threshold.
      Value: !Ref FileSystem
```

References the ID of the filesystem

Each filesystem reports its own PercentIOLimit metric. Therefore, we are configuring a dimension here.

The alarm takes into consideration the last three periods, which is 3x 600 seconds.

The dimension is named FileSystemId.

The alarm evaluates the PercentIOLimit metric by using the maximum.

Next, you will learn about the second factor that affects the performance of an EFS filesystem: the throughput mode.

9.5.2 *Throughput mode*

Besides the performance mode, the throughput mode determines the maximum throughput of an EFS filesystem using the following modes:

- *Bursting Throughput mode*—Comes with a small baseline throughput but is able to burst throughput for short periods of time. Also, the throughput grows with the amount of data stored.
- *Provisioned Throughput mode*—Gives you a constant throughput with a maximum of 1 GiBps. You pay $6.00 per MB/s per month.

BURSTING THROUGHPUT MODE

When using Bursting Throughput mode, the amount of data stored in a filesystem affects the baseline and bursting throughput. The baseline throughput for an EFS filesystem is 50 MiBps per TiB of storage with a minimum of 1 MiBps. For a limited period of time, reading or writing data may burst up to 100 MiBps per TiB of storage, with a minimum of 100 MiBps.

> **WARNING** The discussed limits are labeled default limits by AWS. Depending on your scenario, it might be possible to increase those limits. However, there is no guarantee for that, and AWS does not provide any information on the maximum of a possible limit increase.

A filesystem with Bursting Throughput mode handles up to 1 or 3 GiBps, depending on the region (see http://mng.bz/09Av). Table 9.2 shows the baseline and bursting write throughput of an EFS filesystem in US East (N. Virginia) where the maximum bursting throughput is 3 GiBps.

Table 9.2 EFS throughput depends on the storage size.

Filesystem size	Baseline throughput	Bursting throughput	Explanation
<=20 GiB	1 MiBps	100 MiBps	Minimum baseline throughput is 1 MiBps, and minimum bursting throughput is 100 MiBps.
1 TiB	50 MiBps	100 MiBps	The bursting throughput starts to grow with filesystems larger than 1 TiB.
30 TiB	1500 MiBps	3000 MiBps	The bursting throughput hits the maximum for filesystems in US East (N. Virginia).
>=60 TiB	3000 MiBps	3000 MiBps	Both the baseline and bursting throughput hit the maximum for filesystems in US East (N. Virginia).

As long as you are consuming less than the baseline throughput, the filesystem accumulates burst credits. For every TiB of storage, your filesystem accrues credits of 50 MiB per second. For example, a filesystem with 500 GiB accumulates burst credits for accessing 2160 GiB within 24 hours. That's bursting at the maximum of 100 MiBps for 6 hours.

WARNING   EFS does not support more than 500 MiBps per client, which means an EC2 instance cannot transfer more than 500 MiBps to an EFS filesystem.

Be aware that the maximum credit balance is 2.1 TiB for filesystems smaller than 1 TiB and 2.1 TiB per TiB stored for filesystems larger than 1 TiB. This means filesystems can burst for no more than 12 hours.

It is important to mention that a discount exists for reading data compared to writing data. A filesystem allows 1.66 or three times more read throughput depending on the region. For US East (N. Virginia), the discount is 1.66, which means the maximum read throughput is 5 GiBps. However, be aware that the discount for reading data is not valid for requests returning less than 4 KB of data.

To make things even more complicated, it is worth mentioning that data stored in the Infrequent Access storage class is not taken into consideration when calculating the maximum baseline and burst throughput.

When using the Bursting Throughput mode, you should monitor the burst credits of the filesystem because if the filesystem runs out of burst credits, the throughput will decrease significantly. We've seen many outages caused by an unexpected drop in the baseline performance. The following listing shows how to create a CloudWatch alarm to monitor the `BurstCreditBalance` metric. We've configured the threshold of the alarm to a burst credit of 192 GB, which will allow the filesystem to burst at 100 MiBps for an hour.

Listing 9.7   Monitoring the `PercentIOLimit` metric using a CloudWatch alarm

```
BurstCreditBalanceTooLowAlarm:
  Type: 'AWS::CloudWatch::Alarm'
  Properties:
    AlarmDescription: 'Average burst credit balance over last ...'
    Namespace: 'AWS/EFS'
    MetricName: BurstCreditBalance        The alarm monitors the
    Statistic: Average                    BurstCreditBalance
    Period: 600                           metric.
    EvaluationPeriods: 1
    ComparisonOperator: LessThanThreshold
    Threshold: 192000000000               The threshold of 192000000000 bytes
    Dimensions:                           translates into 192 GB (lasts for ~30
    - Name: FileSystemId                  minutes; you can burst at 100 MiBps).
      Value: !Ref FileSystem
```

If you are running out of burst credits because your workload requires a high and constant throughput, you could switch to the Provisioned Throughput mode or add data to your EFS filesystem to increase the baseline and bursting throughput.

PROVISIONED THROUGHPUT MODE

It is possible to upgrade an EFS filesystem from Bursting Throughput mode to Provisioned Throghput mode at any time. When activating the Provisioned Throughput mode, you need to specify the provisioned throughput of the filesystem in MiBps.

A filesystem will deliver the provisioned throughput continuously. The maximum provisioned throughput is 1 GiBps. Also, you have to pay for the provisioned throughput. AWS charges $6.00 per MB/s per month.

For a filesystem in Provisioned Throughput mode, you pay for throughput only above the baseline performance. So, for example, when provisioning 200 MiBps for a filesystem with 1 TiB, you will pay for only 150 MiBps, because 50 MiBps would be the baseline performance of a filesystem in Bursting Throughput mode.

The following code snippet shows how to provision throughput using Cloud-Formation. Use the efs-provisioned.yaml template to update your `efs` CloudFormation stack:

```
$ aws cloudformation update-stack --stack-name efs \
➥ --template-url https://s3.amazonaws.com/awsinaction-code3/\
➥ chapter09/efs-provisioned.yaml --capabilities CAPABILITY_IAM
```

The next listing contains two differences to the template you used in the previous example: the `ThroughputMode` is set to `provisioned` instead of `bursting`, and the `ProvisionedThroughputInMibps` sets the provisioned throughput to 1 MiBps, which is free, because this is the baseline throughput of a filesystem with bursting throughput.

Listing 9.8   EFS filesystem with provisioned throughput

```
FileSystem:
  Type: 'AWS::EFS::FileSystem'
  Properties:
    Encrypted: true
    ThroughputMode: provisioned        ◁── Sets the throughput mode from bursting to provisioned
    ProvisionedThroughputInMibps: 1    ◁── Configures the provisioned throughput in MiBps. 1 MiBps is free, even for empty filesystems.
    PerformanceMode: generalPurpose
    FileSystemPolicy:
      Version: '2012-10-17'
      Statement:
      - Effect: 'Deny'
        Action: '*'
        Principal:
          AWS: '*'
        Condition:
          Bool:
            'aws:SecureTransport': 'false'
```

With Provisioned Throughput mode enabled, you should keep an eye on the utilization of the throughput that you provisioned. This allows you to increase the provisioned throughput to avoid performance problems caused by EFS becoming the bottleneck of your system. Listing 9.9 shows how to create a CloudWatch alarm to monitor the utilization of the maximum throughput of an EFS filesystem. The same CloudWatch alarm works for filesystems with Bursting Throughput mode as well. This combines the metrics `MeteredIOBytes`, the throughput to the filesystem, and

PermittedThroughput, the maximum throughput of the filesystem, by using metric math (see http://mng.bz/qdvA for details).

Listing 9.9   Monitoring using a CloudWatch alarm and metric math

```
PermittedThroughputAlarm:
  Type: 'AWS::CloudWatch::Alarm'
  Properties:
    AlarmDescription: 'Reached 80% of the permitted throughput ...'
    Metrics:                              ◁──── Uses metric math to
    - Id: m1                          ◁──        combine multiple metrics
      Label: MeteredIOBytes
      MetricStat:                          Assigns the ID m1
        Metric:                            to the first metric
          Namespace: 'AWS/EFS'
          MetricName: MeteredIOBytes   ◁──  The first metric taken
          Dimensions:                       into consideration is the
          - Name: FileSystemId              MeteredIOBytes metric,
            Value: !Ref FileSystem          which contains the
        Period: 60                          current utilization.
        Stat: Sum
        Unit: Bytes
      ReturnData: false
    - Id: m2
      Label: PermittedThroughput
      MetricStat:                          The second metric is the
        Metric:                            PermittedThroughput
          Namespace: 'AWS/EFS'             metric, which indicates
          MetricName: PermittedThroughput ◁ the maximum throughput.
          Dimensions:
          - Name: FileSystemId
            Value: !Ref FileSystem
        Period: 60
        Stat: Sum                          The first metric, m1, returns the
        Unit: 'Bytes/Second'               sum of bytes transferred within
      ReturnData: false                    60 seconds. This expression
    - Expression: '(m1/1048576)/PERIOD(m1)' ◁ converts this into MiBps.
      Id: e1                          ◁──
      Label: e1                            Assigns the ID e1 to the
      ReturnData: false                    metric to reference it
    - Expression: 'm2/1048576'        ◁──  in the following line
      Id: e2
      Label: e2                        Converts the second
      ReturnData: false                metric from bytes/second
    - Expression: '((e1)*100)/(e2)'    into MiBps
      Id: e3
      Label: 'Throughput utilization (%)'  The output of the third expression is
      ReturnData: true                     the only metric/expression returning
    EvaluationPeriods: 10                  data used for the alarm.
    DatapointsToAlarm: 6
    ComparisonOperator: GreaterThanThreshold  The alarm triggers if the
    Threshold: 80     ◁──                     throughput utilization is
                         ...80%.             greater than ...
```

Calculates the throughput utilization in percent

If the CloudWatch alarm flips into the `ALARM` state, you might want to increase the provisioned throughput of your filesystem.

9.5.3 *Storage class affects performance*

The third factor that affects the performance of an EFS filesystem is the storage class used to persist data. By default, read latency to data persisted with standard storage class is as low as 600 microseconds. The latency for write requests is in the low single-digit milliseconds.

But if you choose the One Zone storage class to reduce costs, the read and write latency increases to double-digit milliseconds. Depending on your workload, this might have a significant effect on performance.

9.6 *Backing up your data*

AWS promises a durability of 99.999999999% (11 9s) over a given year for data stored on EFS. When using the Standard storage class, EFS replicates data among multiple data centers. Still, we highly recommend backing up the data stored on EFS, particularly so you can recover from a scenario where someone, maybe even you, accidentally deleted data from EFS.

Luckily, AWS provides a service to back up and restore data: AWS Backup. This service to centralize data protection supports EC2, EBS, S3, RDS, DynamoDB, EFS, and many more. The following three components are needed to create snapshots of an EFS filesystem with AWS Backup, as illustrated in figure 9.4:

- *Vault*—A container for grouping backups.
- *Plan*—Defines when and how to backup resources.
- *Recovery Point*—Contains all the data needed to restore a resource; you could also call it a snapshot.

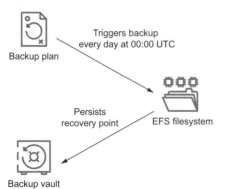

Figure 9.4   AWS Backup creates recovery points based on a schedule and stores them in a vault.

To enable backups for your EFS, update your CloudFormation stack with the template efs-backup.yaml, which contains the configuration for AWS Backups, as shown here. We'll dive into that next:

```
$ aws cloudformation update-stack --stack-name efs \
➥ --template-url https://s3.amazonaws.com/awsinaction-code3/\
➥ chapter09/efs-backup.yaml --capabilities CAPABILITY_IAM
```

Where is the template located?

You can find the template on GitHub. Download a snapshot of the repository at https://github.com/AWSinAction/code3/archive/main.zip. The file we're talking about is located at chapter09/efs-backup.yaml. On S3, the same file is located at https://s3.amazonaws.com/awsinaction-code3/chapter09/efs-backup.yaml.

The following listing is an excerpt from efs-backup.yaml and shows how to create a backup vault and plan. On top of that, it includes a backup selection, which references the EFS filesystem.

Listing 9.10   Backing up an EFS filesystem with AWS Backup

```
BackupVault:                                    Creates a backup vault to
  Type: 'AWS::Backup::BackupVault'              persist recovery points
  Properties:
    BackupVaultName: !Ref 'AWS::StackName'      A backup vault requires a
BackupPlan:                                     unique name; therefore, we
  Type: 'AWS::Backup::BackupPlan'               are using the name of the
  Properties:                                   CloudFormation stack here.
    BackupPlan:                     Creates a
      BackupPlanName: 'efs-daily'   backup plan
      BackupPlanRule:               Each backup plan includes
      - RuleName: 'efs-daily'       at least one rule.
        TargetBackupVault: !Ref BackupVault     The rule defines which
        Lifecycle:                              backup vault should be
          DeleteAfterDays: 30                   used to store backups.
        ScheduleExpression: 'cron(0 5 ? * * *)'
        CompletionWindowMinutes: 1440
BackupSelection:                                The backup plan
  Type: 'AWS::Backup::BackupSelection'          schedules a backup for
  Properties:                                   05:00 UTC every day.
    BackupPlanId: !Ref BackupPlan
    BackupSelection:                            The backup should complete
      SelectionName: 'efs'                      within 24 hours; otherwise,
      IamRoleArn: !GetAtt 'BackupRole.Arn'      it will be cancelled.
      Resources:
      - !GetAtt 'FileSystem.Arn'                References the backup plan
```

The life cycle is configured in a way to delete backups older than 30 days.

Selects the resources to include in the backup

An IAM role is required to grant access to EFS (see the following listing).

Adds the filesystem to the backup selection by using its ARN

Besides this, an IAM role granting access to the EFS filesystem is needed, as shown in the next listing.

Listing 9.11   The IAM role granting AWS Backup access to EFS

```
BackupRole:
  Type: 'AWS::IAM::Role'
  Properties:
    AssumeRolePolicyDocument:
      Version: '2012-10-17'
      Statement:
      - Effect: Allow                          ┐  Only the AWS Backup
        Principal:                             │  service is allowed to
          Service: 'backup.amazonaws.com'  ◁───┘  assume this IAM role.
        Action: 'sts:AssumeRole'
    Policies:                                     The role grants access
    - PolicyName: backup                          to create backups of
      PolicyDocument:                             EFS filesystems...
        Version: '2012-10-17'
        Statement:
        - Effect: Allow                           ...and allows you to describe
          Action:                                 tags of EFS filesystems, which
          - 'elasticfilesystem:Backup'       ◁── is needed in case you define a
          - 'elasticfilesystem:DescribeTags' ◁── backup selection based on tags.
          Resource: !Sub 'arn:${AWS::Partition}:elasticfilesystem
➥ :${AWS::Region}:${AWS::AccountId}:          The policy restricts access to
➥ file-system/${FileSystem}'            ◁──── the filesystem we defined in the
                                              CloudFormation template earlier.
```

AWS Backup allows you to restore an entire filesystem or only some of the folders. It is possible to restore data to the original filesystem as well as to create a new filesystem to do so.

Unfortunately, it will take a while until AWS Backup creates a recovery point for your EFS filesystem. If you are interested in the results, wait 24 hours and check the results as follows:

1. Open the AWS Management Console.
2. Go to the AWS Backup service.
3. Open the backup vault named `efs`.
4. You'll find a list with available recovery points.
5. From here, you could restore an EFS filesystem in case of an emergency.

That's all you need to back up data stored on an EFS filesystem. We should briefly talk about the costs. You are paying for the data stored and if you need to restore your data. The following prices are valid for US East (N. Virginia). For further details, visit https://aws.amazon.com/backup/pricing/:

- Storage: $0.05 per GB and month
- Restore: $0.02 per GB

Cleaning up

First, make sure that the backup vault `efs` does not contain any recovery points like this:

```
$ aws backup list-recovery-points-by-backup-vault --backup-vault-name efs \
  --query "RecoveryPoints[].RecoveryPointArn"
```

If you are getting a list of recovery points, delete each of them using the following command. Don't forget to replace `$RecoveryPointArn` with the ARN of the recovery point you are trying to delete:

```
$ aws backup delete-recovery-point --backup-vault-name efs \
  --recovery-point-arn $RecoveryPointArn
```

After that, use the following command to delete the CloudFormation stack named `efs` that you used while going through the examples within this chapter:

```
$ aws cloudformation delete-stack --stack-name efs
```

Summary

- EFS provides a NFSv4.1-compliant filesystem that can be shared between Linux EC2 instances in different availability zones.
- EFS mount targets are bound to an availability zone and are protected by security groups.
- Data that is stored in EFS is replicated across multiple data centers.
- EFS comes with two performance modes: General Purpose and Max I/O. Use General Purpose if your workload accesses many small files, and Max I/O if you have a few large files.
- By default, the throughput of an EFS filesystem is capable of bursting for a certain amount of time. If you are expecting a high and constant throughput, you should use provisioned throughput instead.
- You need at least two mount targets in different data centers (also called availability zones) for high availability.
- Encryption of data in transit (TLS) and IAM authentication help to protect sensitive data stored on EFS.
- AWS Backup allows you to create and restore snapshots of EFS filesystems.

Using a relational database service: RDS

This chapter covers

- Launching and initializing relational databases with RDS
- Creating and restoring database snapshots
- Setting up a highly available database
- Monitoring database metrics
- Tweaking database performance

WordPress is a content management system that powers substantial parts of the internet. Like many other applications, WordPress uses a relational database to store articles, comments, users, and many other data. It is fair to say that relational databases are the de facto standard for storing and querying structured data, and many applications are built on top of a relational database system such as MySQL. Typically, relational databases focus on data consistency and guarantee ACID (atomicity, consistency, isolation, and durability) database transactions. A typical task is storing and querying structured data, such as the accounts and transactions in an accounting application. If you want to use a relational database on AWS, you have two options:

- Use the managed relational database service *Amazon RDS*, which is offered by AWS.
- Operate a relational database yourself on top of virtual machines.

The Amazon Relational Database Service (Amazon RDS) offers ready-to-use relational databases such as PostgreSQL, MySQL, MariaDB, Oracle Database, and Microsoft SQL Server. Beyond that, AWS offers its own engine called Amazon Aurora, which is MySQL and PostgreSQL compatible. As long as your application uses one of these database systems, it is not a big deal to switch to RDS. The trickiest part is migrating the data, which you will learn about in this chapter as well.

RDS is a managed service. The managed service provider—in this case, AWS—is responsible for providing a defined set of services—in this case, operating a relational database system. Table 10.1 compares using an RDS database and hosting a database yourself on virtual machines.

Table 10.1   Managed service RDS vs. a self-hosted database on virtual machines

	Amazon RDS	Self-hosted on virtual machines
Cost for AWS services	Higher because RDS costs more than virtual machines (EC2)	Lower because virtual machines (EC2) are cheaper than RDS
Total cost of ownership	Lower because operating costs are split among many customers	Much higher because you need your own manpower to manage your database
Quality	AWS professionals are responsible for the managed service.	You'll need to build a team of professionals and implement quality control yourself.
Flexibility	High, because you can choose a relational database system and most of the configuration parameters	Higher, because you can control every part of the relational database system you installed on virtual machines

You'd need considerable time and know-how to build a comparable relational database environment based on virtual machines, so we recommend using Amazon RDS for relational databases whenever possible to decrease operational costs and improve quality. That's why we won't cover hosting your own relational database on VMs in this book. Instead, we'll introduce Amazon RDS in detail.

In this chapter, you'll launch a MySQL database with the help of Amazon RDS. Chapter 2 introduced a WordPress setup like the one shown in figure 10.1 and described next; you'll use this example in this chapter, focusing on the database part:

1 The user sends an HTTP request to the load balancer.
2 The load balancer distributes the incoming request to a fleet of virtual machines.
3 Each virtual machine runs a web server, which connects to a MySQL database as well as a network filesystem.

After the MySQL database is up and running, you'll learn how to import, back up, and restore data. More advanced topics like setting up a highly available database and improving the performance of the database will follow.

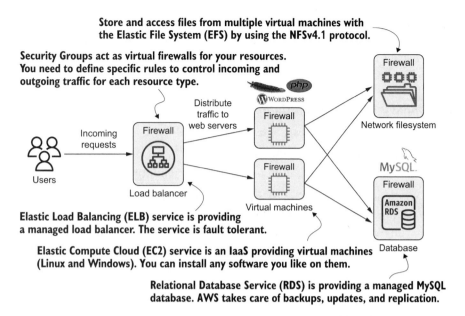

Figure 10.1   The company's blogging infrastructure consists of two load-balanced web servers running WordPress and a MySQL database server.

Not all examples are covered by the Free Tier

The examples in this chapter are not all covered by the Free Tier. A warning message appears when an example incurs costs. Nevertheless, as long as you don't run all other examples longer than a few days, you won't pay anything for them. Keep in mind that this applies only if you created a fresh AWS account for this book and nothing else is going on in your AWS account. Try to complete the chapter within a few days; you'll clean up your account at the end.

10.1   Starting a MySQL database

In the following section, you will launch the infrastructure required to run WordPress on AWS. In this chapter, we will focus on the MySQL database provided by RDS, but you can easily transfer what you learn to other database engines such as Aurora, PostgreSQL, MariaDB, Oracle, and Microsoft SQL Server, as well as to applications other than WordPress.

When you follow the official "How to Install WordPress" tutorial (see http://mng .bz/G1vV), one of the first steps is setting up a MySQL database. Formerly, you might have installed the database system on the same virtual machine that also runs the web server. However, operating a database system is not trivial. You have to implement a solid backup and recovery strategy, for example. Also, when running a database on a single virtual machine, you are introducing a single point of failure into your system that could cause downtimes of your website.

To overcome these challenges, you will use a fully managed MySQL database provided by RDS. AWS provides backup and restore functionality and offers database systems distributed among two data centers as well as the ability to recover from failure automatically.

10.1.1 Launching a WordPress platform with an RDS database

Launching a database consists of two steps:

1 Launching a database instance
2 Connecting an application to the database endpoint

Next, you'll use the same CloudFormation template you used in chapter 2 to spin up the cloud infrastructure for WordPress. The template can be found on GitHub and on S3. You can download a snapshot of the repository at https://github.com/AWSinAction/code3/archive/main.zip. The file we're talking about is located at chapter10/template.yaml. On S3, the same file is located at http://s3.amazonaws.com/awsinaction-code3/chapter10/template.yaml.

Execute the following command to create a CloudFormation stack containing an RDS database instance with a MySQL engine and web servers serving the WordPress application:

```
$ aws cloudformation create-stack --stack-name wordpress --template-url \
➥ https://s3.amazonaws.com/awsinaction-code3/chapter10/template.yaml \
➥ --parameters "ParameterKey=WordpressAdminPassword,ParameterValue=test1234" \
➥ --capabilities CAPABILITY_IAM
```

You'll have to wait several minutes while the CloudFormation stack is created in the background, which means you'll have enough time to learn the details of the RDS database instance while the template is launching. The next listing shows parts of the CloudFormation template used to create the wordpress stack. Table 10.2 shows the attributes you need when creating an RDS database instance using CloudFormation or the Management Console.

Table 10.2   Attributes needed to connect to an RDS database

Attribute	Description
AllocatedStorage	Storage size of your database in GB
DBInstanceClass	Size (also known as instance type) of the underlying virtual machine
Engine	Database engine (Aurora, PostgreSQL, MySQL, MariaDB, Oracle Database, or Microsoft SQL Server) you want to use
DBName	Identifier for the database
MasterUsername	Name for the admin user
MasterUserPassword	Password for the admin user

It is possible to configure a database instance as publicly accessible, but we generally do not recommend enabling access from the internet to your database, to prevent unwanted access. Instead, as shown in listing 10.1, an RDS instance should be accessible only within the VPC.

To connect to an RDS database instance, you need an EC2 instance running in the same VPC. First, connect to the EC2 instance. From there, you can then connect to the database instance.

Listing 10.1   Excerpt from the CloudFormation template for setting up an RDS database

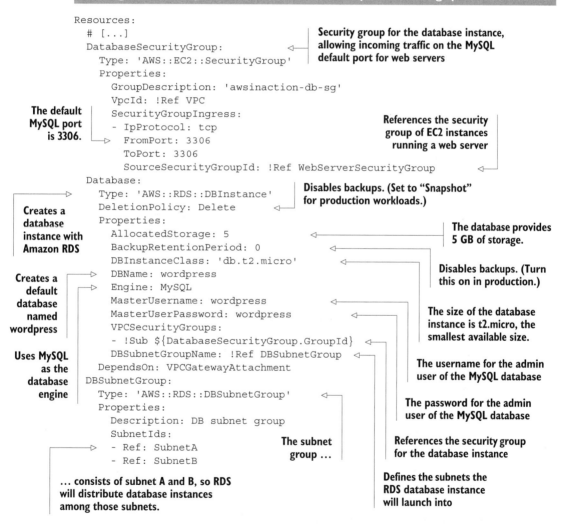

```
Resources:
  # [...]
  DatabaseSecurityGroup:                          ◁──  Security group for the database instance,
    Type: 'AWS::EC2::SecurityGroup'                    allowing incoming traffic on the MySQL
    Properties:                                         default port for web servers
      GroupDescription: 'awsinaction-db-sg'
      VpcId: !Ref VPC
      SecurityGroupIngress:
      - IpProtocol: tcp                                 References the security
        FromPort: 3306                                  group of EC2 instances
        ToPort: 3306                                     running a web server
        SourceSecurityGroupId: !Ref WebServerSecurityGroup   ◁──
  Database:
    Type: 'AWS::RDS::DBInstance'                    Disables backups. (Set to "Snapshot"
    DeletionPolicy: Delete             ◁──          for production workloads.)
    Properties:
      AllocatedStorage: 5              ◁──────────────────────    The database provides
      BackupRetentionPeriod: 0        ◁──                          5 GB of storage.
      DBInstanceClass: 'db.t2.micro'  ◁──
      DBName: wordpress                               Disables backups. (Turn
      Engine: MySQL                                   this on in production.)
      MasterUsername: wordpress       ◁──
      MasterUserPassword: wordpress   ◁──             The size of the database
      VPCSecurityGroups:                              instance is t2.micro, the
      - !Sub ${DatabaseSecurityGroup.GroupId}  ◁──    smallest available size.
      DBSubnetGroupName: !Ref DBSubnetGroup    ◁──
    DependsOn: VPCGatewayAttachment                   The username for the admin
  DBSubnetGroup:                                      user of the MySQL database
    Type: 'AWS::RDS::DBSubnetGroup'   ◁──
    Properties:                                       The password for the admin
      Description: DB subnet group                    user of the MySQL database
      SubnetIds:
      - Ref: SubnetA                                  References the security group
      - Ref: SubnetB                                  for the database instance
```

The default MySQL port is 3306.

Creates a database instance with Amazon RDS

Creates a default database named wordpress

Uses MySQL as the database engine

The subnet group ...

... consists of subnet A and B, so RDS will distribute database instances among those subnets.

Defines the subnets the RDS database instance will launch into

See if the CloudFormation stack named `wordpress` has reached the state `CREATE _COMPLETE` with the following command:

```
$ aws cloudformation describe-stacks --stack-name wordpress
```

Search for StackStatus in the output, and check whether the status is CREATE_ COMPLETE. If not, you need to wait a few minutes longer (it can take up to 15 minutes to create the stack) and rerun the command. If the status is CREATE_COMPLETE, you'll find the key OutputKey in the output section. The corresponding OutputValue contains the URL for the WordPress blogging platform. The following listing shows the output in detail. Open this URL in your browser; you'll find a running WordPress setup.

Listing 10.2   Checking the state of the CloudFormation stack

```
$ aws cloudformation describe-stacks --stack-name wordpress
{
  "Stacks": [{
    "StackId": "[...]",
    "Description": "AWS in Action: chapter 10",
    "Parameters": [...],
    "Tags": [],
    "Outputs": [
        {
            "Description": "WordPress URL",
            "OutputKey": "URL",
            "OutputValue": "http://[...].us-east-1.elb.amazonaws.com"
        }
    ],
    "CreationTime": "2017-10-19T07:12:28.694Z",
    "StackName": "wordpress",
    "NotificationARNs": [],
    "StackStatus": "CREATE_COMPLETE",
    "DisableRollback": false
  }]
}
```

Opens this URL in your browser to open the WordPress application

Waits for state CREATE_COMPLETE for the CloudFormation stack

Launching and operating a relational database like MySQL is that simple. Of course, you can also use the Management Console (https://console.aws.amazon.com/rds/) to launch an RDS database instance instead of using a CloudFormation template. RDS is a managed service, and AWS handles most of the tasks necessary to operate your database in a secure and reliable way. You need to do only two things:

- Monitor your database's available storage, and make sure you increase the allo-cated storage as needed.
- Monitor your database's performance, and make sure you increase I/O and computing performance as needed.

Both tasks can be handled with the help of CloudWatch monitoring, as you'll learn later in the chapter.

10.1.2   *Exploring an RDS database instance with a MySQL engine*

The CloudFormation stack created an RDS database instance with the MySQL engine. Each database instance offers an endpoint for clients. Clients send their SQL queries to this endpoint to query, insert, delete, or update data. For example, to retrieve all rows from a table, an application sends the following SQL request: `SELECT * FROM table`. You can request the endpoint and detailed information of an RDS database instance with the `describe-db-instances` command:

```
$ aws rds describe-db-instances --query "DBInstances[0].Endpoint"
{
  "HostedZoneId": "Z2R2ITUGPM61AM",
  "Port": 3306,
  "Address": "wdwcoq2o8digyr.cqrxioeaavmf.us-east-1.rds.amazonaws.com"
}
```

Port number of database endpoint

Host name of database endpoint

The RDS database is now running, but what does it cost?

10.1.3 Pricing for Amazon RDS

What does it cost to host WordPress on AWS? We discussed this question in chapter 2 in detail. Here, we want to focus on the costs for RDS.

Databases on Amazon RDS are priced according to the size of the underlying virtual machine and the amount and type of allocated storage. Compared to a database running on a plain EC2 VM, the hourly price of an RDS instance is higher. In our opinion, the Amazon RDS service is worth the extra charge because you don't need to perform typical DBA tasks like installation, patching, upgrades, migration, backups, and recovery.

Table 10.3 shows a pricing example for a medium-sized RDS database instance with a standby instance for high availability. All prices in USD are for US East (N. Virginia) as of March 11, 2022. Get the current prices at https://aws.amazon.com/rds/pricing/.

Table 10.3   Monthly costs for a medium-sized RDS instance

Description	Monthly price
Database instance `db.t4g.medium`	$94.17 USD
50 GB of general purpose (SSD)	$11.50 USD
Additional storage for database snapshots (100 GB)	$9.50 USD
Total	$115.17 USD

You've now launched an RDS database instance for use with a WordPress web application. You'll learn about importing data to the RDS database in the next section.

10.2   Importing data into a database

Imagine you are already running WordPress on a virtual machine in your on-premises data center, and you have decided to move the application to AWS. To do so, you need to move the data from the on-premises MySQL database to RDS. You will learn how to do that in this section.

A database without data isn't useful. In many cases, you'll need to import data into a new database by importing a dump from the old database. This section will guide you through the process of importing a MySQL database dump to an RDS database with a MySQL engine. The process is similar for all other database engines (Aurora, PostgreSQL, MySQL, MariaDB, Oracle Database, and Microsoft SQL Server).

To import a database from your on-premises environment to Amazon RDS, follow these steps:

1 Export the database.
2 Start a virtual machine in the same region and VPC as the RDS database.
3 Upload the database dump to the virtual machine.
4 Run an import of the database dump to the RDS database on the virtual server.

We'll skip the first step of exporting a MySQL database, because the RDS instance we created in our example is empty and you may not have access to an existing WordPress database. The next sidebar gives you hints on how to create a database dump in case you need that for your real-world systems later.

> ## Exporting a MySQL database
>
> MySQL (and every other database system) offers a way to export and import databases. We recommend using the command-line tools from MySQL for exporting and importing databases. You may need to install the MySQL client, which comes with the `mysqldump` tool.
>
> The following command exports all databases from localhost and dumps them into a file called dump.sql. Replace $UserName with the MySQL admin user, and enter the password when prompted:
>
> ```
> $ mysqldump -u $UserName -p --all-databases > dump.sql
> ```
>
> You can also specify only some databases for the export, as shown next. To do so, replace $DatabaseName with the name of the database you want to export:
>
> ```
> $ mysqldump -u $UserName -p $DatabaseName > dump.sql
> ```
>
> And, of course, you can export a database over a network connection as follows. To connect to a server to export a database, replace $Host with the host name or IP address of your database:
>
> ```
> $ mysqldump -u $UserName -p $DatabaseName --host $Host > dump.sql
> ```
>
> See the MySQL documentation if you need more information about the `mysqldump` tool.

Theoretically, you could import a database to RDS from any machine from your on-premises or local network, but the higher latency over the internet or VPN connection will slow down the import process dramatically. Because of this, we recommend adding a second step: upload the database dump to a virtual machine running in the same AWS region and VPC, and import the database into RDS from there.

> **AWS Database Migration Service**
>
> When migrating a huge database to AWS with minimal downtime, the Database Migration Service (DMS) can help. We do not cover DMS in this book, but you can learn more on the AWS website: https://aws.amazon.com/dms.

To do so, we'll guide you through the following steps:

1 Connect to the virtual machine that is running WordPress.
2 Download a database dump from S3 to the VM. (If you are using your own database dump, we recommend uploading it to S3 first.)
3 Import the database dump into the RDS database from the virtual machine.

Fortunately, you already started two virtual machines that you know can connect to the MySQL database on RDS, because they're running the WordPress application. Go through the following steps to open a terminal session:

1 Open the EC2 service via AWS Management Console: https://console.aws .amazon.com/ec2/.
2 Select one of the two EC2 instances named wordpress.
3 Click the Connect button.
4 Select Session Manager and click the Connect button.

Because you are connected to a virtual machine with access to the RDS database instance, you are ready to import the database dump. First, change into the home directory of the ssm-user as follows:

```
$ cd /home/ssm-user/
```

We prepared a MySQL database dump of a WordPress blog as an example. The dump contains a blog post and a few comments. Download this database dump from S3 using the following command on the virtual machine:

```
$ wget https://s3.amazonaws.com/awsinaction-code3/chapter10/wordpress-import.sql
```

Next, you'll need the port and hostname, also called the *endpoint*, of the MySQL database on RDS. Don't remember the endpoint? The following command will print it out for you. Run this on your local machine:

```
$ aws rds describe-db-instances --query "DBInstances[0].Endpoint"
```

Run the following command on the VM to import the data from the file wordpress-import.sql into the RDS database instance; replace $DBAddress with the Address you printed to the terminal with the previous command. The Address will look similar to wdtq7tf5caejft.cd0o57zo3ohr.us-east-1.rds.amazonaws.com. Also, type in word-press when asked for a password:

```
$ mysql --host $DBAddress --user wordpress -p < wordpress-import.sql
```

Point your browser to the WordPress blog again, and you'll now find many new posts and comments there. If you don't remember the URL, run the following command on your local machine to fetch it again:

```
$ aws cloudformation describe-stacks --stack-name wordpress \
⇒ --query "Stacks[0].Outputs[0].OutputValue" --output text
```

10.3   Backing up and restoring your database

Over the years, your WordPress site has accumulated hundreds of blog posts and comments from the community. That's a valuable asset. Therefore, it is key that you back up the data.

Amazon RDS is a managed service, but you still need backups of your database in case something or someone harms your data and you need to restore it, or you need to duplicate a database in the same or another region. RDS offers manual and auto-mated *snapshots* for recovering RDS database instances. In this section, you'll learn how to use RDS snapshots to do the following:

- Configuring the retention period and time frame for automated snapshots
- Creating snapshots manually
- Restoring snapshots by starting new database instances based on a snapshot
- Copying a snapshot to another region for disaster recovery or relocation

10.3.1   Configuring automated snapshots

The RDS database you started in section 10.1 can automatically create snapshots if the BackupRetentionPeriod is set to a value between 1 and 35. This value indicates how many days the snapshot will be retained (the default is 1). Automated snapshots are created once a day during the specified time frame. If no time frame is specified, RDS picks a random 30-minute time frame during the night. A new random time frame will be chosen each night.

Creating a snapshot requires all disk activity to be briefly frozen. Requests to the database may be delayed or even fail because of a timeout, so we recommend that you choose a time frame for the snapshot that has the least effect on applications and users (e.g., late at night). Automated snapshots are your backup in case something unexpected happens to your database. This could be a query that deletes all your data accidentally or a hardware failure that causes data loss.

The following command changes the time frame for automated backups to 05:00–06:00 UTC and the retention period to three days. Use the terminal on your local machine to execute it:

```
$ aws cloudformation update-stack --stack-name wordpress --template-url \
➥ https://s3.amazonaws.com/awsinaction-code3/chapter10/\
➥ template-snapshot.yaml \
➥ --parameters ParameterKey=WordpressAdminPassword,UsePreviousValue=true \
➥ --capabilities CAPABILITY_IAM
```

The RDS database will be modified based on a slightly modified CloudFormation template, as shown in the following listing.

> **Listing 10.3   Modifying an RDS database's snapshot time frame and retention time**

```
Database:
  Type: 'AWS::RDS::DBInstance'
  DeletionPolicy: Delete
  Properties:                                   Keeps
    AllocatedStorage: 5                         snapshots for
    BackupRetentionPeriod: 3         ◁──────    three days
    PreferredBackupWindow: '05:00-06:00'   ◁──── Creates snapshots
    DBInstanceClass: 'db.t2.micro'               automatically between
    DBName: wordpress                            05:00 and 06:00 UTC
    Engine: MySQL
    MasterUsername: wordpress
    MasterUserPassword: wordpress
    VPCSecurityGroups:
    - !Sub ${DatabaseSecurityGroup.GroupId}
    DBSubnetGroupName: !Ref DBSubnetGroup
  DependsOn: VPCGatewayAttachment
```

If you want to disable automated snapshots, you need to set the retention period to 0. As usual, you can configure automated backups using CloudFormation templates, the Management Console, or SDKs. Keep in mind that automated snapshots are deleted when the RDS database instance is deleted. Manual snapshots stay. You'll learn about them next.

10.3.2   Creating snapshots manually

You can trigger manual snapshots whenever you need, for example, before you update to the latest WordPress version, migrate a schema, or perform some other activity that could damage your database. To create a snapshot, you have to know the instance identifier. The following command extracts the instance identifier from the first RDS database instance:

```
$ aws rds describe-db-instances --output text \
➥ --query "DBInstances[0].DBInstanceIdentifier"
```

The next command creates a manual snapshot called wordpress-manual-snapshot. Replace $DBInstanceIdentifier with the output of the previous command:

```
$ aws rds create-db-snapshot --db-snapshot-identifier \
➥ wordpress-manual-snapshot \
➥ --db-instance-identifier $DBInstanceIdentifier
```

In case you get a "Cannot create a snapshot because the database instance .. is not currently in the available state." error, retry after five minutes—your database is still initializing.

It will take a few minutes for the snapshot to be created. You can check the current state of the snapshot with this command:

```
$ aws rds describe-db-snapshots \
➥ --db-snapshot-identifier wordpress-manual-snapshot
```

RDS doesn't delete manual snapshots automatically; you need to delete them yourself if you don't need them any longer. You'll learn how to do this at the end of the section.

> **Copying an automated snapshot as a manual snapshot**
>
> There is a difference between automated and manual snapshots. Automated snapshots are deleted automatically after the retention period is over, but manual snapshots aren't. If you want to keep an automated snapshot even after the retention period is over, you have to copy the automated snapshot to a new manual snapshot.
>
> Get the snapshot identifier of an automated snapshot from the RDS database you started in section 10.1 by running the following command at your local terminal. Replace $DBInstanceIdentifier with the output of the describe-db-instances command:
>
> ```
> $ aws rds describe-db-snapshots --snapshot-type automated \
> ➥ --db-instance-identifier $DBInstanceIdentifier \
> ➥ --query "DBSnapshots[0].DBSnapshotIdentifier" \
> ➥ --output text
> ```
>
> The next command copies an automated snapshot to a manual snapshot named wordpress-copy-snapshot. Replace $SnapshotId with the output from the previous command:
>
> ```
> $ aws rds copy-db-snapshot \
> ➥ --source-db-snapshot-identifier $SnapshotId \
> ➥ --target-db-snapshot-identifier wordpress-copy-snapshot
> ```
>
> The copy of the automated snapshot is named wordpress-copy-snapshot. It won't be removed automatically.

10.3.3   *Restoring a database*

Imagine a scary scenario: you have accidentally deleted all of the blog posts from your WordPress site. Of course, you want to restore the data as fast as possible. Lucky for you, RDS has you covered.

If you restore a database from an automated or manual snapshot, a new database will be created based on the snapshot. As figure 10.2 shows, you can't restore a snapshot to an existing database.

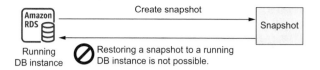

Figure 10.2 A snapshot can't be restored into an existing database.

Instead, a new database is created when you restore a database snapshot, as figure 10.3 illustrates.

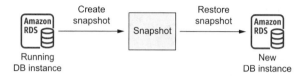

Figure 10.3 A new database is created to restore a snapshot.

To create a new database in the same VPC as the WordPress platform you started in section 10.1, you need to find out the existing database's subnet group. Execute this command to do so:

```
$ aws cloudformation describe-stack-resource \
➥ --stack-name wordpress --logical-resource-id DBSubnetGroup \
➥ --query "StackResourceDetail.PhysicalResourceId" --output text
```

You're now ready to create a new database based on the manual snapshot you created at the beginning of this section. Execute the following command, replacing $Subnet-Group with the output of the previous command:

```
$ aws rds restore-db-instance-from-db-snapshot \
➥ --db-instance-identifier awsinaction-db-restore \
➥ --db-snapshot-identifier wordpress-manual-snapshot \
➥ --db-subnet-group-name $SubnetGroup
```

You might get an "DBSnapshot must have state available but actually has creating" error if your snapshot has not been created yet. In this case, retry the command after five minutes.

A new database named awsinaction-db-restore is created based on the manual snapshot. In theory, after the database is created, you could switch the WordPress application to the new endpoint by modifying the /var/www/html/wp-config.php file on both virtual machines.

If you're using automated snapshots, you can also restore your database from a specified moment, because RDS keeps the database's change logs. This allows you to jump back to any point in time from the backup retention period to the last five minutes.

Execute the following command, replacing $DBInstanceIdentifier with the output of the earlier describe-db-instances command, $SubnetGroup with the output of the earlier `describe-stack-resource` command, and `$Time` with a UTC timestamp from five minutes ago (e.g., `2022-03-11T09:30:00Z`):

```
$ aws rds restore-db-instance-to-point-in-time \
➥ --target-db-instance-identifier awsinaction-db-restore-time \
➥ --source-db-instance-identifier $DBInstanceIdentifier \
➥ --restore-time $Time --db-subnet-group-name $SubnetGroup
```

A new database named awsinaction-db-restore-time is created based on the source database from five minutes ago. In theory, after the database is created, you could switch the WordPress application to the new endpoint by modifying the /var/www/html/wp-config.php file on both virtual machines.

10.3.4 *Copying a database to another region*

When you created the cloud infrastructure for WordPress, you assumed that most readers will come from the United States. It turns out, however, that most readers access your site from Europe. Therefore, you decide to move your cloud infrastructure to reduce latency for the majority of your readers.

Copying a database to another region is possible with the help of snapshots as well. The main reasons you might do so follow:

- *Disaster recovery*—You can recover from an unlikely region-wide outage.
- *Relocating*—You can move your infrastructure to another region so you can serve your customers with lower latency.

The second command copies the snapshot named `wordpress-manual-snapshot` from the region `us-east-1` to the region `eu-west-1`. You need to replace `$SourceSnapshot-Arn` with the Amazon Resource Name (ARN) of the snapshot. Use the following command to get the ARN of your manual snapshot:

```
$ aws rds describe-db-snapshots \
➥ --db-snapshot-identifier wordpress-manual-snapshot \
➥ --query "DBSnapshots[0].DBSnapshotArn" --output text
```

> **COMPLIANCE** Moving data from one region to another may violate privacy laws or compliance rules. Make sure you're allowed to copy the data to another region if you're working with real data.

```
$ aws rds copy-db-snapshot \
➥ --source-db-snapshot-identifier $SourceSnapshotArn \
➥ --target-db-snapshot-identifier wordpress-manual-snapshot \
➥ --region eu-west-1
```

After the snapshot has been copied to the region `eu-west-1`, you can restore a database from it as described in the previous section.

10.3.5 Calculating the cost of snapshots

Snapshots are billed based on the storage they use. You can store snapshots up to the size of your database instance for free. In our WordPress example, you can store up to 5 GB of snapshots for free. On top of that, you pay per GB per month of used storage. As we're writing this book, the cost is $0.095 for each GB every month.

Cleaning up

It's time to clean up the snapshots and delete the restored database instances. Execute the following commands step by step, or jump to the shortcuts for Linux and macOS after the listing:

```
$ aws rds delete-db-instance --db-instance-identifier \
⇨ awsinaction-db-restore --skip-final-snapshot          ◄
$ aws rds delete-db-instance --db-instance-identifier \
⇨ awsinaction-db-restore-time --skip-final-snapshot     ◄
$ aws rds delete-db-snapshot --db-snapshot-identifier \
⇨ wordpress-manual-snapshot                             ◄
$ aws rds delete-db-snapshot --db-snapshot-identifier \
⇨ wordpress-copy-snapshot                               ◄
$ aws --region eu-west-1 rds delete-db-snapshot --db-snapshot-identifier \
⇨ wordpress-manual-snapshot          ◄
```

Deletes the database with data from the snapshot restore

Deletes the database with data from the point-in-time restore

Deletes the manual snapshot

Deletes the copied snapshot

Deletes the snapshot copied to another region

You can avoid typing these commands manually at your terminal by using the following command to download a bash script and execute it directly on your local machine. The bash script contains the same steps as shown in the previous snippet:

```
$ curl -s https://raw.githubusercontent.com/AWSinAction/\
⇨ code3/main/chapter10/cleanup.sh | bash -ex
```

Keep the rest of the setup, because you'll use it in the following sections.

10.4 Controlling access to a database

Every day, you can read about WordPress sites that got hacked. One essential aspect of protecting your WordPress site is controlling access to your cloud infrastructure and database.

The shared-responsibility model applies to the RDS service as well as to AWS services in general. AWS is responsible for the security of the cloud in this case—for example, for the security of the underlying OS. You, the customer, need to specify the rules controlling access to your data and RDS database.

Figure 10.4 shows the following three layers that control access to an RDS database:

- Controlling access to the configuration of the RDS database
- Controlling network access to the RDS database
- Controlling data access with the database's own user and access management features

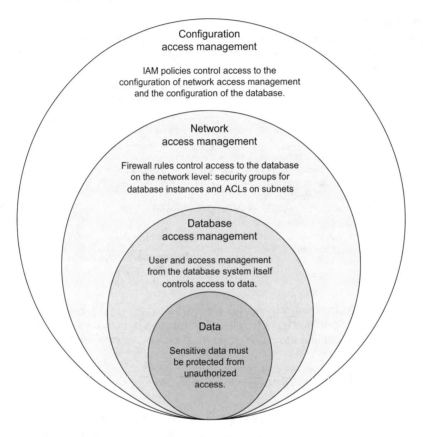

Figure 10.4   Your data is protected by the database itself, security groups, and IAM.

10.4.1   *Controlling access to the configuration of an RDS database*

Access to the RDS service is controlled using the IAM service. IAM is responsible for controlling access to actions like creating, updating, and deleting an RDS database instance. IAM doesn't manage access inside the database; that's the job of the database engine. IAM policies define which configuration and management actions an identity is allowed to execute on RDS. You attach these policies to IAM users, groups, or roles to control what actions they can perform on the database.

The following listing shows an IAM policy that allows access to all RDS configuration and management actions. You could use this policy to limit access by attaching it only to trusted IAM users and groups.

Listing 10.4 Allowing access to all RDS service configuration and management actions

```
{
  "Version": "2012-10-17",        Allows the specified
  "Statement": [{                 actions on the specified
    "Effect": "Allow",      ◁──   resources
    "Action": "rds:*",      ◁──┐
    "Resource": "*"    ◁──┐     All possible actions on
  }]                          │  RDS service are specified
}            All RDS databases   (e.g., changes to the
             are specified.      database configuration).
```

Only people and machines that really need to make changes to RDS databases should be allowed to do so. The following listing shows an IAM policy that denies all destructive actions to prevent data loss by human failure.

Listing 10.5 IAM policy denying destructive actions

```
{                                     Allows access ...
  "Version": "2012-10-17",
  "Statement": [{                     ... to all actions
    "Effect": "Allow",       ◁──┘     related to RDS ...
    "Action": "rds:*",       ◁──
    "Resource": "*"          ◁──      ... and all resources.
  }, {
    "Effect": "Deny",           ◁──   But, denies access ...
    "Action": ["rds:Delete*", "rds:Remove*"],   ◁──
    "Resource": "*"      ◁──                   ... to all destructive actions
  }]                          ... for all      on the RDS service (e.g.,
}                             resources.       delete database instance) ...
```

As discussed in chapter 5, when introducing IAM, a `Deny` statement overrides any `Allow` statement. Therefore, a user or role with the IAM policy attached does have limited access to RDS, because all actions are allowed except the ones that are destructive.

10.4.2 Controlling network access to an RDS database

An RDS database is linked to security groups. Each security group consists of rules for a firewall controlling inbound and outbound database traffic. You already know about using security groups in combination with virtual machines.

The next listing shows the configuration of the security group attached to the RDS database in our WordPress example. Inbound connections to port 3306 (the default port for MySQL) are allowed only from virtual machines linked to the security group called `WebServerSecurityGroup`.

Listing 10.6   CloudFormation template extract: Firewall rules for an RDS database

```
DatabaseSecurityGroup:                    ◁────────┐      The security group for the database
  Type: 'AWS::EC2::SecurityGroup'                  │      instance, allowing incoming traffic on
  Properties:                                              the MySQL default port for web servers
    GroupDescription: 'awsinaction-db-sg'
    VpcId: !Ref VPC                      ┌ The default
    SecurityGroupIngress:                │ MySQL port
    - IpProtocol: tcp                    │ is 3306.                          References the
      FromPort: 3306         ◁───────────┘                                   security group
      ToPort: 3306                                                           for web servers
      SourceSecurityGroupId: !Ref WebServerSecurityGroup   ◁───┘
```

Only machines that really need to connect to the RDS database should be allowed to do so on the network level, such as EC2 instances running your web server or application server. See chapter 5 if you're interested in more details about security groups (firewall rules).

10.4.3 Controlling data access

A database engine also implements access control itself. User management of the database engine has nothing to do with IAM users and access rights; it's only responsible for controlling access to the database. For example, you typically define a user for each application and grant rights to access and manipulate tables as needed. In the WordPress example, a database user called wordpress is created. The WordPress application authenticates itself to the database engine (MySQL, in this case) with this database user and a password.

IAM database authentication

AWS provides an IAM database authentication mechanism for MariaDB, MySQL, and PostgreSQL. With IAM database authentication, you no longer need to create users with a username and password in the database engine. Instead, you create a database user that uses a plug-in called AWSAuthenticationPlugin for authentication. You then log in to the database with the username and a token that is generated with your IAM identity. The token is valid for 15 minutes, so you have to renew it from time to time. You can learn more about IAM database authentication in the AWS documentation at http://mng.bz/z57r.

Typical use cases follow:

- Limiting write access to a few database users (e.g., only for an application)
- Limiting access to specific tables to a few users (e.g., to one department in the organization)
- Limiting access to tables to isolate different applications (e.g., hosting multiple applications for different customers on the same database)

User and access management varies between database systems. We don't cover this topic in this book; refer to your database system's documentation for details.

10.5 *Building on a highly available database*

The availability of our blog cloudonaut.io is key to our business success. That's the case for your WordPress site as well. Therefore, you should avoid downtimes when possible. This chapter is about increasing the availability of your database.

The database is typically the most important part of a system. Applications won't work if they can't connect to the database, and the data stored in the database is mission critical, so the database must be highly available and store data durably.

Amazon RDS lets you launch highly available (HA) databases. Compared to a default database consisting of a single database instance, an HA RDS database consists of two database instances: a primary and a standby database instance. You will be paying for both instances. All clients send requests to the primary database. Data is replicated between the primary and the standby database synchronously, as shown in figure 10.5.

We strongly recommend using high-availability deployment for all databases that handle production workloads. If you want to save money, you can choose not to deploy a highly available database for your test systems.

If the primary database becomes unavailable due to hardware or network failures, RDS starts the failover process. The standby database then becomes the primary database. As figure 10.6 shows, the DNS name is updated and clients begin to use the former standby database for their requests.

RDS detects the need for a failover automatically and executes it without human intervention.

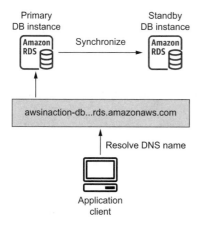

Figure 10.5   The primary database is replicated to the standby database when running in high-availability mode.

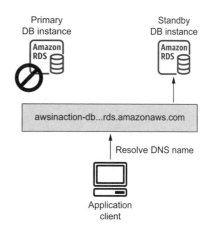

Figure 10.6   The client fails over to the standby database if the primary database fails, using DNS resolution.

Aurora is different

Aurora is an exception to the way that highly available databases operate in AWS. It does not store your data on a single EBS volume. Instead, Aurora stores data on a cluster volume. A cluster volume consists of multiple disks, with each disk having a copy of the cluster data. This implies that the storage layer of Aurora is not a single point of failure. But still, only the primary Aurora database instance accepts write requests. If the primary goes down, it is automatically re-created, which typically takes less than 10 minutes. If you have replica instances in your Aurora cluster, a replica is promoted to be the new primary instance, which usually takes around one minute and is much faster than primary re-creation.

Multi-AZ with two standby instances

AWS introduced a new option for multi-AZ deployments of RDS databases: Multi-AZ with two standby instances. The advantages compared to the single standby instance that we discussed follow:

1   Both standby instances can be used as read replicas to increase capacity for read-only queries. You will learn more about read replicas later.
2   Lower latency and jitter for transaction commits, which improves the write performance.
3   Faster failover in less than 60 seconds.

Right now, this option is available only for PostgreSQL and MySQL engines. Check out https://aws.amazon.com/rds/features/multi-az/ to learn more.

10.5.1   *Enabling high-availability deployment for an RDS database*

WARNING   Starting a highly available RDS database will incur charges, about USD $0.017000 per hour. See https://aws.amazon.com/rds/pricing/ if you want to find out the current hourly price.

Execute the following command at your local terminal to enable high-availability deployment for the RDS database you started in section 10.1:

```
$ aws cloudformation update-stack --stack-name wordpress --template-url \
➥ https://s3.amazonaws.com/awsinaction-code3/\
➥ chapter10/template-multiaz.yaml \
➥ --parameters ParameterKey=WordpressAdminPassword,UsePreviousValue=true \
➥ --capabilities CAPABILITY_IAM
```

The RDS database is updated based on a slightly modified CloudFormation template as shown in the next listing.

Listing 10.7   Modifying the RDS database by enabling high availability

```
Database:
  Type: 'AWS::RDS::DBInstance'
  DeletionPolicy: Delete
  Properties:
    AllocatedStorage: 5
    BackupRetentionPeriod: 3
    PreferredBackupWindow: '05:00-06:00'
    DBInstanceClass: 'db.t2.micro'
    DBName: wordpress
    Engine: MySQL
    MasterUsername: wordpress
    MasterUserPassword: wordpress
    VPCSecurityGroups:
    - !Sub ${DatabaseSecurityGroup.GroupId}
    DBSubnetGroupName: !Ref DBSubnetGroup
    MultiAZ: true
  DependsOn: VPCGatewayAttachment
```

Enables high-availability deployment for the RDS database

It will take several minutes for the database to be deployed in HA mode. There is nothing more you need to do—the database is now highly available.

> **What is Multi-AZ?**
> Each AWS region is split into multiple independent data centers, which are also called availability zones. We introduced the concept of availability zones in chapters 4 and 5, but skipped one aspect of HA deployment that is used only for RDS: the primary and standby databases are launched into two different availability zones. AWS calls the high-availability deployment of RDS Multi-AZ deployment for this reason.

In addition to the fact that a high-availability deployment increases your database's reliability, it offers another important advantage: reconfiguring or maintaining a single-mode database causes short downtimes. High-availability deployment of an RDS database solves this problem because AWS switches to the standby database during maintenance.

10.6 Tweaking database performance

When search engines decide in which order to present the search results, the loading speed of a website is an important factor. Therefore, it is important to optimize the performance of your WordPress site. You will learn how to make sure the MySQL database is not slowing down your website in this section.

The easiest way to scale a RDS database, or an SQL database in general, is to scale *vertically*. Scaling a database vertically means increasing the following resources of your database instance:

- Faster CPU
- More memory
- Faster storage

Keep in mind that you can't scale vertically (which means increasing resources) without limits. One of the largest RDS database instance types comes with 32 cores and 244 GiB memory. In comparison, an object store like S3 or a NoSQL database like DynamoDB can be scaled horizontally without limits, because they add more machines to the cluster if additional resources are needed.

10.6.1 Increasing database resources

When you start an RDS database, you choose an instance type. The instance type defines the computing power and memory of your virtual machine (such as when you start an EC2 instance). Choosing a bigger instance type increases computing power and memory for RDS databases.

You started an RDS database with instance type db.t2.micro, the smallest available instance type. You can change the instance type using a CloudFormation template, the CLI, the Management Console, or AWS SDKs. You may want to increase the instance type if performance is inadequate. You will learn how to measure performance in section 10.7. Listing 10.8 shows how to change the CloudFormation template to increase the instance type from db.t2.micro with one virtual core and 615 MB memory to db.m3.large with two faster virtual cores and 7.5 GB memory. You'll do this only in theory. Don't do this to your running database because it is not covered by the Free Tier and will incur charges. Keep in mind that modifying the instance type causes a short downtime.

> **Listing 10.8 Modifying the instance type to improve performance of an RDS database**

```
Database:
  Type: 'AWS::RDS::DBInstance'
  DeletionPolicy: Delete
  Properties:
    AllocatedStorage: 5
    BackupRetentionPeriod: 3
    PreferredBackupWindow: '05:00-06:00'
    DBInstanceClass: 'db.m3.large'        ◁─┐  Increases the size of the
    DBName: wordpress                         underlying virtual machine
    Engine: MySQL                             for the database instance from
    MasterUsername: wordpress                 db.t2.micro to db.m3.large
    MasterUserPassword: wordpress
    VPCSecurityGroups:
    - !Sub ${DatabaseSecurityGroup.GroupId}
    DBSubnetGroupName: !Ref DBSubnetGroup
    MultiAZ: true
  DependsOn: VPCGatewayAttachment
```

Because a database has to read and write data to a disk, I/O performance is important for the database's overall performance. RDS offers the following three different types of storage, as you already know from reading about the block storage service EBS:

- General purpose (SSD)
- Provisioned IOPS (SSD)
- Magnetic

You should choose general-purpose (SSD) or even provisioned IOPS (SSD) storage for production workloads. The options are exactly the same as when using EBS for virtual machines. If you need to guarantee a high level of read or write throughput, you should use provisioned IOPS (SSD). The general-purpose (SSD) option offers moderate baseline performance with the ability to burst. The throughput for general purpose (SSD) depends on the amount of initialized storage size. Magnetic storage is an option if you need to store data at a low cost, or if you don't need to access it in a predictable, performant way. The next listing shows how to enable general-purpose (SSD) storage using a CloudFormation template.

Listing 10.9   Modifying the storage type to improve performance of an RDS database

```
Database:
  Type: 'AWS::RDS::DBInstance'
  DeletionPolicy: Delete
  Properties:
    AllocatedStorage: 5
    BackupRetentionPeriod: 3
    PreferredBackupWindow: '05:00-06:00'
    DBInstanceClass: 'db.m3.large'
    DBName: wordpress
    Engine: MySQL
    MasterUsername: wordpress
    MasterUserPassword: wordpress
    VPCSecurityGroups:
    - !Sub ${DatabaseSecurityGroup.GroupId}
    DBSubnetGroupName: !Ref DBSubnetGroup
    MultiAZ: true
    StorageType: 'gp2'          ⟵
  DependsOn: VPCGatewayAttachment
```

Uses general-purpose (SSD) storage to increase I/O performance

10.6.2 Using read replication to increase read performance

A database suffering from too many read requests can be scaled horizontally by adding additional database instances for read traffic and enabling replication from the primary (writable) copy of the database instance. As figure 10.7 shows, changes to the database are asynchronously replicated to an additional read-only database instance. The read requests can be distributed between the primary database and its read-replication databases to increase read throughput. Be aware that you need to implement the distinction between read and write requests on the application level.

Tweaking read performance with replication makes sense only if the application generates many read requests and few write requests. Fortunately, most applications read more than they write.

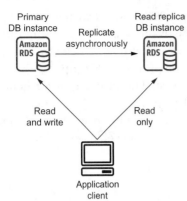

Figure 10.7   **Read requests are distributed between the primary and read-replication databases for higher read performance.**

CREATING A READ-REPLICATION DATABASE

Amazon RDS supports read replication for MySQL, MariaDB, PostgreSQL, Oracle, and SQL Server databases. To use read replication, you need to enable automatic backups for your database, as shown in section 10.3.

> **WARNING**   Starting an RDS read replica will incur charges. See https://aws .amazon.com/rds/pricing/ if you want to find out the current hourly price.

Execute the following command from your local machine to create a read-replication database for the WordPress database you started in section 10.1. Replace the `$DBInstanceIdentifier` with the value from `aws rds describe-db-instances --query "DBInstances[0].DBInstanceIdentifier" --output` text:

```
$ aws rds create-db-instance-read-replica \
  --db-instance-identifier awsinaction-db-read \
  --source-db-instance-identifier $DBInstanceIdentifier
```

RDS automatically triggers the following steps in the background:

1 Creating a snapshot from the source database, also called the primary database instance
2 Launching a new database based on that snapshot
3 Activating replication between the primary and read-replication database instances
4 Creating an endpoint for SQL read requests to the read-replication database instances

After the read-replication database is successfully created, it's available to answer SQL read requests. The application using the SQL database must support the use of read-replication databases. WordPress, for example, doesn't support read replicas by default, but you can use a plug-in called HyperDB to do so; the configuration is tricky, so we'll skip this part. You can get more information here: https://wordpress.org/plugins/hyperdb/.

Creating or deleting a read replica doesn't affect the availability of the primary (writable) database instance.

> **Using read replication to transfer data to another region**
>
> RDS supports read replication between regions for Aurora, MariaDB, MySQL, Oracle, and PostgreSQL databases. You can replicate your data from the data centers in North Virginia to the data centers in Ireland, for example. Three major use cases for this feature follow:
>
> - Backing up data to another region for the unlikely event of an outage covering a complete region
> - Transferring data to another region to be able to answer read requests with lower latency
> - Migrating a database to another region
>
> Creating read replication between two regions incurs an additional cost because you have to pay for the transferred data.

PROMOTING A READ REPLICA TO A STANDALONE DATABASE

Imagine your WordPress site became really popular. On the one hand, that's a great success. On the other hand, you are struggling with handling all that load with your cloud infrastructure. You are thinking about adding read replicas to your database to decrease the load on the primary database.

If you create a read-replication database to migrate a database from one region to another, or if you have to perform heavy and load-intensive tasks on your database, such as adding an index, it's helpful to switch your workload from the primary database to a read-replication database. The read replica must become the new primary database.

The following command promotes the read-replica database you created in this section to a standalone primary database. Note that the read-replication database will perform a restart and be unavailable for a few minutes:

```
$ aws rds promote-read-replica --db-instance-identifier awsinaction-db-read
```

The RDS database instance named awsinaction-db-read will accept write requests after the transformation is successful.

> **Cleaning up**
>
> It's time to clean up, to avoid unwanted expense. Execute the following command:
>
> ```
> $ aws rds delete-db-instance --db-instance-identifier \
>   awsinaction-db-read --skip-final-snapshot
> ```

You've gained experience with the AWS relational database service in this chapter. We'll end the chapter by taking a closer look at the monitoring capabilities of RDS.

10.7 Monitoring a database

To avoid downtime of your WordPress site, it is imperative that you monitor all important parts of your cloud infrastructure. The database is definitely one of the key components. That's why you will learn about RDS monitoring in this section.

RDS is a managed service. Nevertheless, you need to monitor some metrics yourself to make sure your database can respond to all requests from applications. RDS publishes several metrics for free to AWS CloudWatch, a monitoring service for the AWS cloud. You can watch these metrics through the Management Console, as shown in figure 10.8, and define alarms for when a metric reaches a threshold.

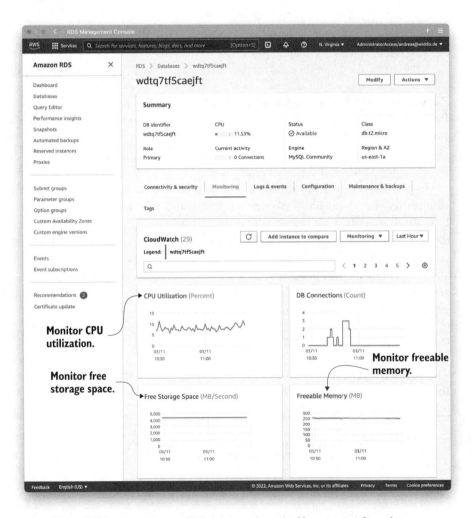

Figure 10.8   Metrics to monitor an RDS database from the Management Console

Table 10.4 shows the most important metrics; we recommend that you monitor them by creating alarms.

Table 10.4 Important metrics for RDS databases from CloudWatch

Name	Description
FreeStorageSpace	Available storage in bytes. Make sure you don't run out of storage space. We recommend setting the alarm threshold to < 2147483648 (2 GB).
CPUUtilization	The usage of the CPU as a percentage. High utilization can be an indicator of a bottleneck due to insufficient CPU performance. We recommend setting the alarm threshold to > 80%.
FreeableMemory	Free memory in bytes. Running out of memory can cause performance problems. We recommend setting the alarm threshold to < 67108864 (64 MB).
DiskQueueDepth	Number of outstanding requests to the disk. A long queue indicates that the database has reached the storage's maximum I/O performance. We recommend setting the alarm threshold to > 64.
SwapUsage	If the database has insufficient memory, the OS starts to use the disk as memory (this is called swapping). Using the disk as memory is slow and will cause performance problems. We recommend setting the alarm threshold to > 268435456 (256 MB).

We recommend that you monitor these metrics in particular, to make sure your database isn't the cause of application performance problems.

Cleaning up

It's time to clean up to avoid unwanted expense. Execute the following command to delete all resources corresponding to the WordPress blogging platform based on an RDS database:

```
$ aws cloudformation delete-stack --stack-name wordpress
```

In this chapter, you've learned how to use the RDS service to manage relational databases for your applications. The next chapter will focus on in-memory caches.

Summary

- RDS is a managed service that provides relational databases.
- You can choose between PostgreSQL, MySQL, MariaDB, Oracle Database, and Microsoft SQL Server databases. Aurora is the database engine built by Amazon.
- The fastest way to import data into an RDS database is to copy it to a virtual machine in the same region and load it into the RDS database from there.
- RDS comes with built-in backup and restore functionality allowing you to create and restore snapshots on demand as well as to restore a database to a certain point in time.

- You can control access to data with a combination of IAM policies and firewall rules and on the database level.
- You can restore an RDS database to any time in the retention period (a maximum of 35 days).
- RDS databases can be highly available. You should launch RDS databases in Multi-AZ mode for production workloads.
- Read replication can improve the performance of read-intensive workloads on an SQL database.
- CloudWatch metrics allow you to monitor your database, for example, to debug performance problems or decide when to increase or decrease the size of your database instance.

Caching data in memory: Amazon ElastiCache and MemoryDB

11

This chapter covers

- The benefits of a having a caching layer between your application and data store
- Defining key terminology, such as cache cluster, node, shard, replication group, and node group
- Using/operating an in-memory key-value store
- Performance tweaking and monitoring ElastiCache clusters

Imagine a relational database being used for a popular mobile game where players' scores and ranks are updated and read frequently. The read and write pressure to the database will be extremely high, especially when ranking scores across millions of players. Mitigating that pressure by scaling the database may help with load but not necessarily the latency or cost. Also, caching relational databases tends to be more expensive than caching data stores.

A proven solution used by many gaming companies is leveraging an in-memory data store such as Redis for both caching and ranking player and game metadata. Instead of reading and sorting the leaderboard directly from the relational database, they store an in-memory game leaderboard in Redis, commonly using a sorted set, which will sort the data automatically when it's inserted, based on the score parameter. The score value may consist of the actual player ranking or player score in the game.

Because the data resides in memory and does not require heavy computation to sort, retrieving the information is incredibly fast, leaving little reason to query directly from the relational database. In addition, any other game and player metadata, such as player profile, game-level information, and so on, that requires heavy reads can also be cached using this in-memory layer, thus alleviating heavy read traffic to and from the database.

In this solution, both the relational database and in-memory layer will store updates to the leaderboard: one will serve as the primary database and the other as the working and fast processing layer. When implementing a caching layer, you can employ a variety of caching techniques to keep the data that's cached fresh, which we'll review later. Figure 11.1 shows that the cache sits between your application and the database.

A cache comes with the following benefits:

Figure 11.1 The cache sits between the application and the database.

- Serving read traffic from the caching layer frees resources on your primary data store, for example, for write requests.
- It speeds up your application because the caching layer responds more quickly than your data store.
- It allows you to downsize your data store, which is typically more expensive than the caching layer.

Most caching layers reside in memory, which is why they are so fast. The downside is that you can lose the cached data at any time because of a hardware defect or a restart. Always keep a copy of your data in a primary data store with disk durability, like the relational database in the mobile game example. Alternatively, Redis has optional failover support. In the event of a node failure, a replica node will be elected to be the new primary and will already have a copy of the data. On top of that, some in-memory databases also support writing data to persistent storage to be able to restore the data after a reboot or outage.

In this chapter, you will learn how to implement an in-memory caching layer to improve the performance of a web application. You will deploy a complex web application called Discourse, a modern forum software application that uses Redis for caching. You will also learn how to scale a cache cluster and how to monitor and tweak performance.

Depending on your caching strategy, you can either populate the cache in real time or on demand. In the mobile game example, on demand means that if the leaderboard is not in the cache, the application asks the relational database and puts the result into the cache. Any subsequent request to the cache will result in a cache hit, meaning the data is found in the cache. This will be true until the duration of the TTL (time-to-live) value on the cached value expires. This strategy is called *lazy-loading* data from the primary data store. Additionally, we could have a job running in the background that queries the leaderboard from the relational database every minute and puts the result in the cache to populate the cache in advance.

The lazy-loading strategy (getting data on demand) is implemented like this:

1 The application writes data to the data store.
2 If the application wants to read the data, at a later time it makes a request to the caching layer.
3 If the caching layer does not contain the data, the application reads from the data store directly and puts the value into the cache, and also returns the value to the client.
4 Later, if the application wants to read the data again, it makes a request to the caching layer and finds the value.

This strategy comes with a problem. What if the data is changed while it is in the cache? The cache will still contain the old value. That's why setting an appropriate TTL value is critical to ensure cache validity. Let's say you apply a TTL of five minutes to your cached data: this means you accept that the data could be out of sync by up to five minutes with your primary database. Understanding the frequency of change for the underlying data and the effects out-of-sync data will have on the user experience is the first step of identifying the appropriate TTL value to apply. A common mistake some developers make is assuming that a few seconds of a cache TTL means that having a cache is not worthwhile. Remember that within those few seconds, millions of requests can be offloaded from your data store, speeding up your application and reducing database pressure. Performance testing your application with and without your cache, along with various caching approaches, will help fine-tune your implementation. In summary, the shorter the TTL, the higher the load on the underlying data store. The higher the TTL, the more out of sync the data gets.

The write-through strategy (caching data up front) is implemented differently to tackle the synchronization problem, as shown here:

1 The application writes data to the data store and the cache (or the cache is filled asynchronously, for example, by a background job, an AWS Lambda function, or the application).
2 If the application wants to read the data at a later time, it makes a request to the caching layer, which always contains the latest data.
3 The value is returned to the client.

This strategy also comes with a problem. What if the cache is not big enough to contain all your data? Caches are in memory, and your data store's disk capacity is usually larger than your cache's memory capacity. When your cache exceeds the available memory, it will evict data or stop accepting new data. In both situations, the application stops working. A global leaderboard will most likely fit into the cache. Imagine that a leaderboard is 4 KB in size and the cache has a capacity of 1 GB (1,048,576 KB). But what about introducing leaderboards per team? You can only store 262,144 (1,048,576/4) leaderboards, so if you have more teams than that, you will run into a capacity issue. Figure 11.2 compares the two caching strategies.

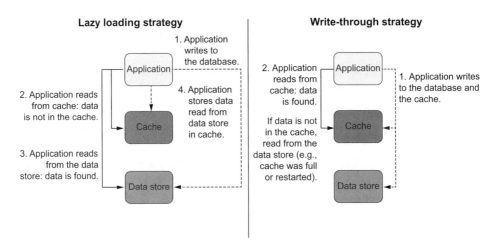

Figure 11.2   Comparing the lazy-loading and write-through caching strategies

When evicting data, the cache needs to decide which data it should delete. One popular strategy is to evict the least recently used (LRU) data. This means that cached data must contain meta information about the time when it was last accessed. In case of an LRU eviction, the data with the oldest timestamp is chosen for eviction.

Caches are usually implemented using key-value stores. Key-value stores don't support sophisticated query languages such as SQL. They support retrieving data based on a key, usually a string, or specialized commands, for example, to extract sorted data efficiently.

Imagine that in your relational database is a player table for your mobile game. One of the most common queries is SELECT id, nickname FROM player ORDER BY score DESC LIMIT 10 to retrieve the top 10 players. Luckily, the game is very popular, but this comes with a technical challenge. If many players look at the leaderboard, the database becomes very busy, which causes high latency or even timeouts. You have to come up with a plan to reduce the load on the database. As you have already learned, caching can help. What technique should you employ for caching? You have a few options.

One approach you can take with Redis is to store the result of your SQL query as a string value and the SQL statement as your key name. Instead of using the whole SQL query as the key, you can hash the string with a hash function like md5 or sha256 to optimize storage and bandwidth, shown in figure 11.3. Before the application sends the query to the database, it takes the SQL query as the key to ask the caching layer for data—step 2. If the cache does not contain data for the key (step 3), the SQL query is sent to the relational database (step 4). The result (step 5) is then stored in the cache using the SQL query as the key (step 6). The next time the application wants to perform the query, it asks the caching layer (step 7), which now contains the cached table (step 8).

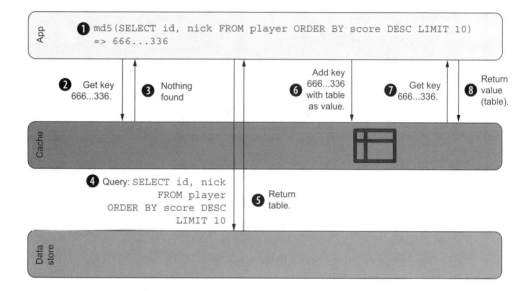

Figure 11.3   SQL caching layer implementation

To implement caching, you only need to know the key of the cached item. This can be an SQL query, a filename, a URL, or a user ID. You take the key and ask the cache for a result. If no result is found, you make a second call to the underlying data store, which knows the truth.

With Redis, you also have the option of storing the data in other data structures such as a sorted set. If the data is stored in a sorted set, retrieving the ranked data will be very efficient. You could simply store players and their scores and sort by the score. An equivalent SQL command would be as follows:

```
ZREVRANGE "player-scores" 0 9
```

This would return the 10 players in a sorted set named "player-scores," ordered from highest to lowest.

The two most popular implementations of in-memory key-value stores are Memcached and Redis. Table 11.1 compares their features.

Table 11.1   **Comparing Memcached and Redis features**

	Memcached	**Redis**
Data types	Simple	Complex
Data manipulation commands	12	125
Server-side scripting	No	Yes (Lua)
Transactions	No	Yes

Examples are 100% covered by the Free Tier

The examples in this chapter are completely covered by the Free Tier. As long as you don't run the examples longer than a few days, you won't pay anything. Keep in mind that this applies only if you created a fresh AWS account for this book and nothing else is going on in your AWS account. Try to complete the chapter within a few days; you'll clean up your account at the end of the sections.

Amazon ElastiCache offers Memcached and Redis clusters as a service. Therefore, AWS covers the following aspects for you:

- *Installation*—AWS installs the software for you and has enhanced the underlying engines.
- *Administration*—AWS administers Memcached/Redis for you and provides ways to configure your cluster through parameter groups. AWS also detects and automates failovers (Redis only).
- *Monitoring*—AWS publishes metrics to CloudWatch for you.
- *Patching*—AWS performs security upgrades in a customizable time window.
- *Backups*—AWS optionally backs up your data in a customizable time window (Redis only).
- *Replication*—AWS optionally sets up replication (Redis only).

Next, you will learn how to create an in-memory cluster with ElastiCache that you will later use as an in-memory cache for a gaming backend.

11.1   *Creating a cache cluster*

In this chapter, we focus on the Redis engine because it's more flexible. You can choose which engine to use based on the features that we compared in the previous section. If there are significant differences to Memcached, we will highlight them.

11.1.1   *Minimal CloudFormation template*

Imagine you are developing an online game. To do so, you need to store sessions that keep the current game state of each user, as well as a highscore list. Latency is important to ensure the gamers enjoy a great gaming experience. To be able to read and write data with very little latency, you decide to use the in-memory database Redis.

First, you need to create an ElastiCache cluster using the Management Console, the CLI, or CloudFormation. You will use CloudFormation in this chapter to manage your cluster. The resource type of an ElastiCache cluster is `AWS::ElastiCache::Cache-Cluster`. The required properties follow:

- `Engine`—Either `redis` or `memcached`
- `CacheNodeType`—Similar to the EC2 instance type, for example, `cache.t2.micro`
- `NumCacheNodes`—1 for a single-node cluster
- `CacheSubnetGroupName`—Reference subnets of a VPC using a dedicated resource called a subnet group
- `VpcSecurityGroupIds`—The security groups you want to attach to the cluster

A minimal CloudFormation template is shown in the next listing. The first part of the template contains the ElastiCache cluster.

Listing 11.1   Minimal CloudFormation template of an ElastiCache Redis single-node cluster

```
---
AWSTemplateFormatVersion: '2010-09-09'
Description: 'AWS in Action: chapter 11 (minimal)'
Parameters:                               Defines VPC
  VPC:                                     and subnets as
    Type: 'AWS::EC2::VPC::Id'             parameters
  SubnetA:
    Type: 'AWS::EC2::Subnet::Id'
  SubnetB:
    Type: 'AWS::EC2::Subnet::Id'          The security group to manage
Resources:                                which traffic is allowed to
  CacheSecurityGroup:                      enter/leave the cluster
    Type: 'AWS::EC2::SecurityGroup'
    Properties:                            Redis listens on port 6379. This allows
      GroupDescription: cache              access from all IP addresses, but because
      VpcId: !Ref VPC                      the cluster has only private IP addresses,
      SecurityGroupIngress:                access is possible only from inside the VPC.
      - IpProtocol: tcp                    You will improve this in section 11.3.
        FromPort: 6379
        ToPort: 6379
        CidrIp: '0.0.0.0/0'               Subnets are defined within a
  CacheSubnetGroup:                        subnet group (same approach
    Type: 'AWS::ElastiCache::SubnetGroup'  is used in RDS).
    Properties:
      Description: cache                   List of subnets that
      SubnetIds:                           can be used by the
      - Ref: SubnetA                       cluster
      - Ref: SubnetB
  Cache:                                   The resource to define
    Type: 'AWS::ElastiCache::CacheCluster' the Redis cluster
```

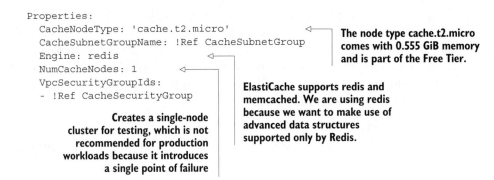

```
Properties:
  CacheNodeType: 'cache.t2.micro'
  CacheSubnetGroupName: !Ref CacheSubnetGroup
  Engine: redis
  NumCacheNodes: 1
  VpcSecurityGroupIds:
  - !Ref CacheSecurityGroup
```

The node type cache.t2.micro comes with 0.555 GiB memory and is part of the Free Tier.

ElastiCache supports redis and memcached. We are using redis because we want to make use of advanced data structures supported only by Redis.

Creates a single-node cluster for testing, which is not recommended for production workloads because it introduces a single point of failure

As mentioned already, ElastiCache nodes in a cluster use only private IP addresses. Therefore, you can't connect to a node directly over the internet. The same is true for other resources as RDS database instances. Therefore, create an EC2 instance in the same VPC as the cluster for testing. From the EC2 instance, you can then connect to the private IP address of the cluster.

11.1.2 Test the Redis cluster

To be able to access the ElastiCache cluster, you'll need a virtual machine. The following snippet shows the required resources:

```
Resources:
  # [...]
  InstanceSecurityGroup:
    Type: 'AWS::EC2::SecurityGroup'
    Properties:
      GroupDescription: 'vm'
      VpcId: !Ref VPC
  Instance:
    Type: 'AWS::EC2::Instance'
    Properties:
      ImageId: !FindInMap [RegionMap, !Ref 'AWS::Region', AMI]
      InstanceType: 't2.micro'
      IamInstanceProfile: !Ref InstanceProfile
      NetworkInterfaces:
      - AssociatePublicIpAddress: true
        DeleteOnTermination: true
        DeviceIndex: 0
        GroupSet:
        - !Ref InstanceSecurityGroup
        SubnetId: !Ref SubnetA
Outputs:
  InstanceId:
    Value: !Ref Instance
    Description: 'EC2 Instance ID (connect via Session Manager)'
  CacheAddress:
    Value: !GetAtt 'Cache.RedisEndpoint.Address'
    Description: 'Redis DNS name (resolves to a private IP address)'
```

The security group does allow outbound traffic only.

The virtual machine used to connect to your Redis cluster

The ID of the instance used to connect via the Session Manager

The DNS name of Redis cluster node (resolves to a private IP address)

Next, create a stack based on the template to create all the resources in your AWS account using the Management Console: http://mng.bz/09jm. You have to fill in the next three parameters when creating the stack:

- SubnetA—You should have at least two options here; select the first one.
- SubnetB—You should have at least two options here; select the second one.
- VPC—You should have only one possible VPC here—your default VPC. Select it.

Want to have a deeper look into the CloudFormation template?

> ### Where is the template located?
> You can find the template on GitHub. Download a snapshot of the repository at https://github.com/AWSinAction/code3/archive/main.zip. The file we're talking about is located at chapter11/redis-minimal.yaml. On S3, the same file is located at http://mng.bz/9Vra.

The following example guides you through storing a gamer's session, as well as populating and reading a highscore list:

1. Wait until the CloudFormation stack reaches status CREATE_COMPLETE.
2. Select the stack and open the Outputs tab. Copy the EC2 instance ID and cache address.
3. Use the Session Manager to connect to the EC2 instance, and use the Redis CLI to interact with the Redis cluster node as described in the following listing.
4. Execute the following commands. Don't forget to replace $CacheAddress with the value from the CloudFormation outputs:

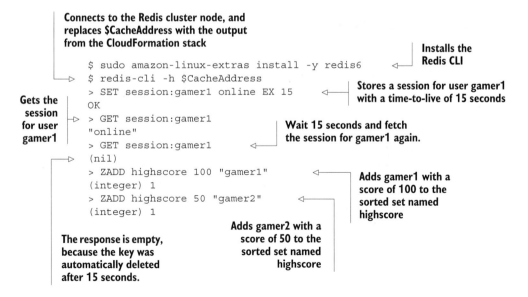

Connects to the Redis cluster node, and replaces $CacheAddress with the output from the CloudFormation stack

Installs the Redis CLI

```
$ sudo amazon-linux-extras install -y redis6
$ redis-cli -h $CacheAddress
> SET session:gamer1 online EX 15
OK
> GET session:gamer1
"online"
> GET session:gamer1
(nil)
> ZADD highscore 100 "gamer1"
(integer) 1
> ZADD highscore 50 "gamer2"
(integer) 1
```

Stores a session for user gamer1 with a time-to-live of 15 seconds

Gets the session for user gamer1

Wait 15 seconds and fetch the session for gamer1 again.

Adds gamer1 with a score of 100 to the sorted set named highscore

The response is empty, because the key was automatically deleted after 15 seconds.

Adds gamer2 with a score of 50 to the sorted set named highscore

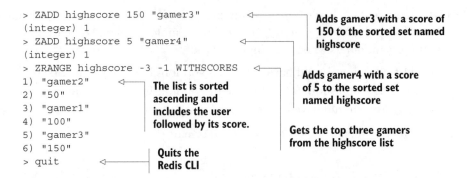

```
> ZADD highscore 150 "gamer3"
(integer) 1
> ZADD highscore 5 "gamer4"
(integer) 1
> ZRANGE highscore -3 -1 WITHSCORES
1) "gamer2"
2) "50"
3) "gamer1"
4) "100"
5) "gamer3"
6) "150"
> quit
```

Adds gamer3 with a score of 150 to the sorted set named highscore

Adds gamer4 with a score of 5 to the sorted set named highscore

The list is sorted ascending and includes the user followed by its score.

Gets the top three gamers from the highscore list

Quits the Redis CLI

You've successfully connected to the Redis cluster and simulated a session store and highscore list used by a typical gaming backend. With this knowledge, you could start to implement a caching layer in your own application. But as always, there are more options to discover.

Cleaning up

It's time to delete the CloudFormation stack named `redis-minimal`. Use the AWS Management Console or the following command to do so:

```
$ aws cloudformation delete-stack --stack-name redis-minimal
```

Continue with the next section to learn more about advanced deployment options with more than one node to achieve high availability or increase the available memory by using sharding.

11.2   Cache deployment options

Which deployment option you should choose is influenced by the following four factors:

- *Engine*—Which in-memory database do you want to use: Memcached or Redis?
- *Backup/Restore*—Does your workload require data persistence, which means being able to backup and restore data?
- *Replication*—Is high availability important to your workload? If so, you need to replicate to at least one other node.
- *Sharding*—Does your data exceed the maximum memory available for a single node, or do you need to increase the throughput of your system?

Table 11.2 compares the deployment options for Memcached and Redis.

Next, we'll look at deployment options in more detail.

Table 11.2   Comparing ElastiCache and MemoryDB engines and deployment options

Service	Engine	Deployment Option	Backup/Restore	Replication	Sharding
ElastiCache	Memcached	Default	No	No	Yes
	Redis	Single Node	Yes	No	No
		Cluster Mode **disabled**	Yes	Yes	No
		Cluster Mode **enabled**	Yes	Yes	Yes
MemoryDB	Redis	Default	Yes	Yes	Yes

11.2.1 *Memcached: Cluster*

An Amazon ElastiCache for Memcached cluster consists of 1–40 nodes. Sharding is implemented by the Memcached client, typically using a consistent hashing algorithm, which arranges keys into partitions in a ring distributed across the nodes. The client decides which keys belong to which nodes and directs the requests to those partitions. Each node stores a unique portion of the key-space in memory. If a node fails, the node is replaced, but the data is lost. You cannot back up the data stored in Memcached. Figure 11.4 shows a Memcached cluster deployment. Remember that a VPC is a way to define a private network on AWS. A subnet is a way to separate concerns inside the VPC. The cluster nodes are distributed among multiple subnets to increase availability. The client communicates with the cluster node to get data and write data to the cache.

Use a Memcached cluster if your application requires a simple in-memory store and can tolerate the loss of a node and its data. For instance, the SQL cache example in the beginning of this chapter could be implemented using Memcached. Because the data is always available in the relational database, you can tolerate a node loss, and you need only simple commands (GET, SET) to implement the query cache.

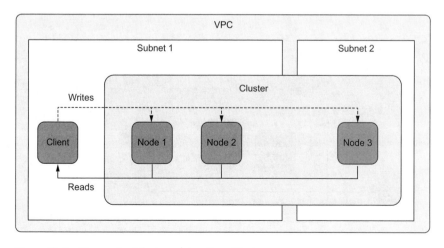

Figure 11.4   Memcached deployment option: Cluster

11.2.2 *Redis: Single-node cluster*

An ElastiCache for Redis single-node cluster always consists of one node. Sharding and high availability are not possible with a single node. But Redis supports the creation of backups and also allows you to restore those backups. Figure 11.5 shows a Redis single-node cluster.

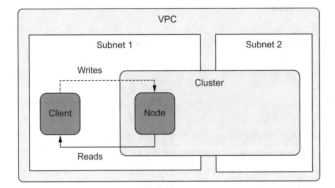

Figure 11.5   Redis deployment option: Single-node cluster

A single node adds a single point of failure (SPOF) to your system. This is probably something you want to avoid for business-critical production systems.

11.2.3 *Redis: Cluster with cluster mode disabled*

Things become more complicated now, because ElastiCache uses two terminologies. We've been using the terms *cluster*, *node*, and *shard* so far, and the graphical Management Console also uses these terms. But the API, the CLI, and CloudFormation use a different terminology: *replication group*, *node*, and *node group*. We prefer the *cluster*, *node*, and *shard* terminology, but in figures 11.6 and 11.7, we've added the *replication group*, *node*, and *node group* terminology in parentheses.

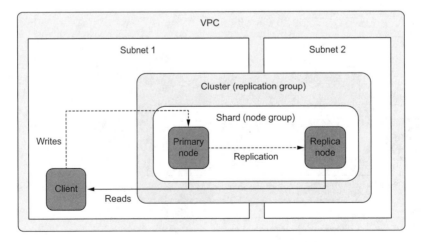

Figure 11.6   Redis deployment option: Cluster with cluster mode disabled

A Redis cluster with cluster mode disabled supports backups and data replication but not sharding. This means there is only one shard containing all the data. The primary node is synchronized to one to five replica nodes.

Use a Redis cluster with cluster mode disabled when you need data replication and all your cached data fits into the memory of a single node. Imagine that your cached data set is 4 GB in size. In that case, the data fits into the memory of nodes of type `cache.m6g.large`, which comes with 6.38 GiB, for example. There is no need to split the data into multiple shards.

11.2.4 *Redis: Cluster with cluster mode enabled*

A Redis cluster with cluster mode enabled, shown in figure 11.7, supports backups, data replication, and sharding. You can have up to 500 shards per cluster. Each shard consists of at least a primary node and optionally replica nodes. In total, a cluster cannot exceed 500 nodes.

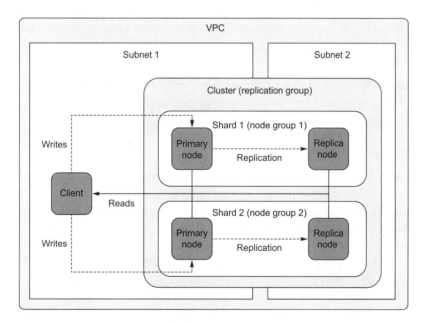

Figure 11.7   Redis deployment option: Cluster with cluster mode enabled

Use a Redis cluster with cluster mode enabled when you need data replication and your data is too large to fit into the memory of a single node. Imagine that your cached data is 22 GB in size. Each cache node has a capacity of 4 GB of memory. Therefore, you will need six shards to get a total capacity of 24 GB of memory. Elasti-Cache provides up to 437 GB of memory per node, which totals to a maximum cluster capacity of 6.5 TB (15 * 437 GB).

Additional benefits of enabling cluster mode

With cluster mode enabled, failover speed is much faster, because no DNS is involved. Clients are provided a single configuration endpoint to discover changes to the cluster topology, including newly elected primaries. With cluster mode disabled, AWS provides a single primary endpoint, and in the event of a failover, AWS does a DNS swap on that endpoint to one of the available replicas. It may take ~1–1.5 minutes before the application is able to reach the cluster after a failure, whereas with cluster mode enabled, the election takes less than 30 seconds.

On top of that, increasing the number of shards also increases the maximum read/write throughput. If you start with one shard and add a second shard, each shard now only has to deal with 50% of the requests (assuming an even distribution).

Last but not least, as you add nodes, your blast radius decreases. For example, if you have five shards and experience a failover, only 20% of your data is affected. This means you can't write to this portion of the key space until the failover process completes (~15–30 seconds), but you can still read from the cluster, given you have a replica available. With cluster mode disabled, 100% of your data is affected, because a single node consists of your entire key space. You can read from the cluster but can't write until the DNS swap has completed.

You learned about the different deployment options for ElastiCache. There is one more thing we want to bring to your attention: AWS offers another in-memory database called MemoryDB, which you will learn about next.

11.2.5 *MemoryDB: Redis with persistence*

Even though ElastiCache for Redis supports snapshots and transaction logs for persistence, AWS recommends using ElastiCache as a secondary data store. AWS also provides an alternative called MemoryDB, a proprietary in-memory database with Redis compatibility and distributed transaction log. MemoryDB writes data to disk and reads from memory. By default, MemoryDB stores data among multiple data centers using a distributed transaction log. Therefore, AWS recommends using MemoryDB as a primary database. Keep in mind that data persistence comes with higher write latency—think milliseconds instead of microseconds.

So, MemoryDB is a good fit when a key-value store is all you need, but data persistency is essential, such as the following situations:

- *Shopping cart*—Stores the items a user intends to check out
- *Content management system (CMS)*—Stores blog posts and comments
- *Device management service*—Stores status information about IoT devices

MemoryDB has been generally available since August 2021. We haven't used MemoryDB for production workloads yet, but the approach sounds very promising to us.

Want to give MemoryDB a try? We have prepared a simple example for you. Create a CloudFormation stack by using the Management Console: http://mng.bz/jAJy.

While you wait for the stack to reach state CREATE_COMPLETE, let's have a look into the CloudFormation template necessary to spin up a MemoryDB cluster, shown here:

```
Resources:
  # [...]
  CacheSecurityGroup:                       ←  The security group
    Type: 'AWS::EC2::SecurityGroup'            controlling traffic to
    Properties:                                the cache cluster
      GroupDescription: cache
      VpcId: !Ref VPC                       ←  The parameter group
  CacheParameterGroup:                         allows you to configure
    Type: 'AWS::MemoryDB::ParameterGroup'      the cache cluster.
    Properties:
      Description: String                   ←  However, we are going
      Family: 'memorydb_redis6'                with the defaults for a Redis
      ParameterGroupName: !Ref 'AWS::StackName'  6–compatible cluster here.
  CacheSubnetGroup:                         ←
    Type: 'AWS::MemoryDB::SubnetGroup'         The subnet groups
    Properties:                                specifies the subnets
      SubnetGroupName: !Ref 'AWS::StackName'   the cluster should use.
      SubnetIds:
      - !Ref SubnetA      ←  We are using two subnets
      - !Ref SubnetB         for high availability here.
  CacheCluster:
    Type: 'AWS::MemoryDB::Cluster'          ←  Disables authentication
    Properties:                                and authorization to
      ACLName: 'open-access'                    simplify the example
      ClusterName: !Ref 'AWS::StackName'
      EngineVersion: '6.2'                  ←  We are using the smallest
      NodeType: 'db.t4g.small'                 available node type.
      NumReplicasPerShard: 0
      NumShards: 1                          ←  A single shard is enough
      ParameterGroupName: !Ref CacheParameterGroup  for testing purposes.
      SecurityGroupIds:                         Adding shards allows
      - !Ref CacheSecurityGroup                 you to scale the available
      SubnetGroupName: !Ref CacheSubnetGroup    memory in the cluster.
      TLSEnabled: false     ←  Disables encryption
                               in transit to simplify
                               the example
```

Annotations:
- **Creates and configures the cache cluster** → CacheSubnetGroup / CacheCluster
- **The Redis engine version** → EngineVersion: '6.2'
- **We are disabling replication to minimize costs for the example.** → NumReplicasPerShard: 0

Want to have a deeper look into the CloudFormation template?

Where is the template located?
You can find the template on GitHub. Download a snapshot of the repository at https://github.com/AWSinAction/code3/archive/main.zip. The file we're talking about is located at chapter11/memorydb-minimal.yaml. On S3, the same file is located at http://s3.amazonaws.com/awsinaction-code3/chapter11/memorydb-minimal.yaml.

We are reusing the gaming example from section 11.1. Hopefully, your CloudFormation stack memorydb-minimal reached status CREATE_COMPLETE already. If so, open the

Outputs tab and copy the EC2 instance ID as well as the cache address. Next, use the Session Manager to connect to the EC2 instance. Afterward, use the steps you used previously in section 11.1 to play with Redis. Make sure to replace $CacheAddress with the value from the CloudFormation outputs:

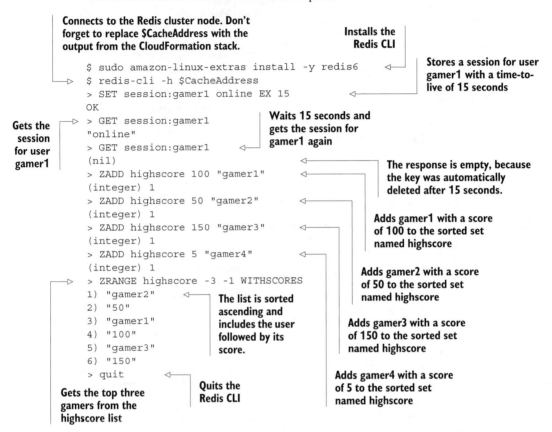

Connects to the Redis cluster node. Don't forget to replace $CacheAddress with the output from the CloudFormation stack.

Installs the Redis CLI

```
$ sudo amazon-linux-extras install -y redis6
$ redis-cli -h $CacheAddress
> SET session:gamer1 online EX 15
OK
> GET session:gamer1
"online"
> GET session:gamer1
(nil)
> ZADD highscore 100 "gamer1"
(integer) 1
> ZADD highscore 50 "gamer2"
(integer) 1
> ZADD highscore 150 "gamer3"
(integer) 1
> ZADD highscore 5 "gamer4"
(integer) 1
> ZRANGE highscore -3 -1 WITHSCORES
1) "gamer2"
2) "50"
3) "gamer1"
4) "100"
5) "gamer3"
6) "150"
> quit
```

Stores a session for user gamer1 with a time-to-live of 15 seconds

Gets the session for user gamer1

Waits 15 seconds and gets the session for gamer1 again

The response is empty, because the key was automatically deleted after 15 seconds.

Adds gamer1 with a score of 100 to the sorted set named highscore

Adds gamer2 with a score of 50 to the sorted set named highscore

Adds gamer3 with a score of 150 to the sorted set named highscore

The list is sorted ascending and includes the user followed by its score.

Adds gamer4 with a score of 5 to the sorted set named highscore

Gets the top three gamers from the highscore list

Quits the Redis CLI

MemoryDB behaves like ElastiCache for Redis, but it comes with persistence guarantees, which make it possible to use it as the primary database.

Cleaning up

It's time to delete the CloudFormation stack named `memorydb-minimal`. Use the AWS Management Console or the following command to do so:

```
$ aws cloudformation delete-stack --stack-name memorydb-minimal.
```

You are now equipped to select the best-fitting in-memory database engine and deployment option for your use case. In the next section, you will take a closer look at the security aspects of ElastiCache to control access to your cache cluster.

11.3 Controlling cache access

Controlling access to data stored in ElastiCache is very similar to the way it works with RDS (see section 11.4). ElastiCache is protected by the following four layers:

- *Identity and Access Management (IAM)*—Controls which IAM user, group, or role is allowed to administer an ElastiCache cluster.
- *Security groups*—Restricts incoming and outgoing traffic to ElastiCache nodes.
- *Cache engine*—Redis >6.0 supports authentication and authorization with role-based access control (RBAC). Memcached does not support authentication.
- *Encryption*—Optionally, data can be encrypted at rest and in transit.

11.3.1 Controlling access to the configuration

Access to the ElastiCache service is controlled with the help of the IAM service. The IAM service is responsible for controlling access to actions like creating, updating, and deleting a cache cluster. IAM doesn't manage access inside the cache; that's the job of the cache engine. An IAM policy defines the configuration and management actions a user, group, or role is allowed to execute on the ElastiCache service. Attaching the IAM policy to IAM users, groups, or roles controls which entity can use the policy to configure an ElastiCache cluster. You can get a complete list of IAM actions and resource-level permissions supported at http://mng.bz/WM9x.

> **SECURITY WARNING** It's important to understand that you don't control access to the cache nodes using IAM. Once the nodes are created, security groups control the access on the network layer. Redis optionally supports user authentication and authorization.

11.3.2 Controlling network access

Network access is controlled with security groups. Remember the security group from the minimal CloudFormation template in section 11.1 where access to port 6379 (Redis) was allowed for all IP addresses. But because cluster nodes have only private IP addresses this restricts access to the VPC, as shown here:

```
Resources:
  # [...]
  CacheSecurityGroup:
    Type: 'AWS::EC2::SecurityGroup'
    Properties:
      GroupDescription: cache
      VpcId: !Ref VPC
      SecurityGroupIngress:
      - IpProtocol: tcp
        FromPort: 6379
        ToPort: 6379
        CidrIp: '0.0.0.0/0'
```

You should improve this setup by working with two security groups. To control traffic as tightly as possible, you will not allow traffic from certain IP addresses. Instead, you create two security groups. The client security group will be attached to all EC2 instances communicating with the cache cluster (your web or application servers). The cache cluster security group allows inbound traffic on port 6379 only for traffic that comes from the client security group. This way you can have a dynamic fleet of clients who are allowed to send traffic to the cache cluster, as shown next. You used the same approach in section 5.4:

```
Resources:
  # [...]
  ClientSecurityGroup:
    Type: 'AWS::EC2::SecurityGroup'
    Properties:
      GroupDescription: 'cache-client'
      VpcId: !Ref VPC
  CacheSecurityGroup:
    Type: 'AWS::EC2::SecurityGroup'
    Properties:
      GroupDescription: cache
      VpcId: !Ref VPC
      SecurityGroupIngress:
      - IpProtocol: tcp
        FromPort: 6379
        ToPort: 6379
        SourceSecurityGroupId: !Ref ClientSecurityGroup
```

> Only allows access from the ClientSecurityGroup

Attach the `ClientSecurityGroup` to all EC2 instances that need access to the cache cluster. This way, you allow access only to the EC2 instances that really need access.

Keep in mind that ElastiCache nodes always have private IP addresses. This means that you can't accidentally expose a Redis or Memcached cluster to the internet. You still want to use security groups to implement the principle of least privilege.

11.3.3 *Controlling cluster and data access*

Unfortunately, ElastiCache for Memcached does not provide user authentication. However, you have two different ways to authenticate users with ElastiCache for Redis:

- Basic token-based authentication
- Users with RBAC

Use token-based authentication when all clients are allowed to read and manipulate all the data stored in the cluster. Use RBAC if you need to restrict access for different users, for example, to make sure the frontend is only allowed to read some of the data and the backend is able to write and read all the data. Keep in mind that when using authentication, you should also enable encryption in-transit to make sure to not transmit secrets in plain text.

In the next section, you'll learn how to use ElastiCache for Redis in a real-world application called Discourse.

11.4 Installing the sample application Discourse with CloudFormation

Small communities, like football clubs, reading circles, or dog schools, benefit from having a place where members can communicate with each other. Discourse is an open source software application for providing modern forums to your community. The forum software is written in Ruby using the Rails framework. Figure 11.8 gives you an impression of Discourse. Wouldn't that be a perfect place for your community to meet? In this section, you will learn how to set up Discourse with CloudFormation. Discourse is also perfectly suited for you to learn about ElastiCache because it requires a Redis in-memory database acting as a caching layer.

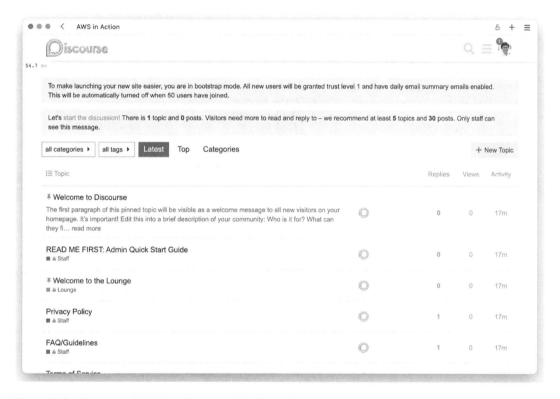

Figure 11.8 Discourse: A platform for community discussion

Discourse requires PostgreSQL as its main data store and uses Redis to cache data and process transient data. In this section, you'll create a CloudFormation template with all the components necessary to run Discourse. Finally, you'll create a CloudFormation stack based on the template to test your work. The necessary components follow:

- *VPC*—Network configuration
- *Cache*—Security group, subnet group, cache cluster

- *Database*—Security group, subnet group, database instance
- *Virtual machine*—Security group, EC2 instance

You'll start with the first component and extend the template in the rest of this section.

11.4.1 *VPC: Network configuration*

In section 5.5, you learned all about private networks on AWS. If you can't follow the next listing, you could go back to section 5.5 or continue with the next step—understanding the network is not key to get Discourse running.

Listing 11.2   CloudFormation template for Discourse: VPC

```
---
AWSTemplateFormatVersion: '2010-09-09'           The email address of
Description: 'AWS in Action: chapter 11'         the Discourse admin
Parameters:                                      must be valid.
  AdminEmailAddress:
    Description: 'Email address of admin user'
    Type: 'String'
Resources:                          Creates a VPC in
  VPC:                              the address range
    Type: 'AWS::EC2::VPC'          172.31.0.0/16
    Properties:
      CidrBlock: '172.31.0.0/16'
      EnableDnsHostnames: true          We want to access Discourse
  InternetGateway:                      from the internet, so we
    Type: 'AWS::EC2::InternetGateway'   need an internet gateway.
    Properties: {}
  VPCGatewayAttachment:                        Attaches the
    Type: 'AWS::EC2::VPCGatewayAttachment'     internet gateway
    Properties:                                to the VPC
      VpcId: !Ref VPC
      InternetGatewayId: !Ref InternetGateway
  SubnetA:                                      Creates a subnet in the address
    Type: 'AWS::EC2::Subnet'                    range 172.31.38.0/24 in the first
    Properties:                                 availability zone (array index 0)
      AvailabilityZone: !Select [0, !GetAZs '']
      CidrBlock: '172.31.38.0/24'
      VpcId: !Ref VPC                    Creates a second subnet in the address
  SubnetB: # [...]                       range 172.31.37.0/24 in the second
  RouteTable:                            availability zone (properties omitted)
    Type: 'AWS::EC2::RouteTable'
    Properties:                       Creates a route table that contains
      VpcId: !Ref VPC                 the default route, which routes all
  SubnetRouteTableAssociationA:       subnets in a VPC
    Type: 'AWS::EC2::SubnetRouteTableAssociation'
    Properties:
      SubnetId: !Ref SubnetA
      RouteTableId: !Ref RouteTable
  # [...]                           Adds a route to
  RouteToInternet:                  the internet via the
    Type: 'AWS::EC2::Route'         internet gateway
```

Associates the first subnet with the route table

```
  Properties:
    RouteTableId: !Ref RouteTable
    DestinationCidrBlock: '0.0.0.0/0'
    GatewayId: !Ref InternetGateway
DependsOn: VPCGatewayAttachment
```

The following listing adds the required network access control list.

Listing 11.3 CloudFormation template for Discourse: VPC NACLs

```
Resources:
  # [...]
  NetworkAcl:                                      ◁──┐ Creates an empty
    Type: AWS::EC2::NetworkAcl                           network ACL
    Properties:
      VpcId: !Ref VPC                                        ┌ Associates the first
  SubnetNetworkAclAssociationA:                     ◁──┘   subnet with the
    Type: 'AWS::EC2::SubnetNetworkAclAssociation'            network ACL
    Properties:
      SubnetId: !Ref SubnetA
      NetworkAclId: !Ref NetworkAcl                    ┌ Allows all incoming traffic on the
  # [...]                                                network ACL. (You will use security
  NetworkAclEntryIngress:                           ◁──┘ groups later as a firewall.)
    Type: 'AWS::EC2::NetworkAclEntry'
    Properties:
      NetworkAclId: !Ref NetworkAcl
      RuleNumber: 100
      Protocol: -1
      RuleAction: allow
      Egress: false                                   ┌ Allows all outgoing
      CidrBlock: '0.0.0.0/0'                            traffic on the
  NetworkAclEntryEgress:                            ◁──┘ network ACL
    Type: 'AWS::EC2::NetworkAclEntry'
    Properties:
      NetworkAclId: !Ref NetworkAcl
      RuleNumber: 100
      Protocol: -1
      RuleAction: allow
      Egress: true
      CidrBlock: '0.0.0.0/0'
```

The network is now properly configured using two public subnets. Let's configure the cache next.

11.4.2 Cache: Security group, subnet group, cache cluster

You will add the ElastiCache for Redis cluster now. You learned how to describe a minimal cache cluster earlier in this chapter. This time, you'll add a few extra properties to enhance the setup. The next code listing contains the CloudFormation resources related to the cache.

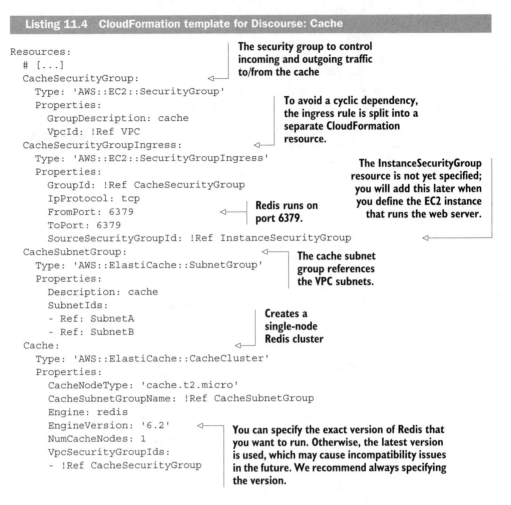

Listing 11.4   CloudFormation template for Discourse: Cache

```
Resources:
  # [...]
  CacheSecurityGroup:                                      ◁─── The security group to control
    Type: 'AWS::EC2::SecurityGroup'                             incoming and outgoing traffic
    Properties:                                                 to/from the cache
      GroupDescription: cache
      VpcId: !Ref VPC                                           To avoid a cyclic dependency,
  CacheSecurityGroupIngress:                             ◁───   the ingress rule is split into a
    Type: 'AWS::EC2::SecurityGroupIngress'                      separate CloudFormation
    Properties:                                                 resource.
      GroupId: !Ref CacheSecurityGroup                             The InstanceSecurityGroup
      IpProtocol: tcp                                              resource is not yet specified;
      FromPort: 6379                      ◁─── Redis runs on       you will add this later when
      ToPort: 6379                             port 6379.          you define the EC2 instance
      SourceSecurityGroupId: !Ref InstanceSecurityGroup           that runs the web server.
  CacheSubnetGroup:                               ◁───
    Type: 'AWS::ElastiCache::SubnetGroup'              The cache subnet
    Properties:                                        group references
      Description: cache                               the VPC subnets.
      SubnetIds:
      - Ref: SubnetA                          Creates a
      - Ref: SubnetB                          single-node
  Cache:                                  ◁─── Redis cluster
    Type: 'AWS::ElastiCache::CacheCluster'
    Properties:
      CacheNodeType: 'cache.t2.micro'
      CacheSubnetGroupName: !Ref CacheSubnetGroup
      Engine: redis
      EngineVersion: '6.2'          ◁─── You can specify the exact version of Redis that
      NumCacheNodes: 1                   you want to run. Otherwise, the latest version
      VpcSecurityGroupIds:              is used, which may cause incompatibility issues
      - !Ref CacheSecurityGroup         in the future. We recommend always specifying
                                        the version.
```

The single-node Redis cache cluster is now defined. Discourse also requires a Post-greSQL database, which you'll define next.

11.4.3 *Database: Security group, subnet group, database instance*

PostgreSQL is a powerful, open source relational database. If you are not familiar with PostgreSQL, that's not a problem at all. Luckily, the RDS service will provide a managed PostgreSQL database for you. You learned about RDS in chapter 10. The following listing shows the section of the template that defines the RDS instance.

Listing 11.5   CloudFormation template for Discourse: Database

```
Resources:
  # [...]                                    Traffic to/from the RDS
  DatabaseSecurityGroup:            ◁───     instance is protected by
    Type: 'AWS::EC2::SecurityGroup'          a security group.
```

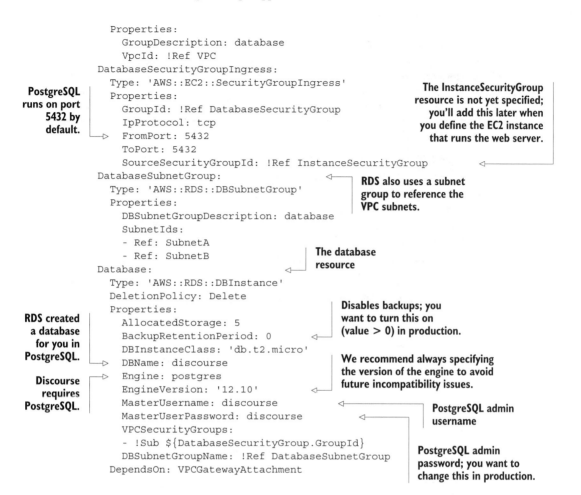

```
          Properties:
            GroupDescription: database
            VpcId: !Ref VPC
      DatabaseSecurityGroupIngress:
        Type: 'AWS::EC2::SecurityGroupIngress'
        Properties:
          GroupId: !Ref DatabaseSecurityGroup
          IpProtocol: tcp
          FromPort: 5432
          ToPort: 5432
          SourceSecurityGroupId: !Ref InstanceSecurityGroup
      DatabaseSubnetGroup:
        Type: 'AWS::RDS::DBSubnetGroup'
        Properties:
          DBSubnetGroupDescription: database
          SubnetIds:
          - Ref: SubnetA
          - Ref: SubnetB
      Database:
        Type: 'AWS::RDS::DBInstance'
        DeletionPolicy: Delete
        Properties:
          AllocatedStorage: 5
          BackupRetentionPeriod: 0
          DBInstanceClass: 'db.t2.micro'
          DBName: discourse
          Engine: postgres
          EngineVersion: '12.10'
          MasterUsername: discourse
          MasterUserPassword: discourse
          VPCSecurityGroups:
          - !Sub ${DatabaseSecurityGroup.GroupId}
          DBSubnetGroupName: !Ref DatabaseSubnetGroup
        DependsOn: VPCGatewayAttachment
```

PostgreSQL runs on port 5432 by default.

The InstanceSecurityGroup resource is not yet specified; you'll add this later when you define the EC2 instance that runs the web server.

RDS also uses a subnet group to reference the VPC subnets.

The database resource

Disables backups; you want to turn this on (value > 0) in production.

RDS created a database for you in PostgreSQL.

Discourse requires PostgreSQL.

We recommend always specifying the version of the engine to avoid future incompatibility issues.

PostgreSQL admin username

PostgreSQL admin password; you want to change this in production.

Have you noticed the similarity between RDS and ElastiCache? The concepts are similar, which makes it easier for you to work with both services. Only one component is missing: the EC2 instance that runs the web server.

11.4.4 *Virtual machine: Security group, EC2 instance*

Discourse is a Ruby on Rails application, so you need an EC2 instance to host the application. Because it is very tricky to install the required Ruby environment with all its dependencies, we are using the recommended way to run Discourse, which is running a container with Docker on the virtual machine. However, running containers is not in scope of this chapter. You will learn more about deploying containers on AWS in chapter 18.

The next listing defines the virtual machine and the startup script to install and configure Discourse.

Discourse requires SMTP to send email

The forum software application Discourse requires access to an SMTP server to send email. Unfortunately, operating an SMTP server on your own is almost impossible, because most providers will not accept emails or flag them as spam. That's why we are using the Simple Email Service (SES) provided by AWS. SES requires verification before sending emails. Start with enabling sandbox mode by adding your email address to the allowlist as follows:

1. Open SES in the AWS Management Console.
2. Select Verified Identities from the menu.
3. Click Create Identity.
4. Choose the identity type Email Address.
5. Type in your email address.
6. Click Create Identity.
7. Check your inbox, and click the verification link.

Please note: you need to request production access to ensure SES is delivering emails to any address. To follow our example, however, this isn't needed.

Listing 11.6   CloudFormation template for Discourse: Virtual machine

```
Resources:
  # [...]
  InstanceSecurityGroup:
    Type: 'AWS::EC2::SecurityGroup'
    Properties:
      GroupDescription: 'vm'
      SecurityGroupIngress:       # Allows HTTP traffic from the public internet
      - CidrIp: '0.0.0.0/0'
        FromPort: 80
        IpProtocol: tcp
        ToPort: 80
      VpcId: !Ref VPC
  Instance:                        # The virtual machine that runs Discourse
    Type: 'AWS::EC2::Instance'
    Properties:
      ImageId: !FindInMap [RegionMap, !Ref 'AWS::Region', AMI]
      InstanceType: 't2.micro'
      IamInstanceProfile: !Ref InstanceProfile
      NetworkInterfaces:
      - AssociatePublicIpAddress: true
        DeleteOnTermination: true
        DeviceIndex: 0
        GroupSet:
        - !Ref InstanceSecurityGroup
        SubnetId: !Ref SubnetA
      BlockDeviceMappings:
      - DeviceName: '/dev/xvda'     # Increases the default volume size from 8 GB to 16 GB
        Ebs:
          VolumeSize: 16
```

```
            VolumeType: gp2
          UserData:
            'Fn::Base64': !Sub |
              #!/bin/bash -x
              bash -ex << "TRY"
                # [...]

                # install and start docker
                yum install -y git
                amazon-linux-extras install docker -y
                systemctl start docker

                docker run --restart always -d -p 80:80 --name discourse \
                  -e "UNICORN_WORKERS=3" \
                  # [...]
                  -e "RUBY_ALLOCATOR=/usr/lib/libjemalloc.so.1" \
                  public.ecr.aws/awsinaction/discourse:3rd /sbin/boot

                docker exec discourse /bin/sh -c /
                  "cd /var/www/discourse && rake db:migrate"
                docker restart discourse
              TRY
              /opt/aws/bin/cfn-signal -e $? --stack ${AWS::StackName} /
                --resource Instance --region ${AWS::Region}
          CreationPolicy:
            ResourceSignal:
              Timeout: PT15M
          DependsOn:
          - VPCGatewayAttachment
```

Installs and starts Docker → `# install and start docker`

Creates and launches a Docker container → `docker run --restart always...`

Runs the database migration script to initialize or migrate the database → `docker exec discourse...`

Restarts the container to make sure the database migration is in effect → `docker restart discourse`

You've reached the end of the template. All components are defined now. It's time to create a CloudFormation stack based on your template to see whether it works.

11.4.5 Testing the CloudFormation template for Discourse

Let's create a stack based on your template to create all the resources in your AWS account, as shown next. To find the full code for the template, go to /chapter11/discourse.yaml in the book's code folder. Use the AWS CLI to create the stack. Don't forget to replace $AdminEmailAddress with your e-mail address:

```
$ aws cloudformation create-stack --stack-name discourse \
 --template-url https://s3.amazonaws.com/\
awsinaction-code3/chapter11/discourse.yaml \
 --parameters \
 "ParameterKey=AdminEmailAddress,ParameterValue=$AdminEmailAddress" \
 --capabilities CAPABILITY_NAMED_IAM
```

> ### Where is the template located?
> You can find the template on GitHub. You can download a snapshot of the repository at https://github.com/AWSinAction/code3/archive/main.zip. The file we're talking about is located at chapter11/discourse.yaml. On S3, the same file is located at https://s3.amazonaws.com/awsinaction-code3/chapter11/discourse.yaml.

The creation of the stack can take up to 20 minutes. After the stack has been created, get the public IP address of the EC2 instance from the stack's output by executing the following command:

```
$ aws cloudformation describe-stacks --stack-name discourse \
➥ --query "Stacks[0].Outputs[1].OutputValue"
```

Open a web browser and insert the IP address in the address bar to open your Discourse website. Figure 11.9 shows the website. Click Register to create an admin account.

Figure 11.9   Discourse: First screen after a fresh install

You will receive an email to activate your account. Note that this email might be hidden in your spam folder. After activation, the setup wizard is started, which you have to complete to configure your forum. After you complete the wizard and have successfully installed Discourse, don't delete the CloudFormation stack because you'll use the setup in the next section.

Congratulations—you have deployed Discourse, a rather complex web application, using Redis as a cache to speed up loading times. You've experienced that ElastiCache is for in-memory databases, like RDS is for relational databases. Because ElastiCache is a relevant part of the architecture, you need to make sure you monitor the cache infrastructure to avoid performance issues or even downtimes. You will learn about monitoring ElastiCache in the following section.

11.5 Monitoring a cache

CloudWatch is the service on AWS that stores all kinds of metrics. Like other services, ElastiCache nodes send metrics to CloudWatch as well. The most important metrics to watch follow:

- `CPUUtilization`—The percentage of CPU utilization.
- `SwapUsage`—The amount of swap used on the host, in bytes. *Swap* is space on disk that is used if the system runs out of physical memory.
- `Evictions`—The number of nonexpired items the cache evicted due to the memory limit.
- `ReplicationLag`—This metric is applicable only for a Redis node running as a read replica. It represents how far behind, in seconds, the replica is in applying changes from the primary node. Usually this number is very low.

In this section we'll examine those metrics in more detail and give you some hints about useful thresholds for defining alarms on those metrics to set up production-ready monitoring for your cache.

11.5.1 Monitoring host-level metrics

The virtual machines running underneath the ElastiCache service report CPU utilization and swap usage. CPU utilization usually gets problematic when crossing 80–90%, because the wait time explodes. But things are more tricky here. Redis is single-threaded. If you have many cores, the overall CPU utilization can be low, but one core can be at 100% utilization. Use the `EngineCPUUtilization` metric to monitor the Redis process CPU utilization. Swap usage is a different topic. You run an in-memory cache, so if the virtual machine starts to swap (move memory to disk), the performance will suffer. By default, ElastiCache for Memcached and Redis is configured to limit memory consumption to a value smaller than what's physical available (you can tune this) to have room for other resources (e.g., the kernel needs memory for each open socket). But other processes (such as kernel processes) are also running, and they may start to consume more memory than what's available. You can solve this issue by increasing the memory of the cache, either by increasing the node type or by adding more shards.

> **Queuing theory: Why 80–90%?**
>
> Imagine you are the manager of a supermarket. What should be the goal for daily utilization of your cashiers? It's tempting to go for a high number, maybe 90%. But it turns out that the wait time for your customers is very high when your cashiers are used for 90% of the day, because customers don't arrive at the same time at the queue. The theory behind this is called *queuing theory*, and it turns out that wait time is exponential

(continued)

to the utilization of a resource. This applies not only to cashiers but also to network cards, CPU, hard disks, and so on. Keep in mind that this sidebar simplifies the theory and assumes an M/D/1 queuing system: Markovian arrivals (exponentially distributed arrival times), deterministic service times (fixed), one service center. To learn more about queuing theory applied to computer systems, we recommend *Systems Performance: Enterprise and the Cloud* by Brendan Gregg (Prentice Hall, 2013) to get started.

When you go from 0% utilization to 60%, wait time doubles. When you go to 80%, wait time has tripled. When you to 90%, wait time is six times higher, and so on. If your wait time is 100 ms during 0% utilization, you already have 300 ms wait time during 80% utilization, which is already slow for an e-commerce website.

You might set up an alarm to trigger if the 10-minute average of the `EngineCPU-Utilization` metric is higher than 80% for one out of one data points, and if the 10-minute average of the `SwapUsage` metric is higher than 67108864 (64 MB) for one out of one data points. These numbers are just a rule of thumb. You should load-test your system to verify that the thresholds are high or low enough to trigger the alarm before application performance suffers.

11.5.2   Is my memory sufficient?

The `Evictions` metric is reported by Memcached and Redis. If the cache is running out of memory and you try to add a new key-value pair, an old key-value pair needs to be deleted first. This is called an eviction. By default, Redis deletes the least recently used key, but only for keys that define a TTL. This strategy is called `volatile-lru`. On top of that, the following eviction strategies are available:

- `allkeys-lru`—Removes the least recently used key among all keys
- `volatile-random`—Removes a random key among keys with TTL
- `allkeys-random`—Removes a random key among all keys
- `volatile-ttl`—Removes the key with the shortest TTL
- `noeviction`—Does not evict any key

Usually, high eviction rates are a sign that you either aren't using a TTL to expire keys after some time or that your cache is too small. You can solve this issue by increasing the memory of the cache, either by increasing the node type or by adding more shards. You might set an alarm to trigger if the 10-minute average of the `Evictions` metric is higher than 1000 for one out of one data points.

11.5.3   Is my Redis replication up-to-date?

The `ReplicationLag` metric is applicable only for a node running as a read replica. It represents how far behind, in seconds, the replica is in applying changes from the primary node. The higher this value, the more out of date the replica is. This can be a problem because some users of your application will see very old data. In the gaming application, imagine you have one primary node and one replica node. All reads are performed by either the primary or the replica node. The `ReplicationLag` is 600, which means that the replication node looks like the primary node looked 10 minutes before. Depending on which node the user hits when accessing the application, they could see 10-minute-old data.

What are reasons for a high `ReplicationLag`? There could be a problem with the sizing of your cluster—for example, your cache cluster might be at capacity. Typically this will be a sign to increase the capacity by adding shards or replicas. You might set an alarm to trigger if the 10-minute average of the `ReplicationLag` metric is higher than 30 for one consecutive period.

Cleaning up
It's time to delete the running CloudFormation stack, as shown here:

```
$ aws cloudformation delete-stack --stack-name discourse
```

11.6   Tweaking cache performance

Your cache can become a bottleneck if it can no longer handle the requests with low latency. In the previous section, you learned how to monitor your cache. In this section, you learn what you can do if your monitoring data shows that your cache is becoming the bottleneck (e.g., if you see high CPU or network usage). Figure 11.10 contains a decision tree that you can use to resolve performance issues with Elasti-Cache. The strategies are described in more detail in the rest of this section.

Three strategies for tweaking the performance of your ElastiCache cluster follow:

- *Selecting the right cache node type*—A bigger instance type comes with more resources (CPU, memory, network) so you can scale vertically.
- *Selecting the right deployment option*—You can use sharding or read replicas to scale horizontally.
- *Compressing your data*—If you shrink the amount of data being transferred and stored, you can also tweak performance.

11.6.1   Selecting the right cache node type

So far, you used the cache node type `cache.t2.micro`, which comes with one vCPU, ~0.6 GB memory, and low to moderate network performance. You used this node type because it's part of the Free Tier. But you can also use more powerful node types on AWS. The upper end is the `cache.r6gd.16xlarge` with 64 vCPUs, ~419 GB memory, and 25 Gb network.

As a rule of thumb: for production traffic, select a cache node type with at least 2 vCPUs for real concurrency, enough memory to hold your data set with some space to

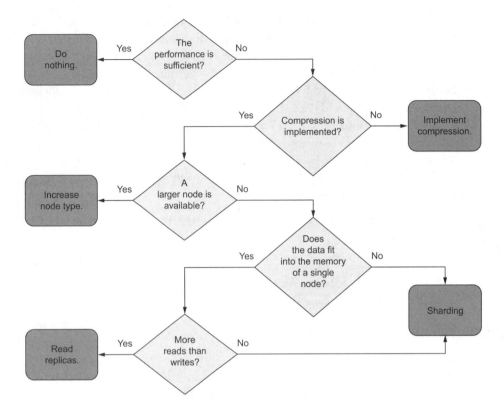

Figure 11.10   An ElastiCache decision tree to resolve performance issues

grow (say, 20%; this also avoids memory fragmentation), and at least high network performance. The cache.r6g.large is an excellent choice for a small node size: 2 vCPUs, ~13 GB, and up to 10 GB of network. This may be a good starting point when considering how many shards you may want in a clustered topology, and if you need more memory, move up a node type. You can find the available node types at https://aws.amazon.com/elasticache/pricing/.

11.6.2 *Selecting the right deployment option*

By replicating data, you can distribute read traffic to multiple nodes within the same replica group. By replicating data from the primary node to one or multiple replication nodes, you are increasing the number of nodes that are able to process read requests and, therefore, increase the maximum throughput. On top of that, by sharding data, you split the data into multiple buckets. Each bucket contains a subset of the data. Each shard is stored on a primary node and is optionally synchronized to replication nodes as well. This further increases the number of nodes available to answer incoming reads—and even writes.

Redis supports the concept of replication, where one node in a node group is the primary node accepting read and write traffic, while the replica nodes only accept read traffic, which allows you to scale the read capacity. The Redis client has to be aware of the cluster topology to select the right node for a given command. Keep in mind that the replicas are synchronized asynchronously. This means that the replication node eventually reaches the state of the primary node.

Both Memcached and Redis support the concept of sharding. With sharding, a single cache cluster node is no longer responsible for all the keys. Instead the key space is divided across multiple nodes. Both Redis and Memcached clients implement a hashing algorithm to select the right node for a given key. By sharding, you can increase the capacity of your cache cluster.

As a rule of thumb: when a single node can no longer handle the amount of data or the requests, and if you are using Redis with mostly read traffic, then you should use replication. Replication also increases the availability at the same time (at no extra cost).

It is even possible to increase and decrease the number of shards automatically, based on utilization metrics, by using Application Auto Scaling. See http://mng.bz/ 82d2 to learn more.

Last but not least, replicating data is possible not only within a cluster but also between clusters running in other regions of the world. For example, if you are operating a popular online game, it is necessary to minimize latency by deploying your cloud infrastructure to the United States, Europe, and Asia. By using ElastiCache Global Datastore, you are able to replicate a Redis cluster located in Ireland to North Virginia and Singapore, for example.

11.6.3 *Compressing your data*

Instead of sending large values (and also keys) to your cache, you can compress the data before you store it in the cache. When you retrieve data from the cache, you have to uncompress it on the application before you can use the data. Depending on your data, compressing data can have a significant effect. We saw memory reductions to 25% of the original size and network transfer savings of the same size. Please note that this approach needs to be implemented in your application.

As a rule of thumb: compress your data using an algorithm that is best suited for your data. Most likely the `zlib` library is a good starting point. You might want to experiment with a subset of your data to select the best compression algorithm that is also supported by your programming language.

On top of that, ElastiCache for Redis also supports data tiering to reduce costs. With data tiering enabled, ElastiCache will move parts of your data from memory to solid-state disks—a tradeoff between costs and latency. Using data tiering is most interesting if your workload reads only parts of the data frequently.

Summary

- A caching layer can speed up your application significantly, while also lowering the costs of your primary data store.
- To keep the cache in sync with the database, items usually expire after some time, or a write-through strategy is used.
- When the cache is full, the least frequently used items are usually evicted.
- ElastiCache can run Memcached or Redis clusters for you. Depending on the engine, different features are available. Memcached and Redis are open source, but AWS added engine-level enhancements.
- Memcached is a simple key-value store allowing you to scale available memory and throughput by adding additional machines—called shards—to the cluster.
- Redis is a more advanced in-memory database that supports complex data structures like sorted sets.
- MemoryDB is an alternative to ElastiCache and provides an in-memory database with strong persistence guarantees. MemoryDB comes with Redis compatibility.
- CloudWatch provides insights into the utilization and performance of ElastiCache.

Programming for the NoSQL database service: DynamoDB

This chapter covers

- Advantages and disadvantages of the NoSQL service, DynamoDB
- Creating tables and storing data
- Adding secondary indexes to optimize data retrieval
- Designing a data model optimized for a key-value database
- Optimizing costs by choosing the best fitting capacity mode and storage type

Most applications depend on a database to store data. Imagine an application that keeps track of a warehouse's inventory. The more inventory moves through the warehouse, the more requests the application serves and the more queries the database has to process. Sooner or later, the database becomes too busy and latency increases to a level that limits the warehouse's productivity. At this point, you have to scale the database to help the business. You can do this in two ways:

- *Vertically*—You can use faster hardware for your database machine; for example, you can add memory or replace the CPU with a more powerful model.
- *Horizontally*—You can add a second database machine. Both machines then form a *database cluster.*

Scaling a database vertically is the easier option, but it gets expensive. High-end hardware is more expensive than commodity hardware. Besides that, at some point, you will not find more powerful machines on the market anymore.

Scaling a traditional relational database horizontally is difficult because transactional guarantees such as atomicity, consistency, isolation, and durability—also known as *ACID*—require communication among all nodes of the database during a two-phase commit. To see what we're talking about, here's how a simplified two-phase commit with two nodes works, as illustrated in figure 12.1:

1 A query is sent to the database cluster that wants to change data (INSERT, UPDATE, DELETE).
2 The database transaction coordinator sends a commit request to the two nodes.
3 Node 1 checks whether the query could be executed. The decision is sent back to the coordinator. If the nodes decide yes, the query can be executed, it must fulfill this promise. There is no way back.
4 Node 2 checks whether the query could be executed. The decision is sent back to the coordinator.
5 The coordinator receives all decisions. If all nodes decide that the query could be executed, the coordinator instructs the nodes to finally commit.
6 Nodes 1 and 2 finally change the data. At this point, the nodes must fulfill the request. This step must not fail.

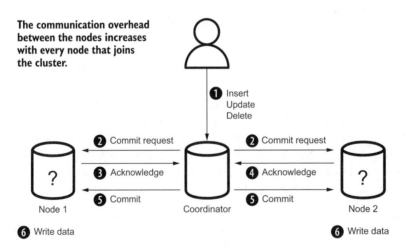

Figure 12.1   The communication overhead between the nodes increases with every node that joins the cluster.

The problem is, the more nodes you add, the slower your database becomes, because more nodes must coordinate transactions between each other. The way to tackle this has been to use databases that don't adhere to these guarantees. They're called *NoSQL databases.*

There are four types of NoSQL databases—document, graph, columnar, and key-value store—each with its own uses and applications. Amazon provides a NoSQL database service called *DynamoDB*, a key-value store. DynamoDB is a fully managed, proprietary, closed source key-value store with document support. In other words, DynamoDB persists objects identified by a unique key, which you might know from the concept of a hash table. *Fully managed* means that you only use the service and AWS operates it for you. DynamoDB is highly available and highly durable. You can scale from one item to billions and from one request per second to tens of thousands of requests per second. AWS also offers other types of NoSQL database systems like Keyspaces, Neptune, DocumentDB, and MemoryDB for Redis—more about these options later.

To use DynamoDB, your application needs to be built for this particular NoSQL database. You cannot point your legacy application to DynamoDB instead of a MySQL database, for example. Therefore, this chapter focuses on how to write an application for storing and retrieving data from DynamoDB. At the end of the chapter, we will discuss what is needed to administer DynamoDB.

Some typical use cases for DynamoDB follow:

- When building systems that need to deal with a massive amount of requests or spiky workloads, the ability to scale horizontally is a game changer. We have used DynamoDB to track client-side errors from a web application, for example.
- When building small applications with a simple data structure, the pay-per-request pricing model and the simplicity of a fully managed service are good reasons to go with DynamoDB. For example, we used DynamoDB to track the progress of batch jobs.

While following this chapter, you will implement a simple to-do application called nodetodo, the equivalent of a "Hello World" example for databases. You will learn how to write, fetch, and query data. Figure 12.2 shows nodetodo in action.

Examples are 100% covered by the Free Tier

The examples in this chapter are totally covered by the Free Tier. Keep in mind that this applies only if there is nothing else going on in your AWS account. You'll clean up your account at the end of the chapter.

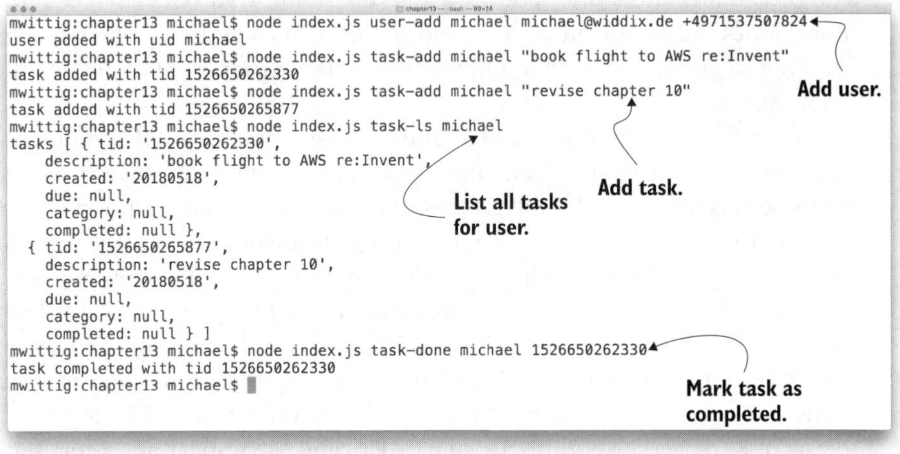

```
mwittig:chapter13 michael$ node index.js user-add michael michael@widdix.de +4971537507824
user added with uid michael
mwittig:chapter13 michael$ node index.js task-add michael "book flight to AWS re:Invent"
task added with tid 1526650262330
mwittig:chapter13 michael$ node index.js task-add michael "revise chapter 10"
task added with tid 1526650265877
mwittig:chapter13 michael$ node index.js task-ls michael
tasks [ { tid: '1526650262330',
    description: 'book flight to AWS re:Invent',
    created: '20180518',
    due: null,
    category: null,
    completed: null },
  { tid: '1526650265877',
    description: 'revise chapter 10',
    created: '20180518',
    due: null,
    category: null,
    completed: null } ]
mwittig:chapter13 michael$ node index.js task-done michael 1526650262330
task completed with tid 1526650262330
mwittig:chapter13 michael$
```

Add user.

Add task.

List all tasks
for user.

Mark task as
completed.

Figure 12.2   Manage your tasks with the command-line to-do application, nodetodo.

12.1   Programming a to-do application

DynamoDB is a key-value store that organizes your data into tables. For example, you can have a table to store your users and another table to store tasks. The items contained in the table are identified by a unique key. An item could be a user or a task; think of an item as a row in a relational database.

To minimize the overhead of a programming language, you'll use Node.js/JavaScript to create a small to-do application, nodetodo, which you can use via the terminal on your local machine. nodetodo uses DynamoDB as a database and comes with the following features:

- Creates and deletes users
- Creates and deletes tasks
- Marks tasks as done
- Gets a list of all tasks with various filters

To implement an intuitive CLI, nodetodo uses *docopt*, a command-line interface description language, to describe the CLI interface. The supported commands follow:

- user-add—Adds a new user to nodetodo
- user-rm—Removes a user
- user-ls—Lists users
- user—Shows the details of a single user
- task-add—Adds a new task to nodetodo
- task-rm—Removes a task
- task-ls—Lists user tasks with various filters

- `task-la`—Lists tasks by category with various filters
- `task-done`—Marks a task as finished

In the following sections, you'll implement these commands to learn about DynamoDB hands-on. This listing shows the full CLI description of all the commands, including parameters.

```
nodetodo

Usage:
  nodetodo user-add <uid> <email> <phone>
  nodetodo user-rm <uid>
  nodetodo user-ls [--limit=<limit>] [--next=<id>]      ◁──┐  The named
  nodetodo user <uid>                                       │  parameters limit and
  nodetodo task-add <uid> <description> \                   │  next are optional.
➥  [<category>] [--dueat=<yyyymmdd>]      ◁──┐  The category
  nodetodo task-rm <uid> <tid>                │  parameter is optional.
  nodetodo task-ls <uid> [<category>] \
➥  [--overdue|--due|--withoutdue|--futuredue]     ◁──┐  Pipe indicates
  nodetodo task-la <category> \                       │  either/or.
➥  [--overdue|--due|--withoutdue|--futuredue]
  nodetodo task-done <uid> <tid>
  nodetodo -h | --help         ◁──┐  help prints
  nodetodo --version                │  information about
                                    │  how to use nodetodo.
Options:
  -h --help      Show this screen.
  --version      Show version.
```

Version information ──▷ `nodetodo --version`

DynamoDB isn't comparable to a traditional relational database in which you create, read, update, or delete data with SQL. You'll use the AWS SDK to send requests to the REST API. You must integrate DynamoDB into your application; you can't take an existing application that uses an SQL database and run it on DynamoDB. To use DynamoDB, you need to write code!

12.2 Creating tables

Each DynamoDB table has a name and organizes a collection of items. An *item* is a collection of attributes, and an *attribute* is a name-value pair. The attribute value can be scalar (number, string, binary, Boolean), multivalued (number set, string set, binary set), or a JSON document (object, array). Items in a table aren't required to have the same attributes; there is no enforced schema. Figure 12.3 demonstrates these terms.

DynamoDB doesn't need a static schema like a relational database does, but you must define the attributes that are used as the primary key in your table. In other words, you must define the table's primary key schema. Next, you will create a table for the users of the nodetodo application as well as a table that will store all the tasks.

330 CHAPTER 12 *Programming for the NoSQL database service: DynamoDB*

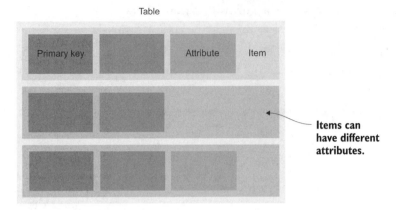

Figure 12.3 DynamoDB tables store items consisting of attributes identified by a primary key.

12.2.1 Users are identified by a partition key

To be able to assign a task to a user, the nodetodo application needs to store some information about users. Therefore, we came up with the following data structure for storing information about users:

```
{
  "uid": "emma",
  "email": "emma@widdix.de",
  "phone": "0123456789"
}
```

A unique user ID

The user's email address

The phone number belonging to the user

How to create a DynamoDB table based on this information? First, you need to think about the table's name. We suggest that you prefix all your tables with the name of your application. In this case, the table name would be `todo-user`.

Next, a DynamoDB table requires the definition of a *primary key*. A primary key consists of one or two attributes. A primary key is unique within a table and identifies an item. You need the primary key to retrieve, update, or delete an item. Note that DynamoDB does not care about any other attributes of an item because it does not require a fixed schema, as relational databases do.

For the `todo-user` table, we recommend you use the `uid` as the primary key because the attribute is unique. Also, the only command that queries data is `user`, which fetches a user by its `uid`. When using a single attribute as primary key, DynamoDB calls this the *partition key* of the table.

You can create a table by using the Management Console, CloudFormation, SDKs, or the CLI. Within this chapter, we use the AWS CLI. The `aws dynamodb create-table` command has the following four mandatory options:

- `table-name`—Name of the table (can't be changed).
- `attribute-definitions`—Name and type of attributes used as the primary key. Multiple definitions can be given using the syntax `AttributeName=attr1`, `AttributeType=S`, separated by a space character. Valid types are `S` (string), `N` (number), and `B` (binary).
- `key-schema`—Name of attributes that are part of the primary key (can't be changed). Contains a single entry using the syntax `AttributeName=attr1`, `KeyType=HASH` for a partition key, or two entries separated by spaces for a partition key and sort key. Valid types are `HASH` and `RANGE`.
- `provisioned-throughput`—Performance settings for this table defined as `ReadCapacityUnits=5,WriteCapacityUnits=5` (you'll learn about this in section 12.11).

Execute the following command to create the `todo-user` table with the `uid` attribute as the partition key:

Prefixing tables with the name of your application will prevent name clashes in the future.

Items must at least have one attribute uid of type string.

```
$ aws dynamodb create-table --table-name todo-user \
    --attribute-definitions AttributeName=uid,AttributeType=S \
    --key-schema AttributeName=uid,KeyType=HASH \
    --provisioned-throughput ReadCapacityUnits=5,WriteCapacityUnits=5
```

The partition key (type HASH) uses the uid attribute.

You'll learn about this in section 12.11.

Creating a table takes some time. Wait until the status changes to `ACTIVE`. You can check the status of a table as follows.

Listing 12.2 Checking the status of the DynamoDB table

```
$ aws dynamodb describe-table --table-name todo-user
{
  "Table": {
    "AttributeDefinitions": [
      {
        "AttributeName": "uid",
        "AttributeType": "S"
      }
    ],
    "TableName": "todo-user",
    "KeySchema": [
      {
        "AttributeName": "uid",
        "KeyType": "HASH"
      }
    ],
    "TableStatus": "ACTIVE",
    "CreationDateTime": "2022-01-24T16:00:29.105000+01:00",
```

The CLI command to check the table status

Attributes defined for that table

Attributes used as the primary key

Status of the table

```
      "ProvisionedThroughput": {
        "NumberOfDecreasesToday": 0,
        "ReadCapacityUnits": 5,
        "WriteCapacityUnits": 5
      },
      "TableSizeBytes": 0,
      "ItemCount": 0,
      "TableArn": "arn:aws:dynamodb:us-east-1:111111111111:table/todo-user",
      "TableId": "0697ea25-5901-421c-af29-8288a024392a"
    }
}
```

12.2.2 Tasks are identified by a partition key and sort key

So far, we created the table `todo-user` to store information about the users of node-todo. Next, we need a table to store the tasks. A task belongs to a user and contains a description of the task. Therefore, we came up with the following data structure:

```
{                                    The task is assigned to         The creation time (number of
  "uid": "emma",                     the user with this ID.          milliseconds elapsed since January
  "tid": 1645609847712,                                              1, 1970 00:00:00 UTC) is used as
  "description": "prepare lunch"                                     ID for the task.
}
                                                                     The description
                                                                     of the task
```

How does nodetodo query the task table? By using the `task-ls` command, which we need to implement. This command lists all the tasks belonging to a user. Therefore, choosing the `tid` as the primary key is not sufficient. We recommend a combination of `uid` and `tid` instead. DynamoDB calls the components of a primary key with two attributes partition key and *sort key*. Neither the partition key nor the sort key need to be unique, but the combination of both parts must be unique.

> **NOTE** This solution has one limitation: users can add only one task per time-stamp. Because tasks are uniquely identified by `uid` and `tid` (the primary key) there can't be two tasks for the same user at the same time. Our timestamp comes with millisecond resolution, so it should be fine.

Using a partition key and a sort key uses two of your table's attributes. For the partition key, an unordered hash index is maintained; the sort key is kept in a sorted index for each partition key. The combination of the partition key and the sort key uniquely identifies an item if they are used as the primary key. The following data set shows the combination of unsorted partition keys and sorted sort keys:

```
["john", 1] => {                    The primary key consists of the uid
  "uid": "john",                    (john) used as the partition key and
  "tid": 1,                         tid (1) used as the sort key.
  "description": "prepare customer presentation"
}
["john", 2] => {                    The sort keys are sorted
  "uid": "john",                    within a partition key.
```

```
      "tid": 2,
      "description": "plan holidays"
}
["emma", 1] => {                    ⟵──┐  There is no order in
   "uid": "emma",                       │  the partition keys.
   "tid": 1,
   "description": "prepare lunch"
}
["emma", 2] => {
   "uid": "emma",
   "tid": 2,
   "description": "buy nice flowers for mum"
}
["emma", 3] => {
   "uid": "emma",
   "tid": 3,
   "description": "prepare talk for conference"
}
```

Execute the following command to create the `todo-task` table with a primary key consisting of the partition key `uid` and sort key `tid` like this:

**At least two attributes are needed
for a partition key and sort key.**

```
$ aws dynamodb create-table --table-name todo-task \
  ⇒ --attribute-definitions AttributeName=uid,AttributeType=S \
  ⇒ AttributeName=tid,AttributeType=N \
  ⇒ --key-schema AttributeName=uid,KeyType=HASH \              The tid attribute
  ⇒ AttributeName=tid,KeyType=RANGE \         ⟵──┘             is the sort key.
  ⇒ --provisioned-throughput ReadCapacityUnits=5,WriteCapacityUnits=5
```

Wait until the table status changes to `ACTIVE` when you run `aws dynamodb describe-table --table-name todo-task`.

The `todo-user` and `todo-task` tables are ready. Time to add some data.

12.3 Adding data

Now you have two tables up and running to store users and their tasks. To use them, you need to add data. You'll access DynamoDB via the Node.js SDK, so it's time to set up the SDK and some boilerplate code before you implement adding users and tasks.

> **Installing and getting started with Node.js**
>
> Node.js is a platform for executing JavaScript in an event-driven environment so you can easily build network applications. To install Node.js, visit https://nodejs.org and download the package that fits your OS. All examples in this book are tested with Node.js 14.
>
> After Node.js is installed, you can verify that everything works by typing `node --version` into your terminal. Your terminal should respond with something similar to `v14.*`. Now you're ready to run JavaScript examples like nodetodo for AWS.

> **(continued)**
>
> Do you want to learn more about Node.js? We recommend *Node.js in Action* (second edition) by Alex Young, et al. (Manning, 2017), or the video course *Node.js in Motion* by PJ Evans (Manning, 2018).

To get started with Node.js and docopt, you need some magic lines to load all the dependencies and do some configuration work. Listing 12.3 shows how this can be done.

> **Where is the code located?**
>
> As usual, you'll find the code in the book's code repository on GitHub: https://github .com/AWSinAction/code3. nodetodo is located in /chapter12/. Switch to that directory, and run npm install in your terminal to install all needed dependencies.

Docopt is responsible for reading all the arguments passed to the process. It returns a JavaScript object, where the arguments are mapped to the parameters in the CLI description.

Listing 12.3   nodetodo: Using docopt in Node.js (index.js)

Loads the fs module to access the filesystem

Loads the docopt module to read input arguments

```
const fs = require('fs');
const docopt = require('docopt');
const moment = require('moment');
const AWS = require('aws-sdk');
const db = new AWS.DynamoDB({
  region: 'us-east-1'
});
```

Loads the moment module to simplify temporal types in JavaScript

Loads the AWS SDK module

```
const cli = fs.readFileSync('./cli.txt',
  {encoding: 'utf8'});
const input = docopt.docopt(cli, {
  version: '1.0',
  argv: process.argv.splice(2)
});
```

Reads the CLI description from the file cli.txt

Parses the arguments, and saves them to an input variable

Next, you will add an item to a table. The next listing explains the putItem method of the AWS SDK for Node.js.

Listing 12.4   DynamoDB: Creating an item

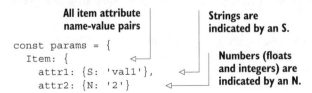

All item attribute name-value pairs

Strings are indicated by an S.

```
const params = {
  Item: {
    attr1: {S: 'val1'},
    attr2: {N: '2'}
```

Numbers (floats and integers) are indicated by an N.

```
        },
        TableName: 'app-entity'          ⟵───┤  Adds item to the
    };                                           app-entity table
    db.putItem(params, (err) => {        ⟵────  Invokes the putItem
      if (err) {                                 operation on DynamoDB
        console.error('error', err);
      } else {
        console.log('success');
      }
    });
```

Handles errors └⟶ (points to `if (err) {` block)

The first step is to add an item to the `todo-user` table.

12.3.1 Adding a user

The following listing shows the code executed by the `user-add` command.

Listing 12.5 nodetodo: Adding a user (index.js)

Item contains all attributes. Keys are also attributes, and that's why you do not need to tell DynamoDB which attributes are keys if you add data.

The uid attribute is of type string and contains the uid parameter value.

```
    if (input['user-add'] === true) {
      const params = {
        Item: {
          uid: {S: input['<uid>']},         ⟵
          email: {S: input['<email>']},     ⟵
          phone: {S: input['<phone>']}      ⟵
        },
        TableName: 'todo-user',
        ConditionExpression: 'attribute_not_exists(uid)'    ⟵
      };
      db.putItem(params, (err) => {
        if (err) {
          console.error('error', err);
        } else {
          console.log('user added');
        }
      });
    }
```

The email attribute is of type string and contains the email parameter value.

The phone attribute is of type string and contains the phone parameter value.

Specifies the user table └⟶ (points to `TableName: 'todo-user'`)

Invokes the putItem operation on DynamoDB ⟶ (points to `db.putItem(params, (err) => {`)

If putItem is called twice on the same key, data is replaced. ConditionExpression allows the putItem only if the key isn't yet present.

When you make a call to the AWS API, you always do the following:

1. Create a JavaScript object (map) filled with the needed parameters (the `params` variable).
2. Invoke the function via the AWS SDK.
3. Check whether the response contains an error, and if not, process the returned data.

Therefore, you only need to change the content of `params` if you want to add a task instead of a user. Execute the following commands to add two users:

```
node index.js user-add john john@widdix.de +11111111
node index.js user-add emma emma@widdix.de +22222222
```

Time to add tasks.

12.3.2 Adding a task

John and Emma want to add tasks to their to-do lists to better organize their everyday life. Adding a task is similar to adding a user. The next listing shows the code used to create a task.

Listing 12.6   nodetodo: Adding a task (index.js)

```
if (input['task-add'] === true) {
  const tid = Date.now();                          ← Creates the task ID (tid) based on the current timestamp
  const params = {
    Item: {
      uid: {S: input['<uid>']},
      tid: {N: tid.toString()},                    ← The tid attribute is of type number and contains the tid value.
      description: {S: input['<description>']},
      created: {N: moment(tid).format('YYYYMMDD')} ← The created attribute is of type number (format 20150525).
    },
    TableName: 'todo-task',                         ← Specifies the task table
    ConditionExpression: 'attribute_not_exists(uid)
    and attribute_not_exists(tid)'                  ← Ensures that an existing item is not overridden
  };
  if (input['--dueat'] !== null) {                  ← If the optional named parameter dueat is set, adds this value to the item
    params.Item.due = {N: input['--dueat']};
  }
  if (input['<category>'] !== null) {               ← If the optional named parameter category is set, adds this value to the item
    params.Item.category = {S: input['<category>']};
  }
  db.putItem(params, (err) => {                     ← Invokes the putItem operation on DynamoDB
    if (err) {
      console.error('error', err);
    } else {
      console.log('task added with tid ' + tid);
    }
  });
}
```

Now we'll add some tasks. Use the following command to remind Emma about buying some milk and a task asking John to put out the garbage:

```
node index.js task-add emma "buy milk" "shopping"
node index.js task-add emma "put out the garbage" "housekeeping" --dueat "20220224"
```

Now that you are able to add users and tasks to nodetodo, wouldn't it be nice if you could retrieve all this data?

12.4 Retrieving data

So far, you have learned how to insert users and tasks into two different DynamoDB tables. Next, you will learn how to query the data, for example, to get a list of all tasks assigned to Emma.

DynamoDB is a key-value store. The key is usually the only way to retrieve data from such a store. When designing a data model for DynamoDB, you must be aware of that limitation when you create tables (as you did in section 12.2). If you can use only the key to look up data, you'll sooner or later experience difficulties. Luckily, DynamoDB provides two other ways to look up items: a secondary index lookup and the scan operation. You'll start by retrieving data by the items' primary key and continue with more sophisticated methods of data retrieval.

> ## DynamoDB Streams
>
> DynamoDB lets you retrieve changes to a table as soon as they're made. A Stream provides all write (create, update, delete) operations to your table items. The order is consistent within a partition key. DynamoDB Streams also help with the following:
>
> - If your application polls the database for changes, DynamoDB Streams solves the problem in a more elegant way.
> - If you want to populate a cache with the changes made to a table, DynamoDB Streams can help.

12.4.1 Getting an item by key

Let's start with a simple example. You want to find out the contact details about Emma, which are stored in the `todo-user` table.

The simplest form of data retrieval is looking up a single item by its primary key, for example, a user by its ID. The `getItem` SDK operation to get a single item from DynamoDB can be used like this.

Listing 12.7 DynamoDB: Query a single item (index.js)

```
const params = {                      Specifies the
  Key: {                              attributes of the
    attr1: {S: 'val1'}                primary key
  },
  TableName: 'app-entity'
};                                    Invokes the
db.getItem(params, (err, data) => {   getItem operation
  if (err) {                          on DynamoDB
    console.error('error', err);
  } else {                            Checks whether an
    if (data.Item) {                  item was found
      console.log('item', data.Item);
    } else {
      console.error('no item found');
    }
  }
});
```

The user <uid> command retrieves a user by the user's ID. The code to fetch a user is shown in listing 12.8.

Listing 12.8   nodetodo: Retrieving a user (index.js)

```
const mapUserItem = (item) => {          ◁──┐  Helper function
  return {                                    │  to transform
    uid: item.uid.S,                          │  DynamoDB result
    email: item.email.S,
    phone: item.phone.S
  };
};

if (input['user'] === true) {            ┌── Looks up a user
  const params = {                       │   by primary key
    Key: {
      uid: {S: input['<uid>']}    ◁──────┤
    },                                   │   Specifies the
    TableName: 'todo-user'      ◁────────┘   user table
  };
  db.getItem(params, (err, data) => {   ◁──┐  Invokes the getItem
    if (err) {                               │  operation on
      console.error('error', err);           │  DynamoDB
    } else {
      if (data.Item) {                 ◁──┐ Checks whether
        console.log('user', mapUserItem(data.Item));  │ data was found for
      } else {                              │ the primary key
        console.error('user not found');
      }
    }
  });
}
```

For example, use the following command to fetch information about Emma:

```
node index.js user emma
```

You can also use the `getItem` operation to retrieve data by partition key and sort key, for example, to look up a specific task. The only change is that the `Key` has two entries instead of one. `getItem` returns one item or no items; if you want to get multiple items, you need to query DynamoDB.

12.4.2 *Querying items by key and filter*

Emma wants to get check her to-do list for things she needs to do. Therefore, you will query the `todo-task` table to retrieve all tasks assigned to Emma next.

 If you want to retrieve a collection of items rather than a single item, such as all tasks for a user, you must query DynamoDB. Retrieving multiple items by primary key works only if your table has a partition key and sort key. Otherwise, the partition key will identify only a single item. Listing 12.9 shows how the `query` SDK operation can be used to get a collection of items from DynamoDB.

Listing 12.9   DynamoDB: Querying a table

```
const params = {
  KeyConditionExpression: 'attr1 = :attr1val
  AND attr2 = :attr2val',
  ExpressionAttributeValues: {
    ':attr1val': {S: 'val1'},
    ':attr2val': {N: '2'}
  },
  TableName: 'app-entity'
};
db.query(params, (err, data) => {
  if (err) {
    console.error('error', err);
  } else {
    console.log('items', data.Items);
  }
});
```

The condition the key must match. Use AND if you're querying both a partition and sort key. Only the = operator is allowed for partition keys. Allowed operators for sort keys are =, >, <, >=, <=, BETWEEN x AND y, and begins_with. Sort key operators are blazing fast because the data is already sorted.

Dynamic values are referenced in the expression.

Always specify the correct type (S, N, B).

Invokes the query operation on DynamoDB

The query operation also lets you specify an optional FilterExpression, to include only items that match the filter and key condition. This is helpful to reduce the result set, for example, to show only tasks of a specific category. The syntax of Filter-Expression works like KeyConditionExpression, but no index is used for filters. Filters are applied to all matches that KeyConditionExpression returns.

To list all tasks for a certain user, you must query DynamoDB. The primary key of a task is the combination of the uid and the tid. To get all tasks for a user, KeyCondition-Expression requires only the partition key.

The next listing shows two helper functions used to implement the task-ls command.

Listing 12.10   nodetodo: Retrieving tasks (index.js)

```
const getValue = (attribute, type) => {
  if (attribute === undefined) {
    return null;
  }
  return attribute[type];
};
```

Helper function to access optional attributes

```
const mapTaskItem = (item) => {
  return {
    tid: item.tid.N,
    description: item.description.S,
    created: item.created.N,
    due: getValue(item.due, 'N'),
    category: getValue(item.category, 'S'),
    completed: getValue(item.completed, 'N')
  };
};
```

Helper function to transform the DynamoDB result

The real magic happens in listing 12.11, which shows the implementation of the task-ls command.

Listing 12.11   nodetodo: Retrieving tasks (index.js)

```
if (input['task-ls'] === true) {
  const yyyymmdd = moment().format('YYYYMMDD');
  const params = {
    KeyConditionExpression: 'uid = :uid',
    ExpressionAttributeValues: {
      ':uid': {S: input['<uid>']}}
    },
    TableName: 'todo-task',
    Limit: input['--limit']
  };
  if (input['--next'] !== null) {
    params.KeyConditionExpression += ' AND tid > :next';
    params.ExpressionAttributeValues[':next'] = {N: input['--next']};
  }
  if (input['--overdue'] === true) {
    params.FilterExpression = 'due < :yyyymmdd';
    params.ExpressionAttributeValues
    [':yyyymmdd'] = {N: yyyymmdd};
  } else if (input['--due'] === true) {
    params.FilterExpression = 'due = :yyyymmdd';
    params.ExpressionAttributeValues[':yyyymmdd'] = {N: yyyymmdd};
  } else if (input['--withoutdue'] === true) {
    params.FilterExpression =
    'attribute_not_exists(due)';
  } else if (input['--futuredue'] === true) {
    params.FilterExpression = 'due > :yyyymmdd';
    params.ExpressionAttributeValues[':yyyymmdd'] = {N: yyyymmdd};
  } else if (input['--dueafter'] !== null) {
    params.FilterExpression = 'due > :yyyymmdd';
    params.ExpressionAttributeValues[':yyyymmdd'] =
      {N: input['--dueafter']};
  } else if (input['--duebefore'] !== null) {
    params.FilterExpression = 'due < :yyyymmdd';
    params.ExpressionAttributeValues[':yyyymmdd'] =
      {N: input['--duebefore']};
  }
  if (input['<category>'] !== null) {
    if (params.FilterExpression === undefined) {
      params.FilterExpression = '';
    } else {
      params.FilterExpression += ' AND ';
    }
    params.FilterExpression += 'category = :category';
    params.ExpressionAttributeValues[':category'] =
      S: input['<category>']};
  }
  db.query(params, (err, data) => {
    if (err) {
      console.error('error', err);
    } else {
      console.log('tasks', data.Items.map(mapTaskItem));
      if (data.LastEvaluatedKey !== undefined) {
        console.log('more tasks available with --next=' +
```

Primary key query. The task table uses a partition and sort key. Only the partition key is defined in the query, so all tasks belonging to a user are returned.

Query attributes must be passed this way.

Filter attributes must be passed this way.

Filtering uses no index; it's applied over all elements returned from the primary key query.

attribute_not_exists(due) is true when the attribute is missing (opposite of attribute_exists).

Multiple filters can be combined with logical operators.

Invokes the query operation on DynamoDB

```
                data.LastEvaluatedKey.tid.N);
        }
      }
  });
}
```

As an example, you could use the following command to get a list of Emma's shopping tasks. The query will fetch all tasks by `uid` first and filter items based on the category attribute next:.

```
node index.js task-ls emma shopping
```

Two problems arise with the query approach:

- Depending on the result size from the primary key query, filtering may be slow. Filters work without an index: every item must be inspected. Imagine you have stock prices in DynamoDB, with a partition key and sort key: the partition key is a ticker like AAPL, and the sort key is a timestamp. You can make a query to retrieve all stock prices of Apple (AAPL) between two timestamps (20100101 and 20150101). But if you want to return prices only on Mondays, you need to filter over all prices to return only 20% (one out of five trading days each week) of them. That's wasting a lot of resources!

- You can only query the primary key. Returning a list of all tasks that belong to a certain category for all users isn't possible, because you can't query the category attribute.

You can solve these problems with secondary indexes. Let's look at how they work.

12.4.3 *Using global secondary indexes for more flexible queries*

In this section, you will create a secondary index that allows you to query the tasks belonging to a certain category.

A *global secondary index* is a projection of your original table that is automatically maintained by DynamoDB. Items in an index don't have a primary key, just a key. This key is not necessarily unique within the index. Imagine a table of users where each user has a country attribute. You then create a global secondary index where the country is the new partition key. As you can see, many users can live in the same country, so that key is not unique in the index.

You can query a global secondary index like you would query the table. You can imagine a global secondary index as a read-only DynamoDB table that is automatically maintained by DynamoDB: whenever you change the parent table, all indexes are asynchronously (eventually consistent!) updated as well.

In our example, we will create a global secondary index for the table `todo-tasks` which uses the `category` as the partition key and the `tid` as the sort key. Doing so allows us to query tasks by category. Figure 12.4 shows how a global secondary index works.

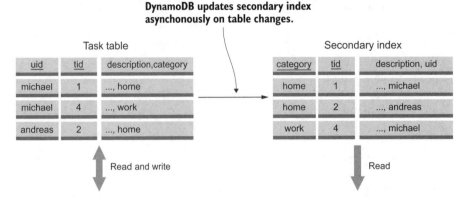

Figure 12.4   A global secondary index contains a copy (projection) of your table's data to provide fast lookup on another key.

A global secondary index comes at a price: the index requires storage (the same cost as for the original table). You must provision additional write-capacity units for the index as well, because a write to your table will cause a write to the global secondary index as well.

> **Local secondary index**
>
> Besides global secondary indexes, DynamoDB also supports local secondary indexes. A local secondary index must use the same partition key as the table. You can only vary on the attribute that is used as the sort key. A local secondary index consumes the read and write capacity of the table.

A huge benefit of DynamoDB is that you can provision capacity based on your workload. If one of your global secondary indexes gets tons of read traffic, you can increase the read capacity of that index. You can fine-tune your database performance by provisioning sufficient capacity for your tables and indexes. You'll learn more about that in section 13.9.

12.4.4   *Creating and querying a global secondary index*

Back to nodetodo. John needs the shopping list including Emma's and his tasks for his trip to town.

To implement the retrieval of tasks by category, you'll add a secondary index to the `todo-task` table. This will allow you to make queries by category. A partition key and sort key are used: the partition key is the `category` attribute, and the sort key is the `tid` attribute. The index also needs a name: `category-index`. You can find the following CLI command in the README.md file in nodetodo's code folder and simply copy and paste:

Creates a new
secondary index

Adds a global secondary index by updating the
table that has already been created previously

```
$ aws dynamodb update-table --table-name todo-task \
   --attribute-definitions AttributeName=uid,AttributeType=S \
   AttributeName=tid,AttributeType=N \
   AttributeName=category,AttributeType=S \
   --global-secondary-index-updates '[{\
   "Create": {\
   "IndexName": "category-index", \
   "KeySchema": [{"AttributeName": "category",
   "KeyType": "HASH"}, \
   {"AttributeName": "tid", "KeyType": "RANGE"}], \
   "Projection": {"ProjectionType": "ALL"}, \
   "ProvisionedThroughput": {"ReadCapacityUnits": 5, \
   "WriteCapacityUnits": 5}\
   }}]'
```

Adds a category attribute,
because the attribute will
be used in the index

The category
attribute is the
partition key, and
the tid attribute is
the sort key.

All attributes are
projected into the index.

Creating a global secondary index takes about five minutes. You can use the CLI to find out if the index is ready like this:

```
$ aws dynamodb describe-table --table-name=todo-task \
   --query "Table.GlobalSecondaryIndexes"
```

The next listing shows the code to query the global secondary index to fetch tasks by category with the help of the task-la command.

Listing 12.12   nodetodo: Retrieving tasks from a global secondary index (index.js)

```
if (input['task-la'] === true) {
  const yyyymmdd = moment().format('YYYYMMDD');
  const params = {
    KeyConditionExpression: 'category = :category',
    ExpressionAttributeValues: {
      ':category': {S: input['<category>']}
    },
    TableName: 'todo-task',
    IndexName: 'category-index',
    Limit: input['--limit']
  };
  if (input['--next'] !== null) {
    params.KeyConditionExpression += ' AND tid > :next';
    params.ExpressionAttributeValues[':next'] = {N: input['--next']};
  }
  if (input['--overdue'] === true) {
    params.FilterExpression = 'due < :yyyymmdd';
    params.ExpressionAttributeValues[':yyyymmdd'] = {N: yyyymmdd};
  }
  [...]
  db.query(params, (err, data) => {
    if (err) {
      console.error('error', err);
    } else {
```

A query against an
index works the
same as a query
against a table ...

... but you must
specify the index you
want to use.

Filtering works the
same as with tables.

```
        console.log('tasks', data.Items.map(mapTaskItem));
        if (data.LastEvaluatedKey !== undefined) {
          console.log('more tasks available with --next='
            + data.LastEvaluatedKey.tid.N);
        }
      }
    }
  });
}
```

When following our example, use the following command to fetch John and Emma's shopping tasks:

```
node index.js task-la shopping
```

But you'll still have situations where a query doesn't work. For example, you can't retrieve all users from `todo-user` with a query. Therefore, let's look at how to scan through all items of a table.

12.4.5 *Scanning and filtering all of your table's data*

John wants to know who else is using nodetodo and asks for a list of all users. You will learn how to list all items of a table without using an index next.

Sometime you can't work with keys because you don't know them up front; instead, you need to go through all the items in a table. That's not very efficient, but in rare situations, like daily batch jobs or rare requests, it's fine. DynamoDB provides the `scan` operation to scan all items in a table as shown next.

Listing 12.13 DynamoDB: Scan through all items in a table

```
const params = {
  TableName: 'app-entity',
  Limit: 50                                    Specifies the
};                                             maximum number
                                               of items to return
db.scan(params, (err, data) => {              Invokes the scan
  if (err) {                                   operation on
    console.error('error', err);              DynamoDB
  } else {
    console.log('items', data.Items);
    if (data.LastEvaluatedKey !== undefined) {    Checks whether there
      console.log('more items available');        are more items that
    }                                             can be scanned
  }
});
```

The following listing shows how to scan through all items of the `todo-user` table. A paging mechanism is used to prevent too many items from being returned at a time.

Listing 12.14 nodetodo: Retrieving all users with paging (index.js)

```
if (input['user-ls'] === true) {
  const params = {
    TableName: 'todo-user',
```

```
    Limit: input['--limit']                ◄────   The maximum number
  };                                                of items returned
  if (input['--next'] !== null) {
    params.ExclusiveStartKey = {
      uid: {S: input['--next']}            ◄────┐   The named parameter
    };                                            next contains the last
  }                                               evaluated key.
  db.scan(params, (err, data) => {       ◄────┐   Invokes the scan
    if (err) {                                    operation on
      console.error('error', err);               DynamoDB          ┌── Checks
    } else {                                                       │   whether the
      console.log('users', data.Items.map(mapUserItem));          │   last item has
      if (data.LastEvaluatedKey !== undefined) {          ◄───────┘   been reached
        console.log('page with --next=' + data.LastEvaluatedKey.uid.S);
      }
    }
  });
}
```

Use the following command to fetch all users:

```
node index.js user-ls
```

The scan operation reads all items in the table. This example didn't filter any data, but you can use FilterExpression as well. Note that you shouldn't use the scan operation too often—it's flexible but not efficient.

12.4.6 *Eventually consistent data retrieval*

By default, reading data from DynamoDB is *eventually consistent.* That means it's possible that if you create an item (version 1), update that item (version 2), and then read that item, you may get back version 1; if you wait and fetch the item again, you'll see version 2. Figure 12.5 shows this process. This behavior occurs because the item is

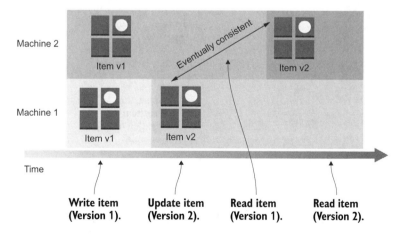

Figure 12.5   Eventually consistent reads can return old values after a write operation until the change is propagated to all machines.

persisted on multiple machines in the background. Depending on which machine answers your request, the machine may not have the latest version of the item.

You can prevent eventually consistent reads by adding `"ConsistentRead": true` to the DynamoDB request to get *strongly consistent reads*. Strongly consistent reads are supported by `getItem`, `query`, and `scan` operations. But a strongly consistent read is more expensive—it takes longer and consumes more read capacity—than an eventually consistent read. Reads from a global secondary index are always eventually consistent because the synchronization between table and index happens asynchronously.

Typically, NoSQL databases do not support transactions with atomicity, consistency, isolation, and durability (ACID) guarantees. However, DynamoDB comes with the ability to bundle multiple read or write requests into a transaction. The relevant API methods are called `TransactWriteItems` and `TransactGetItems`—you can either group write or read requests, but not a mix of both of them. Whenever possible, you should avoid using transactions because they are more expensive from a cost and latency perspective. Check out http://mng.bz/E0ol if you are interested in the details about DynamoDB transactions.

12.5 Removing data

John stumbled across a fancy to-do application on the web. Therefore, he decides to remove his user from nodetodo.

Like the `getItem` operation, the `deleteItem` operation requires that you specify the primary key you want to delete. Depending on whether your table uses a partition key or a partition key and sort key, you must specify one or two attributes. The next listing shows the implementation of the `user-rm` command.

Listing 12.15   nodetodo: Removing a user (index.js)

```
if (input['user-rm'] === true) {
  const params = {
    Key: {
      uid: {S: input['<uid>']}          Identifies an item
    },                                   by partition key
    TableName: 'todo-user'          Specifies the
  };                                user table
  db.deleteItem(params, (err) => {          Invokes the
    if (err) {                              deleteItem
      console.error('error', err);         operation on
    } else {                               DynamoDB
      console.log('user removed');
    }
  });
}
```

Use the following command to delete John from the DynamoDB table:

```
node index.js user-rm john
```

But John wants to delete not only his user but also his tasks. Luckily, removing a task works similarly. The only change is that the item is identified by a partition key and sort key and the table name has to be changed. The code used for the `task-rm` command is shown here.

Listing 12.16 nodetodo: Removing a task (index.js)

```
if (input['task-rm'] === true) {
  const params = {
    Key: {
      uid: {S: input['<uid>']},          Identifies an item
      tid: {N: input['<tid>']}           by partition key
    },                                   and sort key
    TableName: 'todo-task'               Specifies the
  };                                     task table
  db.deleteItem(params, (err) => {
    if (err) {
      console.error('error', err);
    } else {
      console.log('task removed');
    }
  });
}
```

You're now able to create, read, and delete items in DynamoDB. The only operation you're missing is updating an item.

12.6 *Modifying data*

Emma is still a big fan of nodetodo and uses the application constantly. She just bought some milk and wants to mark the task as done.

You can update an item with the `updateItem` operation. You must identify the item you want to update by its primary key; you can also provide an `UpdateExpression` to specify the updates you want to perform. Use one or a combination of the following update actions:

- Use `SET` to override or create a new attribute. Examples: `SET attr1 = :attr1val`, `SET attr1 = attr2 + :attr2val`, `SET attr1 = :attr1val, attr2 = :attr2val`.
- Use `REMOVE` to remove an attribute. Examples: `REMOVE attr1`, `REMOVE attr1, attr2`.

To implement this feature, you need to update the task item, as shown next.

Listing 12.17 nodetodo: Updating a task as done (index.js)

```
if (input['task-done'] === true) {
  const yyyymmdd = moment().format('YYYYMMDD');
  const params = {
    Key: {
      uid: {S: input['<uid>']},          Identifies the item
      tid: {N: input['<tid>']}           by a partition and
    },                                   sort key
```

```
      UpdateExpression: 'SET completed = :yyyymmdd',        ◁──────┐  Defines which
      ExpressionAttributeValues: {                                    attributes should
        ':yyyymmdd': {N: yyyymmdd}        ◁──┐  Attribute values      be updated
      },                                       must be passed
      TableName: 'todo-task'                   this way.
    };
    db.updateItem(params, (err) => {     ◁──┐  Invokes the
      if (err) {                              updateItem operation
        console.error('error', err);          on DynamoDB
      } else {
        console.log('task completed');
      }
    });
}
```

For example, the following command closes Emma's task to buy milk. Please note: the <tid> will differ when following the example yourself. Use node index.js task-ls emma to get the task's ID:

```
node index.js task-done emma 1643037541999
```

12.7   *Recap primary key*

We'd like to recap an important aspect of DynamoDB, the primary key. A primary key is unique within a table and identifies an item. You can use a single attribute as the primary key. DynamoDB calls this a partition key. You need an item's partition key to look up that item. Also, when updating or deleting an item, DynamoDB requires the partition key. You can also use two attributes as the primary key. In this case, one of the attributes is the partition key, and the other is called the sort key.

12.7.1   *Partition key*

A partition key uses a single attribute of an item to create a hash-based index. If you want to look up an item based on its partition key, you need to know the exact partition key. For example, a user table could use the user's email address as a partition key. The user could then be retrieved if you know the partition key—the email address, in this case.

12.7.2   *Partition key and sort key*

When you use both a partition key and a sort key, you're using two attributes of an item to create a more powerful index. To look up an item, you need to know its exact partition key, but you don't need to know the sort key. You can even have multiple items with the same partition key: they will be sorted according to their sort key.

The partition key can be queried only using exact matches (=). The sort key can be queried using =, >, <, >=, <=, and BETWEEN x AND y operators. For example, you can query the sort key of a partition key from a certain starting point. You cannot query only the sort key—you must always specify the partition key. A message table could use a partition key and sort key as its primary key; the partition key could be the user's email, and the sort key could be a timestamp. You could then look up all of user's messages that are newer or older than a specific timestamp, and the items would be sorted according to the timestamp.

12.8 *SQL-like queries with PartiQL*

As the developer of nodetodo, we want to get some insight into the way our users use the application. Therefore, we are looking for a flexible approach to query the data stored on DynamoDB on the fly.

Because SQL is such a widely used language, hardly any database system can avoid offering an SQL interface as well, even if, in the case of NoSQL databases, often only a fraction of the language is supported. In the following examples, you will learn how to use PartiQL, which is designed to provide unified query access to all kinds of data and data stored. DynamoDB supports PartiQL via the Management Console, NoSQL Workbench, AWS CLI, and DynamoDB APIs. Be aware that DynamoDB supports only a small subset of the PartiQL language. The following query lists all tasks stored in table `todo-task`:

> **The command execute-statement**
> **supports PartiQL statements as well.**

```
$ aws dynamo3db execute-statement \          <
⇨ --statement "SELECT * FROM \""todo-task\"""          <
```

> **A simple SELECT statement to fetch all attributes of all items**
> **from table todo-task. The escaped " is required because the**
> **table name includes a hyphen.**

PartiQL allows you to query an index as well. The following statement fetches all tasks with category equals `shopping` from index `category-index`:

```
$ aws dynamodb execute-statement --statement \
⇨ "SELECT * FROM \""todo-task\".\"category-index\""
⇨ WHERE category = 'shopping'"
```

Please note that combining multiple queries (`JOIN`) is not supported by DynamoDB. However, DynamoDB supports modifying data with the help of PartiQL. The following command updates Emma's phone number:

```
aws dynamodb execute-statement --statement \
⇨ "Update \"todo-user\" SET phone='+33333333' WHERE uid='emma'"
```

Be warned, an `UPDATE` or `DELETE` statement must include a `WHERE` clause that identifies a single item by its partition key or partition and sort keys. Therefore, it is not possible to update or delete more than one item per query.

Want to learn more about PartiQL for DynamoDB? Check out the official documentation: http://mng.bz/N5g2.

In our opinion, using PartiQL is confusing because it pretends to provide a flexible SQL language but is in fact very limited. We prefer using the DynamoDB APIs and the SDK, which is much more descriptive.

12.9   DynamoDB Local

Imagine a team of developers is working on a new app using DynamoDB. During development, each developer needs an isolated database so as not to corrupt the other team members' data. They also want to write unit tests to make sure their app is working. To address their needs, you could create a unique set of DynamoDB tables with a CloudFormation stack for each developer. Or you could use a local DynamoDB for offline development. AWS provides a local implementation of DynamoDB, which is available for download at http://mng.bz/71qm.

Don't run DynamoDB Local in production! It's only made for development purposes and provides the same functionality as DynamoDB, but it uses a different implementation: only the API is the same.

> **NoSQL Workbench for DynamoDB**
>
> Are you looking for a graphical user interface to interact with DynamoDB? Check out NoSQL Workbench for DynamoDB at http://mng.bz/mJ5P. The tool allows you to create data models, analyze data, and import and export data.

That's it! You've implemented all of nodetodo's features.

12.10   Operating DynamoDB

DynamoDB doesn't require administration like a traditional relational database, because it's a managed service and AWS takes care of that; instead, you only have a few things to do.

With DynamoDB, you don't need to worry about installation, updates, machines, storage, or backups. Here's why:

- DynamoDB isn't software you can download. Instead, it's a NoSQL database as a service. Therefore, you can't install DynamoDB like you would MySQL or MongoDB. This also means you don't have to update your database; the software is maintained by AWS.
- DynamoDB runs on a fleet of machines operated by AWS. AWS takes care of the OS and all security-related questions. From a security perspective, it's your job to restrict access to your data with the help of IAM.
- DynamoDB replicates your data among multiple machines and across multiple data centers. There is no need for a backup from a durability point of view. However, you should configure snapshots to be able to recover from accidental data deletion.

Now you know some administrative tasks that are no longer necessary if you use DynamoDB. But you still have things to consider when using DynamoDB in production:

monitoring capacity usage, provisioning read and write capacity (section 12.11), and creating backups of your tables.

> **Backups**
>
> DynamoDB provides very high durability. But what if the database administrator accidentally deletes all the data or a new version of the application corrupts items? In this case, you would need a backup to restore to a working table state from the past. In December 2017, AWS announced a new feature for DynamoDB: on-demand backup and restore. We strongly recommend using on-demand backups to create snapshots of your DynamoDB tables to be able to restore them later, if needed.

12.11 Scaling capacity and pricing

As discussed at the beginning of the chapter, the difference between a typical relational database and a NoSQL database is that a NoSQL database can be scaled by adding new nodes. Horizontal scaling enables increasing the read and write capacity of a database enormously. That's the case for DynamoDB as well. However, a DynamoDB table has two different read/write capacity modes:

- *On-demand mode* adapts the read and write capacity automatically.
- *Provisioned mode* requires you to configure the read and write capacity upfront. Additionally, you have the option to enable autoscaling to adapt the provisioned capacity based on the current load automatically.

At first glance, the first option sounds much better because it is totally maintenance free. Table 12.1 compares the costs between on-demand and provisioned modes. All of the following examples are based on costs for us-east-1 and assume you are reading and writing items with less than 1 KB.

Table 12.1   Comparing pricing of DynamoDB on-demand and provisioned mode

Throughput	On-demand mode	Provisioned mode
10 writes per second	$32.85 per month	$4.68 per month
100 reads per second	$32.85 per month	$4.68 per month

That's a significant difference. Accessing an on-demand table costs about seven times as much as using a table in provisioned capacity mode. But the example is not significant, because of the assumption that the provisioned throughput of 10 writes and 100 reads per second is running at 100% capacity 24/7. This is hardly true for any application. Most applications have large variations in read and write throughput. Therefore, in many cases, the opposite is correct: on-demand is more cost-efficient than provisioned. For example, we are operating a chatbot called marbot on AWS. When we switched from provisioned to on-demand capacity in December 2018, we reduced our monthly costs for DynamoDB by 90% (see http://mng.bz/DD69 for details).

As a rule of thumb, the more spikes in your traffic, the more likely that on-demand is the best option for you. Let's illustrate this with another example. Assume your application is used only during business hours from 9 a.m. to 5 p.m. The baseline throughput is 100 reads and 10 write per second. However, a batch job is running between 4 p.m. and 5 p.m., which requires 1,000 reads and 100 writes per second.

With provisioned capacity mode, you need to provision for the peak load. That's 1,000 reads and 10 writes per second. That's why the monthly costs for a table with provisioned capacity costs is $24.75 higher than when using on-demand capacity in this example, as shown here:

```
// Provisioned capacity mode
$0.00065 for 1 writes/sec * 100 * 24 hours * 30 days = $46.80 per month
$0.00013 for 2 reads/sec * 500 * 24 hours * 30 days = $46.80 per month

Read/Writes with provisioned capacity mode per month: $93.60

// On-demand Capacity Mode
(7 hours * 60 min * 60 sec * 10 write) + (1 hour * 60 min * 60 sec * 100
    writes) = 612,000 writes/day
(7 hours * 60 min * 60 sec * 100 reads) + (1 hour * 60 min * 60 sec * 1000
    reads) = 6,120,000 reads/day

$0.00000125/write * 612,000 writes/day * 30 days = $22.95
$0.00000025/read * 6,120,000 reads/day * 30 days = $45.90

Read/Writes with On-demand Mode per month: $68.85
```

By the way, you are not only paying for accessing your data but also for storage. By default, you are paying $0.25 per GB per month. The first 25 GB are free. You only pay per use—there is no need to provision data upfront.

Does your workload require storing huge amounts of data that are accessed rarely? If so, you should have a look into Standard-Infrequent Access, which reduces the cost for storing data to $0.10 per GB per month but increases costs for reading and writing data by about 25%. Please visit the https://aws.amazon.com/dynamodb/pricing/ for more details on DynamoDB pricing.

12.11.1 *Capacity units*

When working with provisioned capacity mode, you need to configure the provisioned read and write capacity separately. To understand capacity units, let's start by experimenting with the CLI, as shown here:

```
$ aws dynamodb get-item --table-name todo-user \        Tells DynamoDB
   --key '{"uid": {"S": "emma"}}' \                      to return the used
   --return-consumed-capacity TOTAL \                    capacity units
   --query "ConsumedCapacity"
{
    "CapacityUnits": 0.5,          getItem requires
    "TableName": "todo-user"       0.5 capacity units.
}
```

```
$ aws dynamodb get-item --table-name todo-user \
  --key '{"uid": {"S": "emma"}}' \
  --consistent-read --return-consumed-capacity TOTAL \          A consistent
  --query "ConsumedCapacity"                                    read ...
{
    "CapacityUnits": 1.0,          ◁─────┐  ... needs twice as
    "TableName": "todo-user"              │  many capacity
}                                            units.
```

More abstract rules for throughput consumption follow:

- An eventually consistent read takes half the capacity of a strongly consistent read.

- A strongly consistent `getItem` requires one read capacity unit if the item isn't larger than 4 KB. If the item is larger than 4 KB, you need additional read capacity units. You can calculate the required read capacity units using `roundUP(itemSize / 4)`.

- A strongly consistent `query` requires one read capacity unit per 4 KB of item size. This means if your query returns 10 items, and each item is 2 KB, the item size is 20 KB and you need five read units. This is in contrast to 10 `getItem` operations, for which you would need 10 read capacity units.

- A write operation needs one write capacity unit per 1 KB of item size. If your item is larger than 1 KB, you can calculate the required write capacity units using `roundUP(itemSize)`.

If capacity units aren't your favorite unit, you can use the AWS Pricing Calculator at https://calculator.aws to calculate your capacity needs by providing details of your read and write workload.

The provision throughput of a table or a global secondary index is defined in seconds. If you provision five read capacity units per second with `ReadCapacityUnits=5`, you can make five strongly consistent `getItem` requests for that table if the item size isn't larger than 4 KB per second. If you make more requests than are provisioned, DynamoDB will first throttle your request. If you make many more requests than are provisioned, DynamoDB will reject your requests.

Increasing the provisioned throughput is possible whenever you like, but you can only decrease the throughput of a table four to 23 times a day (a day in UTC time). Therefore, you might need to overprovision the throughput of a table during some times of the day.

> **Limits for decreasing the throughput capacity**
>
> Decreasing the throughput capacity of a table is generally allowed only four times a day (a day in UTC time). Additionally, decreasing the throughout capacity is possible even if you have used up all four decreases if the last decrease has happened more than an hour ago.

It is possible but not necessary to update the provisioned capacity manually. By using Application Auto Scaling, you can increase or decrease the capacity of your table or global secondary indices based on a CloudWatch metric automatically. See http://mng.bz/lR7M to learn more.

12.12 Networking

DynamoDB does not run in your VPC. It is accessible via an API. You need internet connectivity to reach the DynamoDB API. This means you can't access DynamoDB from a private subnet by default, because a private subnet has no route to the internet via an internet gateway. Instead, a NAT gateway is used (see section 5.5 for more details). Keep in mind that an application using DynamoDB can create a lot of traffic, and your NAT gateway is limited to 10 Gbps of bandwidth. A better approach is to set up a VPC endpoint for DynamoDB and use that to access DynamoDB from private subnets without needing a NAT gateway at all. You can read more about VPC endpoints in the AWS documentation at http://mng.bz/51qz.

12.13 Comparing DynamoDB to RDS

In chapter 10, you learned about the Relational Database Service (RDS). For a better understanding, let's compare the two different database systems. Table 12.2 compares DynamoDB and the RDS. Keep in mind that this is like comparing apples and oranges: the only thing DynamoDB and RDS have in common is that both are called databases. RDS provides relational databases that are very flexible when it comes to ingesting or querying data. However, scaling RDS is a challenge. Also, RDS is priced per database instance hour. In contrast, DynamoDB scales horizontally with little or no effort. Also, DynamoDB offers a pay-per-request pricing model, which is interesting for low-volume workloads with traffic spikes. Use RDS if your application requires complex SQL queries or you don't want to invest time into mastering a new technology. Otherwise, you can consider migrating your application to DynamoDB.

Table 12.2   Differences between DynamoDB and RDS

Task	DynamoDB	RDS Aurora
Creating a table	Management Console, SDK, or CLI `aws dynamodb create-table`	SQL `CREATE TABLE` statement
Inserting, updating, or deleting data	SDK or PartiQL (limited version of SQL)	SQL `INSERT`, `UPDATE`, or `DELETE` statement
Querying data	SDK `query` or PartiQL	SQL `SELECT` statement
Adding indexes to extend the possibility of query data	No more than 25 global secondary indexes per table	Number of indexes not limited per table

Table 12.2   Differences between DynamoDB and RDS *(continued)*

Task	DynamoDB	RDS Aurora
Increasing storage	No action needed; storage grows and shrinks automatically.	Increasing storage is possible via the Management Console, CLI, or API.
Increasing performance	Horizontal, by increasing capacity. DynamoDB will add more machines under the hood.	Vertical, by increasing instance size and disk throughput; or horizontal, by adding up to five read replicas
Distribute data globally	Multiactive replication enables reads and writes in multiple regions.	Read replication enables data synchronization to other regions as well, but writing data is possible only in the source region.
Installing the database on your machine	DynamoDB is available on AWS only. There is a local version for developing on your local machine.	Install MySQL or PostgreSQL on your machine.
Hiring an expert	DynamoDB skills needed	General SQL skills sufficient for most scenarios

12.14 NoSQL alternatives

Besides DynamoDB, a few other NoSQL options are available on AWS as shown in table 12.3. Make sure you understand the requirements of your workload and learn about the details of a NoSQL database before deciding on an option.

Table 12.3   Differences between DynamoDB and some NoSQL databases

Amazon Keyspaces	Columnar store	A fully managed Apache Cassandra–compatible database service	A good fit when dealing with very large data sets. Think of DynamoDB as an open source project. Available as a managed service by other vendors as well.
Amazon Neptune	Graph store	A proprietary graph database provided by AWS	Perfect fit for a social graph, personalization, product catalog, highly connected data sets
Amazon DocumentDB with MongoDB compatibility	Document store	A database service that is purpose-built for JSON data management at scale, fully managed and integrated with AWS. Amazon DocumentDB is compatible with MongoDB 3.6.	A good choice if you are looking for a NoSQL database that also brings flexible query capabilities. A common use case are common CRUD (create, read, update, and delete) applications.
Amazon MemoryDB for Redis	Key-value store	An in-memory database with durability, providing a Redis-compatible interface	A good match for implementing a cache, a session store, or whenever I/O latency is super critical

Cleaning up

Don't forget to delete your DynamoDB tables after you finish this chapter like so:

```
aws dynamodb delete-table --table-name todo-task
aws dynamodb delete-table --table-name todo-user
```

Summary

- DynamoDB is a NoSQL database service that removes all the operational burdens from you, scales well, and can be used in many ways as the storage backend of your applications.
- Looking up data in DynamoDB is based on keys. To query an item, you need to know the primary key, called the partition key.
- When using a combination of partition key and sort key, many items can use the same partition key as long as their sort key does not overlap. This approach also allows you to query all items with the same partition key, ordered by the sort key.
- Adding a global secondary index allows you to query efficiently on an additional attribute.
- The query operation queries a table or secondary indexes.
- The scan operation searches through all items of a table, which is flexible but not efficient and shouldn't be used too extensively.
- Enforcing strongly consistent reads avoids running into eventual consistency problems with stale data. But reading from a global secondary index is always eventually consistent.
- DynamDB comes with two capacity modes: on demand and provisioned. The on-demand capacity mode works best for spiky workloads.

Part 4

Architecting on AWS

Werner Vogels, CTO of Amazon.com, is quoted as saying "Everything fails all the time." Instead of trying to reach the unreachable goal of an unbreakable system, AWS plans for failure in the following ways:

- Hard drives can fail, so S3 stores data on multiple hard drives to prevent the loss of data.
- Computing hardware can fail, so virtual machines can be automatically restarted on another machine if necessary.
- Data centers can fail, so there are multiple data centers per region that can be used in parallel or on demand.

Outages of IT infrastructure and applications can cause a loss of trust and money and are a major risk for businesses. You will learn how to prevent an outage of your AWS applications by using the right tools and architecture.

Some AWS services handle failure by default in the background. For some services, responding to failure scenarios is available on demand. And some services don't handle failure by themselves but offer the possibility to plan and react to failure. The following table shows an overview of the most important services and their failure handling.

Designing for failure is a fundamental principle of AWS. Another is to make use of the elasticity of the cloud. You will learn about how to increase your number of virtual machines based on the current workload. This will allow you to architect reliable systems for AWS.

Table 1   Overview of services and their failure-handling possibilities

	Description	Examples
Fault tolerant	Services can recover from failure automatically without any downtime.	S3 (object storage), DynamoDB (NoSQL database), Route 53 (DNS)
Highly available	Services can recover from some failures automatically with little downtime.	RDS (relational database), EBS (network attached storage)
Manual failure handling	Services do not recover from failure by default but offer tools to build a highly available infrastructure on top of them.	EC2 (virtual machine)

Chapter 13 lays the foundation for becoming independent of the risk of losing a single server or a complete data center. You will learn how to recover a single EC2 instance either in the same data center or in another data center.

Chapter 14 introduces the concept of decoupling your system to increase reliability. You will learn how to use synchronous decoupling with the help of load balancers on AWS. You'll also see asynchronous decoupling using Amazon SQS, a distributed queuing service, to build a fault-tolerant system.

Chapter 15 is about automating the deployment of an application with little or no downtime. It is also a prerequisite for building highly available and fault-tolerant systems.

Chapter 16 uses a lot of the services you've discovered so far to build a fault-tolerant application. You'll learn everything you need to design a fault-tolerant web application based on EC2 instances (which aren't fault tolerant by default).

Chapter 17 is all about elasticity. You will learn how to scale your capacity based on a schedule or based on the current load of your system.

Chapter 18 presents options for running new and existing applications on AWS using containers.

Achieving high availability: Availability zones, autoscaling, and CloudWatch

This chapter covers

- Recovering a failed virtual machine with a CloudWatch alarm
- Using autoscaling to guarantee your virtual machines keep running
- Understanding availability zones in an AWS region
- Analyzing disaster-recovery requirements

Imagine you run an online shop. During the night, the hardware running your virtual machine fails. Your users can no longer access your web shop until the next morning when you go into work. During the eight-hour downtime, your users search for an alternative and stop buying from you. That's a disaster for any business. Now imagine a highly available web shop. Just a few minutes after the hardware failed, the system recovers, restarts itself on new hardware, and your e-commerce website is back online again—without any human intervention. Your users can now continue to shop on your site. In this chapter, we'll teach you how to build a highly available system based on EC2 instances like this one.

Virtual machines are not highly available by default, so the potential for system failure is always present. The following scenarios could cause an outage of your virtual machine:

- A software problem causes the virtual machine's OS to fail.
- A software problem occurs on the host machine, causing the virtual machine to fail (either the OS of the host machine fails or the virtualization layer does).
- The compute, storage, or networking hardware of the physical host fails.
- Parts of the data center that the virtual machine depends on fail: network connectivity, the power, or the cooling system.

For example, if the computing hardware of a physical host fails, all EC2 instances running on this host will fail. If you're running an application on an affected virtual machine, this application will fail and experience downtime until somebody intervenes by starting a new virtual machine on another physical host. In the case of a small outage—for example, when a single physical host fails—AWS will reboot the affected virtual machines and launch them on a new host. However, in the case of a larger outage—for example, when a whole rack is affected—you are in charge of recovering the failed instances. Therefore, to avoid downtime and to build a highly available system, we recommend enabling autorecovery based on a CloudWatch alarm or distributing the workload among multiple virtual machines.

Examples are 100% covered by the Free Tier

The examples in this chapter are totally covered by the Free Tier. As long as you don't run the examples longer than a few days, you won't pay anything for it. Keep in mind that this applies only if you created a fresh AWS account for this book and there is nothing else going on in your AWS account. Try to complete the chapter within a few days, because you'll clean up your account at the end of the chapter.

High availability describes a system that is operating with almost no downtime. Even if a failure occurs, the system can provide its services most of the time. The Harvard Research Group (HRG) defines high availability with the classification AEC-2, which requires an uptime of 99.99% over a year, or not more than 52 minutes and 35.7 seconds of downtime per year. You can achieve 99.99% uptime with EC2 instances if you follow the instructions in the rest of this chapter. Although a short interruption might be necessary to recover from a failure, no human intervention is needed to instigate the recovery.

High availability vs. fault tolerance

A highly available system can recover from a failure automatically with a short downtime. A fault-tolerant system, in contrast, requires the system to provide its services without interruption in the case of a component failure. We'll show you how to build a fault-tolerant system in chapter 16.

AWS provides building blocks for highly available systems based on EC2 instances. Depending on whether you can distribute a workload across multiple machines, different tools come into play, as described here:

- Building a highly available infrastructure by using groups of isolated data centers, called availability zones, within a region.
- Monitoring the health of virtual machines with CloudWatch and triggering recovery automatically, if needed. This option fits best for workloads that need to run on a single virtual machine.
- Using autoscaling to guarantee a certain number of virtual machines are up and running and replace failed instances automatically. Use this approach when distributing your workload among multiple virtual machines is an option.

You will learn how to automatically replace a failed virtual machine in the first section of this chapter. But what happens if you have a data center outage? You will learn how to recover from that in the second section of this chapter. At the end of the chapter, we will discuss how to analyze disaster recovery requirements and translate them into an AWS architecture. In the following section, you'll learn how to protect a workload that can run on only a single virtual machine at a time from failures.

13.1   Recovering from EC2 instance failure with CloudWatch

AWS does recover failed virtual machines under only some circumstances. For example, AWS will not recover an EC2 instance if a whole rack failed. An easy countermeasure is to automate the recovery of an EC2 instance by creating a CloudWatch alarm. You will learn how to do so in this section.

Suppose that your team is using an agile development process. To accelerate the process, your team decides to automate the testing, building, and deployment of the software. You've been asked to set up a continuous integration (CI) server, which allows you to automate the development process. You've chosen to use Jenkins, an open source application written in Java that runs in a servlet container such as Apache Tomcat. Because you're using infrastructure as code, you're planning to deploy changes to your infrastructure with Jenkins as well. (Learn more about Jenkins by reading its documentation at http://mng.bz/BZJg.)

A Jenkins server is a typical use case for a high-availability setup. It's an important part of your infrastructure, because your colleagues won't be able to test and deploy new software if Jenkins suffers from downtime. But a short downtime due to a failure with automatic recovery won't hurt your business too much, so you don't need a fault-tolerant system. Jenkins is only an example. You can apply the same principles to any other applications where you can tolerate a short amount of downtime but still want to recover from hardware failures automatically. For example, we used the same approach for hosting FTP servers and VPN servers.

In this example, you'll do the following:

1 Create a virtual network in the cloud (VPC).
2 Launch a virtual machine in the VPC, and automatically install Jenkins during bootstrap.
3 Create a CloudWatch alarm to monitor the health of the virtual machine and replace the virtual machine when needed.

> **AWS CloudWatch**
>
> AWS CloudWatch is a service offering metrics, events, logs, and alarms for AWS resources. You used CloudWatch to monitor a Lambda function in chapter 6, and gained some insight into the current load of a relational database instance in chapter 10.

We'll guide you through these steps with the help of a CloudFormation template. You can find the CloudFormation template for this example on GitHub and on S3. Download a snapshot of the repository at http://github.com/AWSinAction/code3/archive/master.zip. The file we're talking about is located at chapter13/recovery.yaml. On S3, the same file is located at https://s3.amazonaws.com/awsinaction-code3/chapter13/recovery.yaml.

The following command creates a CloudFormation template that launches an EC2 instance with a CloudWatch alarm that triggers a recovery if the virtual machine fails. Replace $Password with a password consisting of 8–40 characters. The template automatically installs a Jenkins server while starting the virtual machine:

```
$ aws cloudformation create-stack --stack-name jenkins-recovery \
  --template-url https://s3.amazonaws.com/\
  awsinaction-code3/chapter13/recovery.yaml \
  --parameters "ParameterKey=JenkinsAdminPassword,
  ParameterValue=$Password" \
  --capabilities CAPABILITY_IAM
```

While you are waiting for CloudFormation to launch the EC2 instance, we will have a look into the CloudFormation template. The CloudFormation template contains the definition of a private network. The most important parts of the template follow:

- A virtual machine with user data containing a bash script, which installs a Jenkins server during bootstrapping
- A public IP address assigned to the EC2 instance, so you can access the new instance after a recovery using the same public IP address as before
- A CloudWatch alarm based on the system status metric published by the EC2 service

The next listing shows how to create an EC2 instance that runs a script to install Jenkins during bootstrapping. The Elastic IP address ensures a static public IP address for the virtual machine.

Listing 13.1   Starting an EC2 instance using a Jenkins CI server with recovery alarm

```
#[...]
ElasticIP:
  Type: 'AWS::EC2::EIP'        ◁——  The public IP address stays
  Properties:                        the same after recovery when
    InstanceId: !Ref Instance        using Elastic IP address.
    Domain: vpc
  DependsOn: VPCGatewayAttachment
Instance:                      ◁——  Launches a virtual
  Type: 'AWS::EC2::Instance'         machine to run a
  Properties:                        Jenkins server
    ImageId: !FindInMap [RegionMap, !Ref
➥ 'AWS::Region', AMI]          ◁——  Selects the
                                     AMI (in this case,
                                     Amazon Linux)
    InstanceType: 't2.micro'   ◁——  Recovery is
    IamInstanceProfile: !Ref IamInstanceProfile   supported for t2
    NetworkInterfaces:               instance types.
    - AssociatePublicIpAddress: true
      DeleteOnTermination: true
      DeviceIndex: 0
      GroupSet:                ◁——  User data containing a shell
      - !Ref SecurityGroup           script that is executed
      SubnetId: !Ref Subnet          during bootstrapping to
    UserData:                  ◁——  install a Jenkins server
      'Fn::Base64': !Sub |
        #!/bin/bash -ex
        trap '/opt/aws/bin/cfn-signal -e 1 --stack ${AWS::StackName}
        ➥ --resource Instance --region ${AWS::Region}' ERR

        # Installing Jenkins
        amazon-linux-extras enable epel=7.11 && yum -y clean metadata
        yum install -y epel-release && yum -y clean metadata
        yum install -y java-11-amazon-corretto-headless daemonize
        wget -q -T 60 http://.../jenkins-2.319.1-1.1.noarch.rpm
        rpm --install jenkins-2.319.1-1.1.noarch.rpm

        # Configuring Jenkins
        # ...

        # Starting Jenkins   ◁——  Starts
        systemctl enable jenkins.service   Jenkins
        systemctl start jenkins.service
        /opt/aws/bin/cfn-signal -e $? --stack ${AWS::StackName}
        ➥ --resource Instance --region ${AWS::Region}
    Tags:
    - Key: Name
      Value: 'jenkins-recovery'
  CreationPolicy:
    ResourceSignal:
      Timeout: PT10M
  DependsOn: VPCGatewayAttachment
```

Downloads and installs Jenkins (annotation pointing to the "# Installing Jenkins" block)

In case the EC2 instance fails, AWS will not replace the instance automatically under all circumstances. Therefore, you need to create a CloudWatch alarm to trigger the recovery of the virtual machine automatically. A CloudWatch alarm consists of the following:

- A metric that monitors data (health check, CPU usage, and so on)
- A rule defining a threshold based on a statistical function over a period of time
- Actions to trigger if the state of the alarm changes (such as triggering a recovery of an EC2 instance if the state changes to ALARM)

An alarm can be in one of the following states:

- OK—The threshold hasn't been reached.
- INSUFFICIENT_DATA—There isn't enough data to evaluate the alarm.
- ALARM—The threshold has been tripped.

Listing 13.2 creates a CloudWatch alarm based on a metric called StatusCheck-Failed_System (referenced by attribute MetricName) to monitor a virtual machine's health and recover it if the underlying host system fails. This metric contains the results of the system status checks performed by the EC2 service every minute. If the check fails, a measurement point with value 1 is added to the metric StatusCheck-Failed_System. Because the EC2 service publishes this metric, the Namespace is called AWS/EC2 and the Dimension of the metric is the ID of a virtual machine.

The CloudWatch alarm checks the metric every 60 seconds, as defined by the Period attribute. As defined in EvaluationPeriods, the alarm will check the last five periods—the last five minutes in this example. The check runs a statistical function specified in Statistic on the time periods. The result of the statistical function, a maximum function in this case, is compared against Threshold using the chosen ComparisonOperator. If the result is negative, the alarm actions defined in Alarm-Actions are executed: in this case, the recovery of the virtual machine—a built-in action for EC2 instances.

In summary, AWS checks the status of the virtual machine every minute. The result of these checks is written to the StatusCheckFailed_System metric. The alarm checks this metric, and if there are five consecutive failed checks, the alarm trips.

Listing 13.2 Creating a CloudWatch alarm to recover a failed EC2 instance

The name of the metric

The metric to monitor is provided by the EC2 service with the namespace AWS/EC2.

Creates a CloudWatch alarm to monitor the health of the virtual machine

```
RecoveryAlarm:
  Type: 'AWS::CloudWatch::Alarm'
  Properties:
    AlarmDescription: 'Recover EC2 instance when underlying hardware fails.'
    Namespace: 'AWS/EC2'
    MetricName: 'StatusCheckFailed_System'
    Statistic: Maximum
    Period: 60
```

Statistical function to apply to the metric. The minimum is to notify you if a single status check failed.

Duration for which the statistical function is applied, in seconds. Must be a multiple of 60.

```
EvaluationPeriods: 5
ComparisonOperator: GreaterThanThreshold
Threshold: 0
AlarmActions:
  - !Sub 'arn:aws:automate:${AWS::Region}:ec2:recover'
Dimensions:
  - Name: InstanceId
    Value: !Ref Instance
```

Operator for comparing the output of the statistical function with the threshold

The virtual machine is a dimension of the metric.

Threshold triggering an alarm

Action to perform in case of an alarm. Uses the predefined recovery action for EC2 instances.

Number of time periods over which data is compared to the threshold

While you have been reading through the details, the CloudFormation stack should have reached the status COMPLETE. Run the following command to get the output of the stack. If the output is null, retry after a few more minutes:

```
$ aws cloudformation describe-stacks --stack-name jenkins-recovery \
➥ --query "Stacks[0].Outputs"
```

If the query returns output like the following, containing a URL, a user, and a password, the stack has been created and the Jenkins server is ready to use. If not, retry the command after a few minutes. Next, open the URL in your browser, and log in to the Jenkins server with user admin and the password you've chosen:

```
[
  {
    "Description": "URL to access web interface of Jenkins server.",
    "OutputKey": "JenkinsURL",
    "OutputValue": "http://54.152.240.91:8080"
  },
  {
    "Description": "Administrator user for Jenkins.",
    "OutputKey": "User",
    "OutputValue": "admin"
  },
  {
    "Description": "Password for Jenkins administrator user.",
    "OutputKey": "Password",
    "OutputValue": "********"
  }
]
```

Open this URL in your browser to access the web interface of the Jenkins server.

Use this user name to log in to the Jenkins server.

Use this password to log in to the Jenkins server.

Now you'll want to try out whether the Jenkins server works by creating your first build job on the Jenkins server. To do so, you have to log in with the username and password from the previous output. Figure 13.1 shows the Jenkins server's login form.

Figure 13.1   The web interface
of the Jenkins server

The following steps guide you through the process of creating a Jenkins project:

1   Open http://$PublicIP:8080 in your browser, and replace $PublicIP with the public IP address from the output of the previous describe command.
2   Log in with user admin and the password you chose when starting the Cloud-Formation template.
3   Select the Install Suggested Plugins option.
4   Keep the default for Jenkins URL and click Save and Finish.
5   Click Start Using Jenkins.
6   Click New Item to create a new project.
7   Type in AWS in Action as the name for the new project.
8   Select Freestyle Project as the job type, and click OK.

The Jenkins server runs on a virtual machine with automated recovery. If the virtual machine fails because of problems with the host system, it will be recovered with all data and the same public IP address. The URL doesn't change because you're using an Elastic IP for the virtual machine. All data is restored because the new virtual machine uses the same EBS volume as the previous virtual machine, so you can find your AWS in Action job again.

Unfortunately, you can't test the recovery process. The CloudWatch alarm monitors the health of the host system, which can be controlled only by AWS.

13.1.1 How does a CloudWatch alarm recover an EC2 instance?

Now that you've launched an EC2 instance with self-healing capabilities, it's time to take a look at the details. The EC2 service checks the status of every virtual machine automatically. System status checks are performed every minute, and the results are available as CloudWatch metrics.

A *system status check* detects a loss of network connectivity or power, as well as software or hardware problems on the physical host. By default, AWS does not recover failed EC2 instances automatically. You can, however, configure a CloudWatch alarm based on the system status check to restart a failed virtual machine on another physical host.

Figure 13.2 shows the process if an outage affects a virtual machine, described here:

1 The physical hardware fails and causes the EC2 instance to fail as well.
2 The EC2 service detects the outage and reports the failure to a CloudWatch metric.
3 A CloudWatch alarm triggers the recovery of the virtual machine.
4 The EC2 instance is launched on another physical host.
5 The EBS volume and Elastic IP stay the same and are linked to the new EC2 instance.

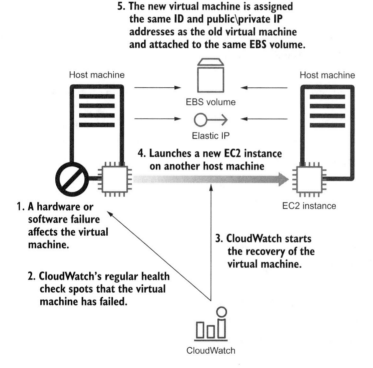

5. The new virtual machine is assigned the same ID and public\private IP addresses as the old virtual machine and attached to the same EBS volume.

Host machine

EBS volume

Host machine

Elastic IP

4. Launches a new EC2 instance on another host machine

EC2 instance

1. A hardware or software failure affects the virtual machine.

3. CloudWatch starts the recovery of the virtual machine.

2. CloudWatch's regular health check spots that the virtual machine has failed.

CloudWatch

Figure 13.2   In the case of a hardware failure, CloudWatch triggers the recovery of the EC2 instance.

After the recovery, a new EC2 instance will run with the same ID and private IP address. Data on network-attached EBS volumes is available as well. No data is lost because the EBS volume stays the same. EC2 instances with local disks (instance storage) aren't supported for this process. If the old EC2 instance was connected to an Elastic IP address, the new EC2 instance is connected to the same Elastic IP address.

Requirements for recovering EC2 instances

An EC2 instance must meet the following requirements if you want to use the recovery feature:

- It must be running on a VPC network.
- The instance family must be A1, C3, C4, C5, C5a, C5n, C6g, C6gn, Inf1, C6i, M3, M4, M5, M5a, M5n, M5zn, M6g, M6i, P3, R3, R4, R5, R5a, R5b, R5n, R6g, R6i, T2, T3, T3a, T4g, X1, or X1e. Other instance families aren't supported.
- The EC2 instance must use EBS volumes exclusively, because data on instance storage would be lost after the instance was recovered.

Cleaning up

Now that you've finished this example, it's time to clean up to avoid unwanted charges. Execute the following command to delete all resources corresponding to the Jenkins setup:

```
$ aws cloudformation delete-stack --stack-name jenkins-recovery
$ aws cloudformation wait stack-delete-complete \
    --stack-name jenkins-recovery
```
Waits until the stack is deleted

The approach you learned about in this section has an important limitation: the CloudWatch alarm will recover a failed instance but can do so only in the same availability zone. If a whole data center fails, your Jenkins server will become unavailable and will not recover automatically.

13.2 Recovering from a data center outage with an Auto Scaling group

Recovering an EC2 instance after underlying software or hardware fails is possible using system status checks and CloudWatch, as described in the previous section. But what happens if the entire data center fails because of a power outage, a fire, or some other disaster? The process for recovering a virtual machine described in section 13.1 will fail because it tries to launch an EC2 instance in the *same data center.*

AWS is built for failure, even in the rare case that an entire data center fails. The AWS regions consist of multiple data centers grouped into availability zones. By distributing your workload among multiple availability zones, you are able to recover from an data center outage. Two pitfalls when building a highly available setup over multiple availability zones follow:

- Data stored on network-attached storage (EBS) won't be available after failing over to another availability zone by default. In this case, you can end up having no access to your data (stored on EBS volumes) until the availability zone is back online (but you won't lose your data in this case).

- You can't start a new virtual machine in another availability zone with the same private IP address. That's because subnets are bound to availability zones, and each subnet has a unique IP address range. By default, you can't keep the same public IP address automatically after a recovery, as was the case in the previous section with a CloudWatch alarm triggering a recovery.

We will deal with those pitfalls at the end of this section. In this section, you'll improve the Jenkins setup from the previous section, add the ability to recover from an outage of an entire availability zone, and work around the pitfalls afterward.

13.2.1 Availability zones: Groups of isolated data centers

As you've learned, AWS operates multiple locations worldwide, called *regions*. You've used the region US East (N. Virginia), also called us-east-1, if you've followed the examples so far. In total, there are 23 publicly available regions throughout North America, South America, Europe, Africa, and Asia Pacific.

Each region consists of multiple availability zones (AZs). You can think of an AZ as an isolated group of data centers and a region as an area where multiple availability zones are located at a sufficient distance. The region us-east-1 consists of six availability zones (us-east-1a to us-east-1f), for example. The availability zone us-east-1a could be one data center or many. We don't know because AWS doesn't make information about their data centers publicly available. So, from an AWS user's perspective, you know only about regions and AZs.

The AZs are connected through low-latency links, so requests between different availability zones aren't as expensive as requests across the internet in terms of latency. The latency within an availability zone (such as from an EC2 instance to another EC2 instance in the same subnet) is lower compared to latency across AZs. The number of availability zones depends on the region. All regions come with three or more availability zones. Keep in mind that AWS charges $0.01/GB for network traffic between availability zones. Figure 13.3 illustrates the concept of availability zones within a region.

13.2.2 Recovering a failed virtual machine to another availability zone with the help of autoscaling

In the first part of the chapter, you used a CloudWatch alarm to trigger the recovery of a virtual machine that was running a Jenkins CI server in case of a failure. This mechanism launches an identical copy of the original virtual machine, if necessary. This is possible only in the same availability zone, because the private IP address and the EBS volume of a virtual machine are bound to a single subnet and a single availability zone. But suppose your team isn't happy about the fact that they won't be able to use the Jenkins server to test, build, and deploy new software in the case of a unlikely availability zone outage. You need a tool that will let you recover in another availability zone.

Failing over into another availability zone is possible with the help of *autoscaling*. You can find the CloudFormation template for this example on GitHub and on S3.

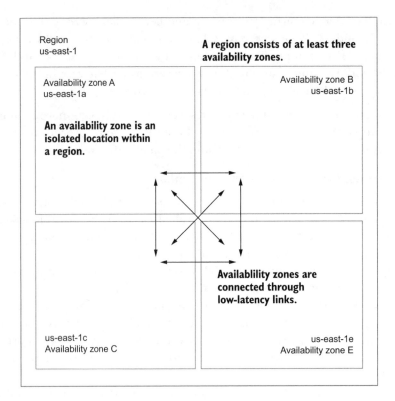

Figure 13.3   A region consists of multiple availability zones connected through low-latency links.

Download a snapshot of the repository at https://github.com/AWSinAction/code3/archive/main.zip. The file we're talking about is located at chapter13/multiaz.yaml. On S3, the same file is located at https://s3.amazonaws.com/awsinaction-code3/chapter13/multiaz.yaml.

Autoscaling is part of the EC2 service and helps you to ensure that a specified number of EC2 instances is running, even when availability zones become unavailable. You can use autoscaling to launch a virtual machine and make sure a new instance is started if the original instance fails. You can use it to start virtual machines in multiple subnets. For example, if you have an outage of an entire availability zone, a new instance can be launched in another subnet in another availability zone.

Execute the following command to create a virtual machine that can recover in another availability zone if necessary. Replace `$Password` with a password consisting of 8–40 characters:

```
$ aws cloudformation create-stack --stack-name jenkins-multiaz \
  --template-url https://s3.amazonaws.com/\
  awsinaction-code3/chapter13/multiaz.yaml \
  --parameters "ParameterKey=JenkinsAdminPassword,
```

```
ParameterValue=$Password" \
--capabilities CAPABILITY_IAM
```

While you wait for CloudFormation to create the stack, you will learn more about the details. To configure autoscaling, you need to create the following two parts of the configuration:

- A *launch template* contains all information needed to launch an EC2 instance: instance type (size of virtual machine) and image (AMI) to start from.
- An *Auto Scaling group* tells the EC2 service how many virtual machines should be started with a specific launch template, how to monitor the instances, and in which subnets EC2 instances should be started.

Figure 13.4 illustrates this process.

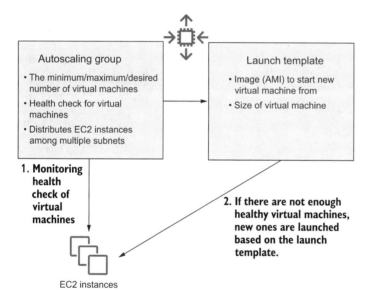

Figure 13.4 Autoscaling ensures that a specified number of EC2 instances are running.

You'll find both a launch template and an Auto Scaling group in the CloudFormation template for launching a Jenkins server, as shown in the next listing. The parameters are explained in table 13.1. You have already used the most important parameters for the launch template when starting a single virtual machine with a CloudWatch recovery alarm in the previous section.

Table 13.1 Required parameters for the launch template and Auto Scaling group

Context	Property	Description	Values
LaunchTemplate	ImageId	The ID of the AMI from which the virtual machine should be started	Any AMI ID accessible from your account

Table 13.1 Required parameters for the launch template and Auto Scaling group (continued)

Context	Property	Description	Values
LaunchTemplate	InstanceType	The size of the virtual machine	All available instance sizes, such as t2.micro, m3.medium, and c3.large
LaunchTemplate	SecurityGroupIds	References the security groups for the EC2 instance	Any security group belonging to the same VPC
LaunchTemplate	UserData	Script executed during bootstrap to install the Jenkins CI server	Any bash script
AutoScalingGroup	MinSize	The minimum value for the DesiredCapacity	Any positive integer—use 1 if you want a single virtual machine to be started based on the launch template.
AutoScalingGroup	MaxSize	The maximum value for the DesiredCapacity	Any positive integer (greater than or equal to the MinSize value); use 1 if you want a single virtual machine to be started based on the launch template.
AutoScalingGroup	VPCZoneIdentifier	The subnet IDs in which you want to start virtual machines	Any subnet ID from a VPC from your account. Subnets must belong to the same VPC.
AutoScalingGroup	HealthCheckType	The health check used to identify failed virtual machines. If the health check fails, the Auto Scaling group replaces the virtual machine with a new one.	EC2 to use the status checks of the virtual machine, or ELB to use the health check of the load balancer (see chapter 16).

One important difference exists between the definition of a single EC2 instance and the launch template: the subnet for the virtual machine isn't defined in the launch template but rather in the Auto Scaling group.

An Auto Scaling group is also used if you need to scale the number of virtual machines based on usage of your system. You'll learn how to scale the number of EC2 instances based on current load in chapter 17. In this chapter, you only need to make sure a single virtual machine is always running. Because you need a single virtual machine, set the following parameters for autoscaling to 1:

- MinSize
- MaxSize

Listing 13.3 Launching a Jenkins virtual machine with autoscaling in two AZs

```
# [...]
LaunchTemplate:
  Type: 'AWS::EC2::LaunchTemplate'          ◁─── The blueprint used by the
  Properties:                                    Auto Scaling group when
    LaunchTemplateData:                          launching an EC2 instance
      IamInstanceProfile:            ◁─── Attaches an IAM role to the
        Name: !Ref IamInstanceProfile      EC2 instance to grant access
      ImageId: !FindInMap [RegionMap,        for the Session Manager
➡        !Ref 'AWS::Region', AMI]
      Monitoring:                    ◁─── By default, EC2 sends metrics to CloudWatch
        Enabled: false                    every five minutes. You can enable detailed
      InstanceType: 't2.micro'            instance monitoring to get metrics every
      NetworkInterfaces:                  minute for an additional cost.
      - AssociatePublicIpAddress: true   ◁───
        DeviceIndex: 0               ◁─── Configures the network
        Groups:                           interface (ENI) of the
        - !Ref SecurityGroup              EC2 instance
      UserData:
        'Fn::Base64': !Sub |       Associates a public IP
          #!/bin/bash -ex          address when launching
          trap '/opt/aws/bin/cfn-signal -e 1 --stack ${AWS::StackName}
➡            --resource AutoScalingGroup --region ${AWS::Region}' ERR
```

Selects the AMI (in this case, Amazon Linux 2)

The instance type for the virtual machine

The EC2 instance will execute the script loaded from user data at the end of the boot process. The script installs and configures Jenkins.

Attaches a security group allowing ingress on port 8080 to the instance

```
          # Installing Jenkins
          amazon-linux-extras enable epel=7.11 && yum -y clean metadata
          yum install -y epel-release && yum -y clean metadata
          yum install -y java-11-amazon-corretto-headless daemonize
          wget -q -T 60 http://ftp-chi.osuosl.org/pub/jenkins/
➡            redhat-stable/jenkins-2.319.1-1.1.noarch.rpm
          rpm --install jenkins-2.319.1-1.1.noarch.rpm


          # Configuring Jenkins
          # [...]


          # Starting Jenkins
          systemctl enable jenkins.service
          systemctl start jenkins.service
          /opt/aws/bin/cfn-signal -e $? --stack ${AWS::StackName}
➡            --resource AutoScalingGroup --region ${AWS::Region}
AutoScalingGroup:
  Type: 'AWS::AutoScaling::AutoScalingGroup'   ◁─── Auto Scaling group
  Properties:                                        responsible for launching
    LaunchTemplate:                                  the virtual machine
      LaunchTemplateId: !Ref LaunchTemplate
      Version: !GetAtt 'LaunchTemplate.LatestVersionNumber'
```

References the launch template

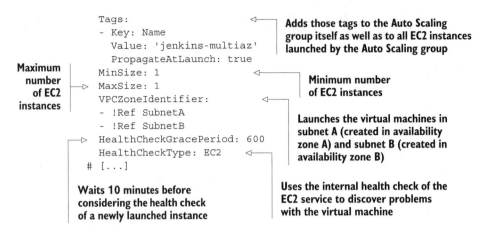

```
          Tags:                                       Adds those tags to the Auto Scaling
          - Key: Name                                 group itself as well as to all EC2 instances
            Value: 'jenkins-multiaz'                  launched by the Auto Scaling group
            PropagateAtLaunch: true
          MinSize: 1                                     Minimum number
          MaxSize: 1                                     of EC2 instances
          VPCZoneIdentifier:
          - !Ref SubnetA                               Launches the virtual machines in
          - !Ref SubnetB                               subnet A (created in availability
          HealthCheckGracePeriod: 600                  zone A) and subnet B (created in
          HealthCheckType: EC2                         availability zone B)
        # [...]
```

Maximum number of EC2 instances

Waits 10 minutes before considering the health check of a newly launched instance

Uses the internal health check of the EC2 service to discover problems with the virtual machine

The CloudFormation stack might be already up and running. Execute the following command to grab the public IP address of the virtual machine. If no IP address appears, the virtual machine isn't started yet. Wait another minute, and try again:

```
$ aws ec2 describe-instances --filters "Name=tag:Name,\
  Values=jenkins-multiaz" "Name=instance-state-code,Values=16" \
  --query "Reservations[0].Instances[0].\
  [InstanceId, PublicIpAddress, PrivateIpAddress, SubnetId]"
[
  "i-0cff527cda42afbcc",          Instance ID of the
  "34.235.131.229",               virtual machine
  "172.31.38.173",
  "subnet-28933375"               Public IP address of
]                                 the virtual machine
```

Subnet ID of the virtual machine

Private IP address of the virtual machine

Open http://$PublicIP:8080 in your browser, and replace $PublicIP with the public IP address from the output of the previous describe-instances command. The web interface for the Jenkins server appears.

Execute the following command to terminate the virtual machine and test the recovery process with autoscaling. Replace $InstanceId with the instance ID from the output of the previous describe command:

```
$ aws ec2 terminate-instances --instance-ids $InstanceId
```

After a few minutes, the Auto Scaling group detects that the virtual machine was terminated and starts a new virtual machine. Rerun the describe-instances command until the output contains a new running virtual machine, as shown here:

```
$ aws ec2 describe-instances --filters "Name=tag:Name,\
  Values=jenkins-multiaz" "Name=instance-state-code,Values=16" \
  --query "Reservations[0].Instances[0].\
  [InstanceId, PublicIpAddress, PrivateIpAddress, SubnetId]"
```

```
[
  "i-0293522fad287bdd4",
  "52.3.222.162",
  "172.31.37.78",
  "subnet-45b8c921"
]
```

The instance ID, the public IP address, the private IP address, and probably even the subnet ID have changed for the new instance. Open http://$PublicIP:8080 in your browser, and replace $PublicIP with the public IP address from the output of the previous describe-instances command. The web interface from the Jenkins server appears.

You've now built a highly available architecture consisting of an EC2 instance with the help of autoscaling. Two problems with the current setup follow:

- The Jenkins server stores data on disk. When a new virtual machine is started to recover from a failure, this data is lost because a new disk is created.
- The public and private IP addresses of the Jenkins server change after a new virtual machine is started for recovery. The Jenkins server is no longer available under the same endpoint.

You'll learn how to solve these problems in the next part of the chapter.

Cleaning up

It's time to clean up to avoid unwanted costs. Execute the following command to delete all resources corresponding to the Jenkins setup:

```
$ aws cloudformation delete-stack --stack-name jenkins-multiaz
$ aws cloudformation wait stack-delete-complete \          Waits until the
⮑ --stack-name jenkins-multiaz                             stack is deleted
```

13.2.3 Pitfall: Recovering network-attached storage

The EBS service offers network-attached storage for virtual machines. Remember that EC2 instances are linked to a subnet, and the subnet is linked to an availability zone. EBS volumes are also located only in a single availability zone. If your virtual machine is started in another availability zone because of an outage, the EBS volume cannot be accessed from the other availability zones. Let's say your Jenkins data is stored on an EBS volume in availability zone us-east-1a. As long as you have an EC2 instance running in the same availability zone, you can attach the EBS volume. If this availability zone becomes unavailable and you start a new EC2 instance in availability zone us-east-1b, however, you can't access that EBS volume in us-east-1a, which means that you can't recover Jenkins because you don't have access to the data. See figure 13.5.

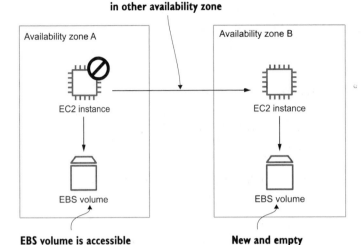

Launch new virtual server in other availability zone

Figure 13.5   An EBS volume is available only in a single availability zone.

EBS volume is accessible from availability zone A only.

New and empty EBS volume

Don't mix availability and durability guarantees

An EBS volume is guaranteed to be available for 99.999% of the time. So if an availability zone outage occurs, the volume is no longer available. This does not imply that you lose any data. As soon as the availability zone is back online, you can access the EBS volume again with all its data.

An EBS volume guarantees that you won't lose any data in 99.9% of the time. This guarantee is called the durability of the EBS volume. If you have 1,000 volumes in use, you can expect that you will lose one of the volumes and its data a year.

You have multiple solutions for this problem:

- Outsource the state of your virtual machine to a managed service that uses multiple availability zones by default: RDS, DynamoDB (NoSQL database), EFS (NFSv4.1 share), or S3 (object store).
- Create snapshots of your EBS volumes regularly, and use these snapshots if an EC2 instance needs to recover in another availability zone. EBS snapshots are stored on S3 and, thus, are available in multiple availability zones. If the EBS volume is the root volume of the ECS instance, create AMIs to back up the EBS volume instead of a snapshot.
- Use a distributed third-party storage solution to store your data in multiple availability zones: GlusterFS, DRBD, MongoDB, and so on.

The Jenkins server stores data directly on disk. To outsource the state of the virtual machine, you can't use RDS, DynamoDB, or S3; you need a file-level storage solution instead. As you've learned, an EBS volume is available only in a single availability zone, so this isn't the best fit for the problem. But do you remember EFS from chapter 9? EFS provides network file storage (over NFSv4.1) and replicates your data automatically between availability zones in a region.

To embed EFS into the Jenkins setup, as shown in listing 13.4, you have to make the following three modifications to the Multi-AZ template from the previous section:

1   Create an EFS filesystem.
2   Create EFS mount targets in each availability zone.
3   Adjust the user data to mount the EFS filesystem. Jenkins stores all its data under /var/lib/jenkins.

Listing 13.4   Storing Jenkins state on EFS

```
# [...]
FileSystem:                                          Creates an Elastic File System
  Type: 'AWS::EFS::FileSystem'          ◄───         (EFS), which provides a NFS
  Properties: {}                                     (network filesystem)
MountTargetSecurityGroup:                ◄───
  Type: 'AWS::EC2::SecurityGroup'                    Creates a security group
  Properties:                                        used to grant network traffic
    GroupDescription: 'EFS Mount target'             from the EC2 instance to EFS
    SecurityGroupIngress:
    - FromPort: 2049                     ◄───         Allows incoming traffic on
      IpProtocol: tcp                                port 2049 used by NFS
      SourceSecurityGroupId: !Ref SecurityGroup
      ToPort: 2049
    VpcId: !Ref VPC                                  The mount target provides
MountTargetA:                            ◄───        a network interface for
  Type: 'AWS::EFS::MountTarget'                      the filesystem.
  Properties:
    FileSystemId: !Ref FileSystem                    The mount target
    SecurityGroups:                                  is attached to a
    - !Ref MountTargetSecurityGroup                  subnet.
    SubnetId: !Ref SubnetA               ◄───
MountTargetB:                            ◄───
  Type: 'AWS::EFS::MountTarget'                      Therefore, you need
  Properties:                                        a mount target per
    FileSystemId: !Ref FileSystem                    subnet.
    SecurityGroups:
    - !Ref MountTargetSecurityGroup
    SubnetId: !Ref SubnetB
# [...]                                              The blueprint used by
LaunchTemplate:                                      the Auto Scaling group to
  Type: 'AWS::EC2::LaunchTemplate'      ◄───         launch virtual machines
  Properties:
    LaunchTemplateData:
      # [...]
      UserData:
        'Fn::Base64': !Sub |
          #!/bin/bash -ex
          trap '/opt/aws/bin/cfn-signal -e 1 --stack ${AWS::StackName}
          ➥ --resource AutoScalingGroup --region ${AWS::Region}' ERR
```

```
                      # Installing Jenkins
                      # [...]

  Adds an             # Mounting EFS volume
 entry to the         mkdir -p /var/lib/jenkins
configuration         echo "${FileSystem}:/ /var/lib/jenkins efs tls,_netdev 0 0"
file for volumes      ⮕ >> /etc/fstab
                      while ! (echo > /dev/tcp/${FileSystem}.efs.${AWS::Region}.
                      ⮕ amazonaws.com/2049) >/dev/null 2>&1; do sleep 5; done
 Mounts the           mount -a -t efs
EFS filesystem        chown -R jenkins:jenkins /var/lib/jenkins

                      # Configuring Jenkins
                      # [...]

                      # Starting Jenkins
                      systemctl enable jenkins.service
                      systemctl start jenkins.service
                      /opt/aws/bin/cfn-signal -e $? --stack ${AWS::StackName}
                      ⮕ --resource AutoScalingGroup --region ${AWS::Region}
              AutoScalingGroup:
                Type: 'AWS::AutoScaling::AutoScalingGroup'
                Properties:
                  LaunchTemplate:
                    LaunchTemplateId: !Ref LaunchTemplate
References            Version: !GetAtt 'LaunchTemplate.LatestVersionNumber'
the launch        Tags:
template          - Key: Name
defined             Value: 'jenkins-multiaz-efs'
above               PropagateAtLaunch: true
                  MinSize: 1
                  MaxSize: 1
                  VPCZoneIdentifier:
                  - !Ref SubnetA
                  - !Ref SubnetB
                  HealthCheckGracePeriod: 600
                  HealthCheckType: EC2
              # [...]
```

Callouts: Creates a folder used by Jenkins to store data if it does not exist yet — Waits until the EFS filesystem becomes available — Changes the ownership of the mounted directory to make sure Jenkins is able to write and read files — Creates the Auto Scaling group

You can find the CloudFormation template for this example on GitHub and on S3. Download a snapshot of the repository at https://github.com/AWSinAction/code3/archive/main.zip. The file we're talking about is located at chapter13/multiaz-efs.yaml. On S3, the same file is located at https://s3.amazonaws.com/awsinaction-code3/chapter13/multiaz-efs.yaml.

Execute the following command to create the new Jenkins setup that stores state on EFS. Replace $Password with a password consisting of 8–40 characters:

```
$ aws cloudformation create-stack --stack-name jenkins-multiaz-efs \
⮕ --template-url https://s3.amazonaws.com/\
⮕ awsinaction-code3/chapter13/multiaz-efs.yaml \
⮕ --parameters "ParameterKey=JenkinsAdminPassword,
⮕ ParameterValue=$Password" \
⮕ --capabilities CAPABILITY_IAM
```

The creation of the CloudFormation stack will take a few minutes. Run the following command to get the public IP address of the virtual machine. If no IP address appears, the virtual machine isn't started yet. In this case, wait another minute, and try again:

```
$ aws ec2 describe-instances --filters "Name=tag:Name,\
  Values=jenkins-multiaz-efs" "Name=instance-state-code,Values=16" \
  --query "Reservations[0].Instances[0].\
  [InstanceId, PublicIpAddress, PrivateIpAddress, SubnetId]"
[
  "i-0efcd2f01a3e3af1d",          Instance ID of the
                                  virtual machine
  "34.236.255.218",
  "172.31.37.225",                Public IP address of
  "subnet-0997e66d"               the virtual machine
]
          Subnet ID of the     Private IP address of
          virtual machine      the virtual machine
```

Next, create a new Jenkins job by following these steps:

1. Open http://$PublicIP:8080/newJob in your browser, and replace $PublicIP with the public IP address from the output of the previous describe command.
2. Log in with user admin and the password you chose when starting the Cloud-Formation template.
3. Select the Install Suggested Plugins option.
4. Keep the default for Jenkins URL and click Save and Finish.
5. Click Start Using Jenkins.
6. Click New Item to create a new project.
7. Type in AWS in Action as the name for the new project.
8. Select Freestyle Project as the job type, and click OK.

You've made some changes to the state of Jenkins stored on EFS. Now terminate the EC2 instance with the following command, and you will see that Jenkins recovers from the failure without data loss. Replace $InstanceId with the instance ID from the output of the previous describe command:

```
$ aws ec2 terminate-instances --instance-ids $InstanceId
```

After a few minutes, the Auto Scaling group detects that the virtual machine was terminated and starts a new virtual machine. Rerun the describe-instances command shown next until the output contains a new running virtual machine:

```
$ aws ec2 describe-instances --filters "Name=tag:Name,\
  Values=jenkins-multiaz-efs" "Name=instance-state-code,Values=16" \
  --query "Reservations[0].Instances[0].\
  [InstanceId, PublicIpAddress, PrivateIpAddress, SubnetId]"
```

```
[
  "i-07ce0865adf50cccf",
  "34.200.225.247",
  "172.31.37.199",
  "subnet-0997e66d"
]
```

The instance ID, the public IP address, the private IP address, and probably even the subnet ID have changed for the new instance. Open http://$PublicIP:8080 in your browser, and replace $PublicIP with the public IP address from the output of the previous describe-instances command. The web interface from the Jenkins server appears, and it still contains the AWS in Action job you created recently.

You've now built a highly available architecture consisting of an EC2 instance with the help of autoscaling. State is now stored on EFS and is no longer lost when an EC2 instance is replaced. There is one problem left: the public and private IP addresses of the Jenkins server change after a new virtual machine is started for recovery. The Jenkins server is no longer available under the same endpoint.

Cleaning up

It's time to clean up to avoid unwanted costs. Execute the following command to delete all resources corresponding to the Jenkins setup:

```
$ aws cloudformation delete-stack --stack-name jenkins-multiaz-efs
$ aws cloudformation wait stack-delete-complete \
       --stack-name jenkins-multiaz-efs          ◁────── Waits until the
                                                          stack is deleted
```

You'll learn how to solve the last problem next.

13.2.4 *Pitfall: Network interface recovery*

Recovering a virtual machine using a CloudWatch alarm in the same availability zone, as described at the beginning of this chapter, is easy because the private IP address and the public IP address stay the same automatically. You can use these IP addresses as an endpoint to access the EC2 instance, even after a failover.

When it comes to creating a virtual network in the cloud (VPC), you need to be aware of the following dependencies, as figure 13.6 illustrates:

- A VPC is always bound to a region.
- A subnet within a VPC is linked to an availability zone.
- A virtual machine is launched into a single subnet.

You can't keep the private IP address when using autoscaling to recover from a EC2 instance or availability zone outage. If a virtual machine has to be started in another

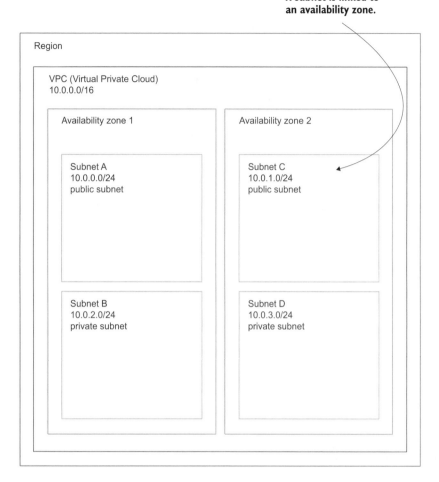

A subnet is linked to an availability zone.

Region

VPC (Virtual Private Cloud)
10.0.0.0/16

Availability zone 1

Subnet A
10.0.0.0/24
public subnet

Subnet B
10.0.2.0/24
private subnet

Availability zone 2

Subnet C
10.0.1.0/24
public subnet

Subnet D
10.0.3.0/24
private subnet

Figure 13.6   A VPC is bound to a region, and a subnet is linked to an availability zone.

availability zone, it must be started in another subnet. Therefore, it's not possible to use the same private IP address for the new virtual machine, as figure 13.7 shows.

By default, you also can't use an Elastic IP as a public IP address for a virtual machine launched by autoscaling. The requirement for a static endpoint to receive requests is common, though. For the use case of a Jenkins server, developers want to bookmark an IP address or a hostname to reach the web interface. Different possibilities exist for providing a static endpoint when using autoscaling to build high availability for a single virtual machine, as described here:

- Allocate an Elastic IP, and associate this public IP address during the bootstrap of the virtual machine.
- Create or update a DNS entry linking to the current public or private IP address of the virtual machine.

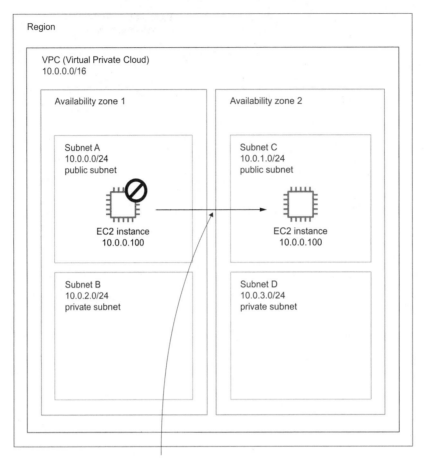

**The private IP address has to change because the
virtual machine is recovered in another subnet.**

**Figure 13.7   The virtual machine starts in another subnet in case of a failover and
changes the private IP address.**

- Use an Elastic Load Balancer (ELB) as a static endpoint that forwards requests
  to the current virtual machine.

To use the second solution, you need to link a domain with the Route 53 (DNS) service; we've chosen to skip this solution because you need a registered domain to implement it. The ELB solution is covered in chapter 14, so we'll skip it in this chapter as well. We'll focus on the first solution: allocating an Elastic IP and associating this public IP address during the virtual machine's bootstrap.

Execute the following command to create the Jenkins setup based on autoscaling again, using an Elastic IP address as static endpoint:

```
$ aws cloudformation create-stack --stack-name jenkins-multiaz-efs-eip \
➥ --template-url https://s3.amazonaws.com/\
```

```
➡ awsinaction-code3/chapter13/multiaz-efs-eip.yaml \
➡ --parameters "ParameterKey=JenkinsAdminPassword,
➡ ParameterValue=$Password" \
➡ --capabilities CAPABILITY_IAM
```

You can find the CloudFormation template for this example on GitHub and on S3. Download a snapshot of the repository at https://github.com/AWSinAction/code3/ archive/main.zip. The file we're talking about is located at chapter13/multiaz-efs-eip .yaml. On S3, the same file is located at https://s3.amazonaws.com/awsinaction-code3/ chapter13/multiaz-efs-eip.yaml.

The command creates a stack based on the template shown in listing 13.5. The differences from the original template spinning up a Jenkins server with autoscaling follow:

- Allocating an Elastic IP
- Adding the association of an Elastic IP to the script in the user data
- Creating an IAM role and policy to allow the EC2 instance to associate an Elastic IP

Listing 13.5 Using an EIP as a static endpoint for a virtual machine

```
# [...]
ElasticIP:                                    Creates a
  Type: 'AWS::EC2::EIP'          ◁──          static public IP
  Properties:                                 address
    Domain: vpc
  DependsOn: VPCGatewayAttachment             Creates an IAM role granting
IamRole:                                      access to AWS services to
  Type: 'AWS::IAM::Role'         ◁──          the EC2 instance
  Properties:
    AssumeRolePolicyDocument:
      Version: '2012-10-17'
      Statement:
      - Effect: Allow                         The IAM role can be
        Principal:                            used only by EC2
          Service: 'ec2.amazonaws.com'  ◁──   instances.
        Action: 'sts:AssumeRole'
    Policies:
    - PolicyName: ec2                         The IAM policy allows access
      PolicyDocument:                         to the EC2 API action called
        Version: '2012-10-17'                 AssociateAddress, which is
        Statement:                            used to associate an Elastic
        - Action: 'ec2:AssociateAddress'  ◁── IP with an EC2 instance.
          Resource: '*'
          Effect: Allow
    - PolicyName: ssm             ◁──
      PolicyDocument:                         The other IAM policy enables
        Version: '2012-10-17'                 access to the Session Manager,
        Statement:                            enabling you to open a terminal
        - Effect: Allow                       connection with the EC2 instance.
          Action:
          - 'ssmmessages:*'
          - 'ssm:UpdateInstanceInformation'
```

```
            - 'ec2messages:*'
              Resource: '*'
IamInstanceProfile:
  Type: 'AWS::IAM::InstanceProfile'
  Properties:
    Roles:
    - !Ref IamRole
LaunchTemplate:
  Type: 'AWS::EC2::LaunchTemplate'
  Properties:
    LaunchTemplateData:
      IamInstanceProfile:
        Name: !Ref IamInstanceProfile
      ImageId: !FindInMap [RegionMap, !Ref 'AWS::Region', AMI]
      Monitoring:
        Enabled: false
      InstanceType: 't2.micro'
      NetworkInterfaces:
      - AssociatePublicIpAddress: true
        DeviceIndex: 0
        Groups:
        - !Ref SecurityGroup
      UserData:
        'Fn::Base64': !Sub |
          #!/bin/bash -ex
          trap '/opt/aws/bin/cfn-signal -e 1 --stack ${AWS::StackName}
          ⮡ --resource AutoScalingGroup --region ${AWS::Region}' ERR

          # Attaching EIP
          INSTANCE_ID="$(curl
          ⮡ -s http://169.254.169.254/latest/meta-data/instance-id)"
          aws --region ${AWS::Region} ec2 associate-address
          ⮡ --instance-id $INSTANCE_ID
          ⮡ --allocation-id ${ElasticIP.AllocationId}
          ⮡ --allow-reassociation
          sleep 30

          # Installing Jenkins [...]
          # Mounting EFS volume [...]
          # Configuring Jenkins [...]

          # Starting Jenkins
          systemctl enable jenkins.service
          systemctl start jenkins.service
          /opt/aws/bin/cfn-signal -e $? --stack ${AWS::StackName}
          ⮡ --resource AutoScalingGroup --region ${AWS::Region}
```

An IAM instance profile is needed to be able to attach an IAM role to an EC2 instance.

The launch template defines the blueprint for launching the EC2 instance.

Attaches the IAM instance profile defined when starting the virtual machine

Gets the ID of the running instance from the metadata service (see http://mng.bz/deAX for details)

The EC2 instance associates the Elastic IP address with itself by using the AWS CLI.

If the query returns output shown in the following listing, containing a URL, a user, and a password, the stack has been created and the Jenkins server is ready to use. Open the URL in your browser, and log in to the Jenkins server with user admin and the password you've chosen. If the output is null, try again in a few minutes:

```
$ aws cloudformation describe-stacks --stack-name jenkins-multiaz-efs-eip \
⮡ --query "Stacks[0].Outputs"
```

You can now test whether the recovery of the virtual machine works as expected. To do so, you'll need to know the instance ID of the running virtual machine. Run the following command to get this information:

```
$ aws ec2 describe-instances --filters "Name=tag:Name,\
➥ Values=jenkins-multiaz-efs-eip" "Name=instance-state-code,Values=16" \
➥ --query "Reservations[0].Instances[0].InstanceId" --output text
```

Execute the following command to terminate the virtual machine and test the recovery process triggered by autoscaling. Replace $InstanceId with the instance from the output of the previous command:

```
$ aws ec2 terminate-instances --instance-ids $InstanceId
```

Wait a few minutes for your virtual machine to recover. Because you're using an Elastic IP assigned to the new virtual machine on bootstrap, you can open the same URL in your browser, as you did before the termination of the old instance.

> **Cleaning up**
>
> It's time to clean up to avoid unwanted costs. Execute the following command to delete all resources corresponding to the Jenkins setup:
>
> ```
> $ aws cloudformation delete-stack --stack-name jenkins-multiaz-efs-eip
> $ aws cloudformation wait stack-delete-complete \
> ➥ --stack-name jenkins-multiaz-efs-eip
> ```
>   ◁─── **Waits until the stack is deleted**

Now the public IP address of your virtual machine running Jenkins won't change, even if the running virtual machine needs to be replaced by another virtual machine in another availability zone.

Last but not least, we want to come back to the concept of an availability zone and dive into some of the details.

13.2.5 Insights into availability zones

A region consists of multiple availability zones. Each availability zone consists of at least one isolated data center. The identifier for an availability zone consists of the identifier for the region (such as us-east-1) and a character (a, b, c, …). So us-east-1a is the identifier for an availability zone in region us-east-1. To distribute resources across the different availability zones, the AZ identifier is mapped to one or multiple data centers randomly when creating an AWS account. This means us-east-1a might point to a different availability zone in your AWS account than it does in our AWS account.

We recommend that you take some time to explore the worldwide infrastructure provided by AWS. You can use the following commands to discover all regions available for your AWS account:

```
$ aws ec2 describe-regions          ◁──── Lists all regions           The endpoint URL,
{                                          available for your          used to access the
  "Regions": [                             AWS account                 EC2 service in the
    {                                                                  region
      "Endpoint": "ec2.eu-north-1.amazonaws.com",      ◁─────────────┘
      "RegionName": "eu-north-1",               ◁──────  The name of
      "OptInStatus": "opt-in-not-required"      ◁──────┘ the region
    },
    {                                                    Newer regions
      "Endpoint": "ec2.ap-south-1.amazonaws.com",        require an opt-in.
      "RegionName": "ap-south-1",
      "OptInStatus": "opt-in-not-required"
    },
    [...]
    {
      "Endpoint": "ec2.us-west-2.amazonaws.com",
      "RegionName": "us-west-2",
      "OptInStatus": "opt-in-not-required"
    }
  ]
}
```

Next, to list all availability zones for a region, execute the following command and replace $Region with RegionName of a region from the previous output:

```
$ aws ec2 describe-availability-zones --region $Region    ◁──┐ Lists the
{                                                              availability zones
  "AvailabilityZones": [                                       of a region
    {
      "State": "available",
      "OptInStatus": "opt-in-not-required",
      "Messages": [],                               The name of the availability zone
      "RegionName": "us-east-1",    ◁──             might point to different data centers
      "ZoneName": "us-east-1a",          ◁──────    in different AWS accounts.
      "ZoneId": "use1-az1",         ◁──────
      "GroupName": "us-east-1",                     The ID of the availability
      "NetworkBorderGroup": "us-east-1",            zone points to the same data
      "ZoneType": "availability-zone"               centers in all AWS accounts.
    },
    {
      "State": "available",
      "OptInStatus": "opt-in-not-required",
      "Messages": [],
      "RegionName": "us-east-1",
      "ZoneName": "us-east-1b",
      "ZoneId": "use1-az2",
      "GroupName": "us-east-1",
      "NetworkBorderGroup": "us-east-1",
      "ZoneType": "availability-zone"
    },
    [...]
    {
      "State": "available",
      "OptInStatus": "opt-in-not-required",
```

The region name ┄┄▷ (annotation pointing to "RegionName": "us-east-1")

```
      "Messages": [],
      "RegionName": "us-east-1",
      "ZoneName": "us-east-1f",
      "ZoneId": "use1-az5",
      "GroupName": "us-east-1",
      "NetworkBorderGroup": "us-east-1",
      "ZoneType": "availability-zone"
    }
  ]
}
```

At the end of the chapter, you will learn how to analyze resilience requirements and derive an AWS architecture from the results.

13.3   *Architecting for high availability*

Before you begin implementing highly available or even fault-tolerant architectures on AWS, you should start by analyzing your disaster-recovery requirements. Disaster recovery is easier and cheaper in the cloud than in a traditional data center, but building for high availability increases the complexity and, therefore, the initial costs as well as the operating costs of your system. The recovery time objective (RTO) and recovery point objective (RPO) are standards for defining the importance of disaster recovery from a business point of view.

Recovery time objective (RTO) is the time it takes for a system to recover from a failure; it's the length of time until the system reaches a working state again, defined as the system service level, after an outage. In the example with a Jenkins server, the RTO would be the time until a new virtual machine is started and Jenkins is installed and running after a virtual machine or an entire availability zone goes down.

Recovery point objective (RPO) is the acceptable data-loss time caused by a failure. The amount of data loss is measured in time. If an outage happens at 10:00 a.m. and the system recovers with a data snapshot from 09:00 a.m., the time span of the data loss is one hour. In the example of a Jenkins server using autoscaling, the RPO would be zero, because data is stored on EFS and is not lost during an AZ outage. Figure 13.8 illustrates the definitions of RTO and RPO.

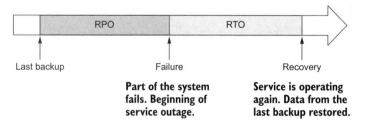

Figure 13.8   Definitions of RTO and RPO

13.3.1   *RTO and RPO comparison for a single EC2 instance*

You've learned about two possible solutions for making a single EC2 instance highly available. When choosing the solution, you have to know the application's business requirements. Can you tolerate the risk of being unavailable if an availability zone goes down? If so, EC2 instance recovery is the simplest solution, where you don't lose any data. If your application needs to survive an unlikely availability zone outage, your safest bet is autoscaling with data stored on EFS, but this method also has performance effects compared to storing data on EBS volumes. As you can see, there is no one-size-fits-all solution. You have to pick the solution that fits your business problem best. Table 13.2 compares the solutions.

Table 13.2   Comparison of high availability for a single EC2 instance

	RTO	RPO	Availability
EC2 instance, data stored on EBS root volume: recovery triggered by a CloudWatch alarm	About 10 minutes	No data loss	Recovers from a failure of a virtual machine but not from an outage of an entire availability zone
EC2 instance, data stored on EBS root volume: recovery triggered by autoscaling	About 10 minutes	All data lost	Recovers from a failure of a virtual machine and from an outage of an entire availability zone
EC2 instance, data stored on EBS root volume with regular snapshots: recovery triggered by autoscaling	About 10 minutes	Realistic time span for snapshots: between 30 minutes and 24 hours	Recovers from a failure of a virtual machine and from an outage of an entire availability zone
EC2 instance, data stored on EFS filesystem: recovery triggered by autoscaling	About 10 minutes	No data loss	Recovers from a failure of a virtual machine and from an outage of an entire availability zone

If you want to be able to recover from an outage of an availability zone and need to decrease the RPO, you should try to achieve a stateless server. Using storage services like RDS, EFS, S3, and DynamoDB can help you to do so. See part 3 if you need help with using these services.

13.3.2   *AWS services come with different high availability guarantees*

It is important to note that some AWS services are highly available or even fault-tolerant by default. Other services provide building blocks to achieve a highly available architecture. As described next, you can use multiple availability zones or even multiple regions to build a highly available architecture, as figure 13.9 shows:

- Route 53 (DNS) and CloudFront (CDN) operate globally over multiple regions and are highly available by default.
- S3 (object store), EFS (network filesystem) and DynamoDB (NoSQL database) use multiple availability zones within a region so they can withstand a data center outage.

- The Relational Database Service (RDS) offers the ability to deploy a primary-standby setup, called Multi-AZ deployment, so you can fail over into another availability zone with a short downtime, if necessary.
- A virtual machine runs in a single availability zone. AWS offers a tool to build an architecture based on EC2 instances that can fail over into another availability zone: autoscaling.

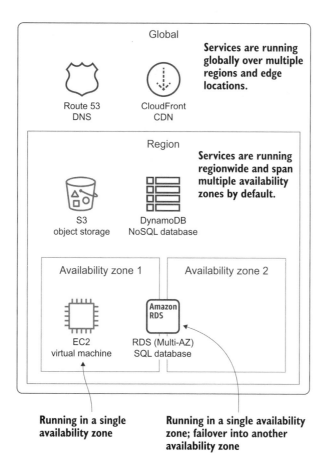

Figure 13.9   AWS services can operate in a single availability zone, over multiple availability zones within a region, or even globally.

When planning for failure, it is also important to consider the service-level objective (SLO) and service-level agreement (SLA) committed to by AWS. Most services define an SLA, which helps you as a customer when estimating the availability of an architecture. You can read them here: http://mng.bz/rn7Z.

When designing a system for AWS, you need to look into the SLA and resilience specifications of each building block. To do so, check the AWS documentation, which includes a section on resilience for most services.

Summary

- A virtual machine fails if the underlying hardware or virtualization layer fails.
- You can recover a failed virtual machine with the help of a CloudWatch alarm: by default, data stored on EBS, as well as the private and public IP addresses, stays the same.
- An AWS region consists of multiple isolated groups of data centers called availability zones.
- Recovering from a data center outage is possible when using multiple availability zones.
- Use autoscaling to replace a failed virtual machine, even in the event of a data center outage. The pitfalls are that you can no longer blindly rely on EBS volumes and, by default, IP addresses will change.
- Recovering data in another availability zone is tricky when stored on EBS volumes instead of managed storage services like RDS, EFS, S3, and DynamoDB.
- Some AWS services use multiple availability zones by default, but virtual machines run in a single availability zone.

14
Decoupling your infrastructure: Elastic Load Balancing and Simple Queue Service

This chapter covers

- The reasons for decoupling a system
- Synchronous decoupling with load balancers to distribute requests
- Hiding your backend from users and message producers
- Asynchronous decoupling with message queues to buffer message peaks

Imagine that you want some advice from us about using AWS, and therefore, we plan to meet in a café. To make this meeting successful, we must:

- Be available at the same time
- Be at the same place
- Find each other at the café

The problem with making our meeting happing is that it's *tightly coupled* to a location. We live in Germany; you probably don't. We can solve that problem by decoupling our meeting from the location. So, we change plans and schedule a Google Hangout session. Now we must:

- Be available at the same time
- Find each other in Google Hangouts

Google Hangouts (and other video/voice chat services) does *synchronous decoupling*. It removes the need to be at the same place, while still requiring us to meet at the same time.

We can even decouple from time by using email. Now we must:

- Find each other via email

Email does *asynchronous decoupling*. You can send an email when the recipient is asleep, and they can respond later when they're awake.

Examples are 100% covered by the Free Tier

The examples in this chapter are totally covered by the Free Tier. As long as you don't run the examples longer than a few days, you won't pay anything for it. Keep in mind that this applies only if you created a fresh AWS account for this book and there is nothing else going on in your AWS account. Try to complete the chapter within a few days, because you'll clean up your account at the end of the chapter.

NOTE   To fully understand this chapter, you'll need to have read and understood the concept of autoscaling covered in chapter 13.

In summary, to meet up, we have to be at the same place (the café), at the same time (3 p.m.) and find each other (I have black hair and I'm wearing a white shirt). Our meeting is tightly coupled to a location and a place. We can decouple a meeting in the following two ways:

- *Synchronous decoupling*—We can now be at different places, but we still have to find a common time (3 p.m.) and find each other (exchange Skype IDs, for instance).
- *Asynchronous decoupling*—We can be at different places and now also don't have to find a common time. We only have to find each other (exchange email addresses).

A meeting isn't the only thing that can be decoupled. In software systems, you can find a lot of tightly coupled components, such as the following:

- A public IP address is like the location of our meeting: to make a request to a web server, you must know its public IP address, and the virtual machine must be connected to that address. If you want to change the public IP address, both parties are involved in making the appropriate changes. The public IP address is tightly coupled with the web server.
- If you want to make a request to a web server, the web server must be online at the same time. Otherwise, your request will be rejected. A web server can be offline for many reasons: someone might be installing updates, a hardware failure, and so on. The client is tightly coupled with the web server.

AWS offers solutions for synchronous and asynchronous decoupling. Typically, synchronous decoupling is used when the client expects an immediate response. For example, a user expects an response to the request to load the HTML of a website with very little latency. The Elastic Load Balancing (ELB) service provides different types of load balancers that sit between your web servers and the client to decouple your requests synchronously. The client sends a request to the ELB, and the ELB forwards the request to a virtual machine or similar target. Therefore, the client does not need to know about the target; it knows only about the load balancer.

Asynchronous decoupling is different and commonly used in scenarios where the client does not expect an immediate response. For example, a web application could scale and optimize an image uploaded by the user in the background and use the raw image until that process finished in the background. For asynchronous decoupling, AWS offers the *Simple Queue Service* (SQS), which provides a message queue. The producer sends a message to the queue, and a receiver fetches the message from the queue and processes the request.

You'll learn about both the ELB and the SQS services in this chapter. Let's start with ELB.

14.1 Synchronous decoupling with load balancers

Exposing a single EC2 instance running a web server to the outside world introduces a dependency: your users now depend on the public IP address of the EC2 instance. As soon as you distribute the public IP address to your users, you can't change it anymore. You're faced with the following problems:

- Changing the public IP address is no longer possible because many clients rely on it.
- If you add an additional EC2 instance (and IP address) to handle the increasing load, it's ignored by all current clients: they're still sending all requests to the public IP address of the first server.

You can solve these problems with a DNS name that points to your server. But DNS isn't fully under your control. DNS resolvers cache responses. DNS servers cache entries, and sometimes they don't respect your time-to-live (TTL) settings. For example, you might ask DNS servers to only cache the name-to–IP address mapping for one minute, but some DNS servers might use a minimum cache of one day. A better solution is to use a load balancer.

A load balancer can help decouple a system where the requester awaits an immediate response. Instead of exposing your EC2 instances (running web servers) to the outside world, you expose only the load balancer to the outside world. The load balancer then forwards requests to the EC2 instances behind it. Figure 14.1 shows how this works.

The requester (such as a web browser) sends an HTTP request to the load balancer. The load balancer then selects one of the EC2 instances and copies the original

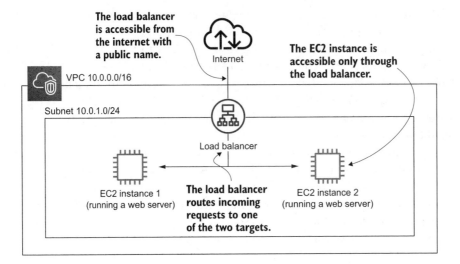

Figure 14.1   A load balancer synchronously decouples your EC2 instances.

HTTP request to send to the EC2 instance that it selected. The EC2 instance then processes the request and sends a response. The load balancer receives the response and sends the same response to the original requester.

AWS offers different types of load balancers through the Elastic Load Balancing (ELB) service. All load balancer types are fault tolerant and scalable. They differ in supported protocols and features as follows:

- *Application Load Balancer (ALB)*—HTTP, HTTPS
- *Network Load Balancer (NLB)*—TCP, TCP TLS
- *Classic Load Balancer (CLB)*—HTTP, HTTPS, TCP, TCP TLS

Consider the CLB deprecated. As a rule of thumb, use the ALB whenever the HTTP/HTTPS protocol is all you need, and the NLB for all other scenarios.

> **NOTE**   The ELB service doesn't have an independent management console. It's integrated into the EC2 Management Console.

Load balancers can be used with more than web servers—you can use load balancers in front of any systems that deal with request/response-style communication, as long as the protocol is based on TCP.

14.1.1 *Setting up a load balancer with virtual machines*

AWS shines when it comes to integrating services. In chapter 13, you learned about Auto Scaling groups. You'll now put an ALB in front of an Auto Scaling group to decouple traffic to web servers by removing the dependency between your users and the EC2 instance's public IP address. The Auto Scaling group will make sure you always have two web servers running. As you learned in chapter 13, that's the way to protect against downtime caused by hardware failure. Servers that are started in the Auto Scaling group can automatically register with the ALB.

Figure 14.2 shows what the setup will look like. The interesting part is that the EC2 instances are no longer accessible directly from the public internet, so your users don't know about them. They don't know if there are two or 20 EC2 instances running behind the load balancer. Only the load balancer is accessible, and it forwards requests to the backend servers behind it. The network traffic to load balancers and backend EC2 instances is controlled by security groups, which you learned about in chapter 5.

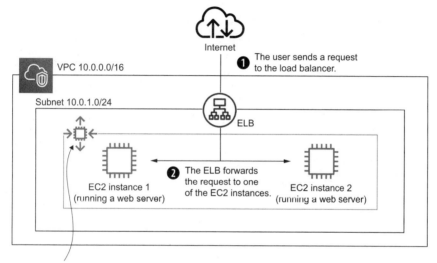

The Auto Scaling group manages two EC2 instances. If a new instance is started, the Auto Scaling group registers the instance with the ALB.

Figure 14.2   The load balancer evaluates rules so it can forward incoming rules to a specific target group.

If the Auto Scaling group adds or removes EC2 instances, it will also register new EC2 instances at the load balancer's target group and deregister EC2 instances that have been removed.

An ALB consists of the following three required parts and one optional part:

- *Load balancer*—Defines some core configurations, like the subnets the load balancer runs in, whether the load balancer gets public IP addresses, whether it uses IPv4 or both IPv4 and IPv6, and additional attributes.
- *Listener*—The listener defines the port and protocol that you can use to make requests to the load balancer. If you like, the listener can also terminate TLS for you. A listener links to a target group that is used as the default if no other listener rules match the request.

- *Target group*—A target group defines your group of backends. The target group is responsible for checking the backends by sending periodic health checks. Usually backends are EC2 instances, but they could also be a container running on Elastic Container Service (ECS) as well as Elastic Kubernetes Service (EKS), a Lambda function, or a machine in your data center connected with your VPC.
- *Listener rule*—Optional. You can define a listener rule. The rule can choose a different target group based on the HTTP path or host. Otherwise, requests are forwarded to the default target group defined in the listener.

Figure 14.3 shows the ALB parts.

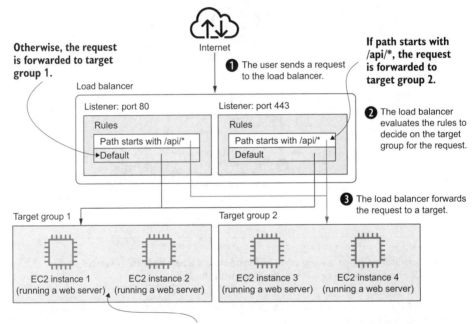

Figure 14.3   Creating an ALB, listener, and target group. Also, the Auto Scaling group registers instances at the target group automatically.

The following three listings implement the example shown in figure 14.3. The first listing shows a CloudFormation template snippet to create an ALB and its firewall rules, the security group.

Listing 14.1   Creating a load balancer and connecting it to an Auto Scaling group A

```
# [...]
LoadBalancerSecurityGroup:
  Type: 'AWS::EC2::SecurityGroup'
```

```
Properties:
  GroupDescription: 'alb-sg'
  VpcId: !Ref VPC
  SecurityGroupIngress:
  - CidrIp: '0.0.0.0/0'
    FromPort: 80
    IpProtocol: tcp
    ToPort: 80
LoadBalancer:
  Type: 'AWS::ElasticLoadBalancingV2::LoadBalancer'
  Properties:
    Scheme: 'internet-facing'
    SecurityGroups:
    - !Ref LoadBalancerSecurityGroup
    Subnets:
    - !Ref SubnetA
    - !Ref SubnetB
    Type: application
  DependsOn: 'VPCGatewayAttachment'
```

> Only traffic on port 80 from the internet will reach the load balancer.

Attaches the ALB to the subnets

> The ALB is publicly accessible (use internal instead of internet-facing to define a load balancer reachable only from a private network).

> Assigns the security group to the load balancer

The second listing configures the load balancer to listen on port 80 for incoming HTTP requests. It also creates a target group. The default action of the listener forwards all incoming requests to the target group.

Listing 14.2 Creating a load balancer and connecting it to an Auto Scaling group B

```
Listener:
  Type: 'AWS::ElasticLoadBalancingV2::Listener'
  Properties:
    DefaultActions:
    - TargetGroupArn: !Ref TargetGroup
      Type: forward
    LoadBalancerArn: !Ref LoadBalancer
    Port: 80
    Protocol: HTTP
TargetGroup:
  Type: 'AWS::ElasticLoadBalancingV2::TargetGroup'
  Properties:
    HealthCheckIntervalSeconds: 10
    HealthCheckPath: '/index.html'
    HealthCheckProtocol: HTTP
    HealthCheckTimeoutSeconds: 5
    HealthyThresholdCount: 3
    UnhealthyThresholdCount: 2
    Matcher:
      HttpCode: '200-299'
    Port: 80
    Protocol: HTTP
    VpcId: !Ref VPC
```

> The load balancer forwards all requests to the default target group.

> The load balancer listens on port 80 for HTTP requests.

> Every 10 seconds …

> … HTTP requests are made to /index.html.

> If HTTP status code is 2XX, the backend is considered healthy.

> The web server on the EC2 instances listens on port 80.

Shown in the third listing is the missing part: the targets. In our example, we are using an Auto Scaling group to launch EC2 instances. The Auto Scaling group registers the virtual machine at the target group.

Listing 14.3   Creating a load balancer and connecting it to an Auto Scaling group C

```yaml
LaunchTemplate:
  Type: 'AWS::EC2::LaunchTemplate'
  # [...]
  Properties:
    LaunchTemplateData:
      IamInstanceProfile:
        Name: !Ref InstanceProfile
      ImageId: !FindInMap [RegionMap, !Ref 'AWS::Region', AMI]
      Monitoring:
        Enabled: false
      InstanceType: 't2.micro'
      NetworkInterfaces:
      - AssociatePublicIpAddress: true
        DeviceIndex: 0
        Groups:
        - !Ref WebServerSecurityGroup
      UserData: # [...]
AutoScalingGroup:
  Type: 'AWS::AutoScaling::AutoScalingGroup'
  Properties:
    LaunchTemplate:
      LaunchTemplateId: !Ref LaunchTemplate
      Version: !GetAtt 'LaunchTemplate.LatestVersionNumber'
    MinSize: !Ref NumberOfVirtualMachines          ◁─────  Keeps two EC2 instances
    MaxSize: !Ref NumberOfVirtualMachines                  running (MinSize ⇐
    DesiredCapacity: !Ref NumberOfVirtualMachines          DesiredCapacity ⇐ MaxSize)
    TargetGroupARNs:          ◁─────  The Auto Scaling
    - !Ref TargetGroup                group registers new
    VPCZoneIdentifier:                EC2 instances with the
    - !Ref SubnetA                    default target group.
    - !Ref SubnetB
  CreationPolicy:
    ResourceSignal:
      Timeout: 'PT10M'
  DependsOn: 'VPCGatewayAttachment'
```

The connection between the ALB and the Auto Scaling group is made in the Auto Scaling group description by specifying TargetGroupARNs.

The full CloudFormation template is located at http://mng.bz/VyKO. Create a stack based on that template by clicking on the Quick-Create link at http://mng.bz/GRgO, and then visit the output of your stack with your browser. Every time you reload the page, you should see one of the private IP addresses of a backend web server.

To get some detail about the load balancer in the graphical user interface, navigate to the EC2 Management Console. The subnavigation menu on the left has a Load Balancing section where you can find a link to your load balancers. Select the one and only load balancer. You will see details at the bottom of the page. The details contain a Monitoring tab, where you can find charts about latency, number of requests, and much more. Keep in mind that those charts are one minute behind, so you may have to wait until you see the requests you made to the load balancer.

> **Cleaning up**
> Delete the CloudFormation stack you created.

14.2 *Asynchronous decoupling with message queues*

Synchronous decoupling with ELB is easy; you don't need to change your code to do it. But for asynchronous decoupling, you have to adapt your code to work with a message queue.

A message queue has a head and a tail. You can add new messages to the tail while reading messages from the head. This allows you to decouple the production and consumption of messages. Now, why would you want to decouple the producers/requesters from consumers/receivers? You can achieve the following key benefits:

- *The queue acts as a buffer.* Producers and consumers don't have to run at the same speed. For example, you can add a batch of 1,000 messages in one minute while your consumers always process 10 messages per second. Sooner or later, the consumers will catch up, and the queue will be empty again.
- *The queue hides your backend.* Similar to the load balancer, message producers have no knowledge of the consumers. You can even stop all consumers and still produce messages. This is handy while doing maintenance on your consumers.

When decoupled, the producers and consumers don't know each other; they both only know about the message queue. Figure 14.4 illustrates this principle.

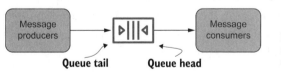

Figure 14.4   Producers send messages to a message queue while consumers read messages.

As you decoupled the sender from the receiver, the sender could even put new messages into the queue while no one is consuming messages, with the message queue acting as a buffer. To prevent message queues from growing infinitely large, messages are saved for only a certain amount of time. If you consume a message from a message queue, you must acknowledge the successful processing of the message to permanently delete it from the queue.

How do you implement asynchronous decoupling on AWS? That's where the Simple Queue Service (SQS) comes into play. SQS offers simple but highly scalable—throughput and storage—message queues that guarantee the delivery of messages at least once with the following characteristics:

- Under rare circumstances, a single message will be available for consumption twice. This may sound strange if you compare it to other message queues, but you'll see how to deal with this problem later in the chapter.
- SQS doesn't guarantee the order of messages, so you may read messages in a different order than they were produced. Learn more about the message order at the end of this section.

This limitation of SQS is also beneficial for the following reasons:

- You can put as many messages into SQS as you like.
- The message queue scales with the number of messages you produce and consume.
- SQS is highly available by default.
- You pay per message.

The pricing model is simple: $0.24 to $0.40 USD per million requests. Also, the first million requests per month are free. It is important to know that producing a message counts as a request, and consuming is another request. If your payload is larger than 64 KB, every 64 KB chunk counts as one request.

We have observed that many applications default to a synchronous process. That's probably because we are used to the request-response model and sometimes forget to think outside the box. However, replacing a synchronous with an asynchronous process enables many advantages in the cloud. Most importantly, scaling becomes much easier when you have a queue that can buffer requests for a while. Therefore, you will learn how to transition to an asynchronous process with the help of SQS next.

14.2.1 Turning a synchronous process into an asynchronous one

A typical synchronous process looks like this: a user makes a request to your web server, something happens on the web server, and a result is returned to the user. To make things more concrete, we'll talk about the process of creating a preview image of a URL in the following example, illustrated in figure 14.5:

1. The user submits a URL.
2. The web server downloads the content at the URL, takes a screenshot, and renders it as a PNG image.
3. The web server returns the PNG to the user.

Figure 14.5   A synchronous process to create a screenshot of a website.

With one small trick, this process can be made asynchronous and benefit from the elasticity of a message queue, for example, during peak traffic, as shown in figure 14.6:

1 The user submits a URL.
2 The web server puts a message into a queue that contains a random ID and the URL.
3 The web server returns a link to the user where the PNG image will be found in the future. The link contains the random ID (such as http://$Bucket.s3 .amazonaws.com/$RandomId.png).
4 In the background, a worker consumes the message from the queue.
5 The worker downloads the content and converts the content into a PNG.
6 Next, the worker uploads the image to S3.
7 At some point, the user tries to download the PNG at the known location. If the file is not found, the user should reload the page in a few seconds.

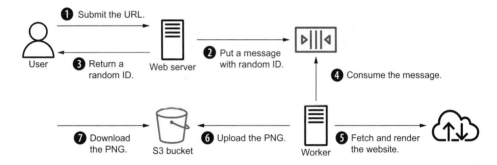

Figure 14.6   The same process, but asynchronous

If you want to make a process asynchronous, you must manage the way the process initiator tracks the process status. One way of doing that is to return an ID to the initiator that can be used to look up the process. During the process, this ID is passed from step to step.

14.2.2 Architecture of the URL2PNG application

You'll now create a basic but decoupled piece of software named URL2PNG that renders a PNG from a given web URL. You'll use Node.js to do the programming part, and you'll use SQS as the message queue implementation. Figure 14.7 shows how the URL2PNG application works.

On the message producer side, a small Node.js script generates a unique ID, sends a message to the queue with the URL and ID as the payload, and returns the ID to the user. The user now starts checking whether a file is available on the S3 bucket using the returned ID as the filename.

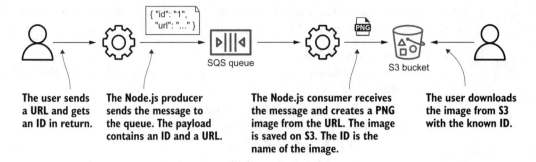

The user sends a URL and gets an ID in return.

The Node.js producer sends the message to the queue. The payload contains an ID and a URL.

The Node.js consumer receives the message and creates a PNG image from the URL. The image is saved on S3. The ID is the name of the image.

The user downloads the image from S3 with the known ID.

Figure 14.7   Node.js producer sends a message to the queue. The payload contains an ID and URL.

Simultaneously, on the message consumer side, a small Node.js script reads a message from the queue, generates the screenshot of the URL from the payload, and uploads the resulting image to an S3 bucket using the unique ID from the payload as the filename.

To complete the example, you need to create an S3 bucket with web hosting enabled. Execute the following command, replacing $yourname with your name or nickname to prevent name clashes with other readers (remember that S3 bucket names have to be globally unique across all AWS accounts):

```
$ aws s3 mb s3://url2png-$yourname
```

Now it's time to create the message queue.

14.2.3 Setting up a message queue

Creating an SQS queue is easy: you only need to specify the name of the queue as follows:

```
$ aws sqs create-queue --queue-name url2png
{
  "QueueUrl": "https://queue.amazonaws.com/878533158213/url2png"
}
```

The returned QueueUrl is needed later in the example, so take note of it.

14.2.4 Producing messages programmatically

You now have an SQS queue to send messages to. To produce a message, you need to specify the queue and a payload. You'll use Node.js in combination with the AWS SDK to make requests to AWS.

> ## Installing and getting started with Node.js
>
> Node.js is a platform for executing JavaScript in an event-driven environment so you can easily build network applications. To install Node.js, visit https://nodejs.org and download the package that fits your OS. All examples in this book are tested with Node.js 14.
>
> After Node.js is installed, you can verify that everything works by typing `node --version` into your terminal. Your terminal should respond with something similar to `v14.*`. Now you're ready to run JavaScript examples like URL2PNG.
>
> Do you want to get started with Node.js? We recommend *Node.js in Action* (second edition) by Alex Young et al. (Manning, 2017), or the video course *Node.js in Motion* by PJ Evans (Manning, 2018).

Here's how the message is produced with the help of the AWS SDK for Node.js; it will be consumed later by the URL2PNG worker. The Node.js script can then be used like this (don't try to run this command now—you need to install and configure URL2PNG first):

```
$ node index.js "http://aws.amazon.com"
PNG will be available soon at
http://url2png-$yourname.s3.amazonaws.com/XYZ.png
```

As usual, you'll find the code in the book's code repository on GitHub https://github.com/AWSinAction/code3. The URL2PNG example is located at /chapter14/url2png/. The next listing shows the implementation of index.js.

Listing 14.4   index.js: Sending a message to the queue

```
const AWS = require('aws-sdk');
var { v4: uuidv4 } = require('uuid');
const config = require('./config.json');        Creates an
const sqs = new AWS.SQS({});                     SQS client

if (process.argv.length !== 3) {                 Checks whether a
  console.log('URL missing');                    URL was provided
  process.exit(1);
}
                                    Creates a
                                    random ID
const id = uuidv4();
const body = {                      The payload contains
  id: id,                           the random ID and
  url: process.argv[2]              the URL.
};

sqs.sendMessage({
    MessageBody: JSON.stringify(body),           Converts the
                                                 payload into a
Invokes the sendMessage                          JSON string
operation on SQS
```

```
    QueueUrl: config.QueueUrl                    Queue to which the message
}, (err) => {                                     is sent (was returned when
  if (err) {                                      creating the queue)
    console.log('error', err);
  } else {
    console.log('PNG will be soon available at http://' + config.Bucket
    ➥ + '.s3.amazonaws.com/' + id + '.png');
  }
});
```

Before you can run the script, you need to install the Node.js modules. Run npm install in your terminal to install the dependencies. You'll find a config.json file that needs to be modified. Make sure to change QueueUrl to the queue you created at the beginning of this example, and change Bucket to url2png-$yourname.

Now you can run the script with node index.js "http://aws.amazon.com". The program should respond with something like PNG will be available soon at http://url2png-$yourname.s3.amazonaws.com/XYZ.png. To verify that the message is ready for consumption, you can ask the queue how many messages are inside as follows. Replace $QueueUrl with your queue's URL:

```
$ aws sqs get-queue-attributes \
➥ --queue-url "$QueueUrl" \
➥ --attribute-names ApproximateNumberOfMessages
{
  "Attributes": {
    "ApproximateNumberOfMessages": "1"
  }
}
```

SQS returns only an approximation of the number of messages. This is due to the distributed nature of SQS. If you don't see your message in the approximation, run the command again and eventually you will see your message. Next, it's time to create the worker that consumes the message and does all the work of generating a PNG.

14.2.5 *Consuming messages programmatically*

Processing a message with SQS takes the next three steps:

1 Receive a message.
2 Process the message.
3 Acknowledge that the message was successfully processed.

You'll now implement each of these steps to change a URL into a PNG.

To receive a message from an SQS queue, you must specify the following:

- QueueUrl—The unique queue identifier.
- MaxNumberOfMessages—The maximum number of messages you want to receive (from one to 10). To get higher throughput, you can get messages in a batch. We usually set this to 10 for best performance and lowest overhead.

- VisibilityTimeout—The number of seconds you want to remove this message from the queue to process it. Within that time, you must delete the message, or it will be delivered back to the queue. We usually set this to the average processing time multiplied by four.
- WaitTimeSeconds—The maximum number of seconds you want to wait to receive messages if they're not immediately available. Receiving messages from SQS is done by polling the queue. AWS allows long polling, for a maximum of 20 seconds. When using long polling, you will not get an immediate response from the AWS API if no messages are available. If a new message arrives within 10 seconds, the HTTP response will be sent to you. After 20 seconds, you also get an empty response.

The following listing shows how this is done with the SDK.

Listing 14.5 worker.js: Receiving a message from the queue

```
const fs = require('fs');
const AWS = require('aws-sdk');
const puppeteer = require('puppeteer');
const config = require('./config.json');
const sqs = new AWS.SQS();
const s3 = new AWS.S3();

async function receive() {                        Invokes the
  const result = await sqs.receiveMessage({       receiveMessage
                                                  operation on SQS
    QueueUrl: config.QueueUrl,
    MaxNumberOfMessages: 1,          Takes the message
    VisibilityTimeout: 120,          from the queue for
    WaitTimeSeconds: 10              120 seconds
  }).promise();
                                     Long poll for 10
  if (result.Messages) {             seconds to wait
    return result.Messages[0]         for new messages
  } else {
    return null;          Gets the one      Checks whether a
  }                       and only          message is
};                        message           available
```

- Consumes no more than one message at once → MaxNumberOfMessages: 1,

The receive step has now been implemented. The next step is to process the message. Thanks to the Node.js module puppeteer, it's easy to create a screenshot of a website, as demonstrated here.

Listing 14.6 worker.js: Processing a message (take screenshot and upload to S3)

```
async function process(message) {
  const body = JSON.parse(message.Body);      The message body is a
  const browser = await puppeteer.launch();   JSON string. You convert it
  const page = await browser.newPage();       back into a JavaScript
                                              object.
                        Launches a
                        headless browser
```

```
await page.goto(body.url);
page.setViewport({ width: 1024, height: 768})
const screenshot = await page.screenshot();                Takes a
                                                           screenshot

await s3.upload({ Uploads screenshot to S3
  Bucket: config.Bucket,
  Key: `${body.id}.png`,                    The S3 bucket to which
  Body: screenshot,                         to upload the image
  ContentType: 'image/png',
  ACL: 'public-read',                       The key, consisting of the
}).promise();                               random ID generated by the
                                            client and included in the
await browser.close();                      SQS message
};
              Allows anyone to read        Sets the content type to
              the image from S3            make sure browsers are
              (public access)              showing the image correctly
```

The only step that's missing is to acknowledge that the message was successfully consumed, as shown in the next listing. This is done by deleting the message from the queue after successfully completing the task. If you receive a message from SQS, you get a `ReceiptHandle`, which is a unique ID that you need to specify when you delete a message from a queue.

Listing 14.7   worker.js: Acknowledging a message (deletes the message from the queue)

```
async function acknowledge(message) {        Invokes the deleteMessage
  await sqs.deleteMessage({                   operation on SQS
    QueueUrl: config.QueueUrl,
    ReceiptHandle: message.ReceiptHandle       ReceiptHandle is
  }).promise();                                unique for each receipt
};                                             of a message.
```

You have all the parts; now it's time to connect them, as shown next.

Listing 14.8   worker.js: Connecting the parts

```
async function run() {
  while(true) {                                An endless loop polling
                                               and processing messages
    const message = await receive();
    if (message) {
      console.log('Processing message', message);
      await process(message);
      await acknowledge(message);             Acknowledges the message by
    }                                         deleting it from the queue
    await new Promise(r => setTimeout(r, 1000));
  }                                                  Sleeps for one second
};                                                   to decrease number of
            Starts                                   requests to SQS
run();      the loop
```

Receives a message → `const message = await receive();`

Processes the message → `await process(message);`

Now you can start the worker to process the message that is already in the queue. Run the script with `node worker.js`. You should see some output that says the worker is in the process step and then switches to Done. After a few seconds, the screenshot should be uploaded to S3. Your first asynchronous application is complete.

Remember the output you got when you invoked node index.js "http://aws .amazon.com" to send a message to the queue? It looked similar to this: http:// url2png-$yourname.s3.amazonaws.com/XYZ.png. Now put that URL in your web browser, and you will find a screenshot of the AWS website (or whatever you used as an example).

You've created an application that is asynchronously decoupled. If the URL2PNG service becomes popular and millions of users start using it, the queue will become longer and longer because your worker can't produce that many PNGs from URLs. The cool thing is that you can add as many workers as you like to consume those messages. Instead of only one worker, you can start 10 or 100. The other advantage is that if a worker dies for some reason, the message that was in flight will become available for consumption after two minutes and will be picked up by another worker. That's fault tolerant! If you design your system to be asynchronously decoupled, it's easy to scale and create a good foundation to be fault tolerant. The next chapter will concentrate on this topic.

Cleaning up

Delete the message queue as follows:

```
$ aws sqs delete-queue --queue-url "$QueueUrl"
```

And don't forget to clean up and delete the S3 bucket used in the example. Issue the following command, replacing $yourname with your name:

```
$ aws s3 rb --force s3://url2png-$yourname
```

14.2.6 Limitations of messaging with SQS

Earlier in the chapter, we mentioned a few limitations of SQS. This section covers them in more detail. But before we start with the limitations, the benefits include these:

- You can put as many messages into SQS as you like. SQS scales the underlying infrastructure for you.
- SQS is highly available by default.
- You pay per message.

Those benefits come with some tradeoffs. Let's have a look at those limitations in more detail now.

SQS DOESN'T GUARANTEE THAT A MESSAGE IS DELIVERED ONLY ONCE

Two reasons a message might be delivered more than once follow:

- *Common reason*—If a received message isn't deleted within VisibilityTimeout, the message will be received again.

- *Rare reason*—A `DeleteMessage` operation doesn't delete all copies of a message because one of the servers in the SQS system isn't available at the time of deletion.

The problem of repeated delivery of a message can be solved by making the message processing idempotent. *Idempotent* means that no matter how often the message is processed, the result stays the same. In the URL2PNG example, this is true by design: if you process the message multiple times, the same image will be uploaded to S3 multiple times. If the image is already available on S3, it's replaced. Idempotence solves many problems in distributed systems that guarantee messages will be delivered at least once.

Not everything can be made idempotent. Sending an email is a good example: if you process a message multiple times and it sends an email each time, you'll annoy the addressee.

In many cases, processing at least once is a good tradeoff. Check your requirements before using SQS if this tradeoff fits your needs.

SQS DOESN'T GUARANTEE THE MESSAGE ORDER

Messages may be consumed in a different order than that in which you produced them. If you need a strict order, you should search for something else. If you need a stable message order, you'll have difficulty finding a solution that scales like SQS. Our advice is to change the design of your system so you no longer need the stable order, or put the messages in order on the client side.

> ### SQS FIFO (first in, first out) queues
>
> FIFO queues guarantee the order of messages and have a mechanism to detect duplicate messages. If you need a strict message order, they are worth a look. The disadvantages are higher pricing and a limitation of 3,000 operations per second. Check out the documentation at http://mng.bz/xM7Y for more information.

SQS DOESN'T REPLACE A MESSAGE BROKER

SQS isn't a message broker like ActiveMQ—SQS is only a message queue. Don't expect features like message routing or message priorities. Comparing SQS to ActiveMQ is like comparing DynamoDB to MySQL.

> ### Amazon MQ
>
> AWS announced an alternative to Amazon SQS in November 2017: Amazon MQ provides Apache ActiveMQ as a service. Therefore, you can use Amazon MQ as a message broker that speaks the JMS, NMS, AMQP, STOMP, MQTT, and WebSocket protocols.
>
> Go to the Amazon MQ Developer Guide at http://mng.bz/AVP7 to learn more.

Summary

- Decoupling makes things easier because it reduces dependencies.
- Synchronous decoupling requires two sides to be available at the same time, but the sides don't have to know each other.
- With asynchronous decoupling, you can communicate without both sides being available.
- Most applications can be synchronously decoupled without touching the code, by using a load balancer offered by the ELB service.
- A load balancer can make periodic health checks to your application to determine whether the backend is ready to serve traffic.
- Asynchronous decoupling is possible only with asynchronous processes, but you can modify a synchronous process to be an asynchronous one most of the time.
- Asynchronous decoupling with SQS requires programming against SQS with one of the SDKs.

15
Automating deployment: CodeDeploy, CloudFormation, and Packer

About 20 years ago, we rented our first virtual machine. Our goal was to deploy WordPress, a content management system. To do so, we logged in to the machine using SSH, downloaded WordPress, installed the scripting language PHP and the web server Apache, edited the configuration files, and started the web server.

To this day, the following steps for deploying software—whether open source, proprietary, or homegrown—have remained the same:

1. Fetch source code or binaries
2. Install dependencies
3. Edit configuration files
4. Start services

These activities are also summarized under the term *configuration management*. The two main reasons for why automating deployments is a must-have in the cloud follow:

- To ensure high availability and scalability, you need to configure an Auto Scaling group to launch EC2 instances automatically. A new machine could spin up at any time, so deploying changes manually is not an option.
- Manual changes are error prone and expensive to reproduce. Automating increases reliability and reduces the costs per deployment.

From what we have learned from our consulting clients, organizations that implement automated deployments have a higher chance of success in the cloud.

In this chapter, you will learn how to automate the deployment of an application. We want to introduce three approaches with different pros and cons, so that you can pick the solution that best fits your situation. We use the following three options and will provide an overview that helps you make a decision at the end of the chapter:

- AWS CodeDeploy to deploy to running EC2 instances
- AWS CloudFormation, Auto Scaling groups, and user data to perform a rolling update
- Bundling an application into a customized AMI for immutable deployments with Packer by HashiCorp

Examples are 100% covered by the Free Tier

The examples in this chapter are completely covered by the Free Tier. As long as you don't run the examples longer than a few days, you won't pay anything. Keep in mind that this only applies if you created a fresh AWS account for this book and nothing else is going on in your AWS account. Try to complete each section within a few days; you'll clean up your account at the end of each section.

Chapter requirements

This chapter assumes that you have a basic understanding of the following components:

- Ensuring high availability by launching EC2 instances with an Auto Scaling group (chapter 13)
- Distributing requests with Elastic Load Balancing (chapter 14)

On top of that, the example included in this chapter makes intensive use of the following:

- Automating cloud infrastructure with CloudFormation (chapter 4)

Let's look at an example to see how this process might play out. Imagine you are the organizer of a local AWS meetup, and you want to provide a service allowing the community members to edit documents collaboratively. Therefore, you decided to deploy Etherpad, a web application, on EC2. The architecture, described next, is straightforward and illustrated in figure 15.1:

- Application Load Balancer forwards incoming requests.
- Auto Scaling launches and monitors exactly one virtual machine.
- The EC2 instance runs Etherpad.
- The RDS database instance stores the documents.

Unfortunately, Etherpad does not support clustering, which means it is not possible to run it on more than one machine in parallel.

You are sold on the idea of automating deployments and are looking for the right tool for the job. The first option might sound familiar to you. We are using a solution that applies changes with the help of agents installed on the virtual machines.

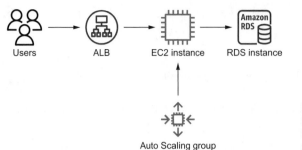

Figure 15.1   Etherpad infrastructure: ALB, EC2 instance, Auto Scaling group, and RDS database instance

15.1   *In-place deployment with AWS CodeDeploy*

You have two main reasons for performing in-place deployments. First, the speed of the deployment matters. Second, your application persists state on the virtual machine, so you try to avoid replacing running machines. So, for example, if you are running a database-like system that persists data on disk, the in-place deployment approach is a good fit.

The purpose of AWS CodeDeploy is to automate deployments on EC2, Fargate, and Lambda. Even on-premises machines are supported. The fully managed deployment service is free for EC2, Fargate, and Lambda and costs $0.02 per on-premises machine update. Figure 15.2 shows how CodeDeploy works for EC2 instances, as described here:

1   An engineer uploads a zip archive, including deployment instructions and the binaries or source code.
2   An engineer creates a deployment by choosing the revision and target instances.
3   An agent running on the EC2 instances pulls deployment tasks from CodeDeploy.
4   The agent downloads the zip archive from an S3 bucket.
5   The agent executes the instructions specified in the deployment artifact and copies the binaries or source code.
6   The agent sends a status update to CodeDeploy.

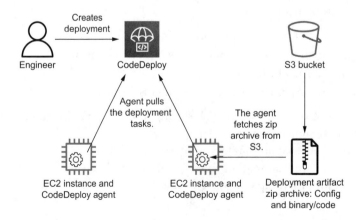

Figure 15.2   CodeDeploy automates deployments to EC2 instances.

This approach is called *in-place deployment.* The EC2 instances keep running while the agent rolls out the change. We want to introduce the following important components of CodeDeploy before we proceed:

- *Application*—Specifies a name and the compute platform (EC2/on-premises, ECS, or Lambda)
- *Deployment group*—Points to the targets (an Auto Scaling group in our example)
- *Revision*—References the code to deploy on S3 or GitHub
- *Deployment*—Rolls out a specific revision to a target group

How do you deploy the web application Etherpad with CodeDeploy? Start with setting up the infrastructure consisting of an Application Load Balancer, an Auto Scaling group, and an RDS database instance. We prepared a CloudFormation template to do just this. As usual, you'll find the code in the book's code repository on GitHub: https://github.com/AWSinAction/code3. The CloudFormation template for the WordPress example is located in /chapter15/codedeploy.yaml.

Use the following command to create a CloudFormation stack based on the template. The command will exit after the stack has been created successfully:

```
aws cloudformation deploy --stack-name etherpad-codedeploy \
  --template-file chapter15/codedeploy.yaml --capabilities CAPABILITY_IAM
```

Besides creating an Application Load Balancer, an Auto Scaling group, and an RDS database instance, the CloudFormation template also creates the following resources required to deploy Etherpad with CodeDeploy:

- *S3 bucket*—Stores the deployment artifacts (zip files)
- *CodeDeploy application*—Manages deployments of Etherpad
- *CodeDeploy deployment group*—Points to the Auto Scaling group
- *IAM role*—Required by CodeDeploy
- *Parameter*—Stores the database endpoint in the Systems Manager Parameter Store

The next listing shows a deeper look into the resources specified in the CloudFormation template /chapter15/codedeploy.yaml.

Listing 15.1 The CodeDeploy application and deployment group

```
# [...]
ArtifactBucket:          ◁───┐  The S3 bucket to store
  Type: 'AWS::S3::Bucket'     │  the deployment artifacts
  Properties: {}
Application:             ◁───┐  The CodeDeploy application—
  Type: 'AWS::CodeDeploy::Application'  a collection of deployment
  Properties:                 │  groups and revisions
    ApplicationName: 'etherpad-codedeploy'
    ComputePlatform: 'Server'      ┐ The CodeDeploy deployment
DeploymentGroup:         ◁───┘  group specifies the targets
                                 for a deployment.
```

```
      Type: 'AWS::CodeDeploy::DeploymentGroup'
      Properties:
        ApplicationName: !Ref Application
        DeploymentGroupName: 'etherpad-codedeploy'
        AutoScalingGroups:
        - !Ref AutoScalingGroup
        DeploymentConfigName: 'CodeDeployDefault.AllAtOnce'
        LoadBalancerInfo:
          TargetGroupInfoList:
          - Name: !GetAtt LoadBalancerTargetGroup.TargetGroupName
        ServiceRoleArn: !GetAtt CodeDeployRole.Arn
    CodeDeployRole:
      Type: 'AWS::IAM::Role'
      Properties:
        AssumeRolePolicyDocument:
          Version: '2012-10-17'
          Statement:
          - Effect: Allow
            Principal:
              Service: 'codedeploy.amazonaws.com'
            Action: 'sts:AssumeRole'
        ManagedPolicyArns:
        - 'arn:aws:iam::aws:policy/service-role/AWSCodeDeployRole'
    DatabaseHostParameter:
      Type: 'AWS::SSM::Parameter'
      Properties:
        Name: '/etherpad-codedeploy/database_host'
        Type: 'String'
        Value: !GetAtt 'Database.Endpoint.Address'
    # [...]
```

The deployment group points to the Auto Scaling group.

Because only one EC2 instance is running, deploys to all instances at once

The IAM role to use for deployments

The IAM role grants access to autoscaling, load balancing, and other services that are relevant for a deployment.

Considers the load balancer's target group when performing deployments

Stores the database hostname in the Systems Manager's Parameter Store

By default, CodeDeploy comes with the deployment configurations defined in table 15.1.

Table 15.1   The predefined deployment configurations for CodeDeploy

Name	Description
CodeDeployDefault.AllAtOnce	Deploy to all targets at once.
CodeDeployDefault.HalfAtATime	Deploy to half of the targets at a time.
CodeDeployDefault.OneAtATime	Deploy to targets one by one.

On top of that, CodeDeploy allows you to define your own deployment configurations, such as deploying to 25% of the targets at a time.

After you have deployed and prepared the infrastructure for Etherpad and Code-Deploy, it is about time to create the first deployment. Before you do so, you need to gather some information. Use the following command to get the outputs from the CloudFormation stack named etherpad-codedeploy:

```
aws cloudformation describe-stacks --stack-name etherpad-codedeploy \
➥ --query "Stacks[0].Outputs"
```

In our case, the output looks like this:

```
[
  {
    "OutputKey": "ArtifactBucket",
    "OutputValue": "etherpad-codedeploy-artifactbucket-12vah1x44tpg7",
    "Description": "Name of the artifact bucket"
  },
  {
    "OutputKey": "URL",
    "OutputValue": "http://ether-LoadB-...us-east-1.elb.amazonaws.com",
    "Description": "The URL of the Etherpad application"
  }
]
```

> Copies the name of the S3 bucket used to store the deployment artifacts

> Opens the URL in your browser to access Etherpad

Note the `ArtifactBucket` output. You will need the name of the S3 bucket in the following step. Also, open the `URL` output in your browser. The ALB shows an error page, because you haven't deployed the application yet.

Creating a deployment artifact, also called a revision, is the next step. To do so, you need to create a zip file containing the source code, the scripts, and a configuration file. You'll find an example to deploy Etherpad in the book's code repository on GitHub: https://github.com/AWSinAction/code3 at /chapter15/etherpad-lite-1.8.17.zip. We encourage you to unzip the file to take a closer look at its contents.

The deployment instruction file needed for CodeDeploy is called an AppSpec file: appspec.yml. The following listing explains the AppSpec file that we prepared to deploy Etherpad.

Listing 15.2 The AppSpec file used to deploy Etherpad with the help of CodeDeploy

> Odd but true: the latest version of the App Spec file format is 0.0.

> CodeDeploy supports Linux and Windows.

```
version: 0.0
os: linux
files:
- source: .
  destination: /etherpad
hooks:
  BeforeInstall:
  - location: hook_before_install.sh
    timeout: 60
  AfterInstall:
  - location: hook_after_install.sh
    timeout: 60
  ApplicationStart:
  - location: hook_application_start.sh
    timeout: 180
    runas: ec2-user
  ValidateService:
  - location: hook_validate_service.sh
    timeout: 300
    runas: ec2-user
```

> Copies all files from the archive to /etherpad

> Hooks allow you to run scripts during the deployment process.

> Triggered before CodeDeploy copies the source files

> Triggered after CodeDeploy copies the source files

> Triggered to start the application

> Triggered to validate the service after starting the application

Now let's inspect the contents of the `hook_after_install.sh` script in the next listing.

Listing 15.3   Executing the script after the install step

```
#!/bin/bash -ex                          Gets a token to access the
                                         EC2 metadata service
                                                                              Fetches the
TOKEN=`curl -X PUT "http://169.254.169.254/                                   availability zone
➥ latest/api/token"                                                          of the EC2 instance
➥ -H "X-aws-ec2-metadata-token-ttl-seconds: 60"`      ◄─                     from the metadata
AZ=`curl -H "X-aws-ec2-metadata-token: $TOKEN" -v      ◄─                     service
➥ http://169.254.169.254/latest/meta-data/placement/availability-zone`
REGION=${AZ::-1}                                        ◄─
DATABASE_HOST=$(aws ssm get-parameter --region ${REGION}  ◄─                  Removes the last
➥ --name "/etherpad-codedeploy/database_host"                                character of the
➥ --query "Parameter.Value" --output text)                                   availability zone
                                                                              to get the region

chown -R ec2-user:ec2-user /etherpad/   ◄─                                    Fetches the
cd /etherpad/                                  Makes sure all                 database host
rm -fR node_modules/                ◄─         files belong to                name from the
echo "                         ◄─              ec2-user instead               Systems Manager
{                                              of root                        Parameter Store
\"title\": \"Etherpad\",
\"dbType\": \"mysql\",                 Cleans up the
\"dbSettings\": {                      Node.js modules
\"host\": \"${DATABASE_HOST}\",        used by Etherpad
\"port\": \"3306\",
\"database\": \"etherpad\",        Generates the
\"user\": \"etherpad\",            settings.json file for
\"password\": \"etherpad\"         Etherpad containing
},                                 the database host
\"exposeVersion\": true
}
" > settings.json
```

Next, create a zip file containing the Etherpad source code as well as the appspec.yml file. As mentioned before, we have already prepared the zip file for you. All you have to do is upload it to S3 by executing the following command. Make sure to replace $BucketName with the artifact bucket name:

```
aws s3 cp chapter15/etherpad-lite-1.8.17.zip \
➥ s3://$BucketName/etherpad-lite-1.8.17.zip
```

Now you are ready to deploy Etherpad. Use the following command to create a deployment. Don't forget to replace $BucketName with the name of your artifact bucket:

```
aws deploy create-deployment --application-name etherpad-codedeploy \
➥ --deployment-group-name etherpad-codedeploy \
➥ --revision "revisionType=S3,
➥ s3Location={bucket=$BucketName,
➥ key=etherpad-lite-1.8.17.zip,bundleType=zip}"
```

Use the AWS Management Console or the following command to check whether the deployment succeeded. Replace $DeploymentId with the deployment ID printed to the console from the previous command:

```
$ aws deploy get-deployment --deployment-id $DeploymentId
```

Reload or open the URL of your Etherpad application and create a new pad. Click the settings icon to check the current version of Etherpad. The version is c85ab49, which is the latest Git commit ID for version 1.8.17.

Next, imagine you want to update to version 1.8.18 of Etherpad to roll out a fix for a security problem. The first step is to upload the revision. Don't forget to replace $BucketName with the name of your artifact bucket:

```
$ aws s3 cp chapter15/etherpad-lite-1.8.18.zip \
➥ s3://$BucketName/etherpad-lite-1.8.18.zip
```

Afterward, create another deployment to roll out version 1.8.18 with the following command:

```
$ aws deploy create-deployment --application-name etherpad-codedeploy \
➥ --deployment-group-name etherpad-codedeploy \
➥ --revision "revisionType=S3,
➥ s3Location={bucket=$BucketName,
➥ key=etherpad-lite-1.8.18.zip,bundleType=zip}"
```

Again, use the AWS Management Console or the following command to check progress, as shown next. Replace $DeploymentId with the deployment ID printed to the console from the previous command:

```
$ aws deploy get-deployment --deployment-id $DeploymentId
```

After the deployment is successful, reload the Etherpad web application. Check the version, which should be 4b96ff6 after the update. Congratulations—you have successfully deployed Etherpad with the help of CodeDeploy.

Cleaning up

Don't forget to clean up your AWS account before proceeding with the next step using the following code. Replace $BucketName with the name of the bucket used to store deployment artifacts:

```
$ aws s3 rm --recursive s3://${BucketName}
$ aws cloudformation delete-stack --stack-name etherpad-codedeploy
```

By the way, CodeDeploy will also make sure that the latest revision is deployed to any EC2 instances launched by the Auto Scaling group, such as if the health check failed and the Auto Scaling group replaced the failed EC2 instance.

Speed is an important advantage of in-place deployments with CodeDeploy. However, applying changes to long-running virtual machines, also called snowflake servers, is risky. A deployment might fail on a machine because of a change applied weeks before. It is difficult to reproduce the exact state of a machine.

That's why we prefer a different approach. To roll out a new revision, instead of modifying a running machine, spin up a new virtual machine. By doing so, each deployment starts from the same state, which increases reliability. You will learn how to implement a rolling update of EC2 instances with the help of CloudFormation in the following section.

> **Blue-green deployments with CodeDeploy**
>
> We have omitted that CodeDeploy supports blue-green deployments. With this method, a new machine is started instead of an in-place update. However, we prefer using CloudFormation for rolling updates because of its simplicity.

15.2 Rolling update with AWS CloudFormation and user data

CloudFormation is the Infrastructure as Code tool designed to manage AWS resources in an automated way. In addition, you can also use CloudFormation to orchestrate a rolling update of EC2 instances in an Auto Scaling group.

In contrast to an in-place update, a rolling update does not cause any downtime for the users. We use this approach whenever the virtual machines are disposable, meaning whenever our application does not persist any data on a local disk or in memory. For example, we use CloudFormation and user data to deploy WordPress, Jenkins, or a homegrown worker to crawl websites.

Back to our previous example: let's deploy Etherpad on EC2 with the help of CloudFormation. Figure 15.3 explains the process, which is laid out here:

1. The engineer initiates an update of the CloudFormation stack.
2. CloudFormation orchestrates a rolling update of the EC2 instance launched by the Auto Scaling group.
3. The Auto Scaling group launches a new EC2 instance based on the updated launch template, which includes a deployment script.
4. The EC2 instance fetches and executes a user data script.
5. The script fetches the source code from GitHub, creates a settings file, and starts the application.
6. The Auto Scaling group terminates the old EC2 instance.

To get started, deploy a CloudFormation stack based on the template we prepared to deploy Etherpad, as shown next. You'll find the CloudFormation template /chapter15/

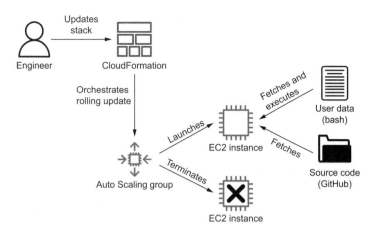

Figure 15.3 Rolling update orchestrated by CloudFormation with the help of a user data script

cloudformation.yaml in the book's code repository on GitHub https://github.com/AWSinAction/code3:

```
aws cloudformation deploy --stack-name etherpad-cloudformation \
  --template-file chapter15/cloudformation.yaml \
  --parameter-overrides EtherpadVersion=1.8.17 \
  --capabilities CAPABILITY_IAM
```

It will take about 10 minutes until the CloudFormation stack has been created and the command returns. Afterward, use the following command to get the URL of Etherpad:

```
aws cloudformation describe-stacks --stack-name etherpad-cloudformation \
  --query "Stacks[0].Outputs[0].OutputValue" --output text
```

Open the URL in your browser, and create a pad. Click the settings icon to check the current version of Etherpad as you did in the previous section. The version is c85ab49, which is the latest Git commit ID for version 1.8.17.

Great, but how did we deploy Etherpad to the EC2 instance? The following listing shows the CloudFormation template chapter15/cloudformation.yaml and answers this question.

Listing 15.4 Adding a bash script to the user data

```
# [...]
LaunchTemplate:                              ◁——  The Auto Scaling group
  Type: 'AWS::EC2::LaunchTemplate'                 uses the launch template
  Properties:                                      as a blueprint when
    LaunchTemplateData:                            launching EC2 instances.
      # [...]
      ImageId: !FindInMap [RegionMap,         Picks the Amazon
  !Ref 'AWS::Region', AMI]        ◁——         Linux 2 AMI dependent
                                              on the current region
```

Selects the instance type applicable for the Free Tier

Here is where the magic happens: the user data defined here is accessible by the EC2 instance during runtime.

```
InstanceType: 't2.micro'
UserData:
  'Fn::Base64': !Sub |
    #!/bin/bash -ex
    trap '/opt/aws/bin/cfn-signal -e 1 --stack ${AWS::StackName}
--resource AutoScalingGroup --region ${AWS::Region}' ERR
```

The operating system will execute this bash script at the end of the boot process.

If any step fails, the script will abort and notify CloudFormation by calling cfn-signal.

```
# Install nodejs and git
curl -fsSL https://rpm.nodesource.com/setup_14.x | bash -
yum install -y nodejs git

# Fetch, configure, and start Etherpad as non-root user
su ec2-user -c '
cd /home/ec2-user/
git clone --depth 1 --branch ${EtherpadVersion}
https://github.com/AWSinAction/etherpad-lite.git
cd etherpad-lite/
echo "
{
  \"title\": \"Etherpad\",
  \"dbType\": \"mysql\",
  \"dbSettings\": {
    \"host\": \"${Database.Endpoint.Address}\",
    \"port\": \"3306\",
    \"database\": \"etherpad\",
    \"user\": \"etherpad\",
    \"password\": \"etherpad\"
  },
  \"exposeVersion\": true
}
" > settings.json
./src/bin/run.sh &'

/opt/aws/bin/cfn-signal -e 0 --stack ${AWS::StackName}
--resource AutoScalingGroup --region ${AWS::Region}
# [...]
```

Fetches Etherpad from the GitHub repository

Creates a settings file for Etherpad containing the database host name

Notifies CloudFormation about a successful deployment

Starts Etherpad

Let's repeat how this deployment works:

1 The launch template specifies a script to add to the user data when launching an EC2 instance.

2 The Auto Scaling group launches an EC2 instance based on the Amazon Linux 2 image.

3 At the end of the boot process, the EC2 instance executes the bash script fetched from user data.

4 The bash script fetches, configures, and starts Etherpad.

In summary, user data is a way to inject a script into the boot process of an EC2 instance—a simple but powerful concept. Note that by default the script is executed only during the first boot of the instance, so don't rely on the script to start services.

> **Debugging a user data script**
>
> In case you need to debug a user data script, use the Session Manager to connect to the EC2 instance. Have a look at the /var/log/cloud-init-output.log log file shown next, which contains the outputs of the user data script at the end:
>
> ```
> $ less /var/log/cloud-init-output.log
> ```

So far, we have deployed Etherpad on EC2 by injecting a bash script into the boot process with the help of user data. But how do we perform a rolling update to update Etherpad from version 1.8.17 to 1.8.18? See the next listing for details.

Listing 15.5   Updating the Auto Scaling group or the referenced launch template

```
AutoScalingGroup:
  Type: 'AWS::AutoScaling::AutoScalingGroup'        The resource defines the
  Properties:                                        Auto Scaling group.
    TargetGroupARNs:
    - !Ref LoadBalancerTargetGroup                   References the launch
    LaunchTemplate:                                  template we saw earlier
      LaunchTemplateId: !Ref LaunchTemplate
      Version: !GetAtt 'LaunchTemplate.LatestVersionNumber'
    MinSize: '1'                                     Etherpad does not support
    MaxSize: '2'                                     clustering; therefore, we are
    HealthCheckGracePeriod: 300                      launching a single machine.
    HealthCheckType: ELB
    VPCZoneIdentifier:                               To enable zero-downtime deployments,
    - !Ref SubnetA                                   we must launch a second machine
    - !Ref SubnetB                                   during the deployment process.
    Tags:
    - PropagateAtLaunch: true
      Value: etherpad
      Key: Name                                      The update policy specifies the
  CreationPolicy:                                    behavior of CloudFormation in case
    ResourceSignal:                                  of changes to the launch template.
      Timeout: PT10M
  UpdatePolicy:                                      That's where the magic
    AutoScalingRollingUpdate:                        happens: the configuration
      PauseTime: PT10M                               of the rolling update.
      WaitOnResourceSignals: true                    The Auto Scaling group waits
      MinInstancesInService: 1                       for a signal from the EC2
                                                     instance.
  The Auto Scaling group awaits
  a success signal from launching       Makes sure the instance is up and
  the EC2 instance within 10            running during the update to ensure
  minutes (see cfn-signal in           zero downtime deployment
  user data script).
```

Let's make the update from version 1.8.17 to 1.8.18 happen. Execute the following command to update the CloudFormation stack. You might want to open the AWS Management Console and watch the running EC2 instances. CloudFormation will spin up a new EC2 instance. As soon as the new EC2 instance is ready, CloudFormation will terminate the old one:

```
$ aws cloudformation deploy --stack-name etherpad-cloudformation \
  --template-file cloudformation.yaml \
  --parameter-overrides EtherpadVersion=1.8.18 \
  --capabilities CAPABILITY_IAM
```

After updating the CloudFormation stack, reload the Etherpad web application. Check the version, which should be `4b96ff6`.

Congratulations! You have deployed a new version of Etherpad without any downtime for the users. Also, you learned how to use user data to bootstrap an EC2 instance in an automated way.

> **Cleaning up**
>
> Don't forget to clean up your AWS account before proceeding with the next step as follows:
>
> ```
> $ aws cloudformation delete-stack --stack-name etherpad-cloudformation
> ```

One flaw with launching an EC2 instance from a base image like Amazon Linux 2 and using a user data script to deploy an application is reliability. Many things can and will go wrong when executing the deployment script. For example, GitHub could be down, so the EC2 instance cannot download Etherpad's source code. The same is true for other repositories, for example, the RPM repository used to install Node.js.

You will learn how to mitigate this risk in the next section by building AMIs, including everything that is needed to start Etherpad without any external dependencies. As an added benefit, this approach allows you to spin up an EC2 instance faster, because the boot process does not include deployment steps.

15.3   *Deploying customized AMIs created by Packer*

In this section, we present using customized Amazon Machine Images (AMIs), also called *immutable servers*. An immutable server starts from an image and is ready to go. To deploy a change, a new image is created, and the old server is replaced by a new one based on the new image.

Because a new image is needed for every change, it is advisable to automate the process of creating it. Usually, we stick to the tools AWS provides. However, we cannot recommend the EC2 Image Builder offered by AWS because it is complicated to use and doesn't seem to be designed to build images when you own the source code.

Instead, we recommend Packer, a tool provided by HashiCorp, which is very easy to use. Figure 15.4 illustrates how Packer works, as described here:

1. Launch an EC2 instance.
2. Connect to the EC2 instance via the Systems Manager.
3. Run the provisioner script.
4. Stop the EC2 instance.
5. Create an AMI.
6. Terminate the EC2 instance.

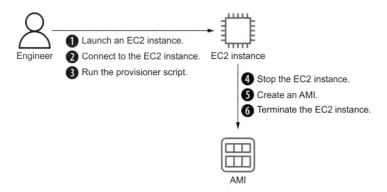

Figure 15.4   Packer automates the process of creating AMIs.

To use Packer, you need to define a template. You'll find the Packer template to build an AMI for Etherpad at chapter15/etherpad.pkr.hcl in the book's code repository on GitHub at https://github.com/AWSinAction/code3. The template starts with configuring Packer and the required plugins, as shown next.

Listing 15.6   The Packer template to build an Etherpad AMI, part 1

```
packer {
  required_plugins {
    amazon = {
      version = ">= 0.0.2"
      source  = "github.com/hashicorp/amazon"
    }
  }
}
```

Next, you need to define a source AMI as well as the details for the EC2 instance, which Packer will launch to build the AMI. By default, Packer uses SSH to connect to the EC2 instance. We are using the Systems Manager for increased security and usability instead.

IAM role ec2-ssm-core

Packer requires an IAM role named `ec2-ssm-core`. You created the role in the chapter 3 section, "Creating an IAM role."

Listing 15.7   The Packer template to build an Etherpad AMI, part 2

Specifies the name for the new AMI adding
{{timestamp}} to ensure uniqueness

```
source "amazon-ebs" "etherpad" {
  ami_name = "awsinaction-etherpad-{{timestamp}}"
  tags = {
    Name = "awsinaction-etherpad"
  }
  instance_type = "t2.micro"
  region        = "us-east-1"
  source_ami_filter {
    filters = {
      name = "amzn2-ami-hvm-2.0.*-x86_64-gp2"
      root-device-type   = "ebs"
      virtualization-type = "hvm"
    }
    most_recent = true
    owners      = ["137112412989"]
  }
  ssh_username        = "ec2-user"
  ssh_interface       = "session_manager"
  communicator        = "ssh"
  iam_instance_profile = "ec2-ssm-core"
  ami_groups = ["all"]
  ami_regions = ["us-east-1"]
}
```

The region used to build the AMI

The instance type for the temporary build instance

The source filter defines the base AMI from which to start.

Searches for Amazon Linux 2 images; the * represents all versions.

Picks the latest version of the Amazon Linux 2 images

Filters only AMIs owned by Amazon; the AWS account 137112412989 belongs to Amazon.

Tells Packer to use the Session Manager instead of plain SSH to connect with the temporary build instance

Adds regions to distribute the AMI worldwide

Attaches the IAM instance profile ec2-ssm-core, which is required for the Session Manager

The last part of the Packer template is shown in the next listing. In the build step, a shell provisioner is used to execute commands on the temporary build instance.

Listing 15.8   The Packer template to build an Etherpad AMI, part 3

```
build {
  name    = "awsinaction-etherpad"
  sources = [
    "source.amazon-ebs.etherpad"
  ]

  provisioner "shell" {
    inline = [
      "curl -fsSL https://rpm.nodesource.com/setup_14.x
  | sudo bash -",
```

References the source; see listing 15.7.

The shell provisioner executes a script on the temporary build instance.

Adds a YUM repository for Node.js

Installs Node.js and Git

```
    "sudo yum install -y nodejs git",
    "sudo mkdir /opt/etherpad-lite",
    "sudo chown -R ec2-user:ec2-user /opt/etherpad-lite",
    "cd /opt",
    "git clone --depth 1 --branch 1.8.17 https://github.com/
 AWSinAction/etherpad-lite.git",
    "cd etherpad-lite",
    "./src/bin/installDeps.sh",
  ]
 }
}
```

Fetches Etherpad from GitHub

Installs Etherpad dependencies

Before you proceed, make sure to install Packer on your local machine. The following commands install Packer on MacOS with brew:

```
$ brew tap hashicorp/tap
$ brew install hashicorp/tap/packer
```

You can also get the binaries from https://packer.io/downloads.html. Check out http://mng.bz/Zp8a for detailed instructions.

After you have installed Packer successfully, use the following command to initialize the tool:

```
$ packer init chapter15/
```

Next, build an AMI with Etherpad preinstalled like this:

```
$ packer build chapter15/etherpad.pkr.hcl
```

Watch Packer spinning up an EC2 instance, executing the provisioner shell script, stopping the EC2 instance, creating an AMI, and terminating the EC2 instance. At the end of the process, Packer will output the AMI ID, which is `ami-06beed8fa64e7cb68` in the following example:

```
==> Builds finished. The artifacts of successful builds are:
--> awsinaction-etherpad.amazon-ebs.etherpad: AMIs were created:
us-east-1: ami-06beed8fa64e7cb68
```

Note the AMI ID because you will need it to deploy Etherpad on AWS soon. As shown in figure 15.5, we are using a similar approach to roll out Etherpad as we did in the previous section. The Auto Scaling group orchestrates a rolling update. But instead of using a user data script to deploy Etherpad, the Auto Scaling group provisions EC2 instances based on the AMI with Etherpad preinstalled.

Use the following command to create the CloudFormation stack to roll out the Etherpad AMI. Replace `$AMI` with the AMI ID from Packer's output:

```
$ aws cloudformation deploy --stack-name etherpad-packer \
 --template-file packer.yaml \
 --parameter-overrides AMI=$AMI \
 --capabilities CAPABILITY_IAM
```

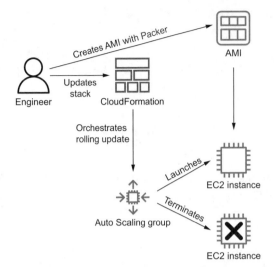

Figure 15.5   Rolling out an AMI with Etherpad preinstalled, built by Packer with the help of CloudFormation

It will take CloudFormation about 10 minutes to provision all the resources. After that, the command will return. Next, use the following command to get the URL to access the Etherpad application:

```
aws cloudformation describe-stacks --stack-name etherpad-packer \
⇨ --query "Stacks[0].Outputs[0].OutputValue" --output text
```

Open the URL of your Etherpad application and create a new pad. Click the settings icon to check the current version of Etherpad as shown in the following listing. The version is c85ab49, which is the latest Git commit ID for version 1.8.17.

The CloudFormation template to deploy the Etherpad AMI built by Packer is very similar to that in the previous section, except a parameter allows you to hand over the ID of your Etherpad AMI. You'll find the Packer template to build an AMI for Etherpad at chapter15/packer.yaml in the book's code repository on GitHub at https://github.com/AWSinAction/code3.

Listing 15.9   Handing over the AMI ID to the CloudFormation template

```
# [...]
Parameters:
  AMI:                              The parameter to
    Type: 'AWS::EC2::Image::Id'     set the AMI
    Description: 'The AMI ID'
Resources:
  # [...]
  LaunchTemplate:
    Type: 'AWS::EC2::LaunchTemplate'
    Properties:
      # [...]
      LaunchTemplateData:
```

```
        ImageId: !Ref AMI              ◁─────  The launch template
        UserData:                              references the AMI
          'Fn::Base64': !Sub |                 parameter.
            #!/bin/bash -ex
            trap '/opt/aws/bin/cfn-signal -e 1 --stack ${AWS::StackName} \
⇒ --resource AutoScalingGroup --region ${AWS::Region}' ERR
            cd /opt/etherpad-lite/
            echo "
            {
              \"title\": \"Etherpad\",
              \"dbType\": \"mysql\",
              \"dbSettings\": {
                \"host\": \"${Database.Endpoint.Address}\",
                \"port\": \"3306\",
                \"database\": \"etherpad\",
                \"user\": \"etherpad\",
                \"password\": \"etherpad\"
              },
              \"exposeVersion\": true
            }
            " > settings.json
            /opt/etherpad-lite/src/bin/fastRun.sh &
            /opt/aws/bin/cfn-signal -e 0 --stack ${AWS::StackName} \
⇒ --resource AutoScalingGroup --region ${AWS::Region}
# [...]
```

Wait what? We are still using user data to inject a script into the boot process of the EC2 instance?

Yes, but only to create a settings file, which requires the database host name; this is not known when creating the AMI …

… and to start the Etherpad application.

There is only one important part missing: the Auto Scaling group. The following listing explains the details.

Listing 15.10 Orchestrating rolling updates with the Auto Scaling group

```
# [...]
AutoScalingGroup:                                      ◁───  The Auto Scaling group ensures
  Type: 'AWS::AutoScaling::AutoScalingGroup'                 that an EC2 instance is running
  Properties:                                               and is replaced in case of failure.
    TargetGroupARNs:
    - !Ref LoadBalancerTargetGroup              References the launch
    LaunchTemplate:                             template explained in
                                          ◁───  listing 15.9
      LaunchTemplateId: !Ref LaunchTemplate
      Version: !GetAtt 'LaunchTemplate.LatestVersionNumber'
    MinSize: 1                          ◁───
    MaxSize: 2                          ◁───    Starts a single machine,
    HealthCheckGracePeriod: 300                because Etherpad cannot
    HealthCheckType: ELB                       run on multiple machines
    VPCZoneIdentifier:                         in parallel
    - !Ref SubnetA
    - !Ref SubnetB                      During a rolling update, the Auto
    Tags:                               Scaling group launches a new
    - PropagateAtLaunch: true           machine before terminating the old
      Value: etherpad                   one; therefore, we need to set the
      Key: Name                         maximum size to 2.
  CreationPolicy:
    ResourceSignal:
      Timeout: PT10M
```

```
  UpdatePolicy:
    AutoScalingRollingUpdate:
      PauseTime: PT10M
      WaitOnResourceSignals: true
      MinInstancesInService: 1
# [...]
```

The update policy configures the rolling update.

The Auto Scaling group will wait 10 minutes for a new EC2 instance signal success with cfn-signal.

Indicates zero-downtime deployments by ensuring that at least one instance is running during a deployment

Enabling waiting for a signal from the EC2 instance during a rolling update

To deploy a new version, you need to build a new AMI with Packer and update the CloudFormation stack with the new AMI ID. Before you do, update the Packer template chapter15/etherpad.pkr.hcl and replace Etherpad version `1.8.17` with `1.8.18`, as shown next:

```
$ packer build chapter15/etherpad.pkr.hcl
$ aws cloudformation deploy --stack-name etherpad-packer \
➥ --template-file chapter15/packer.yaml \
➥ --parameter-overrides AMI=$AMI \
➥ --capabilities CAPABILITY_IAM
```

Hurray! You have deployed Etherpad on immutable servers launched from an image built by Packer. This approach is very reliable and allows you to deploy without any downtime. After updating the CloudFormation stack, reload the Etherpad web application. Check the version, which should be `4b96ff6`.

Cleaning up

Don't forget to clean up your AWS account before proceeding with the next step, as shown here:

```
$ aws cloudformation delete-stack --stack-name etherpad-packer
```

15.3.1 *Tips and tricks for Packer and CloudFormation*

Finally, we want to share the following tips and tricks for deploying an application of your choice with the help of Packer and CloudFormation:

- Launch an EC2 instance based on Amazon Linux 2 or the distribution you want to build on.
- Go through the steps necessary to get the application up and running manually.
- Transfer the manual steps into a shell script.
- Create a Packer template, and include the shell script.
- Run `packer build`, and launch an instance based on the AMI for testing.
- Roll out the AMI with CloudFormation and an Auto Scaling group.
- Use a user data script for dynamic configuration, as shown in our example.

In case you are looking for a way to ship your own source code, check out the file pro-visioner (see https://www.packer.io/docs/provisioners/file), which allows you to upload local files when building AMIs with Packer.

15.4   *Comparing approaches*

In this last section, we will compare the three different options to deploy applica-tions on EC2 that you have learned about while reading through this chapter. We dis-cussed the following three different methods to deploy applications on EC2 instances in this chapter:

- *AWS CodeDeploy*—Uses an agent running on the virtual machines to perform in-place deployments
- *AWS CloudFormation with user data*—Spins up new machines, which will execute a deployment script at the end of the boot process
- *Packer by HashiCorp*—Enables you to bundle the application into an AMI and launch immutable servers

All three options allow zero-downtime deployments, which is a game changer because it allows you to roll out changes without having to ask for a maintenance window in advance. The introduced tools also support deploying changes to a fleet of virtual machines gradually. But the approaches also have differences, as shown in table 15.2.

Table 15.2   **Differences between CodeDeploy, CloudFormation and user data, and Packer**

	AWS CodeDeploy	**AWS CloudFormation and user data**	**Packer**
Deployment speed	Fast	Slow	Medium
Agility	Medium	High	Low
Advantages	In-place deploy-ments work for state-ful machines as well.	Changing the user data script is a flexible way to deploy changes.	Machines are starting really fast, which is important if you want to scale based on demand. Also, you have low risk of failures during the boot process.
Disadvantages	Changes pile up on machines, which make it difficult to reproduce a deploy-ment.	Potential failures during the boot process exist, for example, when third parties like GitHub are down.	Handling the life cycle of AMIs is tricky because you have to clean up unused and old AMIs to avoid storage costs.

We use all three options and choose the approach that best fits a particular scenario.

Summary

- AWS CodeDeploy is designed to automate deployments on EC2, Fargate, and Lambda. Even on-premises machines are supported.
- AWS CloudFormation is actually an Infrastructure as Code tool but comes with features to orchestrate rolling updates of EC2 instances as well.
- By configuring user data for an EC2 instance, you are able to inject a script that the machine will execute at the end of the boot process.
- Packer by HashiCorp is a tool to automate the process of creating Amazon Machine Images (AMIs).
- An immutable server is a server that you do not change after launch. Instead, to deploy changes you replace the old machine with a new one. This approach lowers the risk of side effects caused by former changes or third-party outages.

16

Designing for
fault tolerance

This chapter covers

- What fault-tolerance is and why you need it
- Using redundancy to remove single points
  of failure
- Improving fault tolerance by retrying on failure
- Using idempotent operations to retry on failure
- AWS service guarantees

Failure is inevitable: hard disks, networks, power, and so on all fail from time to time. But failures do not have to affect the users of your system.

A fault-tolerant system provides the highest quality to your users. No matter what happens in your system, the user is never affected and can continue to go about their work, consume entertaining content, buy goods and services, or have conversations with friends. A few years ago, achieving fault tolerance was expensive and complicated, but with AWS, providing fault-tolerant systems is becoming an affordable standard. Nevertheless, building fault-tolerant systems is the top tier of cloud computing and might be challenging at the beginning.

Designing for fault tolerance means building for failure and building systems capable of resolving failure conditions automatically. An important aspect is avoiding single points of failures. You can achieve fault tolerance by introducing redundancy into your system. Instead of running your application on a single EC2 instance, you distribute the application among multiple machines. Also, decoupling the parts of your architecture such that one component does not rely on the uptime of the others is important. For example, the web server could deliver cached content if the database is not reachable.

The services provided by AWS offer different types of *failure resilience*. Resilience is the ability to deal with a failure with no or little effect on the user. You will learn about the resilience guarantees of major services in this chapter. But, in general, if you are unsure about the resilience capabilities of an AWS service, refer to the Resilience section of the official documentation for that service. A fault-tolerant system is very resilient to failure. We group AWS services into the following three categories:

- *No guarantees (single point of failure)*—No requests are served if failure occurs.
- *High availability*—In the case of failure, recovery can take some time. Requests might be interrupted.
- *Fault tolerant*—In the case of failure, requests are served as before without any availability problems.

The most convenient way to make your system fault tolerant is to build the architecture using only fault-tolerant services, which you will learn about in this chapter. If all your building blocks are fault tolerant, the whole system will be fault tolerant as well. Luckily, many AWS services are fault tolerant by default. If possible, use them. Otherwise, you'll need to deal with the consequences and handle failures yourself.

Unfortunately, one important service isn't fault tolerant by default: EC2 instances. Virtual machines aren't fault tolerant. This means an architecture that uses EC2 isn't fault tolerant by default. But AWS provides the building blocks to help you improve the fault tolerance of virtual machines. In this chapter, we will show you how to use Auto Scaling groups, Elastic Load Balancing (ELB), and Simple Queue Service (SQS) to turn EC2 instances into fault-tolerant systems.

First, however, let's look at the level of failure resistance of key services. Knowing which services are fault tolerant, which are highly available, and which are neither will help you create the kind of fault tolerance your system needs.

The following services provided by AWS are neither highly available nor fault tolerant. When using one of these services in your architecture, you are adding a *single point of failure* (SPOF) to your infrastructure. In this case, to achieve fault tolerance, you need to plan and build for failure as discussed during the rest of the chapter:

- *Amazon Elastic Compute Cloud (EC2) instance*—A single EC2 instance can fail for many reasons: hardware failure, network problems, availability zone (AZ) outage, and so on. To achieve high availability or fault tolerance, use Auto Scaling groups to set up a fleet of EC2 instances that serve requests in a redundant way.
- *Amazon Relational Database Service (RDS) single instance*—A single RDS instance could fail for the same reasons that an EC2 instance might fail. Use Multi-AZ mode to achieve high availability.

All the following services are *highly available* (HA) by default. When a failure occurs, the services will suffer from a short downtime but will recover automatically:

- *Elastic Network Interface (ENI)*—A network interface is bound to an AZ, so if this AZ goes down, your network interface will be unavailable as well. You can attach an ENI to another virtual machine in case of a smaller outage, however.
- *Amazon Virtual Private Cloud (VPC) subnet*—A VPC subnet is bound to an AZ, so if this AZ suffers from an outage, your subnet will not be reachable as well. Use multiple subnets in different AZs to remove the dependency on a single AZ.
- *Amazon Elastic Block Store (EBS) volume*—An EBS volume distributes data among multiple storage systems within an AZ. But if the whole AZ fails, your volume will be unavailable (you won't lose your data, though). You can create EBS snapshots from time to time so you can re-create an EBS volume in another AZ.
- *Amazon Relational Database Service (RDS) Multi-AZ instance*—When running in Multi-AZ mode, a short downtime (one minute) is expected if a problem occurs with the master instance while changing DNS records to switch to the standby instance.

The following services are *fault tolerant* by default. As a consumer of the service, you won't notice any failures:

- Elastic Load Balancing (ELB), deployed to at least two AZs
- Amazon EC2 security groups
- Amazon Virtual Private Cloud (VPC) with an ACL and a route table
- Elastic IP addresses (EIP)
- Amazon Simple Storage Service (S3)
- Amazon Elastic Block Store (EBS) snapshots
- Amazon DynamoDB
- Amazon CloudWatch
- Auto Scaling groups
- Amazon Simple Queue Service (SQS)
- AWS CloudFormation
- AWS Identity and Access Management (IAM, not bound to a single region; if you create an IAM user, that user is available in all regions)

Chapter requirements

To fully understand this chapter, you need to have read and understood the following concepts:

- EC2 (chapter 3)
- Autoscaling (chapter 13)
- Elastic Load Balancing (chapter 14)
- Simple Queue Service (chapter 14)

In this chapter, you'll learn everything you need to design a fault-tolerant web application based on EC2 instances (which aren't fault tolerant by default). During this chapter, you will build a fault-tolerant web application that allows a user to upload an image, apply a sepia filter to the image, and download the image. First, you will learn how to distribute a workload among multiple EC2 instances. Instead of running a single virtual machine, you will spin up multiple machines in different data centers, also known as availability zones. Next, you will learn how to increase the resilience of your code. Afterward, you will create an infrastructure consisting of a queue (SQS), a load balancer (ALB), EC2 instances managed by Auto Scaling groups, and a database (DynamoDB).

16.1   *Using redundant EC2 instances to increase availability*

Here are just a few reasons your virtual machine might fail:

- If the host hardware fails, it can no longer host the virtual machine on top of it.
- If the network connection to/from the host is interrupted, the virtual machine will lose the ability to communicate over the network.
- If the host system is disconnected from the power supply, the virtual machine will fail as well.

Additionally, the software running inside your virtual machine may also cause a crash for the following reasons:

- If your application contains a memory leak, the EC2 instance will run out of memory and fail. It may take a day, a month, a year, or more, but eventually it will happen.
- If your application writes to disk and never deletes its data, the EC2 instance will run out of disk space sooner or later, causing your application to fail.
- Your application may not handle edge cases properly and may instead crash unexpectedly.

Regardless of whether the host system or your application is the cause of a failure, a single EC2 instance is a single point of failure. If you rely on a single EC2 instance, your system will fail up eventually. It's merely a matter of time.

16.1.1   Redundancy can remove a single point of failure

Imagine a production line that makes fluffy cloud pies. Producing a fluffy cloud pie requires the following production steps (simplified!):

1   Produce a pie crust.
2   Cool the pie crust.
3   Put the fluffy cloud mass on top of the pie crust.
4   Cool the fluffy cloud pie.
5   Package the fluffy cloud pie.

The current setup is a single production line. The big problem with this process is that whenever one of the steps crashes, the entire production line must be stopped. Figure 16.1 illustrates what happens when the second step (cooling the pie crust) crashes. The steps that follow no longer work, because they no longer receive cool pie crusts.

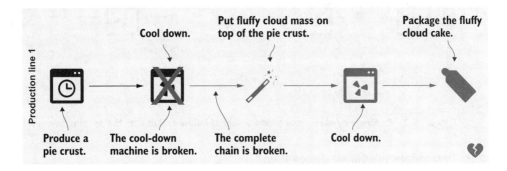

Figure 16.1   A single point of failure affects not only itself but the entire system.

Why not have multiple production lines, each producing pies from pie crust through packaging? Instead of one line, suppose we have three. If one of the lines fails, the other two can still produce fluffy cloud pies for all the hungry customers in the world. Figure 16.2 shows the improvements; the only downside is that we need three times as many machines.

The example can be transferred to EC2 instances. Instead of having only one EC2 instance running your application, you can have three. If one of those instances fails, the other two will still be able to serve incoming requests. You can also minimize the cost of one versus three instances: instead of one large EC2 instance, you can choose three small ones. The problem that arises when using multiple virtual machines: how can the client communicate with the instances? The answer is *decoupling*: put a load balancer or message queue between your EC2 instances and the client. Read on to learn how this works.

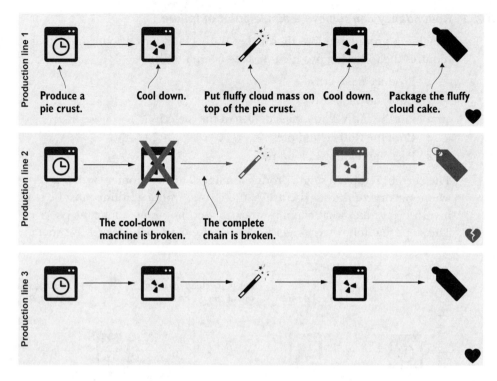

Figure 16.2   Redundancy eliminates single points of failure and makes the system more stable.

16.1.2 *Redundancy requires decoupling*

In chapter 14, you learned how to use Elastic Load Balancing (ELB) and the Simple Queue Service (SQS) to decouple different parts of a system. You will apply both approaches to build a fault-tolerant system next.

First, figure 16.3 shows how EC2 instances can be made fault tolerant by using redundancy and synchronous decoupling. If one of the EC2 instances crashes, the load balancer stops routing requests to the crashed instances. Then, the Auto Scaling group replaces the crashed EC2 instance within minutes, and the load balancer begins to route requests to the new instance.

Take a second look at figure 16.3 and see what parts are redundant:

- *Availability zones (AZs)*—Two are used. If one AZ suffers from an outage, we still have instances running in the other AZ.
- *Subnets*—A subnet is tightly coupled to an AZ. Therefore, we need one subnet in each AZ.
- *EC2 instances*—Two subnets with one or more EC2 instances lead to redundancy among availability zones.
- *Load Balancer*—The load balancer spans multiple subnets and, therefore, multiple availability zones.

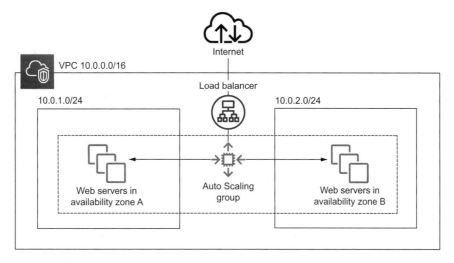

Figure 16.3   Fault-tolerant EC2 instances with an Auto Scaling group and an Elastic Load Balancer

Next, figure 16.4 shows a fault-tolerant system built with EC2 that uses the power of redundancy and asynchronous decoupling to process messages from an SQS queue.

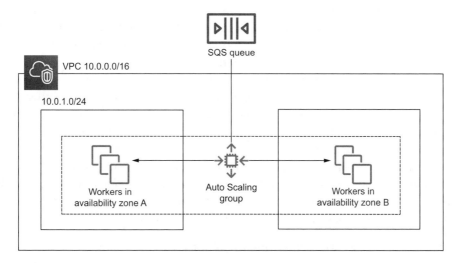

Figure 16.4   Fault-tolerant EC2 instances with an Auto Scaling group and SQS

Second, in figures 16.3 and 16.4, the load balancer and the SQS queue appear only once. This doesn't mean that ELB or SQS are single points of failure; on the contrary, ELB and SQS are both fault tolerant by default.

You will learn how to use both models—synchronous decoupling with a load balancer and asynchronous decoupling with a queue—to build a fault-tolerant system in the following sections. But before we do so, let's have a look into some important considerations for making your code more resilient.

16.2   Considerations for making your code fault tolerant

If you want to achieve fault tolerance, you have to build your application accordingly. You can design fault tolerance into your application by following two suggestions:

- In the case of failure, let it crash, but also retry.
- Try to write idempotent code wherever possible.

16.2.1   Let it crash, but also retry

The Erlang programming language is famous for the concept of "let it crash." That means whenever the program doesn't know what to do, it crashes, and someone needs to deal with the crash. Most often people overlook the fact that Erlang is also famous for retrying. Letting it crash without retrying isn't useful—if you can't recover from a crash, your system will be down, which is the opposite of what you want.

You can apply the "let it crash" concept (some people call it "fail fast") to synchronous and asynchronous decoupled scenarios. In a synchronous decoupled scenario, the sender of a request must implement the retry logic. If no response is returned within a certain amount of time, or an error is returned, the sender retries by sending the same request again. In an asynchronous decoupled scenario, things are easier. If a message is consumed but not acknowledged within a certain amount of time, it goes back to the queue. The next consumer then grabs the message and processes it again. Retrying is built into asynchronous systems by default.

"Let it crash" isn't useful in all situations. If the program wants to respond to the sender but the request contains invalid content, this isn't a reason for letting the server crash: the result will stay the same no matter how often you retry. But if the server can't reach the database, it makes a lot of sense to retry. Within a few seconds, the database may be available again and able to successfully process the retried request.

Retrying isn't that easy. Imagine that you want to retry the creation of a blog post. With every retry, a new entry in the database is created, containing the same data as before. You end up with many duplicates in the database. Preventing this involves a powerful concept that's introduced next: idempotent retry.

16.2.2   Idempotent retry makes fault tolerance possible

How can you prevent a blog post from being added to the database multiple times because of a retry? A naive approach would be to use the title as the primary key. If the primary key is already used, you can assume that the post is already in the database and skip the step of inserting it into the database. Now the insertion of blog posts is idempotent, which means no matter how often a certain action is applied, the outcome must be the same. In the current example, the outcome is a database entry.

It continues with a more complicated example. Inserting a blog post is more complicated in reality, because the process might look something like this:

1 Create a blog post entry in the database.
2 Invalidate the cache because data has changed.
3 Post the link to the blog's Twitter feed.

Let's take a close look at each step.

1. CREATE A BLOG POST ENTRY IN THE DATABASE

We covered this step earlier by using the title as a primary key. But this time, we use a universally unique identifier (UUID) instead of the title as the primary key. A UUID like `550e8400-e29b-11d4-a716-446655440000` is a random ID that's generated by the client. Because of the nature of a UUID, it's unlikely that two identical UUIDs will be generated. If the client wants to create a blog post, it must send a request to the load balancer containing the UUID, title, and text. The load balancer routes the request to one of the backend servers. The backend server checks whether the primary key already exists. If not, a new record is added to the database. If it exists, the insertion continues. Figure 16.5 shows the flow.

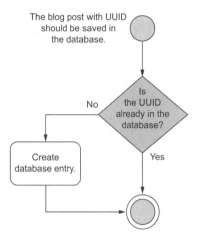

Figure 16.5   Idempotent database insert: Creating a blog post entry in the database only if it doesn't already exist

Creating a blog post is a good example of an idempotent operation that is guaranteed by code. You can also use your database to handle this problem. Just send an insert to your database. The next three things could happen:

- Your database inserts the data. The operation is successfully completed.
- Your database responds with an error because the primary key is already in use. The operation is successfully completed.
- Your database responds with a different error. The operation crashes.

Think twice about the best way to implement idempotence!

2. INVALIDATE THE CACHE

This step sends an invalidation message to a caching layer. You don't need to worry about idempotence too much here: it doesn't hurt if the cache is invalidated more often than needed. If the cache is invalidated, then the next time a request hits the cache, the cache won't contain data, and the original source (in this case, the database) will be queried for the result. The result is then put in the cache for subsequent requests. If you invalidate the cache multiple times because of a retry, the worst thing that can happen is that you may need to make a few more calls to your database. That's easy.

3. POST TO THE BLOG'S TWITTER FEED

To make this step idempotent, you need to use some tricks, because you interact with a third party that doesn't support idempotent operations. Unfortunately, no solution will guarantee that you post exactly one status update to Twitter. You can guarantee the creation of at least one (one or more than one) status update or at most one (one or none) status update. An easy approach could be to ask the Twitter API for the latest status updates; if one of them matches the status update that you want to post, you skip the step because it's already done.

But Twitter is an eventually consistent system: there is no guarantee that you'll see a status update immediately after you post it. Therefore, you can end up having your status update posted multiple times. Another approach would be to save whether you already posted the status update in a database. But imagine saving to the database that you posted to Twitter and then making the request to the Twitter API—but at that moment, the system crashes. Your database will state that the Twitter status update was posted, but in reality, it wasn't. You need to make a choice: tolerate a missing status update, or tolerate multiple status updates. Hint: it's a business decision. Figure 16.6 shows the flow of both solutions.

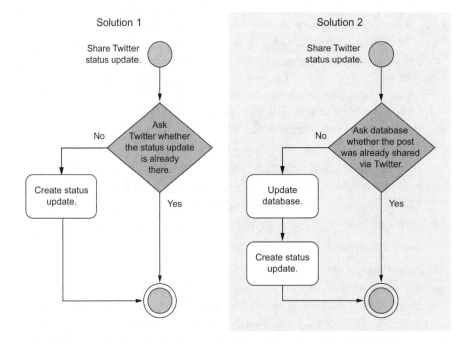

Figure 16.6   Idempotent Twitter status update: Share a status update only if it hasn't already been done.

Now it's time for a practical example! You'll design, implement, and deploy a distributed, fault-tolerant web application on AWS. This example will demonstrate how distributed systems work and will combine most of the knowledge in this book.

16.3   Building a fault-tolerant web application: Imagery

Before you begin the architecture and design of the fault-tolerant Imagery application, we'll talk briefly about what the application should do. A user should be able to upload an image. This image is then transformed with a sepia filter so that it looks fancy. The user can then view the sepia image. Figure 16.7 shows the process.

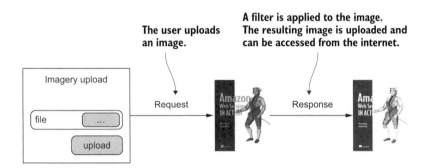

Figure 16.7   The user uploads an image to Imagery, where a filter is applied.

The problem with the process shown in figure 16.7 is that it's synchronous. If the web server crashes during request and response, the user's image won't be processed. Another problem arises when many users want to use the Imagery app: the system becomes busy and may slow down or stop working. Therefore, the process should be turned into an asynchronous one. Chapter 14 introduced the idea of asynchronous decoupling by using an SQS message queue, as shown in figure 16.8.

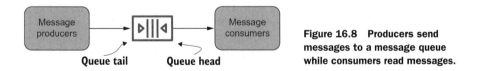

Figure 16.8   Producers send messages to a message queue while consumers read messages.

When designing an asynchronous process, it's important to keep track of the process. You need some kind of identifier for it. When a user wants to upload an image, the user creates a process first. This returns a unique ID. With that ID, the user can upload an image. If the image upload is finished, the worker begins to process the image in the background. The user can look up the process at any time with the process ID. While the image is being processed, the user can't see the sepia image, but as soon as the image is processed, the lookup process returns the sepia image. Figure 16.9 shows the asynchronous process.

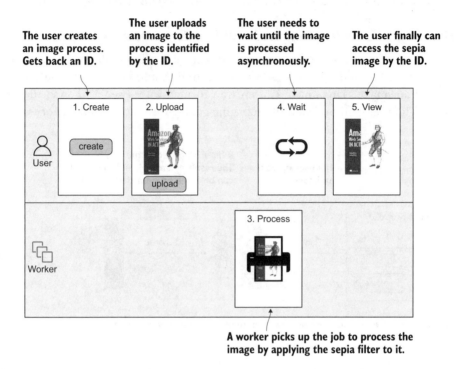

Figure 16.9   **The user asynchronously uploads an image to Imagery, where a filter is applied.**

Now that you have an asynchronous process, it's time to map that process to AWS services. Keep in mind that many services on AWS are fault tolerant by default, so it makes sense to pick them whenever possible. Figure 16.10 shows one way of doing it.

To make things as easy as possible, all the actions will be accessible via a REST API, which will be provided by EC2 instances. In the end, EC2 instances will provide the process and make calls to all the AWS services shown in figure 16.10.

You'll use many AWS services to implement the Imagery application. Most of them are fault tolerant by default, but EC2 isn't. You'll deal with that problem using an idempotent state machine, as introduced in the next section.

> ### Example is 100% covered by the Free Tier
> The example in this chapter is totally covered by the Free Tier. As long as you don't run the example longer than a few days, you won't pay anything for it. Keep in mind that this applies only if you created a fresh AWS account for this book and there is nothing else going on in your AWS account. Try to complete the example within a few days, because you'll clean up your account at the end of the section.

The user creates a process with a unique ID. The process is stored in DynamoDB.

With the process ID, the user uploads an image to S3. The S3 key is persisted to DynamoDB together with the new process state "uploaded." A SQS message is produced to trigger processing.

DynamoDB contains the current state of the process. Wait for the state switches to be processed.

S3 contains the sepia image. DynamoDB knows the S3 key.

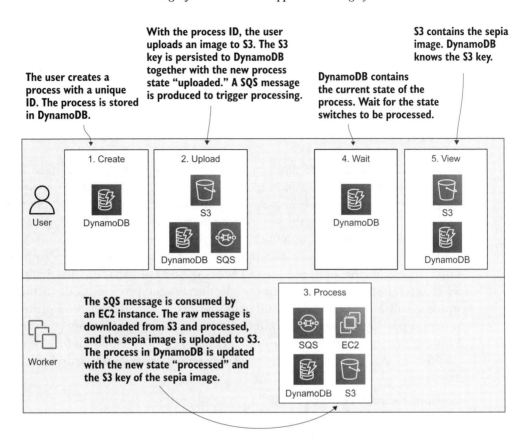

The SQS message is consumed by an EC2 instance. The raw message is downloaded from S3 and processed, and the sepia image is uploaded to S3. The process in DynamoDB is updated with the new state "processed" and the S3 key of the sepia image.

Figure 16.10   Combining AWS services to implement the asynchronous Imagery process

16.3.1 *The idempotent state machine*

An idempotent state machine sounds complicated. We'll take some time to explain it because it's the heart of the Imagery application. Let's look at what a *state and machine* is and what idempotent means in this context.

THE FINITE STATE MACHINE

A finite state machine has at least one start state and one end state. Between the start and the end states, the state machine can have many other states. The machine also defines transitions between states. For example, a state machine with three states could look like this:

```
(A) -> (B) -> (C).
```

This means:

- State A is the start state.
- There is a transition possible from state A to B.

- There is a transition possible from state B to C.
- State C is the end state.

But there is no transition possible between (A) → (C) or (B) → (A). With this in mind, we apply the theory to our Imagery example. The Imagery state machine could look like this:

```
(Created) -> (Uploaded) -> (Processed)
```

Once a new process (state machine) is created, the only transition possible is to `Uploaded`. To make this transition happen, you need the S3 key of the uploaded raw image. The transition between `Created` → `Uploaded` can be defined by the function `uploaded(s3Key)`. Basically, the same is true for the transition `Uploaded` → `Processed`. This transition can be done with the S3 key of the sepia image: `processed(s3Key)`.

Don't be confused by the fact that the upload and the image filter processing don't appear in the state machine. These are the basic actions that happen, but we're interested only in the results; we don't track the progress of the actions. The process isn't aware that 10% of the data has been uploaded or 30% of the image processing is done. It cares only whether the actions are 100% done. You can probably imagine a bunch of other states that could be implemented, but we're skipping that for the purpose of simplicity in this example: resized and shared are just two examples.

IDEMPOTENT STATE TRANSITIONS

An idempotent state transition must have the same result no matter how often the transition takes place. If you can make sure that your state transitions are idempotent, you can do a simple trick: if you experience a failure during transitioning, you retry the entire state transition.

Let's look at the two state transitions you need to implement. The first transition `Created` → `Uploaded` can be implemented like this (pseudocode):

```
uploaded(s3Key) {
  process = DynamoDB.getItem(processId)
  if (process.state !== 'Created') {
    throw new Error('transition not allowed')
  }
  DynamoDB.updateItem(processId, {'state': 'Uploaded', 'rawS3Key': s3Key})
  SQS.sendMessage({'processId': processId, 'action': 'process'});
}
```

The problem with this implementation is that it's not idempotent. Imagine that `SQS.sendMessage` fails. The state transition will fail, so you retry. But the second call to `uploaded(s3Key)` will throw a "transition not allowed" error because `DynamoDB.updateItem` was successful during the first call.

To fix that, you need to change the `if` statement to make the function idempotent, like this (pseudocode):

```
uploaded(s3Key) {
  process = DynamoDB.getItem(processId)
  if (process.state !== 'Created' && process.state !== 'Uploaded') {
    throw new Error('transition not allowed')
  }
  DynamoDB.updateItem(processId, {'state': 'Uploaded', 'rawS3Key': s3Key})
  SQS.sendMessage({'processId': processId, 'action': 'process'});
}
```

If you retry now, you'll make multiple updates to Dynamo, which doesn't hurt. And you may send multiple SQS messages, which also doesn't hurt, because the SQS message consumer must be idempotent as well. The same applies to the transition Uploaded → Processed.

One little thing is still missing. So far, the code will fetch an item from DynamoDB and will update the item a few lines after that. In between, another process might have set the state to Uploaded already. Luckily, the database supports conditional updates, which allows us to reduce all the logic into a single DynamoDB request. DynamoDB will evaluate the condition before updating the item, as shown here (pseudocode):

```
uploaded(s3Key) {
  process = DynamoDB.getItem(processId)
  DynamoDB.updateItem(processId, {
    'state': 'Uploaded',
    'rawS3Key': s3Key,
    condition: 'NOT state IN(Created, Uploaded)'
  })
  SQS.sendMessage({'processId': processId, 'action': 'process'});
}
```

Next, you'll begin to implement the Imagery server.

16.3.2 Implementing a fault-tolerant web service

We'll split the Imagery application into two parts: the web servers and the workers. As illustrated in figure 16.11, the web servers provide the REST API to the user, and the workers process images.

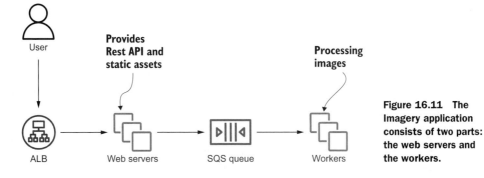

Figure 16.11 The Imagery application consists of two parts: the web servers and the workers.

Where is the code located?

As usual, you'll find the code in the book's code repository on GitHub: https://github
.com/AWSinAction/code3. Imagery is located in /chapter16/.

The REST API will support the following routes:

- POST /image—A new image process is created when executing this route.
- GET /image/:id—This route returns the state of the process specified with the
  path parameter :id.
- POST /image/:id/upload—This route offers a file upload for the process specified with the path parameter :id.

To implement the web server, you'll again use Node.js and the Express web application framework. You'll use the Express framework, but don't feel intimidated because
you won't need to understand it in depth to follow along.

SETTING UP THE WEB SERVER PROJECT

As always, you need some boilerplate code to load dependencies, initial AWS endpoints, and things like that. The next listing explains the code to do so.

Listing 16.1   Initializing the Imagery server (server/server.js)

```
const express = require('express');            ←  Loads the
const bodyParser = require('body-parser');         Node.js modules
const AWS = require('aws-sdk');                     (dependencies)
const { v4: uuidv4 } = require('uuid');
const multiparty = require('multiparty');

const db = new AWS.DynamoDB({});        ←  Creates a
const sqs = new AWS.SQS({});               DynamoDB
const s3 = new AWS.S3({});                 endpoint

const app = express();          ←  Creates an Express
app.use(bodyParser.json());        application

                                ←  Tells Express to
// [...]                            parse the request
                                    bodies

app.listen(process.env.PORT || 8080, function() {   ←  Starts Express on the
  console.log('Server started. Open http://localhost:'    port defined by the
  + (process.env.PORT || 8080) + ' with browser.');       environment variable
});                                                        PORT, or defaults
                                                           to 8080
```

Creates an SQS endpoint → `const sqs = new AWS.SQS({});`
Creates an S3 endpoint → `const s3 = new AWS.S3({});`

Don't worry too much about the boilerplate code; the interesting parts will follow.

CREATING A NEW IMAGERY PROCESS

To provide a REST API to create image processes, a fleet of EC2 instances will run
Node.js code behind a load balancer. The image processes will be stored in DynamoDB.
Figure 16.12 shows the flow of a request to create a new image process.

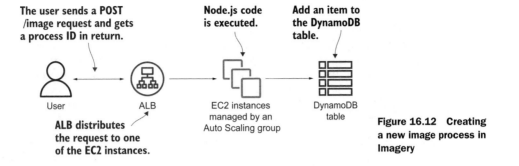

The user sends a POST /image request and gets a process ID in return.

Node.js code is executed.

Add an item to the DynamoDB table.

User

ALB

EC2 instances managed by an Auto Scaling group

DynamoDB table

ALB distributes the request to one of the EC2 instances.

Figure 16.12 Creating a new image process in Imagery

You'll now add a route to the Express application to handle POST /image requests, as shown in the following listing.

Listing 16.2 Creating an image process with POST /image

Uses the version for optimistic locking
(explained in the following sidebar)

```
app.post('/image', function(request, response) {          Registers the route
  const id = uuidv4();              Creates a unique ID     with Express
  db.putItem({                      for the process
    'Item': {
      'id': {               Invokes the putItem
        'S': id             operation on DynamoDB
      },
      'version': {          The id attribute will
        'N': '0'            be the primary key
      },                    in DynamoDB.
      'created': {
        'N': Date.now().toString()          Stores the date and time when
      },                                    the process was created
      'state': {
        'S': 'created'              The DynamoDB table
      }                            will be created later in
    },                             the chapter.
    'TableName': 'imagery-image',
    'ConditionExpression': 'attribute_not_exists(id)'      Prevents the item
  }, function(err, data) {                                 from being replaced
    if (err) {                                             if it already exists
      throw err;
    } else {
      response.json({'id': id, 'state': 'created'});      Responds with
    }                                                     the process ID
  });
});
```

The process is now in the created state:
this attribute will change when state
transitions happen.

A new process can now be created.

Optimistic locking

To prevent multiple updates to an DynamoDB item, you can use a trick called *optimistic locking*. When you want to update an item, you must specify which version you want to update. If that version doesn't match the current version of the item in the database, your update will be rejected. Keep in mind that optimistic locking is your responsibility, not a default available in DynamoDB. DynamoDB only provides the features to implement optimistic locking.

Imagine the following scenario: an item is created in version 0. Process A looks up that item (version 0). Process B also looks up that item (version 0). Now process A wants to make a change by invoking the updateItem operation on DynamoDB. Therefore, process A specifies that the expected version is 0. DynamoDB will allow that modification, because the version matches; but DynamoDB will also change the item's version to 1 because an update was performed. Now process B wants to make a modification and sends a request to DynamoDB with the expected item version 0. DynamoDB will reject that modification because the expected version doesn't match the version DynamoDB knows of, which is 1.

To solve the problem for process B, you can use the same trick introduced earlier: retry. Process B will again look up the item, now in version 1, and can (you hope) make the change. There is one problem with optimistic locking, though: if many modifications happen in parallel, a lot of overhead results because of many retries. But this is a problem only if you expect a lot of concurrent writes to a single item, which you can solve by changing the data model. That's not the case in the Imagery application. Only a few writes are expected to happen for a single item: optimistic locking is a perfect fit to make sure you don't have two writes where one overrides changes made by another.

The opposite of optimistic locking is pessimistic locking. You can implement a pessimistic lock strategy by using a semaphore. Before you change data, you need to lock the semaphore. If the semaphore is already locked, you need to wait until the semaphore becomes free again.

The next route you need to implement is to look up the current state of a process.

LOOKING UP AN IMAGERY PROCESS

You'll now add a route to the Express application to handle GET /image/:id requests. Figure 16.13 shows the request flow.

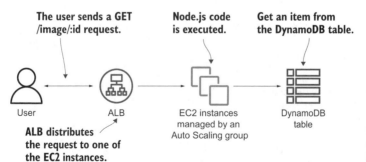

The user sends a GET /image/:id request.

Node.js code is executed.

Get an item from the DynamoDB table.

User

ALB

ALB distributes the request to one of the EC2 instances.

EC2 instances managed by an Auto Scaling group

DynamoDB table

Figure 16.13 Looking up an image process in Imagery to return its state

Express will take care of the path parameter :id by providing it within request
.params.id. The implementation shown in the next listing needs to get an item from
DynamoDB based on the path parameter ID.

Listing 16.3   GET /image/:id looks up an image process (server/server.js)

```
function mapImage = function(item) {          ◁──┐  Helper function to map a
  return {                                          DynamoDB result to a
    'id': item.id.S,                                JavaScript object
    'version': parseInt(item.version.N, 10),
    'state': item.state.S,
    'rawS3Key': // [...]
    'processedS3Key': // [...]
    'processedImage': // [...]
  };
};

                                    ┌─── Invokes the
                                         getItem operation
                                         on DynamoDB
function getImage(id, cb) {
  db.getItem({                       ◁──┘
    'Key': {
      'id': {          ◁──┐  id is the
        'S': id             partition key.
      }
    },
    'TableName': 'imagery-image'
  }, function(err, data) {
    if (err) {
      cb(err);
    } else {
      if (data.Item) {
        cb(null, mapImage(data.Item));
      } else {
        cb(new Error('image not found'));
      }
    }
  });
}
                                                        ┌── Registers the
                                                            route with
                                                            Express
app.get('/image/:id', function(request, response) {     ◁──┘
  getImage(request.params.id, function(err, image) {
    if (err) {
      throw err;
    } else {
      response.json(image);      ◁──┐  Responds with the
    }                                 image process
  });
});
```

The only thing missing is the upload part, which comes next.

UPLOADING AN IMAGE

Uploading an image via a POST request requires several steps:

1 Upload the raw image to S3.
2 Modify the item in DynamoDB.
3 Send an SQS message to trigger processing.

Figure 16.14 shows this flow.

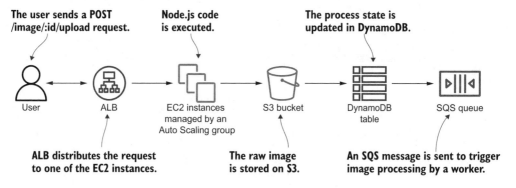

Figure 16.14   Uploading a raw image to Imagery and triggering image processing

The next code listing shows the implementation of these steps.

Listing 16.4   POST /image/:id/upload uploads an image (server/server.js)

The S3 bucket name is passed in as an environment variable (the bucket will be created later in the chapter).

```
function uploadImage(image, part, response) {
  const rawS3Key = 'upload/' + image.id + '-'
   + Date.now();
  s3.putObject({
    'Bucket': process.env.ImageBucket,
    'Key': rawS3Key,
    'Body': part,
    'ContentLength': part.byteCount
  }, function(err, data) {
    if (err) { /* [...] */ } else {
      db.updateItem({
        'Key': {'id': {'S': image.id}},
        'UpdateExpression': 'SET #s=:newState,
 version=:newVersion, rawS3Key=:rawS3Key',
        'ConditionExpression': 'attribute_exists(id)
 AND version=:oldVersion
 AND #s IN (:stateCreated, :stateUploaded)',
        'ExpressionAttributeNames': {'#s': 'state'},
        'ExpressionAttributeValues': {
          ':newState': {'S': 'uploaded'},
```

- **Creates a key for the S3 object** (→ rawS3Key)
- **Calls the S3 API to upload an object**
- **The body is the uploaded stream of data.**
- **Calls the DynamoDB API to update an object**
- **Updates the state, version, and raw S3 key**
- **Updates only when the item exists. Version equals the expected version, and state is one of those allowed.**

```
                 ':oldVersion': {'N': image.version.toString()},
                 ':newVersion': {'N': (image.version + 1).toString()},
                 ':rawS3Key': {'S': rawS3Key},
                 ':stateCreated': {'S': 'created'},
                 ':stateUploaded': {'S': 'uploaded'}
               },
               'ReturnValues': 'ALL_NEW',
               'TableName': 'imagery-image'
             }, function(err, data) {
               if (err) { /* [...] */ } else {
                 sqs.sendMessage({
                   'MessageBody': JSON.stringify({
                     'imageId': image.id, 'desiredState': 'processed'
                   }),
                   'QueueUrl': process.env.ImageQueue,
                 }, function(err) {
                   if (err) {
                     throw err;
                   } else {
                     response.redirect('/#view=' + image.id);
                     response.end();
                   }
                 });
               }
             });
           }
         });
       }
     });
   }
app.post('/image/:id/upload', function(request,
  response) {
    getImage(request.params.id, function(err, image) {
      if (err) { /* [...] */ } else {
        const form = new multiparty.Form();
        form.on('part', function(part) {
          uploadImage(image, part, response);
        });
        form.parse(request);
      }
    });
  });
```

Calls the SQS API to publish a message

Creates the message body containing the image's ID and the desired state

The queue URL is passed in as an environment variable.

Registers the route with Express

We are using the multiparty module to handle multipart uploads.

The server side is finished. Next, you'll continue to implement the processing part in the Imagery worker. After that, you can deploy the application.

16.3.3 Implementing a fault-tolerant worker to consume SQS messages

The Imagery worker processes images by applying a sepia filter asynchronously. The worker runs through the following steps in an endless loop. It is worth noting that multiple workers can run at the same time:

1. Poll the queue for new messages.
2. Fetch the process data from the database.
3. Download the image from S3.

4 Apply the sepia filter to the image.

5 Upload the modified image to S3.

6 Update the process state in the database.

7 Mark the message as done by deleting it from the queue.

SETTING UP THE WORKER

To get started, you need some boilerplate code to load dependencies, initial AWS endpoints, and an endless loop to receive messages. The following listing explains the details.

Listing 16.5   Initializing the imagery worker (worker/worker.js)

```
const AWS = require('aws-sdk');                          ◁──── Loads the
const assert = require('assert-plus');                        Node.js modules
const Jimp = require('jimp');                                 (dependencies)
const fs = require('fs/promises');

const db = new AWS.DynamoDB({});                         ◁──── Configures the
const s3 = new AWS.S3({});                                    clients to interact
const sqs = new AWS.SQS({});                                  with AWS services

const states = {
  'processed': processed                                 This function reads messages
};                                                       from the queue, processes
                                                         them, and finally deletes the
async function processMessages() {               ◁────── message from the queue.
  let data = await sqs.receiveMessage({        ◁──────── Reads one message from the queue;
    QueueUrl: process.env.ImageQueue,                    might return an empty result if
    MaxNumberOfMessages: 1                               there are no messages in the queue
  }).promise();
  if (data.Messages && data.Messages.length > 0) {
    var task = JSON.parse(data.Messages[0].Body);              Makes sure the
    var receiptHandle = data.Messages[0].ReceiptHandle;        message contains all
    assert.string(task.imageId, 'imageId');        ◁────       the required properties
    assert.string(task.desiredState, 'desiredState');
    let image = await getImage(task.imageId);      ◁──────  Gets the process
    if (typeof states[task.desiredState] === 'function') {   data from the
      await states[task.desiredState](image);                database
      await sqs.deleteMessage({                ◁────
        QueueUrl: process.env.ImageQueue,                If the message was processed
        ReceiptHandle: receiptHandle                     successfully, deletes the
      }).promise();                                      message from the queue
    } else {
      throw new Error('unsupported desiredState');
    }
  }
}

async function run() {            A loop running
  while (true) {            ◁──── endlessly
    try {
      await processMessages();
      await new Promise(resolve => setTimeout(resolve,
➡ 10000));
```

Triggers the state machine points to `await states[task.desiredState](image);`

Sleeps for 10 seconds points to the setTimeout line.

```
      } catch (e) {                      ◁──┐   Catches all exceptions,
        console.log('ERROR', e);            │   ignores them, and
      }                                     │   tries again
    }
  }
}

run();
```

The Node.js module `jimp` is used to create sepia images. You'll wire that up next.

HANDLING SQS MESSAGES AND PROCESSING THE IMAGE

The SQS message to trigger the image processing is handled by the worker. Once a message is received, the worker starts to download the raw image from S3, applies the sepia filter, and uploads the processed image back to S3. After that, the process state in DynamoDB is modified. Figure 16.15 shows the steps.

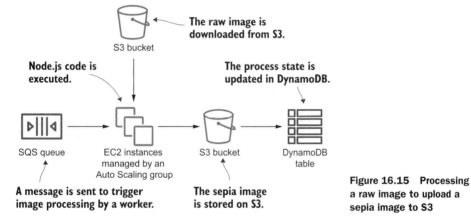

Figure 16.15   Processing a raw image to upload a sepia image to S3

The code to process an image appears next.

Listing 16.6   Imagery worker: Handling SQS messages (worker/worker.js)

```
async function processImage(image) {
  let processedS3Key = 'processed/' + image.id + '-' + Date.now() + '.png';
  let rawFile = './tmp_raw_' + image.id;
  let processedFile = './tmp_processed_' + image.id;
  let data = await s3.getObject({              ◁──┐   Fetches the original
    'Bucket': process.env.ImageBucket,            │   image from S3
    'Key': image.rawS3Key
  }).promise();
  await fs.writeFile(rawFile, data.Body,         ──┐   Writes the original image to
⇒ {'encoding': null});                       ◁──   │   a temporary folder on disk
  let lenna = await Jimp.read(rawFile);        ◁──┐   Reads the file with the
                                                   │   image manipulation
                                                   │   library
```

```
      await lenna.sepia().write(processedFile);
      await fs.unlink(rawFile);
      let buf = await fs.readFile(processedFile,
        {'encoding': null});
      await s3.putObject({
        'Bucket': process.env.ImageBucket,
        'Key': processedS3Key,
        'ACL': 'public-read',
        'Body': buf,
        'ContentType': 'image/png'
      }).promise();
      await fs.unlink(processedFile);
      return processedS3Key;
    }

    async function processed(image) {
      let processedS3Key = await processImage(image);
      await db.updateItem({
        'Key': {
          'id': {
            'S': image.id
          }
        },
        'UpdateExpression':
          'SET #s=:newState, version=:newVersion,
    processedS3Key=:processedS3Key',
        'ConditionExpression':
          'attribute_exists(id) AND version=:oldVersion
    AND #s IN (:stateUploaded, :stateProcessed)',
        'ExpressionAttributeNames': {
          '#s': 'state'
        },
        'ExpressionAttributeValues': {
          ':newState': {'S': 'processed'},
          ':oldVersion': {'N': image.version.toString()},
          ':newVersion': {'N': (image.version + 1).toString()},
          ':processedS3Key': {'S': processedS3Key},
          ':stateUploaded': {'S': 'uploaded'},
          ':stateProcessed': {'S': 'processed'}
        },
        'ReturnValues': 'ALL_NEW',
        'TableName': 'imagery-image'
      }).promise();
    }
```

Applies the sepia filter and writes the processed image to disk

Deletes the original image from the temporary folder

Uploads the processed image to S3

Deletes the processed file from the temporary folder

Reads the processed image

Updates the database item by calling the updateItem operation

Updates the state, version, and processed S3 key

Updates only when an item exists, the version equals the expected version, and the state is one of those allowed

The worker is ready to manipulate your images. The next step is to deploy all that code to AWS in a fault-tolerant way.

16.3.4 Deploying the application

As before, you'll use CloudFormation to deploy the application. The infrastructure consists of the following building blocks:

- An S3 bucket for raw and processed images
- A DynamoDB table, imagery-image

- An SQS queue and dead-letter queue
- An Application Load Balancer (ALB)
- Two Auto Scaling groups to manage EC2 instances running the server and worker
- IAM roles for the server and worker instances

It takes quite a while to create that CloudFormation stack; that's why you should do so now. After you've created the stack, we'll look at the template. After that, the application should be ready to use.

To help you deploy Imagery, we have created a CloudFormation template located at http://s3.amazonaws.com/awsinaction-code3/chapter16/template.yaml. Create a stack based on that template. The stack output `EndpointURL` returns the URL that you can access from your browser to use Imagery. Here's how to create the stack from the terminal:

```
$ aws cloudformation create-stack --stack-name imagery \
   --template-url https://s3.amazonaws.com/\
   awsinaction-code3/chapter16/template.yaml \
   --capabilities CAPABILITY_IAM
```

Next, let's have a look what is going on behind the scenes.

BUNDLING RUNTIME AND APPLICATION INTO A MACHINE IMAGE (AMI)

In chapter 15, we introduced the concept of immutable machines. The idea is to create an Amazon Machine Image (AMI) containing the runtime, all required libraries, and the application's code or binary. The AMI is then used to launch EC2 instances with everything preinstalled. To deliver a new version of your application, you would create a new image, launch new instances, and terminate the old instances. We used Packer by HashiCorp to build AMIs. Check out chapter 15 if you want to recap the details. All we want to show here is the configuration file we used to prebuild and share AMIs containing the Imagery worker and server with you.

Listing 16.7 explains the configuration file we used to build the AMIs for you. Please note: you do not need to run Packer to build your own AMIs. We have done so already and shared the AMIs publicly.

Find the Packer configuration file at chapter16/imagery.pkr.hcl in our source code repository at https://github.com/AWSinAction/code3.

Listing 16.7 Configuring Packer to build an AMI containing the Imagery app

```
packer {                                  ⟵  Initializes and
  required_plugins {                          configures Packer
    amazon = {                            ⟵  Adds the plug-in
      version = ">= 0.0.2"                    required to build
      source  = "github.com/hashicorp/amazon"    AMIs
    }
  }
}
```

Configures how Packer
will create the AMI

The name for the AMI
created by Packer

The tags for the
AMI created by
Packer

The
region
used by
Packer to
create
the AMI

The instance type used by
Packer when spinning up a
virtual machine to build the AMI

Allows
anyone
to access
the AMI

The filter describes how to find
the base AMI—the latest version of
Amazon Linux 2—from which to start.

The username required
to connect to the build
instance via SSH

Copies the AMI to all
commercial regions

Configures the steps
Packer executes while
building the image

The name
for the
build

The sources for the
build (references
source from above)

Copies all files and folders
from the current directory ...

... to the home directory
of the EC2 instance used
to build the AMI

Adds a repository for
Node.js 14, the runtime
for the Imagery server
and worker

Installs Node.js and
the libraries needed
to manipulate images

Installs Node.js
packages for the
server and worker

Executes a shell script on
the EC2 instance used to
build the AMI

```
source "amazon-ebs" "imagery" {
    ami_name       = "awsinaction-imagery-{{timestamp}}"
    tags = {
        Name = "awsinaction-imagery"
    }
    instance_type = "t2.micro"
    region        = "us-east-1"
    source_ami_filter {
        filters = {
            name                 = "amzn2-ami-hvm-2.0.*-x86_64-gp2"
            root-device-type     = "ebs"
            virtualization-type = "hvm"
        }
        most_recent = true
        owners      = ["137112412989"]
    }
    ssh_username = "ec2-user"
    ami_groups = ["all"]
    ami_regions = [
        "us-east-1",
        # [...]
    ]
}

build {
    name    = "awsinaction-imagery"
    sources = [
        "source.amazon-ebs.imagery"
    ]

    provisioner "file" {
        source = "./"
        destination = "/home/ec2-user/"
    }

    provisioner "shell" {
        inline = [
            "curl -sL https://rpm.nodesource.com/setup_14.x | sudo bash -",
            "sudo yum update",
            "sudo yum install -y nodejs cairo-devel
libjpeg-turbo-devel",
            "cd server/ && npm install && cd -",
            "cd worker/ && npm install && cd -"
        ]
    }
}
```

Next, you will learn how to deploy the infrastructure with the help of CloudFormation.

DEPLOYING S3, DYNAMODB, AND SQS

The next code listing describes the VPC, S3 bucket, DynamoDB table, and SQS queue.

Listing 16.8   Imagery CloudFormation template: S3, DynamoDB, and SQS

```yaml
---
AWSTemplateFormatVersion: '2010-09-09'
Description: 'AWS in Action: chapter 16'
Mappings:
  RegionMap:                              ◁──  The map contains key-value
    'us-east-1':                               pairs mapping regions to AMIs
      AMI: 'ami-0ad3c79dfb359f1ba'             built by us including the Imagery
    # [...]                                    server and worker.
Resources:
  VPC:                                    ◁──  The CloudFormation template
    Type: 'AWS::EC2::VPC'                      contains a typical public VPC
    Properties:                               configuration.
      CidrBlock: '172.31.0.0/16'
      EnableDnsHostnames: true
  # [...]                                      A S3 bucket for uploaded and
  Bucket:                                 ◁──  processed images, with web
    Type: 'AWS::S3::Bucket'                    hosting enabled
    Properties:
      BucketName: !Sub 'imagery-${AWS::AccountId}'   ◁──  The bucket name
      WebsiteConfiguration:                                contains the account
        ErrorDocument: error.html                         ID to make the name
        IndexDocument: index.html                         unique.
  Table:                                  ◁──  DynamoDB table
    Type: 'AWS::DynamoDB::Table'               containing the
    Properties:                               image processes
      AttributeDefinitions:
      - AttributeName: id                 ◁──  The id attribute
        AttributeType: S                       is used as the
      KeySchema:                               partition key.
      - AttributeName: id
        KeyType: HASH
      ProvisionedThroughput:
        ReadCapacityUnits: 1
        WriteCapacityUnits: 1
      TableName: 'imagery-image'               The SQS queue that
  SQSDLQueue:                             ◁──  receives messages that
    Type: 'AWS::SQS::Queue'                    can't be processed
    Properties:
      QueueName: 'imagery-dlq'                 The SQS queue to
  SQSQueue:                               ◁──  trigger image
    Type: 'AWS::SQS::Queue'                    processing
    Properties:
      QueueName: imagery                       If a message is received
      RedrivePolicy:                           more than 10 times,
        deadLetterTargetArn: !Sub '${SQSDLQueue.Arn}'   it's moved to the
        maxReceiveCount: 10               ◁──  dead-letter queue.
# [...]
Outputs:                      ┌──  Visit the output with your
  EndpointURL:            ◁───┘    browser to use Imagery.
```

```
Value: !Sub 'http://${LoadBalancer.DNSName}'
Description: Load Balancer URL
```

The concept of a *dead-letter queue (DLQ)* needs a short introduction here as well. If a single SQS message can't be processed, the message becomes visible again on the queue after reaching its visibility timeout for other workers. This is called a *retry*. But if for some reason every retry fails (maybe you have a bug in your code), the message will reside in the queue forever and may waste a lot of resources because of all the retries. To avoid this, you can configure a dead-letter queue. If a message is retried more than a specific number of times, it's removed from the original queue and forwarded to the DLQ. The difference is that no worker listens for messages on the DLQ. You should create a CloudWatch alarm that triggers if the DLQ contains more than zero messages, because you need to investigate this problem manually by looking at the message in the DLQ. Once the bug is fixed, you can move the messages from the dead letter queue back to the original queue to process them again.

Now that the basic resources have been designed, let's move on to the more specific resources.

IAM ROLES FOR SERVER AND WORKER EC2 INSTANCES

Remember that it's important to grant only the privileges that are necessary. All server instances must be able to do the following:

- `sqs:SendMessage` to the SQS queue created in the template to trigger image processing
- `s3:PutObject` to the S3 bucket created in the template to upload a file to S3 (You can further limit writes to the `upload/` key prefix.)
- `dynamodb:GetItem`, `dynamodb:PutItem`, and `dynamodb:UpdateItem` to the DynamoDB table created in the template

All worker instances must be able to do the following:

- `sqs:DeleteMessage`, and `sqs:ReceiveMessage` to the SQS queue created in the template
- `s3:PutObject` to the S3 bucket created in the template to upload a file to S3 (You can further limit writes to the `processed/` key prefix.)
- `dynamodb:GetItem` and `dynamodb:UpdateItem` to the DynamoDB table created in the template

Both servers and workers need to grant access for the AWS Systems Manager to enable access via Session Manager as follows:

- `ssmmessages:*`
- `ssm:UpdateInstanceInformation`
- `ec2messages:*`

If you don't feel comfortable with IAM roles, take a look at the book's code repository on GitHub at https://github.com/AWSinAction/code3. The template with IAM roles can be found in /chapter16/template.yaml.

Now it's time to deploy the server.

DEPLOYING THE SERVER WITH A LOAD BALANCER AND AN AUTO SCALING GROUP

The Imagery server allows the user to upload images, monitor the processing, and show the results. An Application Load Balancer (ALB) acts as the entry point into the system. Behind the load balancer, a fleet of servers running on EC2 instances answers incoming HTTP requests. An Auto Scaling group ensures EC2 instances are up and running and replaces instances that fail the load balancer's health check.

The following listing shows how to create the load balancer with the help of Cloud-Formation.

Listing 16.9 CloudFormation template: Load balancer for the Imagery server

```
LoadBalancer:                                              ◄── The load balancer distributes
  Type: 'AWS::ElasticLoadBalancingV2::LoadBalancer'            incoming requests among a
  Properties:                                                  fleet of virtual machines.
    Subnets:
    - Ref: SubnetA
    - Ref: SubnetB
    SecurityGroups:
    - !Ref LoadBalancerSecurityGroup
    Scheme: 'internet-facing'                               Configures a
  DependsOn: VPCGatewayAttachment                           listener for the
LoadBalancerListener:                                   ◄── load balancer
  Type: 'AWS::ElasticLoadBalancingV2::Listener'
  Properties:                                                        The HTTP listener
    DefaultActions:                                                  forwards all requests to
    - Type: forward                                     ◄──         the default target group
      TargetGroupArn: !Ref LoadBalancerTargetGroup               defined below.
    LoadBalancerArn: !Ref LoadBalancer
    Port: 80                                            ◄──     The listener will listen
    Protocol: HTTP                                              for HTTP requests on
LoadBalancerTargetGroup:                                        port 80/TCP.
  Type: 'AWS::ElasticLoadBalancingV2::TargetGroup'
  Properties:
    HealthCheckIntervalSeconds: 5                       ◄──     The target group will check
    HealthCheckPath: '/'                                        the health of registered EC2
    HealthCheckPort: 8080                                       instances by sending HTTP
    HealthCheckProtocol: HTTP                                   requests on port 8080/TCP.
    HealthCheckTimeoutSeconds: 3
    HealthyThresholdCount: 2
    UnhealthyThresholdCount: 2
    Matcher:                                                 By default, the target group will
      HttpCode: '200,302'                                    forward requests to port 8080/TCP
    Port: 8080                                       ◄──     of registered virtual machines.
    Protocol: HTTP
    VpcId: !Ref VPC                                          A security group for
LoadBalancerSecurityGroup:                           ◄──     the load balancer
  Type: 'AWS::EC2::SecurityGroup'
  Properties:
    GroupDescription: 'awsinaction-elb-sg'
    VpcId: !Ref VPC
    SecurityGroupIngress:
```

The default target group

```
      - CidrIp: '0.0.0.0/0'              ◁────   Allows incoming traffic
        FromPort: 80                             on port 80/TCP from
        IpProtocol: tcp                          anywhere
        ToPort: 80
```

Next, creating an Auto Scaling group to launch EC2 instances and registering them at the load balancer is illustrated in the following listing.

Listing 16.10   CloudFormation template: Auto Scaling group for the Imagery server

```
ServerSecurityGroup:                      ◁──     A security group for
  Type: 'AWS::EC2::SecurityGroup'                 the EC2 instances
  Properties:                                     running the server
    GroupDescription: 'imagery-worker'
    VpcId: !Ref VPC
    SecurityGroupIngress:              Allows incoming traffic on
    - FromPort: 8080              ◁──  port 8080/TCP but only
      IpProtocol: tcp                  from the load balancer
      SourceSecurityGroupId: !Ref LoadBalancerSecurityGroup
      ToPort: 8080
ServerLaunchTemplate:                  ◁──   The launch template used
  Type: 'AWS::EC2::LaunchTemplate'            as a blueprint for spinning
  Properties:                                 up EC2 instances
    LaunchTemplateData:
      IamInstanceProfile:
        Name: !Ref ServerInstanceProfile      Looks up the AMI with the Imagery
      ImageId: !FindInMap [RegionMap, !Ref    server preinstalled from the region
  ⇒  'AWS::Region', AMI]                ◁──    map (see listing 16.9)
      Monitoring:
        Enabled: false                        Launches virtual machines of
      InstanceType: 't2.micro'        ◁──     type t2.micro to run examples
      NetworkInterfaces:              ◁──     under the Free Tier
      - AssociatePublicIpAddress: true
        DeviceIndex: 0                  Configures a network interface (ENI)
        Groups:                         with a public IP address and the
        - !Ref ServerSecurityGroup      security group of the server
      UserData:
        'Fn::Base64': !Sub |
          #!/bin/bash -ex
          trap '/opt/aws/bin/cfn-signal -e 1
  ⇒ --region ${AWS::Region} --stack ${AWS::StackName}
  ⇒ --resource ServerAutoScalingGroup' ERR
          cd /home/ec2-user/server/
          sudo -u ec2-user ImageQueue=${SQSQueue} ImageBucket=${Bucket}
  ⇒ nohup node server.js > server.log &
          /opt/aws/bin/cfn-signal -e $? --stack ${AWS::StackName}
  ⇒ --resource ServerAutoScalingGroup --region ${AWS::Region}
ServerAutoScalingGroup:                       ◁──
  Type: 'AWS::AutoScaling::AutoScalingGroup'          Creates an Auto Scaling
  Properties:                                         group that manages the
    LaunchTemplate:          ◁──      References      virtual machines running
                                      the launch      the Imagery server
                                      template
```

Each virtual machine will execute this
script at the end of the boot process.
The script starts the Node.js server.

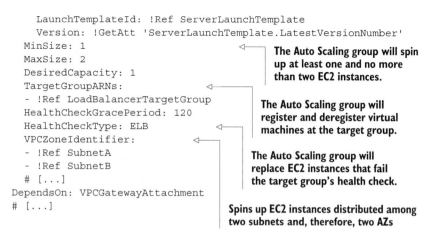

```
      LaunchTemplateId: !Ref ServerLaunchTemplate
      Version: !GetAtt 'ServerLaunchTemplate.LatestVersionNumber'
    MinSize: 1
    MaxSize: 2
    DesiredCapacity: 1
    TargetGroupARNs:
    - !Ref LoadBalancerTargetGroup
    HealthCheckGracePeriod: 120
    HealthCheckType: ELB
    VPCZoneIdentifier:
    - !Ref SubnetA
    - !Ref SubnetB
    # [...]
  DependsOn: VPCGatewayAttachment
  # [...]
```

The Auto Scaling group will spin up at least one and no more than two EC2 instances.

The Auto Scaling group will register and deregister virtual machines at the target group.

The Auto Scaling group will replace EC2 instances that fail the target group's health check.

Spins up EC2 instances distributed among two subnets and, therefore, two AZs

That's it for the server. Next, you need to deploy the worker.

DEPLOYING THE WORKER WITH AN AUTO SCALING GROUP

Deploying the worker works similar to the process for the server. Instead of a load balancer, however, the queue is used for decoupling. Please note that we already explained how to create a SQS in listing 16.8. Therefore, all that's left is the Auto Scaling group and a launch template. The next listing shows the details.

Listing 16.11   Load balancer and Auto Scaling group for the Imagery worker

```
WorkerLaunchTemplate:
  Type: 'AWS::EC2::LaunchTemplate'
  Properties:
    LaunchTemplateData:
      IamInstanceProfile:
        Name: !Ref WorkerInstanceProfile
      ImageId: !FindInMap [RegionMap, !Ref
'AWS::Region', AMI]
      Monitoring:
        Enabled: false
      InstanceType: 't2.micro'
      NetworkInterfaces:
      - AssociatePublicIpAddress: true
        DeviceIndex: 0
        Groups:
        - !Ref WorkerSecurityGroup
      UserData:
        'Fn::Base64': !Sub |
          #!/bin/bash -ex
          trap '/opt/aws/bin/cfn-signal -e 1 --region ${AWS::Region}
--stack ${AWS::StackName} --resource WorkerAutoScalingGroup' ERR
          cd /home/ec2-user/worker/
          sudo -u ec2-user ImageQueue=${SQSQueue} ImageBucket=${Bucket}
nohup node worker.js > worker.log &
```

The launch template used as a blueprint for spinning up EC2 instances

Attaches an IAM role to the EC2 instances to allow the worker to access SQS, S3, and DynamoDB

Looks up the AMI with the Imagery worker preinstalled from the region map (see listing 16.10)

Disables detailed monitoring of EC2 instances to avoid costs

Launches virtual machines of type t2.micro to run examples under the Free Tier

Configures a network interface (ENI) with a public IP address and the security group of the worker

Each virtual machine will execute this script at the end of the boot process. The script starts the Node.js worker.

```
                   /opt/aws/bin/cfn-signal -e $? --stack ${AWS::StackName}
     ➡  --resource WorkerAutoScalingGroup --region ${AWS::Region}
     WorkerAutoScalingGroup:                                    ◁
       Type: 'AWS::AutoScaling::AutoScalingGroup'
       Properties:
         LaunchTemplate:
           LaunchTemplateId: !Ref WorkerLaunchTemplate
           Version: !GetAtt 'WorkerLaunchTemplate.LatestVersionNumber'
         MinSize: 1                             ◁
         MaxSize: 2
         DesiredCapacity: 1
         HealthCheckGracePeriod: 120
         HealthCheckType: EC2                   ◁
         VPCZoneIdentifier:                  ◁
         - !Ref SubnetA
         - !Ref SubnetB
         Tags:
         - PropagateAtLaunch: true
           Value: 'imagery-worker'
           Key: Name
       DependsOn: VPCGatewayAttachment
       # [...]
```

References the launch template

Creates an Auto Scaling group that manages the virtual machines running the Imagery worker

The Auto Scaling group will spin up at least one and no more than two EC2 instances.

The Auto Scaling group will replace failed EC2 instances.

Spins up EC2 instances distributed among two subnets: AZs

Adds a Name tag to each instance, which will show up at the Management Console, for example

After all that YAML reading, the CloudFormation stack should be created. Verify the status of your stack like this:

```
$ aws cloudformation describe-stacks --stack-name imagery
{
  "Stacks": [{
    [...]
    "Description": "AWS in Action: chapter 16",
    "Outputs": [{
      "Description": "Load Balancer URL",
      "OutputKey": "EndpointURL",
      "OutputValue":
  "http://....us-east-1.elb.amazonaws.com"
    }],
    "StackName": "imagery",
    "StackStatus": "CREATE_COMPLETE"
  }]
}
```

Copy this output into your web browser.

Waits until CREATE_COMPLETE is reached

The EndpointURL output of the stack contains the URL to access the Imagery application. When you open Imagery in your web browser, you can upload an image as shown in figure 16.16.

Go ahead and upload some images and enjoy watching the images being processed.

Figure 16.16 The Imagery application in action

Cleaning up

To get the name of the S3 bucket used by Imagery, run the following command in your terminal:

```
$ aws cloudformation describe-stack-resource --stack-name imagery \
  --logical-resource-id Bucket \
  --query "StackResourceDetail.PhysicalResourceId" \
  --output text
imagery-000000000000
```

Delete all the files in your S3 bucket `imagery-000000000000` as follows. Don't forget to replace $bucketname with the output from the previous command:

```
$ aws s3 rm --recursive s3://$bucketname
```

Execute the following command to delete the CloudFormation stack:

```
$ aws cloudformation delete-stack --stack-name imagery
```

Stack deletion will take some time.

Congratulations! You have accomplished a big milestone: building a fault-tolerant application on AWS. You are only one step away from the end game, which is scaling your application dynamically based on load.

Summary

- Fault tolerance means expecting that failures happen and designing your systems in such a way that they can deal with failure.
- To create a fault-tolerant application, you can use idempotent actions to transfer from one state to the next.
- State shouldn't reside on the EC2 instance (a stateless server) as a prerequisite for fault tolerance.

- AWS offers fault-tolerant services and gives you all the tools you need to create fault-tolerant systems. EC2 is one of the few services that isn't fault tolerant right out of the box.
- You can use multiple EC2 instances to eliminate the single point of failure. Redundant EC2 instances in different availability zones, started with an Auto Scaling group, are how to make EC2 fault tolerant.

17

Scaling up and down: Autoscaling and CloudWatch

This chapter covers

- Creating an Auto Scaling group with a launch template
- Using autoscaling to change the number of virtual machines
- Scaling a synchronous decoupled app behind a load balancer (ALB)
- Scaling an asynchronous decoupled app using a queue (SQS)

Suppose you're organizing a party to celebrate your birthday. How much food and drink do you need to buy? Calculating the right numbers for your shopping list is difficult due to the following factors:

- How many people will attend? You received several confirmations, but some guests will cancel at short notice or show up without letting you know in advance. Therefore, the number of guests is vague.
- How much will your guests eat and drink? Will it be a hot day, with everybody drinking a lot? Will your guests be hungry? You need to guess the demand for food and drink based on experiences from previous parties as well as weather, time of day, and other variables.

Solving the equation is a challenge because there are many unknowns. Being a good host, you'll order more food and drink than needed so no guest will be hungry or thirsty for long. It may cost you more money than necessary, and you may end up wasting some of it, but this possible waste is the risk you must take to ensure you have enough for unexpected guests and circumstances.

Before the cloud, the same was true for our industry when planning the capacity of our IT infrastructure. Planning to meet future demands for your IT infrastructure was nearly impossible. To prevent a supply gap, you needed to add extra capacity on top of the planned demand to prevent running short of resources. When procuring hardware for a data center, we always had to buy hardware based on the demands of the future. We faced the following uncertainties when making these decisions:

- How many users need to be served by the infrastructure?
- How much storage would the users need?
- How much computing power would be required to handle their requests?

To avoid supply gaps, we had to order more or faster hardware than needed, causing unnecessary expenses.

On AWS, you can use services on demand. Planning capacity is less and less important. You can scale from one EC2 instance to thousands of EC2 instances. Storage can grow from gigabytes to petabytes. You can scale on demand, thus replacing capacity planning. AWS calls the ability to scale on demand *elasticity*.

Public cloud providers like AWS can offer the needed capacity with a short waiting time. AWS serves more than a million customers, and at that scale, it isn't a problem to provide you with 100 additional virtual machines within minutes if you suddenly need them. This allows you to address another problem: recurring traffic patterns, as shown in figure 17.1. Think about the load on your infrastructure during the day versus at night, on a weekday versus the weekend, or before Christmas versus the rest of year. Wouldn't it be nice if you could add capacity when traffic grows and remove capacity when traffic shrinks? That's what this chapter is all about.

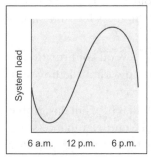 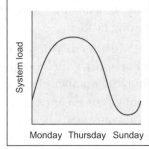 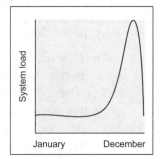

Figure 17.1 Typical traffic patterns for a web shop

Scaling the number of virtual machines is possible with Auto Scaling groups (ASG) and *scaling policies* on AWS. Autoscaling is part of the EC2 service and helps you scale the number of EC2 instances you need to fulfill the current load of your system. We introduced Auto Scaling groups in chapter 13 to ensure that a single virtual machine was running even if an outage of an entire data center occurred.

In this chapter, you'll learn how to manage a fleet of EC2 instances and adapt the size of the fleet depending on the current use of the infrastructure. To do so, you will use the concepts that you learned about in chapters 14 and 15 and enhance your setup with automatic scaling as follows:

- Using Auto Scaling groups to launch multiple virtual machines of the same kind as you did in chapters 13 and 14
- Changing the number of virtual machines based on CPU load with the help of CloudWatch alarms, which is a new concept we are introducing in this chapter
- Changing the number of virtual machines based on a schedule to adapt to recurring traffic patterns—something you will learn about in this chapter
- Using a load balancer as an entry point to the dynamic EC2 instance pool as you did in chapter 14
- Using a queue to decouple the jobs from the dynamic EC2 instance pool, similar to what you learned in chapter 14

Examples are 100% covered by the Free Tier

The examples in this chapter are totally covered by the Free Tier. As long as you don't run the examples longer than a few days, you won't pay anything for it. Keep in mind that this applies only if you created a fresh AWS account for this book and there is nothing else going on in your AWS account. Try to complete the chapter within a few days, because you'll clean up your account at the end of the chapter.

The following prerequisites are required to scale your application horizontally, which means increasing and decreasing the number of virtual machines based on the current workload:

- The EC2 instances you want to scale need to be *stateless*. You can achieve stateless servers by storing data with the help of services like RDS (SQL database), DynamoDB (NoSQL database), EFS (network filesystem), or S3 (object store) instead of storing data on disks (instance store or EBS) that are available only to a single EC2 instance.
- An entry point to the dynamic EC2 instance pool is needed to distribute the workload across multiple EC2 instances. EC2 instances can be decoupled synchronously with a load balancer or asynchronously with a queue.

We introduced the concept of the stateless server in part 3 of this book and explained how to use decoupling in chapter 13. In this chapter, you'll return to the concept of the stateless server and also work through an example of synchronous and asynchronous decoupling.

17.1   *Managing a dynamic EC2 instance pool*

Imagine that you need to provide a scalable infrastructure to run a web application, such as a blogging platform. You need to launch uniform virtual machines when the number of requests grows and terminate virtual machines when the number of requests shrinks. To adapt to the current workload in an automated way, you need to be able to launch and terminate VMs automatically. Therefore, the configuration and deployment of the web application needs to be done during bootstrapping, without human interaction.

In this section, you will create an Auto Scaling group. Next, you will learn how to change the number of EC2 instances launched by the Auto Scaling group based on scheduled actions. Afterward, you will learn how to scale based on a utilization metric provided by CloudWatch. Auto Scaling groups allows you to manage such a dynamic EC2 instance pool in the following ways:

- Dynamically adjust the number of virtual machines that are running
- Launch, configure, and deploy uniform virtual machines

The Auto Scaling group grows and shrinks within the bounds you define. Defining a minimum of two virtual machines allows you to make sure at least two virtual machines are running in different availability zones to plan for failure. Conversely, defining a maximum number of virtual machines ensures you are not spending more money than you intended for your infrastructure. As figure 17.2 shows, autoscaling consists of three parts:

- A launch template that defines the size, image, and configuration of virtual machines
- An Auto Scaling group that specifies how many virtual machines need to be running based on the launch template
- Scaling plans that adjust the desired number of EC2 instances in the Auto Scaling group based on a plan or dynamically

If you want multiple EC2 instances to handle a workload, it's important to start identical virtual machines to build a homogeneous foundation. Use a launch template to define and configure new virtual machines. Table 17.1 shows the most important parameters for a launch template.

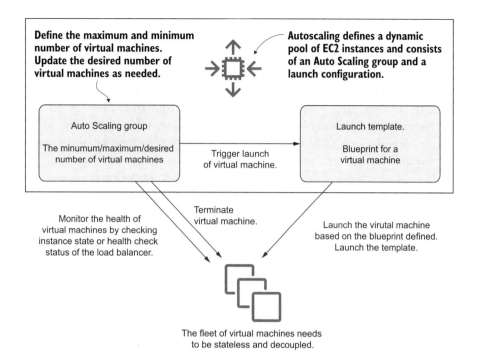

Figure 17.2 **Autoscaling consists of an Auto Scaling group and a launch template, launching and terminating uniform virtual machines.**

Table 17.1 **Launch template parameters**

Name	Description	Possible values
ImageId	Image from which to start a virtual machine	ID of an Amazon Machine Image (AMI)
InstanceType	Size for new virtual machines	Instance type (such as t2.micro)
UserData	User data for the virtual machine used to execute a script during bootstrapping	BASE64-encoded string
NetworkInterfaces	Configures the network interfaces of the virtual machine. Most importantly, this parameter allows you to attach a public IP address to the instance.	List of network interface configurations
IamInstanceProfile	Attaches an IAM instance profile linked to an IAM role	Name or Amazon Resource Name (ARN, an ID) of an IAM instance profile

After you create a launch template, you can create an Auto Scaling group that references it. The Auto Scaling group defines the maximum, minimum, and desired number of virtual machines. *Desired* means this number of EC2 instances should be running. If the current number of EC2 instances is below the desired number, the Auto Scaling group will add EC2 instances. If the current number of EC2 instances is above the desired number, EC2 instances will be terminated. The desired capacity can be changed automatically based on load or a schedule, or manually. *Minimum* and *maximum* are the lower and upper limits for the number of virtual machines within the Auto Scaling group.

The Auto Scaling group also monitors whether EC2 instances are healthy and replaces broken instances. Table 17.2 shows the most important parameters for an Auto Scaling group.

Table 17.2   Auto Scaling group parameters

Name	Description	Possible values
DesiredCapacity	Desired number of healthy virtual machines	Integer
MaxSize	Maximum number of virtual machines; the upper scaling limit	Integer
MinSize	Minimum number of virtual machines; the lower scaling limit	Integer
HealthCheckType	How the Auto Scaling group checks the health of virtual machines	EC2 (health of the instance) or ELB (health check of instance performed by a load balancer)
HealthCheckGracePeriod	Period for which the health check is paused after the launch of a new instance to wait until the instance is fully bootstrapped	Number of seconds
LaunchTemplate	ID (LaunchTemplateId) and version of launch template used as a blueprint when spinning up virtual machines	ID and version of launch template
TargetGroupARNs	The target groups of a load balancer, where autoscaling registers new instances automatically	List of target group ARNs
VPCZoneIdentifier	List of subnets in which to launch EC2 instances	List of subnet identifiers of a VPC

If you specify multiple subnets with the help of VPCZoneIdentifier for the Auto Scaling group, EC2 instances will be evenly distributed among these subnets and, thus, among availability zones.

Don't forget to define a health check grace period

If you are using the ELB's health check for your Auto Scaling group, make sure you specify a `HealthCheckGracePeriod` as well. Specify a health check grace period based on the time it takes from launching an EC2 instance until your application is running and passes the ELB's health check. For a simple web application, a health check period of five minutes is suitable.

The next listing shows how to set up such a dynamic EC2 instance pool with the help of a CloudFormation template.

Listing 17.1   Auto Scaling group and launch template for a web app

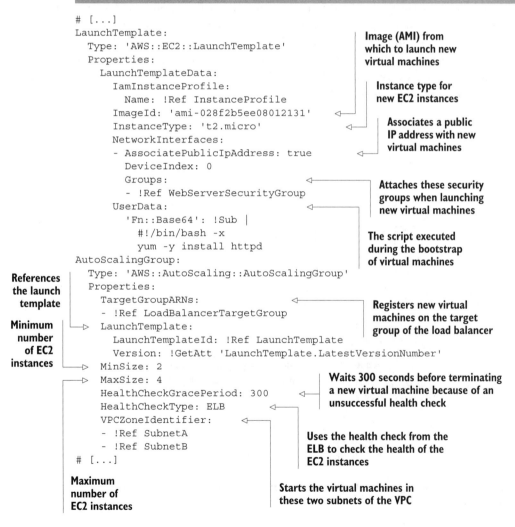

```
# [...]
LaunchTemplate:
  Type: 'AWS::EC2::LaunchTemplate'
  Properties:
    LaunchTemplateData:
      IamInstanceProfile:
        Name: !Ref InstanceProfile
      ImageId: 'ami-028f2b5ee08012131'
      InstanceType: 't2.micro'
      NetworkInterfaces:
      - AssociatePublicIpAddress: true
        DeviceIndex: 0
        Groups:
        - !Ref WebServerSecurityGroup
      UserData:
        'Fn::Base64': !Sub |
          #!/bin/bash -x
          yum -y install httpd
AutoScalingGroup:
  Type: 'AWS::AutoScaling::AutoScalingGroup'
  Properties:
    TargetGroupARNs:
    - !Ref LoadBalancerTargetGroup
    LaunchTemplate:
      LaunchTemplateId: !Ref LaunchTemplate
      Version: !GetAtt 'LaunchTemplate.LatestVersionNumber'
    MinSize: 2
    MaxSize: 4
    HealthCheckGracePeriod: 300
    HealthCheckType: ELB
    VPCZoneIdentifier:
    - !Ref SubnetA
    - !Ref SubnetB
# [...]
```

Image (AMI) from which to launch new virtual machines

Instance type for new EC2 instances

Associates a public IP address with new virtual machines

Attaches these security groups when launching new virtual machines

The script executed during the bootstrap of virtual machines

References the launch template

Minimum number of EC2 instances

Registers new virtual machines on the target group of the load balancer

Waits 300 seconds before terminating a new virtual machine because of an unsuccessful health check

Uses the health check from the ELB to check the health of the EC2 instances

Maximum number of EC2 instances

Starts the virtual machines in these two subnets of the VPC

In summary, Auto Scaling groups are a useful tool if you need to start multiple virtual machines of the same kind across multiple availability zones. Additionally, an Auto Scaling group replaces failed EC2 instances automatically.

17.2 *Using metrics or schedules to trigger scaling*

So far in this chapter, you've learned how to use an Auto Scaling group and a launch template to manage virtual machines. With that in mind, you can change the desired capacity of the Auto Scaling group manually so new instances will be started or old instances will be terminated to reach the new desired capacity.

To provide a scalable infrastructure for a blogging platform, you need to increase and decrease the number of virtual machines in the pool automatically by adjusting the desired capacity of the Auto Scaling group with scaling policies. Many people surf the web during their lunch break, so you might need to add virtual machines every day between 11 a.m. and 1 p.m. You also need to adapt to unpredictable load patterns—for example, if articles hosted on your blogging platform are shared frequently through social networks. Figure 17.3 illustrates two ways to change the number of virtual machines, as described in the following list.

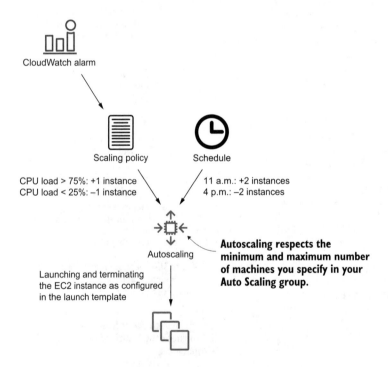

Figure 17.3 Triggering autoscaling based on CloudWatch alarms or schedules

- *Defining a schedule*—The timing would increase or decrease the number of virtual machines according to recurring load patterns (such as decreasing the number of virtual machines at night).
- *Using a CloudWatch alarm*—The alarm will trigger a scaling policy to increase or decrease the number of virtual machines based on a metric (such as CPU usage or number of requests on the load balancer).

Scaling based on a schedule is less complex than scaling based on a CloudWatch metric, because it's difficult to find a metric on which to scale reliably. On the other hand, scaling based on a schedule is less precise, because you have to overprovision your infrastructure to be able to handle unpredicted spikes in load.

17.2.1 Scaling based on a schedule

When operating a blogging platform, you might notice the following load patterns:

- *One-time actions*—Requests to your registration page increase heavily after you run a TV advertisement in the evening.
- *Recurring actions*—Many people seem to read articles during their lunch break, between 11 a.m. and 1 p.m.

Luckily, scheduled actions adjust your capacity with one-time or recurring actions. You can use different types of actions to react to both load pattern types.

The following listing shows a one-time scheduled action increasing the number of web servers at 12:00 UTC on January 1, 2018. As usual, you'll find the code in the book's code repository on GitHub: https://github.com/AWSinAction/code3. The CloudFormation template for the WordPress example is located in /chapter17/wordpress-schedule.yaml.

Listing 17.2   Scheduling a one-time scaling action

```
OneTimeScheduledActionUp:                               Defining a
  Type: 'AWS::AutoScaling::ScheduledAction'     <──┐    scheduled action
  Properties:
    AutoScalingGroupName: !Ref AutoScalingGroup <──   Name of the Auto
    DesiredCapacity: 4                          <──   Scaling group
    StartTime: '2025-01-01T12:00:00Z'           <──
                                                      Sets the desired
              Changes the setting at 12:00          capacity to 4
              UTC on January 1, 2025
```

You can also schedule recurring scaling actions using cron syntax. The code example shown next illustrates how to use two scheduled actions to increase the desired capacity during business hours (08:00 to 20:00 UTC) every day.

Listing 17.3   Scheduling a recurring scaling action that runs at 20:00 UTC every day

```
RecurringScheduledActionUp:                             Defining a
  Type: 'AWS::AutoScaling::ScheduledAction'     <──┐    scheduled action
  Properties:
```

```
    AutoScalingGroupName: !Ref AutoScalingGroup          Sets the desired
    DesiredCapacity: 4                                    capacity to 4
    Recurrence: '0 8 * * *'
RecurringScheduledActionDown:                            Increases the capacity
  Type: 'AWS::AutoScaling::ScheduledAction'              at 08:00 UTC every day
  Properties:
    AutoScalingGroupName: !Ref AutoScalingGroup
    DesiredCapacity: 2
    Recurrence: '0 20 * * *'                 Sets the desired
                                             capacity to 2
         Decreases the capacity
         at 20:00 UTC every day
```

Recurrence is defined in Unix cron syntax format as shown here:

```
* * * * *
| | | | |
| | | | +- day of week (0 - 6) (0 Sunday)
| | | +--- month (1 - 12)
| | +----- day of month (1 - 31)
| +------- hour (0 - 23)
+--------- min (0 - 59)
```

We recommend using scheduled scaling actions whenever your infrastructure's capacity requirements are predictable—for example, an internal system used during work hours only, or a marketing action planned for a certain time.

17.2.2 *Scaling based on CloudWatch metrics*

Predicting the future is hard. Traffic will increase or decrease beyond known patterns from time to time. For example, if an article published on your blogging platform is heavily shared through social media, you need to be able to react to unplanned load changes and scale the number of EC2 instances.

You can adapt the number of EC2 instances to handle the current workload using CloudWatch alarms and scaling policies. CloudWatch helps monitor virtual machines and other services on AWS. Typically, services publish usage metrics to CloudWatch, helping you to evaluate the available capacity. The types of scaling policies follow:

1   *Step scaling*—Allows more advanced scaling because multiple scaling adjustments are supported, depending on how much the threshold you set has been exceeded.

2   *Target tracking*—Frees you from defining scaling steps and thresholds. You need only to define a target (such as CPU utilization of 70%), and the number of EC2 instances is adjusted accordingly.

3   *Predictive scaling*—Uses machine learning to predict load. It works best for cyclical traffic and recurring workload patterns (see "Predictive Scaling for Amazon EC2 Auto Scaling" at http://mng.bz/RvYO to learn more).

4   *Simple scaling*—A legacy option that was replaced with step scaling.

All of the scaling policies use metrics and alarms to scale the number of EC2 instances based on the current workload. As shown in figure 17.4, the virtual machines publish metrics to CloudWatch constantly. A CloudWatch alarm monitors one of these metrics and triggers a scaling action if the defined threshold is reached. The scaling policy then increases or decreases the desired capacity of the Auto Scaling group.

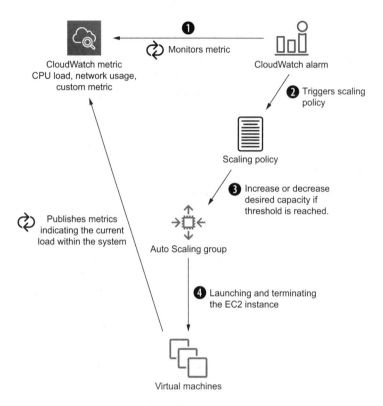

Figure 17.4   Triggering autoscaling based on a CloudWatch metric and alarm

An EC2 instance publishes several metrics to CloudWatch by default: CPU, network, and disk utilization are the most important. Unfortunately, no metric currently exists for a virtual machine's memory usage. You can use these metrics to scale the number of VMs if a bottleneck is reached. For example, you can add EC2 instances if the CPU is working to capacity. The following parameters describe a CloudWatch metric:

- `Namespace`—Defines the source of the metric (such as AWS/EC2)
- `Dimensions`—Defines the scope of the metric (such as all virtual machines belonging to an Auto Scaling group)
- `MetricName`—Unique name of the metric (such as `CPUUtilization`)

CloudWatch alarms are based on CloudWatch metrics. Table 17.3 explains the alarm parameters in detail.

Table 17.3 Parameters for a CloudWatch alarm that triggers scaling based on CPU usage of all virtual machines belonging to an Auto Scaling group

Context	Name	Description	Possible values
Condition	`Statistic`	Statistical function applied to a metric	`Average, Sum, Minimum, Maximum, SampleCount`
Condition	`Period`	Defines a time-based slice of values from a metric	Seconds (multiple of 60)
Condition	`EvaluationPeriods`	Number of periods to evaluate when checking for an alarm	Integer
Condition	`Threshold`	Threshold for an alarm	Number
Condition	`ComparisonOperator`	Operator to compare the threshold against the result from a statistical function	`GreaterThanOrEqual-ToThreshold, Greater-ThanThreshold, LessThanThreshold, LessThanOrEqualTo-Threshold`
Metric	`Namespace`	Source of the metric	`AWS/EC2` for metrics from the EC2 service
Metric	`Dimensions`	Scope of the metric	Depends on the metric; references the Auto Scaling group for an aggregated metric over all associated EC2 instances
Metric	`MetricName`	Name of the metric	For example, `CPUUtilization`
Action	`AlarmActions`	Actions to trigger if the threshold is reached	Reference to the scaling policy

You can define alarms on many different metrics. You'll find an overview of all namespaces, dimensions, and metrics that AWS offers at http://mng.bz/8E0X. For example, you could scale based on the load balancer's metric counting the number of requests per target, or the networking throughput of your EC2 instances. You can also publish custom metrics—for example, metrics directly from your application like thread pool usage, processing times, or user sessions.

You've now learned how to use autoscaling to adapt the number of virtual machines to the workload. It's time to bring this into action.

> ### Scaling based on CPU load with VMs that offer burstable performance
>
> Some virtual machines, such as instance families t2 and t3, offer burstable performance. These virtual machines offer a baseline CPU performance and can burst performance for a short time based on credits. If all credits are spent, the instance operates at the baseline. For a t2.micro instance, baseline performance is 10% of the performance of the underlying physical CPU.
>
> Using virtual machines with burstable performance can help you react to load spikes. You save credits in times of low load and spend credits to burst performance in times of high load. But scaling the number of virtual machines with burstable performance based on CPU load is tricky because your scaling strategy must take into account whether your instances have enough credits to burst performance. Consider searching for another metric to scale (such as number of sessions) or using an instance type without burstable performance.

17.3   *Decoupling your dynamic EC2 instance pool*

If you need to scale the number of virtual machines running your blogging platform based on demand, Auto Scaling groups can help you provide the right number of uniform virtual machines, and scaling schedules or CloudWatch alarms can increase or decrease the desired number of EC2 instances automatically. But how can users reach the EC2 instances in the pool to browse the articles you're hosting? Where should the HTTP request be routed?

Chapter 14 introduced the concept of decoupling: synchronous decoupling with ELB and asynchronous decoupling with SQS. If you want to use autoscaling to grow and shrink the number of virtual machines, you need to decouple your EC2 instances from the clients, because the interface that's reachable from outside the system needs to stay the same no matter how many EC2 instances are working behind the scenes.

Figure 17.5 shows how to build a scalable system based on synchronous or asynchronous decoupling. A load balancer acts as the entry point for synchronous decoupling, by distributing requests among a fleet of virtual machines. A message queue is used as the entry point for asynchronous requests, and messages from producers are stored in the queue. The virtual machines then poll the queue and process the messages asynchronously.

Decoupled and scalable applications require stateless servers. A stateless server stores any shared data remotely in a database or storage system. The following two examples implement the concept of a stateless server:

- *WordPress blog*—Decoupled with ELB, scaled with autoscaling and CloudWatch based on CPU utilization, and data outsourced to a MySQL database (RDS) and a network filesystem (EFS)
- *URL2PNG taking screenshots of URLs*—Decoupled with a queue (SQS), scaled with autoscaling and CloudWatch based on queue length, and data outsourced to a NoSQL database (DynamoDB) and an object store (S3)

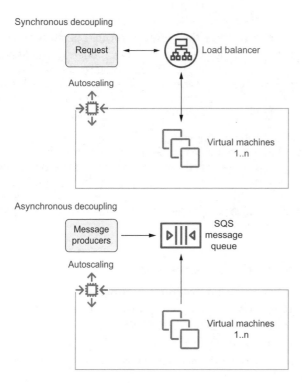

Figure 17.5   Decoupling allows you to scale the number of virtual machines dynamically.

17.3.1 *Scaling a dynamic EC2 instance pool synchronously decoupled by a load balancer*

Answering HTTP(S) requests is a synchronous task. If a user wants to use your web application, the web server has to answer the corresponding requests immediately. When using a dynamic EC2 instance pool to run a web application, it's common to use a load balancer to decouple the EC2 instances from user requests. The load balancer forwards HTTP(S) requests to multiple EC2 instances, acting as a single entry point to the dynamic EC2 instance pool.

Suppose your company has a corporate blog for publishing announcements and interacting with the community, and you're responsible for hosting the blog. The marketing department complains about slow page speed and even timeouts in the evening, when traffic reaches its daily peak. You want to use the elasticity of AWS by scaling the number of EC2 instances based on the current workload.

Your company uses the popular blogging platform WordPress for its corporate blog. Chapters 2 and 10 introduced a WordPress setup based on EC2 instances and RDS (MySQL database). In this chapter, we'd like to complete the example by adding the ability to scale.

Figure 17.6 shows the final, extended WordPress example. The following services are used for this highly available scaling architecture:

- EC2 instances running Apache to serve WordPress, a PHP application
- RDS offering a MySQL database that's highly available through Multi-AZ deployment
- EFS storing PHP, HTML, and CSS files as well as user uploads such as images and videos
- ELB to synchronously decouple the web servers from visitors
- Autoscaling and CloudWatch to scale the number of EC2 instances based on the current CPU load of all running virtual machines

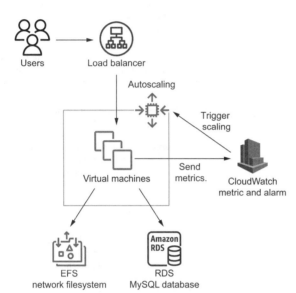

Figure 17.6   **Autoscaling web servers running WordPress, storing data on RDS and EFS, decoupled with a load balancer scaling based on load**

As usual, you'll find the code in the book's code repository on GitHub: https://github .com/AWSinAction/code3. The CloudFormation template for the WordPress example is located in /chapter17/wordpress.yaml.

Execute the following command to create a CloudFormation stack that spins up the scalable WordPress setup. Replace $Password with your own password consisting of eight to 30 letters and digits.

```
$ aws cloudformation create-stack --stack-name wordpress \
  --template-url https://s3.amazonaws.com/\
  awsinaction-code3/chapter17/wordpress.yaml --parameters \
  "ParameterKey=WordpressAdminPassword,ParameterValue=$Password" \
  --capabilities CAPABILITY_IAM
```

It will take up to 15 minutes for the stack to be created. This is a perfect time to grab some coffee or tea. Log in to the AWS Management Console, and navigate to the AWS

CloudFormation service to monitor the process of the CloudFormation stack named wordpress. You have time to look through the most important parts of the Cloud-Formation template, shown in the following three listings.

Create a blueprint to launch EC2 instances, also known as a launch template, as illustrated next.

Listing 17.4   Creating a scalable, HA WordPress setup, part 1

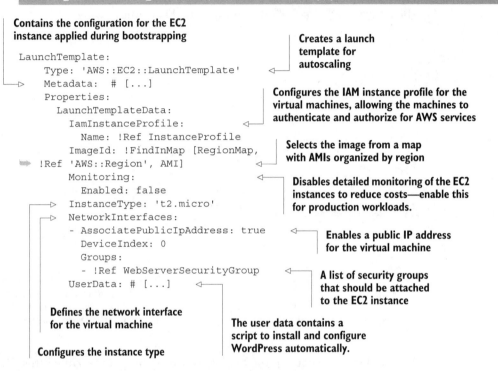

Second, the Auto Scaling group shown in the next listing launches EC2 instances based on the launch template.

Listing 17.5   Creating a scalable, HA WordPress setup, part 2

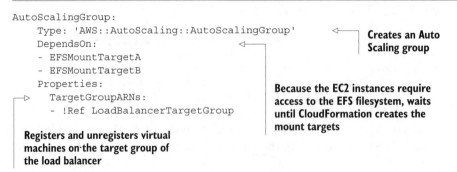

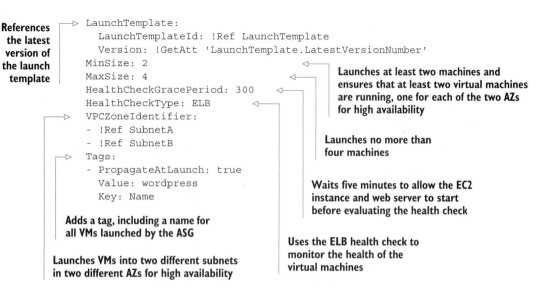

References the latest version of the launch template

```
LaunchTemplate:
    LaunchTemplateId: !Ref LaunchTemplate
    Version: !GetAtt 'LaunchTemplate.LatestVersionNumber'
MinSize: 2
MaxSize: 4
HealthCheckGracePeriod: 300
HealthCheckType: ELB
VPCZoneIdentifier:
- !Ref SubnetA
- !Ref SubnetB
Tags:
- PropagateAtLaunch: true
  Value: wordpress
  Key: Name
```

Launches at least two machines and ensures that at least two virtual machines are running, one for each of the two AZs for high availability

Launches no more than four machines

Waits five minutes to allow the EC2 instance and web server to start before evaluating the health check

Adds a tag, including a name for all VMs launched by the ASG

Uses the ELB health check to monitor the health of the virtual machines

Launches VMs into two different subnets in two different AZs for high availability

You will learn how to create CloudWatch alarms for scaling in the next example. For now, we are using a target-tracking scaling policy that creates CloudWatch alarms automatically in the background. A target-tracking scaling policy works like the thermostat in your home: you define the target, and the thermostat constantly adjusts the heating power to reach the target. Predefined metric specifications to use with target tracking follow:

- `ASGAverageCPUUtilization`—Scale based on the average CPU usage among all instances within an Auto Scaling group
- `ALBRequestCountPerTarget`—Scale based on the number of requests forwarded from the Application Load Balancer (ALB) to a target
- `ASGAverageNetworkIn` and `ASGAverageNetworkOut`—Scale based on the average number of bytes received or sent

In some cases, scaling based on CPU usage, request count per target, or network throughput does not work. For example, you might have another bottleneck you need to scale on, such as disk I/O. Any CloudWatch metric can be used for target tracking as well. Only one requirement exists: adding or removing instances must affect the metric proportionally. For example, request latency is not a valid metric for target tracking, because adjusting the number of instances does not affect the request latency directly.

The following listing shows a target-tracking policy based on the average CPU utilization of all EC2 instances of the Auto Scaling group.

Listing 17.6 Creating a scalable, HA WordPress setup, part 3

```
ScalingPolicy:
    Type: 'AWS::AutoScaling::ScalingPolicy'
    Properties:
```

Creates a scaling policy

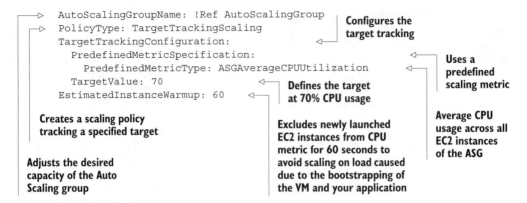

```
AutoScalingGroupName: !Ref AutoScalingGroup
PolicyType: TargetTrackingScaling
TargetTrackingConfiguration:
  PredefinedMetricSpecification:
    PredefinedMetricType: ASGAverageCPUUtilization
  TargetValue: 70
  EstimatedInstanceWarmup: 60
```

Configures the target tracking

Uses a predefined scaling metric

Defines the target at 70% CPU usage

Creates a scaling policy tracking a specified target

Average CPU usage across all EC2 instances of the ASG

Adjusts the desired capacity of the Auto Scaling group

Excludes newly launched EC2 instances from CPU metric for 60 seconds to avoid scaling on load caused due to the bootstrapping of the VM and your application

Follow these steps after the CloudFormation stack reaches the state CREATE_COMPLETE to create a new blog post containing an image:

1 Select the CloudFormation stack wordpress, and switch to the Outputs tab.
2 Open the link shown for key URL with a web browser.
3 Search for the Log In link in the navigation bar, and click it.
4 Log in with username admin and the password you specified when creating the stack with the CLI.
5 Click Posts in the menu on the left.
6 Click Add New.
7 Type in a title and text, and upload an image to your post.
8 Click Publish.
9 Go back to the blog by clicking on the View Post link.

Now you're ready to scale. We've prepared a load test that will send 500,000 requests to the WordPress setup within a few minutes. Don't worry about costs: the usage is covered by the Free Tier. After three minutes, new virtual machines will be launched to handle the load. The load test takes 10 minutes. Another 15 minutes later, the additional VMs will disappear. Watching this is fun; you shouldn't miss it.

NOTE   If you plan to do a big load test, consider the AWS Acceptable Use Policy at https://aws.amazon.com/aup and ask for permission before you begin (see also http://mng.bz/2r8m).

Simple HTTP load test

We're using a tool called Apache Bench to perform a load test of the WordPress setup. The tool is part of the httpd-tools package available from the Amazon Linux package repositories.

Apache Bench is a basic benchmarking tool. You can send a specified number of HTTP requests by using a specified number of threads. We're using the following command for the load test to send 500,000 requests to the load balancer using 15 threads. The

load test is limited to 600 seconds, and we're using a connection timeout of 120
seconds. Replace $UrlLoadBalancer with the URL of the load balancer:

```
$ ab -n 500000 -c 15 -t 300 -s 120 -r $UrlLoadBalancer
```

Update the CloudFormation stack with the following command to start the load test:

```
$ aws cloudformation update-stack --stack-name wordpress \
 --template-url https://s3.amazonaws.com/\
 awsinaction-code3/chapter17/wordpress-loadtest.yaml --parameters \
 ParameterKey=WordpressAdminPassword,UsePreviousValue=true \
 --capabilities CAPABILITY_IAM
```

Watch for the following things to happen, using the AWS Management Console:

1 Open the CloudWatch service, and click Alarms on the left.
2 When the load test starts, the alarm called `TargetTracking-wordpress-Auto-`
   `ScalingGroup-`**AlarmHigh-** will reach the ALARM state after about 10 minutes.
3 Open the EC2 service, and list all EC2 instances. Watch for two additional
   instances to launch. At the end, you'll see five instances total (four web servers
   and the EC2 instance running the load test).
4 Go back to the CloudWatch service, and wait until the alarm named `Target-`
   `Tracking-wordpress-AutoScalingGroup-`**AlarmLow-** reaches the ALARM state.
5 Open the EC2 service, and list all EC2 instances. Watch for the two additional
   instances to disappear. At the end, you'll see three instances total (two web servers and the EC2 instance running the load test).

The entire process will take about 30 minutes.

You've now watched autoscaling in action: your WordPress setup can now adapt to
the current workload. The problem with pages loading slowly or even timeouts in the
evening is solved.

Cleaning up

Execute the following commands to delete all resources corresponding to the Word-
Press setup:

```
$ aws cloudformation delete-stack --stack-name wordpress
```

17.3.2 Scaling a dynamic EC2 instances pool asynchronously decoupled by a queue

Imagine that you're developing a social bookmark service where users can save and
share their links. Offering a preview that shows the website being linked to is an
important feature. But the conversion from URL to PNG is causing high load during

the evening, when most users add new bookmarks to your service. Because of that, customers are dissatisfied with your application's slow response times.

You will learn how to dynamically scale a fleet of EC2 instances to asynchronously generate screenshots of URLs in the following example. Doing so allows you to guarantee low response times at any time because the load-intensive workload is isolated into background jobs.

Decoupling a dynamic EC2 instance pool asynchronously offers an advantage if you want to scale based on workload: because requests don't need to be answered immediately, you can put requests into a queue and scale the number of EC2 instances based on the length of the queue. This gives you an accurate metric to scale, and no requests will be lost during a load peak because they're stored in a queue.

To handle the peak load in the evening, you want to use autoscaling. To do so, you need to decouple the creation of a new bookmark and the process of generating a preview of the website. Chapter 14 introduced an application called URL2PNG that transforms a URL into a PNG image. Figure 17.7 shows the architecture, which consists of an SQS queue for asynchronous decoupling as well as S3 for storing generated images. Creating a bookmark will trigger the following process:

1 A message is sent to an SQS queue containing the URL and the unique ID of the new bookmark.
2 EC2 instances running a Node.js application poll the SQS queue.

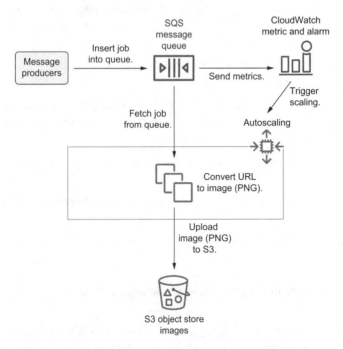

Figure 17.7 Autoscaling virtual machines that convert URLs into images, decoupled by an SQS queue

   3 The Node.js application loads the URL and creates a screenshot.

   4 The screenshot is uploaded to an S3 bucket, and the object key is set to the unique ID.

   5 Users can download the screenshot directly from S3 using the unique ID.

A CloudWatch alarm is used to monitor the length of the SQS queue. If the length of the queue reaches five, an additional virtual machine is started to handle the workload. When the queue length goes below five, another CloudWatch alarm decreases the desired capacity of the Auto Scaling group.

The code is in the book's code repository on GitHub at https://github.com/ AWSinAction/code3. The CloudFormation template for the URL2PNG example is located at chapter17/url2png.yaml.

Execute the following command to create a CloudFormation stack that spins up the URL2PNG application:

```
$ aws cloudformation create-stack --stack-name url2png \
    --template-url https://s3.amazonaws.com/\
    awsinaction-code3/chapter17/url2png.yaml \
    --capabilities CAPABILITY_IAM
```

It will take up to five minutes for the stack to be created. Log in to the AWS Management Console, and navigate to the AWS CloudFormation service to monitor the process of the CloudFormation stack named url2png.

We're using the length of the SQS queue to scale the number of EC2 instances. Because the number of messages in the queue does not correlate with the number of EC2 instances processing messages from the queue, it is not possible to use a target-tracking policy. Therefore, you will use a step-scaling policy in this scenario, as illustrated here.

Listing 17.7 Monitoring the length of the SQS queue

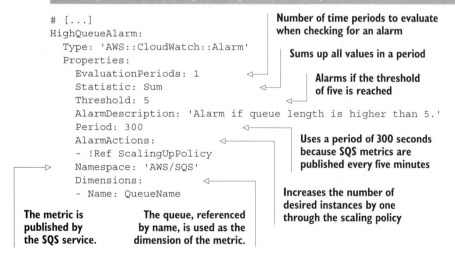

```
# [...]
HighQueueAlarm:
  Type: 'AWS::CloudWatch::Alarm'
  Properties:
    EvaluationPeriods: 1          ◁──  Number of time periods to evaluate
                                        when checking for an alarm
    Statistic: Sum                ◁──  Sums up all values in a period
    Threshold: 5                  ◁──  Alarms if the threshold
                                        of five is reached
    AlarmDescription: 'Alarm if queue length is higher than 5.'
    Period: 300                   ◁──  Uses a period of 300 seconds
                                        because SQS metrics are
    AlarmActions:                       published every five minutes
    - !Ref ScalingUpPolicy        ◁──  Increases the number of
    Namespace: 'AWS/SQS'                desired instances by one
    Dimensions:                         through the scaling policy
    - Name: QueueName             ◁──
```

The metric is published by the SQS service.

The queue, referenced by name, is used as the dimension of the metric.

```
        Value: !Sub '${SQSQueue.QueueName}'
        ComparisonOperator: GreaterThanThreshold
        MetricName: ApproximateNumberOfMessagesVisible
# [...]
```

> **Alarms if the sum of the values within the period is greater than the threshold of five**

> **The metric contains an approximate number of messages pending in the queue.**

The CloudWatch alarm triggers a scaling policy. The scaling policy shown in the following listing defines how to scale. To keep things simple, we are using a step-scaling policy with only a single step. Add additional steps if you want to react to a threshold breach in a more fine-grained way.

Listing 17.8 A step-scaling policy adding one more instance to an Auto Scaling group

> **The aggregation type used when evaluating the steps, based on the metric defined within the CloudWatch alarm that triggers the scaling policy**

```
# [...]
ScalingUpPolicy:
  Type: 'AWS::AutoScaling::ScalingPolicy'
  Properties:
    AdjustmentType: 'ChangeInCapacity'
    AutoScalingGroupName: !Ref AutoScalingGroup
    PolicyType: 'StepScaling'
    MetricAggregationType: 'Average'
    EstimatedInstanceWarmup: 60
    StepAdjustments:
    - MetricIntervalLowerBound: 0
      ScalingAdjustment: 1
# [...]
```

> **Creates a scaling policy**

> **The scaling policy increases the capacity by an absolute number.**

> **Attaches the scaling policy to the Auto Scaling group**

> **Creates a scaling policy of type step scaling**

> **Defines the scaling steps. We use a single step in this example.**

> **The scaling step is valid from the alarms threshold to infinity.**

> **Increases the desired capacity of the Auto Scaling group by 1**

> **The metrics of a newly launched instance are ignored for 60 seconds while it boots up.**

To scale down the number of instances when the queue is empty, a CloudWatch alarm and scaling policy with the opposite values needs to be defined.

You're now ready to scale. We've prepared a load test that will quickly generate 250 messages for the URL2PNG application. A virtual machine will be launched to process jobs from the SQS queue. After a few minutes, when the load test is finished, the additional virtual machine will disappear. Update the CloudFormation stack with the following command to start the load test:

```
$ aws cloudformation update-stack --stack-name url2png \
    --template-url https://s3.amazonaws.com/\
    awsinaction-code3/chapter17/url2png-loadtest.yaml \
    --capabilities CAPABILITY_IAM
```

Watch for the following things to happen, with the help of the AWS Management Console:

1 Open the CloudWatch service, and click Alarms at left.

2 When the load test starts, the alarm called url2png-**HighQueueAlarm**-* will reach the ALARM state after a few minutes.

3 Open the EC2 service, and list all EC2 instances. Watch for an additional instance to launch. At the end, you'll see three instances total (two workers and the EC2 instance running the load test).

4 Go back to the CloudWatch service, and wait until the alarm named url2png -**LowQueueAlarm**-* reaches the ALARM state.

5 Open the EC2 service, and list all EC2 instances. Watch for the additional instance to disappear. At the end, you'll see two instances total (one worker and the EC2 instance running the load test).

The entire process will take about 20 minutes.

You've just watched autoscaling in action. The URL2PNG application can now adapt to the current workload, and the problem with slowly generated screenshots has been solved.

Cleaning up

Execute the following commands to delete all resources corresponding to the URL2PNG example:

```
$ URL2PNG_BUCKET=aws cloudformation describe-stacks --stack-name url2png \
    --query "Stacks[0].Outputs[?OutputKey=='BucketName'].OutputValue" \
    --output text

$ aws s3 rm s3://${URL2PNG_BUCKET} --recursive

$ aws cloudformation delete-stack --stack-name url2png
```

Whenever distributing an application among multiple EC2 instances, you should use an Auto Scaling group. Doing so allows you to spin up identical instances with ease. You get the most out of the possibilities of the cloud when scaling the number of instances based on a schedule or a metric depending on the load pattern.

Summary

- You can use autoscaling to launch multiple identical virtual machines by using a launch template and an Auto Scaling group.
- EC2, SQS, and other services publish metrics to CloudWatch (CPU usage, queue length, and so on).
- CloudWatch alarms can change the desired capacity of an Auto Scaling group. This allows you to increase the number of virtual machines based on CPU usage or other metrics.

- Using stateless machines is a best practice, when scaling the number of machines according to the current workload automatically.
- To distribute load among multiple virtual machines, synchronous decoupling with the help of a load balancer or asynchronous decoupling with a message queue is necessary.

Building modern architectures for the cloud: ECS, Fargate, and App Runner

18

This chapter covers

- Deploying a web server with App Runner, the simplest way to run containers on AWS
- Comparing Elastic Container Service (ECS) and Elastic Kubernetes Service (EKS)
- An introduction into ECS: cluster, task definition, task, and service
- Running containers with Fargate without the need for managing virtual machines
- Building a modern architecture based on ALB, ECS, Fargate, and S3

When working with our consulting clients, we handle two types of projects:

- Brownfield projects, where the goal is to migrate workloads from on-premises to the cloud. Sooner or later, these clients also ask for ways to modernize their legacy systems.
- Greenfield projects, where the goal is to develop a solution from scratch with the latest technology available in the cloud.

Both types of projects are interesting and challenging. This chapter introduces a modern architecture, which you could use to modernize a legacy system as well as to build something from scratch. In recent years, there has hardly been a technology that has spread as rapidly as containers. In our experience, containers fit well for both brownfield and greenfield projects. You will learn how to use containers to deploy your workloads on AWS in this chapter.

We want to focus on the cutting-edge aspects of deploying containers on AWS. Therefore, we skip the details on how to create container images or start a container with Docker. We recommend *Docker in Action* (Manning, 2019; https://www.manning .com/books/docker-in-action-second-edition) if you want to learn about the fundamentals of Docker and containers.

Examples not covered by Free Tier

The examples in this chapter are not covered by the Free Tier. Deploying the examples to AWS will cost you less than $1 per day. You will find information on how to delete all resources at the end of each example or at the end of the chapter. Therefore, we recommend you complete the chapter within a few days.

Chapter requirements

This chapter assumes that you have a basic understanding of the following components:

- Running software in containers (*Docker in Action*, second edition; http://mng .bz/512a)
- Storing data on Simple Storage Service (chapter 7)
- Distributing requests with Elastic Load Balancing (chapter 14)

On top of that, the example included in this chapter makes extensive use of the following:

- Automating cloud infrastructure with CloudFormation (chapter 4)

18.1 Why should you consider containers instead of virtual machines?

Containers and virtual machines are similar concepts. This means you can apply your knowledge gained from previous chapters to the world of containers. As shown in figure 18.1, both approaches start with an image to spin up a virtual machine or container. Of course, differences exist between the technologies, but we will not discuss them here. As a mental model, it helps to think of containers as lightweight virtual machines.

How often do you hear "but it works on my machine" when talking to developers? It is not easy to create an environment providing the libraries, frameworks, and runtime environments required by an application. Since 2013, Docker has made the concept of containers popular. As in logistics, a container in software development is a

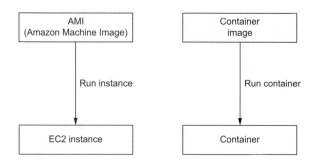

Figure 18.1 From a high-level view, virtual machines and containers are similar concepts.

standardized unit that can be easily moved and delivered. In our experience, this method simplifies the development process significantly, especially when aiming for continuous deployment, which means shipping every change to test or production systems automatically.

In theory, you spin up a container based on the same image on your local machine, an on-premises server, and in the cloud. Boundaries exist only between UNIX/Linux and Windows, as well as Intel/AMD and ARM processors. In contrast, it is much more complicated to launch an Amazon Machine Image (AMI) on your local machine.

Containers also increase portability. In our opinion, it is much easier to move a containerized workload from on-premises to the cloud or to another cloud provider. But beware of the marketing promises by many vendors: it is still a lot of work to integrate your system with the target infrastructure.

We have guided several organizations in the adoption of containers. In doing so, we have observed that containers promote an important competency: building and running immutable servers. An immutable server is a server that you do not change once it is launched from an image. But what if you need to roll out a change? Create a new image and replace the old servers with servers launched from the new image. In theory, you could do the same thing with EC2 instances as well, and we highly recommend you do so. But because you are typically not able to log in to a running container to make changes, following the immutable server approach is your only option. The keyword here is *Dockerfile*, a configuration file containing everything needed to build a container image.

18.2 Comparing different options to run containers on AWS

Next, let's answer the question of how best to deploy containers on AWS. To impress you, let's start with a simple option: AWS App Runner. Type the code in listing 18.1 into your terminal to launch containers running a simple web server from a container image.

> **AWS CLI**
>
> Is the AWS CLI not working on your machine? Go to chapter 4 to learn how to install and configure the command-line interface.

Listing 18.1 Creating an App Runner service

Creates an App Runner service that will spin up containers

Defines a name for the service

Configures the source of the container image

Chooses a public or private container registry hosted by AWS

```
aws apprunner create-service \
  --service-name simple \
  --source-configuration '{"ImageRepository": \
  {"ImageIdentifier": "public.ecr.aws/
  s5r5a1t5/simple:latest", \
  "ImageRepositoryType": "ECR_PUBLIC"}}'
```

It will take about five minutes until a simple web server is up and running. Use the following code to get the status and URL of your service, and open the URL in your browser. On a side note, App Runner even supports custom domains, in case that's a crucial feature to you.

Listing 18.2 Fetching information about App Runner services

The ARN of the service, needed to delete the service later

Opens this URL in your browser

Waits until the status reaches RUNNING

```
$ aws apprunner list-services
{
  "ServiceSummaryList": [
    {
      "ServiceName": "simple",
      "ServiceId": "5e7ffd09c13d4d6189e99bb51fc0f230",
      "ServiceArn": "arn:aws:apprunner:us-east-1:...",
      "ServiceUrl":
"bxjsdpnnaz.us-east-1.awsapprunner.com",
      "CreatedAt": "2022-01-07T20:26:48+01:00",
      "UpdatedAt": "2022-01-07T20:26:48+01:00",
      "Status": "RUNNING"
    }
  ]
}
```

App Runner is a Platform as a Service (PaaS) offering for container workloads. You provide a container image bundling a web application, and App Runner takes care of everything else, as illustrated in figure 18.2:

- Runs and monitors containers
- Distributes requests among running containers
- Scales the number of containers based on load

You pay for memory but not CPU resources during times when a running container does not process any requests. Let's look at pricing with an example. Imagine a web application with minimal resource requirements only used from 9 a.m. to 5 p.m.,

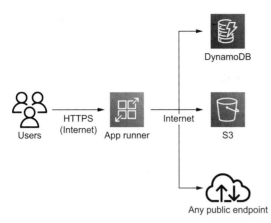

Figure 18.2 App Runner provides a simple way to host containerized web applications.

which is eight hours per day. The minimal configuration on App Runner is 1 vCPU and 2 GB memory:

- Active hours (= hours in which requests are processed)
  - 1 vCPU: $0.064 * 8 * 30 = $15.36 per month
  - 2 GB memory: 2 * $0.007 * 8 * 30 = $3.36 per month
- Inactive hours (= hours in which no requests are processed)
  - 2 GB memory: 2 * $0.007 * 16 * 30 = $6.72 per month

In total, that's $25.44 per month for the smallest configuration supported by App Runner. See "AWS App Runner Pricing" at https://aws.amazon.com/apprunner/pricing/ for more details.

By the way, don't forget to delete your App Runner service to avoid unexpected costs. Replace $ServiceArn with the ARN you noted after creating the service, as shown here.

Listing 18.3 Fetching information about App Runner services

```
$ aws apprunner delete-service \
⇒ --service-arn $ServiceArn
```

That was fun, wasn't it? But simplicity comes with limitations. Here are two reasons App Runner might not be a good fit to deploy your application:

- App Runner does not come with an SLA yet.
- Also, comparing costs between the different options is tricky, because different dimensions are used for billing. Roughly speaking, App Runner should be cheap for small workloads with few requests but rather expensive for large workloads with many requests.

That's why we will introduce two other ways to deploy containers on AWS next. The two main services to manage containers on AWS are Elastic Container Service (ECS) and Elastic Kubernetes Services (EKS).

> **WHAT IS KUBERNETES?** Kubernetes (K8s) is an open source container orchestration system. Originally, Google developed Kubernetes, but nowadays, the Cloud Native Computing Foundation maintains the project. Kubernetes can run on your local machine and on-premises, and most cloud providers offer a fully managed service.

The discussion about which of the two services is better is often very heated and reminiscent of the discussions about the editors vim and emacs. When viewed unemotionally, the functional scope of ECS and EKS is very similar. The both handle the following:

- Monitoring and replacing failed containers
- Deploying new versions of your containers
- Scaling the number of containers to adapt to load

Of course, we would also like to highlight the differences, which we have summarized in table 18.1.

Table 18.1 Launch configuration parameters

Category	ECS	EKS
Portability	ECS is available on AWS. ECS Anywhere is an extension to use ECS for on-premises workloads. Other cloud providers do not support ECS.	EKS is available on AWS. For on-premises workloads, you have EKS Anywhere, which is supported by AWS but requires VMware vSphere and offers the option to deploy and manage Kubernetes yourself. Also, most other cloud providers come with a Kubernetes offering.
License	Proprietary service but free of charge	Open source license (Apache License 2.0)
Ecosystem	Works very well together with many AWS services (e.g., ALB, IAM, and VPC)	Comes with a vibrant open source ecosystem (e.g., Prometheus, Helm). Integration with AWS services exists but is not always mature.
Costs	A cluster is free. Of course, you pay for the compute infrastructure.	AWS charges about $72 per month for each cluster. Also, AWS recommends *not* to deploy workloads that require isolation to the same cluster. On top of that, you are paying for the compute infrastructure.

We observe that Kubernetes is very popular especially, but not only, among developers. Even though we are software developers ourselves, we prefer ECS for most workloads. The most important arguments for us are monthly costs per cluster and integration with other AWS services. On top of that, CloudFormation comes with full support for ECS.

Next, you will learn about the basic concepts behind ECS.

18.3   The ECS basics: Cluster, service, task, and task definition

When working with ECS, you need to create a cluster first. A cluster is a logical group for all the components we discuss next. It is fine to create multiple clusters to isolate workloads from each other. For example, we typically create different clusters for test and production environments. The cluster itself is free, and by default, you can create up to 10,000 clusters—which you probably do not need, by the way.

To run a container on ECS, you need to create a task definition. The task definition includes all the information required to run a container, as shown here. See figure 18.3 for more details:

- The container image URL
- Provisioned baseline and limit for CPU
- Provisioned baseline and limit for memory
- Environment variables
- Network configuration

Please note: a task definition might describe one or multiple containers.

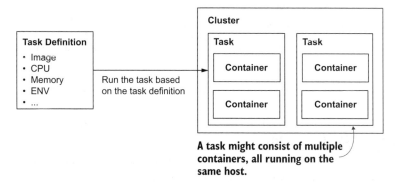

Figure 18.3   A task definition defines all the details needed to create a task, which consists of one or multiple containers.

Next, you are ready to create a task. To do so, you need to specify the cluster as well as the task definition. After you create the task, ECS will try to run the containers as specified. Note that all containers defined in a task definition will run on the same host. This is important if you have multiple containers that need to share local resources—the local network, for example. Figure 18.3 shows how to run tasks based on a task definition.

Luckily, you can, but do not have to, create tasks manually. Suppose you want to deploy a web server on ECS. In this case, you need to ensure that at least two containers of the same kind are running around the clock to spread the workload among two availability zones. In the case of high load, even more containers should be started for a short time. You need an ECS service for that.

Think of an ECS service as similar to an Auto Scaling group. An ECS service, as shown in figure 18.4, performs the following tasks:

- Runs multiple tasks of the same kind
- Scales the number of tasks based on load
- Monitors and replaces failed tasks
- Spreads tasks across availability zones
- Orchestrates rolling updates

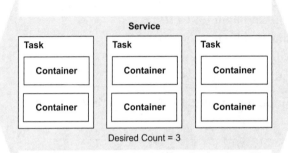

- **Resilience**: replace failed tasks, spread tasks across AZs.
- **Scalability**: add or remove tasks based on current load.
- **Deployment**: roll out new versions without downtime.

Figure 18.4   An ECS service manages multiple tasks of the same kind.

Equipped with the knowledge of the most important components for ECS, we move on.

18.4   *AWS Fargate: Running containers without managing a cluster of virtual machines*

Let's take a little trip down AWS history lane. ECS has been generally available since 2015. Since its inception, ECS has been adding another layer to our infrastructures. With ECS you had to manage, maintain, and scale not only containers but also the underlying EC2 instances. This increased complexity significantly.

In November 2017, AWS introduced an important service: AWS Fargate. As shown in figure 18.5, Fargate provides a fully managed container infrastructure, allowing you to spin up containers in a similar way to launching EC2 instances. This was a game changer! Since then, we have deployed our workloads with ECS and Fargate whenever possible, and we advise you to do the same.

By the way, Fargate is available not only for ECS but for EKS as well. Also, Fargate offers Amazon Linux 2 and Microsoft Windows 2019 Server Full and Core editions as a platform for your containers.

With EC2 instances, you choose an instance type, which specifies the available resources like CPU and memory. In contrast, Fargate requires you to configure the provisioned CPU and memory capacity per task. Table 18.2 shows the available options.

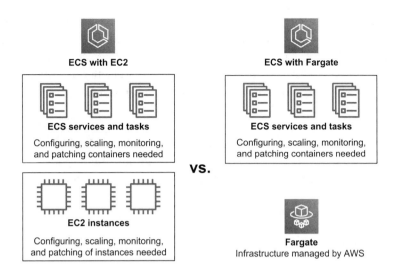

Figure 18.5   With Fargate, you do not need to manage a fleet of EC2 instances to deploy containers with ECS.

Table 18.2   Provisioning CPU and memory for Fargate

CPU	Memory
0.25 vCPU	0.5 GB, 1 GB, or 2 GB
0.5 vCPU	Minimum 1 GB, Maximum 4 GB, 1 GB increments
1 vCPU	Minimum 2 GB, Maximum 8 GB, 1 GB increments
2 vCPU	Minimum 4 GB, Maximum 16 GB, 1 GB increments
4 vCPU	Minimum 8 GB, Maximum 30 GB, 1 GB increments
8 vCPU	Minimum 16 GB, Maximum 60 GB, 4 GB increments
16 vCPU	Minimum 32 GB, Maximum 120 GB, 8 GB increments

Fargate is billed for every second a task is running, from downloading the container image until the task terminates. What does a Fargate task with 1 vCPU and 4 GB memory cost per month? It depends on the region and architecture (Linux/X86, Linux/ARM, Windows/X86). Let's do the math for Linux/ARM in us-east-1:

- 1 vCPU: $0.04048 * 24 * 30 = $29.15 per month
- 4 GB memory: 4 * $0.004445 * 24 * 30 = $12.80 per month

In total, that's $41.95 per month for a Fargate task with 1 vCPU and 2 GB memory. See "AWS Fargate Pricing" at https://aws.amazon.com/fargate/pricing/ for more details.

When comparing the costs for CPU and memory, it is noticeable that EC2 is cheaper compared to Fargate. For example, a `m6g.medium` instance with 1 vCPU and 4 GB memory costs $27.72 per month. But when scaling EC2 instances for ECS yourself, fragmentation and overprovisioning will add up as well. Besides that, the additional complexity will consume working time. In our opinion, Fargate is worth it in most scenarios.

It is important to mention that Fargate comes with a few limitations. Most applications are not affected by those limitations, but you should double-check before starting with Fargate. A list of the most important—but not all—limitations follows. See "Amazon ECS on AWS Fargate" at http://mng.bz/19Wn for more details:

- A maximum of 16 vCPU and 120 GB memory.
- Container cannot run in `privileged` mode.
- Missing GPU support.
- Attaching EBS volumes is not supported.

Now it's finally time to see ECS in action.

18.5   *Walking through a cloud-native architecture: ECS, Fargate, and S3*

We take notes all the time: when we're on the phone with a customer, when we're thinking through a new chapter for a book, when we're looking at a new AWS service in detail. Do you do this too? Imagine you want to host your notes in the cloud. In this example, you will deploy Notea, a privacy-first, open source note-taking application to AWS. Notea is a typical modern web application that uses React for the user interface and Next.js for the backend. All data is stored on S3.

The cloud-native architecture, as shown in figure 18.6, consists of the following building blocks:

- The Application Load Balancer (ALB) distributes incoming requests among all running containers.
- An ECS service spins up containers and scales based on CPU load.
- Fargate provides the underlying compute capacity.
- The application stores all data on S3.

You may have noticed that the concepts from the previous chapters can be transferred to a modern architecture based on ECS easily.

As usual, you'll find the code in the book's code repository on GitHub: https://github.com/AWSinAction/code3. The CloudFormation template for the Notea example is located in /chapter18/notea.yaml.

Execute the following command to create a CloudFormation stack that spins up Notea. Don't forget to replace `$ApplicationId` with a unique character sequence (e.g., your name abbreviation) and `$Password` with a password for protecting your notes.

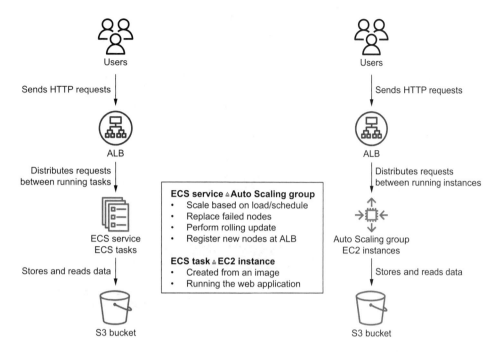

Figure 18.6   ECS is for containers what an Auto Scaling group is for EC2 instances.

Please note: your password will be transmitted unencrypted over HTTP, so you should use a throwaway password that you are not using anywhere else:

```
$ aws cloudformation create-stack --stack-name notea \
  --template-url https://s3.amazonaws.com/\
  awsinaction-code3/chapter18/notea.yaml --parameters \
  "ParameterKey=ApplicationID,ParameterValue=$ApplicationId" \
  "ParameterKey=Password,ParameterValue=$Password" \
  --capabilities CAPABILITY_IAM
```

It will take about five minutes until your note-taking app is up and running (figure 18.7). Use the following command to wait until the stack was created successfully and fetch the URL to open in your browser:

```
$ aws cloudformation wait stack-create-complete \
  --stack-name notea && aws cloudformation describe-stacks \
  --stack-name notea --query "Stacks[0].Outputs[0].OutputValue" \
  --output text
```

Congratulations! You have launched a modern web application with ECS and Fargate. Happy note-taking!

Next, we highly recommend you open the AWS Management Console and go to the ECS service to explore the cluster, the service, the tasks, and tasks definition. Use https://console.aws.amazon.com/ecs/ to jump right into the ECS service.

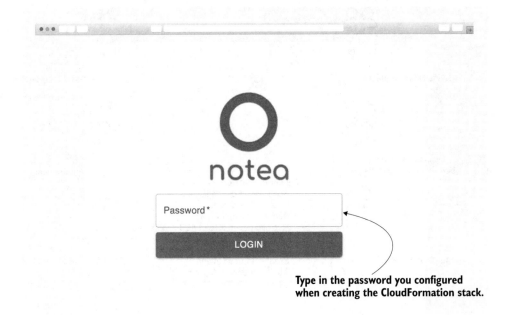

Figure 18.7   Notea is up and running!

What we like about ECS is that we can deploy all components with CloudFormation. Therefore, let's dive into the code. First, you need to create a task definition. For a better understanding, figure 18.8 shows the different configuration parts of the task definition.

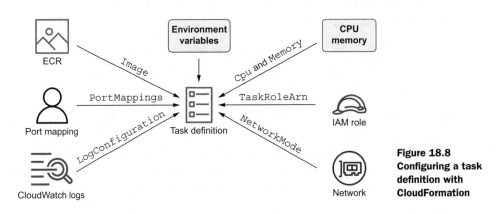

Figure 18.8 Configuring a task definition with CloudFormation

The code in the next listing shows the details.

Listing 18.4   Configuring a task definition

**We will reference
the container named
app later.**

```
TaskDefinition:
  Type: 'AWS::ECS::TaskDefinition'
  Properties:
    ContainerDefinitions:
    - Name: app
      Image: 'public.ecr.aws/s5r5a1t5/notea:latest'
      PortMappings:
      - ContainerPort: 3000
        Protocol: tcp
      Essential: true
      LogConfiguration:
        LogDriver: awslogs
        Options:
          'awslogs-region': !Ref 'AWS::Region'
          'awslogs-group': !Ref LogGroup
          'awslogs-stream-prefix': app
      Environment:
      - Name: 'PASSWORD'
        Value: !Ref Password
      - Name: 'STORE_REGION'
        Value: !Ref 'AWS::Region'
      - Name: 'STORE_BUCKET'
        Value: !Ref Bucket
      - Name: COOKIE_SECURE
        Value: 'false'
    Cpu: 512
    ExecutionRoleArn: !GetAtt 'TaskExecutionRole.Arn'
    Family: !Ref 'AWS::StackName'
    Memory: 1024
    NetworkMode: awsvpc
    RequiresCompatibilities: [FARGATE]
    TaskRoleArn: !GetAtt 'TaskRole.Arn'
```

**Remember that a task
definition describes one or
multiple containers? In this
example, there is only one
container, called app.**

**The URL points to
a publicly hosted
container image
bundling the
Notea app.**

**The
container
starts a
server on
port 3000.**

**The log configuration tells
the container to ship logs
to CloudWatch, which is the
default for ECS and Fargate.**

**The notea container expects a
few environment variables for
configuration. Those environment
variables are configured here.**

**Tells
Fargate
to assign
1024 MB
memory to
our task**

**Tells Fargate
to provision
0.5 vCPUs for
our task**

**The IAM role is used
by Fargate to fetch
container images,
ship logs, and
similar tasks.**

**Specifies that the task
definition should be
used with Fargate only**

**The IAM role used
by the application
to access S3**

**Fargate supports only the networking
mode awsvpc, which will attach an
Elastic Network Interface (ENI) to
each task. You learned about the
ENI in chapter 16 already.**

The task definition configures two IAM roles for the tasks. An IAM role is required to authenticate and authorize when accessing any AWS services. The IAM role defined by ExecutionRoleArn is not very interesting—the role grants Fargate access to basic services for downloading container images or publishing logs. However, the IAM role TaskRoleArn is very important because it grants the containers access to AWS services. In our example, Notea requires read and write access to S3. And that's exactly what the IAM role in listing 18.5 is all about.

Listing 18.5   Granting the container access to objects in an S3 bucket

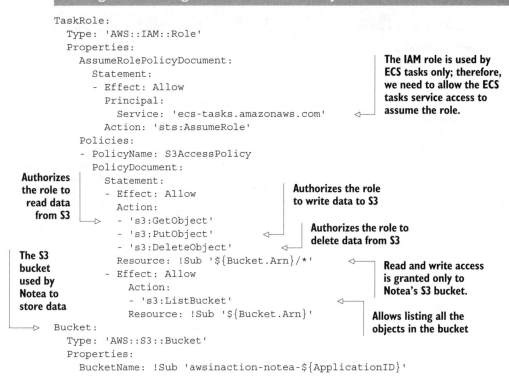

```
TaskRole:
  Type: 'AWS::IAM::Role'
  Properties:
    AssumeRolePolicyDocument:
      Statement:
      - Effect: Allow
        Principal:
          Service: 'ecs-tasks.amazonaws.com'
        Action: 'sts:AssumeRole'
    Policies:
    - PolicyName: S3AccessPolicy
      PolicyDocument:
        Statement:
        - Effect: Allow
          Action:
          - 's3:GetObject'
          - 's3:PutObject'
          - 's3:DeleteObject'
          Resource: !Sub '${Bucket.Arn}/*'
        - Effect: Allow
          Action:
          - 's3:ListBucket'
          Resource: !Sub '${Bucket.Arn}'
Bucket:
  Type: 'AWS::S3::Bucket'
  Properties:
    BucketName: !Sub 'awsinaction-notea-${ApplicationID}'
```

The IAM role is used by ECS tasks only; therefore, we need to allow the ECS tasks service access to assume the role.

Authorizes the role to read data from S3

Authorizes the role to write data to S3

Authorizes the role to delete data from S3

Read and write access is granted only to Notea's S3 bucket.

The S3 bucket used by Notea to store data

Allows listing all the objects in the bucket

Next, you need to create an ECS service that launches tasks and, with them, containers. The most important configuration details shown in the next listing are:

- `DesiredCount`—Defines the number of tasks the service will launch. The `DesiredCount` will be changed by autoscaling later.
- `LoadBalancers`—The service registers and unregisters tasks at the ALB out of the box with this configuration.

Listing 18.6   Creating an ECS service to spin up tasks running the web app

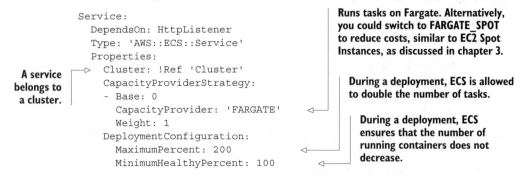

```
Service:
  DependsOn: HttpListener
  Type: 'AWS::ECS::Service'
  Properties:
    Cluster: !Ref 'Cluster'
    CapacityProviderStrategy:
    - Base: 0
      CapacityProvider: 'FARGATE'
      Weight: 1
    DeploymentConfiguration:
      MaximumPercent: 200
      MinimumHealthyPercent: 100
```

Runs tasks on Fargate. Alternatively, you could switch to FARGATE_SPOT to reduce costs, similar to EC2 Spot Instances, as discussed in chapter 3.

A service belongs to a cluster.

During a deployment, ECS is allowed to double the number of tasks.

During a deployment, ECS ensures that the number of running containers does not decrease.

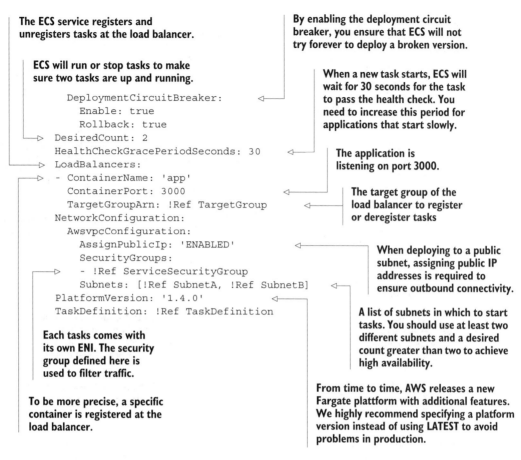

The ECS service registers and unregisters tasks at the load balancer.

By enabling the deployment circuit breaker, you ensure that ECS will not try forever to deploy a broken version.

ECS will run or stop tasks to make sure two tasks are up and running.

When a new task starts, ECS will wait for 30 seconds for the task to pass the health check. You need to increase this period for applications that start slowly.

```
    DeploymentCircuitBreaker:
      Enable: true
      Rollback: true
  DesiredCount: 2
  HealthCheckGracePeriodSeconds: 30
  LoadBalancers:
  - ContainerName: 'app'
    ContainerPort: 3000
    TargetGroupArn: !Ref TargetGroup
  NetworkConfiguration:
    AwsvpcConfiguration:
      AssignPublicIp: 'ENABLED'
      SecurityGroups:
      - !Ref ServiceSecurityGroup
      Subnets: [!Ref SubnetA, !Ref SubnetB]
  PlatformVersion: '1.4.0'
  TaskDefinition: !Ref TaskDefinition
```

The application is listening on port 3000.

The target group of the load balancer to register or deregister tasks

When deploying to a public subnet, assigning public IP addresses is required to ensure outbound connectivity.

A list of subnets in which to start tasks. You should use at least two different subnets and a desired count greater than two to achieve high availability.

Each tasks comes with its own ENI. The security group defined here is used to filter traffic.

From time to time, AWS releases a new Fargate plattform with additional features. We highly recommend specifying a platform version instead of using LATEST to avoid problems in production.

To be more precise, a specific container is registered at the load balancer.

Being able to scale workloads is one of the superpowers of cloud computing. Of course, our container-based infrastructure should be able to scale out and scale in based on load as well. The next listing shows how to configure autoscaling. In the example, we are using a target-tracking scaling policy. The trick is that we need to define the target value only for the CPU utilization. The Application Auto Scaling service will take care of the rest and will increase or decrease the desired count of the ECS service automatically.

Listing 18.7   Configuring autoscaling based on CPU utilization for the ECS service

The upper limit for scaling tasks

```
ScalableTarget:
  Type: AWS::ApplicationAutoScaling::ScalableTarget
  Properties:
    MaxCapacity: '4'
    MinCapacity: '2'
    RoleARN: !GetAtt 'ScalableTargetRole.Arn'
```

The lower limit for scaling tasks

The IAM role is required to grant Application Auto Scaling access to CloudWatch metrics and ECS.

Application Auto Scaling supports all kinds of services. You want to scale ECS in this example.

Scales by increasing or decreasing the desired count of the ECS service

References the ECS service in the ECS cluster created above

A simple way to scale ECS services is by using target-tracking scaling, which requires minimal configuration.

References the scalable target resource from above

```
      ServiceNamespace: ecs
      ScalableDimension: 'ecs:service:DesiredCount'
      ResourceId: !Sub
      - 'service/${Cluster}/${Service}'
      - Cluster: !Ref Cluster
        Service: !GetAtt 'Service.Name'
CPUScalingPolicy:
  Type: AWS::ApplicationAutoScaling::ScalingPolicy
  Properties:
    PolicyType: TargetTrackingScaling
    PolicyName: !Sub 'awsinaction-notea-${ApplicationID}'
    ScalingTargetId: !Ref ScalableTarget
    TargetTrackingScalingPolicyConfiguration:
      TargetValue: 50.0
      ScaleInCooldown: 180
      ScaleOutCooldown: 60
      PredefinedMetricSpecification:
        PredefinedMetricType: ECSServiceAverageCPUUtilization
```

After terminating tasks, waits three minutes before reevaluating the situation

In this example, we scale based on CPU utilization. ECSServiceAverageMemoryUtilization is another predefined metric.

The target is to keep the CPU utilization at 50%. You might want to increase that to 70–80% in real-world scenarios.

After starting tasks, waits one minute before reevaluating the situation

That's it, you have learned how to deploy a modern web application on ECS and Fargate.

Don't forget to delete the CloudFormation stack and all data on S3, as shown in the following code snippet. Replace `$ApplicationId` with a unique character sequence you chose when creating the stack:

```
$ aws s3 rm s3://awsinaction-notea-${ApplicationID} --recursive
$ aws cloudformation delete-stack --stack-name notea
$ aws cloudformation wait stack-delete-complete \
➥ --stack-name notea
```

What a ride! You have come a long way from AWS basics, to advanced cloud architecture principles, to modern containerized architectures. Now only one thing remains to be said: go build!

Summary

- App Runner is the simplest way to run containers on AWS. However, to achieve simplicity, App Runner comes with limitations. For example, the containers aren't running in your VPC.

- The Elastic Container Service (ECS) and the Elastic Kubernetes Service (EKS) are both orchestrating container clusters. We recommend ECS for most use cases because of cost per cluster, integration into all parts of AWS, and Cloud-Formation support.
- With Fargate, you no longer have to maintain an EC2 instance to run your containers. Instead, AWS provides a fully managed compute layer for containers.
- The main components of ECS are cluster, task definition, task, and service.
- The concepts from EC2-based architectures apply to container-based architectures as well. For example, an ECS service is the equivalent of an Auto Scaling group.

index

AWS Security
by Dylan Shields

ISBN 9781617297335
312 pages, $59.99
August 2022

*Serverless Architectures with AWS,
Second Edition*
by Peter Sbarski, Yan Cui, Ajay Nair

ISBN 9781617295423
256 pages, $49.99
February 2022

AWS for Non-Engineers
by Hiroko Nishimura

ISBN 9781633439948
176 pages, $39.99
November 2022

Cloud Native Patterns
by Cornelia Davis
Foreword by Gene Kim

ISBN 9781617294297
400 pages, $49.99
May 2019

For ordering information, go to www.manning.com

A new online reading experience

liveBook, our online reading platform, adds a new dimension to your Manning books, with features that make reading, learning, and sharing easier than ever. A liveBook version of your book is included FREE with every Manning book.

This next generation book platform is more than an online reader. It's packed with unique features to upgrade and enhance your learning experience.

- Add your own notes and bookmarks
- One-click code copy
- Learn from other readers in the discussion forum
- Audio recordings and interactive exercises
- Read all your purchased Manning content in any browser, anytime, anywhere

As an added bonus, you can search every Manning book and video in liveBook—even ones you don't yet own. Open any liveBook, and you'll be able to browse the content and read anything you like.*

Find out more at www.manning.com/livebook-program.

*Open reading is limited to 10 minutes per book daily